The University Libraries at Penn State
and the Penn State University Press, through the
Office of Digital Scholarly Publishing, produced
this volume to preserve the informational content
of the original. This reprint edition was created
by means of digital technology and is printed on
paper that complies with the permanent Paper
Standard issued by the National Information
Standards Organization (z39.48-1984).

2008

THE

MOUNTAIN.

BY

R. M. S. JACKSON, M.D.,

CORRESPONDING MEMBER OF THE ACADEMY OF NATURAL SCIENCES OF PHILADELPHIA;
MEMBER OF THE AMERICAN ASSOCIATION FOR THE PROMOTION OF SCIENCE;
MEMBER OF THE AMERICAN MEDICAL ASSOCIATION; MEMBER OF THE
MEDICAL SOCIETY OF PENNSYLVANIA; MEMBER OF THE CORPS OF
THE GEOLOGICAL SURVEY OF PENNSYLVANIA; CORRESPOND-
ING MEMBER OF THE ACADEMY OF SCIENCES AND
ARTS OF PITTSBURG; MEMBER OF THE LYCEUM
OF JEFFERSON COLLEGE, CANONSBURG,
ETC. ETC. ETC.

"Heaven shortens not the life of man: it is man that does it by his own crimes. Thou mayest avoid the calamities that come from heaven; but thou canst never escape those which thou drawest upon thyself by thy crimes."—CONFUCIUS.

PHILADELPHIA:
J. B. LIPPINCOTT & CO.
1860.

Entered, according to Act of Congress, in the year 1860, by

R. M. S. JACKSON, M.D.,

In the Clerk's Office of the District Court for the Eastern District of Pennsylvania.

A WORD TO THE SUBSCRIBERS

OF

THE MOUNTAIN.

FRIEND SUBSCRIBER:—

Are you a country doctor? Do you "*pull teeth?*" Are you your own cupper, bleeder, leecher? Are you your own druggist, filling out in detail your own prescriptions? Are you surgeon, midwife, general practitioner; and have you no time to get fame and money through any of the specialties of the profession—diseases of eye, ear, lung, stomach and bowel, cerebro-spinal axis, women and children, because you are "boy of all work," and have to treat them all? Are you occasionally pig, cow, and horse doctor for the neighbors? Are your patients scattered over a large and diversified surface, which you must traverse on horseback, through swampy roads, wildernesses of fallen timber, traps, deadfalls of roots, and endless continuities of black forests; and do you really *go* in all sorts of weather? Are your patients so inaccessible that most of your time is consumed in merely destroying space to get to them; and have you actually *anything to do* in your profession; and when you do your work, have you five times as much trouble to get your bills as to make them at first, your patients knowing better than you do, *what you ought* to charge, and just *when they ought* to pay? Possibly, to get along, you may be trying to farm a little, endeavoring to scratch some hard patch of desolation into agricultural propriety, or bravely to make, like the hero of "Life in the Woods," some tough glebe "say beans!" This is all very well, and no doubt you will have your reward in heaven. But permit me to ask you a few more questions, absurd and ridiculous as such questions may appear to common sense—and improbable as it may be to expect any answer: Are you trying to write and publish a book, in the midst of all this horror and distraction—nights of sleepless anguish, days of despair? Are you trying to repose and dream in a drum, or paint a picture seated with your easel on a log-sled hauled by a team of oxen over the rocks, roots, logs, and stumps of a spruce-pine clearing; in short, have you been trying to do in the broils of Bedlam that which, to do aright, you should have quiet, absolute repose from all care and anxiety, still nights of visions, golden mornings of ecstatic influx, and brave days of spiritual wrestling, inspired by the gentle, heroic, and loving sympathy of the living, with solemn beckonings and greetings of grace and holiness from the dead? Then, did I understand you to say that you were two hundred and fifty miles from your publishers, two hundred and fifty miles from libraries of any extent, where you could have access to books of reference and quick facilities for correcting proof, and so on? And you have really, under all these difficulties, been going through the torments of that everlasting stone-rolling of Sisyphus of 1700 ems in a page, i-dottings, t-crossings, commas stuck in by nineteen elaborate rules, colons by five, semicolons by five, periods by five, etc.?

These interrogations you answer all in the affirmative? Well, then, on thy brow be written FOOL! for a "thousand years in heaven cannot recompense your miserable heart" for such a blunder, or "make you capable of one brief joy," after such a hideous folly! "Ah, me! miserable! which way shall I fly?"

Pardon the unfortunate author, then, benevolent subscriber! and, before sending him away from this court under conduct of proper officers, "to be hanged by the neck until dead, dead," (asking the Lord to have mercy on his soul,) allow him to offer for your *reconsideration* a few of the first explanatory words of the announcement to the subscribers, published in the part of the book printed some time since, as some apology for the protracted tedium and delay in the delivery of the whole volume; for now the voice singing the song, the book heralding the claims of the Mountain, so long promised, is actually handed to you. It is, and from the surroundings of the author could not be otherwise, a feeble effort withal, patched up from occasional scribblings of a troubled man,—a tired soldier in the agonizing life-fight,—or squeezed out of heart and brain in weary interludes of the roar and shock of that same battle.

When the rash promise was made to write a Mountain book, the guardian angel of one soul was fast asleep; and when the greater part of the subscription list was made, there was no book in existence. Then it was entirely unknown what kind of book it would be, or, if it had any existence, what sort of thing it was, and various surmises were risked.*

* These surmises, as might be expected, were of a diversified character and coloring, viz.: that it was a "Tragical Romance," a "Narrative," a "Poem," a "Hoax," particularly a—God knows what! It was well known to all the *friends of the author* that years of "storm and pressure" had passed over his head during his labors on the Alleghany Mountain—years of the most disastrous experiences—bitter, mournful, and pointing to the grave as the only relief; torments such as men rarely suffer. At one time the active member of six firms, all of which proved infirm, with results of woe and despair, whether through Satan, Fate, or Folly, it matters not, it was natural for these friends to expect that something of the order of "Sorrows of Werter," "Confessions of St. Augustine," possibly,—"Livingstone's Adventures in Africa," "Border Life, or Wild Sports of the West," "Riley's Narrative," "Robinson Crusoe," "Sinbad the Sailor," or "Romance of the Black Forest," would come off,—surely *anything* but a "Song to Joy." Think of a country doctor practicing medicine in two firms, making fire-brick in one, sawing lumber in another, cutting cross-ties for a railroad in another, selling drugs in another, and speculating in mountain lands and building Health Institutes on his *own hook, all at one time!* Old Father Adam had a good Paradise of a farm, and was no doubt a good farmer. It was extremely foolish in him to try to get into other business, (endeavoring to *know more than he ought to know*,) and deliberately take the chances of that tremendous *Fall*. No doubt he thought, like everybody else,—

"And set it down in his table of forces,
That any *one man* equals any four horses."

Results were inevitable—immeasurable sorrow. In the Prolegomenon some allusions are made to those days of wrath, experiences infernal, things, persons, and consequents, which the friends will understand, knowing all, but which to the stranger will be Greek and darkness. The stranger will kindly pardon and pass all that he does not understand in the category of local and personal allusions. They were merely a sort of chimney, through which escaped the smoke of the hell in which the unfortunate author was roasted, and have no essential connection with the Song of the Mountain. They legitimately belong, however, to the genesis of the book.

It was at first ignorantly and profanely considered a joke for "good fellows," who, as was supposed, had disingenuously, and even feloniously, deluded the author into the vain and stupid conceit that he had something to say that the human race wanted or *needed* to hear.

The *real* motive, it was further imagined, was a wicked experiment to ascertain the exact shade of verdancy afflicting the UNFORTUNATE, and the precise degree of his proclivity to a sell, and not a *veritable delusion* on their part, that he could say a word that ought not to be lost.

Grandly transcended and forgiven are the sages, with whom "wisdom will no doubt die."

A word upon what we have been about must suffice.

The flight to the Mountain was always looked upon by those calling themselves sober, common-sense friends, as an absolute dementia, and constantly stuck, or rather dug, into the tender sensibilities of the unfortunate author of the Alleghany Mountain Sanitarium, as *the prodigious blunder* of his existence.

Any account that might be given of the mountain, especially the unutterable folly of ANY BOOK about that plain old chain of pine-covered knobs and its true significance to men, must meet the unqualified disapprobation of this self-styled, sober, common-sense party; and any delay in the appearance of said book, hailed as a signal manifestation of the merciful interposition of a special Providence.

Earnest in the belief that life in the country is nearest connate with man's organization, securing to him constantly the greatest of all blessings, perfect health and physical development, and standing with outstretched arms a great world of counter-forces or balance-sheet in favor of humanity, against the destructive influence of city life or the fatal results of the swarming instincts, founding the Sanitarium, and uttering a voice from the woods, have become a mission, solemn as a command from Heaven, and with the sternness and reality of life and death.

Is it not time for the Philanthropist, whose highest form is the "healing man," to ask the *significance and end* of the action of the depraved and vitiated gregarious instincts which now impel this race to fix its hopes of earthly happiness on city life alone, and associate its dreams of man's perfection, and the highest ENDS of his existence, with anything but a rational culture, by the love and study of the laws of this beautiful world, and the obeying of the divine behest by executing the humble offices of an industrious and real life?

Can the present tendency to agglomerate in swarms, or accumulate in masses and mobs, be designated by any such agreeable appellations as love of society, association for mutual refinement and exaltation, or Christian compact for the advancement and more perfect development of the social instincts of the soul?

Inspect the present fruit of this wondrous human tree. It is called a composite race, having in it dribblings of all the bloods, but with two varieties of the typical Caucasian form predominating; namely, the Celtic and Teutonic.

The Celt, in the parlance of the ethnological savant, is said to be polytheistic, monarchical, despotic, sensuous, gregarious, frivolous, excitable, etc.; while the Teuton is affirmed to be monotheistic, democratic, self-sufficient, solitary, intense in love of freedom, hating aristocracies, castes, and shams.

Examine this composite fruit (the inhabitants of the United States) of the two tallest branches of the blood-tree, man, and say to which its destiny leans?

Its instincts seem to come from below, and struggle to drag it down still lower.

If the commercial despotism which now holds the world in its grasp will develop warts and wens, cancers and dropsies, on the surface of the planet, in the shape of overcrowded cities, at the expense of the well-being and normal life of the whole race, and persist in catching men, as trout are caught by artificial fancy flies, let it take the responsibility, and answer to the ages for the certain abridgment of the mean duration of human life, and the vitiated and perverted reign of the elements of anarchy and death.

Why do the highest and lowest meet in city life in infernal fellowship? One class dissipates, flourishes, lives fast, sins fast, dies fast; while the other drudges, withers, sinks fast, suffers fast, and also dies fast. One class is vicious, proud, imperial; the other low, menial, degraded,—both guilds forgetting humanity, forgetting God; swallowed by one common fate, ingulfed in one common ruin.

The beckoning from the mountain-top, the significance of the country life, the song of the hill and meadow, have assumed gravity and grandeur.

Man in contact with the healthy *real*, man militant with rocks and trees, snakes and wolves, man ready and willing to work, to dig and to delve for his own blood, especially happy to *do* something, to advance and to grow, stands out in beautiful relief, the king of the planet, sceptred and crowned.

Might not a friendly voice from the woods be heard in the hum and shock, or possibly reach the ear of some haggard sufferer, writhing in the folds and meshes of the artificial life, or flung out scathed and blasted by the wayside, and inspire him with hope that the blue hills and green fields, the cool sequestered forests, the lonely haunts by mountain springs in the stillness of evening or dewy freshness of the morning, might have life, health, and joy for him?

With sweet solicitude the kind earth woos him. Come, my feverish boy! my poor, hot, sinful, sick, and poisoned child! fast horses and champagne, green turtle and terrapin, whisky and oysters, are not the "dream of life" realized. Come, troubled one, "Nature is medicinal;" there is salvation in exercise and honest labor. Come, "grow two blades of grass where one grew;" from the eye of the potato fill your eye and stomach, too; come, grow fruit and bread plants instead of poison weeds and brambles; the rambo apple for the crab; delicious pears instead of knotty haws; the ox and horse in place of deer and elk; but especially, come, regrow thyself, and, with thy body renewed, introduce thyself to the universe with a renewed soul!

"Pass thou through Mount Ephraim, and the land of Shalisha, the land of Shalim, the land of the Benjamites, into the land of Zuph," and there, like Saul, the son of

Kish, hunting his father's asses, thou shalt be "among the prophets," and find a kingdom.

Rebellious transgressor! Science has long struggled for thee; Nature has importuned thee,—come, be a fact, do a thing, be saved!

The struggle has been to set the claims of the mountain to the music of science and nature. It was a presumptuous effort, and much time, labor, suffering, and certain failure were inevitable. Hence, friend subscriber, somewhat annoying, even galling it must be acknowledged, had become your oft-repeated queries: Why don't you print that book we subscribed for? What are you so long about? (as if a book were a "toby cigar," and its leaves could be rolled up in a minute!) What have you found on that old mountain to interest you? What can *you* say about it worth hearing? What scribblings about its old rocks and trees, its air and waters, can you make that any one will read?—For Heaven's sake tell us, *what is the book* about?—and, whatever it is, why don't you print it?

True, they are plain old rocks and trees, plain old crystalline skies, limpid waters, and piny heights—very plain to seared and bleared eyes; plain to benumbed brains and nauseated stomachs; plain as square acres of the old salt sea, monotonous as square miles of Libyan sand deserts. But reflect, profane interrogator, on this sublime fact: a wheelbarrow load of desert fragments, a pailful of ocean water, could not be exhausted by science in a thousand years!

Be patient, then; meditate; be considerate, subscriber! Any undue haste in the narration of the advantages of the rural life, so imposing and beautiful; any undignified hurry in a dissertation on the sacred and sublime theme of the "Paradise regained" by man's physical redemption from vice and disease, and his attainment of the healthy life, the painless death, and blissful transit to immortal joy, would be to ignominiously profane these subjects; and any indecorous precipitancy in the rehearsal of the august oratorio of the mountain, would be almost impious and sacrilegious,—certainly a crime indictable before the high court of Propriety.

In the treatment of these great subjects the solemn watchword throughout has been, EARNESTNESS; and the only desire, as the world's recognition and appreciation of an effort thus humble but sincere, is simply the intelligent and grave conviction, it is HONEST.

The real desire has been to get *something* of the natural science of that piece of the venerable spheroid (the earth) called the Alleghany Mountain, made more generally known to men, also to try to introduce some of its metaphysical elements into the recorded soul of the world; but, above all, to assert its sanitary claims or powers to produce health and happiness.

It will occur to the intelligent thinker, that such an undertaking was *anything but* a *"joke"* to a wretched slave of a country physician, trying to scratch his bread from a surface of naked sand-rocks; and weeks, even months of continuous arrestation of the work, and standing still of all things, were, from the nature of his engagements, inevitable.

The story of the mountain has in this manner, as already stated, been FORCED to crawl slowly and languidly out through a multitude of never-ceasing occupations. Torn by distractions, bewildered by complex functions, will you, subscriber, pardon the delay in the appearance of the book, when you are assured that something really useful has been attempted; some catalogues of facts, even if they are fragmentary and unfinished, some suggestions, however crude and inelaborate, have been made; and that *some earnest* aspirations and prayers have been breathed (however untimely, uncomely, and ungrateful to averted ears) for the well-being, especially of diseased and suffering fellow-sinners?

One thing you WILL accord, and have the justice to acknowledge, that WHATEVER the BOOK may be, a reality is in the Mountain and its Sanitarium, *positive* and *alive*, as the *blood and heart* of *man are alive*.

Be it then what it may, "monstrum horrendum" or "ridiculous mouse," the book of "The Mountain" is now a fact on the stupid list of existing things.

From the tyranny of the hour, and the inexorable despotism of circumstance, it *could not* be a finished *closet* production, sand-papered into extreme smoothness, polished, varnished, and tortured into severest proprieties. Unfortunately, the felicities and graces of the word have not been consulted, nor refinement, finish, and ornamentation of style adhered to. The asperities of the mountain, that rugged, formless, semichaotic old pile of moss-covered rocks, had insinuated themselves into the brain, and overwhelmed, with the intoxication of enthusiasm, the soul of the blundering scribe, and it could not be otherwise but that *roughness* must appear in and characterize the scripture. It is known of a number of popular lecturers that they have delivered their lectures several hundred times, and afterwards published them in a book.* Think of a small patch of garden being weeded every five minutes over and over, all its walks scraped, trees clipped into primmest attitudes, every bush fixed up to be looked at, every grass spot shaped "*so nicely*"—a perfect paradise of proprieties and gentilities elaborately dressed for great occasions!! These lectures, and their consequent books, were of course designed for, and generally delivered to, large, cultivated, and highly refined metropolitan audiences, where intellectually cormorantine men, having swallowed all literatures, arts, and sciences, have become dainty and fastidious; and the world of thought and sentiment, under the "refining suggestions of woman's brain," have been required to be mellowed into divine softness and sublimation, delicacy and grace. Such rasped and burnished production could not be expected from a rude fighter, a common private in the ranks of the sanguine order of knights of the lancet, who was required to be on perpetual duty in actual service, and at constant hand-gripes with the emissaries of death. Alas! beloved subscriber and friend of the sentimental and delicate order, only disappointment awaits you. This rough mountain production is not a thing that could be printed on satin with gold, and that a hypercritical, over-cultivated, morbidly-intensated, intellectual virtuoso, or fastidious liter-

* How charming to read Everett's Lecture on Washington in a book, after hearing it delivered one hundred and eleven times!

ary duenna, would read aloud to a bevy of youthful city blues, lounging on sofas in the regal city parlor; but a story that a rugged man or sensible woman (mother of the Gracchi) might possibly find useful as a cicerone on the Alleghany Mountain, and "worry down" a page or two in the morning twilight, in some grove of God Almighty.

It seems the fate of laboring men to be rough, and work makes not only the hands but the brain hard. It has also always been remarked that men who fight the elements, and come in contact with naked realities, as mule and ox drivers, soldiers, sailors, blacksmiths, and country doctors, are always uncouth, and have a disposition to swear a little. This being a *part of the nature of things*, nothing can be said on the question of refinement of language, and the general roughness of such men, or their productions. Their hearts are sometimes right, if their heads do occasionally require combing.

Need an apology be offered for the rattle of the pill-box in the "Mountain," any more than for the repulsive presence of the quills of the porcupine?

A scraggy bramble-patch at best is this mountain book, troublesome and disagreeable to travel through; the benevolent hope is, however, that nobody's private views will be offended—no petted crotchets scratched—no pap-nursed opinions lacerated—no spiritual skirts, with whatever elements dilated, shall be torn—no cherished formulæ, punctured and collapsed, or horn-lanterns fractured, for "No proposition should *astonish*, no belief should *offend*, however contrary it may be to any man's own, as there is no fancy so frivolous and extravagant that it does not seem to be a very suitable product of the human understanding."

With grateful acknowledgments for patience and sympathy, kindly forbearance and friendly solicitude, will you, my dear subscriber, allow me, after offering greetings of affection, with a benediction, to make my best bow, and say farewell!

R. M. S. JACKSON.

ALLEGHANY MOUNTAIN SPRINGS,
  Cresson, Cambria Co., Pa.,
      July, 1860.

The philosophy of spirit must develop itself out of the philosophy of Nature, as doth the flower out of the stem. For Nature is the spirit analyzed and at rest, which we can handle at our pleasure. It does not appear only for an instant, but, as stone, air, and such like entities, abideth alway, as if to solicit and preserve us for its investigation.

OKEN: *Biology*.

For us the winds do blow,
The earth doth rest, heaven move, and fountains flow.
Nothing we see but means our good,
As our delight, or as our treasure:
The whole is either our cupboard of food
Or cabinet of pleasure.

The stars have us to bed;
Night draws the curtain which the sun withdraws.
Music and light attend our head:
All things unto our FLESH are kind,
In their *descent* and *being;* to our MIND,
In their ASCENT and *cause.*

More servants wait on man
Than he'll take notice of. In every path
He treads down that which doth befriend him
When sickness makes him pale and wan.
Oh, mighty love! Man is one world, and hath
Another to attend him!

GEORGE HERBERT.

WHERE one scale of the balance is quite empty, I let the other waver under the dreams of an old woman.

Nonsense is a scurvy quality; but not to be able to bear with it, and to fret and vex at it, is another sort of disease, altogether as troublesome as nonsense.

Moreover, vulgar and casual opinions, considered in their weight, are indeed something more than nothing in nature.

All such whimsies as are current about us deserve at least to be hearkened unto. As to me, they are all mere vanity; and that is what they really import. As to every opposition, we don't consider whether it be just, but how we shall, right or wrong, disengage ourselves from it. Instead of extending our arms, we thrust out our claws.

I could suffer myself to be roughly handled by my friends telling me I am a fool and a dreamer. I love to hear gentlemen speak as they think, with courage. We must fortify and harden our organ of hearing against this ceremonious sound of words. I love a strong and manly familiarity and conversation,—a friendship that is pleased with the sharpness and vigor of its communications, as love is with biting and scratching. 'Tis not vigorous or generous enough if it be not quarrelsome, if it be civilized and artificial, if it treads gingerly and is afraid of a shock.

Neque enim disputari sine reprehensione potest. I incline towards him who contradicts and instructs me. I enter into a conference and dispute with great freedom and ease, forasmuch as opinion meets in me a soil very unfit for penetration, and too hard for it to take any deep root in. No proposition astonishes me, no belief offends me, how contrary soever it be to my own.

There is no fancy so frivolous and extravagant that it does not seem to me to be a very suitable product of the human understanding.

MICHAEL SEIGNEUR DE MONTAIGNE.

THE Natural Science of a region is the natural language of that region as a habitat or medium of existence for animated beings. Life must develop itself under the absolute conditions of life,—limited on one side by the brute immobility of ponderable bodies, and on the other held by the despotic power of the imponderables. As the special student of the phenomena of *life*, normal and abnormal, the Physician must be intimately acquainted with the science of the fragment of the planet upon which he operates,—namely, its geology and soil, or mineral composition; its hydrography, or geographic distribution of waters; its hydrology, or the QUALITY, COMPOSITION, *and* PHENOMENA of its waters; its meteorology, or constant climatal phenomena, as well as its botany or zoology, or life in the plant and animal. IGNORANT of the great volume whose leaves are open constantly around him and invite him to explore forever their meaning, and of *which disease is but a chapter*, he is unworthy of the respect and confidence of his brother man as high-priest in the great sanctuary of Nature.

ROBERT SMITH.

A MAN being contented with his own particular lot and duty obtaineth perfection. Hear how that perfection is to be accomplished.

The man who maketh an offering of his own works to that being from whom the principles of all beings proceed, and by whom the whole universe was spread forth, by that means obtaineth perfection. The duties of a man's own peculiar calling, although not free from faults, are far preferable to the duty of another, let it be ever so well pursued. A man, by following the duties which are appointed by his birth, doeth no wrong. A man's own calling, with all its faults, ought not to be forsaken. EVERY UNDERTAKING IS INVOLVED IN ITS FAULTS, AS THE FIRE IN ITS SMOKE. A disinterested mind and conquered spirit, who, in all things, is free from inordinate desires, obtaineth a perfection unconnected with works by that resignation and retirement which is called Sănnyās; and, having attained that perfection, learn from me, in brief, in what manner he obtaineth Brăhm, and what is the foundation of wisdom.

BHĂGVĂT-GĒĒTĀ.

LET every one mind his own business and endeavor to be what he was made. Why should we be in such desperate haste to succeed, and in such desperate enterprises? If a man does not keep pace with his companions, perhaps it is because he hears a different drummer. Let him step to the music which he hears, however measured or far away. It is not important that he should mature as soon as an apple-tree or an oak.

There was an artist in the city of Kouroo who was disposed to strive after perfection. One day it came into his mind to make a staff. Having considered that in an imperfect work time is an ingredient, but into a perfect work time does not enter, he said to himself, "It shall be perfect in all respects, though I should do nothing else in my life." He proceeded instantly to the forest for wood, being resolved that it should not be made of unsuitable material; and, as he searched for and rejected stick after stick, his friends gradually deserted him,—for they grew old in their works and died; but he grew not older by a moment. His singleness of purpose and resolution, and his elevated piety, endowed him, without his knowledge, with perennial youth. As he made no compromise with Time, Time kept out of his way, and only sighed at a distance because he could not overcome him. Before he had found a stock in all respects suitable, the city of Kouroo was a hoary ruin, and he sat on one of its mounds to peel the stick. Before he had given it the proper shape, the dynasty of the Candahars was at an end, and with the point of the stick he wrote the name of the last of that race in the sand, and then resumed his work. By the time he had smoothed and polished the staff, Kalpa was no longer the pole-star; and, ere he had put on the ferule and the head adorned with precious stones, Brahma had awoke and slumbered many times. But why do I stay to mention these things? When the finishing-stroke was put to his work, it suddenly expanded before the eyes of the astonished artist into the fairest of all creations of Brahma. He had made a new system in making a staff,—a world with full and fair proportions: in which, though the old cities and dynasties had passed away, fairer and more glorious ones had taken their places. And now he saw, by the heap of shavings still fresh at his feet, that for him and his work the former lapse of time had been an illusion, and that no more time had elapsed than is required for a single scintillation from the brain of Brahma to fall on and inflame the tinder of a mortal brain. The material was pure, and his art was pure: how could the result be other than wonderful?

THOREAU.

PROLEGOMENON.

A PROLEGOMENON, Proem, or Preface to any production of the human mind is defined by lexicographers to be "preliminary observations to a book," "introductory remarks or discourse prefixed to a book," or treatise informing the reader or hearer of the "main design," or whatever is necessary to the *understanding* of the discourse, book, or essay. A Preface, then, ought to be an epitome, a condensation, of the soul or substance of that which is to follow, a shadow cast before; at least a bird's-eye view of the field, or photograph under clearest light of the production itself. In the nature of things, is this possible? Can a leaf preface a tree? a tree preface a forest? or a rock preface a mountain? If the book, essay, or discourse told its own story, why a twice-told tale, in the shape of a preface, to give the "burden of its song," "main design," "introductory remarks," or whatever is necessary to the understanding of the same? To speak a word, to tell a fact, to articulate any secret of the universe, truly and forever, seems to be the great trouble with all books, essays, and discourses. "To speak and to create are one to the Infinite:" for light to be, it is only necessary to say, "Let there be light;" but for man, the finite, poor man!! when he speaks, there is mumbling and confusion; the idea and the symbol, the thought and its dress the word, can scarcely get together: his efforts to create light are generally followed by a painful visibility of his own darkness. The flirtations of the word and the spirit have always been calamitous: witness the reign of horrors and barbarisms in the history of the soul in the past, and even in the present hour, with every lantern and flambeau of the nineteenth century in full blaze of illumination. Here is ever the sad tragedy, "the pale realm of shade;" here is the dim domain of doubt and fear.

All literature seems but the record of blunders, more or less flagrant and pitiable, of the thought trying to get the fatal word. How, then, shall a preface tell the "main design" of a book, essay, or discourse, when most books, essays, and discourses fail to tell it themselves, or succeed but lamely? A preface is often a simple Oyez! to the world, admonishing all persons that there is something for sale in the shape of intellectual merchandise, of which *it* affects to *be* a more or less perfect invoice. More generally the preface appears a forlorn and scraggy creation, in the form of a supplication to the reader to have faith and go on, to screw up his courage to wade through the coming revelation, it may be of chaos and night, of heaviness and sleep; with a solemn assurance that his threshing shall not be of straw alone, but that the winnowing thereof will give some grains of wheat.

Or, again, a preface appears a sheepish, stammering apology, a gawkish, blundering prayer for forgiveness for the impertinence and folly of asking a fellow-sinner to read something that the writer knows, and blushes to feel, is not worth his perusal. More frequently it comes in the shape of a mendicant address, a bow profound, an obsequious display of flags of truce, or some show of the white feather, or acknowledgment of the presence of the carrion-crow, fear. "Authors in their prefaces generally speak in a conciliatory, deprecating tone of the critics, whom they hate and fear; as of old the Greeks spoke of the Furies as the *Eumenides*, the *Benign Goddesses*." One other very important fact about prefaces is, be they what they may, "preliminary discourses," "analytic synopses," camera-obscura pictures-IDEAL of the coming REAL, or precursors however luminous, elaborated, and useful, they are never read. It is sometimes said that the name of a book—its title-page—suggests what it is, or is redolent of its contents. This can scarcely be true; for an inspection of a catalogue of books is frequently a chapter of supremest affectations, and would carry the conviction that the names of books and their title-pages were meant to delude, and conceal the tenor of their discourses; that the genius of whim, as in many other departments, presides here also; and, that in the baptism of the crowd of intellectual infants that appear daily, rhyme and reason have seldom stood hand in hand. A happy title is a happy thing; but most books are like backgammon-boards, with "Hume's History of England" or "Shakspeare" on their backs, or like the saintly dodge of that pious, heaven-inclined soul who had his handsomely done-up leather-cased whisky-bottle arranged with "Holy Bible" on its back. Still, they say there is "magic in a name," although the rose by any other, &c. &c. In the consideration of names, title-pages, &c., is not the "Mountain" as suggestive as a "Sofa," upon which an immortal poem has been written; or a "Tub," another imperishable tale; or the "Louse," which has been the theme of an eternal song? "If it were inquired of an ingenious writer what page of his work had occasioned him most perplexity, he would point to the title-page. That curiosity which we would excite is most fastidious to gratify; yet such is the perversity of man, that a modest simplicity will fail to attract: we are only to be allured by paint and patches, and yet we complain that we are duped! It is too often with the titles of books as with those painted representations exhibited by the keepers of wild beasts; where, in general, the picture itself is more curious and interesting than the enclosed animal."

The name disposed of, and the title fixed, whilst the futility of all preface-writing is admitted, what of the production itself? what of the origin and contents of this book you call the "Mountain"? What excuse have you for imposing upon the world another calamity? Can there be any possible apology for dragging out of limbo another confusion of tongues, or attempting to make discordantly vocal another moment of the harmonious and divine silences which hold the worlds in their spells?

This is the beginning and substance of the story, also something of its "to whom related" and by whom created, of the *why* of its appearance, the *how* it came about, and the *what* it is; or a word on the advent to the Mountain, its *mission* and *motive*, with a cursory notice of some of the *beautiful experiences* involved in that crusade against disease and death. A village Doctor—the "fool of ideas," "poorly tied to a few thoughts," victimized by dreams—discovers himself to be violently seized and carried irresistibly away by a number of despotic perceptions and intense convictions; among which the self-sufficiency of the universe shone forth, and ESPECIALLY the REMEDIAL FORCES *of nature*, and her perpetually divine conatus to *restore* and *reproduce*, as by the curative powers and medicinal virtues of climates, changes of localities, with accompanying changes of *whole habitat*, of air, water, magnetism, heat, and light, of all earthly and heavenly influences upon the body, sanitary impressions of the world through the soul upon the body, of the aromal, the spiritual, as well as material and dynamic, powers of the earth, operating prophylactically and therapeutically upon that darling of Fate, man; nursing him maternally when sick, dandling him like a babe when well, and handling him like a toy perpetually; streaming *through him* like an Æolian harp, rather playing *upon* him as "a STRING of the Æolian harp of the universe." He pursues a hallucination of being an Æsculapian regenerator of his race to a distant mountain-top, the great summit-wave of the Appalachian chain,—a hydrographic axis between the waters of the Atlantic Ocean and Gulf of Mexico, and more than two thousand feet above the level of the sea; where, near a group of springs, surrounded by unbroken masses of primitive forests, he locates, and founds by legal enactment of the Legislature of Pennsylvania, a sanitarium, under the name, style, and title of the "Alleghany Mountain Health

Institute;" the object of the corporation thereby created being to purchase lands, to erect and furnish buildings, to ornament and improve grounds, for the treatment of invalids and for the enjoyment and amusement of others seeking recreation and health; also, to found a museum, library, observatory, and other facilities for the study and promotion of the natural sciences. An institution thus embracing both elements of man, *its end*, the restoration and perpetuation of the soundness of his physical frame, and the culture, development, and sanity of his soul. Thus was the infirm mind as well as diseased body, the spiritual as well as the animal man, to be represented. Not for wine-bibbers, sensual and profane persons, not for the gross and godless, not for seekers and lovers of pleasure *alone* was it to be provided, but for the sick and the suffering, the mournful wanderers in the dismal realms of the pain-world, and to whom is left only weariness of being, sorrow, and the bitter waiting for the great physician, Death. Also for the broken-hearted, the heavy-laden, the oppressed and overworked man, of whatever calling or election,—the diseased, disabled, conscript brother, with "horny hands or wrinkled brow," who with heroic will has grandly accepted the curses of existence, and dared to fight the battle of life manfully. Also the privileged brother, born with golden spoon on lip, to whom existence is a long, long summer day of delight, pleasure, *pleasure only* being the "chief end of man," but to whom also is there a ghastly compensation revealing itself, in the revenge of pound of pain for pound of pleasure, of pound of agony for pound of joy.

A home also was it to be for the wise and the gentle, the cultivated and refined, those whose bodies long for more perfect health, and whose souls also hunger for knowledge; thus offering to the human family almost the whole catalogue of good things left at the fall of man; namely, the pure elements of nature, health and soundness, books, and the joys of wisdom, including the compensation of two fruits of Paradise still growing on that "poison-tree, *the world*, sweet as the waters of life,—love, or the society of beautiful souls, and poetry, whose taste is like the immortal juice of Vishnu." In the pursuit of which idea, he invites the race to new fountains of physical redemption, sings a doctorial song of joy to suffering humanity, asserts the *claims of the mountain*, tells the story of what *it is*, and what it CAN DO; vindicates the ways of Providence to man in the shape of pure earth influences, pure water influences, and pure air influences; proclaiming also the influence of *all good* things upon man, the high, the low, the simple, the complex, the commonplace, the recondite, every-day-by-the-roadside influences, also the power of the high and divine upon the soul, and, through the soul, upon the miraculous machinery of the body. Advocates likewise the combination of all these influences. To pure mountain air and absolute water would add constant exposure to said air, with boundless swallowings of said water, accompanied by arduous walks in pine-groves, heart and brain intonated and inspired by the many-voiced concerts of the forests attuned to the "lays the wood-gods sing;" at the same time knowing surely that the catching of mountain trout must develop the capacity of eating and digesting mountain trout, that the hunting and shooting of squirrels must make the heart jump à-la-squirrel, that a gallop on horseback through the woods will gallop the troubled soul out of the slough of indigestion and despair, and into the gates of light and hope, making the "juices to career through well-strained tubes," and, consequently, to have the Sirens sing.

Thus, whilst the *body* should drink health and life from the charmed goblet of nature, could not the *soul* drink knowledge and wisdom from the fountains of thought?

Would not the excursion of the botanist develop the capacity to digest more perfectly his flowers and mosses? would not the journey of the geologist enable *him* to ASSIMILATE more absolutely his rocks and fossils? would not the mind of the bird-student *appropriate his game* in a higher and BETTER SENSE than his stomach could enjoy its flesh, whilst the overworked artist's sickly face would bloom with the life and light of the picture his hand had wrestled for, and won from the world? Concerning all of which it seemed necessary that *something* should be said. There is also another excuse or apology, an account that may be rendered, for the appearance of this rude, unkempt, uncombed story of the Mountain. Being a regular member of the Old School of medicine for many years, and thus a Priest in the sanctuary of healing, according to the unbroken apostolic descent from Hippocrates and Galen, the Hegira, or flight to the mountain, with the approaching advent of a Hospital or Health-Resort for invalids, had, as supposed by many of the brethren in the faith, an anomalous appearance, an aspect *eminently* suspicious, even rendering the author thereof obnoxious to the charge of apocryphalness in his pretensions to professional soundness. They said, "It has a *questionable shape:* it *looks like* a hydropathic arrangement. Are you really a convert to the water-cure? Have you left the regular profession, and have you ceased to practise secundum artem?" Being immaculate in the faith, and accepting with religious awe the venerable oracles of Delphi as the *true* and *only fountain* of medical inspiration, and having with zeal and piety sworn devoutly and constantly by the beard, dog, and snake of Esculapius, including, in the daily recitation of the calendar of true saints and conservators of the world, the lancet, calomel, and quinine, Spanish flies, and ipecacuanha, it became *painfully incumbent* to utter some word of explanation, some rational account, if possible, for the appearance of an unhappy doctor of medicine in a wilderness where the original elements still reigned, and sand, rocks, trees, water, and air were ALL that Nature had left as implements in the art of healing. The afflux of hydropathic advertisements, pamphlets, and even patients, gave a serious coloring to the impression that some obliquity of position in regard to the infallibility of the ancient school of medicine existed; that the ephemeral popularity among the innocent and gullible, the ignorant and frivolous, of some of the fashionable quackeries of the hour, might have *warped* and even *seduced* him from the original faith of his culture: hence, from the instinct of self-justification, self-preservation, and explication, a small flourish of trumpets, a recitation of the regular orthodox creed with upturned eyes and devout genuflexions,—in short, an explanation of his position, aims, and objects,—was demanded, and lo! the army of his haters (whose name is legion) have an answer to their prayers, "Oh that our enemy would write a book!" and thus is that same forlorn Medicus pinned to the wall to their hearts' content. The folly of thus exposing his unprotected flank, and even surrendering his pneumogastric and umbilicus to the fingers of his enemies, can only be accounted for from the fact that there are innocent and devout men, the greater number of whose original snakes, or *totally depraved faculties*, are *still fast asleep*, and who, in the thick darkness that surrounds them, are as likely to blunder, and fall into the traps and snares of satanic men, as to stand erect, or walk with precision. Included in the foregoing motives and reflections there is another suggestion, which may have been instrumental in bringing about this blunder of the Mountain. There are erected to *Priessnitz*, (an ignorant and unlettered serf,) in the United States, a large number of monuments,—that is, establishments for the "water-cure." There are but FEW country sanitaria or health-establishments under the jurisdiction of the regular profession of medicine. What does this mean? Do the gods nod? Is Olympus asleep? Is Apollo dethroned from the guardianship of the world, and has he retired again, in humility and sorrow, to watch the flocks of Admetus on the "flowery plains of Thessaly," or to wander disconsolate through the "moonlight glades of Paphos"? Have Hippocrates and Galen failed? Have the spirits who watch over the destiny of the earth become nauseated with the odor of drugs? Has the regular profession become fossilized in dead vocables, with its "shops, pestle and mortar," "dried alligators' skins stuffed, and beggarly account of empty boxes"? And is this living, fresh-budding, expanding, reproductive *Nature*, with her divine powers to regenerate and save the bodies of men, to be surrendered to quacks and idiots, who shall place to the credit of humbuggery and charlatanery the power, wisdom, and loving kindness of Almighty God, who has provided for man's sustenance, healing, and ecstasy this "world of goodness, light, and endless love"? Why shall not the regular profession, possessing the knowledge and wisdom of Nature, and holding the *only keys* which *can* unlock her mysteries and scientifically exhaust her resources, profit by her system of goodness and mercy, her scale of rewards and punishments,—reading, with veneration and love, the miraculous intelligence and morality that run hand-in-hand through all things, embracing solar systems as well as stomachs and bowels, and for whose rational elaboration and merciful administration Science stands as gentle handmaid and ministering spirit? Did not the divine Hippocrates, twenty-three hundred years ago, from the depths of his transcendent soul indite a treatise on "Airs, Waters, and Places," decided by a recent astute observer to be the "most philosophical of his works, evincing extended observation, travel, and study"? And does not this wonderful creation, at that hour of the world's progress, evince in the father of medicine an *instinct* of *the spirit* bordering on the inspiration of prophecy? "In it he inquires into the effects of the seasons, winds, and various kinds of waters, localities, nature of the soil, modes of life, and exercise, upon health, and the *necessity of a physician making himself acquainted* with *all these* matters.

"He next points out the influence of climates, and the diseases depending on differences in them. He compares the people of Europe, and especially of Greece, with those of Asia, and shows how the uniformity of the climate and the fertility of the soil in the latter induce a monotonous course of life and thought, and disinclination to exertion, in the inhabitants, who in consequence give themselves up to indolence and love of ease; whereas the Europeans, living on a poorer soil and in a climate of frequent vicissitudes, are compelled for self-protection to exert themselves in various ways, and thus acquire habits of self-reliance, and display greater courage. Hellenic pride, and consciousness of superior advantages, speak through the medical philosopher when he tells us, 'On this account the inhabitants of Europe are more warlike than the Asiatics; and also owing to their institutions, because they are not governed by kings like the latter; for where men are governed by kings there they must be very cowardly, as I have stated before,—for their souls are enslaved, and they will not readily or willingly undergo dangers in order to promote the power of another. But those that are FREE undertake dangers on their *own account*, and not for the sake of others: they court hazard and go out to meet it; for they themselves bear off the rewards of victory: and thus these institutions contribute not a little to their courage.' Ethno-climatic-MEDICAL and political teachings of this nature ought to find willing disciples among the people of the United States." And here the observation might be recorded, that the profession of medicine could certainly profit by an occasional retrospective glance into the past, and even by return to, and some gleanings of, the ancient fields, if only to demonstrate that Priessnitz, Hobensack, Hahnemann, and the whole ravens army of quackdom, have all been surrounded, and the ground preoccupied, by science and reason,—both, it may be admitted, in a state of comparative infancy in those far-off ages, and walking with somewhat tottering and uncertain steps, but still under the influence of the great and healthy instincts of the soul, and under the direction of the great ORGANIC EYE which has progressively opened, and *now* drinks in the strongest sunlight of the mind of the present hour.

This is a subject of surprise: a treatise on "Airs, Waters, and Places" has been in existence twenty-three centuries, and a world of human creatures have been groping their way through life, bowed down by the curse of a host of diseases, existence darkened and imbittered by pain and suffering from infirmities which could have been cured by the magical power of "airs, waters, and places," whose jubilant song of physical redemption had been shouted more than four hundred years before the arrival of the Christian religion upon earth; before the Nazarene youth had ravished the ear of suffering man with the melodies of his voice upon the precious problems of the "blessed life" and the salvation of the soul.

> "Were man to live coëval with the sun,
> The patriarch-pupil would be learning still."

Unhappy star-gazer! he is looking to the heavens for succor, when it is under his feet; he goes through elaborate processes of medication under renowned wisdom, or victimizes himself by the mummeries of quackery, as in the multiplex soakings and pourings of hydropathy, or the delusive efforts at swallowing the fantastic shadows-of-shades of homœopathic globules, whilst *"in every path he treads down that which doth befriend him when sickness makes him pale and wan."* Impressed with the conviction of the infinite wisdom and perfection of all things, that each object is "full of use and duty," that Nature is always man's obedient servant, and as a patient donkey will carry her liege-lord like a king, that she invites him forever to study and learn her ways, which are surely wisdom, and to obey her decalogue, which is always *peace,* and which is written in stars and grass-blades as well as blood-globules and palpitating viscera, and as clearly legible in the laws of health and disease as in sidereal systems and the soul; that man's apparent dislocation with Nature is purely accidental; that he may become a "garden in a paradise," growing with the milk of the corn, flowing with the blood of the grape; that the gulf so deep and wide is not in Nature, but in man himself; that when men are sensible and sound they shall affect the longevity of the patriarchs, and shoot the black stream as quietly and sweetly as now they "walk the waves of sleep," instead of blundering through the grim valley in an agonizing and protracted death-struggle, slowly crushed by pain; and, finally, that the human family was not created solely for evil and suffering, or eternally foreordained to endure the curse of disease and pain; that health is the birthright of every created thing, from the polypus to the man; that the condition called normal—which means perpendicular—is blessed Nature's aim and end.

"Heaven shortens not the life of man: it is *man that does it, by his own crimes.*" Consumption and dyspepsia, neuralgia and gout, mumps and measles, bilious fever and small-pox, are certainly not angels from heaven; and the inevitability undodgable, and that forever inseparable connection of *violation* of *laws* of *life and health with pain and disease,* of the *tax of suffering that must be paid* for infraction of the law by *vicious indulgence,* are written in the experiences of every hour, in every gorged stomach, in every whisky-deranged liver and brandy-boiled brain, in the slabbering salivation of tobacco, or the reekings of its smoke from the human mouth and nostrils, in bread forever sour, in meat converted into indestructible sole-leather, in insane and barbarous habits of life, or wicked murdering of the body by the whole army of devils of Depravity and Vice under the despotic drill of that savage Monkey-Queen of absurdities, Fashion, enthroned on her rocks of ages, "caste-keeping and guild-preserving," and, worst of all, the *eternizing of disease and defective development* in the process of generation profane and ungodly, presided over by the genius of sin and death,—true dust and ashes of the apples of Sodom, the words "hereditary taint" having attained a *fearful significance.* This is that sour curse of the "sins of the fathers" followed by teeth upon edge and heritages of woe in third and fourth generations. This is the true opening of the box of Pandora; this is that "rash hand that in evil hour" still stretches forth to pluck forbidden fruits and "unbar the gates of hell." Thou mayest avoid the calamities that come from heaven by publishing a sound and healthy existence, with temperance and virtue, through the laws of thy normal organization; but thou canst never escape those calamities which thou drawest upon thyself and thine offspring by the introduction of demons of disease and destruction into *thine* own body; for the human form is either a Paradise for angels and temple of the Holy Ghost, a nest of unclean birds, or a den of venomous reptiles. And this brings the recognition of the wise significance of the *uses* and *ends* of *all suffering*,—that it is a schoolmaster's rod and an instrument of goodness and love, the end proposed being the regeneration and salvation of the culprit or criminal, the *reformation* of *the offender* against the law, and thus the *creature of good*, at the same time flouting the profane doctrine of disinterested malignity on the part of the Eternal, and clearly discerning that in the divine economy for each hurt there *must* be a *heal*, for each *smart* a *salve*, for every *woe* a *balm*. Profoundly impressed and overshadowed by the immense reality of this conviction, and held firmly bound by an abiding faith in the healing influences of the *simplest and constantly present* powers of the world, this dominant idea has been pursued, hunted, enthusiastically explored, and wrestled with, until the gospel of "Airs, Waters, and Places," and their power over the human body, has become the universe. Thus one element of success shines conspicuously forth:—Faith, Faith! the soul of every real conquest of the world.

> "The lover may
> Distrust the look that steals his soul away;
> The babe may cease to think that it can play
> With heaven's rainbow; alchymists may doubt
> The shining gold their crucible gives out;
> But *Faith*,—fanatic *Faith*,—once wedded fast
> To some dear *phantom*, hugs it to the last."

The Temple, or Place for the administration and dispensation of the promises and blessings of this evangel, then, became the great desideratum. To get a "Place" with its "airs and waters" for the Sanitarium, or home of healing for all suffering and infirmity, has long been an absorbing effort, the tyrannous thought and constant fight for years, the only aim and motive of action and existence.

Devoured by this vast and overpowering enthusiasm, caught up into the vortex of a celestial ardor, in this chivalric pursuit of an ideal so transcendent, of an end so apparently unattainable, it was inevitable that fearful battles with the *hard actual*, with the material and gross, with wicked and anarchic powers, in all the mournful and wearisome details of the *real* in this vulgar work-a-day world, even mingled with elements of the tragic and marvellous, must come. In short, there must inevitably arrive the bores and tortures inseparable from the unexpected adventures of a village Leech leaving his doctorial puddle in search of benevolent and humane reformations and healing-institutions; involving also quixotic money-tilts with windmill issues, cowing of lions, blanketings, &c., not forgetting frequent collapses towards annihilation. It is a natural query, and has been often made: What could tempt a doctor to leave a bailiwick in which he enjoyed all a country practitioner could or should enjoy, or wish, or deserve to possess upon earth,—namely, common comforts of life, occasionally some money, (every one knows it was semi-occasionally!) very much more reputation and professional ascendency than he deserved,—all that a village, indeed, could give to any one who wished to be an honest worker in the ranks of the guild to which he belonged,—and go a Mazeppa-ride through wastes of hungry wolves and ravens, perhaps to eternal exile and ruin? It might relieve the inquirer slightly if he should reflect for a moment upon the amount of tragic elements in the country physician's life at best, including the whole detail of human suffering to be seen, heard, and felt, with only the hope of some fruits of reward in the shape of credits in heaven;

not to speak of mere terrestrial results, in the form of growth and development from discipline and tuition of the conflict with adversity. Although it cannot be said that village life was at all an approach to Paradise, it must be admitted that it had much in it that sinners want on earth; and much *more* than they deserve, even much more than A COUNTRY DOCTOR DESERVES, which of course, FINALLY, from all sources of conviction and belief, must be that same kingdom of everlasting blessedness.

But there was a dream in that unhappily possessed doctor's head, a monomaniacal thought, a demon idea, which took final possession of the whole mind and heart of its victim. The vision, with its accompanying prayer, shaped itself in this form:—Guardian spirits of the world! grant the power to construct on some mountain-top, some tall "heaven-kissed hill," some Alpine height of the earth's surface, above the plain of perpetual malaria, a hospital, a sanitarium, a retreat for the sick, for those who struggle with disease in the heated plains below, or in the poisoned valleys: vouchsafe this power, and, with the remedial virtues of change of air, climate, water, and exercise, *and the instrumentality of the resources of the regular art of healing*, there shall be results in the sphere of physical regeneration yet undreamed of in medical philosophies. Grant this power, answer this prayer, and judge of the tree by its fruit.

It will be easily discernible that in this enterprise there would be an enlarged sphere of professional power, a more extensive range of observation and influence than a village gave in the world of disease; with less expenditure of animal force, less exhaustion of the animal man, in the process of destroying space through the instrumentality of the horse to get to his business, which makes the laborious life and certain *premature* death of the country practitioner. This scheme of course included incidentally (and it must be acknowledged, with shame, that there was something of selfishness and sin, something of earthliness and cowardice, in this) an escape from the dismal array of tortures which only the country doctor knows: midnight rides of dreary miles in snow and rain storms; lonely struggling with the disorganizing powers of the world; the mournful tragedy of "death life overtaking" in the woodman's lonely cabin, in the ploughman's lowly cot, and the beggar's filthy sty; also, of course, the constant *single-hand fight* with the destroying angel, with none of the band of true brothers near, and the fearful responsibility of the contract to preserve life in all the details of the profession, representing every department, as the *country doctor must*, and be veritable factotum in the profession, executing the institutes of surgery, midwifery, and practice, including, at the same time, the arts of the druggist, dentist, and veterinary surgeon. With hard work, suffering, distractions, and agonies, and perhaps the worst of all experiences to bear, might be included the angry and averted face when asked for the "quid pro quo" for saving life, or the FEE for *services money* could never *pay* for executing, and which only a sense of duty could *command* any man to execute at all. To escape in some way the FULL MEASURE of suffering of a country practice, the extreme agonies and dreary wastes of horror of a country doctor's life, and at the same time to attain the clear mountain-top of a higher force professional, a larger range of power, a more extensive sphere in which to develop the heavenly functions of the art of healing; in short, from its inception the enterprise has been nothing but an enlarged projection of the *country physician's power* in the *relief* of suffering, and the *creation* of health and happiness. A doctorial project in toto, nursed in the heart and brain for years of patient vigilance and solicitude, not unmingled (as has been adverted to and acknowledged, with a sense of shame) with the more terrestrial visions of a better way to the dollar, a clearer track than the thumb-screw or torture process of extracting cents by forceps from the pockets of patients, and presenting a more direct route, as was hoped, to competency, (for here it must be acknowledged, with sorrow for humanity, that the laborer in this department is not generally considered *worthy of his hire*, but is held in profane estimation,—fearful, fatal evidence of the barbarism of the hour!—as a vulgar pill-peddler, monkey-hunter, or swabber of intestines, who should find in the *mere performance* of the interesting details and duties of his profession a sufficient and exceeding great reward for his troubles,) than the forty-and-one swops of chips and whetstones in efforts to touch the penny, in the truck-trade of a country doctor's bill-collecting; practising his art, as supposed by his patients, under the employment of the commonwealth or Heaven, whilst making his bread by his wit in other lines of business-operations, as in the intellectual and refined manœuvres of trafficking in the flesh of horses, or in the scarcely more rational efforts of making brick *without straw*,—it might be, chimerical experiments in the fabrication of lumber by steam: in short, existing by the wit and tricks of common trade or huckstering, and discharging, at the same time, the august duties of the medical profession for the pure, unmixed love of the Father of all and his wretched children, the suffering human family. It will be pardoned, then, in the grand scheme of benevolence and love of the Mountain Sanatarium, if visions of some royal highroad to fortune might have *profanely* mingled a little. Here the unhappy alas!! did and indeed *could* not foresee exactly whither that hallucination might lead him, even into waste spaces and vast abysses of suffering of all orders and degrees, but, most of all, into heart-scaldings and sorrows, in this same line of the dollar, its treacheries and despotisms. The devil seems not to have forgotten his ancient stratagem of trying experiments in the line of money-temptations on tops of mountains, or of attempting to get the dollar, (like the wedge of Achan,) a perpetual element of discord and death, into all the really good, benevolent, and heavenly operations of this lower world. The enterprise in *itself* involved the necessity of sundry and various rencounters with dangerous creatures of the financial deeps,

—awful whales and sword-fish of those bottomless pits and maelstroms of the money-power, including, of course, interesting bouts with the shark,—*the beautiful shark*,—who is the purest and most perfect symbol and representative of the poetic and ecstatic lover of the dollar for its *naked beauty*. The whale is somewhat peculiar and dainty in his appetite and shape of food, (having a gourmand's taste for the "elio borealis,") as are also some other monsters of the deep; but that omnivorous glutton, the all-loving shark, swallows promiscuously—like "Time, the hungry hyena!"—every thing, including grossest elements, but is clearest and most emphatic in his appreciation and epicurean perception of the delicacy of human flesh, which, like that kingly rascal the lion, he always prefers. Very frequent contact with this individual—*all teeth and stomach*—was necessary in the financial department of the Sanatarium, and also, of course, with his friend the pilot-fish, (scomber ductor.) This is a servile but faithful retainer, attendant, and slave of the shark, who is supposed to scent out for and report *to him* the secrets of the ocean on the subjects of garbage, carrion, and "grab-game" in general. He also seems to exercise a kind of guardianship over his sharkish excellency, (an extremely fallen form of the guardian angel,) attending him assiduously, protecting him from dangers of all kinds, fondling with him, and flattering him with devotion. Of this fidelity wonderful instances are recorded, as in the story of Captain Richards, of the Royal Navy. "A shark, attracted by a corpse that had been thrown overboard, followed the vessel. A hook was baited to catch him; but, in the language of the captain, the shark, attended by four pilot-fish, repeatedly approached the bait, and every time that he did so one of the pilots preceding him was distinctly seen from the taffrail of the ship to run his snout against the side of the shark's head to turn it away. After some further play, the fish swam off in the wake of the vessel, his dorsal fin being long distinctly visible above the water. When he had gone a considerable distance, he suddenly turned around and darted after the vessel, and, before the pilot-fish could overtake him and interpose, snapped at the bait, and was taken. In hoisting him up, one of the pilots was observed to cling to his side until he was half above water, and then fall off. All the pilot-fish then swam about for a while, as if in search of their FRIEND, with every apparent mark of anxiety and distress, and afterwards darted suddenly down into the depths of the sea."—CUVIER *Pisces*, p. 637.

Wonderful fidelity and devotion of pilot-fish and sharks, —far transcending the affections of men,—clinging together even in death!

Many persons may know a few singed rats of pettifogging lawyers in the State of Pennsylvania who would here, with their usual *affectation* of infallible cat-smartness, and *real cat* cunningness, treachery, and unholdable eel-sliminess, immediately raise the question, Was it *real love* that actuated that pilot-fish to hold on to the shark, *pure, disinterested personal affection*, or did not the shark, from the evidence of some of the facts of the case, (that *might have been adduced*,) or presumption in the case, *owe the pilot a fee?* This individual—the pilot-fish—represents with miraculous and transcendent fidelity *the legal profession*,—at least the small fry of *scaly* attorneys *always* found bumping their noses obsequiously around the shark, or *money man*.

Abundant issues with this fish and his friend the shark were destined to come off, and in due course of time came; but all this was inscrutably hidden in the future from the vision of that unfortunate doctor lost in his dreams. Having faith larger than a bushel of mustard-seed in this scheme of a Sanitarium, moving a mountain seemed no difficult affair. Sequel inevitable, if the mountain would not move—

* * * * * * * * * *

And this, very unexpectedly certainly, brought also the great tragical issues of history among the pine-roots and rocks of the Alleghany Mountains, and gave solemnity and grandeur to the apparently contemptible events of the hour, to wit: the man and his scheme of benevolence *vs.* some institution of earth under the genius of selfishness and sin; or, it might be, some consolidated power of darkness and death, of other ages, of other worlds, *vs.* light and truth, hope and mercy, progress and the soul. In connection with which, as a totally unpardonable episode, it may be remarked that, however interesting to the archæologist the history of the Middle Ages may be in the organic development of the family of man as the unit or multiplex, conservative or radical, progressive or retrospective, to meet the Middle Ages, with its claws and scales, its tusks and bristles, in the lap of the nineteenth century, with the warm, genial, life-giving sun flashing beauty, fertility, and progress through the hard old rind of the earth, (the arrow-marks pointing forward!) is not so refreshing to the soul of the man whose effort and sympathies are with *the present hour*, and whose hopes and aspirations are *in the future*.

But it was the "previous discourse" to the forthcoming story of the Mountain, and some account of the "Sanitarium," that was being indited, and not a dissertation on the philosophy of history, or even tragical glimpses into the biography of obscure and insignificant personages, forever paltry and pitiable, forever flat and mean, stale and unprofitable, the mere record of earth-troubles, conflicts with evil spirits and vulturous men, and all the wearisome details of that same thrice painful, sober, and even ghastly, actual, but *to* which the philosopher or hero cannot allude, and *of* which much less complain, without signal loss of prestige and divinity.

It scarcely remains to be determined, now, that the establishment of a Sanitarium on the summit of the Alleghany Mountains is not an impossible dream, delusion, or folly, but a glorious substance and reality, full of blessings for suffering man. Can it be said to be premature as a project, or insane as an idea? does it fill the needs of the hour, endorsed by *common sense?* and is it to be furthered, advanced, and published to the world, in the proportions of the vision in the soul, as a *success*, or to drop, half developed, half *made up*, or even *still-born*, into the silence of oblivion? As a project, philanthropic, benevolent, and at *first sight* not having in it the *bone* and muscle of a *common business-enterprise*, must it share the fate of all efforts to bless, regenerate, and save the rebellious savage, man, from sin and degradation, disease and death? Will no enterprise live on earth for the good of humanity unconnected with the *curse* of *gain?* Will men endorse nothing but projects that have three per cent. a month in them secured by real estate? Will they engage heartily in nothing except the organization and creation of cunningly-devised institutions to catch each other, and by which the head-man—the *cunning, sharp man*, whose symbol is the fox—shall subjugate the hand-man, or innocent "creator in the finite," whose symbol is the patient ox bowing his neck to the yoke? And in a world that has been praying for long hundreds of years for the kingdom of heaven to come, that the Great Will might be done on earth as it is in those blissful abodes, and where philosophers and prophets, seers and saints, have heralded the advent of all orders of millenniums, with the reign of peace and good-will, of mercy and love,—will it come at last that men and angels shall tremble to behold the *Dollar* "a solitary God, over ghastly ruin frowning forever from his throne"? Will nothing that has the soul in it succeed on this planet? Have men SWORN to propagate evil and disease only, viciously and insanely hazarding the permanent and eternal degradation of their race? Will no human being try the experiment of publishing a clean and normal life of the body and *heavenly* life of the soul, with soundness of one, and some *disinterested* benevolence in the other? Is the element of *mutual antagonism* and *selfishness* the wax that *sticks* and *holds* the world together, whilst the "love of the neighbor," the "self-denial and renunciation," the kingdom of heaven and its righteousness, which are always to be FIRST, are antediluvian fogyisms, too slow and simple for the rapidly-rushing (*progressive*, *as they are called!*) *man* and social compact of the present hour?

After a life of sorrowful struggling for his race, the melancholy Pestalozzi, whose formula of salvation for man was universal education, was forced to say, "I learned that no man in God's wide earth is either *willing* or *able* to help another man." The good and honest Sandy Mackaye was equally unsuccessful, during his pilgrimage, in finding the heavenly man. He says, "Dinna spier what I believe in: I canna tell ye. I've been seventy years trying to believe in God, and to meet anither man that believed in him: so I am just like the Quaker o' the town o' Redcross, that met *by himsel'* every first day in his ain hoose." The good * * * * also wails, "I have hunted in vain for forty years to find one man who really believed in God, and proved it by loving his neighbor *half as well as himself;* or who would, either from impulse or a sense of duty, do *any thing* for his brother man without the desire of being *paid for it.*" Terrestrial croakers, whose abdomens are near the sod, say that no project that had in it either benevolence or love ever succeeded at all, or was ever enjoyed or realized by its author; that the wicked are *sure* to reap the crops and harvest the labor of the righteous; and that satanic spirits have still their ancient desire to crawl into paradises prepared for angels and men. Passing strange and inconceivable seem the decrees of the Eternal. Did it really *require* the martyrdom of the Divine Carpenter to found a "CHRISTENDOM," with safe and comfortable sea-room, in which money dragons alone could flourish,—(the *only order of creatures he hated whilst upon earth,*)—and has it veritably come to pass that "the sole bond between man and man is cash payment," that the highest achievements of civilization are the issues of money *vs.* love, money *vs.* virtue, money *vs.* blood, and money *vs.* the soul, and that money, as in the case of the thirty pieces of silver given to the only sharp business-man of the Twelve, always *must* win, whilst the noble endowments of generosity and faith in man, and the divine instinct of self-sacrifice, necessarily become curses amidst the treacheries and villanies of men, and that the philanthropist must forever continue to bleed in the future, as he has done in the past, for the good of mankind?

The Mountain Sanitarium, with its overtures of healing and salvation, must not subtend this fatal angle, must not succumb to the evil genius of humanity, must not postpone its promises of joy to the reign of baleful enchantments, or be profaned by vulgarity and sin to gross and common purposes. The faithful have trusted that this could never be; but sometimes, especially in the disastrous approach of the recent oscillations of the earthquake-wave which has shivered the crust of the financial world, somewhat cracked and tottering, *partially* eclipsed, hid slightly in the signless Inane, were its fate and destiny.

In the mean time, with great suffering, great results have been achieved, jostlings and difficulties have occurred and been transcended, rough and ugly places in the road have been passed, fierce battles have been fought with the sordid and benighted, especially in that howling wilderness of doleful things called "*The Law*." This, of course, necessitated occasional contact and companionship (followed, as ever, by somewhat disastrous results) with common publicans and sinners, also frequently the more agreeable communion with those inspirers of hope and solid rocks of anchorage for the troubled, the members of the legal profession, to be followed by vast but somewhat questionable spiritual expansions, inseparable from intercourse with this order of beings, including numberless developments of the vulpine instincts and marauding faculties, (omitting, fortunately, to the great joy of the guardian angel of one soul, the horrors of euchre, cigars, and snuff,—three of the highest intellectual indulgences and moral disciplines of this guild,) coming as fruit natural and inevitable of the tuition of renowned barristers carrying the culture and light, the sharpness and wisdom, of ages in their heads, as well as with smaller fish of the same scale, who carry the still more enormous weight of their own self-sufficiency.

Thus it has come that wheel-within-wheel-to-the-infinite difficulties of legal labyrinths have been threaded through; gordian knots, twisted by legal quibblers, have been untied, or cut through, by legal gentlemen; crotchet within crotchet, dead fall below dead fall, of small-potato attorney-logic have been dissected to the light of day, and whole nests of vipers' eggs destroyed. Verily, this entirely fascinating game of eels in the mud, of bore *vs.* boree, plucker *vs.* pluckee, in all its exquisite details, has been agonizingly squirmed and wriggled through. This involved frequent and ferocious skirmishes before that august potentate, the country justice of the peace, a gorgeous but fatal Juggernaut, in whose presence, and compared with whose overwhelming consciousness of grandeur and assumption of power and self-importance, all forms of the tyrant man submerge instantly. Then came · the more formidable array of the regular legal battle of saws, coming down from the ancients, from other men, under other forms of government, under other circumstances, and in other conditions of human society, but still with the solemnity and awful paraphernalia of obsolete abstractions and dusty rags of the graves of buried formulæ, under the overshadowing dignity of the presidency of courts and juries, in the assumption of the administration of that attribute of the Eternal called Justice. This sublime consummation upon earth is supposed to be fully attained and executed when twelve bean-bags—that is, twelve drowsy men, rudimentary, unlettered, with half-born spiritual bodies, faculties still in chaos, but with their *natural bodies* stuffed with sour-crout, pork, and beans, ruminating upon tobacco-quids, and moping like melancholy owls over a frog-pond—are squeezed into a jury-box, and are silently and grandly brooded over by a trinity of buzzards, also with gorged stomachs, sleeping profoundly on a roost called "the Judges' Bench," whilst the kennel of dogs, "hell-hounds of justice," mongrel pups and "curs of low degree," are permitted to snarl, snap their teeth, and howl,—the crowd of fascinated spectators around this kennel in the mean time being kept under abeyance by that magical wand, the pole of the tipstaff. This is salvation through the *intellect* and *morale* of the jury-box and bench, in legal parlance yclept Courts of Judicatory, supposed to be a close adumbration to the modus operandi of the Divine Being in his jurisdiction of the Universe, and consequently the *most infallible mode* of adjusting difficulties between man and man, and the grandest achievement of that highest and last phasis of development or expansion of the human race *called civilization*, and of whose duration forever there is no doubt in any lawyer's head, or despair in his stomach.

Through this dismal swamp of juridical solecisms years have been sadly and mournfully wandered away, the blind leading the blind an agonizing exodus through dreary wastes of deserts, in the vain and futile effort as potter in that wretched "quicksilver, human clay;" also at squaring circles, making hills without hollows, and other impossibilities to God himself, including interesting endeavors at "shovelling sunshine into shade upon a rainy day;" but, most absurd *of all*, the effort to get, by any earthly appliance or manœuvre yet invented, a bona-fide dollar's worth of work for *three actual dollars paid*, out of any private or even commissioned officer of the rascally brigade of the army of refractory Caucasian men (no division of the more tractable African forces extending in that direction) operating in the wilderness which was to be made to blossom as the rose. Add to these abortive efforts also "will-o'-the-wisp" hunts to get some solid points of fixity in the bottomless quagmires and quicksand-under-quicksand uncertainties of Alleghany Mountain land-titles, with frequent results in the highly-interesting neighborhood of ZERO, and also with occasional culminations truly astonishing to all rational beings,—even decisions of Supreme Courts and "venire de novos." To this classical gymnastics of the soul, "bleeding footprints to the temple of perfection," all absolutely necessary to develop a "man of 'cute parts and polished understanding," called a "business-man," ADD wear and tear of heart, crucifixion of sensibility, disappointment and despair, making life a "galling load, a long, a rough, a weary road," from the enormous promises of friendship, the dwarfish and ignominious failure, the seductive ideal, the INFERNAL REAL, the cold water of the faithless perpetually dropping, the gross weight of sand-bags constantly dragging downwards, the brutal defamation of malignant and unprincipled enemies, venomous scorpions, poisoning the air and putting obstructions in the path, turning life's wine to vinegar, its milk to gall; whilst a crowd of infidels to the progressive expansion of the universe have appeared in the arena with averted faces, shrivelled hearts, and fists eternally shut upon the penny,— wretches without faith or hope, but with the snout of a grovelling selfishness held fast in the mire of the earth. And then there came in due course of heavenly experiences the play of that lovely instinct which man possesses in common with inferior animals, with whom he still delights to "hold his bonds of ancient alliance," and which is constantly observable in herds of buffalo and deer, more *especially in packs of wolves*,—that, with the first appearance of a limp in an unfortunate brother, the whole herd attack and destroy without mercy the wretch who *dares to be lame*. It is also said to be true that "in the woods the leopard knows his kind, the tiger preys not on the tiger's brood, and that man *only* is the uncompromising foe of man." "For our enemies God keeps a standing army: we can manage them: but may the merciful Heavens protect and defend us from *our friends!*"

Was the glory or wretchedness, the majesty or meanness, of the universe to unveil itself to the soul? was fate intent upon developing a misanthrope or unfolding a philanthropist? was *love* or *hate* finally to prevail? Why the

Alleghany Mountain was to become a Golgotha or place of skulls, to be wandered sadly through, instead of "a pleasant walk across the fields of barley;" why, the torments of death were given as a reward for pursuing benevolent aspirations; why gall and wormwood were added in such profusion, and "mene tekel" was written over so much of human nature that appeared divine, so much that SEEMED AMBROSIAL AND ETERNAL; and why, with the threatened down-rushing of material interests, the spiritual should fail, and friendship, love, even common sympathy, should totter and pale, should fade away and perish, and despair would come to be the only comforter, —must ever remain somewhat inexplicable to the purblind sinner charitably supposed to be still in the gall of bitterness and the bonds of iniquity.

Have any of your friends, when you intimated the need of a favor, turned a cold shoulder to you and said, "No; it serves you right: you *ought never to have tasted whisky*,"— perhaps emphasizing some other peccadillo having existence only in their imaginations,—justifying their brutal heartlessness by an agile dodge, the reference to your supposed infirmities being made with an evident chuckle of self-gratulation? These, you will find, are of the ornamental form of the genus amicus or friend; elegant fellows for sunshiny days, harvest-homes, and good times: they grow on every bough. The tough old human blood-and-soul form, sound through weal and woe, through good and bad report, to the bitter end loving and blessing, is not so abundant, but still extant,—a rare bird, alas!—but on hand occasionally for the "tug and the tussle," thanks to the great God of the gods. "Is it in mere death that men *die most?*" Does it not come as bitterest mockery that

"The beautiful seems right
By force of beauty; and *the feeble wrong
By cause of weakness*,"
  and that
"Power is justified,
Though arm'd against St. Michael"?

It were vain, perhaps, to inquire just what ARE the ultimate *moral expansions* derived from the experiences of ingratitude,—a savage axe to the root of the natural man, it seems, but hardest of all to bear, and without redress except the brute's joy of vindictiveness and revenge.

> "The world well known will give our hearts to God,
> Or make us devils, *long* before we die."

Ingratitude is the crime of fiends, and stands alone, abhorred by the meanest worm as well as angel and man. In the thirty-ninth Olympiad, Dracon the Athenian instituted a code of laws so exceedingly rigorous that Herodicus and Damades remarked that "his laws were not those of a *man*, but a *dragon*, [Δραχων,] and that they were not written in ink, but *in blood*." Nevertheless, this Dracon was a sensible man; and although his name is proverbially associated with laws considered vindictive and brutal, yet for the NEEDS of the age they were perfect,—*his laws* being, in his own words, "instruments *for appeasing the anger of the Gods, moral guilt* being the *sole rule of punishment*."

Some of his enactments should be in all codes to this hour, and are certainly divine. He made the punishment of *ingratitude* death, feeling in his soul that eternal truth,—

> "And still on the words of the bard keep a fix'd eye,
> "Ingratum si dixeris omnia dixti,'"—

knowing surely that the man who was capable of INGRATITUDE was capable of *all crime*, and, ipso facto, *worthy of death*.

This is a *verdict of the soul, and forever right*. The laws of the present moment, in their blind and stupid groping after justice, scarcely knowing right hand from left, take fierce revenge for the stealing of the purse; but for the *stealthy stab* of the GOOD NAME, or the treacherous, silent *assassination* of the trusting, sleeping heart, they have no prison or death. They make honorable restitution to the maltreated dollar, but for *faith destroyed* in a brother man's character have no atonement,—"taking savage cognizance of the dagger which slays the *body*, but having no retribution for the *murder* of the *soul*." The wise Dracon went behind the act, and saw in the fountain of the spirit the true causal force of *all acts*, the true origin of all crimes, the perverted elements of fallen humanity; and, as the man who was capable of *ingratitude* was capable of *any crime*, he punished it with *death*. Sound!

The human family have suffered ever since the repeal of this code of Dracon. If virtue is really its *own reward* in the regular decrees of the Eternal, it would seem diabolical bribery and treachery to permit a crime so atrocious as ingratitude to escape condemnation and wrath; and for the law-maker of this time to pass it over without some fearful penalty is to endorse the iniquity of Satan, the enemies of man, and the powers that struggle to destroy the world.

From all of which conflicting chaoses and diabolical experiences came there no fruits, came there no achievements, no results, and was it all suffering? Were there no sequestered spots by the dusty wayside in this struggle, no fresh and dewy meads of hope and consolation, no " fair Rosetta vales," with sparkling waters, where the soul could rest for a weary hour, "the world forgetting, by the world forgot"? Have there been no *progressive friends* to encourage, no souls of "faith, hope, and charity" to inspire confidence, no lovers of the light and beauty of Nature to whisper the peace of sympathy? Have there been no BELIEVERS in the rationality and *good sense* of this *healing project*, of this healing world? Has the Mountain not told its story of fate already? Have not the pale faces of suffering infants been made radiant? have not the countenances of jaded and overworked men become bright and hopeful, whilst bleached and bloodless women have been made to bloom with life and strength from its health-founts, and the ends of the great " primary antagonism of the world," or that of "spirit and matter," of "centre and periphery," of that lofty and "heavenly irradiation" in which the mystery of creation lies concealed, have been beautifully consummated?

In this protracted struggle to achieve a great and beneficent end has there been no support of the wise and generous, have there been no receivers of the truths of righteousness, sound men and good, spirits of faith and friendship, hearts of confidence and trust? To say so would be to ignore the majesty of man, the brightest and purest experiences of existence in genuine friendship and sympathy, and to perpetrate a libel upon the wisdom and goodness of the Infinite unpardonable forever.

And here justice demands that a few statements shall be made, "contrary to *all* experience, and *yet true*," but so entirely incredible that some explanation might seem to be required, as all transcendental affirmations at first hearing are insane. Unutterably astonishing, then, and passing all understanding, as it may appear, especially to small politicians of the "genus croaker," *even* a Corporation with a *soul has been found*, a colossal sea-serpent with human blood in its veins and a human heart beating beneath its scaly ribs. And, what may be equally—*nay, still more*—astounding, in the representative man, the very "figure-head" of this "*monster monopoly*," (favorite phrase in political bugbear-twaddle,) instead of the poison-fangs of the copper-head, the claws of the tiger, or the hide of the rhinoceros, there have been found firm and gentle manhood, wisdom and rectitude, honor and friendship, philanthropy, and world-wide, generous, humanitary sympathies. All of which would fix *emphatically* a *new* and *significant sign* of the times, an augury auspicious, carrying hope and inspiration to the humble and humane workers in the vineyard of the Lord, with the assurance that the dollar is not yet *entirely under* the influence of *the devil*. This corporation, which has been howled against by hungry and disappointed politicians as an immeasurable sponge, into whose interstices the commonwealth was to be suddenly absorbed, but the existence of which the historian and statistician will record as a high-water mark of progress, and its achievements the crowning glory of the State, seems *now* to have become (strangely enough to the ravens who croaked) a steadfast anchor, a haven of *safety*, in the reign of financial chaos, amidst the down-rushing fragments of shivered commercial balloons, exploded paper simulacra, and moribund formulæ of the dollar. This beneficent *monopoly*,—surely with persistent energy and wisdom, has achieved *one of the wonders of its age*, perforating and cleaving mountains as by the fabled throes of the Titans, filling and bridging valleys as by the cosmical masonry of the Cyclops, making smooth the rough and straight the crooked ways, carrying that "magician-wand" the railroad-bar, realized dream of the fires and forges of Vulcan, from the tide of the Atlantic Ocean into the great interior Valley of the Mississippi, by the labor of armies of men and horses and cost of millions of dollars, climbing an accumulated elevation of thousands of feet through an endless range of rugged hills and heights separated by deep-washed ravines and valleys, thus inviting the East and the West to *foregather* and unite hands in the commercial marriage of two sides of a continent on the great culminating-crest of the Appalachian chain. This power, directed by the far-reaching sagacity and transcendent business tact of a distinguished Chief, endorsed by the characteristic philanthropy of the City of Friends, with zeal forever alive and intelligent, has caught the significance of the Alleghany Mountain as the site of an Institution full of promise to suffering man, securing all points of interest and beauty, and representing all elements of life and health, as a great magazine of conservative power *antagonizing* the destroying influences of the city and offering bodily renovation and soundness in opposition to disease and death, and promised, with open eye, heart, and hand, to extend a generous help to the "Mountain Sanitarium," and say to the enemies of Heaven and humanity, in their efforts to postpone forever the advent of the perfections and felicities, *Thus far shalt thou go, and no farther.*

Having waved a charitable and tender farewell (after the cheap and accidental contracts of the hour) to the parasites who flattered and fawned, sucked blood, and then betrayed the confidence of friendship,—to the knaves who crawled in to plunder, and, like the frozen viper of the fable, thawed to life, *stung* FIRST *the breast that* WARMED THEM,—to the *ignoble and cruel,* upon whose heads rests the curse of *ingratitude,*—to the oblique and sinister "slimy things that crawl with legs," who have been guilty of treason to the amenities of life and assassination of the holiest instincts of humanity, not to speak of flagrant infractions of the laws of common honesty, consequently whose moral elements are chaos, treachery, and death,—the consolation comes in the discovery of the angelic society in which sufferers and victims of the *machinations* of evil spirits are always found; that it is good to be hated by the mean and cowardly, that rats and reptiles by affinity love rats and reptiles, and bad men by attraction *mix* with *bad* men, good with good.

Then it is WELL for the obscure and humble, the vilified and despitefully-used, to reflect that true benefactors and lovers of the race have always been the targets for the HATERS and the malignant; that all men cursed with the self-sacrificing impulses of the soul and zeal for realizing ideals must *continue* to suffer as the martyrs of faith, science, and sentiment of all ages *have done.*

The great and good Linnæus, in his scientific labors for the well-being of man, made the confession, "I must surely admit that, as I have wandered [in scientific pursuits] through the forests of the world, the monkeys [*meaning ignorant* and *wicked men*] have constantly grinned, chattered their teeth, and laughed at my efforts, even throwing stones and clubs at me: still was I happy,— knowing that I did a good thing, and that the *world* even would approve, when it LEARNED TO UNDERSTAND."

After all, it would surely be a broken-hearted and mournful man who could say, *All men are bad; I hate them all* and distrust the world: I have fought for long years ferociously the doctrine of *total depravity*, but at last I surrender. "There is none that doeth good, *no, not one.*" "Behold, I was shapen in iniquity, and in sin did my mother conceive me."

> "There is no man of Nature's worth
> In the circle of the earth;
> And to mine eye the vast skies fall,
> Dire and satirical,
> On clucking hens and prating fools,
> On thieves, on drudges, and on dolls.
> And I can say to the Most High,
> 'Godhead! all this astronomy,
> And fate, and practice, and invention,
> Strong art, and beautiful pretension,
> This radiant pomp of sun and star,
> Throes that were, and worlds that are,
> Behold! are in vain, and in vain;
> And Nature has miscarried wholly
> Into failure, into folly.'"

Rather say to this disconsolate and hopeless soul,—

> "Alas! THINE is the bankruptcy
> *Blessed Nature so to see.*"

Having no heroic determination on hand *seriously* to reinstitute the WHOLE *code of Dracon*, but only that enactment punishing ingratitude with death,—having no essay to write on "original sin" or the refreshing and ambrosial doctrine of "eternal reprobation," no additions to offer to the Ten Commandments, (unless it might be that eleventh commandment suggested by the progress and NEEDS of the times, and which, critically considered, is the sum and substance of all the rest,—viz.: Thou shalt attend to thine own business and allow thy neighbor to attend to his; for the Lord thy God hath sometimes made *rich* those who were found attending to their own concerns, but will not bless with prosperity, or even hold guiltless, sinners who give themselves exclusively to the affairs of their neighbors,) —having no ambition to improve the "sayings of the Seven Wise Men of Greece" or "the similitudes of Demophilus," —having no patent-extension reforms to suggest to the morals or maxims of Confucius, including the "eighteen sacred *edicts of the Chinese*," no hydrostatic force or elements of gravity and decorum to offer to the oracles of Zoroaster, or special wrinkles of sanctity to impose upon the theology of the Phœnicians, or even scientific critiques to make on the "Cosmogony of Sanchoniatho," or poetical splurges on "the moral grandeur and sublimity of the Bhagvat-Geeta," and especially no additional wailings to affix to the "Lamentations of Jeremiah," much less " Odes to Dejection to compose," not to speak of alligators' eggs either to break or hatch, or rats to pet or poison,—but only a few RESPONSIVE SHOUTS to make from the Alleghany Mountain top in answer to numerous inquiries:—Where are you? what are you about? HOW did you GET THERE? what ENDS do you propose? what have you DONE? what particular landing does the Infinite expect to make through YOUR manipulations on the Appalachians? and *how do you* THINK, really, you are making out *yourself?*

Let it be resolved that dogs, as it is their nature too, "shall delight to *bark and bite;*" that Satans shall *howl* their *rages out;* that because *things are so* they *shall be so, and not otherwise;* that ancient feminines shall continue to drink tea and say *what they please* about their neighbors; and that "little men with little souls shall still say, Little souls, let us try, try,"—not forgetting that, " till you hedge in the sky, starlings will fly, and evil tongues will not refrain from God himself."

And, further, let it be resolved that there is a wide difference between the heaven-intoxicated victim of a beautiful dream full of benign promises and good ends to man, and efforts to carry them out by the organization and construction of hospitals and institutions of learning, and being the author of man-traps baited with whisky and fun, operating as a vulgar builder on the common principles of money speculations, of taverns, hotels, or summer resorts for brandy-suckers and hunters of good times, or bear-pens for the regular worship of the devil.

And, further, that the space is infinitely extended between the physician, or healing man, set apart by the sacredness of his calling from the ordinary motives and pursuits of men, with his prayers for the suffering, and his aspirations to cure the sick and infirm, to save men from disease and death and give them comfort and health, and the profane stuffer of the human intestine with vulgar viands barbarously tortured, and poisonous liquors villanously compounded, the whole system promulgated on the common tricks of the trade of the most profitable and economical feeding and swelling of swine for money alone; and especially must it be entirely obvious, even to a "wayfaring man, though a fool," that said physician, or projector of Hospitals or Healing Institutions as part of the special strategy of the regular profession of medicine in its efforts to surround the Author of evil and his "regiments of the line," must be immeasurably removed from the shadow of suspicion of being implicated, or in any way compromised, as a stool-pigeon, or decoy-duck, for the seduction or inveiglement of friends *particularly*, and the world in general, into said whisky-traps or pigeon-nets, to be plucked by the vandal man-feeders of the same.

Episode unpardonable No. 2. Have you ever approached, with burning throat and parched lips, a clear, cool, mountain-spring to take a drink, when—bolt!—a bull-frog pitches into the spring, and kicks, squirms, and flounders round until the clear spring is a mud-puddle, and in your agonies you see nothing but muddy water to mock your thirst? You ask, What is he after? why muddy the whole spring? His frogship is simply endeavoring to CONCEAL by the mud he stirs up his ugly form, and spoil the spring for *your use*, supposing, no doubt, that the *spring belongs to him*. The man-feeders, or rather *man-eaters,* of the "Health Institute" have thus far followed the example of the frog, and been found quietly concealed in the mud they had kicked up for the purpose of concealing their own rascality,—said mud and trouble to be charged to the general account of "Sundries" of the institution, and the blunders and *misplaced confidences* of its unhappy Author.

And, still further, let it be resolved that, besides the issues of honesty and truth in making a fair pronunciamento and declaration of ends, motives, and designs in terrestrial operations, it is a laudable desire in human nature to set itself right on *all questions,* to escape the odium of the imputation of softness or verdancy, a veritable effort of *instinct* to avoid the calamity of being misunderstood, or split on the rock of fools, or caught, like the hare in the race with the tortoise, sleeping, when the *race could have been* so easily *won,* and thus a natural aspiration toward common sense and reason, and in all things of being acquitted of the charge of absolute fatuity or mental obtuseness, not to speak of being made sound on the more delicate questions of justice and righteousness, of honor and manhood.

And let it be still further resolved, in the mean time, that the prayers of the righteous shall ascend forever, that the kingdom of heaven shall descend in the shape of the perfectly-published, exquisitely-arranged, and totally-appurtenanced, Health Institute or Mountain Sanitarium. Taking all past troubles as innocent experiments on the quality of metal, practical jokes on the part of the supernals at the expense of the most amiable soul now working out its sad duration rapidly in the thongs of the flesh,—permitting the sand-bags to repose, and "leaving the dead to bury the dead,"—it is well ever to grasp the hand of the true man, to progress and grow, to trust and fight, to fight and trust, and in the mean time the Mountain and its claims stand a clearly-pronounced excuse for their own appearance, a sufficiently patent manifestation of the grace and grandeur of the Eternal, to be admitted to a hearing without special plea, and to fill the formulæ of the ends of Divine Love and Divine Wisdom in the universal economy.

Which also being taken for granted and held in the clear light of a revelation, it is fully apparent that it is chiefly in its aspects of benignity, and its promises of good to humanity, that the Mountain asserts its claim to the consideration of men. Those rushing streams of purest water, those ever-green solitudes of piny forests fresh with the verdure of immortal youth, those mountain-heights bathed by the waves of an ocean of air unmingled with an earthly taint and pure as ether, are surely not meant to fade and pass away as the fantastically-arranged *phenomenal*, to vanish as useless visions and cloud-pictures in the sky, or shimmer as ornamental appendages for dramatic purposes, floating on the artist's easel only, in a world of soberest uses and savagest realities, with the single apology that "beauty is its own excuse for being. NOTHING WE SEE BUT MEANS OUR GOOD." Mingled ever with the radiant form of the beautiful is the earnest and sober dowdyism of the useful and necessary. Use, *use* in *all things* would seem in certain attitudes of Nature to be her only object; for "*all the goods which exist* are *called uses,* and by these uses are meant all things which appear upon the earth,—as animals of every kind, vegetables of every kind, nourishment, clothing, habitation, recreation, delight, *protection,* and *preservation.*" Under the despotism of *this light,* insignificant seem all other aspects of things: this is the fierce realization which all men and animals make of the world, and to whose tyrannizing instincts the earth has no *other end.* To the consciousness of most men, the homely mantle of utilitarianism covers all things, and of other or higher purposes in existence there are simply none.

But the globe is round, the atom is round, and Nature revels in spheres; and to take, as representative integers, arcs of her circles or segments of her orbs, is to lose the unity of her purpose, the totality of her end, to avert the grandeur of her face and pervert the integrity and symmetry of her meaning. Thus Nature exists for the health and rectitude of *both body and soul,* for the highest as well as the lowest, *for time and forever.* Mere utilitarianism, then, cannot be all. The world will not resolve itself into a chapter of economics alone. This organic globe, travelling through azure spaces, related with perfect harmony and eternal laws to solar and sidereal systems, is certainly too richly furnished with forms of beauty, with elements of grace and light, of joy and sweetness, to have been designed for a kitchen or barn, a warehouse or machine-shop.

Ever in the din and clangor of its mechanisms, the monotonous homeliness of its utilities, steal in the far-off symphonies of a profounder world of attractions,—"a deeper music, whose tones are ideas,"—a world made aromatic and divine by the Beautiful as well as great and glorious by the Good and the True. Whilst the Mountain invigorates and regenerates the outward man by its healthful powers and restorative influences upon the body, it can also feed the inner man, and give vitality to the streams and currents of spiritual forces that descend from the Infinite to the soul, and by sanity and reason nourish and save them both. The influence of Nature, aside from economics, is to love and worship, through veneration of what is high and holy in the universe, as well as to bless by the affections through objects of sweetness and purity in the sphere of taste and beauty. As the world stands an exponent of the Eternal Mind, "whom Nature veils, clothes, and manifests," now "vocal in a tone, now visible in a gleam," the Mountain still must be the highest thought, the strongest will, the deepest love. Its promises, then, come a song of joy, with a voice of hope and a word of peace for all the children of men.

Here the overworked artist and artisan from the confined air of the city, the care-eaten merchant, the charred and lacerated banker, the wan and feverish man of books and thought, the exhausted professional slave, the haggard hunter of pleasure, can come, and in the depths of original forests, in the presence of the loveliest and grandest forms of Nature, and under the ecstasy and healing of her divine wings, again fall into the "charmed circle" of life and health. In bountiful profusion the saving elements are here poured forth; and the victim of disease and suffering, of care and pain, can drink healing and happiness, soundness and strength, from exhaustless fountains, and both body and soul be delivered from the tyranny of the "gloomy powers which reign in tainted sepulchres" and a sinful world.

It is obvious, then, that some shape of Bill of Fare for this same soul and body was necessary to be rendered,—some statement of the availables of the Mountain in all its aspects of use, health, beauty, and teaching, or worship, ecstasy, progress, and salvation. Thus, of course, there would be demanded a recitation of "what Heaven had done for that delicious land," what the Earth-spirit meant when that patch of the "garment thou readest" was woven, something of this "fragment of the broad creation," "this divine improvization," some song of its *what*, its *where*, its *wherefore*. Clearly devolving, then, was some account of the Mountain, of its science or Natural History, of its final cause, or end for which created, or Supernatural History.

Commencing at the foundation must come the book "Atlas," the great mountain, the great mountain-holder, the great heaven-holder,—he " whose brawny back supports the starry skies, whose head with piny forests crowned." Hence the " Geology of the Mountain" was necessary, as the basis or substratum of its story,—*the skeleton*, the great primordial framework, of its wondrous body.

Naturally upon this would come the enveloping mineral mass, earth-cloak, or integument of the same,—that is, the *Soil*. Then the circulating fluids would attract attention, and the story of the Waters, mineral, thermal, and pure, would appear in due order of sequence. In the chain of rational connection with this would follow the "Flora," the plant or vegetable life-clothing of the mountain, which is again dependent upon the soil, water, climate, &c. of the same,—associated with all of which would arrive a chapter of its "Fauna," or animal life.

A catalogue of animals—namely, mammals, birds, reptiles, and fishes—which inhabit the mountain, or a hurried enumeration of the different orders of creation in that department, would be required.

Then would arrive the consideration of the ocean of air above, upon which all created things depend,—the great medium of existence, the reservoir of vitality or life-currents; for, as "all life comes from the sea," so the sea itself, in the "nebular theories" of philosophers, came from the air. The story of this air-ocean, its MACHINERY, as they call it, its *organization*, or systematic order of movements, as vital to the planet, to animal, to vegetable,—to all living things,—would constitute the "Climatology of the Mountain." Succeeding this would come the aspect of the same as a great SANITARY CREATION, an immeasurable depository of healing forces, curative agencies, acknowledged therapeutic powers in every shape,—as the great exponent of all which elements of the world stands the son of Apollo and Coronis, the laurel-crowned god of physic and physicians, "Æsculapius."

It occurred that a book in his name, dedicated to him as a votive offering, would be the end fulfilled, would be appropriate and comely, would be an expression of the fitness and perfection of things. The fables of his life point to him as the "personification of the healing powers of Nature," in the formula of the God as physician, the function and end of whose existence is health, physical regeneration, and well-being,—the God who uses the world as an hospital, and to whom all objects *must* classify themselves as medicinal or not-medicinal, plus or minus in the scale of healing properties, the world simply existing for the *ends* of health and ecstasy, or soundness and the enjoyment thereof, and *no other*. Thus, a book dedicated to the God of medicine was necessary to a full expression of the attitudes of the Mountain to man, also as *definitive of the position of the healing man*, the truly honest, science-abiding, reason-directed Physician, using *all things to achieve his ends,—nature, art, all substances, all forces, all matter, all spirit, ponderable elements, imponderable agents.*

It occurred as pertinent in the present apparently disastrous aspect of the medical world, split, as it seems to outside observers, into warring factions or squabbling schools, into orthodox and heterodox, regular and quack, to say, once for all, that there is but *one school, one regular profession, one orthodox church of science,* and that is the *old,* which is also the *new,*—embracing and surrounding *all other pretences, ignoring all other affectations* of knowledge,—to wit: the *regular scientific knowledge of man,* commencing with the anatomy of the human body, which must be the "future grammar of every school which gives real instruction to mankind." Embracing also all existences surrounding it in the shape of the influences of the earth and its furniture, material and dynamic agencies,—in short, *all the related natural sciences,* which, of course, comprise those elements of knowledge that have been grouped, from time immemorial, under the head of *Medical Science* and practice as advocated by the ancient brotherhood, *appropriately called the Regular Profession.*

The story of the Doctor, or representative healing man, and his connection with the Mountain, would naturally arrange itself in the form and substance of the chapter "Æsculapius."

Then there are fables of the primitive vigor of man, of the terrible strength of Samson and Hercules, of human lives almost indestructible, stretching into long hundreds of years, as in the proximate immortality of the body of Methuselah and the wellnigh invulnerability of the form of Achilles, all of which would typify a splendor and perfection of his physical nature now unknown and beyond belief or aspiration.

Is the present squalor or walking catalogue of disease and infirmity to be superseded by a more perfect incarnation of the soul? is the present loafer—the "eat-all, do-nothing"—to be succeeded by the normal and sound man, with erect body and determined will, whose works and labors shall shine as the acts of apostles and demigods of history?

There are hopes for humanity which have taken different forms in prophetic souls, in different regenerators of the race,—divine vaticinations of the advent of the new and more perfect splendor, vague articulations of the voice of the Destinies; all of which would herald the dawn of a new world and realize the prayer for the *new* and *perfect man* to be *born*. It is clearly apparent that the man dimly foreshadowed is the perfect physical man, who must *also be the perfect metaphysical* man; for "to FORM man is predicated of the *external* man when made alive, or when he becomes celestial; and as the natural forms of things, both animate and inanimate, are representative of spiritual and celestial things in the Lord's kingdom," so the perfect natural man from divine correspondence will become the perfect supernatural man.

What wisdom is in the fable of Antæus! He was a Giant whose strength was invincible as long as his body was the perfect culmination of the somatic forces derived from Nature, or, as the fable deposeth, from *his mother Earth*, so long as he remained in *contact with his mother*. Now, man is that giant Antæus bereaved of his strength and invincibility by the vicious habitudes of civilized life. He congregates in towns and cities, builds for himself an artificial and morbid world, lives in marble palaces, breathes the mephitic gases and pestilential emanations inseparable from all concentrated accumulations of animal life, with their necessary accompaniments of gutters, sinks, and sewers,—inhaling perpetually the dead and effete air of heating-furnaces, mingled with reekings of rum and tobacco;

walks upon carpets and pavements, consumes disease in the shape of poisonous and luxurious food, lifted into the air by the savage force of the giant Vice,—a terrible Hercules.

Bruised and mangled, his only hope is to touch the bosom of his Mother and receive again his life and strength. Let him seek the regeneration and salvation of the country life; let him leave those seething caldrons of vice and death, towns and cities; let him ignore that fatal gregarious instinct,—old bond of veriest animality, ancient despotism of his brutehood,—and return to the woods and fields still fresh with the fragrance and dews of the dawn of the world, retouched with the sweetness of immortal youth each morning of time; let him rush to the hills and mountains,—

"Where health with health agrees,
And the wise soul expels disease;"

let him return to the wisdom, the reason, and the faith of Nature; let him inhale the odor of the soil; let him walk the field and see how his *blood grows* in apple and potato, in wheat and Indian corn; let him wash his feet in the running brook from the sordes and pollution, the sensuality and disease, of the pathway of the transgressor, and walk upon the sod with bared soles, a humiliated and mournful, but beloved and forgiven prodigal, knowing that his Mother the Earth is kind to her rebellious children, and always receives the penitent who returns from the swine-husks of sin, within the sphere of *her benign* influence, with fat things and bountiful benedictions.

Thus it seemed that the chapter Antæus might embrace the promises of the gospel of physical regeneration, and serve as a pivotal centre around which to rally some of the overtures of healing and bodily perfection held out by inspired souls and Nature to her erring creatures. Symbolizing all earthly influences, then, the Giant invincible, the terrible wrestler of Libya who slew all men who contended with him, stands the incarnation of the perpetually restorative power of the world, the genial, saving forces, which circulate only through the Earth and *are to be received only by coming in contact with the great Mother of all created beings.*

The *blessing* of the Mountain is, then, the prophecy not yet heard; the *glory* of the Mountain is the legend of poesy not yet sung; for the Mountain is the golden age restored: it is the end of the journey of the Queen of Sheba to the King of the Jews, when she received "from his royal bounty all her desires." The Mountain is the great *circle* of health *squared,* the philosopher's stone at last found, the elixir of life surely bottled, more miraculous in its overtures of mercy and happiness than the Utopia of More, the Republic of Plato, or the Heaven of Mahomet.

The perfect publication of the body of man in health and strength seems the highest achievement of all science, of all philosophy.

It comes at last that sound digestion is the "golden key that opes the palace of *felicity,*" sound digestion is Al-Sirat's bridge, sound digestion is the oyster whose shell is the world. Make existence a divine experiment, make the universe a perpetual enchantment, make thy body an instrument of celestial melodies, by looking through eyes that are *not* turned within upon a stomach that groans, like the Titan of old, "pain ever, forever." That cancer of the pylorus is a ghastly joke; that mania from drink is a bitter mockery of the Lord, the tragedy of the soul *lost;* inflammation and ulceration of mucous membranes are fearful accomplishments of the fire-eater. Alas that this should ever be! for have not those evil days most surely come when love of money, love of eating and drinking, love of excitement from the nether flames, are the vultures that devour the liver of this fierce-rushing, fire-stealing, heaven-hating, God-defying, Yankee Prometheus?

Vicious and insane, long has he wandered far from Nature; rebellious and ungrateful, he must return again to her charmed influence or perish. The woods and mountains have healing for him: let him flee from the wrath to come.

The story of the god of the woods is no figment of the

imagination. It means the health and strength of man's own youth; it means his *life-power* in *contact with Nature*, and stands a record of his force revealed by the immortal soundness of his unprofaned, unfallen organism. The God of the woods to the ignorant and uninitiated is a *monster*, savage in his attributes, hideous in his form and mien, the object of fear and detestation. This is superficial and profane; for " PAN is a symbol of the world. In his upper part he resembles a man, in his lower part a beast,—because the supreme and celestial part of the world is beautiful, radiant, and glorious, as is the face of this god, whose horns resemble the rays of the sun and horns of the moon; the redness of his face is like the splendor of the sky; and the spotted skin that he wears is an image of the starry firmament. In his lower parts he is shagged and deformed,— which represents the shrubs and wild beasts and the trees of the earth below; his goat's feet signify the solidity of the earth; and his pipe of seven reeds that celestial harmony which is made by the seven planets. He has a sheephook, crooked at the top, in his hand,—which signifies the turning of the year into itself.

"The nymphs dance to the music of the pipe,—which instrument he first invented; and, as oft as he blows it, the dugs of the sheep are filled with milk, for he is the god of shepherds and hunters, the President of the Mountains and of the Country Life, and the guardian of flocks that graze upon the mountains."

Withal, it is evident from this wondrous story that the great god Pan is a most excellent fellow. He lives in grottos, the shade of rocks, and sylvan solitudes, presiding as deity over forests, pastures, flocks, shepherds, and huntsmen,— especially happy in the glories of the chase, frequenting tops of mountains, indulging in the ecstasies of drinking the blood of wolves and bears, with the unspeakable raptures of eating wild honey and dancing to the music of the syrinx with the nymphs of the woods. Given to snoring sullenly and drowsily when the sun is in the zenith, he is clearly awake when the dews of evening or morning are on the grass. Filled with the loveliness of groves and the beauty of rural haunts, to utter the melodies of his heart he *had* to *invent the shepherd's* flute, and, being in his soul musical, performed upon it to perfection himself. As the favored lover of the nymph Echo, and permitted the honor of instructing Apollo in the art of divination, he must have possessed transcendent attractions: else *how* could he have become the sire of Iynx, "the symbol of passionate and restless love," also deemed worthy of *respect* among the supernals? else *why* the teacher of a great god of Olympus in an art so important as prophecy ?

Decidedly exquisite and charming he must be, then, with his "horns, beard, puck-nose, tail, goat's feet, and covering of hair," notwithstanding his own mother did flee from him with disgust and horror at his birth. The nymphs cared for him, nursed, and brought him up,—which perhaps accounts for the fact of the nymphs liking such fellows ever since. Pan is good to the nymphs: they were very good to him. The fir-tree (hemlock) is sacred to him; for reasons, ask "Pitys," the beautiful and beloved, whose spirit still sadly breathes through its boughs the moan of a suffocated, desolate, and broken heart. They say he is sensual and voluptuous, given much to dancing and revelry. Evidence, *this*, of *health* and *soundness*,—no derangements local or general, acute or chronic, no tuberculous deposits, gouts, dyspepsias, or neuralgias,—having the immortal vigor of the woods in his bones and in his blood, still the vitality of the crystalline air of Arcadia. A proper son of Uranus and Ge, (Heaven and Earth,) with the boundless self-sufficiency of health and strength, he could well afford to live in forests and be the god of shepherds and huntsmen.

Weary of the degeneracy of his ancient habitations, where the haunts of divinities, "mid ruins old," are changed into poultry-roosts and shambles for the flesh of dogs, and a peculiar gout is given to the fat of turkeys by feeding them upon olives, whilst cities of orators, poets, and demi-gods have become doleful dens of fallen races,—

> "The servile offspring of the free,
> Greece being living Greece no more,"—

he has retired to the Alleghany Mountains, where the splendor of his youth has been restored; and he invites, as in golden days of eld, to worship in his first temples, promising his votaries that, if they *devoutly seek, they shall be endowed with his attributes*, in the form of health, toughness and vigor, of which the wolf-murderer and dancer to the music of reeds is the proper incarnation and veritable symbol.

R. M. S. JACKSON.

ALLEGHANY MOUNTAIN SPRINGS,
    Cresson, Cambria county, Pa.

ERRATA.

In the Natural History Catalogues of Book Atlas the *capital letters* to specific names should be lower case or *common letters*.

Page 24 of Prolegomenon, 7th line, for *elio* read *clio*.

Page 100, 31st line, for *haven* read *heaven*.

Page 256, last line, for 2668 read 2928.

Page 342, 3d line, for *Comes south* read *Comes from the South*.

Page 355, 13th line, for *are* read *is*.

Page 379, 8th line, for *literal* read *littoral*.

Page 410, the star refers to note at bottom of page with double cross; the single cross to note star; and the double cross to the note single cross.

Page 440, 21st line, for *hundred* read *hundreds*.

Page 445, 31st line, for the second *as* read *on*.

Page 494, 24th line, for *in matter* read *in ponderable matter*.

Page 525, at bottom of page the Note should read *Wilkinson*.

CONTENTS.

BOOK ATLAS.

NATURAL SCIENCE OF THE MOUNTAIN, OR WHAT THE MOUNTAIN IS IN A CRITICAL INVENTORY OF THE PLANET, SKELETON, SKIN, APPENDAGES, AND CIRCULATING FLUIDS.

CHAPTER I.

GEOLOGY OF THE ALLEGHANY MOUNTAIN.

PAGE

Geography and topography of the Appalachian group; separate Chains; geographic nomenclature; discrepancies; geological and topographic continuities; topography of the Alleghany Mountain *proper;* Appalachian ranges east and west of the Alleghany Mountain; general geology of the Appalachian group with intervening valleys; general distribution and topography of the great sedimentary series of rocks; Appalachian waves and wrinkles; general style of fracture and distribution, with law thereof; anticlinal and synclinal axes; mountains, valleys, denudation, crimping of strata, laws thereof; rending and crushing; geological classification; geology of Old and New Worlds; parallelism of rocks in Europe and America, or geological equivalence; identity, etc.; European and American geologists; theorists; geological suggestions; Silurian and Devonian groups; Americans geologists; recitation of the formations of Pennsylvania from below upward; numerical series; how it forms the surface of the State; whole contour of the surface; geographic distribution; fractures; topographic style of distribution of the rocks in different parts of the State; upper portion of the series of rocks; coal-fields and underlying formations, how arranged; special geology of the Alleghany Mountain; mineral masses forming the body of the mountain; why the mountain is there; bituminous coal-fields; scientific significance of the mountain as a fragment of the globe; how related; song of the rocks; whence, whither, and how related to the whole; scenery of the mountain; elements of use and beauty; glory and grandeur of the mountain; great depository of life-forces; health; disease; final cause of the creation of the mountain.......................... 69

CHAPTER II.

SOIL.

Character; composition; origin of the mineral elements of the same.......... 103

CHAPTER III.

WATERS OF THE MOUNTAIN.

General hydrography of Appalachian axes or water-sheds; special hydrography of the Alleghany Mountain, its springs and streams; how distributed as to shedding surfaces; hydrology; character of waters mineral, thermal, and pure; classification of waters; special details of waters; mineral springs of Pennsylvania; hydrography of the same, or geographic distribution; classification; analysis; origin of mineralization; association of mineral springs with geological formations; medicinal virtues of waters, whence derived; individual springs of Pennsylvania; Bedford; Frankfort; Fayette; Blossburg; Bath; York; Perry County Springs; Doubling Gap; Yellow; Ephrata; Caledonia; Alleghany Mountain Springs; individual springs of this group; analysis; characters of the same, their healing virtues; Bradywine Springs.

Catalogue of mineral springs of the United States and Territories, Canada and New Mexico; Dissertation on mineral and pure waters; prophylactic and therapeutic virtues, medical agents in the great chapter of uses; significance to mankind... 109

CHAPTER IV.

FLORA OF THE MOUNTAIN.

Vegetable cell; the plant, its significance, and where in the Divine economy; laws; distribution; the tree, what is it? significance; symbolical; substantive; the woods; man; love; worship; Tropical Flora; Arctic Flora; Flora of Temperate Zones; Flora of Alleghany Mountain; trees and forests; special portraiture of trees; style of growth of the forests of the Alleghanies; style of forests peculiar to each species of tree; character of mixed forests; description, special, general, of the cone-bearing trees or great pine family; amentaceous or cat-kin bearing trees; mixed woods; laws of distribution; soil, air, water, necessities of; succession of forests; vernal expression, sights and sounds; Summer expression, sights and sounds; Autumnal enchantments; change of leaf; death of leaf-world; Fall; Winter; shrub or heath growth of mountain; plants forming the underwood; "heath," or bush, description of the same; beauty of flowering species; peculiarities of the bush of the mountain; herbaceous plants; flowers of the mountain; crops of different seasons; extreme beauty of the same; cryptogamic plants; ferns; mosses, special home of; lichens; hepaticæ; algæ 203

CHAPTER V.

ANIMAL LIFE OF THE MOUNTAIN.

PAGE

FIRST GREAT DIVISION OF THE ANIMAL KINGDOM.—Animalia Vertebrata: Class 1, Mammalia; Mammals. Class 2, Oviparous Vertebrata; Aves, or Birds. Class 3, Reptilia, or Reptiles. Class 4, Pisces, or Fishes.. 289
SECOND GREAT DIVISION OF THE ANIMAL KINGDOM.—Animalia Mollusca; Soft Animals.. 390
THIRD GREAT DIVISION OF THE ANIMAL KINGDOM.—Animalia Articulata.. 406
FOURTH GREAT DIVISION OF THE ANIMAL KINGDOM.—Animalia Radiata.. 426

CHAPTER VI.

CLIMATE OF THE MOUNTAIN.

Meteorology; laws of atmospheric motions; philosophy of; metereology of North America compared with Old World; climate of coasts; climate of the interior valley of North America; climate of Atlantic and Pacific ranges of mountains; extreme fluctuations of temperature; is of the class of excessive climates of Buffon; magnetic intensities; variations; isothermal lines; climate of Alleghanies; low mean annual temperature of the same; thermometric; magnetic vicissitudes; hygrometric states; hygrometeors in general; rains of the mountain; whence the falling waters; comparison with other portions of the world; quantities of rain in different ports of the planet; Alleghany Mountains atmospheric modifiers; quantity of rain on the Alleghanies; dew precipitations; hygrometric and electric phenomena; local special causes of the same on Alleghanies; supposed moisture of the mountain surfaces, with its streams, deep forests, soaked soils, undried surfaces, etc.; no undue humidity of the atmosphere of the mountain; seasons on the mountain; cloud-forming; fogs; diurnal and nocturnal variations; caloric, hygrometric, electric; Indian summer; great problem, change of climate as a modifier of disease; therapeutics of climates; medicines of airs; positive demonstrable laws of habitats.. 429

BOOK II.—ÆSCULAPIUS.

CHAPTER I.

SIGNIFICANCE OF THE ALLEGHANY MOUNTAINS AS THE SITE OF A SANITARIUM, OR RETREAT FOR THE SICK, ARRANGED BY INFINITE WISDOM—DOCTORIAL USES OF THE MOUNTAIN.

Who is the healing man? origin of the medical profession; critique on fixity and progress; reverence for the past; the word; old medicine too material, too faithful to the preponderables; imponderables the movers, builders, and destroyers; veritable show-masters; ponderables the puppets; imponderables prophylactic and therapeutic, or disorganizing and lethiferous; the vast realities of power sleep in the trace of the divine incubus of law UNDER the *outward phenominal;* hygienics and dynamics of imponderables; efforts to attain the spiritualities of things through the imponderables; medical spiritualities; spirit manifestations; medical theories of the same; plagues of Egypt following regular profession; homœopathy; fantastic tricks of infinitesimals; humbugability of the race; general formula of molecules; philosophy of NOTHING; oracular bard of the sciences; Hahnemann a new revelation; his last formula; new modus operandi of vis medicatrix naturæ; homœopathy; Croelius; hydropathy; Chaldean oracles; Preissnitz; mankind in darkness; arrival of the inspired one; glory of water; gods of waters in old mythology; Preissnitz knocks them all; man clearly amphibious; Maine liquor law; chemistry; water, cleanliness, godliness; water as cure-all; Americans grab worn-out crotchets of Old Word; trot them out Young America; hoaxes run through the mill again and again; after all Yankee easily sold; the thing a little musty from age; must be foreign, however; portentous humbugs: Mesmer, of Swabia; shoots *a la* Jonah's gourd, for a time in heaven with Barnum, Jo Miller, Jo Smith & Co.; disposition to glorify quacks; nemesis; murdered kings of quackery; exploded Barnum's; Yankee not a religious animal—won't worship monkeys, even God, long at a time; tired of Barnum and the inspired Josephs; did print Barnum's book, and inflict a nausea on the solar system; rap! shades of the dead, rise! or speak without getting up, if you prefer; spiritual drummers; healing media; secrets of —— feloniously wormed out; miracles to order; rap! the dead move—beds are taken up, eyes are opened; cancers, avaunt! regular faculty flung; old medicine in trouble; hair dyes, artificial teeth, miracles among the dull catalogue of common things; Hume nods; interruptions of the laws of nature always on hand; peace no longer in the grave; stop singing Psalms in Heaven—go to work, glorified spirits, no time for loafing; be useful; tell us about cancer and consumption; help us through with obstinate constipation; horn of Monker; issues in court; Plato and Zoroaster, Hahnemann and Paracelsus, Rappers and Swedenborg;

CONTENTS. 59

scald head, diarrhœa, oil of dead men; infernal dream; no rest in the grave—must wake up and watch the table business —worse, attend to Dennis O'Flaherty's bowels; horrors of fish and whisky in the Irish intestine; new formula of Gehenna; new patent-rights of torments in Pandemonium; "after death by bilious fever," rapper, won't you let us sleep well "a few days"? other birds of prey—owls and vultures—some obscene, all villanous; get your dictionary; kinesipathy; hypnotism; what of them? "Swedish gymnastics" theory of 2000 movements—all diseases cured—practiced for years in Sweden; hypnotism; James Braid, of Manchester; Wilkinson on Phrenopathy; hypnotism sound on marriage of mud and spirit— pours physical salvation into the animal man through his soul, as follows: * * * * * *

To list of horrors add Uroscopy and Thompsonianism—same birds, sired by "Prince of the Air;" strong family resemblance; nostrums and nostrum makers; new order of dragons; dukes of Sarsaparilla antediluvian saurians; coprolites; the evil spirit in the shape of quack medicines; Hobensack, Swain & Co.; maggot in the head; vermifuge; fearful power to tap the streams of life; satanic issues; blood; money; transportation of granite; humanity; Choctaw wigwams; horrors of Dante's hell; assassination of fraternal instincts; Yankee vultures enthroned, oh weary earth; quack princes; goddess of revenge; nostrum makers and venders; poisonous mixture of quack and felon; what of the doctors, the army of knights of the rueful countenance? is all uncertainty, both quack and regular? net results of systems of medication; Hahnemann; masterly inactivity; grand science of Laissez Faire; nature illimitable, infallible; let things alone; gas away homœopathy, one sell will do, let the patient dream; faith, immortal faith; slander of the druggists; old dragons not discarded by homœopathy.

Hydropathy, real merit, song of the waters—as panacea, egregious humbug; certain conditions, real death power; water a good thing in its place: good in a mug when thirsty; bad as a home for sharks when you are floating on a plank a thousand miles from shore; spirit rapping; unmitigated fraud upon the race; quackeries bet on strong will of conservation; delude man, sell forever; Swain's panacea; Hobensack; tickle the trout; nature's wings are healing; steals feathers of the regular profession; tacit acknowledgment of the corn.

Sickening array of strategies of the devil; where can the sufferer look? REGULAR PROFESSION Rock of Ages; true brazen serpent in the wilderness of life; time honored; the Greek; art of healing; god of medicine sound; regular profession great maternal fount of science of man; what it *has* done; what it *can* do; *use medicinal of all things;* regular profession must not surrender the greatest powers of the world to quacks, who shall fiddle some delusion and put the sick man asleep, while nature cures him; intelligent use of the universe; therapeutics of all things; chemistry; drugs; habits of life; change of habitat; curative virtues of climates; Hygeia, daughter of Æsculapius, true to the teachings of her father; regular profession only hope of humanity; flee to the mountains—their rocks will not cover thee; tears of the last sick man dried.. 481

CHAPTER II.

HYGEIA.

Æsculapius, the father of Hygeia; interpretations of classical writers; is a personification of the healing powers of nature; Hygeia, mild virgin, goddess of health and sound mind; sphere, preservation of health and prevention of disease; fields of labor presided over by her; art of prolonging life; laws of health; philosophy of living; great prophylactic; must not rob her father; Mayo on Hygiene; not original, new, or just in stricture; his dig at the profession; no renegade; faint praise; a word on Prof. Mayo's work, the "Philosophy of Living," and Mayo; table of contents of his book; Hufeland on the macrobiotic life; medical art, hygiene; mixed definitions; troublesome distinctions; art of prolonging life; art of medicines, strictures on; use of medicine and physicians; Hufeland's table of contents; state of science; art of prolonging; extent of literature of medicine in this department; professional books, books not professional—both significant; man and his surroundings; preventive elements simple; all the surroundings of man involved; the bodies we have; what we eat; gastronomy; the stomach; universal consanguinity; only indispensable organ to all animals; all embracing affinities; its ills the full circle of torments; diseased, it is Pandora's box; catalogue of fissures in base of pyramid; Tantalus; waters we drink; pure water great hygienic water; mineral waters; nonsense of promiscuous spring going; organs addressed by mineral waters; what can they do? great impression made first on digestive machinery; real use great new impression; indiscriminate application to diseases absurd; great mineral water, rationally medicated pure water; Dr. Struve; factitious mineral waters; preferable to natural; fabulous powers of natural; mysterious and inexplicable qualities suspicious; special pleading of particular advocates; how in bronchial diseases; mucous surfaces, etc.; in other diseases; great water, pure water, assisted by all surroundings; air we breathe; pure air greatest prophylactic; sleep; heavenly force to cure and prevent; mind and body both saved by sleep; what we wear; importance of philosophy of clothes; despotisms and follies of husk-man's instincts; clothes as preventives; ignorance, if true philosophy of clothes; vice, *crime* of fashionable dressing; slavery to conventionalisms in dress; sin; when will we wake up; what we do; hygiene of work; virtues of work; medicine of work; of all exercise, saving elements; varieties; active; passive; all have special ends; discriminate use of; on the side of the soul, great world of prophylactic powers; closes the circle man on this subject; involves all his surroundings of body and soul; extent of this one attribute of the god of medicine represented by his daughter; *he represents all;* medical profession not confined to cobbling humanity; not restricted to pill-driving; it is great to *prevent* disease, greater to cure when in existence; Æsculapius personification of all powers; Hygeia must *lean* on him; all are parts of one great whole—Anatomy, Physiology, Pathology, Hygiene; pillars of one grand temple; equal in significance all; unity, spirit of the world 537

BOOK III.—ANTÆUS THE GIANT.

CHAPTER I.

THE MOUNTAIN TELLING ITS WHOLE STORY OF FATE TO MAN, CREEPING IN HIS BONES, BOILING IN HIS BLOOD, FLASHING IN HIS BRAIN.

The man of poetry and fable; man of present hour different; rather a failure; vulturous scavenger sinking toward annihilation; man primeval; Methuselah; man once tasted the life everlasting, is now a toad-stool; threescore and ten hold him; gone stomach and loins; some good men in modern times; anatomy and physiology of Methuselah; wisdom of myths; paradises and falls of the races; instincts of the soul; men still turn to those beautiful dreams; mournful Egypts; heavenly Canaans; vague longings have eternal radicles; fallen splendor; "memory will bring back the feeling;" have the doctrines of despair a necessary origin in the nature of things? sins, falls, sufferings; is he lost? sorrowful garden; age of gold departed; crushed giant; a broken-hearted Adam; will the wrathful sword flame on? is all gone? vain efforts of thousands of years; is this a correct rendering of the ways of Providence to men? where does disease come from? catalogues of infirmities; death's bill-of-fare; best medical treatise; best doctor; is man a likeness of the world? living soul; what is the world? dogmas of death; dragon fights; mournful position; lives in tombs; sticks to the past; will he ever look into the future? a small number of world-wide men; only reformers, only true lovers of humanity; had no past; marched straight forward to future; inspired; shall they speak to the deaf and dead always? their words are seed; from the prophets of regeneration turn to the now extant individual; is the man of the present hour plus, minus, or zero? is he fulfilling the divine economy, or playing the fool? at $2.17\frac{1}{2}$ where will he land? with greasy and hypertrophied liver, with cancerous stomach, effete blood, gouty feet, and tuberculated lungs, hadn't he better stop under the first shade-tree and perform a prayerful self-analysis? if there be no water near him, let him perform his ablutions with sand, in manner and form prescribed by the Koran; his Mother Nature, great benevolent cow, for him the rebel, has dry dugs, hollow horn, and wolf in the tail; grass, fresh grass, salvation *through grass;* if a run at grass won't cure him, you need try nothing else, (see N. M. on diseased and worn-out horses); right about face, oh dragon-torn sinner; must leave the cauldrons in which you boil, leave your hot-beds of vice and luxury, towns and cities; dream no more of the flesh-pots of Egypt, or the delicious leeks of the Nile; with muffled drum and trailing arms, forward, march! TOWARD God; too long wandering from Paradise; flaming sword extinguished; may re-enter the hallowed haunts of sound digestion and perennial youth; longevity; golden rules of health; may stay in the body a hundred, *possibly* a thousand years—"CERTAINLY A FEW DAYS;" body of man a divine crucible; universe the ore of gold; fire up, but beware; modern physical degeneracy; clear case; comparative longevity of ancient and modern man; Methuselah; views of Haller and Buffon on the long life; their explanation; Hufeland on Methuselah; Hensler's views; the extreme ancient year; present year of Eastern nations; the patriarchs; Methuselah reduced to near 200 years; period of Abraham; lives of patriarchs; Hebrew record; Hufeland's tables; Abraham, Isaac, and Jacob, etc; Egyptians, ages of; Chinese; Greeks; Romans; catalogues of ancient worthies; of Roman women; actresses; records of Pliny; census, time of Vespasian; Ulpian bills of mortality; Rome compared with London; duration of life the same in time of Moses, Greeks, and Romans; probably men live as long as ever; views of Flourens; ordinary, extraordinary life; Buffon's views—life 100 years; Haller's views—life 200 years; Thomas Parr, Hufeland's account of him; Henry Jenkins; Bacon and Hufeland's list of veterans; ages; vocations of the same; facts of life of same; habits of life; Anglo-Americans, can they be acclimatized? the negro race, Dunglison and Prichard on; Humboldt on Indians; Hufeland's conclusions on duration of human life; Haller's conclusions; general formula; classes of mankind who live longest; emperors, popes, monks, and hermits; doctors shortest livers; table of Wilson; countries most favorable to longevity; general conclusions synopsized; who, how, when, where? all facts of long life; longest livers always followers of nature; conditions of long life; country life; city and town life; tables of Haller and Hufeland; Haller and Buffon on laws of longevity; formulæ; Hufeland on same; life should be 200 years; Flourens on the physiological law; ages of animals; laws of growth; gestation; duration of; will live eight, or seven, or five times as long as they grow; why the rarity of patriarchs; death's regular harvest; is man the giant Antæus? the doctrine of attainability of great age demonstrable; agreeable hope inspired; everybody may live to be as old as Methuselah; historical side of subject; scientific and physiological side; live 200 years if you wish; history, science; means of

CONTENTS. 63

PAGE

attaining age of patriarchs; gist and soul of the fable of Antæus; stick to Mother Nature; recitation of the records who lived longest, how, why, from Methuselah down; modern tables approach ancient; table of Easton of Salisbury, England; several lives 185; regular record of courts, and Harvey's post-mortem; habits of life all point in one direction; nature; open air; fishing, swimming; daily-labor; digestive organs treated with consideration by *them all;* modern patriarchs, sailors, soldiers, workers of some kind; hopeful record; only condition indispensable, *touch the earth;* material side of question all in this; soul, or spirit side of question through the sire of Antæus. Poseidon, who was a "personification of the fertilizing power of water"—a symbol of thought, spirit, genius —creator of the horse, and great water-god; on the side of spirit what comes of the fable: same story from philosophers, saints, anatomists, poets, moralists, *especially physicians; temperance* and *virtue* absolutely the only conditions of PHYSICAL REGENERATION; perfect rectitude a preventive for smallpox and ague; the life of man may become cleaner, brighter, sweeter, and certainly LONGER; the sum total of all prophecies, of all philosophies, of all religions, all sciences, natural, supernatural, is the body of man a perfectly sound implement, absolutely plastic clay in the FINGERS of the PURE, INTELLIGENT, LOVING SOUL; secret of the universe told; great problem of nature solved by the physical regeneration and salvation of the human race; the Mountain the first shore; the first LIFE-THEATRE; the sun first kisses, dawn first bathes the Mountain; lo! for the Son of Man, is it coming day?.................. 567

CHAPTER II.

PAN A SYMBOL OF THE UNIVERSE.

Is nature a unit? ancient atomic theory; strange coincidence; modern atom; what has the intellect done for the atom, from Leucippus to Dalton? souls of great dreamers identical in their instincts; logic of nature; primordial types; fascination of the atom; temptation to brave spirits to exhaust; struggles from Democritus to Schleiden; ancient "atom impenetrable;" modern cell; all organisms necessarily microscopic in structure; all organisms come from infusoria; everything must *flow;* Descartes' vortices celestial; Cuvier's vortices terrestrial; perpetual motion of the cell; life and death dance; motion—motion everywhere; organic, inorganic, imponderable; organs, functions; metamorphoses; immaterial essence; naturel history; supernatural history; the atom, the soul; silent gliding; heavenly soaring; what is pain? what is disease? of the sound cell; diseased cell; physiology, pathology; atom sound; atom morbid and morbific; origin of evil; the cell and general pathology; great functions, great lesions; in nature all things united; the cell the imponderable; old actors in the tragedies of life and death; the ether, the heat, the light; normal, abnormal life; jokes of nature; eternal

CONTENTS.

change; death; body of man bag of water; vibrations; ponderable and imponderable; health, disease; renovation; rejuvenescence, philosophy of; the cell the focus of all renewal; the fountain of youth; implements of renovation, *all medical science* and all nature; chronic disease; change of habitat; vicious despotisms of local causes; voice of nature, come to me, come to the woods, frequent the haunts of Pan; renovation, gospel of; "primordial utricle;" small details—"no great, no small;" Malpighi, Ehrenberg, Brown, Mohl; Galileo, Kepler, Newton, Herschel; brain of Shakspeare; Monas termo; Pan, the cell; details of things cared for on Olympus; the mean and vulgar represented as well as elegant and divine; great forms of matter; kingly and queenly deities; lowly gods, big heads, small heads; Jupiter and Minerva, Pan and Vulcan; no comfort in the world without Pan and Vulcan; the god of "pastoral life" and god of furnaces indispensable; trumps of the hour; iron and milk; thanks and eternal honors due to the humble deities—they superintend the drudgeries, and make earth comfortable; style of the god of the woods; not prepossessing, not beautiful; uses, ends, ghastly needs; represents the great kingdoms of man's both lower and higher nature; significance of the clever ugly god; cloven foot, radiant face, leopard's *skin;* Pan a symbol of the universe; grateful worship due to this god of the woods; let him flourish, and the sacrifices of the seekers of renovation and youth shall burn forever on his altars; god of the woods symbol of the cell, original germ, always perfect; represents the formative nutrient process of the organic world; the great herald of the cell, the microscope, and the philosophy of rejuvenescence..... 607

ATLAS.

Now sees the top of Atlas as he flies,
Whose brawny back supports the starry skies;
Atlas, whose head with piny forests crowned,
Is beaten by the wind, with foggy vapors bound.
Snow hides his shoulders; from beneath his chin
The founts of rolling streams their race begin.
                                    VIRGIL.

A potter, who understood neither Latin nor Greek, was the first, who, toward the end of the sixteenth century, dared to say at Paris, and in the face of all the learned doctors, that fossil shells were real shells, deposited formerly by the sea in the places where they were then found; that animals, and especially fishes, had given to the figured stones all their different figures; and he defied all the school of Aristotle to attack his proofs.—*Histoire de l'Académie des Sciences, annee* 1720, p. 5.

FONTENELLE.

This potter, who defied the school of Aristotle, was Bernard Palissy, "as great a philosopher as Nature alone can produce;" as was said by a writer of his own time, "a man of marvelously quick and acute mind."

FLOURENS.

I have never had any other book than heaven and earth, which is known to every one, and it is given to all to read this beautiful book.

And because there are found stones filled with shells, even at the summits of the highest mountains, you must not think that these shells are formed, as every one says, *by nature pleasing to do something new*. When I have closely examined the forms of stones, I find that none of them could have taken the form of shells, or of any other animal, *if the animal itself* had not constructed its form. We must conclude that before these said shells were petrified, the fishes that formed them were living in the water; and that both the water and the fish were petrified at the same time, *and of these there can be no doubt*.

ŒUVRES DE BERNARD PALISSY. 1575.

There are shapes in the earth *unfinished; things* that are the *forms* of life *without* ever having been the *recipients of life*. They are called fossils.—*Opera Philosophica et Mineralogica.* 1721.

EMANUEL SWEDENBORG.

554.—The earth has without doubt originated according to the laws of the polyhedron, which represents in the nearest manner the globe. The polyhedron of the globe is the rhomboidal dodecahedron.

555.—The land cannot therefore have an equal elevation everywhere above the water, because the crystal consists of edges, angles, and surfaces or sides. The mountain tops are probably the angles, the mountain ridges or chains the edges, the plains the lateral surfaces of the crystal.

557.—Although the earth may be regarded as originally a crystal, that consists of level surfaces, edges, and angles, wide fissures may still have originated between its laminæ, such as we see in large crystals of felspar. These fissures or gaps are the primary valleys.

558.—There must be, therefore, valleys or parallel valleys, which probably extend for hundreds of miles, and are many miles deep—longitudinal valleys.

559.—The laminæ of the earth had without doubt transverse fissures, which have been called hidden passages. These transverse fissures are the transverse valleys, which are consequently less long and deep.

560.—The mountains originate of themselves. They do not properly originate, but valleys only originate, and the ridges of the crystal laminæ afford the mountains. The mountains have not been originally upheaved above the surface of the earth, nor the valleys depressed. A valley, which is several miles broad, must originally have been several miles deep, and the mountain wall consequently several miles high. The earth at its origin was a cloven and jagged polyhedron, a polyhedric star, such as the moon is still.

561.—The mountains are not, therefore, large crystals, which crystallized above the surface of the earth. They are only crystal laminæ, and may be as irregular as possible in form, for they are ruptured crystals.

The constituent forms of the earth are consequently arranged in laminæ. What in the crystal is called the cleavage of the laminæ, is in the earth *stratification*. The strike of the strata combined with their dip determines the crystal nucleus of the earth.—*Physiophilosophy*.

OKEN.

In his strivings, who arrived at the clearest light,—who came nearest the core or heart of the truth,—the humble Potter, the pious Mystic, or the philosophical Poet?

The true Naturalist should not possess in excess any spiritual endowment. With too much imagination and sensibility, he floats off into the region of Transcendental Idealism, intoxicated with the gorgeous ineffability of the "grotto of dreams;" or overwhelmed by the *infinite suggestiveness* of Nature which must *remain forever* unutterable and incommunicable by words, he babbles like one mad. On the other hand, with *too much* of the *senses* and *understanding*, he *congeals* Creation into the "concrete"—under the "wintry moonlight of the Intellect." and the profound necessities revealed in the inseparable connection of Life, Form, and Substance, are lost in a ghastly formula of Mechanism, Chemistry, and Death. The Naturalist must not be the bird that never alights on his feet, and sleeps on his wings, but rather the mole of the ground, or true creature of the earth, penetrated and held by earthly affinities.

Let him, in the blackness that enshrouds him, creep like the humble caterpillar, measuring-worm, or serpent prone, touching Nature lovingly on all her points, rather than leap like the salient grasshopper into unknown spaces, or plunge like an eyeless fish through cavernous deeps of the world.

ROBERT SMITH.

ALLEGHANY

OR

APPALACHIAN MOUNTAINS.

CHAPTER I.

GEOLOGY OF THE ALLEGHANY MOUNTAINS.

This group of mountains of the North American Continent, also called the Atlantic range, as described by some geographers, extends through eleven degrees of latitude, in a direction nearly parallel to, and from fifty to one hundred miles west of the Atlantic Ocean, comprising a belt of from fifty to one hundred and fifty miles wide.*

Other geographers do not give so extensive a range to this chain, but describe it as extending from thirty-five to forty-one degrees north latitude, between the mouth of the St. Lawrence and the source of the Alabama;† while others represent it as extending from thirty-three to fifty-three degrees of north latitude. It is again stated that the Appalachian range "begins in the northern part of Alabama and terminates in the valley of the Hudson;"‡ and also that it extends "from the Gulf of the St. Lawrence to middle Alabama, fifteen hundred miles in length, and from one hundred to two hundred miles broad."§ The most recent and elabo-

---

* Malte Brun. † Phys. Atlas. ‡ Drake. § H. D. Rogers.

rate Gazetteer describes it as "that vast mountain system in the southeastern part of North America, extending, under various names, from Maine southwestward to the northern part of Alabama. In New Hampshire, near the northern termination of this chain, it is less than one hundred miles from the Atlantic coast, but it gradually diverges as it advances southward, so that toward its southern extremity it is about *three hundred* miles from the sea."*

In these delineations there is a discrepancy in geographic and topographic description of the continuance of lines of elevation, necessarily involving also mooted questions as to the unbroken geological continuity of formations; geological equivalency being affirmed by some, while it is alleged that the superficial geology is manifestly different, whatever the more profound and invisible ranges of telluric fracture, or folding together with geological metamorphosis, might reveal; the statement being distinctly recorded, that "the different ridges are distinguished from each other not only in external features, but also in their geology." This fact alone, leaving out the manifest identity of formations as geological equivalents, would account for the disagreement in geographic nomenclature, and the apparent error of generalization; the separate portions of the ranges being considered dissimilar in mineralogical composition, or, at least, geological arrangement of elements, and topographic characters.

Certain associated groups of mountains would be more correctly designated "geographical dependencies of the system."

Thus, the Green Mountains of Vermont and the White Mountains of New Hampshire are described as belonging to this range.

They are crystalline in structure, and some of their peaks attain the elevation of 6500 feet above the level of the ocean. At the southwest, where the group embraces the Alleghany, Blue Ridge, and Smoky mountains, they also attain a great

* J. T. Hodge.

height, their most considerable altitude being 6470 feet above the sea level. This is the height of Mount Mitchell, in North Carolina, which is also said by some geographers to be the "highest mountain summit east of the Mississippi River." Some of these mountain ranges, as the Blue Ridge, are also composed of the old metamorphic strata, gneiss, and altered slates, and sandstones, embracing even the formations characterized by the presence of fossils, or organic forms; while the principal part of the belt of the Appalachian chain is composed exclusively of the sedimentary paleozoic division low in the geological series. And thus from geological mutation, and consequent topographic change, it comes that different members of the chain, in the same lines of continuity of elevation, are called by different names in the course of their range through the United States.

Their height is from two thousand five hundred to six thousand feet, with an approximate average of three thousand feet, above the level of the sea. They form a range of hydrographic axes, which separate the waters that flow into the great interior valley of North America and Gulf of Mexico from those which flow over the Atlantic plain into that ocean: as the Rocky Mountains, on the west, separate those majestic streams which flow to the east and south through the trough of the Mississippi River, from the west or Pacific water-shed.

In their middle and southwestern range, this group of mountains, with its large, rich, and fertile intervening valleys, in its transit through the States, presents a series of chains, or lines of elevation, with great regularity of crests and acclivities, and more or less uniformity of geographic features.

That portion of the Appalachian group, the individual ranges of which are called by different names, east of the Alleghany proper, exhibits a series of sharp, symmetrical mountains, presenting long lines of parallelism, with crests as regularly defined in outline as the ridges of a well-plowed field, separated by valleys as regular as furrows in the same.

Their crest-lines display regular and beautiful horizons, which are almost mathematical lines for miles; while the valleys between the mountains show somewhat diversified surfaces.

The mountain ranges west of the proper Alleghany are not so regular and sharp in outline, and the valleys between are of a different character. These ridges, as they are generally styled, are also called by different names in separate portions of their extent, even when there is no interruption of continuity of elevation.

The whole group, with its characteristic scenery, its splendid system of foldings of the surface, or waves of mountain and valley, upon minute exploration, is discovered to be in strict conformity with the rock structure beneath. The topography of a given portion of the earth's crust, with its contour of outlines and surfaces, is necessitated by its geology, as absolutely as the form of an animal's body is fixed by its skeleton, or stony foundation.

The sharp regular mountains east of the Alleghany itself are formed of different materials, and have a different character from the western collateral parallel ridges. The former are made of the larger and more uniform members of the geological series, those masses which preserve homogeneous mineralogical composition through great extent of their thickness, also sameness of mechanical constitution, or strength of substance, over large geometric areas, and exhibit great uniformity in the style of fracture and plication of the strata.

Those west of the Alleghany are more irregular and indefinite in their outlines, from the more heterogeneous mineralogical constitution and mechanical properties of the rocks of that portion of the group of which they are formed.

What is called especially the Alleghany Mountain (the term Appalachian indicating the whole eastern oceanic system) is the range of knobs, or irregularly serrated edge of the summit-line of that vast plateau, or elevated range of table lands, (much more correctly designated ranges of alpine hills,) which forms the chain of water-sheds of the eastern side of the continent. It is formed of a series of high outstanding geological watch-towers, which coalesce in a crest-

THE MOUNTAIN.

line, irregular, undulating and zigzag, and when approached closely from the east, give the appearance of a chain of separate, short mountains, and knobs almost isolated, towering above the region at their bases; but approached from a greater distance, or from the west, present horizons of straight lines or gentle undulations. The depressions between these knobs are called gaps of the mountain. They are of every shape and form, from simple flexures in the general line of trend, scooped out depressions, or notches cut into the side of the mountain mass, to short, abruptly terminating, or irregular, tortuous and divided valleys, the bottoms of which are the conduits, or rocky beds of the streams which flow southeast from the steep escarpment of the mountain. These gaps or gorges are sometimes cut into the mountain several miles, and even clear through the entire mountain mass, as in the gaps of some of the considerable creeks and rivers. They penetrate the coal-bearing rocks, giving to the eastern margin of the great bituminous coal-field a notched or irregular rim, as points of the coal-seams with accompanying rocks stretch out toward the knobs, forming the sinuous and jagged edge of the great basin.

The knobs, or swells of the mountain themselves, are stratified piles of rocks left between the deep cuts or gorges of denudation made into the side of the elevated mass of broken heights called the Alleghany Mountains. The mineral masses forming the summits of the high buttresses or outstanding peaks of the mountain are constituted of the large group of silicious rocks at the base of the coal series, including the conglomerate, or its representative in coarse sandstone layers, forming the floor of the coal measures.

The gaps referred to between these peaks are simply deep cuts, or sinuosities gouged by the denuding forces out of the groups of rocks which make the mountain, and which are here found with gentle dips, in some places approaching nearly to the horizontal position.

Westward of this range of knobs and gaps, and between

them and the next lines of elevation, forming ridges called by different names, the region presents the character of elevated broken and irregular valleys. The surfaces of these valleys (which, however, can scarcely with propriety be called valleys) is constituted of a series of hills, separated by deep-washed gulleys and ravines, of every conceivable shape and dimension, from steep and precipitous gorges to gentle and flowing vales.

These hills have something of a mountainous character, and the whole surface between the highest ranges of the ridges and mountains is sometimes, though very incorrectly, called "the Mountains."

The whole group of Appalachians, with its intervening valleys, has for its bone-structure or skeleton, that magnificent system of palæozoic or fossiliferous rocks which are so largely developed in North America, and which have scarcely a parallel in any portion of the earth's crust yet subjected to geological scrutiny.

To this immense mass of sedimentary deposits, embraced between the horizon of the crystalline, hypozoic, or gneissic rocks and the top of the coal series, the general term, "Appalachian," has been applied by some geologists. "This series of rocks, more than thirty-five thousand feet thick in some districts, is made up of a number of separate formations, characterized by distinctive features in mineral composition and organic contents," revealing in majestic hieroglyphics the history of an immeasurable chain of phenomena occurring through unreckoned centuries of time, in an unbroken sequence of deposits, closely united by a continuous affiliation of organic forms and general geological characters.

"The whole pile is the demonstrable record of an immeasurable and continuous epoch, the deposit of one vast oceanic basin."*

As the strata are in the main conformable, they constitute a series, divisible into a number of *separate members*, or for-

---

* Rogers.

THE MOUNTAIN. 75

mations, which preserve their mineralogical and fossiliferous identity over extensive geographic surfaces.

They vary from a few feet to several thousand feet in thickness, and generally show a uniformity of mineralogical elements through their entire thickness.* Thus in one formation the silicious element predominates, presenting a series of hard indestructible quartzose strata; whilst, in another, the softer aluminous element forms a series of shaly, slaty, or argillaceous layers.

Sometimes the calcareous or lime material alone predominates, and is found in ponderously stratified masses.

The coals, or fossil carbon formations, make (see vertical section) the upper portion of this series, and are mingled with all the other elements in a stratified group of rocks. The mode and style of distribution of this pile of rocks, (forming the surface of the geological tally-board of the ages,) where it extends over the different States, is a chapter of beauty and wonder. Being all of them mechanical sedimentary rocks, and deposited originally, with exception of the local undulatory and oblique lines of original deposit, in a horizontal position, constituting vast geological scales or laminæ on the surface of the globe, they are now found folded and wrinkled, the strata reposing at every angle of inclination, and presenting a system of gigantic waves or lines of elevation, running parallel and with great regularity for hundreds of miles.

They present a topography of the most curious and interesting character in the middle and eastern portions of the range, forming long, narrow, keel-boat shaped valleys, with abrupt cul-de-sac terminations, surrounded by high, sharp mountains running like immense levees around them, and which are only broken by the gorges of the streams which flow through this region.

This is the wild and picturesque scenery of the Appalachian mountains and valleys, the gaps of whose beautiful rivers are so celebrated by the Traveler, Artist, and Poet.

* See vertical section and description of separate formations.

These waves of rocks are called by geologists "anticlinal," and the troughs between are called "synclinal axes," and everywhere the connection between topography and geology is revealed. Where the rocks are soft and destructible we are presented with valleys of denudation, or washing, and where the rocks are harder and less destructible, mountains are left, monuments of the war of the elements.

Where the stata are spread out with gentle inclinations, or horizontal, there are no mountain ranges, and the valleys are drains or washes cut through the strata, the hills between being simply piles of rocks left by the denuding forces.

Where they are folded and wrinkled, the appearance and disappearance of the same formations, at different points, always show the same topography, as well as geology. Thus all the mountains in the .eastern portion of the range are formed of two or three groups of rocks brought to the surface by frequent foldings of the strata, whilst the valleys between are also made of a few formations which are as constantly cut out and washed away.*

Thus in this apparently much diversified range of mountains and valleys, we have a few rocks continually appearing and disappearing, the out-cropping edges of the different fractured foldings forming long, narrow, parallel belts,—the less destructible masses projecting in mountain lines, the more destructible swept away out of the valleys.

This remarkable folding or plication of the strata is the most distinguishing characteristic of the geology of the Appalachian group of rocks and mountains. Apparently a confusion of interminable waves, arches, and troughs, of anticlinal elevations and synclinal depressions, with continual bending and twisting of the strata,—there is still a regularity and a system, an order of relative position which is never violated.

The foldings of this portion of the skin of the world have but a few general formulæ in their mode of development and distribution. They have a southwestern direction, with

---

* See transverse section

slightly deviating lines; some geologists having numbered and described specifically the alterations of the line of trend. They are from a few miles to several hundred long, and as a general fact show steeper dips on their western sides, while they decrease in abruptness of inclination on both sides of lines of fracture, from east to west, or in a line transverse to the line of fracture, thus demonstrating that the violence of the forces which have ruptured the strata diminishes most obviously proceeding westward toward the central line of the continent. This will be seen by contrasting the gentle arches of the bituminous coal-measures with the abrupt and, in some places, vertical and collapsed, even overturned and crushed axes of the lower part of the series, as exhibited in the eastern range of mountains approaching the great foci of volcanic or earthquake action.

One region reveals violent crimping, wrinkling, or foldings, with steep dips, and great crushing of the strata from flexures and fractures, showing evidence of vast oscillations, followed by fissures and chasms, splitting and rending of rocks, with injections of trap and crystalline metamorphosis of sand layers and mud masses: the other showing increased respect for the law of gravitation, with preponderance of inertia, allowing the rocks to repose with gentle dips, or in horizontal position, —comparative immobility or sleep of the elements predominating over extensive ranges of quiet and undisturbed basins, the waves gradually subsiding from violent tossings to gentlest undulations, and dying away into absolute repose.

It is a natural inquiry, Where do these rocks belong? what are they? and, is the geological structure of this Continent the same as that of the Old World? Have we the same order of position of mineral masses, the same lithological characters, and organic remains?

Many American observers, struck with the beauty and perfection of the classification of the English geologists, have been explaining the geology of this country by reference to that classification.

They seem to be successful in identifying species of organic remains, and have satisfied themselves as to the parallelism of the formations of Europe and America, having, as they suppose, made out the geological equivalents on both continents.

In this category are a number of the authors of the different geological surveys of the United States, two of whom,* after enumerating several species of fossils answering descriptions in the New York reports of what they call their "Clinton" group, and also in Murchison's silurian system,—say, "If our fossils be really identical in species,—*of which we entertain no doubt,*—then the rocks in question may be referred to the upper part of the Lower Silurian system, and may be considered the western representatives of the 'Clinton group of New York' and the 'Caradoc of England.'" This is arriving quickly but surely at a sweeping generalization.

They then proceed to describe their fossils, identifying many with the fossils of New York, and also of Europe, establishing—as they think, without doubt—their identity with the Silurian and Devonian groups, together with the Carboniferous limestone; and this also appears to have been the opinion of M. De Verneuil, after his visit to the localities mentioned.

On the subject of the identity of American and European rocks, the list of species now accumulated is a most interesting achievement.

Mr. Lyell constantly speaks of our rocks as referable to the classification of Europe. In his travels through this country, the terms "Silurian group of the Transition rocks," or the "Devonian," are as familiarly applied to our formations, as if he were traveling and describing them in England.

By examining the reports of the geological surveys of this country, it will be seen that many of our geologists endeavor to get our rocks classified after the formulæ of the European geologists.

In the second annual report of the Geological Survey of New York, we are presented with their different groups of

* Yandell and Shumard.

rocks all bearing some particular name, generally of the locality where they are most largely developed. For example, Mohawk and Trenton limestone, Salmon River limestone and shales, Rochester shales, etc. etc.; or they are again named from some striking character, as Pentamerus limestone, Gypseous shales, Gray Brachiopodous sandstone, Olive sandstone, etc. etc.

These are again classified according to European nomenclature, as different members of the Transition series, Cambrian, or Silurian, etc. etc. Speaking of this classification, Mr. Lyell says,—" Their grouping of the subordinate members of the Devonian and Silurian systems, has been based on *sound principles,* on mixed geographical, lithological, and paleontological considerations; and the *analogy of European Geology* teaches us that minor subdivisions—however useful and important within certain limits—are *never applicable* to countries extremely remote from each other, or to areas of indefinite extent. The thinning out and disappearance of the mud-stones and sandstones of the more Eastern States, causing limestones, such as the Helderberg and Niagara, so widely separated in New York, to unite and form single and indivisible masses in Ohio, affords no argument against the classification of the New York geologists."

He then proceeds to enumerate the species of fossils which he had inspected that were common to the rocks of Ohio, Sweden, and Russia.

These are a number of Trilobites, as the Isotelus gigas, Paradoxides, Trinucleus, Asaphus, etc. etc. Also of shells, as the Spirifer lynx, regarded by Murchison and De Verneuil as very characteristic of the Silurian beds of Sweden and Russia; also others of the same order, Leptœna sericea, Orthis-striatula, Pterinea, Cypricardia, Orthoceras, and Bellerophon bilobatus. He also enumerates the Crinoideæ or Stone Lilies, and then proceeds,—" In regard to the proportion of the species common to the Silurian beds of Europe and America, whether of the lower or upper divisions, I may confidently affirm that it is not greater, than would be expected from the analogy of the laws governing the distribution of living invertebrate animals. A contrary opinion has prevailed very widely, it being rashly assumed that at remote epochs the majority of species were far more *cosmopolite* than in modern times."

He further proceeds,—"The recent researches of Murchison and De Verneuil, point to the conclusion that the fossil shells, corals, and trilobites of the Silurian system of Scandinavia and Russia *greatly resemble* those of the British Isles; yet nearly half the species which they collected there were *different* from ours, and the departure from a common type was far more conspicuous in the lower Silurian fossils of Britain and Russia than in those of the upper division.

"When the same fossils of Northern Europe were compared by De Verneuil with those brought by me from America, the distinctness was *obviously much greater*, although the representation of generic forms in the organic remains of the upper and lower Silurian strata, *was not clear and satisfactory.*"

He then adduces the negative evidence which would tend to the conclusion of the identity of the ancient fossiliferous rocks of Europe and America, and seems to have no difficulty in demonstrating their parallelism.

To the Onion-Peel formula there have been some dissenters. They object to the classification now existing as "not possessing scientific elements of generalization sufficiently *universal.*" That the out-cropping edges of groups of geological formations, such as appear in the British Islands, the mere rim of vast basins like the old continent,—that an insignificant fragment, as England is, of so vast an area as the eastern hemisphere, should give a classification to the geology of whole continents, and the whole world, and this in a nomenclature derived from a purely geographic origin, without any elements of geological science at its foundation, they have objected to.

Of course, this objection can also be made to *any attempt* to identify by name all the rocks of this country.

The vertical section of Pennsylvania rocks shows the

number and something of the geological and mineralogical character of the separate masses called formations.*

Some American geologists who object to *old names and classes* have attempted a new nomenclature of the pile. These efforts are somewhat fanciful and far-fetched, but at the same time contain suggestions founded in reason upon which to base its terminology.†

In this hasty enumeration of the rocks of the mountain, it would not be desirable to dwell on points of *purely theoretical or scientific import*, as an elaborate treatise in this department would require a volume or volumes, and then leave the subject unexhausted.

The simple statement of what *is actually there*,—the far-off *hows, whys,* and *wherefores* omitted,—is all that can be required or be of interest to the general observer. Some account of the material fitting in and forming a certain part of the rocky circle of the globe,—that segment of the great arch in the district called the Appalachian mountain-chain, —is all that would be expected or demanded in a general schedule of the Mountain's effects. On far-reaching, world-wide geological theories, or *all-embracing formulæ* of the organization of planets or primordial patterns of habitable globes, there is no excuse for dwelling in this recitation. The philosophy of the wrinkled and wonderfully-plicated, the waved and folded condition of the earth's crust in the region under consideration, whether from the result of "actual billows in the fluid mass upon which the crust floated, excited by the sudden rupturing and instantaneous collapsing of the crust, rent by the tension of highly elastic vapors, etc.,"‡ or from the power of "earthquakes to raise permanent anticlinals," or "from the contortions produced by subsidence from the collapse of larger arcs upon smaller segments of the sphere of the earth," belongs to the student's chapter of theories in geological dynamics. But a short and hurried recitation of the formations may be necessary

* See vertical section.

† For an attempt of this kind, see the Messrs. Rogers's Classification, page 101.   ‡ H. D. Rogers.

to a proper understanding of the exact geological position of the Mountain.

The whole mass of rocks has been separated into nine groups, by some observers; again, from careful analysis, into forty-eight formations, none of which are coextensive with the great palæozoic or fossil-bearing basin in which they are found, and many of them of quite circumscribed range.

The old number of thirteen formations, of the geological reports of Pennsylvania, will suit all purposes here, the numerical series commencing below and counting upward.

In contact with the lower crystalline rocks, and to a certain extent mingled therewith, is the formation at the base of the great sedimentary pile, designated in the annual reports of the Pennsylvania survey as

No. 1.

It is a sand-rock formation, composed of fine-grained, white quartzose strata, sometimes of a gray color, especially dark, loose-grained, and full of cherty concretions where it passes into the formation above.

In other regions this is called Potsdam and Calciferous sand-rock. Thickness sometimes 1000 feet.

No. 2.

Reposing on No. 1 is a large mass of limestone, generally of a blue color, with layers of chert. Some parts of the formation are a light blue, or dove-color, even of a fawn tint, containing a quantity of magnesia. Where it passes into the formation above the layers are argillaceous and nearly black. When it mingles with the formation below it presents siliceous limestones and calcareous sandstones. The group is replete with fossil corals, encrinites, trilobites, numerous bivalves, and orthocerata, etc., of the Silurian rocks of England. This is the Trenton limestone of some geologists, and forms the long, boat-shaped, limestone valleys of Pennsylvania, called also "coves." The largest caves or caverns of the State are in this formation.

Formation 3.

Upon 2 reposes a slate and shale formation. It is usually black, dark blue, sometimes gray, olive, and drab-colored. It is a valuable mass, in some places giving roofing-slate. It also contains sand layers, gray and white, occasionally conglomeritic.

It is one of the mud-stones of the East, spoken of by Mr. Lyell. It gradually mingles with the formation above and below, in layers of calcareous slate and argillaceous sandstone. It is filled with fossils in some parts of the mass. Thickness from 200 to 6000 feet.

Formation 4.

Succeeding the last formation is a sandstone group. It is made up of a series of layers, white and gray, sometimes fine-grained, compact; again coarse and conglomeritic. Many of its layers are full of fossil marine plants called "Fucoides." It is from 400 to 2000 feet thick.

This is the formation which gives the belt of sharp, symmetrical Appalachian mountains east of the Alleghany range and which are parallel with it. They run like majestic waves from northeast to southwest in lines as straight for miles, often, as they could be run by the compass. Where these mountains are *entire anticlinal* axes, they present broad, gentle slopes; but where the axes are split or cracked open, and the two sides separate to surround valleys of the subjacent formations, as around the large limestone valleys of Formation 2, the mountains are narrow and abrupt, with steep and precipitous escarpments, covered with stone slides, and spaces of loose, massive fragments, in rugged confusion, with no vegetation except the lichen and moss.

The material of this formation being hard and indestructible, the mountains which it always forms run like immense dikes through the country, cut by numerous water-gaps, through which the streams and roads of the region pass from valley to valley.

These mountains are often but a few yards wide at their summits, and resemble huge walls in ruin; their sides the talus of long ages of gnawing by the teeth of time; but their majestic cliffs, still imperial, proud, and defiant, offering battle, as if forever, to the elements that seek to destroy them. Where the rocks in them have a gentle inclination they are high, attaining the elevation of 1400 to 1600 feet above the waters in the gaps. Where the rocks are in a vertical position, the mountains are low. The cause of this is obvious; the gently-inclined strata resisting like the slope of a dam, while the vertical rocks had to contend against the direct action of the denuding currents by cohesion alone, the abrading force operating at *right-angles* to the resisting surfaces.

Above, this formation passes by degrees into the superincumbent formation, showing, as usual, a mingling of the characters of both.

The philosophy of the structure of valleys of Formation 2 surrounded by this rock, will be understood by observing its relation to that Formation, and applying the common laws of *natural philosophy*.

Formation 5

Is the next in the ascending order.

It is composed of a series of variegated slates, shales, and sandstones of all colors, generally light, as olive, yellow, gray, and red. In the lower part of the formation the siliceous element of the subjacent group mingles, presenting sand strata, which contain fossils, animal and vegetable, or trilobites and fucoides.

This Formation is always found on the flanks of mountains of Formation 4; sometimes making gradual slopes high up the mountains; and again, partially denuded, it gives more precipitous declivities, and is covered by fragments of the sandstone of Formation 4.

This is the formation which contains the celebrated fossiliferous iron ore, upon which so many furnaces of the State are built. In the upper part of the group there is a mass of red shale and a series of yellow, bluish, olive, and chocolate slates with limy layers, which is the passage of this mass into the next Formation above, a limestone.

These layers are full of fossil shells and encrinites, and it is one of these bands which has been altered into the principal stratum of ore, of which, however, there are several. In some places the Formation is 2000 feet thick; at the bases of the mountains of Formation 4, it is from 600 to 900 feet thick.

The Formation is especially interesting to the geologist, on account of the great abundance of fossils which it contains. It is nearly on the same horizon as the Niagara limestone of the New York survey.

FORMATION 6.

This is a limestone group, with some intermingling of other elements. It contains argillaceous, magnesian, and siliceous layers; the former, where it passes into the rocks below, and the latter, where it mingles with the formation above, or No. 7, a sand group. It is full of fossils, presenting a great variety of corals, encrinites, and shells. Many of the strata appear to be almost entirely composed of organic remains. This is the equivalent of the cliff limestone of the Western geologists. It ranges through all the valleys of denudation, with

FORMATION 7

Which is a sandstone mass, composed of coarse-grained, loosely-accreted, yellow and white sand layers. It is full of fine casts of shells, and also a variety of corals, among which are beautiful stone lilies. Where this Formation is exposed to gradual erosion and denudation, it washes away irregularly, leaving columns of the harder part of the rock standing like strange and grotesque productions of art, called "Pulpit Rocks," etc.

In some places it has attained the thickness of 600 feet, but in other places it is not more than 50 feet thick.

Formation 8

Is a large mass of rocks, called the "olive slate group, or the Hamilton, Portage, and Chemung groups" of the New York reports. It is composed of a series of dark-gray and olive slates and sandstones, sometimes yellow, greenish, and brown. The sandstones are argillaceous and fine-grained, showing extensive and peculiar lines of cleavage.

At the base of the mass it abounds in fossils; but fossils are found through the whole formation, some localities giving several species of trilobites. There are also in it shells and corals in abundance. It is from 5000 to 8000 feet thick, and, wherever distributed, presents a characteristic style of topography, with great sameness of soil, quality of surface, etc. etc.

Formation 9

Reposes upon the last group described, and is a large mass of rocks composed of red slates and shales, red, gray, and brown argillaceous sandstones and slates. This is the group which forms the southeastern slopes of the Alleghany Mountain, and is extensively exposed in all the gaps or cuts of the mountain.

It also forms the slopes of the mountains in the anthracite regions. Some of the northern counties have a considerable portion of their surfaces formed of this and associated masses, as Pike, Wayne, and Monroe counties. It contains fossil shells, and beautiful vegetable fucoïdal forms in abundance, as cock's-comb fucus, etc.

It is frequently 6000 feet thick, and sometimes more; and is the Catskill group of the New York reports. The whole is a mass of sand and mud rocks, a bright-red being the predominating color. It also contains an iron ore of value, and some copper.

Formation 10

Is a mass of gray, brownish, coarse, and fine-grained sandstones, with sometimes coarse, siliceous conglomerates. It also contains blackish, carbonaceous slates and coal shales, sometimes with one or two small coal-seams. It is a hard, indestructible group, and consequently forms mountains. It is the rock which makes up and caps the first range of Alleghany spurs. It also forms many other mountains, as Shickshinny, Nescopeck, Peter's, Berry's, and Mahantongo mountains in Pennsylvania. It contains fossils, both animal and vegetable. In some localities the formation is 2000 feet thick; but generally, throughout Pennsylvania, it is not more than 300 feet thick.

Formation 11.

On No. 10 there is a mass of red shale and sandstone, also gray sandstone, sometimes compact, but generally soft and argillaceous; containing also some lime layers, with fossils, and a peculiar calcareous sand mass, which, from its style of weathering, is easily identified, and is always a key for fixing the position of masses above and below. Its weathered surfaces have a remarkable oblique-lined appearance, and the mass is full of water-worn cavities, enlarging, in some places, into considerable caverns. The Formation generally produces slight depressions behind the first peaks or butresses of the mountains of Formation 10, its soft shales being easily abraded and destroyed.

It is sometimes, in the anthracite region, 2900 feet thick, but in the bituminous measures it is not more than 250 or 300 feet thick. It contains an iron ore of value in some places. It also contains, in certain parts of the bituminous coal-region, a thin seam or two of coal, and in the south, one or two large workable beds of coal, although its place is under the conglomerate, the proper floor of the coal.

Formation 12.

On the red shales of No. 11 repose the coarse sandstones and quartzose conglomerates, called generally, "the conglomerate," as it is considered the floor of the coal measures proper. In the anthracite region it attains the thickness of 1400 feet, but in the bituminous region or Alleghany Mountain, it is generally not more than from 100 to 250 feet thick; whilst occasionally, a few coarse-grained, massive strata, are all that stand as its representative. There are occasionally thin layers of dark carbonaceous slate and shale in this formation, the representatives of imperfect coal-seams, the formation being the inauguration of that splendid group of which it forms the base.

Formation 13

Is the true carboniferous division of the great sedimentary pile. Upon the conglomerate rests the series of sandstones of all colors, generally gray and white, slates of all colors, and shales of all colors, limestones, and coal-seams, called the coal series or "carboniferous group." In the anthracite region, as estimated on the vertical section, it is near 6000 feet thick. In the bituminous coal measures, the whole group gives a thickness of some 3000 or 3500 feet of sandstones, shales and slates, limestones, iron ores, with beds of coal through the whole group. In the whole series there are about twenty coal-seams, many of which are workable; together with a number of other insignificant layers, the aggregate of coal being about 55 feet in all.

The *true significance* of this division of the series of rocks, the carboniferous group, in the great chapter of uses of the world and its connection with the progress and well-being of humanity, it is impossible to estimate.

The patient toil of centuries has here accumulated reservoirs of power that seem exhaustless, and the genius of the hour having subdued the fire-king, having chained, tamed, and harnessed the most terrible of the brute forces of the earth to do his work, finds food and sustenance for the conquered dragon, for thousands of years.

The scientific elaboration into well-fixed formulæ of this one member of the great geological series, was well *worth* the effort and *worthy of* the ambition of a true and gifted student and lover of science, whose unique and beautiful Monograph on coal leaves little to be said for the present on that subject.*

A short and hurried enumeration has been made of the thirteen separate formations or geological groups in the ascending series, its base boiled, burned, and crystallized by the long-exhausted primitive central fires of the planet, and its summit regally crowded by a diadem of slumbering flames in endless depositories of fuel, or world-fires, heat and light for a globe, still untouched and inexhaustible in a buried flora, whose gorgeous forms scientifically restored, would be a "midsummer night's dream" of wonders. Neptune and Pluto are no longer fables; they have become stereotyped symbols in the language of science, recording the past achievements of time. The imagination ("reason *using the external world*") striding forward over hundreds of years, her delicate instinct prophesying the *inevitable*, has at last hailed and united with the understanding in her conquest of the actual, in the stern demonstrations of the intellect.

A glimpse at this majestic pile, whose whole thickness aggregated some six or seven miles of solid rocks, is all that has been or could be attempted here. But it is that portion of the group forming the Alleghany Mountain, in its transit of the State of Pennsylvania, that is the special subject of consideration in this place.

The Alleghany Mountain crosses the State from northeast to southwest, dividing it into two approximately equal districts. The region to the southeast of the line of elevations called the Alleghany,—with the exception of a small

---

* Manual of Coal and its Topography, by J. P. Lesley, Topographical Geologist. Published by J. B. Lippincott & Co.

portion of the southeastern corner of the State, perhaps one-seventh of the entire surface of the State, and which is constituted of the highly-crystallized metamorphic hypozoic rocks,—is made of the middle and lower part of this vast pile of unaltered sedimentary strata which forms the elevated and wrinkled plateau of the eastern side of the continent. The manner in which the rocks are bent and contorted, forming this rugged but highly-interesting and wonderful mountain region of the middle and southeastern counties, is a subject of the highest scientific attraction and exhaustless intellectual speculation. It has already been adverted to a number of times, and will be readily understood by reference to the sections; especially the transverse section showing the style of plication of the rocks. In some parts of this region the whole group of rocks from the crystalline to the coal measures inclusive, is presented for inspection. The series already described as constituted of thirteen easily-separable groups of strata, are recognizable and easily identified over vast extents of geographic distribution by a wonderful homogeneity of mineralogical, geological, and palaozoic or fossilliferous characters. In the region west and northwest of the Alleghany Mountains, we are presented with but few of the members of this group of formations, the surface of the state being here made of the carboniferous division and two or three of the underlying formations, the strata being in a different geological position from the southeastern division of the State, and consequently, it shows a different topography, and one which forms a striking contrast with that portion of the State. This difference would strike the most superficial observer. The rolling surface of the northwestern region has through its extent only these uppermost formations stretching over the whole region, that tumultuous tossing of the strata with regular crest lines which characterizes the southeastern range of sharp mountains, and those deep-washed regular parallel valleys, here cease, the waves of that magnificent system of the regular Appalachian mountains and valleys gradually subsiding. The axes or arcs of the waves or wrinkles of the rocks flatten out, and the strata show a tendency to assume a horizontal position, approaching the quiet basin of the centre of the continent. These gentler undulations retain the general features of the abrupt eastern axes, that is, they run in lines northeast and southwest, and preserve their usual parallelism, and the relationship of the inclination of strata on the different sides of the axes. The two great natural agents which give external geology and geography to a country,—namely, the deep subterranean or upheaving, and the superficial disintegrating and abrading forces, have very clearly acted with much less intensity in this region. The dips of the strata do not change often, and the inclination of the rocks is never great, whilst the fracturing and grinding of the strata and the sweeping force of currents appear to have acted with much less violence, and consequently, the destruction of the valuable contents of this region has been prevented, over any considerable extent. It is thus that the coal and iron of this highly-gifted portion of the earth has been saved from destruction. Instead of wide-sweeping valleys of denudation, such as we are presented with in the southeastern part of the State, destroying and carrying to the rebuilding of new continents vast quantities of mineral matter, we have small narrow valleys and ravines, natural excavations as it were, designed to bring into man's power the immeasurable wealth of the rocks below. And here, in the small, as in the largest thing that is, the wisdom and perfection of the Universe is revealed. By this apparently accidental distribution of the surface into hill and hollow there is the most perfect access to the mineral contents of the region; and a large and comprehensive view of the geological structure of the northwestern half of the State presents an extensive basin, or rather, the termination of an immense basin which extends southwestwardly from the northern border of Pennsylvania, almost to the centre of Alabama. This coal field, remarkable for its vast extent, continues uninterruptedly from northeast to southwest, a distance of some seven hundred and forty miles, presenting a width of sometimes one hundred and eighty miles. One estimate of its superficial area gives sixty-three thousand square miles. Its original limits, as suggested by geologists, must have measured, before they were reduced by denudation, nine hundred miles in length, and two hundred miles in breadth.

In the State of Pennsylvania, from its southern line in Somerset county, to the north branch of the Susquehanna River in Luzerne county, the Alleghany Mountain forms the eastern margin of this basin. Between that limit and the State of New York on the north, and Lake Erie on the northwest, all the rocks belong to three or four formations, as already described, including the carboniferous group. The two large formations that underlie the silicious masses under the coal series, the olive slate group, and the red sandstone and slate group, run along with and form the southeastern escarpment of the Alleghany Mountain and the range of hills at its base, between the points designated, and sweep in a wide curve around the northeastern terminations of the upper rocks in Susquehanna and Bradford counties, and are traceable, although thinning down, westward, in a long belt nearly parallel with the north line of the State from Towanda into the State of Ohio. Immediately within the belt thus traced, there is found a bold escarpment, formed of hard sandstones, conglomerates, and silicious slates, directly underlying and forming part of the carboniferous formation, which is the actual northeastern margin of the great bituminous coal basin. The anthracite and semi-bituminous coals are found in the more disturbed and broken belt of the Appalachian range, east of the basin thus designated, but occupying the same geological position; in other words, being true geological equivalents. The Alleghany Mountain, as an individual chain, is the rim, margin, or eastern escarpment of the crops of the sands, conglomerates, and slates of this vast basin, presenting many flexures, but all with general southwest line of trend. The summits

THE MOUNTAIN. 93

of its highest knobs, as already remarked, are formed of these rocks, which are all here found dipping in one general direction, exhibiting a vast monoclinal axis of gentle inclinations. The northern and western range of these silicious masses give a more broken, undulating, and irregular chain of heights, extending west from Towanda by Blossburg, in Tioga county, the northeastern limit of the bituminous coal, and north of Smithport, in McKean county, and Warren, in Warren county, from which it is slightly deflected, with greatly reduced altitude, somewhat to the south, in the region of Meadville, in Crawford county, and crossing into Ohio through the county of Trumbull. Along the northern side of this basin all the formations, from the olive slate to the coal measures inclusive, have gentle southern dips, and the passage into the large basin is successively over higher and higher strata from the New York line, where the slates, shales, and argillaceous sandstones of the olive (Formation 8) slate formation are the predominating rocks. In Crawford and Mercer counties, where the lower strata crop out northwest of the coal, the general dip is southeast; while on the southeastern margin, or in the range of the Alleghany, the prevailing inclination is north of west; thus inward all round toward the centre of the great trough containing the coal. While this is true with regard to the edge of the large basin, *within this* boundary there are a number of arches or anticlinal axes, some of which are of great length and considerable elevation, others low, with slight inclinations, giving to the entire mass of the basin a series of more or less gentle undulations. Many of these lines of elevation lift the formations below the coal to the surface, sometimes causing the latter to be washed away over considerable extents of country, thus dividing the region of the large basin into a number of subordinate coal basins. These anticlinal lines sometimes rise into the height of mountainous ridges, called by different names, as Elk Mountain, Chestnut Ridge, Laurel Hill, Negro Mountain, etc. The whole number of these anticlinal axes, or western parallel Appalachian ranges, which are large enough to impress any striking features on the topography of this region, or to have caused the coal to be removed from their lines of elevation, are not generally of any considerable size, further than forty miles into the basin across the strata.

Between these higher ranges of ridges are the wide and irregular valleys, already described in the topographical part of this chapter, scarcely conveying the idea or impression of valleys, from their surfaces being perpetually broken up by hills of greater or less magnitude. Through these basins the crops of the coal-seams are found on the hill-sides and in the ravines, extending from hill to hill, and rising gradually toward the anticlinal axes, or plunging below the watercourses and levels of denudation, toward the invisible ranges of the synclinal troughs.

The smaller valleys, or minor depressions, are generally the courses of the streams which drain this district, and are extremely irregular, presenting every imaginable variety of configuration of surface.

This fact alone gives variety unequaled, and an element of surprise and enchantment to the landscapes of this interesting region.

The coal series, designated and characterized as a separate formation, is made up, as has been already said, of a variety of sandstones, slates, and shales, with limestone and coal-seams, forming, as will be easily understood by reference to the vertical section, the upper part of that majestic pile of sedimentary rocks constituting almost the entire geological structure of Pennsylvania, as well as a considerable portion of the Atlantic and Middle United States.

In Pennsylvania the region made of these coal rocks presents throughout the broken and hilly surface already described; the higher lines, or chains of hills, showing the position of the geological masses below, and revealing the ranges of fracture, and of elevation, and depression; the system of drainage also showing the lines of washing, toward the larger valleys of denudation, in which the creeks and rivers continue to flow. Some of these streams cleave into the mountain ranges so deeply as to bring forth geological formations below the coal series. This is apparent in the gaps of the Susquehanna and its tributary streams through the Alleghany Mountains; also in the gaps of the Conemaugh, Youghiogheny, and other streams, through the collateral ranges of Laurel Hill and Chestnut Ridge. Stretching westward from the Alleghany, the region between it and its parallel ridges presents a continued series of undulating surfaces, or labyrinth of hills, with certain features of sameness, yet with a forever-renewed variety of landscape, surprising in its diversity, and exceedingly beautiful. The traveler, who has passed through this country, will not forget the continually-recurring delight with which there arose before him a perfectly new and heretofore unseen combination of hill and valley; each variety of soil exhibiting its characteristic clothing or vegetable dress, thus giving rise to an endless succession of the most exquisite and diversified pictures of nature. This is the general character of the Alleghany with the region west of it.

It is the Alleghany Mountain itself, however, which presents claims of the greatest interest in the world of uses and beauties for man. The great sweep of its eastern range of knobs, with steep southeastern declivities, overlooks, like a range of observatories, the region stretching for miles in front toward the sea; the picturesque gorges and ravines cut abruptly into the mass forming the mountain, are the courses of fresh, rushing mountain streams, with their craggy sides covered by forests of evergreen pines and laurels; while westward it gradually mingles with an interminable extent of rolling hills. It is this wild and majestic character that attracts and holds spell-bound with visions of beauty the lovers of nature, and makes the mountain and its groups of landscapes of every style of grandeur and beauty the glory of the world, a region of never-failing attraction and delight.

Standing on its highest knobs, in the central part of Pennsylvania, the beholder is presented with the most exquisite and sublime panoramas of the earth. North and south, the range of spurs stretches off into the distance, the parallel chains east and west sweeping in majestic curves to unite apparently in vast circular mountains.

To the west, the table-land valleys extend a rolling surface between the Alleghany and parallel ridges; and succeeding this are the western mountains, with slightly undulating crests rising in succession until lost in the distance.

Looking east toward the Atlantic Ocean, the vision is one for the expression of whose beauty there is, as yet, no voice or word.

Immediately below reposes the range of beautiful valleys at the southeastern base of the Alleghanies, their northwestern margins sloping up to the mountain in a range of round, soft, billowy hills,—as it were, the gentle heavings of a summer sea, breaking against the shore upon whose rocky heights the beholder stands. Rising from the southeast side of these valleys is the first chain of sharp, regular, Appalachian mountains, formed by the hard rocks in the lower part of the series. Succeeding this is another of the same kind of mountains, and beyond this others still of the same order, the spaces between the lines which are made of their crests becoming less and less, as the obliquity of the lines becomes greater and greater.

It is also beautiful to perceive that, in the space between each of these lines which represents the distance between the mountain summits, the tint, from the increased distance, becomes deeper and deeper, until lost in the clear blue of ether. As the eye follows the azure steps of this kingly portal to the skies, line rising above line, it can scarcely be realized that, within each of these tints of deeper blue, there reposes a range of the richest and loveliest limestone valleys of Pennsylvania. Often, with bars of clouds reposing on the horizon, it is impossible for the eye to distinguish the distant lines, or fix where the earth ceases and the heavens commence.

The poet and painter are here presented with a boundless field, as the element of beauty seems alone to have been recognized and consulted in its creation. Let the artist then bathe his soul forever in this river of enchantments and play like an exstatic child in this sea of heavenly forms. Descending from this ethereal element,—the "dread power" of beauty,—the economist or utilitarian finds immeasurable reservoirs of wealth and power in mineral resources; whilst the savan finds also a field of endless study and contemplation, exhaustless depositories of organic forms, rocks teeming with fossils, leaves of the miraculous volume filled with the eventful history of a planet struggling into being, into peace, order, beauty, and light, from war, chaos, brutality, and darkness.

The elaborate scientific details of the history of the geological genesis and exodus of the mountain is not the chapter proposed to be indited here. To the sphere of the special geologist, whose end is the stern and severe inductions of science alone, this belongs, a world of rich and inspiring visions, a universe of grand and gorgeous suggestions, eloquent with the music of "starry spaces and long thousands of years." The mountain dissolved, like Cleopatra's pearl, would be a drink for a whole sanhedrim of geological gods. It would seem, in one aspect, a very small page of a very vast volume, being an insignificant fragment or protuberance on a globe twenty-five thousand miles in circumference; yet to comprehend it with clear intelligence, to illuminate it with perfect scientific precision, would be to read all the secrets of Nature, make vocal the silent and infinite, give the key to open the mysteries of eternity, and explain the riddle of the Universe to the soul. Its true story would be the philosophy of creation, its true song the beatitude of humanity.

A part is related to the whole, and to apprehend it fully, would be to apprehend the whole; for "every natural part is an emanation, and that from which it emanates is also an emanation," the world of effects reflecting the world of causes,—as "by the sea, reflected is the sun," too glorious to be gazed at,—in their own sphere of transcendent brightness.

There is clear and perfect wisdom in the seeming chaos; and although multiform and diverse, confused and irregular to the uninitiated the world and its fragments appear, still there is a system in them, a meaning that can be read; the labyrinth has a clue and Dædalus has told the secret. "The wondrous maze is not without a plan." There is an organization, an intelligible order in the arrangement of the materials of the earth and its mountains, and this order is never violated; for, being the first law of Heaven, it is the last of Earth.

It would then be a pleasing, an enchanting task to follow the mountain in its progress through the dreams of fabulous geology, when it was a mystery and miracle, why "shells were found on mountain-tops, but *not* surprising why shells were found at all;" when it was the ceaseless wonder how those "forms," so like the recipient of life, should be where life could never be, the wondrous imagination, with its creative power, having solved all things into strange mimic creatures,—a "lusus naturæ having sported herself with a useless creation of needless beings."

What story has the mountain to tell of world-wide geological cataclysms, of immeasurable flourishings and sportings of earthquakes and volcanoes, long sleeping and silent, but still convenient and useful to geological theorists? What has the mountain to say of Noah's grand water-spout, of floods of Deucalian, of Ptolemaic and Mosaic systems? When did this veritable Alleghany actually crack the shell and protrude its spine from that mysterious mundane egg of Egyptian cosmogony?

It would surely be a glorious privilege to follow the mountain to the dizzy heights of bewildered speculations, of fiery pictures of whirling flame-worlds travelling through celestial spaces; also to follow it through lofty visions of immeasurable times, of unreckoned centuries, of vast periods, contrasted with which the date of the first dawn of primeval history is as yesterday, or any assignable period for the origin of our race as to-day! A great romance that would be, a pedigree of the mountain's rocks; or the chronicles of the war of Pluto and Neptune, of water and fire, the congelation of primary crystalline masses, or the pulverizing, washing, and hardening of secondary sediments! Then it would be curious to know what the mountain would say to the ambitious intellectual game-fowls, who are always so anxious to fight the battles of orthodoxy and heterodoxy, and settle the wondrous difficulties of the problem: was Omnipotent Power six *actual* days, or six millions of *actual* years building these hills and laying the foundation of these everlasting rocks? Thanking the Infinite profoundly for the sacred vessels of thought turned off from the "marvellously quick and acute mind" of the divine potter, Bernard Palissy, whilst his hand fabricated the lowly implement of clay; and accepting with deepest love and veneration the shining and immortal jewels chiseled from the soul of the miraculous stone-cutter, Hugh Miller, whilst his hand made plastic the humble rock,— we can certainly with joy surrender theoretical fogs to be sliced by intellectual Quixotes, never ceasing to utter gratitude and pæans of gladness to find that the *mountain is really here*, arranged as a structure for the ages, and clothed in everlasting beauty,—standing an absolute and irrefragible fact, its significance in a system of goodness and love shining beautifully and peacefully out upon the last and greatest achievement of time, the last most precious consummation of the world, "that crowning of creation's birth," man himself. Grand and beneficent are the gifts Nature has provided for him in the finish and furniture of this his glorious home. Long has been the pilgrimage of her tortured elements, through fire and through water, to their present perfection of arrangement for the comfort and exstacy of this, her darling child. A protracted warfare of the dragons, a long, a lonely, *barren road*, from fiery vapors to solid rocks, from the lichen and moss clinging to the naked lava or granite, to the corn-stalk and apple-tree in the prairie sod. Ages must struggle to feed the plant, ages again to nourish the animal, and ages upon ages to fill the streams which circulate through this wondrous creature, man. Incandescent crystallines would have been a troublesome home for the cereals, and only decades of centuries of wear and tear could give nourishment to their roots. Where shall the elephant browse? where shall the horse make his manger? and wherewithal, especially, his rider be clothed and fed?

The gods were at work, primeval powers forged the refractory elements into propriety, and life and light flashed upon the world. The lichen stirred the stillness and was a fact; the trilobite became an individual, and soon had brothers and cousins; the saurian flourished an animated rock, the incarnation of the brute or dragon forces of the world, and made the deep to boil; and the tread of the mastodon was heard in the forest. At last, with order and beauty a teeming earth, wrapt by a mantle of delicious crystalline air, wandered a docile and obedient satellite through ethereal spaces, and the hand of Praxiteles brought forth the imperishable beauty slumbering in the marble's heart; Plato talked, amidst the groves of Academus, of divine virtue and the immortal soul; and Cuvier dreamed over that wondrous bone to the music of a galaxy of morning stars shouting together the great song of a reclaimed earth and the science of geology! The divine end seems to have arrived. With quiet and majestic steps this system of illimitable goodness and unspeakable beauty has been approaching the haven of its perfection, and the lover of Nature is now left to contemplate and admire forever the bountiful provision which has been made for his enjoyment and delight on "this green ball which floats him through the heavens."

GEOLOGY.

THE ROGERS' CLASSIFICATION

OF

PENNSYLVANIA ROCKS.

In "Second Visit" of Lyell, page 249, we are presented with the following startling utterance, (conveying despair to many an aspiring genius, no doubt, who had been imagining his direct connection, and blood and bone alliance, with the stock of Shakspeare and Milton,) viz. *"Since experience has now proved that there is, in the Anglo-Saxon mind, an* INHERENT POVERTY OF INVENTION IN MATTERS OF NOMENCLATURE, ETC." Taking up this glove, with the full determination of wiping out so hideous a stain from the genius of the Anglo-American, or Yankee wing, at least, of this *omniscient* and *omnipotent Anglo-Saxon race*, the Rogers-brotherhood (Anglo-Saxons, of course,) have made a plunge into the chaos of "inherent poverty," with the following result, in the shape of a nomenclature of the palæozoic rocks of the State of Pennsylvania.

Primal series,	No. 1.
Auroral series,	
Matinal series,	Nos. 2 and 3.
Levant series,	No. 4.
Surgent series,	No. 5.
Scalent series,	" "
Pre-Meridian series,	No. 6.
Meridian series, (or Medidial,)	No. 7.

Post-Meridian series, (or Post-Medidial,)	No. 8.
Cadent series,	" "
Vergent series,	" "
Ponent series,	No. 9.
Vespertine series,	No. 10.
Umbral series,	No. 11.
Seral series,	Nos. 12 and 13.

This symbolical category is predicated on the dream of the "deposits of a prodigious sea," and the intercalation, in the eternity a parte-ante, of an extraordinary day, computed to be seventeen millions of millions of years long, from morning until evening twilight. The poets are not all dead, and the "*inherent poverty*" of the Anglo-Saxon mind is not so positively "proved by experience," after all.

There being a considerable row on hand, with regard to the appropriation of the glory of baptizing the great system of sedimentary rocks of North America, it has been thought best to wait for a subsidence of the mud stirred up by the fury (we mean, of course, scientific zeal!!) of the intellectual Saurians, who are now contending for the honor of depositing that shining and eternal coprolite in the sediment of the ocean of *fame*, to wit, the "NOMENCLATURE" of said illustrious palæozoic pile. After clear water has been established, and we can see through the turbid boil and battle of *words*, there will be substituted for the humble numbers, 1, 2, 3, etc., the elaborated French, Latin, Greek, Hebrew, or Sanscritism, finally arranged by the *individual*, or *Congress* of savans, to be THE THING, fixed and established *forever*.

CHAPTER II.

SOIL OF THE MOUNTAIN.

The term soil applies to the film forming the surface of the pulverulent mineral mass composed of, and covering the rock formations of the crust of the earth, and floating like a mantle, or folded like an outward integument around certain portions of the body of the planet uncovered by water. The soil is the point of contact and union of two separate elements of creation,—the worlds of organic and inorganic matter. In the soil, the rock, weary of its brute immobility and long, deep slumber, tries to awaken into the more delightful dance of the organic elements, and to introduce itself to the higher sphere of life; "strives to become a different and attain the light." In the soil the ponderable and imponderable commence the mystic circulation of organic existence. Soils derive their constituent principles from the earth and the air; the plant, or special possessor thereof, being characterized as "organic water which is polarized upon two sides towards the earth and the air." From the earth comes the *body*, or mineral elements forming the substance of soils; from the air certain chemical principles, without which plants could not grow. Given then, simplicity and homogeneity in component elements of soils, there will follow simplicity and homogeneity of vegetable forms; and, as a necessary corollary, with greatly diversified geological, mineralogical, and chemical elements, will arrive complexity and exaltation in structure and composition of the plant world, existing as a medium within and upon the same.

Thus, from thin barren cuticles of sand, forming the covering of mountain heights, to the deep loam, rich with chemical and organic elements, of the alluvial and diluvial deposits of plains and valleys, the growth of the plant marks the advancement of an eternal and divine progress.

The soil of the Alleghany Mountain and its parallel ridges exhibits the characters, mineralogical and chemical, of the rock masses composing them. This may be asserted of almost every country, to a certain extent, but it is especially true of mountain regions where there are no alluvial or diluvial deposits. The material which forms the inorganic mineral part of soils, comes, of necessity, originally from the disintegration or wearing away of rocks which have been previously fractured and crushed.

The soil of valleys, of drift formations, alluvial deposits, and diluvial flats, show a more heterogeneous composition from the diversity of the materials composing them, as they exhibit the lithological characters of the regions through which the waters depositing them flow, or have flowed, and from which they have been derived.

The superficial deposit of crushed rocks, of gravel and earth, supply these washings. They extend, with different depths, from a few inches to several hundred feet over the fractured surfaces of the rock-formations. From any given portion of country were this deposit removed, there would be presented the naked edges, jagged angles, and severed faces of the different varieties of stratified or amorphous rocks, from which the mass of superficial disintegration was originally derived.

Of course, the prevailing mineral and geological elements will give prevailing characters to this mass. If silicious rocks predominate, the soil will be silicious; if argillaceous or calcareous rocks are in excess, the superficial deposits of soil and fragments will show the predominance, with all the characteristics, of these elements. The Alleghany and its associated ridges have, as their geology reveals, the sand or silicious element the great prevailing item; the largest and most ponderous masses of the geological formations of these chains being silicious rock. This is especially true of the Alleghany Mountain itself, which has been formed, as has been shown, of the heavy sand group at the base, and in the lower part of the coal series. These rocks form the barren heights and precipitous gorges of its knobs and gaps. The surface, in many of the ravines, is formed almost exclusively of deposits of coarse fragments, and sometimes ranges of enormous boulders of these sand masses. This occurs on both sides of the mountain, very large extents of the surface being frequently strewed over with these fragments. They are often of great size, exhibiting the dimensions of 40 by 60 feet, and sometimes 30 feet in thickness. They are frequently found a considerable distance from the summit line, in chains or ranges of smaller fragments of the conglomerate and sand rocks, and generally correspond to the deeper notches in the crest line of the mountain. As these drifts are several miles from the original rocks from which they are derived, the precise history or mode of transportation affords subject-matter for contemplation, interesting to the geologist.

The argillaceous or slate material is also abundant in the masses of the mountain, giving a clayey character to the soil of many districts, and a general intermixture of clay and sand to almost all the soils of the mountain. The extreme summits of the knobs and ridges are sometimes but slightly covered with a soil of almost pure sand. Proceeding from the southern line of the State to the northeastern termination of the Alleghany, there is a gradual increase of the silicious element, with an accompanying predominance of the same in the soils of the regions through which it ranges. This is shown in the wilderness counties, especially the region of the outcropping masses, forming the terminating ledges or rim of the great Bituminous Coal Basin.

The limestone material is not found in great abundance in the rocks of the mountain. The layers of this rock are thin; and those impure, from intermixture with iron, clay, and sand. Proceeding from the *northern* line of the State towards the southwest, where the valleys between the Alleghany and its collateral ridges are deeper, the limestone formations and softer shales and slates thicken, and become much more important, giving, as usual, an increase of value to the soils of those districts, and a corresponding *change* to the whole surface of the country.

As a general thing, then, the soils of the mountain heights are sandy and clayey, but have, withal, a susceptibility of improvement through the application of the principles of scientific agriculture, which has not attracted sufficient attention and examination.

On the highest knobs the sand soil prevails, and is barren, except to plants which affect such soils; but *some distance off* these heights, the coal rocks of the western side give good soils, and the slates and shales of the eastern base of the mountain are also susceptible of successful cultivation. Of course, there is a gradual modification and amelioration of ALL *these soils* of the mountain and its slopes going on, as has been since the elevation of the rocks to the surface, and the fracturing, wearing, softening, and pulverizing of the same, with the gradual intermingling of the more complex pabulum of plants derived from the atmosphere, namely, water, carbonic acid, ammonia, with the mineral soil nourishment also of potash, soda, lime, magnesia, silica, alumina, iron, sulphuric acid, phosphoric acid, etc. This is shown by the natural succession of plants,—the lichen, the moss, the fern, the conifers, and, lastly, catkin-bearing trees and Rosaceæ. The gradual succession, change, and death of forests can now be seen, as parts are dying while other portions are green and flourishing, showing a gradual surrender of the pioneer forest-trees, and their supercession by trees with membraneous leaves, or those requiring a richer or more compound soil. Different parts of the mountain, then, show all the geological changes and soil metamorphoses from bare rocks with lichen and moss, to sand soil with pine-tree and huckleberry, or clay and loam with the oak, walnut, and apple-tree.

It would seem to be a habitat adapted to a variety of the gramineæ or grass family. These include nearly all of the common starch-bearing, introduced and naturalized plants or

SOIL OF THE MOUNTAIN.

cereals, the ordinary food of men and animals. Of this class a number seem to have an obvious affinity for or adaptation to the soil of the mountain ranges, as the oats, (*Avena sativa;*) timothy, (*Phleum pratense;*) barley, (*Hordeum vulgare;*) etc.

The proper bread cereals, wheat, (*Triticum vulgàre,*) and rye, (*Secale cereale,*) are grown with facility, especially among the coal-bearing rocks in the basins or elevated valleys, where limestone is found mingled with slates and shales. In the arenaceous soils of the heights, the crops of these grains are thin. The red clover (*Trifolium pratense*) is found growing with the grasses; but, as this plant contains lime, potash, soda, phosphoric acid, sulphuric acid, chlorine, silica, magnesia, and peroxide of iron, soils entirely destitute of these elements, especially lime and potash, are not well adapted to its growth.

That superb and kingly grass, the Zea Mays, or Indian corn, does not flourish very well in the soils of the mountain. One or two varieties sometimes ripen well, but the seasons are too short for all those generally cultivated to attain perfection, *some* of them being invariably caught by the frost before being fully matured.*

The soil of many parts of this region seems particularly adapted to the growth of a number of indigenous and introduced pasture-grasses. It is to be deplored that this subject, and the growing of stock adapted to such regions, has not as yet received the attention which it merits from the

---

* It may not be amiss to notice another plant which seems to possess a strong attraction to the soil of the mountain, viz. the Solanum tuberosum, commonly called potato.

Notwithstanding the story of the botanists, that this plant was originally native or indigenous to Peru, South America, many inhabitants of certain districts of the mountain are fully and solemnly impressed with the conviction that it belongs to those particular regions from the Creation, having appeared *there first*, a primordial gift of love from the supernals to a heaven-favored race, which was finally to occupy that promised land.

noble and hardy cultivators of the mountain; and the traveller is impressed with pain to observe how few flocks and herds graze upon its grass-grown sides.

Its perfect adaptation to the growth of one domestic animal, the sheep and its varieties, alone would secure to the mountain a precious specialty, and one of inestimable value.

Leaving out the question of a wool crop, it is well known that the grasses of the mountain will, in a given time, develop more *mutton-tallow* than any other pasture upon which the sheep can feed. Sixty days of mountain grass converts the sheep from a skeleton covered with skin into a mass of the finest, newly-infiltrated mutton; its hide, stretched over angular bones, metamorphosed into a round, distended sack of snow-white fat.

In the vegetable world, however, and its soil affinities, its vital relations to earth, air, and water, the chapter on the Flora of the mountain will show the connection of cause and effect in this order of things.

One other record must be made with emphasis, and that is, the entire FREEDOM of the surface of the mountain from morasses, swamps, and boggy soils, with large accumulations of vegetable matter in a state of decomposition, and the consequent immunity of the Alleghany heights, in Pennsylvania, from the WHOLE CLASS of malarial diseases. This star fact alone, reposing upon the mountain's brow, is a sufficient crown of glory.

CHAPTER III.

WATERS OF THE MOUNTAIN.

"Each thing is full of duty;
   Waters united are our navigation;
   Distinguished, our habitation;
    Below, our drink; above, our meat:
Both are our cleanliness.   Hath one such beauty?
   Then how are all things neat!"

HERBERT.

The water of hills and mountains differs in quality, according as it filters through banks of pure rock, of schist, of quartz, or of sand, from all which substances it can scarcely derive any property whatever; or as it flows over beds of potter's earth, which it neither draws along with it nor dissolves; or, lastly, as it traverses ground which is calcareous, marly, gypseous, impregnated with magnesia, salt, or bitumen. Waters of the kind last mentioned are always very much mixed with heterogeneous substances, and for the greatest part of the year are hard, turbid, and unwholesome, at least if daily used. Hippocrates, Homer, and Plutarch have long ago condemned the use of them. Those waters which have clayey bottoms are most common; they unite those qualities which are essential to salubrity. Those which flow from the *hard rock* are still more pure and limpid, as they must undergo a process of *filtration* in wearing their way over a stony bed.

MALTE-BRUN.

HYDROGRAPHY.

Prefatory to the chapter on the waters of the mountain, it may not be irrelevant to take a cursory view of the general system of water-distributions, of which it forms a fraction. By consulting the maps and charts of physical geographers, this will be found the most extraordinary feature of the Western Hemisphere. It will soon be discovered that the hydrography of the New World has been projected upon a scale of unparalleled magnitude, and in dimensions truly colossal. In its rivers,—unequaled for length and volume of waters on any other division of the earth, draining the richest and largest basins in the world, terminating in "bays and gulfs which are more like wide arms of the ocean" than rivers; in her broad, inland seas or lakes, chained together, many of them, by equally remarkable streams and straits, the whole embosomed in a soil exhaustlessly productive, and washing a geological and mineralogical crust of incompatible wealth,—there is presented a chart of distribution of bodies of water or system of mundane hydraulics, which exhibits a base line for the maritime and commercial department of a social structure or pyramid, of which the imagination of man has as yet no dream.

The large lake-chain itself presents features of great interest in every aspect of contemplation. Many of their beds extend hundreds of feet below the level of the sea, while their surfaces are several hundred feet above; the whole containing an aggregated mass of "more than one-half of all the fresh water on the surface of the globe."[*] As objects of admiration, they are unparalleled in beauty and grandeur. In the chapter of utilities, this system of waters exhibits illimitable resources and expansions in the whole

---

[*] Johnston's Physical Atlas.

sphere of uses to man, revealing worlds of economics, of which the present chapter of statistics gives no shadow of intimation.

It would seem from the geological and geographic structure of the continents, as parts of the architecture of the globe, and their connection with the oceans of water on both sides, together with their relationship to the meteoric elements and forces, or ocean of air above, that some primordial contract must have existed on the question of water as one of the few original trustworthy elements of the world, and that an infinite supply as a planetary agent was required to fill the bond for the honest pronunciation and realization of the destiny of this hemisphere. The prophet who has its special details to foretell, the political economist who has its tariffs to fix, or the statistician who has its tables of forces to establish, have each an exhaustless theme; and the happy genius of the hydrography and hydrology of the Americas has the side of a planet upon which to project his diagrams.

In this place there is only a verse to recite of the grand old poem of waters called Appalachian, it might be said still less, a single line to spell out, viz. the waters of the

ALLEGHANY MOUNTAIN MINERAL AND PURE.

The wrinkled swell on the Atlantic side of the continent, forming the Appalachian mountain range, as referred to in the chapter on geology, forms a series of hydrographic axis, to which the rivers on that side of North America owe their origin. And here the rock-skeleton of the globe shows its usual despotism in necessitating geographic features, style of topography, and consequently hydrography.

As a result, we find that from certain points of elevation, or Appalachian centres, there are presented a series of watersheds between the inclined plane which stretches from the Atlantic Ocean to the highest range of Alleghany peaks, and the inclined plane which stretches westward and south-

HYDROGRAPHY.

westward from that range of elevations to the bed of the Mississippi River, which is the great drain of the streams which flow over the southern declivity of the vast central basin, or the Mississippi and the Mackenzie plane of the interior valley.

The Alleghany Mountain, as the dividing ridge in the midst of the eastern plateau, is the separating line or range of centres of the streams flowing through the planes above designated. In New York and Pennsylvania, we are presented with the third of the five Appalachian hydrographical centres on the eastern side of the continent, proceeding from the north, described by physical geographers. The water-systems of these axes, and their general connection with the hydrography of the continent, is a subject of extreme interest. Leaving the parallel Appalachian mountains and their groups of streams, the waters of the Alleghany demand a brief but special notice.

The true fountains of the streams being the heavens, or in other words, the waters which they convey being all meteoric in their origin, as from the falling of rain and snow, with the precipitation of vapors, it follows that the higher in the mountain, and the nearer to their springs or points from which they emerge after percolating the soil and rocks, the freer and more perfect will be their waters from earthy elements, and the least changed will they be from their original meteoric condition. After falling, the waters soon burst forth in springs on the heights of the ranges, and seek by the first declivity to flow east or west, as the lines of denudation may necessitate.

The first springs which rise near the summits in the gaps or gorges of the mountain, or in the valleys or washes from its sides, form swift and rushing streams which fall over rocky beds, broken by frequent rapids.

It is often observed that these rivulets in the heights of the mountain, rising from the same spring, separate and flow in opposite directions, into the Gulf of Mexico and Atlantic Ocean.

Separating at their cradle, the young streams part to traverse a whole continent, before they again unite in the great mother's bosom of the ocean from whence they came. The waters which flow east into the Atlantic, have generally steep and rocky beds from the mountain-summit to the first range of valleys, after which they take their courses with slower and more regular currents to the sea.

Their channels are sometimes in the line of the valleys, and again cleave the groups of parallel mountains by a series of water gaps, forming that most extraordinary combination of the picturesque and grand found only in the startling landscape pictures of this beautiful region.

The cause of the greater rapidity of the currents of the eastern streams is obvious, as the eastern side of the mountain presents a bold and precipitous escarpment,—a wall, as it were, rising above the valleys at its base.

Through the notches, ravines, and gaps cut into this jutting buttress or rampart, rush the streams that flow directly east. It would be difficult to conceive anything more attractive, wild, and wonderful than these swift and arrowy streams pouring over falls and rapids, or rushing and boiling through their rocky channels.

On the western side of the Alleghany Mountain the streams have slower and gentler currents, presenting irregular courses, and with more winding and circuitous channels. As the high table-lands fall off more gradually from the Alleghany spurs westward to the Mississippi, the streams flow through the irregular washes of denudation which separate the labyrinth of hills more slowly. Many of these streams are quiet and sluggish, appearing as mere passive and dead drains of the surface. Their waters appear different from those of the eastern shed, where they flow through the beds of the larger currents. Descending these streams the waters become turbid from the intermingling of the softer mineral elements which form this region.

The larger bodies of water here show the well-known muddy and turbid character of western rivers. They form

HYDROLOGY.

a striking contrast with the crystalline and limpid currents of the eastern drainage. In the heights of the mountains, however, both sets of brooks near their fontal springs present the same characters, frequently, as we have seen, flowing from the same rock. The western streams, from the above designated characters of tortuousness and sluggishness, are also more liable to dry up at a distance from their springheads in the mountains.

The springs, themselves, are not generally very large, as there are not in the mountain any extensive limestone formations or soluble rocks through which water can make subterranean caverns, consequently there are not any considerable bodies of water suddenly emerging from the earth in fullborn creeks and rivers, as in the large limestone districts east and west.

As might be expected in the rocky heights of the mountain,

> "From beneath whose chin
> The FOUNTS of rolling streams
> Their race begin,"

the waters are of exceeding purity.

The rain and snows fall, and after short percolation through the different rock formations break out in fresh and beautiful springs. As to the mineralization of their waters they show the characters of the rocks through which they flow. If the mineral substances composing these formations are soluble, their waters will *show their presence;* if *insoluble*, they will be more or less free of stony contents, the earth elements of waters being derived from the filters or rocks through which they pass, some of their gaseous substances being retained from the air.

This point in the treatment of the subject introduces another division of the chapter on waters, namely, its

HYDROLOGY,

or the chemical character, therapeutic *virtues*, and other properties of waters. For besides the purposes of irrigation, navigation, and other mere mechanical values of the vast and wonderful circulatory system of the Americas, (to which slight allusion has been made,) for the commodities of trade, and the perpetually expanding world of life, a full estimate of the uses of the waters of the New World present another phase of great significance. This is the consideration of the hygienic and therapeutic value of waters, pure, mineral, and thermal, in their relationship to human health, and consequently to human happiness.

In this department we are presented with a rich and extensive variety; and here also has Nature been lavish in her gifts of value. Almost every water that has been the subject of scientific analysis,—and the catalogue comprises all that have been styled mineral waters,—are here found in profusion. In some of the oldest inhabited points of the continent there are springs *whose reputed virtues*, descending by tradition from the *aborigines* of *the country*, science has discovered to contain quantities of mineral elements.

Romance and imagination have had much to do in this department, as the half-fabulous stories of the virtue of many springs, as recorded by *their special historians*, would amply testify; still the *real virtues* of a *number* are *undeniable*, and their efficacy as remedial agents unquestionable. Throughout the United States this class of waters is abundant, sometimes characterized by the predominance of *one element, sometimes* by *another*. The leading items in the chemical inventory of their contents decides the character or class to which they belong. They are variously classified by different writers on the subject. That of Dr. Bell* in his recent work being perhaps the most sensible for practical purposes, will serve our purpose, being plain and simple and founded on obvious qualities addressing the senses of all.

These are, first, acidulous or carbonated; second, saline;

---

* Dr. Bell's excellent little book on "mineral springs" should be in the hands of every traveller, invalid, *and especially every physician*.

HYDROLOGY.

third, sulphureous; fourth, chalybeate. Ioduretted, Bromuretted, and acid waters are by some writers added to these classes. Still further defined, they stand thus:—

FIRST.

The acidulous waters contain and evolve gases, principally carbonic acid, making them pungent to the taste and sparkling. They hold in solution saline substances, mostly *carbonates of lime, magnesia, soda,* and *iron*, with common salt.

SECOND.

Saline waters abound in salts, sulphate of magnesia or Epsom salts, sulphate of soda or Glauber salts, the medicinal properties of which are well known to all. Chloride of sodium or common salt, and carbonic acid are sometimes found in them.

THIRD.

The sulphureous, which are characterized by a gas charged with sulphur, called sulphuretted hydrogen, or sulphohydric acid gas. The presence of this gas is recognized by well-known and familiar tests. This class is again subdivided into those waters which contain free sulphuretted hydrogen gas, those which contain carbonic acid or acidulo-sulphureous and those which contain carbonic acid and sulphuretted hydrogen, and those also which contain iron with other sulphureous combinations.

FOURTH.

This class embraces the chalybeate or ferruginous waters. The iron in most of these waters is in a state of a carbonate of protoxide dissolved in carbonic acid. They also contain the sulphate of iron, or common copperas.

The medicinal qualities of these waters are of course the therapeutic properties of iron in general. There is another division of waters into cold, and thermal or heated. All the four classes of mineralized waters are found in either of these classes; there being cold and thermal waters holding all of the above chemical elements in solution. The mineral and gaseous contents of these waters are often in great quantities and in almost every conceivable proportion. Some of them have attained world-wide reputations in the modification, alleviation, and cure of different classes of diseases. Many of them are peculiar and rare in the combination of their mineral contents; whilst some of the thermal waters of the southern, interior, and western side of the continent have scarcely a parallel for intensity of heat, in any other part of the world. The attempt to perpetrate anything like an elaborate treatise on mineral waters would of course be out of place here, but a hurried enumeration or catalogue of the most important mineral waters of Pennsylvania, and of the continent as far as analyzed by science and registered, may not be deemed so.

The highest knobs of the Alleghany being composed of hard silicious and argillaceous masses, the materials of which are only slightly soluble *at low temperatures*, the waters which emerge from them are nearly in the same condition in which they fell from the clouds. Many of this class of springs are almost perfectly pure water with all the characters of rain-water, and a near approach to absolute or chemical water. This is the character of the higher or summit springs. The other members of the rock-group forming the mountain, have each their class of characteristic springs. Throughout the coal series we are presented with a variety of mineral elements in the waters. Common salt or the chloride of sodium abounds in great quantities in some of the rocks. Where they are depressed in the synclinal troughs further in the coal measures, salt is manufactured from them by perforating the masses containing it. Where they crop out, the rocks sometimes show the presence of salt by effloresence and sloughing on their surfaces. These formations also contain bromine and iodine, or the elements of sea-water, the water used at the salt-wells showing their presence in considerable proportions.

HYDROLOGY. 119

The coal-seams and associated shales contain sulphur and iron in a state of chemical combination, called sulphuret of iron, or pyrites. The chemical decomposition of this material, in these rock masses, gives rise to several varieties of mineral waters. First, to waters containing the salts of iron, or proper chalybeate waters. Secondly, to acidulous waters, or those which contain free sulphuric acid; and thirdly, to proper sulphur waters, or those which contain sulphuretted hydrogen in a state of solution, constituting the celebrated sulphur waters of writers on mineral springs. From some of the calcareous and magnesian masses we have waters of another character, namely, waters containing salts of the alkaline bases, or the class of aperient waters.

We are thus presented, in the spring system of the Alleghany, with an interesting group, showing almost every stage of mineralization, from the pure and limpid water of the sand-rock, to the highly-charged, earthy salt solutions of the coal-seam and its accompanying slates. The mountain, then, stands in the chapter of uses *also as* a great laboratory, in which a number of waters, mineral and pure, are produced; and this alone would seem a sufficient end or final cause for its existence. The student of another order of values might pass its song of the waters with indifference, and find in its coal-seams—those magazines of wealth and power to man, in its valuable forests and soil, its masses of iron, and useful rocks—the only objects worthy of his attention, and the only *end* for which it was desirable to create the mountain at all. 'Tis thus to the partial and one-sided, the narrow and utilitarian, that the world ever appears. But such is the order of things, that "each *end* is a *beginning;*" *there are no private contracts,—favoriteism and selfishness being unknown in nature.* The worm borer in the stick of timber, and the human borer in the coal-seam; the sap-sucker penetrating the bark of the sugar-tree, and the salt-boiler perforating the brine-rock; the caterpillar eating the leaves of the linden for bread, and the painter sketching its foliage for beauty, may *each suppose that the important individual* has a universe to himself,—"is unrelated, unallied." "See, *all things for* MY *use*," especially *this thing;* but the worm's log must make the coal-digger a prop for the roof of his drift; the sap-sucker's maple must make the salt-sucker a handle for his drill; while the caterpillar's linden-tree will make an excellent bowl, from which the hungry artist might eat his mush and milk. Need the brook-trout, sporting in the mossy rock-bed of the crystal torrent, quarrel with the pale valetudinarian who drinks new life from its pure waters?* "*All things* are kind to our flesh, in their *descent and being*," and of one wondrous web, although cut in different patterns, and *apparently* for *different* ends, are all the creatures of the earth.

A scientific estimate of the intrinsic and perpetual worth of things will give to the pure freestone or soft water of the mountain the greatest consideration; this is its crowning blessing—the true heal-all and specific for the maladies of men. Springing, as we have observed, from the large silicious formations which make the highest spurs of the mountain, the waters have the mean annual temperature of the rock from which they issue; and they are frequently so pure that chemical tests give but traces of any foreign element whatever, thus demonstrating their constitution to be as nearly as can ever occur in nature, absolute or pure water.†

---

* Provided always, of course, that said valetudinarian be not in fell purpose intent on predatory invasion of the sacred haunts of said trout, or be armed with cruel, barbed instruments of death, wickedly concealed by worm writhing in the tortures of longitudinal transfixation, or seductively hidden within the treacherous folds of brilliant feathers, stolen from the neck of chicken-cock, styled, in Waltonian phrase, "*The Fly.*"

† Absolutely pure natural water does not exist. Water falling from the clouds contains carbonic acid gas and ammonia. "Decomposition of silicious and other rocks occurs from the action of water holding in solution carbonic acid, and the organic acids arising from the decay of vegetable matter." Silica is never absent from natural water, and is greater in surface waters slightly impregnated with mineral ingredients. The analysis of Sterry Hunt, of the waters of

HYDROLOGY.   121

It follows, from this, that for all the multifarious order of uses to which man applies this indispensable element, from the building up of his "heaven-labored form, erect, divine," to the humblest of domestic uses, pure water is the great and indispensable *want;* pure water is the best, under *all* conditions, to bathe in, consequently the best to wash the human integuments or skin in; it is the best water to wash his outer covering or clothes in; and *emphatically* the best to supply the perpetually wasting vital streams within, or blood currents of his body.

The question of temperature or thermalism is one of interest and importance. As a general thing, the springs of the mountain have the general mean of their localities. Some of the waters which are highly mineralized, and which flow from the coal-bearing rocks, have a *slight elevation* of their temperature. This is, no doubt, attributable to the chemical changes of decomposition which occur within the masses, from which the water derives its mineral contents. Of this order is the well-known heat arising from the decomposition of pyrites, which has been known to ignite coal and other substances in contact with it. Of the class of warm and hot springs, or those having a temperature over one hundred degrees, there are no representatives in the mountain, as yet discovered in Pennsylvania.

Farther southwest the Appalachian range of fractures and axes give some true thermal waters. See Moorman's book on Springs of Virginia, and Geological Reports.

Of the *individual springs* of medicated waters of Pennsylvania, a short notice will be in place. Some of these waters have been the subject of extravagant encomiums, and fictitious chemical analysis, purporting to possess fabulous and

the Ottawa and St. Lawrence rivers, gives the presence of chloride of sodium and potassium, sulphate, carbonate, and bromate of soda, carbonate of lime and magnesia, silica, and a trace of alumina. The analysis of Schuylkill water, by Booth, Garrett, and Camac, gives the presence of silex, lime, soda, potash, magnesia, alumina, or oxide of iron, the acids being sulphuric and carbonic.

impossible, because *incompatible*, elements, with extensive manifestoes or representations, in the ordinary mode of publication of such things. Many have received *no notice*, or but slight and comparatively insignificant attention. The true worth of these unknown and neglected waters will soon be declared to the world, as their effects are being clearly pronounced by critical observation and experience. As the need of them shall be felt, they will attract attention and experimentation until their true character shall be demonstrated, and their great value declared.

PENNSYLVANIA MINERAL SPRINGS.

SEVERAL members of the series of geological formations, constituting the surface of this State, give origin to valuable mineral springs. When a full, minute, and perfect exploration, such as has now been partially achieved by the geological survey of the State, shall be made known to the world, it will be discovered that Pennsylvania, so munificently provided with mineral resources of so great a variety, and so exhaustless in quantity, is also as richly furnished with a diversity of mineral waters. This would follow as a necessary consequence; the source of all mineralization of water being, as we have seen, the rock formations of the earth, which are the medicated media or sieves, through which it passes after its descent from the clouds. Diversity of composition in mineral masses would then give, consequently, a variety of mineralized waters. This we find to be eminently the case throughout the State of Pennsylvania; and thus it ultimately will be discovered that the State which persists with such obstinate pertinacity to call herself, and *insists upon being called by everybody else*, the EMPIRE STATE, with her large catalogue of mineral waters, will only have enjoyed her pre-eminence in this particular because the Yankee has been sharp enough to endeavor to ascertain the true character of things about him, and *smart enough to tell it to the world* when he did—the splendid final report of the Geological Survey of New York, and its beautifully elaborated division—on the chemistry of her rocks and mineral springs, having long been before the world.*

In this department it is to be deeply deplored that Pennsylvania has so long remained in darkness, and her indus-

---

* Mineralogy of New York, by Dr. Beck.

trious, intelligent, and enterprising people, anxious to develop her mineral resources of every order, after the expenditure of immense sums of money, and the laborious efforts for years of some twenty gentlemen of highly respectable intellectual endowments and undoubted scientific attainments, have been denied access to the results of the explorations of this corps, until the existence of such results was mythical, and they had come to be regarded as eternally forbidden fruits.

The aggregated labors of the accomplished and indefatigable men forming the corps of the Geological Survey of Pennsylvania, will soon appear in the form of the final report of that survey, which, with the original survey, has now, strange to say, been in progress nearly a *quarter of a century*.

When this achievement, so long and ardently prayed for, shall have been fully realized and actually accomplished, by the *finished, final report* being *handed at last to the people* of Pennsylvania, it is to be hoped it will awaken a new spirit of inquiry with regard to her mineral resources, and reproduce, in these times of despondency and industrial paralysis, a new tidal wave of healthy progress and sound expansion. Will it not also excite a new interest in, and impart a new impetus to, the practical application of the *waters* of the State,—to the whole class of uses originally designed by nature?

Commencing below, and at the base of the group of palæozoic formations, we are presented with a few valuable springs in the metamorphic rocks or gneissic group.

The waters of these rocks have not attracted the attention they deserve, and have received, in some of the neighboring States, where they are found to be of a valuable character. Proceeding upward, in the rock series, we find in the first large limestone formation, (No. 2,) a number of springs. Some of these are of great volume; the rocks being soluble, the waters which fall in the valleys gradually wear deep subterranean sewers and caves; the springs are frequently of immense size. These are generally common springs of limestone water, or holding in solution the salts of lime. There are some true mineral springs which have attracted attention in this group, both in Pennsylvania and Virginia.

In the *transition* between this formation and the one below, the waters are also frequently mineralized. In the *passage into* the formation above, the dark slate group, which contains a number of mineral elements, there have been noticed some valuable waters, as also *in* No. 3 itself.

In the fourth formation, (No. 4,) which we have seen, is a large accumulation of silicious strata, there is but little variety in the water, as the quartzose elements, constituting almost the entire substance of the formation, are but slightly soluble in water at the temperature of the earth. The waters of this formation are generally, then, soft and pure, containing few mineral or organic substances in solution or suspension. The next formation above, or fifth of the series, being a slate group with lime, magnesian, and iron-ore strata intermingling, the springs are consequently more diversified in their character than the preceding, and belong to the classes carbonated, saline, and chalybeate. The next formation, sixth in the ascending series, is a limestone, (No. 6,) with a few interlayers of slate. Some valuable waters emerge from this formation. Succeeding this is a small sand group with some slate layers, too limited generally in its development to give character to the waters which pass through it. The next formation, olive slate, (No. 8,) of the series is an enormous mass of slate or argillaceous strata with silicious interminglings. There are also in the lower part of the formation some calcareous layers; also a quantity of the carbonate and sulphuret of iron. That portion of the formation containing these substances is a soft black friable slate. As would be expected from the number of mineral elements above enumerated, most of which possess strong chemical affinity for decomposition, and of course the reproduction of new compounds, many of which are soluble in water, it would of course follow that the springs of this mass would exhibit diversity in mineral characters. The next formation above, (No. 9,) is a slate and sand group of large extent with few soluble elements. In some portions of the State it contains iron in different forms, and here of course mineral waters might be looked for. The formation succeeding this (No. 10 of the series) being constituted principally of coarse heavy silicious masses, almost insoluble, gives consequently common unmineralized springs. The next is the shale formation, (No. 11,) with lime layers, and succeeding this is the *Conglomerate and Coal Series*, constituting the summit of the whole group. It is made up, as we have seen in the chapter on geology, of sandstone layers, slate and shale strata, limestone layers, and coal-seams. From this extensive range of mineral elements it would naturally be inferred that we would be presented with a corresponding number of mineral waters. This we accordingly discover to be the fact. In the lower part of the carboniferous group we find true saliferous or salt-bearing strata. In certain portions of the State these are perforated by boring from a few hundred to many hundred feet in depth, and from these borings, or wells, as they are called, large quantities of the finest common salt are manufactured. They are situated in the bituminous coal series upon the tributaries of the Alleghany and Monongahela rivers. Of these the Conemaugh and Kiskiminetas and Sewickly are the most extensively worked. The water of these salt-wells also contains iodine and bromine, which have been made from them in small quantities, also salts of magnesia and lime in appreciable quantities; they are classified, however, among the pure brine or salt waters. The shales, limestones, and coal-seams give rise to other classes of waters containing mineral elements. We consequently find in this region, as has been remarked in the general observations on the hydrology of the mountain, representatives of most of the classes of medicated waters,—the acidulous and carbonated occurring where the alkaline bases prevail, and the saline in the region where the rocks containing salt can be penetrated. It is, however, the classes of sulphureous and chalybeate waters that this formation supplies most abundantly. The origin of these materials in the waters is obvious. Free sulphuric acid is found in many springs coming from coal-seams, forming true sour or acid waters. The association of mineral waters in Pennsylvania with fractures and dislocations of the rock strata, or axes and faults, shows the same law as observed by geologists in New York and Virginia. The recent report of Sterry Hunt to Mr. William E. Logan, in the Geological Survey of Canada for 1857, presents an emphatic confirmation of the same law, all the mineral springs reported issuing from the palæozoic formations of the Lower Silurian in the line of axes, fractures and dislocations, as at other places. Whether the suggestions of the geologists, many of which appear wise, are the real philosophy on the subject, may require some more observation of facts to demonstrate. The suggestions have the highest plausibility to support them, and are ardently advocated by Forbes, Daubeny, and some American geologists.

Although the mineral waters of Pennsylvania have not received the attention they deserve, still there are a number of springs which have acquired justly merited celebrity; they belong to the classes already enumerated. Some of them have been in use for many years, and have enjoyed a wide and extended reputation; whilst others, more recently discovered, enjoy a more limited popularity, and have a more restricted and local faith attached to their virtues. Among those longest known and best established in their reputation are the

BEDFORD SPRINGS.

They are among the first-noticed springs of the State, and are situated near the town of Bedford, in the county of the same name. Their waters flow into one of the tributaries of the Juniata River. There are here several springs which are asserted to possess different characters, and all flow from *the same geological formation.* This is the *limestone* situated between the large slate formations; the Corniferous Limestone of the New York Geological Reports, and the sixth formation in the Pennsylvania group, (No. 6.) Above this formation is the thin porous sandstone of Formation 7; succeeded by the large slate and shale groups already spoken of. As we have seen, the *lower* part of Formation 8 contains quantities of sulphuret of iron, and the decomposition of this substance with the consequent liberation of sulphuric acid, (the limestone itself containing strata of a peculiar fetid rock, full of organic remains and magnesia,) is undoubtedly the origin of the salts of the springs which issue from it. There are here several minor foldings or waves of the rocks between the large axes of the mountains surrounding the valley in which the springs are situated. These form small anticlinal axes and synclinal troughs, some of which contain the black slate above alluded to in Formation 8, and it is here that the meteoric water is first impregnated and afterwards breaks out, after traversing the channels of the lime rock for some distance, in one of the anticlinal arches at the springs. The principle spring,

"ANDERSON'S,"

Is designated a "Saline chalybeate." The substances which possess the active qualities which have given character to the spring are the sulphate of magnesia, the muriates of soda and lime, and carbonates of *iron* and *lime.* The quantity of carbonic acid gas in a quart of the water is stated by Dr. Church to be *eighteen and a half cubic inches (!!!)* the temperature of the spring being 55° Fahr.: somewhat higher than that of other springs in the neighborhood. Their reputation is, that they possess certain powers over diseases of the stomach and bowels, also over renal affections; and in chronic, cutaneous, gouty, and rheumatic derangements, they are said to be beneficial. A critical analysis by Dr. Church gives in a quart of the water thirty-one grains of residuum, of which Epsom salts is 20 grains, the balance being constituted of the already enumerated elements.*

FLETCHER'S SPRING

Is a short distance from Anderson's, and shows more iron and common salt, with less magnesia, but in other respects like the last-named spring. Quite a range of morbid states are supposed to be benefited by these waters; especial advocates of their virtues giving lengthy catalogues of the affections over which they exert their power, commencing with the stomach and including the whole range of the primæ viæ, with offended associated organs; also of skin, with "secondary diseases of lungs originating from sympathy of those *organs* with the *stomach* and *liver*, over which conditions these waters, *together with the bracing vigor of the mountain air*, are *said to effect most happy changes.*" Sulphur Spring is also within a short distance of Anderson's. It is said to contain carbonic acid and sulphuretted hydrogen gas, lime, magnesia, and *common salt*.

SWEET SPRING,

Also near Anderson's, is pure water, containing very little mineral substance in any shape.

Three miles from Anderson's and one and a half from Bedford, northeast, there is a chalybeate spring. This is a small spring exhaling the odor of sulphuretted hydrogen, said to contain carbonic acid, sulphuretted hydrogen, carbonate of iron, muriate of soda, and magnesia. The waters of Bedford have long enjoyed a deserved celebrity. The place,

---

* The analysis of Dr. Chester J. Morris, of Philadelphia, shows a wide discrepancy, compared with this old analysis of Dr. Church, in *quantity* of chemical contents, in the *proportion* of the *substances*, and even in the *existence* of *some items*. They agree, however, on the presence of some of the leading elements in the waters, in some shape and proportion.

situated in a pleasant valley, among the mountains east of the Alleghany range, offers elements of attraction found at few summer retreats.

HUNTINGDON SPRINGS.

Five miles north of the town of Huntingdon, in Huntingdon County, are some springs called the "Warm Springs." They have been a place of resort for many years. Their exact temperature, whether really above the annual mean of the place or their chemical contents, have not yet been made the subject of scientific investigation. The waters of these springs issue from the base of a monoclinal axis with eastern dips of Formation 7, which here forms the Warrior Ridge, on the summit of which are isolated shafts or needles of this formation, left by denudation, called Pulpit Rocks.

FRANKFORT MINERAL SPRINGS

Are situated in Beaver County, near the village of Frankfort. They emerge from rocks which belong to the carboniferous group.

CAVE SPRING, of this place, contains carbonic acid, carbonate of iron, and magnesia, sulphuretted hydrogen, muriate of soda, and a *minute portion of bitumen*. This is the analysis of Dr. Church. LEIPER SPRING, near the above, contains more iron and soda, less magnesia, and about the same proportion of sulphuretted hydrogen and carbonic acid. These waters are prescribed in a variety of diseased conditions: dyspeptic derangements of the stomach, rheumatism and skin diseases, with general debility.

There is a chalybeate spring a few miles from Pittsburg. Dr. Mead's analysis gives muriate of soda, muriate of magnesia, oxide of iron, sulphate of iron, sulphate of lime, carbonic acid gas, 18 cubic inches to the quart!!

FAYETTE SPRINGS

Are in Fayette County, near the National Road's crossing of Laurel Hill. They emerge from shales and sandstones, belonging to the carboniferous group a short distance above the conglomerate. Coal and iron ore abound in the neighborhood; the water is a *pure, strong chalybeate*, with the properties and virtues of iron waters generally.

They are situated in the second bituminous coal-basin west of the Alleghany, in a mountainous region, surrounded by beautiful scenery, and with a most enchanting atmosphere.

BLOSSBURG MINERAL SPRINGS

Are in Tioga County, at the town named; and, according to Dr. E. Hartshorne, the waters are acid.

Besides the excess of sulphuric acid, they contain sulphates of iron and alumina, with sulphate of magnesia, and possess the properties of these substances.

BATH CHALYBEATE SPRINGS, near Bristol, on the Delaware River, were noticed as early as 1773, by Dr. B. Rush.

The Artesian well of Petty's Island, opposite northern Philadelphia, is a chalybeate. Booth's analysis "gives bicarbonate of iron, lime, magnesia, and soda, silica, organized matter, and carbonic acid."

YORK SPRINGS

Are in Adams County, within a few hours' travel of a number of large towns. One of the springs contains sulphate of magnesia, sulphate of lime, and muriate of soda. There is also here an iron spring, possessing the usual properties of those springs.

PERRY COUNTY SPRINGS.

The waters of these springs are 70° F., and said to be aperient and diuretic. They are upon Sherman's Creek, eleven miles from Carlisle.

Carlisle Springs.

Near this town there is a sulphureous spring. There are also fine common springs here.

Doubling Gap Springs

Are called sulphureous and chalybeate. They are situated in Cumberland County, eight miles from Newville. They contain sulphuretted hydrogen, carbonate of soda, and magnesia, Glauber salts, Epsom and common salt. The chalybeate shows bicarbonate of iron as a principal ingredient, also Epsom salts, common salt, and carbonate of magnesia. Of course they possess the medicinal properties of elements contained.

Yellow Springs,

In Chester County, are not reputed to possess any medicinal properties, but are very pure, and the place attractive.

Ephrata Springs,

In Lancaster County, is also a place of considerable resort. *Common spring* water is supplied in every way to visitors, and the place extremely attractive.

Caledonia Springs

Are within fifteen miles of Chambersburg, at the base of South Mountain. The delights as well as sanitary advantages of this retreat are eloquently advocated by Dr. Bell, although *only a pure water*, with a temperature 52° F. *The springs have great reputation for the cure of divers grave maladies.* Speaking of them, Dr. Bell has the following observations:—"Without *meaning to undervalue the efficacy of mineral waters*, the writer can recommend invalids, or the WEAK, who wish to become *stronger*, to make the regular drinking of the SINGULARLY PURE WATER of one of the springs before breakfast and before dinner, a part of the pleasant regimen of good eating, sound sleeping, and *varied exercise*, which he will enjoy at this favored spot."

Other springs of the world, not medicinal, have acquired the *same reputation "for the cure of a large number of diseases."* Of these are the Malvern springs, in England, alluded to by Dr. Bell and others. The Malvern, acknowledged to be of *extreme purity,* is said to "SOMETIMES PURGE," *and be serviceable in "chronic cutaneous diseases, used externally* and internally." The waters of Caledonia are recommended to be used both by bath and internally.

THE ALLEGHANY MOUNTAIN SPRINGS

Are situated near the summit of the Alleghany, in Cambria County, at the point of crossing of the great thoroughfare of the State, the road of the Central Rail-Road Company, Cresson Station, near the contemplated mountain village of Rhododendron. These springs are more than two thousand feet above the level of the sea, surrounded by original forests, amidst the range of vertebral knobs or spinous processes constituting the highest line of water shedding, and the true summit of the great Appalachian chain. There are here a number of springs, which rise and flow from a small mountain vale scooped out of the western side of the crest of the Alleghany. At this elevated spot the tributaries of two large rivers have their origin; some of the rivulets flowing east into the Atlantic through the channel of the Susquehanna and Chesapeake Bay, while others flow west through the Conemaugh and Mississippi to the Gulf of Mexico. The springs of this new watering-place exhibit the general character of the waters of the Alleghany Mountain heights.

The greatest point of interest and attraction, the truly invaluable quality of a number of these springs, is their almost absolute purity. The geological position of the place, or the rock formations from which they flow, as already explained, is among the silicious and argillaceous masses in the lower barren part of the bituminous coal series. Those which *flow exclusively through* sand masses and slate, are of course almost free from the presence of all earthy substances, as these rocks are but slightly soluble in *cold water.*

It occurs then, that by these vast and perfect filters of nature, all surface-washings of vegetable and other substances are effectually arrested in the process of percolation. The greater number of the springs at this place are of this character, some being so pure that chemical tests show only *traces of any mineral substances whatever*, or water as nearly absolute as possible. There are, however, some of the springs which are highly charged with chemical elements; these come from the calcareous layers and pyritous shales associated with the lower group of coal-seams. Some of these are gently aperient, more of them tonic, from the intermingling of the salts which possess those powers. The true *mineral waters* of this place, which excel all others, are the chalybeates. This class of waters is found, as we have seen, in the greatest perfection in the coal series.

Of the *individual* springs which have received attention at this new establishment, chartered by the Legislature of Pennsylvania, in the name of the Alleghany Mountain Health Institute, a few may be selected as the subject of special notice.

RHODODENDRON SPRING.

This is a large, pure water spring, emerging in a considerable volume from a group of crushed strata, which is formed almost exclusively of silicious elements or sand. It is the drain of an extensive bench of this rock, and the spring is perhaps 1000 feet northeast of the large hotel. The volume of water is never changed much during the dryest season, and retains a mean temperature of 43° F. The water of this spring is limpid and sweet, and as near water in purity, or distilled water, as can occur naturally. It is used for all domestic purposes, and its extremely low temperature makes it a perfect luxury at the hottest seasons, without ice. This spring is invaluable as an absolute or nearly perfectly pure water.

A few hundred yards north of this spring there is a group called the

"HEMLOCK SPRINGS."

These springs emerge from slate strata, and contain some iron, with carbonate of lime. They have a temperature of 45° Fahr., and are situated in a dense forest of hemlock-trees.

"CAKATION SPRING"

Is five or six hundred yards east of "Hemlock Springs." It is higher up in the geological series, emerging from slate, and sandstone interlayers, does not contain appreciable quantities of any earthy salts, being a water of exceeding purity.

West of Rhododendron Spring, perhaps one hundred rods, is QUEMAHONING SPRING, the water containing, according to Booth, Garrett, and Camac, a trace of sulphate of lime and magnesia. It is nearly a pure water, emerging from a group of slate rocks and sandstones.

"MEADOW SPRING"

Is still farther west than Quemahoning, and possesses the same general character, according to the tests of the laboratory.

"DISCORD SPRING"

Emerges from a mass of slate and shale, containing traces of salts of lime, and iron.

"BRANDY SPRING."

This spring derives its name from the generous flow of that beverage which occurred at the time of its discovery. It is a pure freestone water at the temperatute of 45° Fahr., and, according to Booth, Garrett, and Camac, contains only the smallest appreciable traces of lime and magnesia. It is a few hundred yards south of the Mountain House, supplying that house and its baths with water, and, according to the above chemists, who tested it, "may be termed a water of great purity."

Of the class of proper chalybeate waters there are several springs in the neighborhood of the hotels, coming from slates and shales lower down in the series, the most distinguished of which is

"Ignatius' Spring."

This is a strong iron water, depositing, as it flows, quantities of ochery precipitates of hydrated peroxide of iron, from escape of the carbonic acid gas. It has been named after the venerable huntsman (Ignatius Adams) who first discovered its life-preserving powers, and gave to the world, in his own person, a revelation of the secret of its true medicinal properties. By drinking this water, dwelling in the woods, and eating venison, he has lived to near the good old age of one hundred years. It seemed but a just tribute to his worth to give his name to the spring. It has, however, always been called the "Sulphur Spring," although chemical analysis has given the presence of *no sulphuretted hydrogen gas* in its waters. It was supposed to be sulphureous from its depositing the *bright-yellow* ochery oxide of iron, imagined *to be sulphur*, and also from a tradition connected with Ignatius, as one of the intrepid Nimrods of the Alleghany Mountain, and his well-known love for, and *faith in gun-powder*. The tradition of the origin of its sulphureous character has never been considered an idle tale, as it was generally believed by the natives that "Old Ig.," as he is sometimes profanely called by the boys, had, on some occasion of glory, spilled the contents of his powder-horn into the spring, and that it has tasted of gunpowder and been depositing sulphur ever since. If they had substituted ink-horn for *powder-horn*, the association of its sensible properties with the tradition of their origin would have been very close to the fact as it now exists, possessing, as it does, the actual taste of *ink*, but it would not have *fitted so appropriately* the character of the old huntsman.

PENNSYLVANIA MINERAL SPRINGS.

The analysis made in the laboratory of Booth, Garrett, and Camac, of Philadelphia, shows the presence of *iron, lime, magnesia, carbonic and sulphuric acid*. In their report of the examination of this water they say, "One gallon contains 144 *grains* of mineral matter, consisting of sulphate of iron, sulphate of lime, *carbonate of iron*, and *sulphate* of magnesia. It is, therefore, a CHALYBEATE or iron spring of GOOD QUALITY, and will exhibit decided medicinal properties when employed fresh from the spring."

This water has fixed a well-established character in a range of cures of maladies requiring tone and exaltation *of the life of tissues and organs*. Its virtues have long been appreciated and appropriated by the inhabitants of the neighborhood and strangers who have visited the mountain springs.

This spring is one half-mile south of the "Mountain House," the principle hotel of the Sanitarium or Health Institute Association. It arises from the earth near one of the lower group of coal-seams, and deposits its yellow sediment from precipitation of iron for some distance as it flows over the surface. The walk to this spring is through a forest of ancient hemlock, birch, and chestnut trees, woods called primeval, from whose cool, sequestered shades the weary invalid can absorb life and strength as he wanders to the charmed fountain of "Ignatius."

There are *other springs* in this interesting locality; they will, however, fall into the classes described under the head of the *general notice of the waters of the mountain*.

There are many mineral springs in Pennsylvania but little known to the public, which it is hoped will soon be analyzed, and recorded in the list of regular medicated waters of the State. *Pre-eminent* in valuable minerals in the *solid state*, shall *she not also be pre-eminent in the fluid, or springs* of minerals possessing medicinal properties?

BRANDYWINE SPRINGS, *in Delaware*, are a few miles from Wilmington. They belong to the class of chalybeates.

MAINE SPRINGS.

Passing in rapid review the mineral springs of the continent, those only which have been most frequently described, and whose contents have been the subject of more or less chemical investigation, will be catalogued; and first those of the United States will be noticed, commencing at the northeast and pursuing, to a certain extent, the obvious geographic range, followed by Dr. Bell, in the work already alluded to, and from which frequent quotations will be made in this synopsis.

Mineral Springs of Maine.

In the first report of the Geological Survey of Maine, Dr. C. T. Jackson gives an account of "Lubeck Saline Spring:" water colorless; specific gravity 1·025; analysis of 100 grains of dried salt gives, in a pint of water,—

Chloride of sodium,	64·1 grs.
Sulphate of lime,	3·6 "
Chloride of magnesium,	20·2 "
Sulphate of soda,	9·0 "
Carbonate of iron,	0·8 "
Carbonate of lime,	2·0 "
Chloride of calcium,	trace.
Carbonic acid gas,	———

At *Dexter* there is a chalybeate spring, described as an excellent iron water, by Dr. Jackson. It is said to be a good tonic in digestive disorders.

SPRINGS OF VERMONT.

In this State there are sulphureous springs within a few miles of St. Alban's Bay, called "HIGHGATE SPRINGS." East of Montpelier is the "NEWBURG SULPHUREOUS SPRING." The water of this spring is impregnated with sulphuretted hydrogen gas.

ALBURGH SPRINGS are of the same character.

Professor Hitchcock describes a spring called the "BENNINGTON THERMAL SPRING," containing *nitrogen and oxygen gases* (*!!!*)

"CLARENDON GASEOUS SPRINGS" give slightly acidulous waters. Dr. Hayes's analysis shows the presence of nitrogen, carbonic acid, and atmospheric air.

MASSACHUSETTS MINERAL WATERS.

Of these waters not much has yet reached the world at large. This is the more surprising, as the progressive Yankee State is given to *finding things out;* but on this subject we have very little, even under the overshadowing formula of the infinite GUESS, of that peculiarly sharp and wide-awake people. As recorded, it stands thus: BERKSHIRE SODA SPRINGS are acidulous, containing carbonic acid, soda, chlorine, and alumina. Location near Great Barrington, Berkshire County, —said to be in a region attractive for *more than* its water and air.

HOPKINTON SPRINGS show, from Dr. Gorham's analysis, carbonates of lime, magnesia, and iron; and another spring gives the presence of sulphur in its waters.

Notwithstanding the suggestions of Professor Mather, that geological investigations would reveal in certain lines of disturbances and fracturing, or upheaval of strata, northeast of New York, mineral springs similar to those in that State, there have, as yet, however, been made no discoveries of such springs, either in Vermont, New Hampshire, or Massachusetts. This is all the more astonishing, bearing in mind the present received doctrines of geologists on continuity of original formations.

MINERAL SPRINGS OF NEW YORK.

THAT same "Empire State," ambitious to be EMPIRE IN ALL THINGS, has certainly distinguished herself by her attention to her mineral springs, and by the invitation she has so long extended to the world to appreciate and enjoy the same. She is plentifully supplied with different kinds of mineral waters. Some of the mineral springs of New York are more celebrated than any others in the United States, and rival the far-famed springs of Europe. They are considered to possess more medicinal properties, and more rare and distinguished endowments in the sphere of sanitary attractions, than any other springs in this country. The *names* of SARATOGA and BALLSTON alone suggest not only the memory of gunpowder, or sulphur, and victory, but of health, fashion, and splendor.

The mineral springs of New York belong, as the list will show, to a number, or indeed all of the classes of waters, namely, carbonated, saline, sulphureous, and chalybeate. The geological position of the gaseous springs, the most celebrated of which are the Saratoga and Ballston range, according to Professor Mather, is in the transition of the Trenton limestone and superimposed slate, or Formations 2 and 3 of Pennsylvania. He also suggests, that the "source of the mineral qualities may be *deeper than* the junction of the Trenton limestone and slate, and even as far down in the series as the Calciferous Sandstone." (No. 1 of Pennsylvania.)

The waters of the Saratoga group are *carbonated saline*. This class of waters is very numerous in a certain part of the State, restricted, it is alleged, however, by the geologists of New York, to a *particular line* of disturbance and faults of the geological formations, all of which possess the same general character of water, or at least a strong resemblance. The springs at Saratoga form the centre of this range.

They have here a larger chain of distinctive features, and more clearly pronounced qualities, although the other springs possess the same chemical elements, differing only in quantity and proportion. A critical estimate of the whole range would show identity of character. Certain springs have, however, by common consent, been distinguished for superior qualities, and the Saratoga group is of that number. Of the origin of these waters, various geological theories have been suggested that scarcely concern us here, although the problem is intensely interesting to geologists, and one of paramount value in the final rendering of the natural history of these objects. The minute geology of the localities and surroundings decides the whole question; the waters, even of deep and thermal origin, deriving their mineral elements from the rock structures below the surface, and through which they flow. The reports of the Saratoga and Ballston springs exhibit almost perfect identity of chemical composition, and the superiority of the former, especially of the celebrated "CONGRESS SPRING," is only based upon an accidental character, or notoriety, whose shade of color is extremely questionable.

Of "Congress Spring," the analysis of Dana (Dr. Steel's being nearly the same) gives the following substances in a pint of the water:—

	DANA.	STEEL.
Chloride of sodium,	54·30 grs.	———
Hydriodate of soda,	———	0·44
Carbonate of soda,	2·00	———
Bicarbonate of soda,	———	1·12
Carbonate of magnesia,	4·00	———
Bicarbonate of magnesia,	———	11·97
Carbonate of lime,	18·00	———
Carbonate of iron,	———	0·68
Silica,	trace, with iron,	———
Hydrobromate of potassa,	trace,	———

They also contain carbonic acid gas, nitrogen, and atmospheric air. Temperature, 50, Steel; 51, Daubeny.

The PAVILION SPRING exceeds it in carbonic acid.

UNION SPRING shows greater quantity of saline elements, and carbonic acid less than in the last spring.

The PUTNAM SPRING is said, by Dr. Bell, to be among the richest of the Saratoga springs in iron, but nearly the same as the rest in other elements.

WALTON or IODINE SPRING contains hydriodate of soda, three grains to a gallon. Temperature, 47° F.

A number of other springs, HIGH ROCK, FLAT ROCK, WASHINGTON, and COLUMBIAN, are like those already enumerated, with the addition of iron. HIGH ROCK was the first spring discovered, according to Dr. Steel, and a sprinkling of Indian tradition mingles with its history, which extends back nearly ninety years.

There are also other springs enumerated as medicinal, as HAMILTON, JACKSON, ALEXANDER, RED, and SULPHUR SPRINGS, with temperatures from 47 to 51° F. Dr. Bell asserts that "all the mineral springs of the valley may be considered as, to a certain extent, *thermal*."

BALLSTON SPRINGS are seven miles from Saratoga, and have been used since 1787. The springs are the FRANKLIN SULPHUR, FULTON CHALYBEATE, UNITED STATES, PARK, and LOW'S WELL. The water of the UNITED STATES, according to Dr. Beck's analysis, contains in the pint,

Chloride of sodium,	53·12 grs.
Carbonate of soda,	2·11 "
Carbonate of lime, with iron,	3·65 "
Carbonate of magnesia,	0·72 "
Sulphate of soda,	0·22 "
Silica,	1·00 "
Carbonic acid,	30·50 cubic inch.

They contain less salt and gas than Saratoga. Some of the other springs contain iron in addition to the saline elements.

The Ballston and Saratoga waters have long been in use,

and have been the subject of great experimentation; also, the objects of a great amount of fabulous exaggeration; also worthy of attention as possessing positive merit as healing agents. In certain diseases, the profession is satisfied that their virtue is real, and their effects undoubted. The catalogue of their fancied and absolute healings would be a nosological table of almost the whole *range of human infirmities*. The *real* powers of these waters are those usually ascribed to all saline and aperient waters. A discriminating survey shows their chief force to be in their effects upon the organs contained in the cavity of the abdomen. This embraces the stomach, liver, small and large intestines, kidneys, etc., a large number of whose functional, and even organic derangements, are said to be curable by these waters. The special advocates of their powers give extensive tables of diseases within their control. Omitting what is obviously false and fraudulent in these statements and suggestions, a critical reading of the testimony in favor of their powers, points out the great abdominal region, with enclosed viscera, as the special theatre of their action, and its extensive class of diseases as the legitimate subjects of trial with them.

As these derangements are the horrors that hang, like the sword of Damocles, or the skull at the Egyptian banquet, over the classes of society diseased by luxurious indulgences, that division of the human family to whom it has become fabulous and absurd that the *chief end of man* is self-sacrifice and crucifixion of the flesh, but that the more tangibly good ends, the stuffing the human bread-basket, and having a good time generally, are demonstrably sound as a religious creed and system of salvation; it would follow, that any waters that have a tendency to swab out or deterge the great sacks and sewers of the body would be beneficial. It being the law, that swift and sure upon the heels of the indulgence comes the expiatory suffering, it would occur, even to the unthinking, that a clear navigation being effected in the tortuous canal of membranes that undoubtedly occupies the interior of the human body, (however *beautiful* and

MINERAL SPRINGS OF NEW YORK. 145

angelic the expression of the *outer husk* may be,) by the purgative action of the Saratoga waters upon said intestines of the fashionable world that resort to its famed fountains, would be followed by the most brilliant results.* We accordingly find that it *is thus* that this great assimilative cavity, with its contained organs, *are impressed;* also, the long complicated chains of sympathetic connections with other parts of the system modified and rearranged healthfully,—Epsom salts and common salt being the great sanitary forces. Much is said of the alterative properties of these waters, as great reorganizers upon all the tissues and organs, by the use of those said to contain iodine and iron, in connection with those containing salts and gases. In all this catalogue of distinguished achievements of Congress and other waters, it might be desirable to know *just the influence* of certain excursions to Saratoga Lake, Long Lake, and Lake George, together with *fishing excursions, and exercise of all kinds*, assisted by the "*balsamic and turpentine qualities of the air, impregnated with the pine and other forest-trees,*" in the assistance and furtherance of the action of said waters.

There are still other acidulous waters, varying slightly in

---

* On this subject, as involving literary and scientific issues in the great problem of the incarnation of the soul, it may be remarked that the effects of castor-oil upon the intellect and moral sentiments have long been known, at least to medical philosophers. How much of the heavens, in certain directions, could have been cleared up by the judicious application of vegetable or saline cathartics—how much of the atra-bilious tint bleached out of the theologies by blue-mass and Seidlitz powders; and how many of the gases, of the offensive and poisonous order, at least, could have been kept from penetrating the philosophies, by the chewing of rhubarb or aloes, and securing the perfectly regulated function of the large intestine.

This is a ghastly realm of human thought, carrying the mind into fearful abysses of speculation; but, at the same time, immensely rich in its resources, startling in its *suggestions*, and *portentous* in its *revelations* and *demonstrations*, especially in the departments of Theology, Metaphysics, and Poetry.

the proportion of their chemical elements. Of these are the Albany Artesian Mineral Wells; also Reed's Mineral Spring, in South Argyle, and Halleck's, in Oneida County, near Hampton.

Of chalybeate waters, New York claims also to possess a number of springs; of these are Sandlake Village Spring, in Rensselaer County, and others in Columbia, Dutchess, and Delaware counties.

Of the class of *sulphureous waters* New York has a large supply, as, according to Dr. Bell, "There is scarcely a single county in the State in which the springs of this class, impregnated with sulphuretted hydrogen, are not found;" and the geologists report a large number in some of the districts. Though widely separated, they have one common character with regard to temperature and mineral composition which would seem to point to a *common geological origin.* Besides sulphuretted hydrogen, these waters contain carbonic acid, carbonate and sulphate of lime, and some of them carburetted hydrogen.

SHARON and AVON are the most celebrated sulphur springs in New York.

SHARON SPRINGS are near Leesville, Schoharie County. They are called the "White Sulphur," and "Magnesian;" they come, according to Dr. Beck, "from the pyritous slates beneath the Helderburg limestone series." Dr. Chilton reports White Sulphur to contain, in a pint of water,—

Sulphate of magnesia,	2·65 grs.
Sulphate of lime,	6·68 "
Chloride of sodium,	0·14 "
Chloride of magnesium,	0·15 "
Hydro-sulphuret of sodium and calcium, each	0·14 "
With one cubic inch of sulphuretted hydrogen gas.	

Drs. Beck and North differ in this analysis.

MAGNESIAN SPRING has a slightly different composition, containing, like the other, sulphuretted hydrogen, according to the analysis of Professor Reed, of New York.

The AVON SPRINGS are near the town of Avon, eastern branch of Genesee River, in Livingston County. These springs have been used for more than half a century; they differ but slightly in chemical composition, and their general temperature is about 50° to 51° Fahr.

The Avon New Spring contains, in a pint,—

Carbonate of lime,	3·37 grs.
Sulphate of lime,	0·44 "
Magnesia,	1·01 "
Soda,	4·84 "
Chloride of sodium,	0·71 "
Sulphuretted hydrogen,	3·90 cubic inches.

Another spring, according to Professor Hadley, contains, in a pint,—

Sulphuretted hydrogen,	12·00 inches.
Carbonic acid,	5·00 cubic inches.
Carbonate of lime,	1·00 gr.
Sulphate of lime,	10·00 grs.
Sulphate of magnesia,	1·25 "
Sulphate of soda,	2·00 "
Chloride of sodium,	2·30 "

The third spring is said to be richer in salts than the last noticed.

The IODINE or SILVAN SPRINGS, according to the analysis of Dr. Chilton, contain an appreciable quantity of iodine, with other of the more ordinary combinations of saline elements.

Of the special virtues of the Avon and Sharon waters much has been said, both in separate treatises and also in works of a more general character. Their therapeutic qualities are those of sulphur waters generally. They are supposed to exert their force *emphatically* upon chronic diseases of the skin, mucous membranes, and rheumatism. Their claims are well set forth by Sallisbury, Francis, Bell, and others, whose detailed accounts of the waters used both internally and externally, qualities, modus operandi, etc., are certainly worthy of the greatest respect and most attentive consideration of all invalids and *physicians* who are desirous of being posted in the resources of their art. There are other sulphur springs in New York of considerable celebrity.

CLIFTON SPRING, in Ontario County, is said to be "so impregnated with gas that the odor is perceptible for *one-fourth of a mile.*" Temperature, 51° Fahr.

CHITTENANGO SPRINGS are in Madison County; they contain carbonate and sulphate of lime, sulphate of magnesia and chloride of sodium, sulphuretted hydrogen and carbonic acid gas; temperature, 49° Fahr. One of the springs also contains sulphate of soda. Dr. Beck speaks highly of these springs.

MANLIUS LAKE and SPRING, in Onondaga County, are charged with sulphuretted hydrogen.

The SALINE SPRINGS, of Salina and Syracuse, are also charged with sulphuretted hydrogen.

MESSINA SPRING also contains sulphur.

Near Auburn, in Cayuga County, there are springs called "AUBURN SPRINGS." From Chilton's analysis they contain, in a pint,—

Sulphate of lime,	15·00 grs.
Sulphate of magnesia,	3·20 "
Chloride of magnesium,	0·25 "
Chloride of sodium,	0·75 "
Sulphuretted hydrogen,	1·05 cubic inches.

ROCHESTER SPRING contains, in a pint,—

Carbonate of lime and magnesia,	1·48 grs.
Chloride of sodium,	6·52 "
Sulphate of soda,	6·97 "
Sulphuretted hydrogen and carbonic acid,	2·16 cubic inches.
Temperature, 52° Fahr.	

MINERAL SPRINGS OF NEW YORK.

There are a number of springs of the same character in Monroe County, whose waters have reputation as mineral.

VERONA SPRING, in Oneida County, according to Professor Noyes, contains, in a pint,—

Chloride of lime and magnesia,	8·50 grs.
Chloride of sodium,	90·00 "
Sulphate of lime,	7·50 "

Sulphuretted hydrogen in large quantities.

SAQUOIT SPRINGS, a few miles from Utica, are represented to be highly charged with sulphuretted hydrogen, also carburetted hydrogen, and chloride of sodium and magnesium, with sulphate of lime and iron.

Niagara County contains a number of sulphur springs, as in the vicinity of Lewistown and Pendleton.

SENECA SPRINGS contain quantities of gas, also saline substances.

Northern New York has sulphur springs in the counties of Clinton and St. Lawrence.

The valley of the Hudson contains, in the space of one hundred and fifty miles, a number of sulphur springs. There are, in other portions of the State, springs of this class, as HARROWGATE SPRINGS, in Rensselaer County, NEWBURG, in Orange County, CATSKILL, in Green County, also in Dutchess County, and NANTICOKE, in Broome County, and DRYDEN SPRINGS, in Tompkins County. There are sulphur springs in Chenango, Tioga, Stephen, and Cattaraugus counties. There are found in Chatauqua County a number of sulphur springs which evolve carburetted hydrogen.

There is still another class of springs in New York, viz. acid springs. They contain sulphuric acid in excess, with sulphate of alumina or alum, and sulphate of iron. At Byron, Genesee County, two of these springs are found, according to Dr. Beck, "containing nearly pure sulphuric acid, and not a solution of acid salts." Other acid springs are found in this county.

Near the village of Medina, in Genesee County, are the "OAKORCHARD ACID SPRINGS." Analyses by Chilton and Emmons give the presence of saline materials with the acid. Chilton's analysis gives free sulphuric acid in the proportions of 82·96 grs. to the gallon; also,

Sulphate of lime,	38·60 grs.
Alumina,	9·68 "
Magnesia,	8·28 "
Protosulphate of iron,	14·32 "

Emmons gives free sulphuric acid, to the pint, 31·50 grs.; also, sulphate of iron, lime, and magnesia. Other springs give 24·25 grs. free acid in a pint, and some only 19·30. The therapeutic properties of these springs are of course derived from their chemical contents. According to Drs. White and Spring, they are practically curative of quite a number of diseases, the catalogue of which they render.

LEBANON SPRING, in Columbia County, is thermal, its waters being 70° Fahr. It also contains saline impregnations and nitrogen gas.

Besides the springs already enumerated as medicinal waters, there are, in New York, a number of brine or salt springs. According to Dr. Beck, "they show a great sameness of composition. They all contain chlorides of calcium and magnesium, with common salt. They also contain bromine and iron, and are of great value, the State deriving considerable revenue from the salt springs of Onondaga County."

Springs containing nitrogen gas are found in Seneca, Rensselaer, and Franklin.

The FREDONIA SPRINGS, as observed, are highly charged with carburetted hydrogen. This gas occurs in quantities, and is extensively used for ordinary purposes of illumination.

Those who may wish fuller and more detailed accounts of the mineral springs of New York and their geological connections, may find them in Dr. Beck's "Mineralogy of New York;" Dr. Bell's "Mineral Springs;" also in Emmons, Hall, and geological reports, essays, and contributions. However interesting, really useful, and instructive it might be to dwell, especially upon their therapeutic properties and the question of their *real power over disease*, it would be out of place in a mere catalogue.

NEW JERSEY SPRINGS.

The principal mineral spring of New Jersey which has any reputation as medicinal, is Schooley's Mountain Spring. According to Dr. McNevin, the characteristic ingredients are muriate and sulphate of lime, and carbonated oxide of iron. As a carbonated chalybeate this is a valuable water, its indications being those which call for the use of iron generally; temperature, 50° Fahr.

Much is said of the delightful character of this retreat, and the *power* of *its water; not enough* of the *power of exercise and pure air.*

OHIO MINERAL WATERS.

There are many mineral springs in Ohio, according to Dr. Drake, but they have attracted little notice and been the subject of little scientific investigation. W. W. Mather, in the Geological Report of Ohio, asserts, "mineral springs may be found in almost every county." Those observed are of the classes of chalybeate, saline, and sulphureous waters.

"Yellow Spring" is in Green County, on the Cincinnati and Sandusky Railroad, sixty-four miles north of Cincinnati. It is described as proceeding from the same geological filter as the "chalybeate springs of the Olympian Valley, in Kentucky." The water, possessing the temperature of the springs of the surrounding country, 52° Fahr., is clear, and has a "slight chalybeate taste." Drake asserts it to be a tonic of "reputed powers in convalescent conditions from severe disease."

"WESTPORT SPRING" is in Deer Creek. Its chemical elements are "sulphate of magnesia, iron, and carbonic acid, its properties being cathartic."

There are mineral springs in Crawford County.

CAREY'S SPRING contains sulphuretted hydrogen and common salt.

WYANDOT SULPHUR SPRING, two miles below Upper Sandusky, contains sulphuretted hydrogen, sulphuric and muriatic acids, lime, and magnesia.

ANNAPOLIS SULPHUR SPRING contains sulphuretted hydrogen.

KNISLEY'S or CRAWFORD SULPHUR SPRING contains sulphuretted hydrogen, sulphate of magnesia, and lime, and promises to be an attractive watering-place.

DELAWARE SPRINGS, and springs at Cleveland and Medina, are mentioned by Mather, as also gas and petolium springs at several localities.

Salt springs are numerous in Ohio, and those of Muskingum County, Hocking and Sciota valleys, have long been known. Other springs are mentioned in the Geological Report, as CHALYBEATE SPRING, near Darrtown, SULPHUR SPRING, near Zoar, and NEW PHILADELPHIA, etc.

ILLINOIS SPRINGS.

Of the springs of this State there is an extremely meagre supply of facts. In a recent report, Dr. Norwood has given a number of analyses, but not of mineral waters. Dr. Bell enumerates a few, quoting from Professor Shepard.

UPPER ILLINOIS SPRINGS contain carbonate of lime and soda, chlorides of sodium, calcium, and magnesium, sulphate of lime, magnesia, and soda, carbonic acid and nitrogen gases. They possess a higher temperature than the surrounding springs. There is a sulphureous spring in the bank of the Illinois, said to contain "sulphuretted hydrogen and *hydrosulphuret* of *sodium.*" Sulphur springs are also found in the bed of Vermilion River.

IOWA SPRINGS.

Above the Raccoon Fork, on the Des Moines, associated with the carboniferous rocks of that region, there is a mineral water referred to by Owen in his Geological Report. It oozes from the argillaceous layers associated with the coal, and is described as "having a faint-brown tinge, acid reaction, and strong styptic taste."

According to Mr. Owen, "chemical reagents show that it is an acid solution of sulphate of alumina, sulphate of potash, and sulphate of protoxide of iron, and a little chloride of potassium and sodium. It is, in fact, a double alum of potash and protoxide of iron. The same kind of water was observed at several other localities on the Upper Des Moines."

MISSOURI MINERAL SPRINGS.

G. C. SWALLOW, the geologist of this State, has reported some mineral waters. "North River Lick," in Marion County, is a strong brine water. There are chalybeate springs and sulphur waters also reported, as "SULPHUR SPRING," on Lick Creek, "CHELTENHAM SULPHUR SPRING," etc.

VIRGINIA MINERAL SPRINGS.

PROCEEDING south, the next springs which attract attention are the mineral and thermal springs of Virginia. This State has been peculiarly blessed in this order of gifts. These springs have long been known, and justly esteemed; many of them belonging to the carbonated class of true thermal waters. And first on the subject of thermalism, the facts, and not the philosophy thereof, occupying the moment, a word on theories may be tolerated, nevertheless.

"THE VALLEY," as it is called, between the Blue Ridge and the Alleghany Mountain, is the location of a number of the most celebrated of the Virginia springs. They are quite numerous, and belong to several of the classes described. The region is delightful, possessing beauty of scenery and salubrity of atmosphere, and, as a spring region, has become celebrated; the marked effects of its waters and climate, as great hygienic and therapeutic powers of the world, having long been the subject of scientific interest to the medical profession of the United States.

In the geological theory of thermal springs, the observations of Professor Forbes and Dr. Daubeney find some confirmation in the position of the Virginia springs, according to Dr. W. B. Rogers, the geologist of that State, who points out the association of thermal springs with anticlinal axes and faults, showing that of "fifty-six springs mentioned in twenty-five distinct localities within an area of 15,000 square miles, forty-six springs are *on* or *near axes*, seven on faults and inversions, and three—the only group of this kind yet known in Virginia—near point of contact of hypogene, or primitive with Appalachian rocks."

The observations were made in the great limestone valley of Virginia, upon *springs decidedly thermal*, according to ordinary acceptance, applying the term *thermal*, as *Bischof does*, to "springs with temperature *above* the atmospheric mean of the region in which they are situated."

Professor W. B. Rogers considers that the "great proportion of the copious and constant springs of the vast belt of mountains occupied by the Appalachian range, especially those of the great limestone valley of Virginia, are *truly* though *slightly thermal*, and that they owe to a deep subterranean source the remarkable *uniformity they exhibit.*"

This excludes the formula of volcanism, as there are "no volcanic or igneous rocks over the vast surface of the Appalachian region;" the source of heat being *"hot strata in the interior;* the fractures and arches of the rocks being the mere appliances mechanical, by which the water is admitted to the region of constant fires."

Similar observations have been made by other geologists in different parts of the world.

The views of the New York geologists on this subject have been already noticed, and Professor Mather's suggestions on the range of continued northeast disturbances alluded to.

On the subject of the connection of mineral springs with axes, we have also some interesting facts in the recent report (for 1857) of Sterry Hunt to Sir William E. Logan, of the Geological Survey of Canada. He says:—"There are few mineral springs in the *undisturbed portion* of the western basin of Canada. *Almost all* of the mineral springs issue from *palæozoic formations*, and the *greater part* from the lower silurian rocks of Lower Canada. They are connected, as elsewhere, *with disturbances, axes, dislocations, faults, and intrusive rocks.*"

Of the springs of Virginia, of the class Thermal, a number are quite celebrated.

"WARM SPRINGS," in Bath County, are fifty miles from Staunton, and one hundred and seventy from Richmond. The temperature is 98–99° F. The solid contents are small in quantity, some twenty grains in the gallon. The water also contains nitrogen, carbonic acid, and sulphuretted hydrogen gases. It is used both internally and externally, in a number of diseases, as in joint and skin-diseases, paralysis, scrofulous degenerations, and glandular obstructions. These waters are delightful in the extreme for bathing, also, truly medicinal in quality. They have been long in use, and have been much extolled by writers on this subject. They have reputation in an extensive catalogue of diseases, embracing that multifarious variety of conditions for which warm bathing is recommended. The gases of this water are nitrogen, sulphuretted hydrogen, and carbonic acid; and the saline contents, muriate of lime, sulphate of magnesia, carbonate and sulphate of lime, with soda. Temperature, 98° F.

HOT SPRINGS are also in Bath County, five miles west of Warm Spring. The water is from 98 to 100° F. They are used in cases of disease alone, as gout, chronic rheumatism, debility positive, together with chronic derangements of stomach and intestine; also, glandular obstructions, chronic ulcers, scrofulous swellings, diseases of skin, and paralytic cases. They are used internally also as excitants, in weak conditions of the stomach and bowels, chronic disease of bowels and stomach, also as diuretics and diaphoretics. According to Dr. Goode, the water of Hot Springs is not a simple, pure hot water, but contains sulphate and carbonate of lime, sulphate of soda and magnesia, muriate of iron, carbonic acid, sulphuretted hydrogen, nitrogen, and are useful, internally administered.*

BATH SPRING is situated in Berkley County, and has been styled a "mild, carbonated, thermal water." It contains salts of lime and magnesia, and has a temperature of 73° F. It is said to be useful in rheumatic affections, and in several chronic derangements.

Virginia is furnished with a number of extremely valuable springs of the class of *sulphureous waters*. This group is one of much interest. The springs are called by different names, indicative of some noticeable fact about them, as White Sulphur, Blue Sulphur, Salt Sulphur, and Red Sulphur.

WHITE SULPHUR SPRINGS are in Greenbrier County, on Howard's Creek, in the midst of the famous region of springs. According to Augustus H. Hayes, of Roxbury, they contain nitrogen, oxygen, carbonic acid, and hydrosulphuric acid gases, 16 inches to 237 inches or a gallon of the water. Of saline matter, they contain sulphate of lime in large quantity, sulphate of magnesia, chloride of magnesium, carbonate of lime, organic matter, with some silicates. This is of the order of saline sulphuretted waters. Much is said of a "*certain organic substance*" by the chemist, who also suggests that the "*medical property* of the waters *are due to this substance.*" In the analysis of Professor W. B. Rogers, of Virginia, the list is a long one of the mineral contents, embracing, in 100 cubic inches of water,—

Sulphate of lime,	31·680 grs.
Sulphate of magnesia,	8·241 "
Sulphate of soda,	4·050 "
Carbonate of lime,	1·530 "
Carbonate of magnesia,	0·506 "
Chloride of calcium,	0·010 "

* Moormann's "Mineral Springs of Virginia."

Chloride of magnesium,	0·070 grs.
Chloride of sodium,	0·226 "
Protosulphate of iron,	0·069 "
Sulphate of alumina,	0·012 "
Iodine,	——
Azotized organic matter,	0·005 "

Gases, sulphuretted hydrogen, nitrogen, oxygen, and carbonic acid.

Of the special application of these waters to disease, or mode of operating, and the whole catalogue of infirmities curable thereby, also on manner of administration, see Dr. John J. Moormann's clever little book on the "Mineral Springs of Virginia." It is considered "the strongest water of the spring region."

BLUE SULPHUR SPRING is twenty-two miles west of White Sulphur, on Muddy Creek, one of the waters of Greenbrier River. This spring has a fine reputation, and is prescribed in all diseases for which sulphur waters are used. Professor Rogers's analysis of 100 cubic inches of water gives the presence of—

Sulphate of lime,	20·150 grs.
Sulphate of magnesia,	2·760 "
Sulphate of soda,	9·020 "
Carbonate of lime,	2·180 "
Carbonate of magnesia,	0·481 "
Chloride of magnesium,	0·407 "
Chloride of calcium,	0·005 "
Chloride of sodium,	1·868 "
Hydrosulphate of sodium and magnesium,	——
Oxide of iron, existing as protosulphate,	0·015 "
Iodine,	——
Sulphur, organic matter,	3·000 "

Dr. Moormann speaks very favorably of this spring as a remedial agent. Temperature variable, from 46° to 56° F. Drs. Hunter and Martin give favorable reports of this water.

SALT SULPHUR. There are three of these springs in Monroe County, near *Union*, and twenty-four miles south of White Sulphur. They are, according to Dr. Moormann, "encircled by mountains on every side, having Peters's Mountain on the south and east, Alleghany to the north, and Swope's Mountain to the west, near the base of which are the three springs." The waters of this place possess great and deserved notoriety as medicinal, and the place is extremely attractive. Professor Rogers's analysis gives, in 100 cubic inches of water,—

Sulphate of lime,	36·755 grs.
Sulphate of magnesia,	7·883 "
Sulphate of soda,	9·682 "
Carbonate of lime,	4·445 "
Carbonate of magnesia,	1·434 "
Chloride of sodium,	0·683 "
Chloride of magnesium,	0·116 "
Chloride of calcium,	0·025 "
Oxide of iron,	0·042 "
Iodine,	———
Azotized organic matter, blended with sulphur,	0·004 "
Earthy phosphates,	trace,
Gases:	
Sulphuretted hydrogen,	1·50 cubic inches.
Nitrogen,	2·05 " "
Oxygen,	0·27 " "
Carbonic acid,	5·75 " "

One of the springs contains a larger quantity of iodine; said to be useful in scrofula, goitre, and diseases of skin. Dr. Mütter speaks of the salt sulphur waters as efficient in a variety of diseases, as chronic affections of nervous centre, chronic kidney and bladder diseases, rheumatism, gout, and skin disease, chronic liver and bowel disorders. Dr. Moormann also speaks highly of the salt sulphur waters in a number of complaints.

RED SULPHUR SPRINGS are in the southern part of Monroe County, south of White Sulphur forty-two miles. This has been a celebrated watering-place for many years. The temperature of the spring is 54° F. Professor Rogers's analysis gives sulphate of soda, lime, and magnesia, carbonate of lime, and muriate of soda. It also contains a "peculiar organic substance, mingled with sulphur." Gaseous contents are,—

Sulphuretted hydrogen,	4·54 inches to gallon.
Carbonic acid,	8·75 " " "
Nitrogen,	4·25 " " "

This is "the least stimulating of the sulphur waters," and represented as *even sedative*. It has a *"peculiar and distinguished reputation for diseases of the thoracic viscera,* INCLUDING CONFIRMED CONSUMPTION" (! ! ? ?) Has undoubted efficacy as a mineral water, but on the subject of its curing *confirmed consumption??* see Moormann.

SWEET SPRINGS, also in Monroe County, are twenty-two miles from Salt Sulphur Springs. These springs attracted attention early (1764) to their waters. They were analyzed by Bishop Madison, in 1774; said to be a tonic, "with just celebrity." Their temperature is 73° F. The analysis of Rowelle "gives saline substances, earthy salts, and iron, sulphate of magnesia, muriate of soda, and lime, with silicious earth." Sweet Spring is a popular and fashionable resort. The name is not appropriate, as the water has the usual taste of saline waters. It possesses excess of carbonic acid, and is said to be useful in a number of diseases, used both by bathing and internally. The water is *especially lauded* for bathing purposes, as a luxury, and for medicinal qualities.

SWEET CHALYBEATE SPRING is in Alleghany County, west of Sweet Spring. One of the springs here has the same character as the last-named spring, and the other contains a larger quantity of iron. Rowelle gives, in one quart of water,—

Carbonate of lime,	4 grs.
Carbonate of magnesia,	3 "
Carbonate of iron,	2 "
Silex,	1 "
Sulphate of magnesia,	1 "
Muriate of soda,	½ "
Iron, combined with carbonic acid,	1 "

Professor Rogers gives sulphate of lime, magnesia, and soda, carbonate of lime, chloride of magnesium, sodium, and calcium, oxide of iron, organic matter, and iodine. The iron, he says, is dissolved in the water as a carbonate. The gases in this water are nitrogen, oxygen, sulphuretted hydrogen. The bubbles which rise from the spring are nitrogen and carbonic acid; temperature of the spring being 77° to 80° F. Waters possess the same therapeutic properties as other springs of the class; as a tonic extremely celebrated. *Dr. Moormann* is *enthusiastic in his admiration* of and belief in *their efficacy.*

DIBRELL'S SPRING is in Botetourt County, nineteen miles from the Natural Bridge, and forty-four miles from the White Sulphur Springs, on the stage-road.

Professor Rogers's analysis gives carbonate of soda, sulphate of soda, chloride of sodium, carbonate of magnesia, peroxide of iron, silica dissolved, "*organic matter*, containing chloride of potassium, nitrogen, carbonate of lime, and carbonate of ammonia. Gases: carbonic acid, oxygen, sulphuretted hydrogen, nitrogen,—this spring possessing the usual character of sulphur waters, and used medicinally the same way."

RAWLEY'S SPRING is in Rockingham County, northwest of Harrisonsburg twelve miles; water pure, chalybeate, and strong, good tonic. According to Dr. Moormann, "as a pure tonic, it deserves to stand at the very head of that class of medicines." No analysis of the water yet made.

HEALING SPRINGS are, according to Dr. Burke, "in the gorge of the mountains, near the road to the celebrated

Falling Spring, one of the curiosities of this region, and three and a half miles south of Hot Springs." In chemical contents they are apparently very much like the "SWEET SPRINGS," or perhaps more like the Red Sweet, since the chalybeate taste is more distinct than in that of the former. Medical virtues transcendent; curing scrofulous and skin affections, and fibrous diseases in the shape of "*rheumatisms* and *sprains.*" Temperature of spring, 84° Fahr. As a luxury and real healthful operative, the bath waters of this spring are to be commended largely.

HOLSTEIN SPRINGS are found in Scott County, southwest part of the State, and belong to the saline class. They are thermal, having a temperature of 68° Fahr., and 16° above the mean temperature of the springs about. The water is charged with sulphur, magnesia, and lime, to the extent of 41·14 grains to the gallon. Their action is directed to kidneys and skin, and especially *whole digestive tube.*

CHURCH HILL ALUM SPRING is in the city of Richmond. Mineral elements, Epsom salts, leading force also in large quantities of salts of iron and alumina. Thus the water is tonic from aluminous and ferruginous qualities of great value, consequently it is serviceable in a number of affections as a giver of tone and a condenser of tissue. (See Bell.)

Seventeen miles above Richmond, near James River, in Powhattan County, are the two

HUGUENOT SPRINGS, one sulphureous, the other chalybeate. The sulphur spring has the properties of others of the class, the chalybeate, also, possessing qualities of its class.

WARRENTON WHITE SULPHUR SPRINGS are near that town, in Farquier County. They are described as a mild sulphureous water, applicable to certain derangements of the stomach, and bowels, and rheumatism.

CAPON SPRINGS are some thirty miles from Winchester. This place is represented as a charming retreat. No analysis has been made of the waters, said to be useful in stomach derangements and glandular disorders.

JORDAN'S WHITE SULPHUR SPRINGS are near the Winchester and Harper's Ferry Railroad. They are said to possess curative properties over cutaneous diseases, chronic affections of the stomach and rheumatism.

SHANNONDALE SALINE SPRINGS are near Charleston, Jefferson County, and near the banks of the Shenandoah River. They are said to possess diuretic and aperient properties.

The BATH ALUM SPRINGS are at the eastern base of Warm Spring Mountain, on the road from Richmond to the Ohio River. Dr. Hayes's analysis of these springs give the presence of carbonic and sulphuric acids, with the salts of iron and alumina. They possess, of course, the medicinal properties of those substances, being tonic and astringent. They are used in various chronic affections, diseases of mucous surfaces, and general debility, also used in cutaneous diseases, scrofula, and chronic ulcerations.

ROCKBRIDGE ALUM SPRINGS are situated between the North Mountain and Mill Mountain, seventeen miles from Lexington. Dr. Hayes's analysis gives an excess of free sulphuric acid and sulphate of alumina. This is of the order of sour springs already spoken of, useful in diseases in which these chemical elements are usually applied.

KENTUCKY SPRINGS.

In the Second Report (1857) of the Geological Survey of this State, by David Dale Owen, thirty-eight mineral and other waters are stated to have been examined and analyzed; twenty-five qualitatively and thirteen quantitatively, by Dr. Peter. There is great sameness in the mineral contents of these springs, which are generally lime, magnesia, soda, with acids carbonic, sulphuric, iron, all of which are combined in endless proportions and quantities.

YELVINGTON SPRING, in Daviess County, shows the presence of these substances; also, OLIVER SPRING, in same county.

Owen quotes Professor J. Lawrence Smith's analysis of PAROQUET SPRING. This consists of *nineteen substances*, or different combinations, to wit, sodium, calcium, magnesium, potassium, with chlorine,—these substances also in combination with sulphuric and carbonic acids, iodine, and bromine. It also contains organic matter, silica and sulphuretted hydrogen.

ALUM SPRING, at the base of Burdett Knob, contains sulphate of alumina and protoxide of iron, bicarbonates of lime and magnesia, with strong and deleterious properties, said to be poisonous. Near this, a well contains water of much the same character.

Yates's mineral water contains lime, magnesia, soda, chlorine, sulphuric and carbonic acids.

NEVIEN'S SULPHUR SPRING, in Lincoln County, at the sources of Salt River, contains the same ingredients, with sulphuretted hydrogen.

ROCHESTER SPRINGS, in Boyl County, shows a large amount of sulphate of magnesia; also, soda, lime, alumina, and iron.

In Washington and Nelson counties are springs containing the same ingredients.

WHITE SULPHUR and MAMMOTH WELL contain the same items, in somewhat modified proportions. Mr. Owen recites the names and contents of a great many springs of Kentucky called mineral and sulphur waters. Their constituent principles are in the above-named substances repeated over again, with occasionally a new item or two.

Dr. Peter's Table of the thirteen waters of Lincoln County shows, with slightly modified proportions, the following materials:—carbonate of iron, carbonate of *manganese*, carbonate of lime, carbonate of magnesia, sulphates of lime, magnesia, potash, and soda, chlorides of magnesium and sodium, with silica. Of their connection with geological formations, Mr. Owen speaks of some having their "origin in the *black shales* of the Devonian Epoch," or rocks of the "Lower Silurian Period," whilst "HOWELL MINERAL SPRING issues in a copious flow from the *sub-carboniferous limestone* of the 'Barrens' of Hardin County." Many of the sulphur and magnesian waters are associated with the rotten sandstone or silicious mudstone, and the Blue Limestone Formation. His analysis differs slightly from that of Dr. Raymond, procured by Dr. Drake, and gives sulphates of magnesia and lime, bicarbonates of magnesia and lime, with a trace of chlorides, and carbonate of iron in the "HARRODSBURG SALOON SPRING."

The GREENVILLE SPRING, at Harrodsburg, has a trace of sulphuretted hydrogen and iron, otherwise like Saloon Spring.

In the Third Geological Report of Kentucky (1857,) Owen notices twenty-six mineral waters; qualitative analyses and testings at fountain-heads of many, and quantitative analyses of a few. This list includes some springs already examined and reported by Drake and others. From the great prevalence of mineral springs in Kentucky, it might occur to inquire, whether it may not be difficult to *find any pure water* in a region so crowded with "licks" and mineral fountains. In this Report (volume third) the Harrodsburg group is again reviewed. The chemical contents nearly the same as already quoted for the Saloon and Greenville Springs, the latter retaining *the trace of sulphuretted hydrogen*. It is stated that these "springs issue from the beds of blue limestone near its junction with the underlying marble rocks." These springs of Kentucky, reported by Mr. Owen, have a stereotype resemblance,—all containing the same salts of the same bases.

Jones's Mineral Water, Washington County, contains lime, soda, magnesia, sulphur, with chlorine, carbonic and sulphuric acids.

In Nelson County there are a number of mineral waters, as Grigsby's White Sulphur, Mammoth Well, Bell's Mineral Water, and others, their contents being common salt, lime, magnesia, iron, and sulphur, with great sameness in style of combination.

In Shelby and Henry counties there are sulphur and chalybeate waters, and in Owen County, a weak saline. Some springs are quoted as poisonous to cattle from excess of the salts of magnesia.

The waters of BLUE LICK, ESCULAPIAN, and ALUM SPRINGS, are reported with usual salts of lime, magnesia, soda, and sulphur. Qualitative analyses are also given of OLYMPIAN SPRINGS, in Bath County. They differ but little from the large number noticed, containing lime, magnesia, soda, with some sulphuretted hydrogen, and *sulphate of magnesia in quantities*.

Sudduth Springs on Mud Lick, Sweet Lick Estill Springs, Irvine's Sulphur, Russell's Sulphur and Chalybeate, in Russell County, are also reported. They contain the regular routine of ingredients characterizing KENTUCKY MINERAL SPRINGS.

"A strong sulphuretted saline" is reported in Kettle Creek, Cumberland County; also, strong sulphur springs in Marion and Taylor counties. These springs are represented to contain large amounts of sulphuretted hydrogen, in addition to the salts of lime, magnesia, and soda.

Lindsey's Mineral Water, in Christian County, is also

strongly impregnated with sulphuretted hydrogen. These waters are highly commended by Owen as medical waters, except those reputed to be poisonous, in connection with which he suggests the geological origin of the somewhat mysterious milk-sickness.

The State of Kentucky owes, also, to the genius and labor of the illustrious Dr. Drake an elaborate and world-extended notice of her mineral springs. This indefatigable lover of, and worker for man, in his splendid critique on the Nosology, or Table of Diseases of the Mississippi Valley, has left no subject of science, connected with this department of human knowledge, untouched. His account of Kentucky Springs, scenery, and resources, whilst rigidly scientific, has all the charm of romance, even mounting to the sphere of poetry or the witchery of song. For particulars on mineral springs especially, and *everything else*, see one of the most interesting books printed in several hundred years, viz. "Principle Diseases of the Valley of North America," by Daniel Drake, M.D.

According to Dr. Drake, HARRODSBURG SPRINGS are in "the basin of Salt River," near the town of Harrodsburg. This is an elevated spot near the origin of several veinlets of rivers. To use his own words, "*it is not in a volcanic district.* In every direction, for several miles round, the country is as free from drained lands, marshes, swales, and ponds, as any other equal area in the Ohio Basin." According to Professor Yandell, they issue from the magnesian limestone "which rests upon the oldest formations known in the Ohio Basin." There are here two springs: first, GREENVILLE SPRING. Dr. Raymond, of Cincinnati, gives an analysis of this spring, which, in the pint of water, contains,—

Bicarbonate of magnesia,	2·87 grs.
" " lime,	0·86 "
Sulphate of magnnesia, crystallized,	16·16 "
Sulphate of lime,	11·6 "
Also a trace of chloride of sodium.	

Of the other "SALOON" or CHALYBEATE SPRING, the same gentleman gives, in same quantity of water,—

Bicarbonate of lime,	4·31 grs.
Magnesia,	11·43 "
Bicarbonate of iron,	0·50 "
Sulphate of magnesia, crystallized,	27·92 "
Sulphate of lime,	10·24 "
Chloride of sodium,	1·20 "

The predominating salts are those of lime and magnesia, containing neither *free carbonic* acid, nor *sulphuretted hydrogen gases.**

These waters are prescribed in an extensive catalogue of diseases, including derangements of the contents of the large splanchnic cavities,—abdomen, thorax, and head. Of the value of these waters hygienically, also of the delights of the place as a resort for luxury, Dr. Drake is eloquent in his praises. He thinks they will "compare advantageously with any to be found in Europe or America." Certainly, from his account, few places possess a tithe of the charms of this favored spot. Of the environs of Harrodsburg he speaks with extravagance, as possessing all elements of the romantic and beautiful, while its medicinal waters are represented as possessing healing powers over a large number of diseases, the whole locality having been favored by nature with a rare and wonderful combination of select and valuable things.

ROCHESTER SPRING is situated one mile from Perrysville. From Dr. Drake's Report it is of the same character as the Harrodsburg in "sensible qualities, composition, and effects." The following group has been noticed by Owen, as already quoted.

OLYMPIAN, or MUD LICK SPRINGS are in Bath County,

---

* The analysis procured by Owen, as we have just seen, *does contain some sulphuretted hydrogen.*

fifty miles from Lexington east, on Licking River. This, according to Dr. Drake, is "one of the oldest and most noted watering-places in Kentucky." There are several springs of different characters at this place, which are designated, by Drake, "*salt sulphur, white sulphur,* and *chalybeate.*" The salt sulphur has a temperature of 58° F. It is a weak lime-water charged with sulphuretted hydrogen. The quantity of salt is smaller than many or most of the springs in the West. "It contains sulphuretted hydrogen, chloride of sodium, or common salt, muriate of lime, and carbonate of soda." The WHITE SULPHUR is half a mile from this, and "said to have made its first appearance in the earthquakes of 1811." Composition like the Salt Sulphur, with "difference in proportion of elements." There is, in the SULPHUR, a much larger quantity of sulphuretted hydrogen, but less chloride of sodium, with some carbonate of soda. Temperature, 59° F.

The IRON SPRINGS are two in number, half a mile from the last, with temperature 52° F., and contain "carbonate of iron, with the proportion of muriates and carbonates which our common springs afford."

VITRIOL SPRING contains "muriates and carbonates only, and these in such moderate quantities that it is used for culinary purposes, although *spoken of as medicinal.*" The medical properties of this spring are not lauded exceedingly, although the place is described as a broken surface, peculiar from irregular hills and ravines, and consequently attractive for its beauty of scenery and the wildness of its landscapes. According to Dr. Peter, "there are *six springs belonging to the Olympian group,*—three sulphuretted hydrogen, two iron saline, and *one* acidulous saline; the contents not great in quantity."

Of the *Olympian group,* Bath County, Owen gives qualitative testing of five springs. The first is a weak chalybeate, with salts of lime, magnesia, soda. The second contains more iron, with many of the same salts. The third is a good saline alkaline chalybeate. The fourth contains a large list of salts of lime, magnesia, soda, iron, with sulphuretted hydrogen and iodide *of sodium.* Owen suggests that this "is a very valuable mineral water, from the fact that it contains iodine." The fifth is described as a good alkaline sulphur water, containing also the ordinary salts of the waters of this region.

At BLUE LICKS, Drake reports that there are several springs, all saline sulphur. They are on the Licking River, twenty-four miles from the Ohio. Salt was formerly made from these waters, but being weak, they were abandoned.

In the Third Geological Report of this State, already quoted, Mr. Owen has an extended and valuable account of the "Lower Blue Lick Spring," Nicholas County. From a minute examination of the spring, it is discovered to have a temperature of 62° F., or seven degrees above the mean temperature of the region. A quantitative analysis has been made of this water by Mr. Owen, which is found to contain sulphuretted hydrogen and carbonic acid gases, carbonate of lime and magnesia, alumina, phosphate of lime and oxide of iron, chloride of sodium, magnesium, and potassium, bromide of magnesium, *iodide of magnesium*, sulphate of lime and *potash*, silicic acid, oxide of manganese, crenic and apocrenic acids. He enumerates a long list of diseases, "as chronic disorders of liver, dyspepsia, chronic cutaneous diseases, rheumatism, gout, scrofulous affections, and also speaks of the water as a *nervous stimulant*, diaphoretic, and diuretic." The value of this water, as highly medicinal, is insisted upon by Mr. Owen. (See Third Geological Report, from page 361 to page 368.)

According to Peter, LOWER BLUE LICK SPRING is a saline sulphur. "It emerges from the *Great Blue Limestone Formation of the West,*—a formation of great extent, composed of limestone layers of greater or less thickness, hardness, and purity, with beds of bluish, marly clay, presenting sometimes a shaly structure; all rich in the fossil remains of the inhabitants of the deep, primeval ocean, under which they were evidently deposited." The *Spring of the Big Bone Lick* is in this formation, and exhibits the same general character as the Blue Licks, that is, *salt sulphur.* A number of salt springs are found in this formation, also salt wells. At the BLUE LICKS there are several springs, all of which are very similar in composition, according to Professor Peter. The salt wells or deep waters contain chlorides of sodium, potassium, calcium, and magnesium, sulphate and carbonate of lime, impregnated with sulphuretted hydrogen, while the surface springs are simply limestone water with little salt or gas.

In Keene, Jessamine County, there is a well in the Limestone Formation containing a sulphureous salt water, with medicinal properties. Contents, sulphuretted hydrogen and carbonic acid gases, bicarbonates of lime, magnesia, and soda, chlorides of sodium, magnesium, calcium, with potassium, and some iron. The water is not so strong as BLUE LICK, containing 16 grains of salt in 1000 grains of water. (Peter.)

In Scott County there is a well, in this Formation, 176 feet deep, the water of which contains chlorides of sodium, calcium, and magnesium, with the odor of sulphuretted hydrogen.

Another well, in Harrison County, also in the "Blue Limestone Formation," 105 feet deep, contains a water with sulphureous odor, and sixteen parts in a thousand of saline matter, chloride of sodium, calcium, magnesium, and potassium, sulphate of lime, bicarbonates of lime, magnesia, and iron, with some iodine. (Peter.) It resembles *Blue Lick waters.*

Other wells, in the same formation, exhibit the same character of waters; there being also a number in Lexington with the elements above enumerated. There are none of the waters of the Lime Formation so valuable as the "*Lower Blue Lick.*" (Peter.) At this place the principal spring is near Licking River; temperature of water, 62° F. "The water is of a yellowish-green tint, depositing a yellowish-gray sediment. This color comes from the decomposition of the chemical elements of the water,—the hydrogen, oxygen,

KENTUCKY SPRINGS. 173

sulphur, iron, and carbon, undergoing certain changes of position from the original composition of the water." The water also contains nitrogen gas, with carbonic acid, and sulphuretted hydrogen. For saline contents, see analysis just quoted from the third volume of the Geological Survey of Kentucky.

The medicinal properties are those of salt sulphur waters generally, and used in all chronic derangements to which sulphur waters are prescribed, both internally and externally. (See Owen.) This water is distributed extensively by barreling and bottling. Being, according to Dr. Drake, in a region of perpetual malaria, the place is *thus doomed* for certain seasons of the year.

Of ESTILL SPRINGS, in Estill County, Kentucky, see also Report, page 245. Two springs, called "*White* and *Red* Sulphur," give, in the first, carbonic acid and sulphuretted hydrogen gases, carbonates of soda, lime, magnesia, and iron, sulphates of lime, magnesia, and soda, chloride of sodium, and hydrosulphate of soda; specific gravity, 1·001; saline contents, 0·09 per cent.

The "RED SULPHUR" contains carbonic and sulphuretted hydrogen gases, carbonates of lime, magnesia, soda, and iron, sulphates of soda, lime, and magnesia, chlorides of sodium, calcium, and magnesium, and hydrosulphate of soda. The composition is similar to White, only differing in proportion of elements and specific gravity, 1·0002; saline contents 0·04 per cent. (Peter.)

The Kentucky springs have each special advocates, who speak emphatically of the power of their waters. Some of these authorities are so high that the medicinal properties of the waters as represented, stand, with *certain qualifications which apply to all springs*, accredited by the profession at large; as do those of the other States, which have been made the subject of special examination. When the Geological Survey, now progressing under Professor Owen, shall have been finished, no doubt the mineral springs of Kentucky will appear with the last chemical details and geological associations, perfected for the inspection of the world. This is a reasonable expectation, bearing in mind the high position of the principal of the Survey of that State, and his accomplished assistants.

TENNESSEE SPRINGS.

But few reports have been made of the mineral springs of Tennessee. Dr. Troost, the geologist of the State, gave an account, some time ago, of a number of them. These are mostly of the sulphureous class; several of them are in Davidson County, French Lick, Sam's Creek, and White's Creek.

In Franklin County are Winchester and Brown's springs; Maysfield, in Williamson County; Terrie's, in Rutherford County. These waters contain sulphate of lime, chloride of sodium, and sulphuretted hydrogen. The sulphuretted hydrogen is said to be in larger quantity than most of the sulphur waters of the United States.

Twelve miles from the City of Nashville is WHITE'S CREEK SPRING, said to contain sulphates of iron, magnesia, and sulphur. This water has reputation in skin diseases and calculous derangements. Dr. Troost gives, to 20 ounces of this water,—

Sulphuretted hydrogen,	6·25 cubic inches.
Carbonic acid,	5·90 " "
Solid matter, 16 grains, viz.—	
Carbonate of lime,	5·50 grs.
Sulphate of lime,	3·05 "
Sulphate of soda,	2·05 "
Sulphate of magnesia,	3·00 "
Hydrosulphate of soda,	1·01 "

TENNESSEE SPRINGS. 175

Twenty miles from Nashville are ROBINSON'S SPRINGS, which are saline.

At or near Nashville mineral springs are reported.

Dr. Bell speaks of East Tennessee as exceedingly delightful, and recommends the climate and watering-places.

LEE SPRINGS are twenty miles east of Knoxville, one of which is a strong iron water, the other two are sulphur. There are also sulphur springs in Granger County.

In Franklin County, near Winchester, are the WINCHESTER SPRINGS, some seventy miles from Nashville. There are several varieties of water here that have attained some celebrity. They are pure iron and sulphur waters, and said to be actively medicinal; some of the waters give 6 cubic inches of gas to 20 ounces; situated in an interesting region and solidly attractive to invalids. Near these springs are ALLIANCE SPRINGS, which are reported to possess the same qualities as those last mentioned.

Near Knoxville are MONTVALE SPRINGS. The spot is described as being very beautiful, and the waters truly medicinal.

On French Broad River there are springs with a temperature of 96° Fahr. Troost notices a number of other springs.

CASTILIAN SPRING, in Sumner County, contains sulphuretted hydrogen, sulphate of magnesia and lime, and hydrochlorate of soda.

HAGER'S SPRING, in this county, contains sulphuretted hydrogen, carbonic acid, and sulphate of lime.

SAM'S CREEK SPRINGS, Davidson County, contains, in 20 fluid ounces,—

Sulphuretted hydrogen,	8·05 inches.
Carbonic acid,	1·05 "

Solid contents, 6 grains, composed of sulphate of lime and hydrochlorate of soda.

MAYSFIELD SPRING, in Williamson County, contains, in 20 fluid ounces,—

Sulphuretted hydrogen,	6 cubic inches.
Hydrochlorate of soda,	6 grs.
Sulphate of lime,	———

TERRIE'S SPRING, in Rutherford County, gives, in 20 fluid ounces,—

Sulphuretted hydrogen,	10 cubic inches.
Sulphuric acid,	5·00 grs.
Hydrochloric acid,	2·21 "
" lime,	5·34 "

DUNN'S SPRING, in Davidson County, gives sulphuretted hydrogen and hydrochlorate of soda.

TYRE'S SPRING, in same county, contains, in 20 fluid ounces of water,—

Sulphuretted hydrogen,	3 cubic inches.
Carbonic acid,	1 " inch.
Solid matter,	30 grs.

Sulphate of lime and magnesia, carbonate of lime and hydrochlorate of soda.

FRENCH LICK, in same county, gives sulphuretted hydrogen, carbonic acid, hydrochloric acid, sulphuric acid, magnesia, and hydrochlorate of soda.

BROWN'S SPRING contains, in 20 fluid ounces,—

Sulphuretted hydrogen,	8 cubic inches.
Solid matter,	3·25 grs.

Composed of hydrochlorate of lime and soda.

NORTH CAROLINA SPRINGS.

Emmons seems to carefully avoid the subject of mineral springs in his report on the Geology of North Carolina for 1856. There are, however, some springs in North Carolina which have been noticed. Of these, the most celebrated are the Warm and Hot Springs, in Buncombe County. They are on French Broad River, and have a temperature from 94° to 104° Fahr. The region about these springs is said to be beautiful.

Professor Smith's analysis gives the following substances in the water:—muriates of magnesia and lime, sulphate of magnesia, *sulphate of lime* in larger proportions than any other element. The waters are used both internally and externally, and possess great importance as therapeutic agents; but, according to Dr. Bell, they should be used with discretion. They are applicable to cases of palsy and chronic rheumatism, rigidity of joints, etc.

SOUTH CAROLINA SPRINGS.

According to Tuomey, "this State is not favorable to mineral springs," but some have attained notoriety.

Glenn's Spring, in Spartanburg District, has waters charged with salts of lime. Professor Shepard gives, in these waters, chloride of calcium, supercarbonate of lime, sulphate of lime, and magnesia, alleging that "they are strongly impregnated with sulphur."

West's Spring, near this, is chalybeate.

Chick's Spring, near Greenville, resembles Glenn's.

In Laurens there "are three or four springs, sulphur and chalybeate, in hornblende slate."

There is a spring at Estatoe Mountains, also in Abbiville District, and one near Parson's Mountain.

Murray's Spring, near Pinson's Ford, is charged with salts of lime and iron.

In "Flat Woods," are springs containing iron, lime, magnesia, and sulphur.

M. Tuomey, the geologist of South Carolina, reports springs worthy of notice, as saline, sulphureous, and chalybeate, which are "confined to certain geological formations."

GEORGIA SPRINGS.

Not much is known of the mineral springs of this State.

The Indian Springs, in Butts County, are sulphureous. They have reputation, according to Professor Arnold, of Savannah, who reports to Dr. Bell all the noticed springs of Georgia, in the alleviation of rheumatic diseases, deranged conditions of stomach, liver, and intestines, of the order chronic.

In Merriwether County are warm springs, which contain salts of magnesia, and have a temperature of 90° Fahr. The forte of their powers is over gout and rheumatism.

In Madison County are the Madison Springs, which are pure iron waters, and useful as a tonic. The claims of these are warmly urged by Professor Arnold, for persons seeking a decidedly marked impression from change of climate, with mineral water action.

In Cass County there is a chalybeate spring.

In Murray County several springs are reported by Dr. Arnold, and reputed to possess medicinal powers. No analysis yet published.

ALABAMA SPRINGS.

THE geology of Alabama is principally tertiary. There are several springs noticed by writers on the subject; these are saline springs, also sulphuretted hydrogen.

TALLAHATTA SPRING contains sulphur, salts of iron, lime, and magnesia.

BAILEY'S SPRING is in Lauderdale County, nine miles from Florence. According to Dr. Currey, the water contains carbonic acid and sulphuretted hydrogen gases, carbonates of soda and magnesia, oxide of iron, with carbonic acid, chloride of sodium, and carbonate of potash. Tuomey's analysis shows carbonates of iron and soda, chloride of sodium, and a trace of carbonate of potash and sulphur; said to be curative in "dropsy, scrofula, and dyspepsia," as an alterative and gentle tonic. This acidulo sulphur-iron water is valuable.

The most celebrated are "BLADON SPRINGS." The analysis of their waters shows the presence of sulphuretted hydrogen and carbonic acid gases, chloride of sodium, carbonates of soda, lime, and magnesia, oxide of iron, sulphate of lime, silica, and alumina, crenic and apocrenic acid. The carbonate of soda is the leading element of this water. It has been examined by Professor Brumby, and has reputation in stomach and kidney derangements. These springs are in Clarke County, near Coffeeville.

There are other mineral springs in this State reputed to possess medicinal items.

MISSISSIPPI SPRINGS.

In the Geological Report of Mississippi for 1857, by L. Harper, we are presented with some facts with regard to the mineral springs of that State. First are the springs of the carboniferous formations. These are sulphur and chalybeate, or waters containing sulphate of iron and sulphuretted hydrogen, and depositing yellow hydrated peroxide of iron. Other springs contain iron, lime, magnesia, alumina, and carbonic acid; and one is reported in these formations containing sulphate of magnesia and iron, with chloride of sodium. Near Warren's Mill, on Mackey's Creek, is a spring containing sulphate of iron and sulphuretted hydrogen. In Tishamingo, Itawamba, Chickasaw, and Tippah counties, there are springs which contain the salts of iron, lime, magnesia, alumina, and soda.

"The Eocene formations of this State contain more mineral springs than any of the other rocks." At LAUDERDALE there are five or six sulphur and chalybeate springs. They are near the line of the Eocene and Miocene formations. These are copious founts, and, according to Mr. Harper, "create, morning and evening, in the surrounding region, a a sulphuric atmosphere."* Quitman's Red Sulphur is valuable, containing sulphuretted hydrogen, lime, magnesia, chlorine, and apocrenic acid. Mineral springs are also reported in the Miocene of Mississippi.

---

* Harper gives a minute analysis of the Lauderdale Springs. He represents them as containing of volatile ingredients, sulphuretted hydrogen, carbonic acid, oxygen, nitrogen, carburetted hydrogen; acids, sulphuric, carbonic, silicic, apocrenic, also, chlorine, iodine, bromine, *inappreciable* (*!!!*) bases, iron, lime, magnesia, potassa, alumina, soda, and *ammonia*.

In Yallabusha County, near Grenada, a spring is reported containing chlorine, sulphuric acid, iron, sulphate of alumina; used in diseases of the bowels, etc In Winston and Nashoba counties there are chalybeate and sulphuretted hydrogen springs. In Yazoo County, near Yazoo City, there is said to be an "*alkaline spring*," and one containing sulphate of iron, carbonic acid, chlorine, alumina, lime, magnesia, and soda. In La Fayette, Panola, and Calhoun counties, chalybeates are said to exist. In Clarke County, near Chickasawhay River, and also near "*Enterprise*," there are springs containing sulphate of iron and sulphuretted hydrogen.

"Cooper's Well" is twelve miles from Jackson, in Hinds County. "It comes from an Artesian well, in sand rock, one hundred and seven feet deep, and is in a region attractive and salubrious." It is described as a salt iron water, and contains oxygen, nitrogen, and carbonic acid gases, sulphate of lime, magnesia, soda, alumina, and potash, chloride of soda, lime, and magnesia, peroxide of iron, and crenate of lime and silica. Said to be useful as iron water, in abdominal diseases of the chronic type, as chronic diarrhœa, dyspepsia, renal and hepatic diseases.

Dr. Bell notices another spring in Mississippi, which has acquired considerable reputation for medicinal qualities. This is

"Ocean Spring," in Lynchburg, Jackson County, which contains carbonic acid and sulphuretted hydrogen gases, chlorides of calcium, sodium, and magnesium, protoxide of iron, iodine, *organic matter*, chloride of potassium a trace, and alumina a trace. Leading elements, chloride of sodium, sulphuretted hydrogen, and iron. "The iron is united with carbonic acid and sulphuretted hydrogen." The medical properties lean to the values of iron and sulphuretted hydrogen, and may be useful in chronic derangements in which such elements are indicated; and, on the authority of Dr. Austin, "they have been successful in the cure of dyspepsia, skin diseases, scrofula, and strumous ophthalmia." According to Dr. Austin, "the springs are situated among pine hills, five miles from the town of Biloxi, and half a mile from the east shore of Biloxi Bay," and said, by its special advocates, to be attractive and beautiful.

ARKANSAS SPRINGS.

The Washitaw Hot Springs are in Hot Spring County, fifty miles south of Arkansas River, near Washitaw River. The springs are at the foot of a mountain called *Hot Mountain*. The streams of hot water are numerous and of considerable volume. They have a temperature, according to "Schoolcraft," of 200° F. The water will vesicate the surface, and boil an egg in a few minutes, and is described as pure and clear.

According to Judge Watts, the springs have a temperature of 145° F. As might be inferred, the waters of these springs have much power as a therapeutic agent, administered both internally and externally. They are used in vapour, hot and warm baths, by cooling down the temperature, and, from well-known laws of the economy, exert their influence as those classes of baths are known to do. They contain salts of lime and magnesia; but a minute and critical analysis is wanting.

The special advocates of these waters as medicinal, represent them as almost specifics in the cure of "the whole order of chronic diseases," including scrofula, gout, rheumatism, also the consequences or sequelæ of acute diseases, vicious drugging, and affections of the skin.

A few miles from Hot Springs there is an *Iron Spring* of reputed powers, and also some other springs, said to be of the *carbonated class;* but the springs of *real significance*

ARKANSAS SPRINGS.

are the thermal or *hot springs* of this curious region. Mr. Featherstonehaugh, the geologist, reports these waters to emerge from a red sandstone formation, which he designates "OLD RED." The numerous springs flow into one stream, which retains its heat for a great distance from the heads of the springs.

The waters, through the intelligent notices of Southern physicians and others, have attained great and just celebrity in a large class of diseases,—waiving the question of their being "absolute specifics in the whole class of chronic diseases."

They belong to the celebrated order of thermal waters of Europe; Carlsbad, Baden-Baden, Wisbaden, and Teplitz, in Bohemia. These have long enjoyed great reputation as bathing waters, also for internal use in a variety of diseases, skin and joint affections, chronic rheumatism, and gout, *chronic skin* diseases, chronic derangements of the glands, and certain nervous affections. The waters of Washitaw Springs contain an *azotized or organic* substance. This, as has been already noticed, is *common* with other hot springs in the United States. The vapor bathing of these springs is highly spoken of by Dr. Bell and others.

FLORIDA SPRINGS.

The mineral springs of Florida are spoken of by some writers, but few *authentic details given*.

Near Tampa there is a SULPHUR SPRING, said to be "white sulphur." There is also at the MAGNOLIA SPRINGS, which are said to be sulphureous, a winter retreat for the sick. A few more springs of the same class are mentioned in this region.

CANADA SPRINGS.

HAVING noticed the most prominent mineral springs of a number of the United States, it may be as well to finish *here* the record, as far as the Eastern side of the continent is concerned, by some account of the springs of Canada, belonging to that class.

In the Report of Sir William E. Logan, Provincial Geologist, and his assistant, Sterry Hunt, of the Survey of Canada, (for 1857,) many mineral springs are registered and described. It appears that the great palæozoic basin of Canada is divided into two secondary basins by an axis extending from Daschambault, on the St. Lawrence, in a direction west to Lake Champlain. The eastern part is affected by undulations and different kinds of disturbances, and is the region already noticed as being the site of nearly all the mineral springs of Canada; the western or *undisturbed* basin having but few medicated waters. Hunt arranges the waters in two classes, "*neutral and alkaline;*" the first with chlorides of magnesium, calcium, sodium; and the second, all of these earthy bases in the form of carbonates and silicates, the water *being alkaline* from the *presence of carbonate of soda.* The few waters of the "upper silurian are all neutral, as also those from the limestone of lower part of lower silurian; while the alkaline waters characterize the schistose strata which constitute its upper portion." The schists of "*Hudson River group*" are "argillaceous, the analysis showing them to be of Feldspathic rocks, containing 3 or 400ths of alkalies, which they slowly give up to the decomposing action of infiltrating waters." In this way the neutral waters of the underlying limestone have their earthy chlorides decomposed, and are converted into alkaline waters, which are still strongly saline. Another class of alkaline waters, with alkaline carbonates and silicates, have a small portion of common salt, derived from argillaceous strata, but no connection with limestone. Such are the springs of Ours, of the grand coteau of Chambly, and some of the waters of Nicolet. About this place, six springs issue from the schists of Hudson River group, along same line of disturbance, the whole within distance of three or four leagues. Of these, two are strongly saline and neutral; two others saline, but alkaline; the *other two* characterized by predominance of alkaline carbonates; the *last* from schists, the *former* from limestone. There are two strong saline neutral waters in West Canada. One is at "BOWMAN'S MILL," the spring being copious, with temperature of 50°, which is perhaps above the mean. The waters are highly saline, very *bitter*, almost *acrid* when concentrated, depositing by boiling, carbonates of lime and magnesia, a little strontia, traces of iron, bromine, and iodine. Analysis of 1000 parts of this water:—

Chloride of sodium,	18·9158
Chloride of calcium,	17·5315
Chloride of magnesium,	9·5437
Bromide of sodium,	·2482
Iodine,	·0008
Carbonate of lime,	·0411
Carbonate of magnesia,	·0227
Salts of strontia, potash, and iron, traces,	
	46·3038

The spring at Whitley's issues from Trenton limestone, (No. 2) in the Township of Hallowell. There are two salt wells on the land of Amos Hubbs, with chlorides, bromine, and iodine. At St. Genevieve, on Bastican River, there are several springs issuing from the lower limestone, strongly saline and neutral; there being two quantitative analyses, the first on the land of Olivier Trudel, of Riviere Veillethe. The spring has abundance of water, with bubbles of sulphuretted hydrogen; also, strongly saline, containing quantities of earthy chlorides and carbonates, but no *sulphates;* 1000 parts of this water contain,—

Chloride of sodium,	17·2671
Chloride of potassium,	·2409
Chloride of calcium,	·6038
Chloride of magnesium,	2·0523
Bromide of sodium,	·0587
Iodide of sodium,	·0133
Carbonate of lime,	·0120
Carbonate of magnesia,	·7506
	20·9987

At the ferry, opposite the church of St. Genevieve, is a spring containing carburetted hydrogen, also, with largest amounts of iodides of any waters in the Province; 1000 parts of this water contain,—

Chloride of sodium,	11·5094
Chloride of calcium,	·2264
Chloride of magnesium,	·8942
Bromide of sodium,	·0273
Iodide of sodium,	·0183
Carbonate of lime,	·0180
Carbonate of magnesia,	·4464
	13·1400

All these waters contain small portions of *oxide* of iron, silica, and alumina. "Any water with excess of hydrochloric acid, gives precipitates of alumina, with oxide of iron, and phosphoric acid."

Berthier, in Parish of Berthier, (Leinster,) is a copious saline spring, with bubbles of inflammable gas; waters neutral, with small portion of earthy chlorides; bromine, (considerable,) iodine, *not so much*. Near this is a slightly chalybeate spring, which can scarcely be called a mineral water.

In RAWDON TOWNSHIP there are two springs, both of which are alkaline, and the first a water containing earthy and alkaline carbonates, with alkaline chlorides, and small portions of sulphates, borates, and a trace of bromine, but no iodine. The second spring is strongly saline, and distinctly alkaline to the taste. Plantagenet new saline springs, neutral, strongly saline, carbonates small, earthy chlorides strong, also iodine and bromine.

In JOLY TOWNSHIP there is an interesting spring on the banks of the Pouisseau Magnea, giving three or four gallons a *minute* of water, with sulphur taste and smell, depositing a "white matter," and exhibiting the "purple vegetation generally met with in sulphur waters." Temperature, 46° F.; air, 52°; also strongly saline; when concentrated, very alkaline and salt to the taste. Analysis of 1000 parts of this water give,—

Chloride of sodium,	0·3818
Chloride of potassium,	·0067
Sulphate of soda,	·0215
Carbonate and borate of soda,	·2301
Carbonate of lime,	·0620
Carbonate of magnesia,	·0257
Silica and alumina, traces,	
	0·7523

It contains, also, boracic acid, and sulphuretted hydrogen.

Mineral springs are rare, as observed, in the undisturbed portion of the western basin of Canada. There are some springs of local reputation in the Township of Scarborough. They contain only a little sulphate of lime and traces of chlorides.

In Toronto is also a well of similar composition; also a

spring at Spadina, remarkable for the quantity of lime deposited. There is also a spring in the village of Brompton "regarded as mineral, with smoky taste; the waters of which become putrid and sulphureous in closed bottles."

Another at Brompton contains a small quantity of chloride and sulphate of lime, magnesia, and alkalies. Perhaps none of these springs rise from the "*Lower Silurian,*" but "owe their mineral contents to clays and muds, covering the palæozoic rocks."

There are also a number more springs enumerated by Dr. Bell and others, in Canada, with analyses proximate and otherwise. The following are the most conspicuous and important noticed by writers on the subject.

TUSCARORA ACID SPRINGS. These springs are in the Township of Tuscarora, twenty miles south of Pass Dover. They contain, according to Mr. Hunt, the sulphates of iron, lime, magnesia, alumina, and a large amount of free sulphuric acid. It is asserted by geologists that "this spring is in the same geological relationship in which the same character of springs in New York are found." It has also the *smell* and *taste* of sulphuretted hydrogen, with an extremely acid and styptic taste.

There are several smaller basins in the neighborhood with the same character of waters. They all contain sulphates of potash, soda, lime, magnesia, iron, and alumina, and sulphuric acid in quantities.

A few miles south of Port Dover, on Lake Erie, is CHARLOTTEVILLE SULPHUR SPRING. Temperature, 45° Fahr. The water is clear, with a sulphureous taste and a strong sulphur odor, and contains sulphates of soda, potash, lime, and magnesia, chlorides of magnesium, carbonate of lime, magnesia, and iron, sulphuretted hydrogen, and carbonic acid. The sulphuretted hydrogen is in the quantity of 26·8 cubic inches to the gallon. (Hunt.)

ANCASTER SPRING is near the village of Ancaster. It is a salt spring, with a temperature of 48° Fahr., the water containing chloride of sodium, chloride of potassium, chlorides of magnesium and calcium, bromide of magnesia, and sulphate of lime. The leading elements are chlorides of sodium, magnesium, and calcium. (Hunt.)

The CALEDONIA SPRINGS are about forty miles from Montreal, near the Ottowa River. There are four founts, three known as Saline Spring, Gas Spring, and White Sulphur Spring.

GAS SPRING has a temperature of 44° F., and is highly charged with carburetted hydrogen, also containing chlorides of sodium and potash, sulphates of potash, bromide of sodium, *iodide* of *sodium*, (? ?) carbonates of soda, lime, magnesia, iron, and manganese, with alumina, silica, and carbonic acid. This extensive catalogue of ingredients embraces half the pharmacopœia, and, like some of the more ancient formulæ or medical prescriptions, contains a small touch of everything. A SAFE WATER under all circumstances, as a widely scattering shot will certainly hit something.

This is Gas Spring, (certainly gaseous ! !)

SALINE SPRING is said to be similar to the one last described in chemical composition ; temperature being 45° F. Differs from last in quantity of free carbonic acid, otherwise qualitative analysis same as above.

SULPHUR SPRING. This spring is in the immediate vicinity of the last, and contains a smaller quantity of sulphur, " a *trace* of *sulphur rather than a quantitative return.*" It also contains carbonates of soda and magnesia, with traces of iron, iodine, and silica. The leading element is the soda, the water being described as "strongly alkaline." There is an intermitting spring a few miles from the others mentioned. The water contains chlorine, bromine, and iodine, with potassium, sodium, calcium, and magnesium, some of these existing as chlorides, with traces of iron and alumina.

At ST. CATHARINES, Canada West, there is an Artesian well of most *miraculous composition* and *consequent power*. The water has more solid contents than fluid, and is manifestly an extraordinary product of Nature. Its "table of forces is a *little stronger* than *any four horses,"* and is bountifully brought out by the highly critical, scientific, and veracious author of Robinson Crusoe, endorsed by three Mud Angels. It is bottled, and can be had in places *for sale.* Said to contain chlorides of sodium, magnesium, calcium, protochloride of iron, sulphate of lime, carbonate of lime and magnesia, bromide and iodide of magnesia, silica and alumina; solid contents in 16 ounces of water, $10\frac{1}{2}$ *ounces of salts: chloride of calcium* being present. For medical properties, see Paracelsus, on the virtue of chicken fat, and Bulgarius, on the final cause of the creation of soft soap.

Seventeen miles from Montreal, on the St. Lawrence, are the VERENNES SPRINGS. "There are two springs, saline and gas, near together, both containing chloride, iodide, and bromide of soda, carbonates of soda, baryta, strontia, lime, magnesia, and iron." The Gas Spring evolves carburetted hy-hydrogen, with temperature of the water, 46° to 47° Fahr.

CAXTON SPRING is in Caxton Township, on the Yannachicke River, near the same named village. It is a saline chalybeate water, with large quantities of carburetted hydrogen gas escaping.

ST. LEON SPRING is a salt iron spring also, with large quantities of carburetted hydrogen gas escaping from the water.

MINERAL SPRINGS OF THE INTERIOR AND WESTERN SIDE OF THE CONTINENT OF NORTH AMERICA.

The vast region stretching from the Mississippi channel to the Pacific Ocean, from the reports of travelers, possesses a large number of springs, mineral and thermal. These are of an extensive variety and interesting character, but the information with regard to them is meagre, there being but few analyses of contents, and the accounts of explorers, who were intent upon other purposes, are necessarily vague and unspecified.

The more recent Reports of the Pacific Ocean Railroad parties have given much additional information with regard to the geography, geology, and climatology of this part of the continent; but *few* of the *mineral* springs have attracted much attention, or been the subject of careful chemical tests or quantitative analyses. Enough, however, has been reported to stimulate inquiry, and warrant the conviction that we have as yet *scarcely* an *intimation* of the real extent of our resources in this department. For full details in this interesting field, see the valuable Reports of Fremont, Stansbury, Gunnison, and others, which have been published for some time; also, the splendidly-illustrated Reports of the Pacific Railroad Routes, which have recently been given to the world.

On the Southern line, or the Pimas villages, Gila, and Rio Grande Route, near the thirty-second parallel of north latitude, Lieutenant Parke has reported mineral springs. On Buenaventura River there is a spring which deposits a large quantity of sulphur. It gave a temperature of 64° F., the air being 55° F. "Along with the spring is an overflow of bitumen, covering the soil twenty feet around with a depth of two feet." "COOK'S SPRING, at foot of Picacho, is a pool of sulphur water forty feet wide."

Aqua Caliente is a spring of remarkably warm water, its temperature being 130° F. The water is full of carbonic acid gas bubbles, and flows from the spring in a large body, depositing quantities of lime. According to Parke, "were it situated within the limits of civilization, it might be made *invaluable* for medical and economical uses." "The water at Vallicitas is hard and sulphureous." Other waters in this region are noticed, which contain mineral substances, as in the valley of Mimbres River, and neighborhood of San Diego and Fort Yuma.

NEBRASKA AND OREGON SPRINGS.

NEAR Fort Laramie there is a thermal spring, described by Fremont and Stansbury. Its temperature is 74° F., but nothing is said of the mineral contents of its water. The spring is between the north fork of the Platte and Laramie rivers, in Nebraska Territory.

Not far from the Oregon line of Nebraska, in Sweetwater River valley, there are ponds of saline water. This is the region of salt plains, the waters being highly charged with carbonate of soda, sulphate of soda, and chloride of sodium.

SODA, or BEER SPRINGS, are in the northern part of Oregon Territory, on Bear River. The region is full of saline springs, Bear River finally discharging itself into Great Salt Lake. The temperature of the water is from 56 to 67° F. They are in 42° 40' north latitude, 111° 46' west longitude. According to Fremont, they contain sulphate of magnesia and lime, carbonate of magnesia and lime, chloride of sodium, lime and magnesia, with vegetable extractive matter. The leading chemical substance is sulphate of magnesia; it also contains carbonic acid in large quantities. There is a large number of springs here of this character, and the region is described by Fremont as containing many curious and peculiar features, and the different springs show some strange forms and remarkable characters.

Near the Beer Spring is Steamboat Spring. "This is a jet of water thrown from the surface, accompanied by a subterranean noise." The water is thermal, having a temperature of 87° F.

The "taste is pungent, disagreeable, and metallic, leaving a burning effect on the tongue." It contains carbonate of lime and magnesia, with oxide of iron, silica, and alumina. The rocks are not critically described by Fremont, who speaks in general terms of a "carbonate of lime and oxide of iron; compact rocks of a dark-blue color, and strata of heavy, hard, micaceous basalt, having a bright metallic lustre when broken." The springs are represented by him as very numerous, and of a diversified character, but, as a general thing, *thermal and saline.*

In the recent Reports of Railroad Surveys, there is a thermal spring spoken of in Des Chutes Valley, Oregon Territory. The spring is said to "give a peculiar character to the region around for some miles in extent." The temperature of the water is 145° F.; and the basin into which it flows is represented as "being filled with floating jelly-like masses of silica."

At Pike's Peak are located the carbonated or boiling springs, which are 6350 feet above the level of the sea, in latitude 38° 25', longitude 105° 22' west. The springs here are large and beautiful, boiling and bubbling with the quantity of gas contained. They are acidulous and much impregnated; have a temperature of 54·3° F.; others 57° F.; and contain carbonate of lime and magnesia, sulphate of lime, chloride of calcium and magnesium, silica, and vegetable matter. Carbonate of lime is the leading element of the mineral substances.

SALT LAKE REGION SPRINGS.

UTAH, in its history, as far as science has yet recorded its wonders in the domain of nature, or common fame reported its political and spiritual phases of development, (only calculable by the philosophy of the *extreme ancients*,) is to the illuminated side of the continent a region of perpetual fable. It would seem, in its geological relationship, from the heat of its rocks and waters, not far from the region of original fire; still closer, in the estimation of the Christian world, to the region of original sin, from the ardency of its social code, and the anomalously distracted religion and morality which prevails in the only effort which this progressive American has as yet made to reclaim these wonderful deserts, humanize the wilderness, and assert the presence of man on a spot of the earth's surface apparently, from physical limitations and spiritual perversions, accursed of the living God. It is thus that the yarn of the tourist through this peculiar region, in the report of its natural history, seems Munchausen, romantic, and impossible; while the historian of the present version of the social contract, or organization of society patriarchal, at that point of the globe, is as inconceivable and fanciful in his narrative as the story of the fictitious commonwealth of the "NEW ATLANTIS," or the wonders of the "CITY OF THE SUN."

It is to be regretted that a more critical exploration of the geology of this wonderful region has not been made. The precise substratum or rock-structure of the valleys, mountains, and deserts of the territory of Utah, has not been made the subject of scientific dissection. It is thus that the origin of the calorification and mineralization of the innumerable springs of this region, charged with all the salts of the pharmacopœia, is the subject of distant and shadowy speculation. A few meagre and fragmentary sections of its rocks, vaguely and unsatisfactorily described,—a few specimens without intelligible association, with the general statement that the region is primitive and volcanic, is all that has been reached in the investigation of the mineral composition of this part of the continent. Thus it is stated that the Hot Springs, near Bear River, issue from between "different strata of conglomerate and limestone," which exceedingly precise description leaves the geologist free sea-room to imagine the origin of their heat and mineral contents; again, "they gush out together beneath a *conglomerate* consisting principally of fragments of grayish-blue limestone, efflorescing a salt upon the surface, the rocks in the bed being colored with a *red deposit.*" Again, "the *strata* are *here contorted*, and in some places nearly perpendicular, whilst not far away there are piles of scoriaceous basalt." The philosophy of the predominance of volcanisms and other isms in this department is left in the interesting limbo of theory. One astonishing fact which stares out upon every traveler is, that here is a region in which there prevails a multitudinous class of the waters of the earth in a *most extraordinary state* of thermal and mineral combination almost without a parallel on any other part of its surface.

In the vicinity of Salt Lake City there are a number of thermal springs.

WARM SULPHUR SPRING, near the city, contains sulphuretted hydrogen, chloride of calcium, sulphate of soda, chloride of sodium, carbonates of lime and magnesia. It is used by the inhabitants of Deseret, and reputed by them to possess remarkable properties, almost the power of the restoration of perpetual youth. "They make a boast of their good health, and attribute it to bathing in those springs; many that I saw declaring that they came to the *Valley perfect cripples*, and were *restored to their health and agility by frequenting them.*"

One of the wonderful thermal springs of the valley is a

SALT LAKE REGION SPRINGS.

white sulphur water of the temperature of 102° Fahr., with a volume "the thickness of a man's body, which has already been brought into the town for the purpose of bathing, and all have learned the habit of indulging in it."

Hot Springs, also in the neighborhood, have a very high temperature. Their water contains chlorides of sodium, magnesium, and calcium, sulphate and carbonate of lime, and have a temperature of 128° Fahr.

The Warm Fountains are very numerous, and situated near the Lake. They contain chloride of sodium in excess, also sulphates of lime and magnesia; and, according to Lieutenant Gunnison, "they deposit gypsum and other sulphates, the waters being of a delightful temperature for bathing."

Some miles north of Salt Lake City are the Hot Iron Springs. They are called Red Springs, from the iron which they deposit. There are a number of these springs at one place, some with a temperature of 136° Fahr. The chemical contents of the waters are iron, lime, magnesia, sodium, and alumina. The predominating ingredients are peroxide of iron and carbonate of lime.

At the northern end of the lake are a number of salt and sulphur springs, which are also strongly impregnated.

The Bear River Hot Springs, described by Gunnison, are near the river of that name. One of the springs is a salt spring; the other a hot sulphur spring. The spring that contains salt is a strong solution, and deposits it upon the surface. The temperature of these springs is 134° Fahr., and, according to Fremont, they are in latitude 41° 42'; longitude 112° W. Salt springs are numerous around the northern end of this lake.

Warm Saline Springs are described by Stansbury as possessing a temperature of 74 to 84° Fahr. "They break out of the mountain at the northern end of the Lake." The western shore of Salt Lake presents numerous springs of salt and sulphureous waters, together with springs of fresh pure water.

SPRING VALLEY derives its name from its abundance of springs, which are mostly thermal or saline; many of them being a saturated solution of common salt, and having a temperature of 70 to 80° Fahr.

Near the mouth of the river Jordan are the *Warm Springs of Lake Utah*. The water of the Great Salt Lake, according to Fremont, is a "*saturated solution of common salt.*" The water is perfectly limpid, and has a specific gravity of 1·170. It contains, besides chloride of sodium, sulphate of soda, chloride of magnesium, and chloride of calcium.

Northwest of BEER SPRING, and 230 miles from Fort Hall, there are a number of hot springs. They emerge from the rocks with considerable force, and have a temperature of 164° Fahr. They contain chloride of sodium, sulphates of soda and lime, magnesia, and oxide of iron. The rocks of the neighborhood seem to be volcanic. They are near latitude 42° 10′ N., and longitude 115° 10′ W.

Northwest of Hot Springs, 120 miles, in latitude 44° 17′ N., and longitude 117° W., are the HOT SPRINGS OF MALHEUR RIVER. Their temperature is 193° Fahr. They are 1880 feet above the level of the sea, and are strongly charged with common salt.

West of Malheur River, 200 miles, are the HOT AND WARM SPRINGS OF FALL RIVER. They are in latitude 44° 40′ N., and 121° 5′ W. Some of these springs are 89° F., others being 134° F. The region here, according to Fremont, exhibits "striking features of volcanic character."

"The HOT SPRINGS OF PYRAMID LAKE," says Fremont, "are the most remarkable of all the western mountain region. The water boils up from some of these springs like immense caldrons, sometimes with smoke or gas escaping. The water is clear, and has a temperature of 208° Fahr. It is strongly impregnated with common salt." According to Dr. Bell, the temperature of some of these springs have scarcely a parallel in the world. They resemble, to a certain extent, the Great Geyser, the Stokkr, and Spouting Springs of Reikum, Reikeiavik, and the hot springs of Azores, New Zealand, and Fejee Islands, both in temperature and chemical contents." These springs are near the western limits of Utah. Pyramid Lake is but a short distance from these boiling springs.

CALIFORNIA SPRINGS.

THE HOT SPRINGS OF SHASTY'S PEAK are in Upper California, west of the foot of Shasty's Peak. The water is hot enough to boil an egg. The peak is 14,000 feet high, and the whole region volcanic, the peak itself being considered as an extinct volcano. The spring is at the foot of the peak, and boils up among the rocks to the height of two or three feet. Near this peak there is also an acid iron spring, containing a large quantity of carbonic acid and iron, having an agreeable acidulous taste, mixed with the taste of iron.

In the desert of the Colorado, in Southern California, there are springs described by Dr. Bell, who quotes Dr. Le Conte, as

VOLCANIC SPRINGS. "They are in a muddy plain, bordering on a salt lake." Near this lake there are numerous hills, described as "volcanic mounds, composed of lava and pumice, with a number of circular caldrons containing boiling mud, exhaling vapor as steam, sulphur, and sal ammoniac, and throwing up jets of salt water. Some of them are surrounded by stalagmites and concretions of remarkable shape."

"Near Vallecitas there are mounds of cinder and pumice, evidently volcanic. Near Fort Yama there are spouting springs. The region here has suffered from earthquake action."

Near Warner's Rancheria, on the mountain west of a desert on the Colorado, in Southern California, there is a *salt sulphur spring*, with a temperature of 137° Fahr., which issues from a granite rock. Of the chemical composition and character generally not much has been said or known.

There are a number of mineral and thermal springs in New Mexico. Thermal and sulphureous waters are found near the river Del Norte, some miles from Santa Fé.

MERE catalogues are, of course, always intolerable, and "dry details," even on mineral springs and waters in general, have just been abundantly demonstrated to be among the things possible. After the precipitant recitation of the water distribution of a portion of North America just attempted, will not the beholder, in a quiet retrospection of the field, be struck by a few obvious convictions, and among them will not these be prominent? If water is a good thing, if it be one of the few primeval indispensables, if it *has* played an *important part* in the *past experiences* of the *planet*, and *is to play a still more* significant agency in the great future mundane programme of the drama of time and space, have not the sister continents been bountifully cared for, divinely apportioned? What means this intense and immense communion of the land and the sea, this prodigious transportation of water on the wings of the wind, these rivers of air which are rivers of water, those mighty Mississippis and Amazons pouring back the deposits of ærial currents into the great ocean reservoir from which they came? A significant fact this 40-inch precipitation over so much of the exposed side of a world,—so much of the earth's surface thus made alive by springs of water of every order,—those wonderful basins of wonderful rivers, what means this array of "water, water everywhere"? Other divisions of the globe have one of the great original elements in excess,—as, too *much fire* in burning deserts,—too much air, monsoons, siroccos, and tornadoes,—too much earth in vast spaces of dead stone, the rugged bones of the world projecting,—or too much water in paludal spaces unreclaimed. But on these wonderful Americas see the harmonious play of those great old creatures, earth, air, fire, and water! By a closer inspection, see also the list of medicated waters, fountains of healing forces,—the earth, the water, and the air in strange communion again.* Is this another cosmical contract on the question of health and soundness? Quantity the Infinite cared not for, but quality, quality!! must play a more refined and delicate part in the onward progression, ultimation, and perfection of the world. Matter was great, but spirit was greater; *organic life was great, but* CONSCIOUS LIFE WAS GREATER. This HIGHER LIFE, then, seems the *end* for which the *lower* life exists, and health of body and soul, which is the harmonious marriage of the higher and the lower, is the condition of true ecstasy, the gorgeous beatitude, the absolute perfection, that which was originally pronounced by God himself to be the "all good, the all fair." For this triumphant attitude of health, for this strange normality, this *miraculous equipoise*, magazines of forces, reservoirs of power, were required; and hence the play of waters mineral, thermal, and pure, forms an integral part of the machinery of the life of all things. Without, within organic bo-

---

* It must be acknowledged and regretted that the medical profession at large has given but little attention to the subject of mineral springs. Very few physicians know *where to send their patients*, or have detailed information sufficient to fill the indications of their cases in the momentous points of climate and water; and especially what instructions to give them when the last prescription, in getting clear of troublesome cases, is made, "Go to the springs." Dr. Bell's valuable little work, so often quoted, and from which so much important information has been derived in this synopsis, fills a need long felt by the profession. It is to be hoped that the work on the "Mineral Springs of the World," promised by this faithful laborer in the literature and science of medicine, will soon appear, and be fully appreciated, at least by his professional brethren.

dies, life plays beneath the surface or "moves upon the face of the waters." Hence the medicine of springs. The Americas have an immeasurable supply of *all waters.**
Great hint of Nature; the laws of the physical world point out a *fate for man commensurate* with the force of water on earth. All that waters (steam, it must not be forgotten, is a union of the two old friends, fire and water) can do, *is to be done* for humanity on this theatre, and hence the true significance of the great water arrangements of the Americas to mankind.

* One might readily think, from observation of his habits, that the Yankee animal had failed to discover the meaning of the water arrangement, amidst which he lives, and had arrived at the conclusion that *whisky* was the greatest element of the world; and that if rum is not the true medium of his existence, his body is the true medium of rum, and hence, that the vast supplies of water prepared for him are an intimation pointing to the conclusion that corresponding quantities of rum (*fire?*) should thereby be quenched, to preserve the delicate state of *parboiledness* which he has come to regard as the proper condition, or true earthly *blessedness.*

FLORA;

OR,

VEGETABLE LIFE OF THE MOUNTAIN.

> "Many such there are,
> Fair Ferns and Flowers, and chiefly that tall Fern
> So stately, of the Queen Osmunda named;
> Plant lovelier in its own retired abode
> On Grasmere's beach, than Naiad by the side
> Of Grecian brook, or Lady of the Mere
> Sole sitting by the shores of Old Romance."
>
> WORDSWORTH.

> "Who hath the virtue to express the rare
>   And curious virtues both of herbs and stones?
> Is there an *herb for that?* Oh that thy care
>   Would show a root that gives expressions!
>
> "And if an herb hath power, what have the stars?
>   A rose, besides his beauty, is a *cure.*
> Doubtless our plagues and plenty, peace and wars,
>   Are there much surer than our art is sure."
>
> "Herbs gladly *cure our flesh*, because that they
>   Find their acquaintance there."
>
> HERBERT.

The plant may be characterized as organic water which is polarized upon two sides, towards the earth and the air. The vegetable vesicle must, therefore, maintain two poles. While it would represent in itself the magnetic pole, it endeavors to identify itself, to obey gravity, and merge into the darkness toward the mediate point of the earth; but that it may remain a galvanic pole it becomes excited by the air, strives to become a Different and to attain the light.

Animals are entire heavenly bodies, satellites or moons, which circulate independently about the earth; all plants, on the contrary, taken together, are only equivalent to one heavenly body. An animal is an infinity of plants.

PHYSIOPHILOSOPHY.

"As sunbeams stream through liberal space,
And nothing jostle or displace,
So waved the pine-tree through my thought,
And fanned the dreams it never brought.

"Who leaves the pine-tree, leaves his *friend*,
Unnerves his strength, invites his end.

"Whether is better the gift or the donor?
Come to me,
Quoth the pine-tree,
I am the giver of honor:
He is great who can live by me.
The rough and bearded forester
Is better than the lord;
God fills the scrip and canister,
Sin piles the loaded board.

"Whoso walketh in solitude,
And inhabiteth the wood,
Choosing light, wave, rock, and bird,
Before the money-loving herd,
Into that forester shall pass,
From these companions, power and grace.
Clean shall he be, without, within,
From the old adhering sin."

EMERSON.

CHAPTER IV.

FLORA OF THE MOUNTAIN.

To the Naturalist the tree stands the kingly record of the triumph of the vegetable life-principle. A transcendental cell, even the imagination can scarcely conceive that from the simplest vital monad such form of loveliness and majesty could ever arrive.

The stately palm in solitary beauty, the gigantic sequoia and lofty pine spiring to the realms of the clouds, the sturdy "everlasting oak" and imperial magnolia, the banyan-fig-tree and mangrove, must acknowledge brotherhood with the humble lichen on their trunks, or the fragile parasite on their leaves, under the overshadowing unity and tyranny of the law of "organic vesicles." It is thus that the primordial formula of the tree appears to the eye of science, under the profane microscope, the ruthless knife, and that despotic *law*.

But there *are* "Trees of Jehovah and Cedars of Lebanon," (Ps. civ. 16,) signifying the spiritual man. (A. C., 776.) "Tree also signifies man; and as man *is* man by virtue of affection which is of the will, and perception which is of the understanding, therefore these also are signified by tree. There is also a correspondence between man and a tree; wherefore, in heaven there appear paradises of trees, which correspond to the affections and consequent perceptions of the angels; and in some places in hell there are also forests of trees, which bear evil fruits, correspondent with the concupiscences and consequent thoughts of those who are there." (A. R., 400.)*

"The tree is man; the effort to produce means is with man, from his will in his understanding; the stem or stalk, with its branches and leaves, are in man its means, and are called the truths of faith; the fruits, which are the ultimate effects of the effort in a tree to fructify, are in a man uses; in these his will exists. (F. 16.) Man, who is re-born, in like manner as a tree, begins from seed; wherefore, by seed in the Word, is signified the truth which is from good; also, in like manner as a tree, he produces leaves, next blossoms, and finally fruit, for he produces such things as are of intelligence, which also in the Word are signified by leaves; next such things as are of wisdom, which are signified by blossoms; and finally, such things as are of life, namely, the goods of love and charity in act, which, in the Word, are signified by fruits. Such is the representative similitude between the fruit-bearing tree and the man who is regenerated, insomuch that from a tree may be learned how the case is with regeneration, if so be, anything be previously known concerning spiritual good and truth." (A. C., 5115.)

"The tree of life signifies perception from the Lord, and the tree of *knowledge of good and evil*, perception from the world. (Ap. Ex., 739.) Trees of Eden (Ezek. xxxi.) signify scientifics, and knowledges collected from the *Word* profaned by reasonings." (A. C., 130.) "And the Tree of Knowledge signifies the pride of one's own intelligence." (D. P., 328.)

The culmination of a vast vital series, the imperial organism of that wondrous chain between death and life,— between the organic and *inorganic* worlds, "man and nothingness," profoundly significant as an emblem of expression or symbol of utterance between the *Finite* and *Infinite*, for the tree also is a type of man, and there is a "corre-

---

* Swedenborg.

spondence between man and the tree;" thus an indispensable element in that shining web of uses which is the universe, the mystical and scientific representations of the tree seem to be numberless.

"All life is figured as a tree. Igdrasil, the Ash-tree of Existence, has its roots deep down in the kingdoms of Hela or Death; its trunk reaches up heaven-high, spreads its branches over the whole *Universe:* it is the Tree of Existence. At the foot of it, in the Death-Kingdom, sit three nornas, Fates,—the Past, Present, and Future,—watering its roots from the sacred Well. Its boughs, with their buddings and disleafings—events, things suffered, things done, catastrophes—stretch through all lands and times. Is not every leaf of it a biography, every fibre there *an* act *or* word? Its boughs are Histories of Nations. The rustle of it is the noise of Human Existence, onward as from of old. It grows there, the breath of human passion rustling *through* it; or storm-tossed, the storm-wind howling through it like the voice of all the gods. It is Igdrasil, the Tree of Existence. It is the Past, the Present, and the Future; what was done, what is doing, what will be done; the infinite conjugation of the verb *to do*. Considering how human things circulate, each inextricably in communion with *all*,—how the word I speak to you to-day is borrowed, not from Ulfila the Mæsogoth only, but from all men since the first man began to speak,—I find no similitude so true as this of a Tree. Beautiful; altogether beautiful and great. The *Machine of the Universe;*—Alas!! do but think of that in contrast!!"*

"The incorruptible being is likened unto the tree Azwăttha, whose root is ABOVE and whose branches are BELOW, and whose leaves are the vĕds. He who knoweth that, is acquainted with the vĕds. Its branches growing from the three Gŏŏn or qualities, whose lesser shoots are the objects of the organs of sense, spread forth some high and some

---

* "Heroes in History;" Thomas Carlyle.

low. The roots which are spread abroad below, in the regions of mankind, are restrained by action. Its form is not to be found here, neither its beginning, nor its end, nor its likeness. When a man hath cut down this Azwăttha, whose root is so firmly fixed, with the strong axe of *disinterest*, from that time that place is to be sought from whence there is no return for those who find it; and I make manifest that first Pŏŏrŏŏsh from whom is produced the ancient progression of all things."*

Does not the oracular tree whisper to each ear the answer to the prayer it wants to hear? To the shepherd boy in the raptures of love,—love only, as when the "Milk-white thorn that scents the evening gale," breathes out *for* him *his* "tender tale;" to the poet, dreaming, it speaks of beauty and ecstasy, a wave of that sea of glittering globules which plays forever before his soul, "a flash of light in the infinite and eternal night;" to the savant, armed with microscope, it gives an invitation, beckoning forward to explore and contemplate forever; and to the pious devotee, in the fervors of devotion, is it not a "stream of consecrated glory, which heaven ardent opens, and lets down on man in audience with the Deity"?

It is thus that the Hebrew prophet's far-reaching adumbrations attain to final organic utterance in the transcendent soul of the Swedish seer through the spiritual interpretation of the Word; and thus, also, that the Myths, of Scandinavian Scalds, find soil for their roots in Scottish heads, and "Heimskringlas" and "Heroes in History" unite in the infinite beauty and significance of the tree. So, in far-off symbolisms and correspondences, in vague and shadowy but living and suggestive thoughts, does the *tree* stretch forth its roots, trunk, branches and leaves, flowers and fruit, into that more spiritual and ethereal world the consciousness of *man*. From ancient bibles and vedas, in inspirations of Hebrew and Hindoo bards, from mysterious Druidical sha-

---

* Of Pŏŏrŏŏshŏttămă. B. V., page 111.

FLORA OF THE MOUNTAIN.

dows, and the first mutterings of poetry and song, steals out the mysterious *life-thought*, as "Tree of Knowledge," "Tree of Jehovah," "Tree of Life," the essential celestial—"and, in a supreme sense, the Lord himself,"—"Tree of Existence," wonderful Igdrasil!! and the still more mystical and divine Tree Azwăttha̓, Symbol of the "Incorruptible Being."

Even to the first opening intelligence of barbarous and semi-barbarous tribes, there was discovered that "occult relation between man and the vegetable," as from his earliest history a reverence for trees and forests was a marked characteristic. The primitive home of the uncivilized man, they gave the first sense of protection and comfort; the first temples of the gods, groves overwhelmed him with awe, and impressed upon him veneration for the supernals.

> "Who haunts the lonely coverts of the grove:
> To these, and these of all mankind alone,
> The gods are *sure reveal'd*, or *sure unknown*."*

Old in story are the woods of the Druids; old are the fables of Pan, and trees sacred to the deities of the forests; and ancient are the groves of Silvanus and Dodona. The love of woods, then, comes as a revelation of the profoundest instincts of the soul; for by no accident could appear this constant fidelity, this inevitable worship.

The retreat of the SAVAGE, the home of the POET, the temple of the PRIEST, the ancient faith and primeval worship of NATURE, was a phasis of man's development stretching down to necessary and immortal affinities, rooted in inevitable placental relationships, sacred as bonds of a divine maternity, and is still *inseparable* from the *duration* of his *normal life*, as air from his lung or blood from his heart. The forest must continue to be the heaven of ecstasy for contemplation and worship, and the haven of rest for the

---

* Rowe.

wounded and wearied from the dusty roads and burning fields of the world; and while the sacred retreat of the devotee of religion and beauty, they invite the sick and suffering in body and soul, the lacerated and riven in spirit and heart, to wander in their life-renewing shades. Why were the temples of Æsculapius built in groves and on mountains outside of towns and cities? A profound wisdom looms forth from the institutions and rites of the ancients, and dear perpetually to the gods is the soundness of the bodies and souls of mortals; the classical dream of Æsculapius and his daughter Hygeia shining as the prophecy of the light of true science dawning and to beam forever.

Leaving the poetry, symbolism, and far-off spiritual significance of the tree, turn to the tree itself. Botanists have distributed the trees that grow on the surface of the planet into a series of belts or zones; as "certain climatal conditions are requisite for the growth of trees, there exist certain portions of the earth's surface destitute of woods, chiefly on account of cold. The tree-limit illustrates this.* At the north this limit is sometimes 71° north latitude, and in the "southern hemisphere it extends as far as the continents."† These zones are named, commencing at the north, 1st, The zone of conifers; 2d, The zone of amentaceous or catkin-bearing trees; 3d, The zone of multiform woods; and 4th, The zone of the rigid-leaved woods.‡

These belts are again designated, by others, the zone of conifers, the zone of deciduous, and the zone of evergreen woods.§

By examining this highly interesting and attractive subject, it will be discovered that with the geographic distribution of plants is connected the whole destiny and progress of the human being, and if "necessity is (*not*) the mother of the world," she *establishes eternal limitations to all things*, and is at least that dread power that fixes the fates of men.

---

* Schouw. † Idem. ‡ Idem. § Schleiden.

FLORA OF THE MOUNTAIN. 213

Within the Tropics or Zone of Multiform Trees a boundless exuberance of vegetative force, with endless diversity of structure, prevails. Rich and varied in color of inflorescence and foliage, the forests of the equatorial regions are masses of life and light. The closely-packed trunks of an extensive variety of eccentric and beautifully-formed trees are chained into continuities of woods by interwoven masses, or networks of vines, which knot and rope the whole together, while their bodies, branches, and leaves are alive with parasitic plants clinging to their surfaces, or trailing in pendant festoons from stem to stem. From the disposition of the leaves, and whole style and character of the foliage, a ghastly light permeates every recess of these forests, which are also filled with a corresponding multitude of animal forms, revelling in the heat and glare which constitute the horrors of the woods of the tropics. With this light and splendor, this flaunting array of fantastic figures and brilliant coloring, the forests of the temperate zone present a most entire and perfect contrast. Leaving the brilliant but noxious display of the vegetation of the torrid spaces, the change to the cool recesses of the mixed woods of the temperate climates is one of the most striking phenomena of Nature. These forests are composed principally of deciduous trees, as the oak, beech, chestnut, maple, etc., with smaller trees mixed, and sometimes with different species of the coniferæ. They have frequently a bush-underwood or heath-growth beneath the larger trees, which is composed of a number of interesting plants, but presents nothing like the labyrinth of vines and smaller shrubs that fill the interspaces of the forests of hot climates. This is explained by the deeply-shading foliage of these woods obstructing the light from their recesses, so that few plants can grow beneath them for want of heat and light, the great life-elements of the tropics. With markedly distinguished features, this zone of plants is widely separated both from the belt of "rigid-leaved," the multiform, and the woods of the exclusive coniferæ. It contains some of the most imposing and interesting forms within the tree-limit. Sometimes single species occupy extensive surfaces, almost to the exclusion of others, their groves stretching in dense and serried ranks over large spaces.

Again, a number of species grow together,—plants widely separated in botanical affinities,—as, for example, the cone-bearers and deciduous tribes, thus giving all the elements of variety and graceful combination to this order of woods. These mixed growths of trees are of surpassing beauty, some of them exhibiting a grandeur and solemnity found only in the dark recesses of the magnificent forests of the temperate latitudes. They are the great woodlands, possessing so much value as reservoirs of timber, for all purposes, and whose importance to man, in *every aspect*, it is impossible to compute.

The Alleghany Mountain, in Pennsylvania, in its botanical developments through planetary affinities, falls, in its general relationship to the world of vegetable-life, into this belt or zone of geographic distribution of plants.

The history of this life and its diversity of types, or the "Flora" of the mountain, especially in the department of trees, is one of extreme attraction.

As the direct and necessary consequence of the geography and geology, or soil and climate of a region, as already shown, the vegetable world unfolds itself by its own fixed and unalterable laws. Next to topographic distribution of surface, hill, valley, mountain, and stream, "the vegetable clothing makes the distinctive features of a country, the tree-world, or arborescent vegetation, being especially concerned in imparting *expression* and *character* to *surfaces*."*

The mixed soils of the different tracts of the Alleghany range, in Pennsylvania, and its mixed climate from elevation above the level of the sea and the medium latitudinal geographic position in the temperate belt of the planet, marks the meeting of separate vegetable classes, and gives great diver-

* Schouw.

FLORA OF THE MOUNTAIN. 215

sity of phytological life. There is, in this region, the combination of two zones of plants just described, namely, the Terebinthinate trees, (coniferæ,) or those possessing slender stems, of great height, and needle-shaped leaves which are evergreen, with the exception of a few species, and the zone of amentaceous trees, which are plants with spreading branches and diffuse spray, bearing wide, tender, and membranous leaves, which drop every year and leave the stems and branches bare through the frost months. The mingling of these two belts, which are representative worlds, and unite widely-separated chapters of the history of the planet, with laws of media, soil, and climate, distinct and peculiar, gives a special charm and interest to the forests of the Alleghany.

A notice of some of the most striking trees composing these forests may not be found uninteresting. This recitation need not be made in the strictly scientific order of the botanist, but in the natural succession in which they might be supposed to attract the attention of the traveler. A catalogue of the most commonly observed and extensively distributed plants of the mountain, including the several departments of botany, will be appended to this chapter. The object of this must be obvious, especially to the physician, to whom the great laws of "Habitats," and the dread necessities which superintend the devevelopment and perpetuation of *Life* in all its forms, reveal themselves in the character, qualities, entire nature of the proper legitimate earth-children rooted in and united by bonds of parental affinity to special localities and in special media.

The trees and woods of this range of mountains have some distinguishing features, all of which will be apparent after a special portraiture of them shall have been made.

The mountain is clothed with an extensive and beautiful variety of trees. In their distribution upon the surface, these trees seek the most congenial localities, affecting the soil and exposure made healthful and agreeable by oldest affinities and home sympathies. Rocky height or rugged ravine, alpine table-land or sloping mountain vale, have each their primal clothing of vegetation. The southeastern slopes of the mountain, also its range of summit-knobs, are generally covered by a variety of oaks, chestnut, firs, and pines, and a number of other trees, those with deciduous leaves greatly predominating. In winter the aspect of this side of the mountain is stark and bare, the monotonous gray of the forests destitute of foliage, prevailing, with occasional spots of pines, their dark-green hue visible at all seasons of the year. Other parts of the mountain, especially the ranges of depressions of the western sides, on the contrary, show great extents of evergreen forests. Its eastern slopes and summit in full summer costume present an unrivaled array of verdure in an endless ocean of leaves,—the foliage of the hardier members of the oak family, as the chestnut oaks, with white, red, and black oaks prevailing. To these may be added the chestnut, beech, and several varieties of birch and maple, with linden, poplar, cucumber, hickory, and walnut.

As the forest is composed of an aggregate of individual trees, and the exact mode of growth of the individual giving at last a general character to the forest, some notice of the manner in which the different trees of the mountain grow may assist in the truthful rendering of its woods. This special portraiture of trees, or the study of the growth and mode of development of each kind of tree, properly belongs to the artistic department of natural science, and is especially attractive to the naturalist who is not a mere cataloguemaker. Besides the exhaustless beauty of the variety of form, and the special attraction of specific styles of growth, this study of the individual tree reveals great laws of science in the necessities which superintend the unfolding of its structure. This style of growth is thus a theme of twofold attraction, interesting to botanical physiologists, and especially interesting to the artist or student of form,—for the different varieties of trees have forms and expressions as different and characteristic as the separate races of animals; indeed, each individual tree, flower, or rock, is a unit as per-

FLORA OF THE MOUNTAIN.

fect as any other unit, whether animal or man. All men are more or less alike, so are all blades of grass; all trees are more or less alike, so are the birds in their branches. But the artist who works from Nature had better forget his patterns or stereotype trees of different orders, his *model men, birds, and plants;* for in the *living universe* they are *all*, also, exceedingly *unlike each other*. Each man and grass-blade is an *individual* having all those modifications of external or secondary qualities which mark him or it from all other men and grass-blades, and makes it that *individual*, unlike all *other men* or grass-blades of the universe. So must the *real artist* paint the individual tree; and thus is the world endless in opulence of resources, and each form of each new tree is a study, and its integrity and beauty renewed forever. Hence, also, is this worshiper in "God's first temple" enveloped in a perpetually new atmosphere of light and loveliness; and thus does he drink from fresh rivers of ethereal wine, and in the deep beatitude of the artist's love of beauty feels that he could be entranced for a thousand years.

No contrast can be more striking than that which exists between the evergreen trees and the deciduous, or those which assume only a summer dress, being arrayed for occasions. Their forms are as differently suggestive as the substances which constitute their bodies. Different members of the pine family affect the shape of the pyramid, yielding to the imagination the idea of duration, by giving a base which no storm can uproot or turn over, their tapering summits, at the same time, presenting the smallest surfaces for the attacking winds. The oak and the beech, very different from the pine, fling out their arms into wide, umbrageous, overshadowing masses of limbs and twigs, which only seem to wish to grow on and cover the largest space. Thus the pine-tree sings its song and has its dance of joy in the war of the winds, and the tempest's roar is its frolic, while the branches of the oak and beech are whirled and twisted like withs in its fury, their leaves being torn to rags and scattered like dust in the tornado's path. One class represents the hardy pioneers of a world in a process of reclamation from chaos, for

> "My garden is the cloven rock,
>   And my manure the snow,
> And drifting sand-heaps feed my stock,
>   In summer's scorching glow."

Thus a full-armed warrior, ready for battle at a moment's warning, stands the pine-tree; the other the representative, also the fruit of a riper time, belonging to a more progressed system, requiring richer soil and fatter provender, can only sport destructible leaves for a short time, soft and evanescent, and requires constant protection and care.

Something of the individual tree or species, its style of development or architecture; something of the fashion of tree-building on the Alleghanies, may introduce the inquirer to a clearer recognition of the laws of organic life under the despotism of physical conditions and the grave necessities of habitats.

In noticing the trees of the mountain, without reference to scientific classification or precedence, we commence with the white ash, as a representative of use and beauty. This is the FRAXINUS AMERICANA of the botanists, and is certainly a family connection of Igdrasil, the Ash-tree of Existence, but just where, in botanical, natural, or artificial systems, is not recorded.

The books quote it as "a large tree, fifty or sixty feet high." This description will not apply to the tree as it grows on the mountain. It there frequently attains to five feet in diameter, with a height of 120 feet; its close-ribbed, deeply and finely sulcated light-gray bark covering a trunk as straight as a granite shaft sometimes for eighty feet, and without a branch. At this height it separates into branches, forming a head of finely divided limbs and spray, its small, green pinnate leaves pubescent and glaucous beneath in 3–4 pairs, giving to its delicate foliage an expression strange and unsuitable for a tree of such majestic proportions. One other less stately species of this genus grows on the mountain, the FRAXINUS PUBESCENS.

MAGNOLIA ACUMINATA.—This is the mountain magnolia, or cucumber-tree. Beck describes it as a "middle-sized tree, sometimes, however, attaining the height of seventy feet;" and Darlington represents it as a "majestic and symmetrical species, sixty to eighty feet high," which would convey but a remote idea of the proportions assumed by this splendid plant on the Alleghanies. It frequently exhibits a diameter of four and a half feet, with a beautiful undivided stem of ninety feet, as straight as a plumb-line, covered by a laminated white bark, with narrow but not deep grooves, the whole tree attaining the height of 120 feet. The leaves of this tree are of exceeding beauty, dark-green and glossy above, and beneath bluish and pubescent, often twelve inches long by six inches in width. The flowers are large and handsome, but not gayly colored, and are followed by a reddish fruit, like a small cucumber, possessing a highly aromatic taste and smell. It is found in considerable abundance in the depths of the forests on the western sides and table-lands of the mountain, and grows mixed with other trees. Its style of foliage and growth gives the tree a peculiar and distinguished cast, its large dark-green leaves attracting the eye, as if some majestic stranger had wandered into the forest; so exotic and foreign in its aspect that the beholder is reminded of tropical palms and mangroves. The lumber of this tree classes in value with that of the poplar or tulip-tree. Gray suggests that, "possibly the Magnolia Fraseri (the long-leaved cucumber-tree) grows in the mountains of Pennsylvania." He also quotes the Magnolia umbrella as being found on the mountains of Pennsylvania. On the Alleghanies they have not yet been seen.

ÀCER.—This is the family of maples, several of which are found on the mountain.

ÀCER SACCHARINUM, or the sugar maple, grows here into a large tree. Both varieties (the saccharinum and nigrum) are found growing sometimes five feet in diameter and 110 feet high. Its trunk is rough and twisted, with rugged, scaly bark, when it grows in open woods, but slender, straight, and smoother when it grows in deep forests with other trees, or in dense groves of its own species. The white silvery wood of this tree is much valued as fuel, also for cabinet purposes, especially when that freak, or "fantastic trick" of the woody fibre occurs, producing what is called "bird's-eye maple." Its well-known sugar-sap gives one of the staples of the mountain.

Àcer rubrum is also found here. This species is called "rock maple," and furnishes the variety of cabinet lumber called "curly maple."

The Àcer Pennsylvánicum, striped maple, moosewood, or striped dogwood, is a small, slender tree, with beautiful foliage, and dark-green, handsomely-striped branches. It grows abundantly on the mountain, but has no value as timber, its trunk never attaining more than a few inches in diameter.

"Àcer spicàtum" is a tall shrub which grows in clumps and thickets in the gorges and ravines of the mountain. This little plant is called "mountain maple," and, although only a bush, it bears a most striking resemblance to its imperial brothers, the arborescent species.

There are several indigenous cherry-trees on the mountain. These are of the genus Cérasus.

Cérasus Pennsylvánica is a graceful little tree, quoted by the botanists at twenty to thirty feet high, but often twice that height. It bears snow-white blossoms on thin, bright-red, and purple branches and twigs, followed by a red, sour little cherry.

Cérasus Virginiàna is the choke-cherry. This is rather a bush, scarcely ever aspiring to the tree form, and grows along streams, bearing abundance of astringent fruit on short, close racemes.

The Cérasus serótina is the wild black-cherry, said to grow "thirty to sixty feet high." On the Alleghanies this

FLORA OF THE MOUNTAIN.

plant is a superb tree, often five feet in diameter and 125 feet high. It grows in groves or mingled with other tall trees, and rivals the tallest of them in height. When it grows in this manner it exhibits the peculiar shape of the mountain trees growing in dense woods. This form of trees has been brought about by the circumstance of their original growth. The mass of foliage rises in a plane forming the tops of the trees. As the lower limbs become shaded and atrophied, they die and drop off, and at last branch-buds cease to be developed and branches to grow, the trunks or stems extending upward as naked symmetrical shafts of mathematical regularity, the terminal branches forming a leafy summit or canopy, which continues to mount higher and higher as the mass of the forest rises in the air.

In open woods and low-lands of the State, this tree grows in a widely-spreading umbrageous mass, the stem dividing into a number of branches, the whole tree scarcely attaining half the height of the same plant struggling in the depths of the mountain forests. A stem without a branch for ninety feet, and as straight as a gun-barrel, is a common form of the plant in these woods. This is the "cherry-lumber" tree, so much valued as cabinet material.

Of the allied genus PRUNUS, the mountain has one species, the "Americana." It has the ordinary characters of the tree elsewhere.

BEECH-TREE.—Of the genus FAGUS, the continent, and, consequently, the Alleghany, has but one species, and that is the FAGUS FERRUGINÉA, or American beech. The mode of growth of this tree in the mountain forests is so entirely different from the shape of the tree elsewhere that it seems to have lost its identity. This is so markedly the case that common observers have made several beeches of the botanical *one species*, as "white" and "red," "mountain" and "water" beech.* These varieties are of course produced by

---

* When the heart-wood, (*duramen*,) which is a flesh-red color, is large in proportion to the white, (*alburnum*,) or sap-wood, it is called

the circumstances of growth, as of the soil, air, moisture, and other special surroundings of the plant. As it grows on the mountain, the tree, an object of loveliness, is especially attractive, and it would seem that in the beech the spirit of grace and beauty had found its most appropriate image and symbol of perfection. It grows in extensive continuous forests, the rugged web of interwoven roots forming almost a floor for miles, while the white symmetrical stems, uninterrupted by branches to a great height, present the appearance of Grecian columns, giving an expression of art to these vast and leafy sylvan temples. In striking contrast with the hemlock forests, the beech groves appear in gay and fanciful antagonism. They grow everywhere on, but seek the flatter slopes of the mountain, and seem to affect the gentle undulating surfaces of the table-land. These forests, with their series of white columnar trunks sporting long, thin, and graceful branches, covered with delicate, green, membranous leaves, half translucent, present an array always festive and beautiful. In the early spring, when the tender tissue-paper young leaves are unfolding, and present their soft and delicate surfaces to the air, it is hard to imagine anything more ethereal and exquisite than a waving grove of this lovely tree. In autumn, when the leaves have turned yellow, they appear almost to possess a self-luminous or phosphorescent power, for, at this time, however dark the night may be, or dense the forests, the traveler sees his path illuminated by a mild, diffused light, each object integrated as by a hazy moon or snow. The effect of this mystic and peculiar light is enchanting. After being for a time in beech woods the contrast is fearful, if the pathway lies through a hemlock

---

"*red beech*." This occurs when the tree is old, but with small diameter, the annual layers being *very thin*, and the limbs and foliage small in quantity and proportion. With a large amount of limbs and leaves the white wood predominates, and a tree of a given diameter may exhibit only half the number of concentric annual sheets, and be of only half the age, of a red or heart-wood tree of the same dimension of trunk.

forest. Almost perfect darkness seems at once to reign, and the journey must be groped through as in a region of absolute night. In mixed forests of these two trees the effect is always charming in the extreme, as they suggest different orders of associations and reveal different phases of the elements of life and beauty.

Of the Cone-Bearers, or Pine Family, there are not many species on the mountain. A few pitch pines (*Pinus rigidia*) and yellow pines (*Pinus mitis*) on the eastern declivities and summits, also an occasional spot on the western slopes, together with the white pine and hemlock, which are very abundant on the whole range, constitute the representatives of the evergreen, or terebinthinate order of plants.

Genus ABIES.—On the Alleghany proper there is but one species of Spruce in great abundance. There are several species of this genus on the parallel Appalachian ridges and intervening elevated valleys of Pennsylvania. Asa Gray cites this State as the locality of several species of Abies, viz., the Frasèri, Nigra, Canadénsis; and it is in the well-known botanical range of the "Balsamea" and "Alba." Some rare localities contain several of these beautiful species, with the Hackmatack. One of these localities is a delightful little "garden of the blest" among the "seven mountains" of Centre and Huntingdon counties, called the "Bear Meadows." It is a small, elevated synclinal trough, surrounded by high, sharp, white sandstone (Formation 4) mountains on all sides, with one outlet or gorge, through which flows the stream draining the valley. It is evidently the bed or rich bottom of a mountain tarn or lake, the waters of which have escaped by a rupture of the wall surrounding it. A wild, exquisite, and secluded spot, it would seem to be the fantastic Arcadia of some dreaming artist or lover of nature, hidden from the world's vulgar gaze, and consecrated to beauty. Fresh glimpses of green carpet-spots of prairie, with osier beds and clumps of stately, solemn evergreens, black, silver, and balsam firs, with pines, cedars, and laurels, open into vistas of tall, deciduous trees, artistic and surprising in their exclusiveness and grace. A dark amber-colored stream, the water stained from vegetable infusion, and exhibiting throughout the year the tint of the mountain waters during the fall of the leaf, wanders, with a thousand curves and foldings, through wastes of reeds, sedges, azaleas, alders, and andromedas, cardinal flowers, "vegetable satyrs," and the more imperial Orchis, with weird Sarracenias and gold-thread Coptis. An ancient and deserted garden of rare and lovely evergreens, varied shrubbery, and beautiful flowers, this little valley seems, in its isolation and sequestered beauty, to be a fragment of Paradise left unprofaned, to remind us of the splendor of the pristine home and of glories departed.

ABIES CANADENSIS.—The Canadian fir-tree, familiarly known as the "hemlock" of the mountain, is a very abundant species. It delights in northern exposures, as if seeking to battle with the coldest winds, asking no sympathy from the more genial gales of the south. It forms large forests, thick and compact, taking a savage and exclusive possession of the surface, and destroying all other forms of vegetable life beneath them. These hemlock forests have a striking and unique appearance, unlike the forests of any other tree. Like the gloomy isles of dark, half-subterranean temples, enveloped in sepulchral gloom, the wanderer feels, as he treads their lonely and sequestered solitudes, that the darkness of night surrounds him at noonday. In sleepy silence, with hushed footsteps, he treads their labyrinths of majestic columns as if veritably in the "land of shades." In the winter they assume an extremely sombre aspect, appearing, in very cold weather, the ground being covered with snow, as if smoked or painted black. Like the forests of the "Inferno," gloomy and peculiar, the tree has a funereal hue, and chills while it invites and offers the protection of its shade. It seems exclusive, and holds its title to the surface by actual possession for hundreds of years.

The hemlock of the mountain grows sometimes to an enormous size, frequently attaining the circumference of 20 feet,

FLORA OF THE MOUNTAIN. 225

with a height of 130 feet. These vast towers of woody fibre are the records of ages of labor of the vegetable life-powers, reclaiming the carbon, earth, and water of the world from chaotic floating. They fill the observer with astonishment, their massive forms, "like pillared props of heaven," suggesting the limbs of "Atlas, whose brawny back supports the starry skies." Their scraggy and rugged trunks give more the idea of rocky shafts than trees, and, like granite needles or stone obelisks, they seem to say they will stand forever. The lumber of this tree is of great value.

PINUS STRÒBUS.—The white pine, like the hemlock, is scattered over the whole mountain in almost every position, rocky height, or ravine, but only prevails in extensive continuous groves along the valleys of the streams, or the cold undulating surfaces of the table-lands. It grows in dense close-set masses, which have an expression, *sui generis*, from the specific shape or style of the tree. It is the loftiest of our indigenous trees, quoted by some of the books at from 80 to 100 feet, but in primitive mountain forests its straight thin columns often attain a height of nearly 200 feet, with an exceedingly narrow diametric base. These small, tapering stems look like masts of ships or lightning-rods, their delicate hair-leaf foliage giving the appearance of green mist in their tallest boughs, the whole woods waving like a grove of colossal plumes in the wind. The sharp, tapering summits of these trees do not intercept the rays of light as occurs in the interlocked canopy of the hemlock forests, but give a green and airy lightness, diffused through their densest groves, without the oppressive sense of shade and darkness which prevail on surfaces covered by their more gloomy brother.

When the white pine grows scattered in forests of other trees, it does not shoot up in single thin stems, but frequently forks or divides into groups of stems, which spring generally from a single, massive, knotty stump, or short trunk, which rises alone from the earth. The size of this basis or pedestal of the miniature forest above is often of enormous dimension and exceedingly irregular in contour, but it is evidently most generally the result of the germination of single seeds, some of them exhibiting, however, the appearance of two or three seeds having germinated in contact. The philosophy of the growth of this particular form is, apparently, that the different species of trees forming these groves have started from the earth's surface at the same time, but somewhat scattered, and, when the first branches of the infant pine were developed, the surrounding growth prevented a lateral expansion of the limbs, each of the primitive branches afterwards becoming a separate trunk or tree, and projecting itself upward, as the pine does in other crowded forests. From the point of separation at the forks, the limbs, each a noble tree itself, spring together, frequently of one size, like an immense chandelier, and rise in the air, the whole bundle of stems being supported and nourished by one large root-base. Many of these *forked-pine* trees have quite a celebrity, and have attained the character of *individuals*, and are visited as curiosities of the mountain. The lumber of the white pine is of great value, and forms one of the chief staples of the mountain.

ULMUS.—Along the flats of some of the streams the elm often attains to a great size, sometimes dividing into regular clumps of thin trunks, which bend outward from the centre, the whole summit being flat, and the tree of the shape of an inverted bell. Three species of the genus Ulmus grow on the mountain, viz., the "*Americana*," the "*fulva*," and "*racemosa.*" They seek, as elsewhere, with their characteristic instinct, the moist flats and neighborhood of streams. Many of these elms are of enormous size, and of exceedingly fantastic and eccentric forms, appearing to have, by some sylvan sorcery, been led to violate all sober and common-sense laws of tree-building, and to have grown by freaks of the vegetative forces into "monsters of such frightful mien," that, to be *remembered*, "need but to be seen."* To have introduced the photographic tran-

* An exact and perfectly-elaborated portrait of an elm of rare and grotesque form and immense proportions has been painted for the

scripts of some of these trees into ANY "Midsummer Night's Dream," would scarcely have been "to have stolen the impression of the fantasy" of Shakspeare's most ultra imaginative creations. Surely, in the presence of one of these fanciful forms, one would say, that the artist who should forget or deny that a tree can be an *individual*, in its contour and lineaments as specific and unique as a statue of Phidias or a church of Michael Angelo, had better drop his pencil, or satisfy his aspirations by transcribing the stereotype trees of his first lesson-book, and by the transference to his canvas of the pictures of fence-rails or timber-posts.

With a sense of shame the forgiveness of the wood-gods must be implored for having neglected so long one of their special admirations, a true splendor of the vegetable world, the LYRIODENDRON-TULIPIFERA, or tulip-tree, sometimes also called the *wild poplar*. The mountain sports this plant in a state of greatest perfection, its trunk attaining the largest proportions by the species anywhere achieved. A proud and lofty monarch of the American woods, it is admired as a beauty of the earth by all who have seen it. With a broad, lobed, and truncated smooth leaf giving a spe-

American Academy of Music of Philadelphia, by Russel Smith, the well-known American landscape-painter. Every limb, twig, and almost every leaf, of this remarkable tree has been fixed on a canvas forty feet square, by the wonderful power and genius of this gifted artist. The original of this picture stands on the "everglades," or what was originally the beaver-dams of one of the tributaries of Clearfield Creek, three miles northwest of the "Alleghany Health Institute." It may not generally be known, even to Pennsylvanians, that many of the finest artistic combinations in the magnificent scenography of the Academy, the grandest histrionic temple in the world, were taken from the recesses of the Alleghany Mountain forests, in their native State, by the magical pencil of Russel Smith, a *native artist*. To more intimately and thoroughly study and *work from* the beautiful models of the mountain, Mr. Smith has secured a rural cabin and piece of land near the "Alleghany Springs" and Pennsylvania Railroad summit, where, in his own words, "some of the brightest and grandest moments of my life have been passed."

cial feature to its foliage, it bears a superb flower, as rich and varied almost, in its tints and style, as the tulip of the gardens. "Erect as a sunbeam" its stem sometimes shoots into a splendid shaft, almost a hundred feet in height without a limb, and then branches into a kingly diadem, or veritable CROWN of leaves and flowers. This shape has been frequently described already as *peculiar* to the trees growing in deep forests. In the tulip-tree it is perhaps the most striking of all. As its enormous trunk, fluted by a deeply-grooved bark of a silver-gray color, carries an almost unaltering thickness throughout its entire height, the imagination requires no assistance to behold its mass of verdure and beauty growing from the summit of some majestic marble column "on Grecian wold." It is one of the valuable *lumber-trees* of the mountain.

TILIA AMERICANA.—This is the linden or bass-wood, "lime-tree," and "white wood," a beautiful and noble tree, attaining to over 100 feet in height. In deep groves it has also the characteristic form of mountain trees, that is, with tall, straight, branchless stem, terminating in a mass of boughs, spray, and leaves, which, together with its smooth, graceful trunk covered by white finely-ribbed bark, presents one of the most striking and beautiful denizens of the woods. The species "*heterophylla*" is also found on the mountain. The lumber of the linden sells under the name of "*whitewood*," with poplar and cucumber.

BETULA.—The Birch Family have several representatives here. These are the BETULA LÉNTA, "*nigra*," "excelsa," and "*papyràcea*." Some of them grow into large trees, as the "*lenta*" and "*nigra*," which are often found ninety feet high. The wood of the well-known sweet, or cherry-birch, the "*lenta*," is valuable, giving a fine-grained red lumber, and good fuel.

QUERCUS.—Several of the oak group are found here, and among them the QUERCUS ALBA, or familiar and valuable white oak. It does not grow in these localities, as in the Appalachian valleys, in continuous groves, but is found mixed in forests of other trees of the noblest proportions, which it ever assumes in any soil.

QUERCUS MONTANA affects the eastern slopes and summits, having a taste, as its common name indicates, (*rock chestnut-oak,*) for rugged and stony surfaces. Associated with the last species is the "*castanea,*" and scattered in different localities over the mountain are the "*nigra,*" "*tinctoria,*" "*coccinea,*" "*rubra,*" and "*falcàta.*" From the size to which many of these species grow, it would seem that here must be a special home of the oaks.*

CASTANEA.—The chestnut has a special affinity for the mountain. The CASTANEA VESCA grows here to a prodigious size, living ages. It bears the familiar well-known sweet nut, and has an extremely rugged bark, covering a coarse-grained, light wood, especially prized for its *indestructibility* as a fencing material. The CASTANEA PUMILA or chinquepin, grows here also.

NYSSA MULTIFLORA.—The tupelo, black or sour gum, grows sparsely over the mountain, presenting its ordinary characters in other localities.

PLATANUS OCCIDENTALIS.—The American plane, sycamore, or buttonwood, is found on the streams at the base and on the table-lands of the Alleghanies, but not on its

---

* In connection with oaks, a word on the progressive instincts of the Pennsylvanians may be in place. It has arranged itself on the record that it required the lumber-men of Maine to come to Pennsylvania to show her mountaineers the value of their forests, the "Yankee stave-cutter" having been a pioneer in one of the most valuable lumber specialties of the mountain and the State. Transcendent Yankee!! his sharpness is past finding out; he cuts the "trees that twist with the sun," saying, that those which "twist against the sun will not hold *molasses.*" Curious problem in the philosophy of *kinks;* it seems that the *refractory saccharine* principle of the South requires a special twist of a special Northern oak to hold it level, and this, too, by the *special twist* "*with the sun,*" *and* not "*against it.*" When will Pennsylvanians wake up to the special twists of Northern Fanatics and Southern Salamanders, both *with* and *against* the *sun?*

summits. Its snow-white stems, mingled with the sombre hemlock, forms one of the finest and most striking contrasts in nature. Its lumber is valued for some purposes.

The MORUS RUBRA, or "*Mulberry-tree*," grows in perfection here.

JUGLANS.—The species cinerea (butternut) of this genus is found in great abundance along the streams in the gorges, also higher up the mountain. The "*nigra*," or "*black walnut*," is also found, but not in such quantity.

CARYA.—There are several species of *hickory* on the mountain. The "*alba*," or shell-bark, grows here with its usual characters, but is not abundant. The "*sulcata*" grows along the base of the mountain, and in the little valleys of the streams. The "*tomentosa*" and "*microcarpa*" are here, but not abundant. The species "*glabra*" is very common on the Alleghany and some of its parallel ridges, constituting quite an article of commerce, the young, tough sprouts being sold for hoop-poles in immense quantities. The "*amara*" is also found here. Several of this genus are but small and insignificant trees on the mountain.

POPULUS.—Of this genus there are several species, as the "*tremuloides*," or "aspen," the "*grandidentata*," or long-toothed aspen, the "*cándicans*," and "*heterophylla.*" These are graceful and attractive trees, generally with smooth stems and beautiful foliage, but do not grow in the deep forests with the large, rough, mountain trees.

The ROBINIA PSEUDACACIA, or common locust, grows in profusion on the mountain. It frequently achieves the proportions of a considerable tree, and is *valuable* as an *indestructible timber.**

SÀLIX.—A number of willows have made their home on the mountain, both of the tree and bush form. Several of

---

* On the question of its indestructibility, see Canal Commissioners' Reports generally of the Portage Railroad of the State, on the eternity of locust crossties, under the jurisdiction of the ship, the horses, and the plough, overshadowed by the protective wings of the American eagle—Virtue, Liberty, and Independence.

FLORA OF THE MOUNTAIN.

the trees are familiar and handsome, but more of the genus are plain unostentatious shrubs.

These are the principal trees which are found in the forests of the Alleghany Mountains in Pennsylvania. The poet might make a book of biography, and the artist a gallery of paintings of these splendid trees alone. An enumeration of some of the most striking trees or larger forms of the vegetable world is all that has been produced as the living mantle or robes of life and organic appendage to the mountain, viewed individually, and in the concrete, or masses of woods. What fills with amazement the explorer of these forests is the thickness or density of the growth, and enormous size of the trees. He is troubled to conceive how these huge and thickly-planted trunks, which seem to have scarcely room to stand, are nourished, or grow in the limited space allotted to each tree. Such pyramids of wood might be supposed to require some base to support them, but the trees are so crowded, that were not the surface of the earth the chained continuity of interlocked roots that it is, they *could not* stand. Where the axe commences to fell these forests, and trees are left standing alone, they soon fall to the earth for want of the support and protection of the surrounding mass. The woods are so dense as to be almost impenetrable, the under-growth frequently having disappeared entirely, the branchless and naked trunks, supporting, only on their summits, a canopy of leaf-bearing branches. In some of these forests the fallen stems of immense trees, that have died of old age, half cover the ground. Here, in deep shadows and silence, sleep the monarchs of the forest, silent and sequestered, the dark solitudes furnishing a suitable graveyard for these heroes of a thousand storms, each one reposing as he fell, for now

> "Low lies the plant to whose creation went
> Sweet influence from every element;
> Whose living towers the *years* conspired to build,
> Whose giddy top the morning loved to gild."

They sleep, while ever-busy Nature clothes each prostrate form with a shroud of verdant mosses,—thus it is

> " Out of sleeping, awaking,
> Out of waking, asleep;
> *Life death overtaking;*
> Deep *underneath deep!*"

The general aspect of these forests, with their different changes in the procession of the seasons, must strike the most careless observer. During the winter they are stark and stern, the evergreen forests affording but a gloomy contrast, their dark-green foliage scarcely suggesting the thought of *life*, while the ceaseless moan of the cold and naked stems speaks only of death to the wolfish winds.

Occasionally, in the winter forests, a phenomenon occurs of surpassing wonder. This is the sudden transition or transmutation, frequently during the night, as if by some magical power, of the whole forest of trees into a forest of glass. The mists, rains, and air charged with moisture, invest the tree-trunks, branches, and twigs with a clothing of ice, clear as crystal, so that the woods seem invested with an unrivaled splendor. This glittering and phantasmal array must be seen to be appreciated or conceived.

The phenomenon of the hoar-frost is allied to this glass metamorphosis. This is the investment of each finest fibre of the woods with a snowy, crystalline, and sparkling velvet of frost, the air being filled with floating and brilliant spangles, detached by the slightest breath of wind.

The vernal change is most genial and striking. After the long death-sleep of the winter, as is the case in northern latitudes, the leaves and flowers, with the first sun-fires, flash out upon the air with an endless succession of tints, forms, and outlines. The shades of green of the young foliage are numerous, giving a different appearance to each newly-arrayed tree. Each plant is peculiar in the character of its new-born leaves; sometimes, as in the case of the beech, dropping from the twig a soft and delicate membrane that floats like a cobweb in the air; again, as in the chestnut, hanging sullenly as if wilted; or, again, as in the oak and maple family, obtruding their more angular leaflets, which stick out rigidly from the terminal twigs. Each tree has a form or physiognomy for its *new-born* leaf, also for the perfect organ or full-grown leaf, and these different aspects show trees as entirely unlike each other, in the different stages of unfolding, as the callow bird in the nest is unlike the full-plumed and perfect adult. Even the grave evergreens assume a new countenance in the spring from the protrusion of their annual growth of twigs which are covered with exceedingly delicate light-green leaves, giving to the tree, at this time, a gay and cheerful look. This fresh livery of the vernal forests forever inspires with joy and hopefulness; for it is the time when the world and the soul are full of promise. With electrical enchantment the spirit of the woods reaches the spirit of the man, and he expands and vibrates with the budding and unfolding leaf, "for man is one world, and hath another to attend him."

The vernal *sounds* of the woods are also striking and characteristic, appropriate and fit, as are all the harmonies of the wild. The soft, young leaf has not yet arrived at firmness enough to rustle or creak, and the boiling, simmering, far-off storm and ocean-sound is not distinctly heard at this season. A soft, muffled whisper, a wavy, stifled murmur, is all that the wind can make, the delicate, drooping leaflet having no vibratory consistency, and consequently the accumulated sound is a simple, monotonous breathing of the air through the moist, sappy lungs of the forest.

As the foliage is perfected, and the summer change comes on, the whole leaf-garment assumes an entirely different expression. The monotonous dark-green of the fully-developed summer-dress of the trees gives the wood, with its different plants, a more uniform aspect. In full array the forest is certainly richer and grander in this display of the life-powers, but it lacks the variety of the vernal tints. The color of all the leaves gradually darkens in hue as they are perfected for the execution of their work,—the nourishment and re-creation of the tree. This darkened tint is gradually increased as the leaf hardens and approaches its death-hour—the arrival of the frost. Some time before this, however, the woods present, for an interval, a sameness of feature, as if the leaves were silently at work, and had no time to give to the phases of beauty, but were hurrying up the execution of their function to pass away into the sleep of death. At this time the full-grown, hard, and stiffened leaves give to the woods the sounds or characteristic summer-voices,—that seething and singing which is the result of infinite friction and vibration of the hard, turgid, and perfectly developed foliage of *all* the trees. The roar of the woods, that great respiratory murmur, has now assumed a tone that cannot be mistaken, and the storm-winds can "howl with the voices of all the gods." The hour of dissolution arrives as the autumn approaches. At this season a change occurs, the most extraordinary of all in the life of the leaf, and gives to the forests of the mountain a richness of expression, an endlessness of variety unrivaled upon the earth. This first touch of the destroyer is, perhaps, the most extraordinary phenomenon of the whole vegetable-world, and, indeed, the most wonderful aspect which Nature reveals.

> "So fair, so calm, so softly seal'd,
> The first, last look by death reveal'd,
> Before Decay's effacing fingers
> Have swept the lines where beauty lingers."

The pageantry of the American forest in autumn has ever been the theme of the poet's song and subject of the painter's pencil. It is exhaustless, as beauty is ever that fresh-water jet, that divine *halitus*, that ever-living sap of existence, circulating *up* "from the far-away centre of all things," and which each moment of time *creates* for the soul a rapture, brightly renewed forever. As this element of Nature is *intangible, ethereal,* and cannot be *appropriated*, it is consequently, to the spirit of man, unattainable, inexhaustible, divine.

FLORA OF THE MOUNTAIN.

It is especially the Alleghany Mountain which reveals the perfect and perpetual wonder of the American autumn,—a chapter of the beauty of the world for which the *old continents have no parallel*, and the earth's surface but *one* such spectacle. This comes of the extensive variety and mixture of deciduous trees, also of the mingling of this numerous class with the evergreen trees, in the woods of the mountain. Each tree has a regular series of colors, or *hues* and *shades of color*, through which its leaf passes, after the *death-stroke* of the frost. These are of an endless variety, and of the most extraordinary *brilliancy*. The solar spectrum is exhausted in this fantastic display of colors. A single tree sometimes stands a pillar of fire, or a glittering cloud of gold and purple, while again, the crimson blood-dye is succeeded by a tree which has taken its hue from the gaudy yellow of the nasturtion's cup, or the "dolphin's back of gold."

Thus the brilliant and diversified phenomenal has taken its most gorgeous robes from the tints of the autumnal forest. These phantom-pictures, like the other multiform phases of the woods, are transitory, and soon pass away, this whole world, vivid and flashing, being remembered like the pomp and pageantry of some splendid dream. Once seen it can never be forgotten. To the bright coloring of the groves gradually but quickly succeeds the russet hue of the *dead* and *withered leaf*, the dark-*brown*, in which it moulders away into dust. At length the death-dirge of the vanishing foliage is sung, and the monotonous gray of naked trees, relieved only by the dark-green of the pines, is the color of the woods, while the ceaseless whistle of the winter winds chills the heart with the thought of that coldness which shall know no warmth, and of that *sleep which* shall know no *waking*.

The forests of the Alleghany, in utility and beauty, are as exhaustless as its rocks and coal, its ocean of air, and streams of water, and present a chapter of ceaseless and perfect attractions.

THE UNDERWOOD, BUSH, OR HEATH-GROWTH OF THE MOUNTAIN.

The transition, from the regular forest-tree to the shrub or bush, is gradual. That portion of the forest which is called heath, or coppice, is composed of true woody plants— that is, plants formed of woody fibre, with perennial roots and stems, and either evergreen or deciduous leaves.

On the mountain the representatives of this department are numerous. Some of these plants have the dimensions of small trees, but never grow to what are called forest-trees, and many of them are of exceeding beauty, and some of value. Where the growth of other larger trees permits it, they form clusters highly ornamental, filling the mid-air spaces of the taller trees with an array of foliage sometimes in fine contrast with the leaves of the larger varieties. As a class, they are comely and attractive, and occupy spaces that seemed otherwise to be vacant. Many of them belong to classes of larger trees, and have been already enumerated among them, as the smaller species of Àcer, Cérasus, but never grow beyond a few inches in diameter of stem. To them, in the descending scale, succeeds the order of true shrubs. Of this class of small, woody plants there is an extensive and diversified field. A perfect catalogue in this department would be an agreeable undertaking, but such a task could not be attempted in a running schedule. A few of the prominent species are all that can be enumerated now, and, to commence with some of the smaller plants connecting the bush of the mountain with the forest-tree, take the genus Ostrya. This is the hop-hornbeam, or iron-wood. The species Virginica grows here, often achieving forty-five feet in height. The hard, compact wood of this little tree is useful, and the tree graceful in its form.

Carpinus Americana is an allied plant, smaller in dimen-

FLORA OF THE MOUNTAIN. 237

sions, and with smoother bark, but resembling the Ostrya in foliage, inflorescence, and fruit.

CRATÆGUS.—Several of the hawthorns grow on the mountain. The shape of this hardy little scavenger family is uniform, whatever may be its locality. On the mountain it shows its usual *noli-me-tangere* roughness of thorns and scraggy branches, bright, beautiful blossoms with pleasant odors knotty, and blood-red fruit, etc. As they are not used for hedges or anything else, they seem, like many other objects, to exist for beauty and sweetness *alone*. The species here are *coccinea*, *tomentosa*, *crus-galli*, and *punctata*.

CORNUS.—Species "*Flórida*" of this genus is found on the eastern slopes of the mountain, but not on the summits or western sides in any quantity. Its flashing white flowers are occasionally seen in the ravines, where the plant grows with other trees. It exhibits its usual characters.

The "*Serícea*" and "*circinátá*" are also found there. The "Canadénsis," or "dwarf cornel," is found on the parallel Appalachian ridges.

CÉRCIS CANADÉNSIS, or Judas-tree, is found sparingly distributed, low on the slopes of the mountain. It is a small, handsome tree, showing its usual characters.

ARALIA SPINOSA is a low, rough little tree, called sometimes the "devil's club." It grows abundantly in a variety of localities on different parts of the mountain. Its large, prickly, pinnate leaves, and rugged spiniferous stem, has so strange an expression as to attract much attention and remark.

ALNUS.—Species "*incàna*," is a small tree, often twenty-five feet high. It is found along the streams of the table-lands.

Leaving the small trees, and descending to the bushes proper, we are presented with a large number of interesting plants on the mountain. The most distinguished group of this smaller class of plants which does not exhibit the tree form, is the order ERICÁCEÆ, or Heath Family. Some of the genera of this order are deciduous plants, but of extreme beauty and splendor of flowering. Others are evergreen, and give a characteristic expression to woods of which they are the undergrowth.

Of the SUB-ORDER I. VACCINEÆ, or Whortleberry Family, the mountain has a number of genera.

GAYLUSSACIA.—Of this genus there are three species, "*resinòsa,*" "*frondòsa,*" and "*dumòsa,*" on the Alleghany, the two first named being highly esteemed for their delightful fruit.

In many of the mountain districts the huckleberry is considered not only innocent as an article of food, but to be endowed with certain medicinal properties. Many of the bare knobs and barren heights of the mountain are covered by the whortleberry, giving varieties of fruit, which ripen in different seasons. The family is very hardy, requiring only the "drifting sand-heap" for a resting-place.

VACCINIUM, or bilberry. Species "*Macrocárpon,*" or American cranberry, is found on many of the parallel mountains, and in some localities on the Alleghany itself, (from report,) but is not abundant. The *stamíneum, Canadénse, Pennsylvánicum, pállidum, fuscátum,* and *corymbósom,* grow there. Some of these species are tall, graceful bushes, twelve feet high, and bear large, black and blue berries. The large, delicious, "*blue huckleberry,*" is obtained from the *Pennsylvánicum.* The *Vitis-Idœa* bears a red, flesh-colored berry, but bitter and acid, without much flavor. Some of these "big huckleberries," as they are called, are found in moist places, others on dry hills and open woods.

SUB-ORDER II.—ERICINEÆ, or Proper Heath Family. Tribe, ANDROMEDEÆ. Two genera of this tribe are small, creeping plants. They are the *Gaultheria procúmbens,* creeping wintergreen or mountain-tea, and the *Epigœa repens,* ground-laurel. The genus ANDRÓMEDA contains a number of handsome bushes, and one tree, *arborea.* The species on the mountain are the *calyculáta, racemósa, Mariána, Ligustrina,* several of which are tall and comely shrubs.

FLORA OF THE MOUNTAIN.

Some of the Andromedas are found in moist, barren spaces or sandy tracts, and, like the whortleberries, seem to have strong affinities for desolate and unreclaimed wastes. Some of them are found in sphagnous swamps, and altogether realize, in the habits of growth of some of the species at least, the spirit of the poetry of the name they bear, "the fabled exposure of Andromeda the unhappy."

Tribe RHODOREÆ.—Several genera of this noble tribe are found on the Alleghanies.

AZALEA, False Honeysuckle.—There are here several species of this plant, generally fine flowering bushes, with a brilliant array of colors in their inflorescence, and possessing delicate odors, which fill the air of the woods with a charming perfume. They are extensively distributed over the mountain, and are frequently mingled in dense brakes or heaths of other bushes of the same natural order.

AZÀLEA ARBORÉSCÉNS is a fine bush, twelve feet high, bearing large, red, fragrant blossoms.

"VISCOSA," Clammy, or White Honeysuckle, is here. It is a beautiful shrub, ten feet high, with white rose-tinted flowers in large clusters, which are very fragrant.

"NUDIFLORA," or Purple Azàlea, is a bush five feet high, bearing a purple and showy flower. It is one of the handsomest species, and has a great many varieties.

The "CALENDULACEA," or Yellow Azàlea, also grows on the mountain. It is a tall bush, twelve feet high, bearing orange-colored blossoms, and giving brilliancy and light to the copse where it grows.

Of evergreen shrubs or bushy-plants of this order, the "KALMIA" and "RHODODENDRON" are the principal.

The "KALMIA," or American Laurel, is a well-known plant, growing on all the mountains of the Middle and Northern States. It is much esteemed for its richly-varnished evergreen leaves, and its splendid array of delicately-tinted flowers. It frequently grows in dense brakes in cool, moist forests, forming what are called "laurel thickets."

The KALMIA LATIFOLIA, or Mountain Laurel, abounds on the Alleghanies, and is the only species of the genus found here. In the dense thickets in which it grows it is frequently seen twenty feet high, with long, knotty roots and twisted stems. It grows abundantly on almost every part of the mountain, and is found in immense continuous brakes, frequently under dense masses of forest-trees, seeming not to be affected by the absence of light in such places. It bears a profusion of beautiful white and rose-colored flowers, which are much admired. The leaves and fruit of this plant are poisonous.

But by far the most beautiful individual of this order, the real pride of the mountain, is the "RHODODENDRON," or Rose-Bay tree. This splendid plant, which is generally called "big laurel," is not a laurel, but closely allied to it. It belongs, with the laurel, as we have just seen, to the family of heaths, or natural order Ericaceæ, sub-order Ericineæ, and tribe Rhodoreæ. It differs from the laurel very essentially, forming a separate genus called Rhododendron, the proper botanical name of the laurel, as has just been stated, being Kalmia. Unlike the latter, it is not poisonous, and differs in its foliage and inflorescence, being a much more imperial and distinguished plant. With the common laurel it covers considerable tracts of the mountain forests, and, like that plant, it seeks the cool, sequestered shades of the deepest wilds, preferring the banks of mountain streams and unfrequented places. A splendid savage, he lives upon the sand-soil in the roughest parts of the mountain, flourishing, like an imperial chief of his order, in unapproachable seclusion. Sometimes, with the common laurel, it forms dense groves, called "*laurel swamps*,"—very improperly, however, as they are not *water plants*, and will not grow in swamps. Together, they form *thickets*, so dense and interwoven that it is almost impossible for man or animal to pass through them, thus making a wall as impenetrable as a Mexican chaparral. They have been, from time immemorial, the terror of the huntsman, as his life was in danger if he

FLORA OF THE MOUNTAIN. 241

attempted to penetrate their inextricable labyrinths.* They are also the horror of the husbandman who has the audacity to attempt to clear the surface where they grow; but especially are they the trouble of the surveyor, who, with transit and compass, axe and chain, intrudes upon them. Many a youthful engineer will remember the days of his chain-carrying and rod-fixing through these thickets, and how frequently he found himself enveloped to the chin by a net of iron thongs, which held him like the jaws of an insidious trap.

The style of growth of the Rhododendron is peculiar. The stems writhe and twist themselves together in every conceivable shape of knots and tortuosities, and wherever the branches touch the ground they strike root, and the plant grows afresh from this point; it is thus that an interlaced web of stems, almost as stiff and hard as iron, is stretched over large extents, which are as impassable as cane-brakes. The traveler who attempts to traverse these thickets finds himself continually caught by loops and dead-falls. The lover of the beauty of the woods, however, will find in these sylvan labyrinths, these evergreen seas of living plants, an attractive department of the Mountain Flora. During the inflorescence of this plant it is impossible to conceive of anything more splendid than its mass of flowers, which are borne in large showy terminal corymbs or clusters. They are of a pale-rose color, and sometimes snow-white, the greenish throat of each blossom being spotted with yellow or red. Its large, thick, coriaceous leaves frequently attain the length of a foot. During winter and in intense cold, they fold or coil up longitudinally, each leaf showing a roll not much larger than a cigar, which drops down close along the terminal twigs of the plant. When a

---

* The engineer corps who located the railroads across this mountain chain, discovered the skeletons of several men who had been lost and starved to death in these thickets of Laurel and Rhododendron.

branch in this condition is carried into a heated chamber, the leaves may *be seen expanding* and rising from the close compact bunch, and assuming the flat or patent attitude, the points stretching upward as in the summer air. Under the influence of very severe frost, with the folded condition of the leaf described, the plant exhibits the same blackened, gloomy appearance, which characterizes the evergreen trees under the same conditions.

In full foliage and inflorescence the Rhododendron stands the monarch of the American heath, and always impresses the beholder with emotions of delight, from its presenting a striking contrast with the more homely and familiar forms of the other tribes of bushes. Of this less imposing, but graceful and beautiful department of the mountain forests, constituting the true underwood of the woodsman, there are many plants which are objects of attraction.

The HYDRANGEA ARBORÉSCENS is a bush found in many parts of the mountain. This plant, like some of the evergreens described, seeks the gloom of the depths of forests, its white flowers and dark-green leaves, in shady ravines and woody solitudes, effecting a perpetual surprise.

HAMAMELIS VIRGINICA, the "Witch Hazel," a tall shrub, is here, as elsewhere, a common plant. Late in the autumn its yellow flowers may be seen among the dead and withered leaves of other plants, affording a strange and startling contrast with the surrounding forms, blooming, when their blossoms and foliage are dead. This "weird" shrub stands the noblest symbol of the true and loving heart, blooming with promise and joy in the midst of desolation and death.

CORYLUS AMERICÀNA and ROSTRÀTA are found in the mountain. They grow on its slopes and the vales at its base. This filbert group seem to have an affinity for the mountain.

DIRCA PALUSTRIS.—This plant grows abundantly along the streams in ravines and small vales. It is interesting on account of the peculiar kind of bark of the plant,

FLORA OF THE MOUNTAIN.

which is as tough as leather, consequently, called "leatherwood."

EUONYMUS ATROPURPUREUS, or Spindle-tree, is found here. It is a showy shrub with waxy, crimson fruit hanging by long fruit-stalks.

CEANOTHUS AMERICANUS grows on the mountain, in certain districts quite abundantly. It affords excellent browsing for the deer, and is the plant used by the soldiers of the Revolution for tea.

ROSA.—Several wild roses abound, as the Lucida blanda and Carolina, with the introduced species Rubiginosa and Micrantha.

RUBUS.—Several species of this interesting genus flourish here.

RUBUS ODORATUS, or Flowering Raspberry, grows in great abundance and in the finest proportions. It shows a profusion of splendid purple flowers from June until August. These flowers often exhibit a disk of two inches in diameter, and are of great beauty. The Strigosus and Occidentalis are found with their usual characters.

The VILLOSUS, or High Blackberry, is found in the greatest quantity. This hardy bramble flourishes wherever any kind, even the poorest and roughest soil, exists. Its fruit is produced in such abundance that it forms one of the crops of the mountain. Some varieties occur.

Species CANADÉNSIS (Dewberry) grows profusely.

RHUS.—There are several species of this genus here, as the "typhina," or stag-horn sumach, "glabra," smooth sumach, "copallina," dwarf sumach, and "aromatica," or fragrant sumach. They are handsome shrubs with graceful, delicate foliage and acid crimson fruit. The poisonous species, Venenata and Toxicodrendron, are rarely found on the mountain.

TAXUS BACCÀTA, variety CANADÉNSIS, is the American Yew or Ground Hemlock. It is a prostrate trailing bush, found in the gorges and on shaded precipices of the mountain. It has handsome, shining evergreen leaves, and bears a berry-like fruit of a blood-red color.

Vitis.—The grape family has established itself on the mountain. The "labrusca" is found in moist places, developing a large fruit with coarse and acrid qualities. This is said to be the parent stem of the Isabella grape, a variety much improved by cultivation.

Species Æstivalis grows in great profusion.

Species Cordifolia, or Frost Grape, grows also well.

Ampelopsis quinquefolia, Virginian Creeper, is found here. Its crimson foliage in autumn, clinging around stumps and trees, gives a marked feature to the woods.

Celastrus scándens, or "wax-work," occurs, but is not abundant. Its yellow pods, displaying scarlet-covered seeds, are esteemed ornamental.

Amelánchier Canadénsis, or Shad Bush, grows profusely on the mountain. Several of the varieties described prevail, as the "botryapium" and "oblongifolia."

Sambucus Canadénsis, or Common Elder, abounds.

Species Pubens, Red-berried Elder, is found in great quantities, especially on the eastern slopes of the mountain. Its bright-scarlet berries, ripening in June, are borne in great profusion, looking like bunches of blood-red coral, and mingling frequently with the array of plants in bloom at this season, the splendid Epilobium, Phlox, Lobelia, and Flowering Raspberry with broad purple petals, give variety and unrivaled splendor to these floral groups.

Pyrus Coronaria.— The American Crab-Apple was omitted in the list of small trees. It sometimes grows to twenty-five feet in height, bearing rose-colored blossoms which possess a delightful fragrance. A variety, not so brambly and scraggy as the common crab, occurs here, with taller trunk, cleaner limbs, and much larger apple.

The Sassafras and Benzoin are also found here, the latter growing profusely.

Pyrularia (Mich.) Oleifera, Oil Nut, is said to be found

FLORA OF THE MOUNTAIN.

on the "mountains of Pennsylvania, near the Alleghanies." (Mich., Gray.)

The water-courses and humid tracts show large quantities of several small species of the genus SALIX, or Willow. They fringe the banks of mountain brooks and springs, and form close, compact waving masses, or osier beds, in swampy spots. The Common Alder (*Alnus Serulata*) is also found in some places covering the banks of streams and moist places, seeking with characteristic instinct the trails of springs and fountains. With the Willow, being essentially aquatic, or lovers of water in their propensities, their presence is always the harbinger of the appearance of that element, their groves being thus the true haunts of the aquatic gods, or "Water-walkers." These plants form a beautiful and characteristic order of copse, or under-bush, their wand-like stems and peculiar foliage marking them distinctly from the other species of bush. Thus *variety*, which seems to be Nature's perpetual trick to enchant her children with forms of beauty and elements of use, here finds a stripe of newness wherewithal to demand attention and admiration. A descriptive catalogue of all the mountain copse would be an attractive chapter, but a glimpse at this beautiful department must satisfy us here.

After dwelling on the lofty and imperial dendroid forms of the vegetable world, also its royal families of smaller shrubs, with their artistic beauty and almost regal pomp of ornament and extravagance of dress, another class of plants, still less imposing, but more graceful and lovely, press upon the attention of the wandererer in the mountain woods. This is the world of flowers, so called, as if perhaps they *existed* to *flower alone*, and had no account to render of themselves, but that they were revelations of the splendor and perfection of things, and brought messages of light and gladness to the soul. Of this numerous class many are found distributed over the Alleghany. They are the fairest, frailest, and most evanescent of all vegetable forms, springing from the earth each season, germinating, flowering, and seeding, then withering and dying, having but one short summer to publish their little lives, "sparkle, and expire." These many-painted forms rise as if by magic; endless variety in unity, and unity in endless variety, is the song they sing. In this world the graces and loves seem to reign, for of the grace and beauty of posies, and the positive loves of flowers, who has not heard? Why this untold riches, why this infinite diversity of form, why this exhaustless profusion of dyes,—only for beauty, only for thought and spirit? So would sing the poet the secret of their spirit and life which "the ages have kept."

> "If I knew
> Only the herbs and simples of the wood,—
> Rue, cinquefoil, gill, vervain, and agrimony,
> Blue-vetch, and trillium, hawkweed, sassafras,
> Milkweeds, and murky brakes, quaint pipes, sundew,
> And rare and virtuous roots, which in these woods
> Draw untold juices from the common earth,
> Untold, unknown, and I could surely spell
> Their fragrance, and their chemistry apply
> By sweet affinities to human flesh,
> Driving the foe and 'stablishing the friend,—
> Oh, that were much! and I could be a part
> Of the round day related to the sun
> And planted world, and full executor
> Of their imperfect functions."

This "sweet affinity to human flesh" is the *great fact* of their being, and is quite a sufficient excuse for their existence. The mountain is rich in its array of flowering plants, some of which are Alpine in their characters. In the order of their appearance, the first that attract attention are the vernal flowers. These, as in all high mountain localities, rush rapidly into life the moment the frost has liberated the surface from its *power*. They spring from the soil in a multitude of graceful forms. Some of them are peculiar, and belong exclusively to mountains, seeming to find their proper life-medium in the cool fresh air of elevated districts, and withering when removed from those regions. The vernal flowers are numerous in this range of heights, and to be known and enjoyed in all their sweetness, must be seen and studied in their native haunts. The snows have scarcely disappeared before the first plants put forth their leaves and delicate petals upon the cold, raw air, and are especially prized and hailed with joy by the botanist as the prophets of the coming world of life. And first in rocky nooks and dripping springs, creep out, as if fearful that the winter winds might return, the Saxifrages, Draba, Heuchera, Hepatica, and Caltha, or Marsh Marigold, in quick succession. Then follow the Wind Flowers, the Wake Robin, the Spring beauty, or Claytonia, Houstonia, and Columbine, Sanguinaria, Bellwort, Corydalis, and Erythronium; mingled with these are delicate violets of almost every hue, and of which numerous and petted family the mountain has many representatives.

The little humble earth-gem "Mitchella," soon dots the green surface with its minute snow-white twin flowers, and the lovely Epigæa, with its graceful trailing stem, and foliage like painted parchment hiding clusters of delicate flowers with faint but delightful ordor, is soon found creeping among the dead and fallen leaves as if to conceal its beauty and sweetness, and give it all to the earth upon whose bosom it clings so closely. More showy plants soon flash out their light upon the air, as flaming Phloxes, Cardinal Lobelias, the Epilobium, or Great Willow Herb, with wand of showy flowers, the proud Lily, and fanciful Orchideæ, among which are the imperial purple-fringed Platanthera, with eccentric and anomalous Cypripedium, or Lady's Slipper, the bizarre form of which remarkable flower is the perpetual joke of the woods, a shape so odd, fantastic, and unexpected, that one asks if it were not created in derision. The mountain's show of summer and autumnal flowers is equally extensive and beautiful. As the summer, or sun months, are a short season on the mountain, this world of plants seem to hurry on to the full publication of their lives, and especially to render glorious a short and brilliant career, with extravagant demonstration of ornament and show.

The scythe of the first frost finds a rich and abundant harvest. The summer plants bloom on and mingle with the autumnal flowers, which seem smiling and unconscious of their coming doom. Of the autumnal flowers the Compositæ, or compound flowers, are the most numerous. Rough and hardy, they appear at the close of the flower season, proud and defiant, as if they braved the hour of dissolution. A number of this class, after slumbering in the soil nearly through the summer, suddenly start and bloom, to be as quickly nipped and destroyed. These plants seem to defy the seasons and to have resolved that they *will*, at all hazards, *bloom*. This immense order has numerous genera* and species on the Alleghany as elsewhere. Many of them are large, showy plants, and strike the most careless observer by the brilliancy of the tints of their flowers, and jantiness of their style of growth. Some of them are the largest and most conspicuous of annual plants, and are considered rough and intrusive weeds, possessing, however, rare and real beauties, as the Helianthus, Eupatorium, Actinomeris, Heliopsis, Vernonia, Lactuca, Hieracium, etc. Others of the order are more delicate and attractive in the style of their beauty, as the Asters, or star-flowers, which present a flashing array of shining faces, radiant as jewels, and of every dimension and tint of color, from white specks, minute and sparkling as snow-flakes, to broad dark-red and azure rays, until the far-famed star-flower of the celestial empire is rivaled in its perfections.

Imperial and proud, the sun-flower (Helianthus) flaunts his colors, as if he were veritably "a son of the sun," and would shine as long as his sire. The Golden-rod, (solidago) its delicate wands studded with flowers, contributes to the "mute music," and makes gay the forest and mountain's

---

* See catalogue of genera at end of chapter "Flora."

sides in those "bright September days." The Gnaphalium, Coreopsis, and Rudbeckia, mingle their silver and gold with the pageantry which heralds the advent of autumn and waves the *first farewell* to departing summer. Winter concludes the story of the flower, and its "little life is rounded with a sleep."

Need the observation be made that the full and elaborate biography of the flowers of the mountain, with their special habits, phases of life-manifestation, and instincts, would be a labor of delight? Here, again, the real lover of nature will find that she is ever true and faithful to her accredited devotees. Coy and cruel, with a face of adamant and steel to selfishness and profane intrusion, she is approachable, gentle, and pliant, to earnestness and love. Thus it will be found, that the life and habits of one plant, read and studied with devout and careful seeking, is a key to the history of earth and air, and a pass-word to the intellectual throne of the knowledge of the realms of organic life.

SERIES II.—PLANTS WITHOUT FLOWERS.

Leaving the first great division of the vegetable kingdom, the series of Phænogamous Botany, or those having definite and clearly marked organs for the reproduction of specific forms, and descending in this chain of organisms, we arrive at another order of plants with marked and distinctive features, called the Cryptogamous, or flowerless plants, or those the *mechanism* of *whose* reproduction was formerly supposed to be concealed, or even non-extant. The first division embraces the imperial forms, the great trees of the ages, the myriads of flowers which beautify the earth; also the useful plants, the companions of man, the proper bread or human-flesh grasses, or cerealia, plants furnished with easily discoverable generative systems, and all propagated by definitely organized seeds. The other division (Cryptogamic) is a more humble series,—organizations of simpler and more homogeneous elements, revealing a less intricately complicated morphology, or, in other words, fewer of the wonder-workings of that same strange cytoblast, from "those minims of the vegetable world," single-cell plants, to the more complicated structure of tree ferns, but all propagated by spores, or simple reproductive cells.

These CELLULARES, or cellular plants, are an interesting department of the vegetable world. Here commences the mysterious circulation of "organic water," and the protean power of that magical "protoplasm," with generative fiat, starts the whirl of the brute elements through the harmonious gyrations of Life. Here the formative forces of vitality assume their simplest attitudes of nutrition and reproduction; and here the "vegetable vesicle" stands the witness of the first erotic approach of the ponderable and imponderable. This is also the realm in which the two great kingdoms, the vegetable and animal, approximate and touch circles in a series of surprising analogies, in the first simple mechanisms of life, for the cell is the result of the *ultimate* analysis of *both*.

"The starting-point of both is the same; for the embryo of the animal up to a certain grade of its development, consists, like that of a plant, of nothing else than an aggregate of cells. The lowest class of animals, the microscopical animalcula, or the invisible inhabitants of stagnant water, appear to be *identical* with the simple cellular plants, already referred to (Volvox globator.")*

"Kutzing does not admit any essential distinction between animals and vegetables.† He maintains that the same being may, at various periods of its development, assume one nature or the other. The following is his theory in a few words:—Every organic being is constituted of vegetable elements and animal elements, and, according as one or other prevails, the being becomes an animal or a vegetable;

* Goadby.
† See quotation from Robert Smith, at end of catalogue.

in the first stages of development of superior beings, and permanently in those of inferior rank, the two elements are equally balanced, and this is the case, in the author's opinion, with the Diatomeæ, which, on this account, cannot be absolutely referred either to one series or the other, but constitute the ring or circle which unites together all organic beings into one kingdom. Long controversies have sprung up between the supporters and opponents of this doctrine, who, to obtain victory, mutually accuse one another of logical errors, of sophisms, and of paradoxes."*

With the exception of the tree Ferns, (Tropical,) whose trunks sometimes attain to the height of forty feet, the cryptogamic plants are lowly structures, the feathers, hair, and microscopic down of the skin of the world.

This division of plants is constituted of three classes, viz.: the ACROGENS, the ANOPHYTES, and THALLOPHYTES. The first of these classes contains four orders, the Equisetaceæ, Filices, Lycopodiaceæ, and Hydropterides. The second two orders, the Musci and Hepaticæ; and the third four orders, the Lichenes, Fungi, Characeæ, and Algæ.

ACROGENS.

Of this class the mountain has the following representatives:—

ORDER EQUISETACEÆ, (Horse-tail Family.)

GENERA.	SPECIES.
Equisetum, (Horse-tail. Scouring Rush,)	2

ORDER FILICES, (Ferns.)

Polypodium, (Polypody,) Tree Fern Family,	2
Allosorus, (Rock Brake,)	1
Pteris, (Brake. Bracken,)	1
Adiantum, (Maiden Hair,)	1
Cheilanthes, (Lip Fern,)	1

* Meneghini, Botanical and Physiological Memoirs, Ray Society, 1853.

GENERA.	SPECIES.
Woodwardia, (Woodwardia,)	1
Camptosorus, (Walking Leaf,)	1
Asplenium, (Spleenwort,)	4
Dicksonia, (Dickson's Fern,)	1
Woodsia, (Woodsia,)	1
Aspidium, (Shield Fern, Wood Fern,)	2
Onoclea, (Sensitive Fern,)	1
Osmunda, (Flowering Fern,)	2
Botrychium, (Moonwort,)	1

The ferns are the most showy, and generally attractive of the cryptogams. Many of them are tall feather-shaped plants, their broad spreading fronds, the ornamental and imperial plumage of the earth, producing the perpetual impression of beauty. Some of them are humble and lowly plants, but possessed of exceeding delicacy and grace. The more imposing species frequently occupy extensive spaces of the mountain heath, forming brakes, or matted continuities, which cover the surface sometimes to the entire exclusion of other small plants. These fern forests have frequently a striking and characteristic expression, from the large fronds all assuming one position, by that instinct which turns the leaves of plants to the sun. The tall plumes are marshaled in order, and stand with a gentle northern inclination, their spreading pinnæ, or leaflets, looking to the south, or facing the sun, and held in file by the strong attraction of his rays. Some of the species are shy and retiring in their habits, and are rarely seen; others are found almost as common as grass, occupying large spaces, growing in the woods and swamps, while others invest the rocks and cliffs, festooning their edges and surfaces with rare and picturesque fringes and wreaths. In most of this family of delicate and comely plants, the light and spiritual forms of the vegetable world, it would seem that *beauty*, or the transcendent element of taste was *alone* consulted; while the "homely utilities" or economical relationships, with a few exceptions, had been ignored.

The ferns seem to be attracted to mountains, and, from

the shyness of their habits, their lonely, retired haunts, in rocky nook or "bosky dell," they speak constantly of sequestered solitudes, walks sacred to the wood-gods, of the isolation and self-sufficiency of nature, and of the mountain spirit, wild and indomitable in all its forms.

The man who has no memory of fern islands mingled with his boyhood's dreams, has not yet drained all the enchanted goblets of the universe, and may have still the ecstasy of a new experience in the revelation of the delicacy and sentiment of nature in her most touching attitudes of wildness, sweetness, and seclusion.

By consulting the catalogue of genera, it will be seen that most of the prominent and interesting forms of the order Filices are represented on the Alleghanies.

ORDER LYCOPODIACEÆ, (Club-moss Family.)

GENERA.	SPECIES.
Lycopodium, (Club-moss,)	5

The species of ground pines, or club-mosses, are found extensively distributed over the mountain in shaded woods and moist places. They are among the most beautiful and striking of the cryptogamic plants.

ANOPHYTES.
ORDER MUSCI, (Mosses.)

This interesting class of cryptogamic plants is extensively distributed over the world. The greater number require a certain humidity of atmosphere, and they are more numerous in temperate latitudes than the tropics. They are lowly and minute, but graceful and beautiful, and are among the first plants which take possession of rocks and sterile soils,— appearing even on volcanic slags and lifeless earth-crusts. Many of them occupy extensive swampy tracts, (the Sphagna,) and form, by their accumulations of leaves and stems, large deposits of carbonaceous mould, (modern formula of the *coal seam,*) while others climb the highest mountains, and penetrate the coldest arctic spaces. Hardy cosmopolites! they are found wherever light and moisture can penetrate, and ornament by their graceful foliage the most forsaken nooks, crannies, and, neglected places. In summer their vivid velvet-mantles and verdant cushions gleam through the forests, investing nearly every prostrate trunk or living tree, bank, rock, and bed of brook. In winter their fragile bright-green leaves may be found fresh and smiling beneath frost and ice, and their tiny fruit-bearing stems carrying fantastic caps on bursting spore-cases, are often seen penetrating the snow with a reproductive energy that defies the most intense cold. This is a floral chapter that seems perennial in its fascinations, and the bryologist is especially happy as even winter gives no interruption to his attractive labors. Mountains seem to be the special home of the moss family, as the valleys, cultivated lowlands, and prairies, do not appear to attract this little race of rock and desert-taming pioneers of the vegetable kingdom. The Pennsylvania Alleghany range is a rich and varied moss district, and has been examined, to a certain extent, by a number of cryptogamic botanists.* It seems to possess the condition of elements most favorable as a habitat of this class of plants. In its cool air, its widely extended forests with interminable shades, and quantities of fallen and decaying timber, its extents of surface covered with fragments of rock, its moist ravines and gorges with projecting cliffs, its sequestered dells and shady precipices, its swampy places and fresh running-streams,—we are presented with a medium of special adaptation to the life-affinities of the Bryaceæ. Embracing several geological formations with diversity of mineral composition, which gives origin to a variety of soils from disintegration, and to the exposure for moss-growing

---

* Of the number who have visited the mountain for moss-gathering purposes, are the accomplished bryologists Leo Lesquereux and Thomas P. James, two indefatigable workers in this department of science, to whom the American student of botany owes much, and, it is to be hoped will owe more, before their labors are ended.

FLORA OF THE MOUNTAIN. 255

surfaces of different kinds of rock, at the same time stretching up through a considerable calorical scale, or height of climatal *variations*, it would be natural to expect that the mountain would reveal extensive botanical affinities in this and other departments. Here, to the common observer, the variety would appear to be infinite, but the drilled eye of the naturalist soon classifies and catalogues them all.

Of the ORDER MUSCI, William S. Sullivant and his co-laborers in this department, have reported three hundred and ninety-four indigenous species, of which two hundred and fifty-five are common to Europe.

No introduced European species are recorded. Some cursory observations of the mosses of the Alleghany give the following list of genera:—

Sphagnum, (Peat-moss.)
Phascum, (Earth-moss.)
Gymnostomum.
Aphanorhegma.
Physcomitrium, (Bladder-moss.)
Hedwigia, (Beardless-moss)
Tetraphis, (Fourtooth-moss.)
Grimmia.
Schistidium.
Racomitrium, (Shredcap-moss.)
Fissidens, (Splittooth-moss.)
Dicranum, (Fork-moss.)
Leucobryum, (Pallid-moss.)
Ceratodon.
Campylopus, (Swanneck-moss.)
Weisia.
Rhabdoweisia, (Streak-moss.)
Drummondia.
Tetraplodon, (Collar-moss.)
Trichostomum, (Fringe-moss.)
Barbula, (Beard-moss.)
Atrichum, (Smoothcap-moss.)
Dicranodontium, (Swanneck-moss.)
Trematodon.
Pogonatum, (Haircup-moss.)
Polytrichum.
Encalypta, (Extinguisher-moss.)
Orthotrichum, (Bristle-moss.)
Diphyscium.
Bartramia, (Apple-moss.)
Aulacomnion, (Furrowcap-moss)
Mnium, (Thymethread-moss.)
Bryum, (Thread-moss.)
Funaria, (Cord-moss.)
Leskea.
Thelia.
Neckera.
Cylindrothecium, (Cylinder-moss)
Leucodon, (Whitetooth-moss.)
Leptodon, (Wing-moss.)
Anomodon
Climacium, (Tree-moss.)
Homalothecium.
Hypnum, (Feather-moss.)
Fontinalis, (Fountain Moss.)
Zygodon, (Yoke-moss.)
Dichelyma.
Pylaisæa.
Platygyrium.

This imperfectly elaborated catalogue of genera embraces more than half of the described North American mosses. It will be increased, no doubt, largely by future and more critical explorations, as many of them are exceedingly minute plants, with shy habits, and requiring great patience and vigilance to discover them. These genera contain a number of species, many of which are found on the mountain, thus giving an extensive list of mosses for that locality. A number of them are of great beauty, and widely distributed. Sometimes they show matted masses resembling forests of miniature pines; again, microscopic cane-brakes, or laurel thickets, investing with their delicate tree-shaped stems the rocks and ground. Considerable spaces of the surface are grown over by some of the species, as the earth is covered by grass. Others, again, are found on trees, covering their trunks and branches, while there are those that inhabit fountains and brooks, and occupy the surfaces of rocks and fallen timber, enveloping whole prostrate trunks with mantles of variously tinted plush, or robes of delicate light-green feathers. Thus, as objects of grace and beauty, they constitute an interesting field of investigation, dressing the myriad shapes of the woods with elaborate and fanciful decorations. Being very retentive of life, and hardy, they resist extremely low temperatures, many of them fructifying, as we have seen, in the snow, and exhibiting their bright foliage when other plants are sleeping or dead. The moss thus appears a silent witness, in the slumber of winter, that life has not been extinguished in the whole world of vegetation, or animation even suspended *in all*, but that in some forms it is imperishable, blooming with the freshness of evergreen youth through all times and seasons.

Another point of interest in this class, as of other cryptogamic plants, is their world-wide or cosmopolitan range. Thus we have seen that of 394 described species of indigenous moss, 255 are common to Europe, while of the whole number of species, including Phænogamous plants, enumerated by Gray, 2668, only 676 are common to Europe.

Order Hepaticæ, (Liverworts.)

This order of cryptogamic plants has many representatives on the Alleghany Mountain. They are small cellular plants, some of them resembling mosses, and presenting many points of similarity, in form and habits, with that order. They are diversified in their forms of vegetation and reproduction, the quaint and peculiar style of which is striking, even to the ordinary observer, and possesses marked attractions for the botanist. In Gray's Manual, William S. Sullivant has reported 38 genera, and 108 species. For the clever monograph, with beautifully elaborated figures of the genera of this order, by this distinguished cryptogamist, the student of American botany must feel under perpetual obligation. A heretofore comparatively closed book is now unsealed, and the student can walk with open eyes into a new and enchanting region. The Alleghany, as already remarked, is a rich Hepatic field, and will give an abundant harvest to the laborer in this department.

THALLOPHYTES.

Order Lichenes, (Lichens.)

The class of organic forms called THALLOPHYTES, are the simplest vegetable structures. They have no distinction into stems, roots, or leaves, as the higher cryptogamic plants exhibit, but are composed of a mass of cells accumulated in a parenchymous plane, called a *Thallus* or *Frond*. The order Lichenes is in this group. They are peculiar, both as to their nutrition and reproduction, and show a strong bearing toward that troublesome region of speculation in which commence the great questions of UNIVOCAL and EQUIVOCAL generation. On SPONTANEOUS generation, or "matter assuming organization under the influence of water and light," the following observations of Lindley may seem to savor of an unorthodox philosophy to many who are given to intellectual stampedings on the announcement of the great generalizations of science:—*

"On this subject the investigations of Meyer are exceedingly interesting. By sowing Lichens he arrived at some curious conclusions, the chief of which are that, like other imperfect plants, they *may owe* their origin either to an *elementary* or a *reproductive* generating power,—the *latter* capable of development like the plant by which they are borne: that decomposed vegetable and some *inorganic* matter, are *equally* capable of *assuming organization* under the influence of *water and light;* and that the pulverulent matter of Lichens is that which is subject to this kind of *indefinite propagation*, while the spores lying in the shields are the only part that will really multiply the species. He further says, that he has ascertained, by means of experiments from seed, that *supposed* species, and even some genera of Acharius, are all forms of the same; as, for instance, Lecanora cerina, Lecidea luteo-alba, and others, of the common Parmelia parietina."†

Of the character, habits of distribution, general nature of the Lichens, Lindley proceeds to observe:—"Pulverulent Lichens are the first plants that clothe the bare rocks of newly-formed islands in the midst of the ocean; foliaceous Lichens follow these, and then Mosses and Liverworts. (D'Urville, Ann. Sc. 6, 54.) They are found upon trees, rocks, stones, bricks, pales, and similar places; and the *same species* seem to be found in many different parts of the world: thus the Lichens of North America differ *little* from *those* of Europe. They are not met with on *decaying mat-*

---

* The mountain being a page of the venerable tome, perhaps a whole leaf of "that elder Scripture writ by God's own hand, Nature," would not desire to appear, except as witness or attorney for plaintiff in issues against those profane burglars, pick-locks, and spies, in the private workshop of the Almighty, called *men* of *science*, (wicked rogues of *nescience!!*) and the municipal corps, or regularly organized simon-pure orthodox police of Heaven.

† Vegetable Kingdom, John Lindley, Lichenales.

ter where they give way to fungi; but they often occupy the surface of living plants, especially their bark. In the tropics they lay hold of evergreen leaves. Their chosen climate is one that is temperate and moist; aspects to the north or west are also their favorite resort, for they shun the rays of the noon-day sun. No place seems to be a more constant haunt than the surface of sandstone rocks, and buildings in cool and moist countries. They are met with, in one place or other, from the equator to the pole, and from the sea-shore to the limits of eternal snow. The finest species are found near the equator; the most imperfect, such as the crustaceous genera, which can hardly be distinguished from the rocks they grow upon, are chiefly observed on mountain-tops, and near the pole. The Idiothalami are most abundant in tropical America."

The Lichen appears, then, the pioneer of that splendid world of forms which seems, from its entire dissimilarity of structure, to ignore its affinity or alliance by any conceivable nexus with it, and as the first blundering effort of inorganic matter to enter the higher sphere of life. The mountain's rocks and forests present an extensive field of research in this department of botany, from the same causes which give exuberance of growth to the other orders of cryptogamic plants. From the lower varieties of pulverulent and crustaceous lichens covering stones, fences, and walls, with white, gray, or yellow scurf, to the more complex structures of fronds, they are found picturing the surfaces of all fixed objects with every conceivable shape of spots and markings, clinging to the bark of trees, investing their branches with fantastic scales and gelatinous skins, or floating festoons of hair; destitute of roots, but eroding at last the hardest vitreous slags. Drawing their nourishment from the air, they adhere to the naked surfaces of everything, clothing the rock and tree with an endless variety of dress and ornament.

In the class of uses, the order abounds in valuable elements, nutritive, medicinal, and chemical coloring-principles.

Something of the extent of the alliance as distributed over the earth, and enumerated by Lindley, may be inferred from the fact that the species, long since described, amounted to 2500.

The ORDER FUNGI, of the class Thallophytes, is one of the most curious and interesting of the whole vegetable series. Viewed with reference to their complex structure, their strange and eccentric habits; their peculiar economic function in the organic world; their chemical composition and special relations,—they constitute a wonderful order of plants.

"A full account of the diversified modifications of structure that Fungi display, and of the remarkable points of their economy, would require a volume."* Something of this vastness of range in numbers and affinities may be imagined from the general enumeration of the "Vegetable Kingdom,"† (Alliance 11 Fungales,) amounting to 598 genera and 4000 species. The forests of the Alleghany Mountain, with their extensive variety of decomposing vegetable matter, give a large catalogue of mushrooms.

The last, but not least wonderful of the THALLOGENS, is the ORDER ALGÆ. It is a vast family, swarming in myriads through seas, rivers, brooks, and pools, and growing sometimes on wet and humid earth. The Algals are of all dimensions, forms, and colors, from microscopic points floating in water as motes swim in the sunbeam, to trailing, leathery masses, hundreds of feet in length, and from transparent mucus scums, to brilliantly tinted sheets dyed with all the colors of the rainbow. This order and its subdivisions also occupy a singular and questionable position in the scale of organisms. Of this ambiguity Lindley observes:—"It is here that the *transition* from animals to plants, whatever its true *nature may* be, occurs; for it is incontestable, as the varying statements of original observers testify, that no man can certainly say whether many of the organic bodies

---

* Asa Gray.   † John Lindley.

placed here belong to the one kingdom of nature or the other. Whatever errors of observation may have occurred, these very errors, to say nothing of the true ones, show the extreme difficulty, not to say the impossibility, of pointing out the exact frontier of either kingdom."* Whereupon the Rev. M. J. Berkeley, startled "by these astounding statements," remarks:—" The same species may assume a vast variety of forms according to varying circumstances, and it is highly instructive to observe these changes; but that the *same spore* should, under different circumstances, be capable of *producing* beings of almost *entirely different nature*, each capable of producing its species, is a matter which ought not to be admitted generally without the strictest proof." In the Zoogeny of Oken it is written, (paragraph 1775,) "Every organic originates from a mucus-point. If this mucus-point occur in the darkness, it thus becomes a terrestrial organism, a plant; if it enter into the light, which is only possible in the water and in air, it thus becomes a solar organism, independent of the planet, self-moving around itself like the sun, an *animal*." "The animal is a whole solar-system, the *plant* only a *planet*. The animal is, therefore, a whole universe, the plant only its half; the former is microcosm, the latter micro-planet." (*Idem*, paragraph 1780.) So sparkle the philosophers on the origin of things, particularly of plants and animals, and all this from the contemplation of the wonderful life-manifestations of the Algals. The streams, pools, springs, and moist spots of the mountain, abound in numerous fresh-water genera and species of this widely-distributed order of plants.

Thus endeth the story of the plant. In stately and majestic repose the mountain folds about itself this many-tissued, many-tinted garment of living fibres, each microscopic alga, each imperial tree, quickened by that worker of perpetual miracles, *life*. For what ends exist this immea-

---

* See observations of Meneghini and Goadby, p. 250.

surable array of attractive objects? First as a vast expanse of living, normal, and beautiful forms, it shall address the senses of the physical man, and by healing sympathies and recuperative vitalizing forces, invite him to a larger, more genial, and healthful world of sensuous emotion. Secondly, it shall, by a purer, more subtle, ethereal and Divine force, penetrate the depths of his spiritual nature, and by sentiment and thought, intelligence and love, magnify and ennoble his soul.

The forest, the heath, the flower, the fern, the moss, the lichen, form thus for man a recipe of health, a concert of harmony, a lesson of wisdom, a transport of beauty.

CATALOGUE OF

FLOWERING PLANTS.

A FULL or descriptive catalogue of *all* the *species* of flowering plants would occupy more space than can be allotted to this department of the natural history of the mountain. An enumeration of the most prominent genera, or common families, with a number of the most *prominent species*, will indicate something of the predominating influences grouped under the name of habitat of the region, as shown by the plant. With the plants already named in the text, we are presented with the following:—*

SERIES I.—FLOWERING OR PHÆNOGAMOUS PLANTS.

CLASS I.—EXOGENOUS OR DICOTYLEDONOUS PLANTS.

SUB-CLASS I.—ANGIOSPÉRMÆ.

1. ORDER RANUNCULÀCEÆ, (Crow-foot Family.)

GENERA.	SPECIES.
Atràgene, (Atragene)	1
Clématis, (Virgin's-Bower)	1
Anemòne, (Wind-Flower)	3
Hepática, (Liver-Leaf)	2
Thalictrum, (Meadow-Rue)	2
Ranúnculus, (Crow-foot Buttercup)	4
Càltha, (Marsh Marigold)	1
Aquilègia, (Columbine)	1
Zanthoriza, (Yellow-root)	1

* This enumeration is the order pursued by Professor A. Gray in his admirable and invaluable "Manual of Botany." Nearly all the plants of this catalogue are common in the interior, middle, and western part of the State of Pennsylvania, as well as on the Alleghany range of mountains.

GENERA.	SPECIES.
Actæa, (Baneberry, Cohosh)	1
Cimicífuga, (Bugbane)	2

2. Order Magnoliàceæ, (Magnolia Family.)
(Already enumerated.)

4. Order Menispermàceæ, (Moonseed Family.)
Menispérmum, (Moonseed)	1

5. Order Berberidàceæ, (Barberry Family.)
Caulophyllum, (Blue Cohosh)	1
Podophyllum, (May-apple, Mandrake)	1

8 Order Nymphæaceæ.
Nuphar	1

10. Order Papaveràceæ, (Poppy Family.)
Papaver, (Poppy,) from Europe	1
Chelidonium, (Celandine,) from Europe	1
Sanguinaria, (Blood-root)	1

11. Order Fumariàceœ, (Fumitory Family.)
Adlùmia, (Climbing Fumitory)	1
Dicentra, (Dutchman's Breeches)	3
Corydalis, (Corydalis)	1

12. Order Cruciferæ, (Mustard Family.)
Nastúrtium, (Watercress)	3
Dentaria, (Pepper-root, Toothwort)	2
Cardámine, (Bitter-cress)	2
Árabis, (Rock-cress)	3
Barbarèa, (Winter-cress)	1
Erysimum, (Treacle-mustard)	1
Sisymbrium, (Hedge-mustard)	1
Sinapis, (Mustard)	2
Dràba, (Whitlow-grass)	2
Lepídium, (Pepper-grass)	1
Capsélla, (Shepherd's Purse)	1
Raphanus, (Radish)	1

15. Order Violàceæ, (Violet Family.)
Sòlea, (Green Violet)	1
Viola, (Violet Heartsease)	10

16. Òrder Cistàceæ, (Rock Rose Family.)
Lechea, (Pinweed)	1

FLORA OF THE MOUNTAIN.

19. Order Hypericàceæ, (St. John's-wort Family.)

GENERA.	SPECIES.
Hypéricum, (St. John's-wort)	4
Elodèa	1

21. Order Caryophyllàceæ, (Pink Family.)

Dianthus, (Pink) introduced	
Saponària, (Soapwort) from Europe	1
Silène, (Catchfly Campion)	3
Agrostémma, (Corn-cockle) from Europe	1
Stellària, Chickweed, Starwort)	1
Cerástium, (Mouse-ear Chickweed)	2
Spergula, (Spurrey) from Europe	1

22. Order Portulacàceæ, (Purslane Family.)

Portulàca, (Purslane) from Europe	1
Claytònia, (Spring-Beauty)	2

23. Order Malvàceæ, (Mallow Family.)

Althæa, introduced from Europe	
Málva, (Mallow) from Europe	2

24. Order Tiliàceæ, (Linden Family.)
(Enumerated.)

27. Order Oxalidàceæ, (Wood-sorrel Family.)

Oxalis, (Wood-sorrel)	3

28. Order Geraniàceæ, (Geranium Family.)

Geranium, (Crane's Bill)	1

29. Order Balsaminàceæ, (Balsam Family.)

Impàtiens, (Jewel-weed)	2

32. Order Anacardiàceæ, (Cashew Family.)

Rhus, (enumerated)	

33. Order Vitaceæ, (Vine Family.)

Vitis, (enumerated)	
Ampelópsis, (enumerated)	

34. Order Rhamnàceæ, (Buckthorn Family.)

Ceanòthus, (enumerated)	

35. Orer Celastràceæ, (Staff-tree Family.)

Celastrus, (enumerated)	
Euonymus, "	

36. Order Sapindàceæ, (Soapberry Family.)

GENERA.	SPECIES.
Acer, (enumerated)	

37. Order Polygàlaceæ, (Milk-wort Family.)

Polygala, (Milkwort)	4

38. Order Leguminosæ, (Pulse Family.)

Lupìnus, (Lupine)	1
Trifòlium, (Clover)	3
Robinia, (enumerated)	
Tephròsia, (Hoary Pea)	1
Hedysarum, (Hedysarum)	1
Desmodium, (Tick Trefoil)	
Lespedèza, (Bush-Clover)	
Stylosanthes, (Pencil-Flower)	
Vicia, (Vetch)	
Lathyrus, (Vetchling)	
Phaseolus, Kidney Bean)	
Ápios, (Ground-nut)	1
Baptísia, (False Indigo)	1
Cercis, (enumerated)	
Cássia, (Senna)	1

39. Order Rosàceæ, (Rose Family.)*

Prunus, (enumerated)	
Cerasus, (enumerated)	
Spiræa, (Meadow-Sweet)	3
Gillènia, (Indian Physic)	2
Agrimònia, (Agrimony)	1
Gèum, (Avens)	
Potentílla, (Cinque-foil)	3
Fragària, (Strawberry)	1
Dalibárda, "	1
Rùbus, (enumerated)	
Ròsa, "	
Cratægus, "	
Pyrus, (Pear Apple)	1
Amelánchier, (enumerated)	

42. Order Lythràceæ, (Loosestrife Family.)

Cùphea, (Cuphea)	1

43. Order Onagraceæ, (Evening Primrose Family.)

Epilòbium	2

* See end of catalogue.

GENERA.	SPECIES.
Œnothèra, (Evening Primrose)	3
Gaùra, (Gaura)	1
Ludwígia, (False Loosestrife)	
Circæa, (Enchanter's Nightshade)	2

46. Order Grossulàceæ, (Currant Family.)

Rìbes, (Gooseberry) 4

48. Order Cucurbitàceæ, (Gourd Family.)

All the cultivated members of this family flourish here, except a few of the delicate melons, which never ripen, although they grow well.

49. Order Grassulàceæ, (Orpine Family.)

Sèdum, (Stone Crop)
Pènthorum, (Ditch Stone-Crop)

50. Order Saxifràgeæ, (Saxifrage Family.)

Saxífraga, (Saxifrage)	
Heùchera, (Alum-root)	2
Mitélla, (Bishop's Cap)	1
Tiarélla, (False Mitre-wort)	1
Hydrángea, (Hydrangea) enumerated	1

51. Order Hamamelàceæ, (Witch-Hazel Family.)

Hamamèlis, (Witch-Hazel,) enumerated

52. Order Umbelliferæ, (Parsley Family.)

Hydrocótyle, (Marsh Pennywort)
Sanícula, (Sanicle)
Daùcus, (from Europe)
Angélica, (Angelica)
Zizia
Cicuta

The cultivated species of this order grow well on the mountain, as the parsley, celery, dill, fennel, and coriander.

53. Order Araliaceæ, (Ginseng Family.)

Aralia 6

53. Order Cornaceæ, (Dogwood Family.)

Cornus, (enumerated)
Nyssa,   "

Division II.—MONOPETALOUS EXOGENS.

55. Order Caprifoliàceæ, (Honeysuckle Family.)

GENERA.	SPECIES.
Lonicera, (Woodbine)	
Triosteum, (Horse-gentian.)	1
Sambucus, (Elder,) enumerated	2
Vibúrnum, (Arrow-wood)	4

56. Order Rubiaceæ, (Madder Family.)

Gàlium, (Bed Straw)	5
Cephalánthus, (Button-bush)	1
Mitchélla, (Partridge-berry)	1
Oldenlandia, (Bluets)	2

58. Order Dipsàceæ, (Teasel Family.)

Dipsacus, (introduced)	1

59. Order Compositæ, (Composite Family.)

Vernonia, (Ironweed)	1
Liatris, (Blazing Star)	2
Eupatorium, (Thoroughwort)	5
Aster, (Starwort)	12
Erigeron, (Fleabane)	4
Solidago, (Golden-rod)	13
Inula, (Elecampane) introduced	1
Ambrosia, (Ragweed)	2
Xanthium, (Clotbur)	1
Heliopsis, (Ox-eye)	1
Rudbeckia, (Cone-flower)	3
Helianthus, (Sunflower)	7
Actinómeris, (Actinomeris)	1
Coreópsis, (Trickseed)	1
Bidens, (Bur-marigold)	4
Helènium, (False Sunflower)	1
Maruta, (Mayweed,) introduced	1
Achillèa, (Yarrow)	1
Leucánthemum, (Ox-eye Daisy)	1
Tanacètum, (Tansy,) introduced	1
Gnaphalium, (Cudweed)	3
Antennaria, (Everlasting)	1
Erechthites, (Fireweed)	1
Cacalia, (Indian Plantain)	1

FLORA OF THE MOUNTAIN.

GENERA.	SPECIES
Senècio, (Groundsel)	1
Centaurea, (Star-thistle) from Europe	2
Cirsium, (Common Thistle)	3
Lappa, (Burdock,) from Europe	1
Krigia, (Dwarf Dandelion)	1
Hieracium, (Hawkweed)	4
Nabalus, (Rattlesnake-root)	2
Taráxacum, (Common Dandelion,) from Europe)	1
Lactuca, (Lettuce)	1

60. Order Lobeliaceæ, (Lobelia Family.)

Lobelia, (Lobelia)	4

61. Order Campanulàceæ, (Campanula Family.)

Campanula, (Bell-flower)	2

62. Order Ericaceæ, (Heath Family.)

Gaylussacia, (enumerated)	
Vaccinium, "	
Epigæa, (Trailing Arbutus)	1
Gaultheria, (Wintergreen, or Mountain Tea)	1
Andromeda, (enumerated)	
Kalmia, (American Laurel,) enumerated	
Menziesia	1
Azalea, (enumerated)	
Rhododendron, (Rose Bay) enumerated	
Pyrola, (False Wintergreen)	3
Chimaphila, (Pipsissewa)	2
Monotropa, (Indian Pipe)	2

64. Order Aquifoliaceæ, (Holly Family.)

Prinos, (Black-alder)	2

68. Order Plantaginaceæ, (Plantain Family.)

Plantago, (Ribgrass)	3

70. Order Primulaceæ, (Primrose Family.)

Lysimàchia, (Loosestrife)	3

71. Order Lentibulaceæ, (Bladderwort Family.)

Utricularia	

73. Order Orobanchaceæ, (Broom-rape Family.)

Epiphegus, (Cancer-root)	1
Conopholis, (Squaw-root)	1
Aphyllon	

74. Order Scrophulariàceæ, (Fig-wort Family.)

GENERA.	SPECIES.
Varbascum, (Mullein)	2
Linaria, (Toad-flax)	1
Scrophularia, (Fig-wort)	1
Chelòne, (Snake-head)	1
Pentstemon, (Beard-tongue)	1
Mímulus, (Monkey-flower)	1
Gratiola, (Hedge-hyssop)	1
Veronica, (Speedwell)	5
Gerárdia, (Gerardia)	3
Castillèia, (Painted-cup)	1
Pediculàris, (Louse-wort)	1
Melampyrum, (Cow-wheat)	1

76. Order Verbenàceæ, (Vervain Family.)

Verbena, (Vervain)	2
Phryma, (Lopseed)	1

77. Order Labiatæ, (Mint Family.)

Teùcrium, (Wood-sage)	1
Isanthus, (False Pennyroyal)	1
Mentha, (Mint)	2
Lycopus, (Water Horehound)	1
Pycnánthemum, (Mountain Mint)	3
Thymus, (Thyme,) from Europe	
Hedeòma, (Mock Pennyroyal)	1
Collinsonia, (Horse-balm)	1
Monarda, (Horse-mint)	3
Nepeta, (Cat-mint,) from Europe	1
Brunella, (Self-heal)	1
Scutellaria, (Skull-cap)	4
Marrubium, (Horehound) from Europe	1
Stachys, (Hedge-nettle)	2
Leonurus, (Motherwort) from Europe	1

78. Order Borraginàceæ, (Borage Family.)

Èchium	1
Mertensia, (Lungwort)	1
Myosotis, (Scorpion-grass)	2
Cynoglossum, (Hound's-tongue)	2

79. Order Hydrophyllàceæ, (Water-leaf Family.)

Hydrophyllum, (Water-leaf)	2

FLORA OF THE MOUNTAIN.

80. Order Polemoniaceæ, (Polemonium Family.)
GENERA.	SPECIES.
Phlox, (Phlox)	4

81. Order Convolvulaceæ, (Convolvulus Family.)
Ipomœa, (Man-of-the-Earth)	1
Cúscuta, (Dodder)	1

82. Order Solanaceæ, (Nightshade Family.)
Solanum, (Nightshade,) from Europe	3
Physalis, (Ground Cherry)	1
Datùra, (Thorn Apple) introduced	1

83. Order Gentianàceæ, (Gentian Family.)
Sabbátia,, (American Centaury)	1
Gentiàna, (Gentian)	2

84. Order Apocynaceæ, (Dogbane Family.)
Apocynum, (Indian Hemp)	2

85. Order Asclepiadaceæ, (Milkweed Family.)
Asclepias, (Silk-weed)	4

86. Order Oleàceæ, (Olive Family.)
Fraxinus, (enumerated)	

87. Order Aristolochiaceæ, (Birthwort Family.)
Asarum, (Wild Ginger)	1
Aristolòchia, (Birthwort)	1

80. Order Phytolaccàceæ, Pokeweed Family.)
Phytolácca, (Pokeweed)	1

90. Order Chenopodiaceæ, (Goosefoot Family.)
Chenopodium, (from Europe)	3

91. Order Amarantaceæ, (Amaranth Family.)
Amarantus, (Amaranth,) introduced	3

92. Order Polygonàceæ, (Buckwheat Family.)
Polygonum, (Knotweed)	7
Fagopyrum, (Buckwheat,) from Europe	1
Rumex, (Sorrel)	3

93. Order Lauraceæ, (Laurel Family.)
Sassafras, (Sassafras)	1
Benzoin, (Wild Allspice)	1

94. Order THYMELEACEÆ, (Mezereum Family.)

GENERA. SPECIES.

Dirca, (Leather-wood) enumerated ....

98. Order SAURURACEÆ, (Lizard's-tail Family.)

Saururus, (Lizard's-tail).. 1

100. Order CALLITRICHACEÆ, (Water Star-wort Family.)

Callitriche,.. 1

102. Order EUPHORBIACEÆ, (Spurge Family.)

Euphorbia, (Spurge).. 2
Acalypha,.. 1

104. Order URTICACEÆ, (Nettle Family.)

Ulmus, (Elm) enumerated..
Morus, (Mulberry) enumerated..
Urtica, (Nettle).. 1
(2 introduced.)
Pilea, (Clear-weed).. 1
Cannabis, (Hemp,) from Europe... 1
Humulus, (Hop).. 1

105. Order PLATANACEÆ, (Plane-tree Family.)

Platanus, (Button-wood,) enumerated ....

106. Order JUGLANDACEÆ, (Walnut Family.)

Juglans, (Walnut,) enumerated ....
Carya, (Hickory,)   "   ....

107. Order CUPULIFERÆ, (Oak Family.)
(Enumerated.)

108. Order MYRICACEÆ, (Sweet-Gale Family.)

Comptonia, (Sweet Fern)... 1

109. Order BETULACEÆ, (Birch Family.)
(Enumerated.)

Alnus, (enumerated)..

110. Order SALICACEÆ, (Willow Family.)

Salix, (enumerated)..
Populus, (Poplar, Aspen,) enumerated....................................

Sub-class II.—GYMNOSPERMÆ.

111. Order Coniferæ, (Pine Family.)

GENERA.	SPECIES.
Pinus, (Pine,) enumerated	
Abies, (Spruce, Fir,) enumerated	
Cupréssus, (White Cedar)	?
Juniperus, (Juniper)	?
Taxus, (Yew,) enumerated	

Class II.—ENDOGENOUS, or MONOCOTYLÉDONOUS PLANTS.

112. Order Araceæ, (Arum Family.)

Arisœma, (Indian Turnip)	2
Symplocárpus, (Skunk Cabbage)	1
Orontium, Golden-club)	1

113. Order Typhaceæ, (Cat-tail Family.)

Typha, (Cat-tail)	2
Sparganium, (Bur-reed)	2

114. Order Lemnaceæ, (Duckweed Family.)

Lemna, (Duck's-meat)	1

115. Order Naiadàceæ, (Pondweed Family.)

Potamogèton, (Pondweed)	5

116. Order Alismaceæ, (Water-plantain Family.)

Alisma, (Water-plantain)	1
Sagittaria, (Arrow-head)	2

119. Order Orchidaceæ, (Orchis Family.)

Orchis, (Orchis)	1
Platanthera, (False Orchis)	7
Goodyèra, (Rattlesnake-plantain)	2
Spiranthes, (Lady's Tresses)	1
Listera,	1
Arethusa, (Arethusa)	1
Micróstylis	1
Corallorhìza, (Coral-root)	1
Cypripedium, (Lady's Slipper)	3

120. Order Amaryllidaceæ, (Amaryllis Family.)

GENERA.	SPECIES.
Hypoxys, (Star-grass)	1

121. Order Hæmodoraceæ, (Bloodwort Family.)

Aletris, (Colic-root)	1

123. Order Iridaceæ, (Iris Family.)

Iris, (Flower-de-Luce)	1
Sisyrinchium, (Blue-eyed Grass)	1

125. Order Smilaceæ, (Smilax Family.)

Smilax, (Greenbrier)	4
Trillium, (Wake Robin)	3
Medeola, (Indian Cucumber-root)	1

126. Order Liliaceæ, (Lily Family.)

Asparagus, (from Europe)	1
Polygonatum, (Solomon's Seal)	2
Smilacina, (False Solomon's Seal)	3
Clintonia, (Clintonia)	2
Allium, (Onion, Garlic)	2
Lilium, (Lily)	2
Erythronium, (Dog's-tooth Violet)	1

127. Order Melanthaceæ, (Colchicum Family.)

Uvularia, (Bellwort)	2
Streptopus, (Twisted-stalk)	1
Melanthium	1
Veratrum, (False Hellebore)	1
Helonias, (Helonias)	1

128. Order Juncaceæ, (Rush Family.)

Juncus, (Bog Rush)	7

129. Order Pontederiaceæ, (Pickerel-weed Family.)

Schollera, (Water Star-grass)	1

131. Order Xyridaceæ, (Yellow-eyed Grass Family.)

Xyris, (Yellow-eyed Grass)	?

133. Order Cypèraceæ, (Sedge Family.)

Cyperus, (Galingale)	?
Scirpus, (Bulrush)	?
Eriophorum, (Cotton-grass)	?
Rhynchóspora	

FLORA OF THE MOUNTAIN.

GENERA.	SPECIES.
Sclèria	?
Carex, (Sedges)	30

This extensive genus of obscure and intricately related plants is largely represented on the mountain. In moist spots and along spring streams, pursuing the general habits of the genus, they are found in fringes and tufts, scattered almost ubiquitously over humid and other spaces. Of the 132 species contributed by John Carey to Gray's Manual, casual observations have brought into notice some thirty species.

134. ORDER GRAMINEÆ, (Grass Family.)

Alopecùrus, (Foxtail Grass)	2
Phlèum, (Cat's-tail Grass, Timothy) from Europe	1
Sporobólus, (Drop-seed Grass)	1
Agrostis, (Bent-Grass)	1
Muhlenbérgia	?
Calamagróstis, (Reed Bent-Grass)	2 ?
Stipa, (Feather-Grass)	?
Tricúspis, (Tall-red-top)	
Kœlèria, (Kœleria)	
Eatònia	
Glycèria, (Manna-Grass)	2 ?
Pòa, (Meadow-Grass, Spear-Grass)	6
Bromus, (Brome-Grass,) from Europe	3
Triticum, (Wheat)	
Hordeum, (Barley)	
Elymus, (Wild Rye)	1
Aira, (Hair-Grass)	2
Danthònia, (Wild Oats)	
Avèna, (Oat)	
Hólcus, (Meadow Soft-grass) from Europe	1
Phalaris, (Canary-Grass)	
Mílium, (Millet-Grass)	
Panicum, (Panic-Grass)	7
Sórghum, (Broom Corn)	

THE MOUNTAIN.

(See ante, p. 250.)

"Given, the head of Socrates, the wisest philosopher of Greece, and a Protococcus pluvialis, a microscopic single-cell plant, is there no '*essential* distinction,' and to which does the word *incomprehensible* most justly apply? Of the creation and destiny (genesis, exodus) of a cell, or a limitless congeries of cells, (organic bodies,) of the how and why of their getting *into* special shapes or living forms from the sleep of inorganic matter, and staying there to circulate for a time within the 'ring' of *natural affinities*, then dropping *out* of that circulation into another apparently temporary sleep, called death,—or of the creation and destiny (genesis, exodus) of a man or numberless congeries of men, (Humanity,) of the how and why of *their* assuming particular styles of existence and circulating for a time within the grasp of *supernatural affinities* (supersensuous, quondam spiritual,—immaterial forces,—will, intellection, sensation, and affection, entities, real as iron or stone, but not on the chemist's table, or naturalist's catalogue,) and also, getting *out* of that material and spiritual circulation, into an apparent sleep, called, likewise, death, what has the microscopic atom, the proud mote, the wise monad, man, *the Philosopher*, to say?

"Place the dry skulls of Plato and Shakspeare beside the ruptured and effete cells of the Protococcus pluvialis and Volvox globator, and say which are the most inconceivable existences, which are the everlasting wonder of wonders. Does not the cell stand the most imposing mystery, the most incomprehensible miracle? The two problems, vast towers!! loom up from the Infinite, their summits and bases both hidden in darkness and unapproachable solitude. The broad gulf between them can only be passed upon the wings of a purer and nobler philosophy, and the deep abyss can only be fathomed by the plumb-line of a profounder and more earnest Faith."— Robert Smith, *Philosophical and Religious Meditations*, vol. vii. p. 472.

FRUIT-TREES AND ESCULENT VEGETABLES.

FRUIT-TREES.

THAT the Alleghany could supply itself with fine fruit of almost every kind there is not the slightest doubt. The indifference of the mountain counties to this department of earth cultivation, as well as many other "cultures," is to be much regretted by all the friends of progress of that region. This indifference or carelessness is not confined, however, to the mountain districts of the State. The following observations of the venerable Dr. Darlington, the justly celebrated botanist of Chester County, are, it would seem, as applicable to his district as to the one here alluded to. Looking, as the inhabitants of the wilderness counties do, to the East for evidences of civilization and light, it was to be hoped that the cultivated county of Chester had passed the "*thoughtlessness*" at least, not to speak of the rudeness and barbarism deplored by the Doctor in one part of his observations on this subject. He says: "Indeed, it is melancholy to reflect how thoughtless and negligent mankind generally are with respect to providing fruit for themselves. There are few persons who do not own or occupy sufficient ground to admit of three or four choice fruit-trees and a grapevine; such, for instance, as an apricot, a peach, a May-duke cherry, a Catharine pear, and a Catawba grape; yet the great majority seem never to think of planting such trees, while they are ready enough to invade the premises, and revel on the fruits of some more provident neighbor! It is due to the *minor morals* of the community that such disreputable negligence and such marauding practices should cease to be tolerated."—*Flora Cestrica*, p. 72.

PYRUS COMMUNIS, common Pyrus, or Pear-tree.—This tree is a native of Europe. There are many varieties of this delightful fruit, which should be cultivated wherever it will grow. The mountain counties have not given the care they should to the cultivation of this tree. The seedling plant grows well on the Alleghany, and the improved varieties would of course flourish equally well. Some fine pears have been produced on the range, and it is to be hoped the subject will receive more attention.

PYRUS MALUS, Apple Pyrus, common apple-tree.—This species is also a native of Europe. Pomologists have produced and described almost innumerable varieties of this wholesome fruit. It will grow every place in Pennsylvania, both mountain-tops and valleys; but little attention has been given to this interesting department on the Alleghany. Some fine apples have been produced, and every variety and quality of that fruit can be grown there, after a time of acclimation of buds and shoots.

CYDONIA VULGARIS, Quince-tree.—This well-known tree is a native of Southern Europe. It grows well on the Alleghany.

PERSICA VULGARIS, common Peach-tree.—This member of the almond family is a native of Persia. It does not find on the Alleghany Mountain a very genial clime. Persia and the Alleghany are widely-sundered habitats, but as that mountain has a vital connection with the whole globe it must necessarily unite with Persia on some issue of fate and nature. The peach, it seems, is this happy bond, not to mention other equally interesting radicles of association!!! The juices of the fruit, as grown on the mountain, are not exactly Persian, or even Jersey-an in their deliciousness of flavor, nevertheless, it produces a peach of respectable dimension, and decidedly agreeable character. It requires constant watching and renewing by planting, as the frost frequently kills it entirely to the ground.

ARMENIACA VULGARIS, Apricot.—This delicious fruit is a native of Armenia. Very little attention is given to its cultivation in the mountain region of Pennsylvania, and on the Alleghany none.

PRUNUS DOMESTICA, common plum, Gage or Damascene.—The cultivated plums are natives of Europe.* Several of the varieties might be cultivated here with success, if attention were given to them. Those that have been tried grow well.

CERASUS, or Cherry genus.—Professor de Candolle distributes the commonly cultivated cherry into four species; Dr. Darlington and others into two. These are the Prunus (cerasus) avium, English, or heart cherry, (sweet;) and the Prunus cerasus (vulgaris,) sour red cherry, or Morello cherry. The heart cherry grows well on the Alleghany, and with a *special luxuriance* in the red shales of the eastern base and slope of the mountain. The Morello cherry also grows finely, the whole cherry family seeming to have the most friendly relations to the mountain.†

RIBES.—The current family are produced in quantities on the mountain. These are the Ribes Uva-crispa, or gooseberry, (Europe,) the Ribes rubrum, or red currant, (Europe,)‡ and Ribes nigrum, or black currant, (also Europe.) Like the native species of Ribes, the introduced species seem to flourish as if at home.

---

* Prunus domestica, L., the cultivated plum, is now deemed by the best botanists to have sprung from the sloe.—*Gray's Manual*, p. 113.

† See wild cherry, or Serasus Serotina, now Prunus Serotina, p. 220.

‡ Gray recites a "rubrum" which is found in New Hampshire as identical.

ESCULENT VEGETABLES.

Of the introduced esculent, garden, or kitchen vegetables, the mountain produces nearly all the ordinarily cultivated species and varieties. The season for growing pot-herbs, or edible plants, is short here, and also late, as the frosts of spring and fall come close together. They almost all, however, grow profusely with any care, and many varieties assume proportions which the same plant rarely attains in the lowlands. Between the valleys of the eastern and western parts of the State and the mountain heights, knobs, and table-lands, there is a difference in the time of growth and perfection of garden vegetables (this difference applying more or less to the whole vegetable world) of from two to four weeks. The results of forcing plants, as achieved in the east and west by hot-beds, hot-houses, and protected sites, is not considered in this general statement. By the use of artificial appliances, hot-beds, hot-houses, and the selection of sheltered situations in the mountain vegetables could be brought very much earlier to perfection, and grown there with the finest qualities and proportions. This subject will receive more attention, in certain parts of the mountain, soon, and extensive experiments will be made.

At the present time the farmers of that district have only small patches of a few yards in extent for kitchen-gardens, and cultivate only such plants as will grow without much care. The amount of vegetables produced in many of these little gardens is quite extraordinary, and shows that the mountain's climate and soil, with any industry, are very favorable and friendly to the class of edible plants. One point of advantage possessed by this region is, that when the staple products of the garden have passed their season, and are withered and dried in the valleys and lowlands east and west, the mountain has them green and fresh, and in the highest perfection.

The following vegetables grow well on the mountain:—

BRASSICA OLERACEA, Cabbage.—This is a native of Europe, and thrives here with several of its varieties or sub-species. These are the "acephala," or tree-cabbage, (leaves not forming heads,) the "bullata," or savoy cabbage, with finely crisped leaves, and the "capitata," or York cabbage, with *dense head*. The variety Caulo-rapa, (Kohl-Rabi,) bulked-stalked cabbage, grows finely, also variety "cauliflora."

The BRASSICA RAPA, sub-species "depressa," or common turnip, grows well also.

Raphanus sativus, Garden Radish.—This plant, a native of China, is hardy, and grows almost every place. There are several varieties or sub-species, as "radicula," "rotunda," "turnip radish," oblonga, common radish, also varieties of the "niger."

Hibiscus esculentus, Okra.—This plant will grow here, but has not been cultivated much. It is a native of India.

Pisum sativum, Garden Pea, and its varieties, are produced in abundance.

Phaseolus vulgaris, String Bean, common pole-bean, and Lunata or Lima Bean, grow well, but the latter will scarcely ripen on account of the shortness of the season.

The Apium Graveolens, Celery, Petroselinum sativum, Parsley, Carum and Fœniculum, Caraway, and Fennel, as already remarked in the catalogue, grow well. The Daucus carota, Garden Carrot, variety Sativa, and Pastinaca sativa, Garden Parsnip, also Umbelliferous plants, flourish equally well.

Cucumis sativus, Common Cucumber.—This plant is a native of Asia. It grows well, but the Cucumis melo, Musk Melon, will not ripen on the mountain.

Cucurbita pepo, Pumpkin; varieties do well, also the Cucurbita melopepo and Verrucosa.

Tragopogon, Oyster Plant, grows well.

Lactuca sativa, Common Lettuce, Salad, a native of India, and Helianthus tuberosus, Jerusalem Artichoke, a Brazilian plant, also flourish.

The Beta vulgaris, Common Garden Beet, has several varieties, all of which, including the Mangel-wurzel, cultivated for cattle, grow well.

Spinacia oleraceæ, Spinach, and Asparagus officinalis, Asparagus, (from Europe,) grow well.

Allium.—Several onions are easily produced, as Allium cepa, Garden Onion, Porium, Garden Leek, Sativum, Garlick, and Scœnoprasum, or Chives.

The Lycopersicum esculentum, or Tomato, grows well, but the seasons are too short to produce or ripen the fruit without a hothouse to develop the plants largely before planting out.

The Solanum melongenum, or Egg Plant, might be cultivated if the same care were taken.

The Solanum tuberosum, or Common Potato, is particularly adapted to the soil of the mountain.

Rheum rhaponticum, or Pie Rhubarb. This plant, a native of Scythia, grows luxuriantly.

FAUNA;

OR,

ANIMAL LIFE OF THE MOUNTAIN.

"THE Animal Kingdom is only a dismemberment of the highest animal, *i.e.* of man."

OKEN.

"Few views of the relations existing in the organic world have received so much approbation as this: that the higher animal forms, in the several stages of development of the individual, from the beginning of its existence to its complete formation, correspond to the permanent forms in the animal series, and that the development of the several animals follows the same laws as those of the entire animal series; that, consequently, the more highly organized animal, in its individual development passes in all that is essential through the stages that are permanent below it, so that the periodical differences of the individual may be reduced to the differences of the permanent animal forms. The different animal forms do not present one uniserial development, from the monad up to man."

K. E. VON BAER.

"All these divisions blend into each other at their confines, and form a circle. In this manner we proceed, beginning with the higher groups, and descending to the lower, until at length we descend to the genera, properly so called, and reach, at last, the species; every group, whether large or small, forming a circle of its own. Thus, there are circles within circles, wheels within wheels,—an infinite number of complicated relations; but all regulated by one simple and uniform principle, that is, the circularity of every group."

MCLEAY.

"The attempt at representing graphically the complicated relations which exist among animals has, however, had one good result: it has checked, more and more, the confidence in the uniserial arrangement of animals, and led to the construction of many valuable maps exhibiting the multifarious relations which natural groups, of any rank, bear to one another."

AGASSIZ on McLEAY.

"Let it, therefore, never be supposed, that because one genus, or one family, is placed before another, we consider it more perfect or superior to the others in the system of beings. He alone could build up such a pretension, who would attempt to place animal nature on a single line; such a project we have long since renounced as one of the most false that can be entertained in natural history. We should, on the contrary, consider each being, each group of beings, in itself and in the character it sustains by its properties and organization, and abstract none of its relations or connections with other beings, whether they be near or remote."

HAMILTON SMITH on BARON CUVIER.

"We are, indeed, free to admit that Swedenborg's tools have been handled and improved since his own time. The law of series, to which he attributed so much, has been set in a new light, and made into a machine of tenfold power, by Charles Fourier; and analogy has been only too prolific in the hands of the German Oken. The latter, we may remark, is all analogy, with no roots. The day of railroads has been preceded by railroads in thought, with all the excesses and expenses of their material types, and these mental iron-ways are the analogies between different provinces of nature, whereby sciences, incommunicable hitherto as Japan or China, are now running into each other for mere lust of travel."

WILKINSON on FOURIER, OKEN, and SWEDENBORG.

―――――

"Control your language or your language will control you."

WASHINGTON MCCARTNEY on ROBERT SMITH.

"Now that the current is setting so strongly against everything which recalls the German physiophilosophers and their doings, and it has become fashionahle to speak ill of them, it is an imperative duty for the impartial reviewer of the history of science to show how great and how beneficial the influence of Oken has been upon the progress of science in general and of Zoology in particular. It is, moreover, easier, while borrowing his ideas, to sneer at his style and his nomenclature than to discover the true meaning of what is left unexplained in his mostly paradoxical, sententious, or aphoristical expressions; but the man who has changed the whole method of illustrating comparative Osteology; who has carefully investigated the embryology of the higher animals, at a time when few physiologists were paying any attention to the subject; who has classified the three kingdoms of nature upon principles wholly his own; who has perceived thousands of homologies and analogies among organized beings entirely overlooked before; who has published an extensive treatise of natural history, containing a condensed account of all that was known at the time of its publication; who has conducted for twenty-five years the most extensive and most complete periodical review of the natural sciences ever published, in which every discovery made during a quarter of a century is faithfully recorded; the man who inspired every student with an ardent love for science, and with admiration for his teacher,—that man will never be forgotten, nor can the services he has rendered to science be overlooked, so long as thinking is connected with investigation."

AGASSIZ on OKEN.

"No animal, excepting man, inhabits every part of the surface of the earth. Each great geographical or climatal region is occupied by some species not found elsewhere; and each animal dwells within certain limits, beyond which it does not range while left to its natural freedom, and within which it always inclines to return, when removed by accident or design. Man alone is a cosmopolite. His domain is the whole earth. For him, and with a view to him, it was created. His right to it is based upon his organization and his relation to Nature, and is maintained by his intelligence and the perfectibility of his social condition.

"A group of animals which inhabits any particular region, embracing all the species, both aquatic and terrestrial, is called its Fauna; in the same manner as the plants of a country are called its Flora.

"There is an evident relation between the fauna of any locality and its temperature, although, as we shall hereafter see, similar climates are not always inhabited by similar animals. Hence, the faunas of the two hemispheres have been distributed into three principal divisions, namely, the arctic, the temperate, and the tropical faunas; in the same manner as we have arctic, temperate, and tropical floras. Hence, also, animals dwelling at high elevations upon mountains, where the temperature is much reduced, resemble the animals of colder latitudes rather than those of the surrounding plains."

AGASSIZ and GOULD.

"The Rocky Mountains, rising through the level of vegetable barrenness to that of perpetual snow, are, at their highest elevations, unsuitable to the existence and support of animal life; and constitute a barrier impenetrable to nearly every class of animals. The country westward of those mountains is therefore separated, zoologically as well as geographically, from that eastward of them; the species common in the more eastern divisions are there replaced by other and different forms; and it is thus a distinct zoological region.

"The Apalachian ranges, on the other hand, of moderate elevation, covered for the most part to their summits with forests, and presenting no limit to the support of animal life, are easily penetrated at many points through their defiles, and present but few obstacles to the extension of species. They constitute NO *zoological barrier* to the land mollusks, although *they do to some other animals;* and if, owing to their altitude and consequent diminution of temperature, individuals are less numerous on their summits than in the valleys, this effect is climatic alone."

AMOS BINNEY,
Terrestrial Air-Breathing Mollusks of the United States, vol. i. p. 106.

CHAPTER V.

FAUNA OF THE MOUNTAIN.

The animal life of the mountains of Pennsylvania is embraced within the division of temperate faunas of the globe, or that portion of the surface of the planet included between the arctic and tropical parallels. The forms of this fauna are not much diversified, and present a medium variety between the region north of the tree limit or isothermal zero, the line of perpetual ground-frost, and the tropical zone of plants and animals. Extending from the vast desolate plains surrendered to the tyranny of the frost-power to the region of the sun's fires, with its arid extents of sand-deserts, this temperate region presents an interesting series of animal structures. A transition from the dreary monotony of one belt to the brilliant diversity of the other, the temperate regions are the theatre of life-manifestations, free from excessive contrasts, the intensation of the action of pure physical forces, and the absolute despotism of the laws of matter, as shown by the multitudinous, eccentric, and peculiar forms of plant, bird, quadruped, fish, and reptile of the equatorial regions, and the excessive but somewhat monotonous animality of the maritime fauna of the arctic world. The predominance of the plain and useful types of the temperate region, as shown in the large, quiet mammals, the ox, the bison, the deer, the horse, the hog, the tribes that follow the bread cereals, must strike the most unobservant when contrasted with the enormous reptiles, the groups of quadrumana or monkeys, felines or cats, in the shape of tigers and lions, pachyderms, as elephants, hippopotami, and tapirs of the equatorial belts, or with the peculiar forms of the Arctic, as the Esquimaux man, with the reindeer and northern fox, or the vast whales, walruses, and seals of the frozen seas of polar spaces. It need scarcely be observed, that the great representative of all the kingdoms and of all the zones and habitats of Nature, man himself, shows, in the temperate region, the supreme perfection of his organization, and the fullest development of his power as a physical, moral, and intellectual being, having attained in this golden mean of existence a shadowy approach to the ideal splendor of his destiny, free from the enervating and sensualizing flames of the tropics, and the deadening and paralyzing frosts of the Arctic circles. As already remarked, the mountain ranges of Pennsylvania are within this highly favored portion of the earth's surface, and its fauna has thus the common characteristics of that region of Divine perfections.

An extensive recitation of the natural history of its indigenous races cannot be attempted, however interesting and valuable such a chapter might be, not only to the lover of nature, but to the student of the economical significance of things.

A thorough exploration of this enchanted realm may be reserved for a future effort, to be elaborated in detail for its own attraction.

FIRST GREAT DIVISION OF THE ANIMAL KINGDOM.

CLASS I.—MAMMALIA.

Order Bimana, (Man.)

The original or indigenous man, as the head of this order, has disappeared some time since. In the scientific distribution of the races he belongs to a type somewhat down in the scale of classification of the varieties of man, and is included in the family of "American mongolidæ."

Of this type he is an evanescent and infirmly rooted race,

peculiar in his instincts and habitudes, not juvenile but apparently senile, showing the tendency of some of his cotemporaries of the lower animal world to vanish from the earth; unallied to other races, unprolific, unfitted to civilization and progress, he seems like the deer and the beaver, the elk and the wolf, destined to extermination. He has left scarcely any traces of himself in the mountains of Pennsylvania, or any record that he has ever been there. The Indian graveyards, somewhat numerous in the valleys of the State, that are now rich agricultural districts, are scarcely met with on the mountain ranges at all. Perhaps these valleys were better original hunting-grounds, and more thickly peopled by the red man and the animals upon which he fed, which accounts for the greater number of relics of him being left in those localities than elsewhere. His present successor is a different order of man, coming from the mixed varieties of another style of immortals, the now dominant Anglo-American race becoming prominent in history for its energy, sharpness, lawlessness, go-a-headism, and general diabolism.

He is the issue of numberless fusions or crosses of diversified varieties of the great typical Caucasian form, the *predominating mixture* being that of Teutone and Celt. In the range of mountainous counties there is a variety in this mixture. In the southwestern part of the chain in the State of Pennsylvania there is a preponderance of the Teutonic element. The middle portion of the range shows an excess of Celt. The northeastern continuation brings in again the Teutone as the prevailing variety. A critical observation of the results brought about by human efforts in the reclamation of these mountain ranges from the dominion of savage nature, will discover the characteristic features of each variety, as revealed by the condition of the surface: roads and fields, ditches and fence-rows, houses and churches, bridges and barns, and demonstrate the prevailing material and spiritual forces at work in the industrial operations of those regions.

As the mountains reveal an excess of the mineral elements which form the deserts of the world, the great sand or silicious formations, the true skeleton material of the globe, and show smaller quantities of pulverulent slates, shales, and limestone, it follows that the soil is not so promising or inviting to the Teutone, with his instincts for growing wheat and Indian-corn. This would not deter the more reckless, romantic, erratic, and unthrifty Celt, with his native affinities for adventures, improvidence, hostility to culture, clannish habitudes and gregarious instincts. These elements have so impressed certain of the mountain counties as to be easily discoverable to the most careless observer.

It is in these mountain regions, however, that some of the most perfectly developed specimens of men have been produced, Herculean in form and strength, and who have lived, or are living, to be near a century old, and have shown characters as manly and noble as their physical frames.

MONKEYS.
Order Quadrumana.

Descending from man, as the great prince of mammals, the next order of creation is the quadrumana or monkeys. There are no indigenous monkeys on the Alleghany Mountain in Pennsylvania, but quite a number of animals bearing so strong a resemblance to that order that it might be embarrassing to the future naturalist to include them in that order, and at the same time omit to mention the fact that they are generally supposed to belong to the order Bimana, genus Homo, or Man. Of the numerous order quadrumana, as described by Martin in his great work on "Man and Monkeys," the genus of anthropoid apes, to which this animal is allied, is either the Pithecus satyrus (orang,) the Hylobates leucogenys (Gibbon,) or Troglodytes (chimpanzee.) They have many points in common with the semi-terrestrial baboons, but their connection with the niam niams, or Ghilanes* is problematical, as they are of a differ-

---

* For an account of this race, see the French traveler, C. L. du Couret's—or Hadji-abd-el-Hamed-Bay (as he called himself)—

ent color, and have rougher skins, and the caudal prolongation of the vertebral column has been abraded by an obstinate indulgence in the sitting posture, the animal being given much to contemplation, and quietly beholding the flow of the river of time. The great predominance of the bones and muscles of the face, the protrusion and magnitude of the jaws, constituting the prognathous muzzle, or countenance which may be taken hold of, together with the extreme minuteness of the brain-box or skull, would point rather to the Hylobates. Its chief characteristics are love of potatoes and whisky, indolence and ease, being proverbially improvident and disposed to let things alone, with the exception of an occasional affectionate surveillance of the neighboring hen-coops and sheep-pens.*

BATS.

Family of Cheiroptera, (Bats.)

This is a peculiar group of animals, and one which would seem, at first sight, to belong to anything but the class of mammals. They are, however, in that class, and have not the organization of the bird. Their leathery wings are expansions of the skin over the enormously elongated bones of the arm and fingers. Although in the order carnivora, some of the family are frugivorous, the others being insectivorous. Their habits of whirling through the air at twilight and night in pursuit of their insect prey, their

description of a specimen he saw in 1842, who was a slave of an Emir of Mecca, published in the Annual of Scientific Discovery for 1850, article Zoology, p. 318. Consult also the Lucubrations of the venerable Banks, of Indiana, on the influences which hold in arrested development the "unlettered" varieties of man.

* The missionary who attempts to evangelize this "variety" ought to be provided with a goodly number of steel traps of sufficient strength to hold a bear; also with a quantity of cat-o'-nine-tails, and commence the work of regeneration by a direct address, vigorously applied, to the skin of the back.

custom of long winter-sleeping in caves, together with their singular and revolting forms, are familiar to all. There are a number of bats on the mountain. The venerable Le Conte, whose wonderful mind seems to have left no department of nature unexplored, has given the best descriptive catalogue of North American bats.* Of the fifteen species of the genus Vespertilio described by him, five are found on the Alleghanies in Pennsylvania.

VESPERTILIO noveboracensis, (Linn.)—This is a universally diffused and common member of the family. It is generally found about houses and other buildings, so that this bat is as familiar almost as the common rat. It is found from Canada to Florida, and numerous everywhere.

VESPERTILIO cinereus, (Pal de B.)—This is not so common a species here. "It is the largest of all the bats found in the United States," its length being six inches.

VESPERTILIO fuscus, (Pal de B.)—"This species is common in the Northern States."

VESPERTILIO pulverulentus, (Tem.)—"Inhabits from New York to Georgia."

VESPERTILIO subulatus, (Say.)—This is the common little brown bat, flapping about every place at night, even pursuing its prey into houses.

Where bats accumulate in caves for their winter lethargy their number is almost incredible. They seek the dry parts of the caverns, sticking to the walls and hanging in enormous bunches by their hooks to each other. They no doubt cling together for mutual comfort, thus preserving their natural temperature by contact with the furry and hairy covering of each other's bodies. These living, black, ghastly festoons, give quite an expression of infernalism to the caves in which they congregate; and myriads thus collecting together and

* See "Observations on the North American species of Bats," Proceedings of the Academy of Natural Sciences of Philadelphia, vol. vii. p. 431.

remaining in a torpid dozy state, fill the air of those caverns with a peculiar and offensive odor.

The different species hybernate together. In the openings of the woods on the mountain during the summer, they are seen in numbers circling about in pursuit of their prey. They pass the day in the loose bark of, and hollows in, the trees.

SHREWS.

Sub-order Insectivora, (Family Soricidæ.)

Genus Sorex, (Linn.) Species Fimbripes, (Bach.)—The fringed shrew is quoted by Baird* as being found on the Alleghany Mountain in Pennsylvania. The specimen referred to was sent by Professor Johnson to the Academy of Natural Sciences, Philadelphia.

De Kay enumerates a list of several species of the genus Sorex, whose geographic range would include Pennsylvania. These are "Sorex de Kayi," to which he gives a range of "Atlantic States from Massachusetts to Virginia," "Sorex brevicaudus," "Sorex parvus," "Sorex Carolinensis," (which *he admits to be extremely doubtful,*) and "Sorex Fosteri." The last named, or "Foster's shrew," is said to be found as far north as the sixty-seventh parallel, and was observed by Richardson where the thermometer descended to forty and fifty degrees below zero. It is an inhabitant of the mountain, and is the animal which makes tracks in the snow with a groove made by its tail between the foot-prints. It constructs tunnels through the snow on the surface of the ground, frequently several yards in length, which, when the snow is melted, remain icy tubes, curved and twisted in all directions. An intrepid and hardy little Esquimaux, no intensity of cold prevents him from leaving his mark on every snow that falls.

Sorex platyrhinus.—Baird gives this species a Pennsyl-

* Mammals of North America, by S. F. Baird, Smithsonian Institute, Pacific report, vol. viii.

vania range. Several of the shrews are inhabitants of the mountain.

Genus BLARINA. Species Talpoides, (Sorex Talpoides, Gupper.)—According to Baird, "this is the most abundant of North American shrews. For the present," he says, "I shall refer *all the large shrews*, with short tails, from the Atlantic States, to the Talpoides." He considers this shrew as identical perhaps with several species of Sorex referred to by authors, as De Kayi, brevicandus, Carolinensis, brachy sorex, etc. He gives it a range from Halifax, Nova Scotia, and Montreal to Columbus, Ohio, and west, also south to Georgia, and from "latitude 45·30 to 32·30; longitude 63·30 to 81·30." He also quotes the Blarina Cinerea, or ash-colored mole, as ranging geographically from South Pennsylvania to Florida.

MOLES.

Genus SCALOPS, (Cuvier.) Species Aquaticus.—The common shrew mole has a wide range, said to be found from 50° north latitude to Carolina, and from the shores of the Atlantic to the Pacific. It is not abundant on the mountain, which may be accounted for by the roughness of the soil, stony and rugged surfaces not being favorable to its habits of life. It prefers to inhabit moist, loose earth occupied by multitudes of insects, worms, etc. It is a great annoyance to the gardener, turning up and tunneling his walks, and also (as is said) devouring the planted seeds. (?) Godman has made his biography an interesting chapter, in the Rambles of a Naturalist.

SCALOPS Breweri.—The hairy-tailed mole has a range from "Connecticut and New York to Cleveland, Ohio." Mr. John Cassin, the distinguished ornithologist, (who is also an accomplished naturalist in other departments of science,) observed this mole near the Chestnut Ridge, one of the western parallel ranges of the Alleghanies in Westmoreland County. It is found in the table-land flats along streams, but not high upon the mountain.

Genus CONDYLURA, (Illiger.) Species Cristata. — The star-nosed mole is found in Pennsylvania, having a "range from Hudson's Bay to Virginia."—D. K. It is an inhabitant of the mountain.

CATS.

ORDER RAPACIA, (Family Felidæ.)

FELIS Maniculata, or domestic cat, abounds.

FELIS Concolor, (Linn.,) panther, cougar, or northern catamount.—The range of this powerful and beautiful feline is from "47° north latitude to 54° south." (?) It is still found in numbers in the wilderness part of the Alleghany range, in Pennsylvania. It is a very formidable animal, and the memories of the first inhabitants, many of whom survive, are full of thrilling adventures and incidents connected with their hunts of the panther, and close ungenial proximity with a forester for whom they entertained the most sincere hatred, and against whom they waged eternal war.*

LYNX Rufus, (Felis Rufa, Temminck,) "Mountain cat," "American wild cat."—This cat is found in considerable numbers on the Alleghanies. It has a wide range from the "Atlantic to the Pacific and from the waters of the Mississippi to the Gila river."

---

* Felis Malta, (I. O. S. M.)—This species of cat is not abundant on the Alleghany. It is said to be a descendant of a regal and far-famed race, even the primeval pre-Adamite Cat of cats. The inconceivably rapid propagation of this species in many places is one of the profoundest scientific problems of the hour, and seems to be a perpetual and inscrutable mystery. Myriads are springing up in certain localities as if by some spontaneous and prolific teeming of the earth. Very little is known of their habits, except that their prowlings and caterwaulings are eminently nocturnal. They are said, by those who pretend to know something about them, to be like other felines, predatory, carnivorous, and somewhat diabolical; but others who have observed their habits as closely as practicable, assert that where the soft foot of the "Maltese" falls, the celestial manna of charity is left, with the blessings of heavenly love.

DOG.

(Family Canidæ.)

CANIS Familiaris, domestic dog.—Some thirty varieties of dog are said to be introduced. Of these the most common are, Molossus, or bull-dog, Sagax, or hound, Avicularis, or pointer, Graius, or greyhound, several kinds, the Extrarius, or spaniel, the Aquaticus, or poodle, and the Danicus, or spotted carriage-dog. Most of these varieties are on the mountain, as man is generally accompanied by this domestic wolf wherever he goes.

De Kay remarks: "Of those peculiar to North America, we find variety borealis, Esquimaux, lagopus, and terra-novæ, Newfoundland, Canadensis, and novæ-Caledoniæ."

CANIS Occidentalis, (Canis Lupus, Harlan,) variety Griseo-albus.—This is the common gray wolf, the type of indigenous North American dogs, and has the range of the continent. A few still linger in the remote and deepest fastnesses of the Alleghanies, and indulge in their ancient love of mutton at the expense of the husbandman. As a victim of the hunt, he is still pursued with vindictive hatred by the new occupant of the soil.

FOX.

VULPES Fulvus, red fox. — The common red fox is abundant on the mountain. He hides in inaccessible places, burrowing in caverns, rocks, hollow logs, and the darkest ravines. He is thus protected from his greatest enemy, man, as an object of diversion. The hound can still penetrate his retreats, but the horseman must arrest his pursuit in the rougher parts of the mountain. In other portions of the table-lands, or elevated valleys between the mountains, there is fine ground for fox-hunting. From the abundance of the red fox, he can be started at any time by hounds, and from his well-known habit of "circling" (as the hunters style the movement) about his native den or thicket, and running for a great length of time in circumscribed spaces, the richest and rarest sport may be enjoyed by those who love the excitement of that regal indulgence, the fox-hunt.

The hunt being a "note in the gamut of ambition," and involving the extreme physical tension and culminating forces of four of the most wonderful animals of the earth,—the man, the horse, the dog, and his brother the fox,—has ever been the grand recreation of monarchs and princely men, and its achievements recorded as the true and only absolute criterion of the actual power of each. In this aspect, the "fox-hunt" ceases to be a vulgar and noisy nuisance, (as supposed by the ignorant and uninitiated!) engaging the lowest form of man and animal, and becomes a great dynamic revelation, involving the spiritual and physical capabilities of four of the highest organisms of the world.

Dull must be the ear to which the voice of the hound in the freshness of the morning, with all nature flashing in the brilliancy of an autumn sunrise, is not music, and the "huntsman's horn," the "mellow, mellow horn," has nothing of that harmony which is the spirit and joy of life, existing in man as well as every object that surrounds him, and in another form "glitters in the wave, the rainbow, the lightning, and the star." The red fox's range, Atlantic States to Missouri, Pennsylvania to Canada and south.

VULPES Virginianus, (Rich.) gray fox.—This species does not abound, although it is found on the mountain. It is alleged by hunters that the gray and red fox will not inhabit the same woods, from some ancient spirit of antagonism. The probable cause is, that the gray fox, possessing neither the swiftness, wind, or lung, (foot and bottom, as the sportsmen say!) nor the sharpness, cunning, and intellect of the red fox, leaves the field from a sense of inequality in competition for game, notwithstanding De Kay's assertion that "it is bolder and more astute than the red fox."

The light, swift, well-trained fox-hound will capture the gray fox often in an hour or two, while eight, twelve, or twenty-four agonizing hours of effort on the part of the best pack is required to fairly beat the red fox, ungorged and in

good condition, the surface being equally propitious to both
dog and fox. Range of the gray fox, "Pennsylvania to
the Southern States and from the Atlantic to the Pacific."

MINK, WEASEL.

(Family Mustelidæ.)

Genus PUTORIUS, (Cuvier.) Species Vison, (Syn. Mustela Vison, Linn.)—The brown mink is a mischievous little animal, and quite abundant on the Alleghany. He is a fatal visitant of the hen-roost; but is much esteemed for his fur.

PUTORIUS Noveboracensis. Common weasel, white weasel, (Syn. Mustela erminea, Harlan.)—Is occasionally seen on the Alleghany; range, New York, Pennsylvania, Illinois to Arkansas.

OTTER.

(Family Lutridæ.)

Genus LUTRA. Species Canadensis, common otter of Pennant, and Lutra Braziliensis of Harlan. The American otter has a range of North United States west to Rocky Mountains, or "from the Atlantic to the Pacific and from the Gulf of Mexico to the shores of the Arctic Sea."—D. K. This sagacious and wary animal is occasionally found on the mountain, but is rare in Pennsylvania, and fast disappearing, on account of its valuable fur. From the shyness of its habits it is difficult to take; sometimes, however, it is captured when its foot-prints are discovered in the sands of the mountain streams. It feeds upon fish and aquatic animals.

SKUNK.

MEPHITIS Mephitica, skunk, pole-cat.—This detestable creature is found on the mountain, but not abundant; and being an offensive and ignominious thief, the less said about (in hearing of "ears polite"!) or done with him, the better. De Kay records the fact, that Dr. Wiley, of Black Island, "smelled him twenty miles at sea." He also seems to regard him with considerable complacency, observing, "the flesh, when carefully prepared, is *very sweet*. A person in my neighborhood took nineteen from one burrow, and salted them down for *family* use during the winter."* The Alleghaniens in Pennsylvania do not seem to regard the polecat as a very great dainty; at least it is not found on the bills of fare of the hotels of that range. The skunk is generally regarded as the essence of all that is disgusting and abominable in nature.†

The pole-cat is found all over the United States east of Missouri Plains and north of Texas.

RACCOON.
(Family Ursidæ.)

Procyon lotor, (Storr.) or common raccoon.—This animal is found throughout the Apalachian range, in Pennsylvania. It abounds on the Alleghany, frequenting water courses and springs, hunting frogs, lizards, and fresh water shells. It is peculiar and interesting‡ in its habits, and seems to have friendly feelings for man, enjoying much a visit to his growing corn-fields, and being easily domesticated. Its flesh is esteemed a delicacy as an article of food in the wilder and more primitive regions, but like many other delicacies it requires a certain drill and conspiracy of circumstances to develop an appreciation of its qualities. Like the god Pan, the huntsman has a taste for the flesh of the woods,

* New York Fauna, p. 30.

† In the spiritual world there are men who assume the form of the skunk. These men on earth were skunkish men, that is, the loves or active principles within them were developed in the skunkish sphere, or in acts the odor of which for intensity of meanness, gave disgust forever to all manly men. "All that is deformed and foul in nature is already in the hells whose loves it effigies, and whose outward kingdom it is."

‡ See note at end of catalogue of "Mammals."

and the vigor of digestion which comes from life in the forest, gives a sublime zest to anything, and thus the "coon," finely frosted and roasted, might, under certain circumstances, for a moment abolish the nausea which comes with the thought (which it certainly inspires) of eating an animal so nearly human as the dog.* The coon night-hunt is among the established sports of the woods. Geographic range, from Massachusetts to Florida and west to Fort Kearny.

BLACK BEAR.

Of the Ursidæ there is another representative, the Ursus Americanus, or black bear. This bear is frequently found in numbers on the Alleghanies, and in some portions of the more savage part of the range the species breeds. They sometimes migrate from one part of the mountain to another, directed in their journeyings by the instinct of self-preservation on the subject of food. The sport of taking this animal is greatly enjoyed by the huntsman, the danger of capture giving zest to the chase. The flesh is esteemed a great dainty by many persons, but its coarse fibre, bathed in grease of a peculiar flavor, must perpetually exclude it from the list of genuine luxuries.† The bear hybernates, passing three or four months in a state of torpidity; range, United States generally.

OPOSSUM.

ORDER MARSUPIATA, (Family Didelphidæ.)

DIDELPHYS, (Linn.,) Virginiana, opossum.—This is a common wild animal of Pennsylvania, and is found on the Alleghanies. Its habits are well known, and some of them peculiar. It is sometimes eaten, and considered a delicacy;

---

* "The coon's flesh, when young, is savory, not unlike pig, but in adults it is rank and disagreeable."—De Kay.

† "The flesh of the bear is savory, but rather luscious, and tastes not unlike pork."—De Kay.

abounding in grease, it is said by its lovers to possess a flavor strongly resembling a mixture of pig and rat, and is consequently one of the rarest combinations of sapors indulged in by omnivorous man. It is the only marsupial on the continent, and has a range from Southern United States to Hudson's River.

SQUIRREL.

Order Rodentia, (Family Sciuridæ.)

Sciurus, species Cinereus, (Linn.) — This is the large squirrel, called fox squirrel. It is not abundant, but sometimes taken on the mountain.

Sciurus, (Gmelin.) Species Carolinensis, (Godman.) — This is the common gray and black squirrel. Possessing a geographic range of the whole United States to the Missouri River, it is of course on the mountain. This squirrel is very abundant during seasons when the mast of the mountain abounds. This abundance is sometimes increased to an enormous extent by immigration of large swarms from the districts where the supply of food has failed. It is a beautiful and interesting species.

Sciurus Hudsonius, (Pallas,) is the Chickaree Pine, or red squirrel of the woods. It has a range from Labrador (lat. 65) to Mississippi. This lively and noisy little squirrel has also quite a range of instincts and affinities. He lives in barns, deserted houses, and hollow trees, and is also found in the deepest and darkest forests, and in the most lonely and unfrequented places. He is familiar and almost impertinent, allowing a near approach, and assuming, with quick and jerking movements of body, all styles of fantastic attitudes—sometimes sitting upright, with his tail over his back, in the crook of a pine limb, or hanging, head downward, by his hind claws; again twirling spirally around the tree, or plunging fearlessly among its topmost boughs.

During all this time there is kept up a perpetual chatter, and saucy querulous complaint. This characteristic bark and rattle (a noise like the sound produced by a boy's small watchman's rattle) may be heard almost at any time during the daylight in the woods. He is a hardy, tireless, and self-sufficient little animal, full of fun, and, like all industrious busy persons, happy. He flashes about at all seasons, from midsummer to dead winter, leaving no nut untasted and no snow untracked. He has no disposition to hybernate, like the little striped squirrel of the ground, or even stay within doors, like the gray squirrel, in inclement weather. He is a special favorite of the woodsman, and his form and voice suggest perpetually pine groves and the beauties of the wilderness.

PTEROMYS, (Cuv.) Sciurus Volucella, (Gmelin.) Pteromys Volucella, or flying squirrel.—This curious little animal is found here. It has a range of the United States to the Mississippi River. It is not abundant, is shy, and found only in solitary places.

TAMIAS, (Illiger.) Sciurus Striatus, (Linn.) Tamias striatus is the Chip Munk, or ground squirrel. This familiar little creature is found every place from Canada to Virginia and the Missouri River. Being earthy in his habits, and held by terrestrial affinities, like other proper earth animals, he hybernates, taking leave of absence during the deep winter months. He is a great favorite with children who frequent the woods and fields, his striped coat and lively motions being much admired.

GROUND-HOG.

ARCTOMYS, (Schreber.) Mus-monax, (Linn.) Arctomys monax, woodchuck, or ground-hog. Abundant; range, Canada to Virginia and from Massachusetts to Wisconsin. He becomes very fat, is eaten, and said to be good, but suggests pup or cat to the imagination.

BEAVER.

Castor Fiber, (Linn.) Castor Canadensis, (Kuhl,) or American beaver.—This animal is said still to be found in the wildest parts of the Alleghany in Pennsylvania. His history, habits, and the wisdom of his instincts are well known. He is fast disappearing. Original range, the continent of North America.

JACULUS.

Jaculus, (Wagler.) Jaculus Hudsonius, or jumping mouse.—This strange little animal is found from Nova Scotia, Labrador, to Southern Pennsylvania, and west to Pacific Ocean.

MOUSE, RAT.

Mus Musculus, common mouse. Range, every place on the continent. Introduced.

Mus Decumanus, (Pallas,) or brown rat, has a continental range. It is an introduced species.

Mus Rattus, or black rat, is found every place. Introduced.

Arvicola Hirsutus and Arvicola Pennsylvanica have a Middle State range.

"Hesperomys Leucopus, (Wagner,) white-footed mouse. Range, Nova Scotia and (Labrador) to Virginia, and west to the Mississippi River."—Baird.

"Hesperomys Nuttalia, red mouse. Range, Southern Pennsylvania to Georgia, and west to St. Louis."—Idem.

MUSK-RAT.

Fiber, (Cuv.) Fiber Zibethicus, musk-rat.—This rat has a continental range, and is said to increase in numbers as the country is improved, which is unlike the other fur tribes, which decrease with the advancement of man. It abounds.

PORCUPINE.

(Family Hystricidæ.)

ERETHIZON, (Cuv.) Erethizon dorsatus, Hystrix Hudsonius, Brisson, white-haired porcupine.— This animal is found on the Alleghany. Its range is said, by Baird and Girard, to be Eastern United States to Mississippi River, and North Pennsylvania to Canada, (and 67° Rich.)

RABBIT.

(Family Leporidæ.)

LEPUS, (Linn.) Lepus Americanus, northern hare, or white rabbit, is said to range from Virginia to Labrador. It is found in the forests, laurel and rhododendron thickets, of the Alleghany in Pennsylvania. It is very shy, and rarely seen, from its vigilant habits and inaccessible retreats, although quite numerous in some places. Hunted with hounds it affords a rare and exciting sport, eluding the dogs like a "will-o'-the-wisp," and requiring sometimes hours to capture him.

LEPUS Sylvaticus, (Bach.) The gray, or common rabbit, is found abundantly through all the States from Massachusetts to Texas and west to Missouri River. It abounds in numbers on the mountain where the red fox has been partially banished or exterminated.

ELK.

ORDER RUMINANTIA, (Family Cervidæ.)

CERVUS, (Linn.) Cervus Canadensis, American elk.— The elk still lingers in the wildest recesses and fastnesses of Pennsylvania Alleghanies. Once abundant on this range, western table-lands, and valleys, it is now found only in the most inaccessible places. Occasionally perfect specimens are taken, but this splendid animal, one of the noblest of American mammals, is destined soon to disappear before advancing civilization, like the human representative or indigenous man of the continent. The huntsman may still hope, as he treads the mountain forests, to be startled by the presence of this superb king of stags. The range of the American elk is Northern United States to Upper Missouri, and west to the Pacific; said also to extend to 57° north latitude, according to Richardson.

DEER.

CERVUS Virginianus, Virginia, or common deer.—This animal is still abundant on the Alleghanies, and said to have a range of the United States generally east of Missouri and north to Maine. Quantities of the flesh of the deer (venison) are sent from the Alleghanies to the cities of the State both east and west.

OX.

(Family Bovidæ.)

Bos, Bison, (Linn.)—This native species has long disappeared from the eastern side of the continent.

Bos, Taurus, introduced.—The common ox has many varieties, some of which are the most useful and interesting animals. The species is susceptible of extensive modification by careful cultivation; and, as the constant friend of man, now almost necessary to his existence, this attention and cultivation seem a sure evidence of his progress. Whether patiently bearing the yoke,* a helper in the field, as in

---

* Although apparently the simplest and easiest of all operations, the driving and management of oxen perfectly is one of the most critical and triumphant of human achievements. They seem to think on the mountain, and they are right, that the real subduer of the ox must possess a special genius, or original influx of force in that direction. As no man, even with any amount or sum-total of ordinary human faculties, can be a poet, a painter, an orator, or a fisherman, so certainly cannot any commonly endowed mortal become a driver of oxen. A special dodge of Fate is required to produce these

the work ox, sacrificing his life for food and luxury, as in the fatted beef, or yielding daily tribute from the secretions of the blood in the shape of milk and cream, in the gentle, beneficent, and motherly cow, this great ruminant would appear

results. A genius, a rage, a transcendent specialty of force in one sphere, is absolutely necessary. The thing must be born in a man. And then, is it not strange to reflect how rarely the great power is revealed, and how long the heavenly gift may remain without being discovered, even by the possessor himself? It would seem that the *genius* of *occasion* is also required to rouse the soul to recognition of itself. Poets have heard the echoes of the magic lyre, and been inspired even in old age to sing immortal songs; painters have caught the enchanting sheen, blind to its power through life, and touched the canvas with undying beauty; and orators, whose youth had passed in silence, have startled a listening world with their eloquence. So on the banks of the Kiskimineas, a foreordained fisherman, who had never baited a hook or felt the nibble of a chub in all his life, was startled, at the age of eighty, into the discovery that he was a natural-born Waltonian priest, anointed from the beginning of all things, and with religious awe assumed the solemn functions of his calling, but died with the raptures of catching pike within sixty days of his ordination. Thus, also, was it that an ancient physician of the Alleghany Mountain, at an advanced age, accidentally discovered that his person was the residence of a beautiful but terrible demon, that he was in fact a poetically inspired, an enthusiastically inebriated ox driver. This strange passion, this wonderful power in a particular drift, had remained hidden deep down in the undeveloped elements of his consciousness for long years, when a bright casualty revealed the faculty divine, and astonished himself and the world. Necessity, (maternal authoress of many things!) on an occasion, directed his attention to the subjugation (under-the-yoking) of two tremendous bulls. That accomplished, two others were added, and yet two others, until, grandly culminating, a team of eight horned monsters, dragging enormous logs, were guided with dexterity and ease through the labyrinths of an intricate forest. Thus, apparently accidental, his illumination came, and he discovered that an imperfectly developed country doctor, (who had committed violence against his organization by beating the bars of his limitations in false directions, through a subversive torture, called *regular education*,) had been forced out of the mournful ruin of perverted elements of an original primordial king, whose indefeasible sceptre was the ox gad.

to be one of "Heaven's best gifts to man." The mountain, with its good grass-growing surfaces, might produce the best varieties of cattle, but it is to be regretted that not much attention has been given to raising the finer stocks. This will apply to all the State, and it would certainly be of great advantage to the ambitious Pennsylvania agriculturist who imagines we are at the top of the ladder in all things, to visit, for instance, an annual fair of our sister State of Ohio. The common varieties alone are found on the mountain, which, however, sometimes produce milk-cows of extraordinary qualities.

SHEEP.

(Family Capridæ.)

Genus OVIS, (Linn.) Species Aries, common sheep.— Few or none of the highly improved varieties of sheep are raised on the mountain. It is more favorable than any other part of the State to the growth of this domestic animal, as has been stated in the chapter on soil and grasses. This is undoubtedly true with regard to both flesh and fleece. The common sheep is the only variety to which any attention has been given. It multiplies rapidly, and produces, as already remarked, a superior quality of mutton. A cross of the Southdown and common sheep is said, by an experienced shepherd,* to be the best animal to grow, both for wool and mutton, as it retains the hardiness of one, (the common,) and imparts the more delicately flavored fat and flesh-fibre of the other, (Southdown,) together with its finer

---

* This allusion is to the renowned man-feeder, Robert Harmer, of Philadelphia. Mr. H. was formally an English shepherd, possessing great practical knowledge of the sheep, and much wisdom in the details of breeding and management of that animal, Of the qualities of mutton there is not extant a better judge than Mr. H., as indeed of all other material used in the sublime art of cooking and feeding, (his new vocation,) since he left behind his dog and crook, and ceased "to watch his flocks by night, all seated on the ground."

fleece. With some enterprise and attention, the mountain may become the mutton-growing region of the State. Will the mountaineers look at this subject a little?

HOG.
PACHYDERMATA, (Family Suidæ.)

Genus SUS. Species Scrofa, variety Domestica.—Many varieties of the common hog exist, the most detestable of which is, perhaps, the mountain wood-hog. It is composed principally of bristles, gristles, legs, and snout,* producing indestructible pork, which is also destitute of lard. The form of the animal is that of a fish, with long legs, constituting the true land-pike, to which no fence is impenetrable. A cross with the Berkshire and China modify the creature to a certain extent in his leading attributes, furnishing a pork that may be partially masticated by first-class natural grinders. This animal is undoubtedly a return (illustration of the fatal and eternal unalterability of type) to the original wild boar, Sus Scrofa.

JACKASS.
(Family Equidæ.)

Genus EQUUS, (Linn.) Species Asinus, Jackass.—This is a native of the East, a hardy and useful animal, valuable for more purposes than the degradation of the horse by the production of monsters in the shape of mules. It thrives well on the mountain.

HORSE.

EQUUS Caballus, the horse.—The present horse cultivated on the continent, as is well known, is not indigenous. It was long supposed that there was no American horse, and

* This is a close connection of the Crawford County hog, a slab-sided brute, flat as a shingle, with large predominance of the above materials, particularly bristles and jaws, with the addition of an excessively long, straight, characteristic tail. This is the variety well known to everybody as the hog which is prevented passing through fences by tying knots on his tail.

never had been. There is no living native horse in America, the wild horse of the Southwest being the introduced European or Asiatic horse, which has run wild. Recent discoveries of Professor Leidy, through explorations of Messrs. Hayden and Holmes in the South and West, have brought to light a number of fossil horses belonging to the continent. They amount to five genera and seven species, cotemporary with the mastodon. When it is remembered that all the different shaped horses which we see, from the Shetland pony, weighing three hundred pounds, to the massive Conestoga wagon-horse of a ton weight, and from the greyhound-shaped turf-horse, fleet as the wind, to the clumsy cob or lunk-head with globular carcass, slow and unwieldy as a fatted hog, are all varieties of one species, E. caballus, the announcement will strike with surprise that there have been five different genera, and seven species of American horses. Many of them have been very peculiar animals, possessing interesting characters. For an account of fossil horses of America, see "Contributions to the Paleontology of North America," published through the Academy of Natural Sciences of Philadelphia, by the distinguished comparative anatomist, Joseph Leidy.

But few of the varieties, strains, or bloods of horses, have received any attention in the mountain districts of the State. This is to be deplored, as the commonest kinds of horses grown there have discovered remarkable qualities of action, speed, and endurance. This indifference, it must be acknowledged, however, characterizes the whole State of Pennsylvania. Some of the Southern and Southwestern States have shown a laudable zeal in this department, and have produced horses possessing as noble qualities of the animal, in all vital and artistic points, as have been bred upon earth.

Pennsylvania has never distinguished herself in this line, with the exception, perhaps, of having grown good draught-horses, and some fine trotters. Eminently utilitarian and common sense, the exclusive turf-horse has had but few patrons in that State, and the desperate fanciers of horses of special powers have not been numerous. Still the State can boast of many intelligent and spirited horsemen, not only as growers, breakers, and dealers, but men to whom the science of the horse, his varieties and functions, is a precious domain of knowledge.

The general apathy and indifference to, and profound ignorance of, this noble animal,—from the blacksmith who carelessly nails a rim of iron around his wonderfully organized hoof,* crippling and deforming one of the most interesting vital mechanisms in the whole animal kingdom, to the quack farrier calling himself "veterinary surgeon," who maltreats and destroys him, having but *one* name (bots) for all his complicated catalogue of diseases ; or from the fool who drives him to death for want of knowledge of his capacity to destroy space and carry loads, to the Cockney who prostitutes his powers to uses never designed by Nature, and who murders† him to gratify his pride or gambling lust,—is a subject of surprise, and constitutes the lowest blunder and inappetency of the man and the hour. Let him reflect with earnestness and intelligence on the horse and his human associations, his significance and true meaning, his laws and his destiny, and he will no longer stand confused for his ignorance of, or condemned for his crimes against him.

To this splendid creature's majestic form, Nature seems to have affixed the high and distinguished marks of the perfection of organic structures. Alone, in the style and grandeur of his proportions, he stands the incarnation of the

---

* See note at end of catalogue of "Mammals."

† "The Mongolic nations eat horse-flesh. Wild horse meat, butchered for the market, is still sold daily in many parts of China." *Hamilton Smith.*

Which is the most rational savage, Cockney or Mongole? Mongole certainly, for he would give, no doubt, the excuse of the cannibal for eating his grandmother, "she was *very good.*" But the Cockney! what has he to say why sentence of death shall not be pronounced upon *him?* Nothing; the verdict stands: "murder in the *first degree.*"

marriage of the soul of the dumb-brute forces of the universe, with the shining and ethereal elements of grace and beauty. Almost human in his capacity of thought or docility and affection, his long-established companionship with man is no accident. The primitive huntsman,* with his bow and arrow, living by the spoils of the chase, or the wandering herdsman and shepherd, existing from the proceeds of their flocks, were feeble, impotent. The infant man developing the first phasis of his earthly career, seemed, by the limitations of his force as an animal, to be doomed to a state of perpetual childhood. When the happy idea arrived of subduing the horse to his uses, he had with that thought the key to an incomputable power.† The command "advance!" was given, and the word Progress came into existence, and had significance. In this arm of strength he realized the meaning of the fable of the Centaur :‡ his power to subdue

* "With regard to mental qualifications, the nations of North America not having passed beyond the state of hunters, show, for want of the laboring ox and *conquering horse*, the characteristics of others in the same condition."—*Hamilton Smith.*

† "It appears that the present Mongolic tribes were long ignorant of the real use of the horse; while, in the Arctic regions, the white wooly race of the Jakoutsk was not deemed serviceable except for food.

"From the subaltaic Yuchi, who were the first rulers, they no doubt learned the art, and became conquerors, by the sole acquisition which changes the relations of every people on earth accessible to this animal."—*Natural History of the Human Species, by Colonel Hamilton Smith.*

‡ "Cheiron was the wisest and justest of the Centaurs." (Hom. Il., xi. 831.) "He was the instructor of Achilles, and had himself been instructed by Apollo and Artemis, and was renowned for his skill in hunting, *medicine*, music, gymnastics, and the art of *prophecy*." (Xen. Cyneg. ! !) "Cheiron is the noblest specimen of a combination of the human and animal forms in the ancient works of art; for, while the Centaurs generally express the sensual and savage features of a man combined with the strength and swiftness of a horse, Cheiron, who possesses the latter likewise, combines with it a mild wisdom. He was represented on the Amyclæan throne of

nature was multiplied by a miraculous implement, and the irresistible mythical monster, half horse half man, became the symbol of a disenthralled and advancing humanity.*

The domesticated and educated horse, then, appears a standard achievement, his body a perfect concentration of the powers of the earth. Gentle, docile, and humble as a slave, his muscles have made the desert to blossom; and the plow stands an everlasting record of man's escape from the horrors of barbarism, and his passage into the enjoyment of the blessings of civilization.

"As in the art of poetry all arts have been blended, so in the art of war have all sciences and arts. The art of war is the highest and most exalted art; the art of freedom and right, of the blessed condition of man and of humanity,— the Principle of Peace."

In this art of arts, in the grand achievements of this "Principle of Peace," the horse has been a primary instrument.† Gentle and loving as a pet and slave, he becomes

---

Apollo, and on the chest of Cypselus." (Pausan, iii. 18.) "Some representations of him are still extant, in which young Achilles, or Erotes, is riding on his back." (Mus. Pio-Clement, i. 52.)

* Thanks to Ixion and his magnesian mares; many thanks to the "bull-killers of the mountains and forests of Thessaly;" thanks eternal to the cloud-begotten Centaurus, "hated by gods and men," for "*benefactors shall be honored.*"

† The worst doom of the horse is not his slaughter on the battle-field. Of the abuse and maltreatment of this invaluable domestic, too much animadversion cannot be expressed; from his brutal oppression for money in races against time and distance, his destruction from abuse in the form of the hired hack, or the still more agonizing death by slow oozing of sweat (blood) from the jaded and worn-out body (rather tottering skeleton!!) of the treadmill omnibus horse. The insane destruction of this noble animal is the vilest form of lawless annihilation of value, and man, in his selfish perversion of the use, and diabolical abuse of him, is indirectly destroying himself.

"Diomedes, the son of Ares and Cyrene, was king of the Bistones in Thrace, and was killed by Hercules on account of his mares, which he fed with human flesh." (Apollod. ii. 5, § 8.) The ninth

in the battle-field an object of terror. United as one with man, he "descends to the harvest of death;" terrible is his might, his "neck clothed with thunder." Imparting to his rider a demoniac force and aspect of grandeur, he too revels in the carnage, as if he had a taste for blood, and fed upon flesh, instead of being an innocent eater of herbs, building his tower of strength from the grass of the field. From the roar of the battle he quietly bows his proud neck and becomes a worker in the sod, and with the plow reproduces the blood

"great and memorable action" or "labor" of Hercules was, "He overcame Diomedes, the most cruel tyrant of Thrace, who fed his horses with the flesh of his guests. Hercules bound him, and threw him to be eaten by those horses to which the tyrant had exposed others." A lesson of wisdom this to profane and reckless handlers of the horse.

"Is not each fast young man,
  With his costly span,
A veriest tyrant Diomedan?
Feeding his mares on human ham—
Spilling dollars as fast he can,
And going to —— at 2.20, slam!
By the wrath of Hercules or the whisky ram, (dram?)"

Beware! if thou art born "seized" of a violent and wicked rage for horses, or mere lust of pleasure or gain in the horse, or fraudulent conquests through the horse, (glory of the turf!) thou art a King Diomedes, a "cruel tyrant of Thrace," and the revenge of the strong Hercules of justice and compensation shall surely be, that thou shalt be eaten up by thine own horses. (It is not distinctly stated that Diomedes ever swapped horses, or maintained at any one time a large number of stallions for the benefit of the farmers of Thrace, but certainly both issues are included in the gist of this Fable.)*

---

* For the fate of horse-breeders in Pennsylvania, and the carelessness and ingratitude of farmers toward agricultural benefactors, see Robert Smith's work, ("Earth Culture and its Consequences," chap. x., "The Draught Horse," p. 311,) for the history of the cost, profit, and loss, of his four stallions, "Governor," "Common Sense," "Boanerges," and "Hellgrimite." It appears from this disastrous experience, that if the husbandmen of Thrace allowed their horse-loving king to be devoured by his own stud, the farmers of a certain part of Pennsylvania were equally cruel, ungrateful, and wicked toward Smith, in his benevolent efforts to improve their stock.

and life he has assisted his infuriated master to destroy. Administering to all his wants, his most coveted luxury, bearing him upon his imperial form in pursuit of pleasure, he is the companion of princely gentlemen; destroying space on the wings of the wind in the ardor of the hunt, or, humble and subdued, he carries the mill boy with the widow's corn to be ground; wise, good, and humanly working, like a creature of reason and thought. Thus, from the king to the serf, he has become an inseparable friend of man. The romance of the Arab's love for him seems ideal and exaggerated, a story of the fancy only; but every genial and spirited boy who has wearied of his rocking-horse, and dreams of the gallant steed he aspires to ride, knows it to be *true* and *real*. The perfected splendor of the whole animal world, his place in the system of uses demonstrates him to be an indispensable element in the progressive development* of the races of men; and in his ancient alliance, through bonds of fraternal love, with the perpetually dominant tribes and nations, he has come at last to be endowed, in imagination and affection, almost with the transcendent faculties of a human being.

* Of the horse, as a sanitary resource, or of horseback exercise as a therapeutic agent, in the cure of many obstinate forms of disease, see chapter Hygieia. The records of medicine show that a number of physicians have been earnest and enthusiastic on the subject of exercise on horseback as a remedy for many morbid conditions. Its power is undoubtedly very great in some conditions, and specifically *assistant* in many more.

(SEE ANTE, p. 311, at *)

The horse's foot is an interesting anatomical structure. In the domesticated state, this living, elastic mass, is used as a sledge-hammer for pulverizing rocks, that is, the hoof is driven over, and jammed against stony surfaces, impelled by the enormous momentum of from seven to eighteen hundred pounds (the range of weights of the animal in general use) in rapid motion. This living mallet (foot) is composed of bones, ligaments, blood-vessels, nerves, and a laminated elastic fibro-cartilaginous structure, (with anatomical characters peculiar to the solipeds,) in the form of plates, or blades, which coalesce or dovetail with a similarly laminated extension of the horny elements of the hoof, uniting the last bone of the extremity with the hoof, which is also alive or full of nerves and blood-vessels to a point called the "quick," all being enveloped in a dead insensible, but still elastic crust, the outer layer of the foot, to which free expansion is given by a spongy cushion or hinge called the frog, also destitute of sensibility, uniting the sides of the sole of the foot, or point of contact of the animal, with the earth. This body receives all the vibrations of the crust, and is the centre of all contractions and expansions of the hoof. To prevent the destruction of the whole mallet, it is faced with a rim of iron, as a hammer is rendered indestructible by a facing of steel. The *elasticity* of the hoof destroyed, the foot becomes lame, and is finally useless. To the reflecting mind, then, the arming of the horses foot with iron is no longer a mere mechanical nailing of a curved bar of metal on a stick of timber. The shoeing of the horse is an *art*, requiring scientific knowledge and great mechanical skill, scarcely ever possessed by the common smith. Hence the wholesale destruction of the hoof and constantly fatal damaging of that noble animal.

CLASS II.—AVES.

Oviparous Vertebrata, (Birds.)

Visions of sentiment and beauty come with the bird, for his life is embalmed in aroma and love, thoughts of gladness gleam from his pinions, for his motions are like the "swift-winged arrows of light;" but his voice! the wild, sweet voice of the bird, that *song*, heard through far-away deeps as a sacred trance of the soul, and delicious revery of the heart, as the memory of other days, and the joys of youth, touches with emotions "that chain the spirit to the gates of Paradise."

> "Yet has each soul an inborn feeling
>   Impelling it to mount and soar away,
> When, lost in heaven's blue depths, the lark is pealing
>   High overhead her airy lay;
> When o'er the mountain pine's black shadow
>   With outspread wing the eagle sweeps,
> And, steering on o'er lake and meadow,
>   The crane his homeward journey keeps."

Swift gliding harbingers of lovely dreams, these fragments of the perfection of the world, come, a sweet and touching mediation between the dumb, inarticulate, uncommunicating animal, and the high speaking consciousness of man. As creatures of beauty their suggestions are exhaustless in artistic intimations, as instruments of the miracles of instinct, they open abysses unfathomable by human thought, and as organs of musical ecstasy they speak of "that which, in all this mortal life, we have not seen, and *never shall see*." "The bird is thoroughly, or out-and-out, organized as an animal of song. In it nature attains unto a definite hearing and speech. The bird speaketh the language of nature. With the bird, the voice, properly speaking, breaks forth for the first time, and that, too, in a high grade of perfection, as melody."

In the bird, nature seems to have ultimated her first most delicate and elaborate form of sensuous existence. Whether we contemplate the furnishing of its structure by special styles of organic mechanisms, adapting its body to existence, and motion in a gaseous medium, and a life of ethereal suspensions, or the wisdom of its wonderful instincts, far transcending the deductions of reason, or the intuitions of the intellect in executing migrations almost circum-mundane in their extents, or other extraordinary endowments, as of love and fidelity almost human, or of music, beyond all imitations of science in depth and touching compass, the bird appears the sure and ineffable consummation and earnest fruitage, of the whole lower or purely animal domain.

"In the bird, also, all the spiritual or mental faculties make their appearance for the first time, and suddenly, whereas, in the preceding classes, (Reptiles, Fishes, etc.,) but slight traces of them are observed. Such, for example, are their mechanical instincts, varied modes of nidification, powers of imitation, susceptibility to instruction, knowledge of their benefactors, sentiment of joy, wheedling or coaxing manners, and so on. We have no example of fishes and reptiles having learned any artificial tricks." (?)

Surely human are these revelations, certainly detached and individual, as endowed with organic will, comes this wonderful being, elevated and ennobled by the enchanting elements and specific attributes of *character*. Hence the enthusiasm of its lovers; hence the devotion and life-long faithfulness of its scientific votaries, and the deep absorption of the true student of ornithology. The names of zealous worshipers come with the voice of the bird and the murmur of the woods, and Wilson, Audubon, Bonaparte, and Cassin, are aptly associated in the imagination with musical groves, and the lives and habitudes of the light-winged denizens of the air. Of the

BIRDS.

economical relationships of birds to man, of their friendly associations with him, making bright and cheerful his surroundings, of their intelligent and curious habits, presenting ceaseless objects of study and observation, the works of the bird biographers are beautiful records; stories redolent of picturesque solitudes and the enchantments of the grove.

This interesting class of animals is found from the Equator to the Poles. Their forms and plumage are as widely different and as wonderfully diversified as their habits and habitats. There are arctic, temperate, and tropical birds, and they all strikingly reveal the influence of the medium in which they exist. Arctic ornithology, like arctic mammalogy, is peculiar in style and color, being generally white or light colored, aquatic birds abounding. The temperate birds have not much variety of color generally, but the tropical birds exhaust every pigment of the chemist and painter, and sport all colors, not only of the rainbow, but every *undescribed* and *indescribable* tint, metallic sheen, or hue. It is, likewise, one of the most extensive classes of animals. Some conception of the immensity of this department may be obtained by a visit to the invaluable museum of the Academy of Natural Sciences, Philadelphia. Of this collection, Dr. Ruschenberger, in his clever notice of the academy, says " It has grown to be the *most extensive* and the very *best* in the *world.*" In 1852 there were 27,000 specimens in this collection. Mr. Cassin now alleges that this number has been largely increased, and is constantly being added to from all quarters. He supposes there may now be in the academy 7500 distinct species, which constitute most of the known birds of the world.

After a walk through the galleries of this magnificent collection, the brain is absolutely dizzy, and the mind stunned and confused by the infinite array of every imaginable style, form, and color of bird obtained from every point of the surface of the planet.

The Alleghany Mountain being the highest line of knobs, or range of Alpine points, of the Appalachian chain, separates, as by a comb, the inclined planes of the East Mississippi Valley and Atlantic slope. In their migrations north and south, following the brush of the sun, many birds journey through the interior valley, as their track of travel, but perhaps a larger number take the Atlantic side, finding in both these regions milder climate, and more food than the mountain crests afford. This applies both to land and water birds, but especially the latter. The larger aquatic birds having oceanic affinities, of course take the Atlantic side, while the birds that have lacustrine and river habits prefer the interior valley in their transits. These points are arranged by the harmonious economics on the question of food and comfort. The bird that breeds on the shores of Hudson's Bay and passes the winter on the shores of the Gulf of Mexico, will make the journeys between these points over the route on which he finds the best "bed and board." The rivulets of the Mississippi and Atlantic running from the mountain form but few bodies of water on those heights, consequently, the aquatic birds avoid these ranges in their journeyings. This is also the case with the land birds that breed *far north*, and consequently, the Alleghany is not visited by as large a number of birds, both land and water, as the other lines of surfaces above designated.

To the thoughtful observer, one of the most imposing experiences of the deep forests of this range, is their unbroken silence from the absence of animal life in every shape, particularly birds. Frequently, for great extents, a stillness as of the grave reigns; no life, no motion, but a solemn and oppressive calm broods over the wilderness. If there is no wind, which always gives motion and the semblance of life, from creaking branches and rustling leaves, a fragment of bark, a limb, or a tree falling, startles as if the spirit-world were invaded and the seclusion and quiet of death profaned. At certain seasons this cheerlessness and solitude is more striking than at others. This scarcity of birds is, no doubt, accounted for by the want of the variety of food required by the different species in these woods, especially throughout the extents of pine and hemlock forests.

A number of birds of far northern migratory range are found during the winter on the mountain, and the traveling crowds stop here on their passage north and south, spring and fall. In these instances, the mountain is of course only "a tent of the night," the birds being strangers and visitors merely.

The catalogue of the birds of the mountain will include some notice of constant visitors, but particularly those species that remain there during the breeding season, or that pass the summer there, building their nests as regular homes, producing their young, and thus establishing permanet citizenship by actual settlement. Many of the shy solitary species seem to prefer the mountain fastnesses for their lines of migration and permanent homes, and make glad the most savage places. They will be noticed in the hasty catalogue which follows, with something occasionally of their habits and peculiarities.

As already observed, the mountain is visited by many birds that remain there during the summer, and breed there, some in the forests and glens, others in open and cultivated parts, while others seek the most rugged knobs and inaccessible spots. The following list comprises many of the most commonly observed birds of the range, either as migrating travelers or regular inhabitants.

RAPACIOUS BIRDS.

HAWKS.

(Family Falconidæ.)

FALCO Columbarius, (Linn.) Pigeon hawk.—This is a shy and wary little hawk, very wild, watchful, and rarely seen. Nuttall states that it has been met as far north as 48°, "even extending its migrations as far as Hudson's Bay," although chiefly an inhabitant of the Southern States, and rearing its young there; color, dusky-brown, breast whitish, with blackish stripes longitudinal. Not at all abundant.

FALCO Sparverius, (Linn.) American sparrow-hawk.—This is a less hawk than the Columbarius, and is the smallest of his tribe. He is a beautiful little bird, with striking marks, and gallant bearing, and sometimes gets as far north as 53°. Color, rufous, beneath nearly white, spotted with brown; seven black curved spots around head; wing covers slate-blue, etc. Prey, mice, small birds, lizards, etc. It is common.

HALIAETUS Leucocephalus, (Linn.) Bald eagle.—This beautiful eagle has an extremely wide range, and is sometimes seen on the knobs and in the water gaps of the mountain. As his general prey is fish, he haunts the larger streams. He is occasionally seen soaring around the spurs near the gaps of the important water-courses. "Color, dark-brown, head and tail white, feet, bill, and cere yellow." This eagle is a regular pirate, his mode of capturing his booty being a subject of interest.*

PANDION Haliæetus, (Linn.) Fish-hawk.—This splendid hawk is rare. A short distance from the slopes of the Alleghany, along the streams, he is sometimes found. He is a regular fisher, and has an extensive range. Color, "dark-brown, beneath white, feet and cere blue." He is a great favorite with some of the old ornithologists, who give him high qualities, and mark his life with sentiment and romance. He is the constant victim of the marauding propensities of the bald eagle.

BUTEO Borealis, (Gmel.) Red-tailed hawk, American buzzard.—This beautiful bird is found over the whole United States. It is a bold and predatory species, often invading the barn-yard, but generally finding his prey in the woods, devouring squirrels, birds, and occasionally condescending to feed upon mice, moles, and frogs. Color, "dark-brown above, white, with dark spots beneath, tail reddish, with

---

* He is the far-famed "American Eagle."

black terminal bands." "One of the most common and easily recognized of the North American species."—Cassin.

ARCHIBUTEO Sancti-johannis. Black hawk, rough-legged buzzard.—This bird is not often seen on the mountain. Mr. Cassin remarks, "This is one of the most abundant birds of this family in all the Atlantic States, and is one of the most variable in plumage." Color, black, with brownish mottling; length, twenty-two to twenty-four inches.

ACCIPITER Fuscus, (Gmel.) Sharp-shinned hawk, chicken-hawk.—This courageous hawk has an extensive range. He is interesting for his daring and reckless valor, following his prey any place without fear. Feeds upon birds, poultry, and squirrels. "Color, dark-slate, beneath white, barred with reddish."—Nutt. "Upper part dark brownish-black, tinged with ashy, occiput mixed with white."—Cas. Length, twelve to fourteen inches. Cassin observes that this little hawk is one of the most common North American species.

ACCIPITER Cooperii, (Bon.) Cooper's hawk.—This fine species, according to Cassin, has for a habitat the "entire territory of the United States." It visits the mountain, but is rare. It is larger than the sharp-shinned hawk. "Color, upper part dark ashy-brown, shafts of feathers brownish-black, an obscure rufous collar on neck behind, beneath rufous and white, transversely barred; length, female, eighteen to twenty inches; male, sixteen to seventeen."—Cas. The females of predatory birds are larger and finer looking than the males, reversing the order of things with many other classes of birds and animals, where the male sports all the ornamental additions to the species.*

BUTEO Lineatus, (Gmel.) Red-shouldered hawk, winter falcon.—This is a noble-looking bird, "some twenty-two to twenty-four inches in length,"—Cas. He has not a far

* "The first spiritual want of the barbarous man being *decoration*," does he take the hint from the streamer of the chicken-cock and mane of the stallion? The *last spiritual want* of the *civilized woman* being also, and only decoration, does *she* take the hint from the superior plumage of the feminine eagle and hawk?

northern range, and is very abundant in the winter at the South. He is frequently seen on the tall pines along water-courses, watching for frogs and small animals. Color, "brown, beneath white, tail red, with bands." "An abundant and very difficult species to the student."—Cas.

CIRCUS Hudsonius, (Linn.) Hen-harrier.—This bird has a far northern range, traveling from Hudson's Bay to the southern part of the United States. Its prey consists of frogs, lizards, and small birds. Color, "bluish-gray, female brown;" length, twenty inches. It is sometimes seen along the streams and marshy places of the mountain.

Many of these rapacious birds are fine noble-looking creatures, but the imagination in endowing them with magnanimous qualities, or estimable characters, commits a blunder unwarrantable by a critical study of their true natures. An accomplished observer of the bird world, and withal a reflecting and philosophical naturalist, with an eye to the law and spirit which speaks the meaning of the deep soul underlying the outward phenomenal, remarks,—"It is, however, entirely erroneous to attribute a noble or generous character to any of the predatory animals, though from an early period of history several species have been so regarded. On the contrary, there is, in all these classes, whether of birds or of other animals, a marked absence of the very traits which are in some measure assigned to them, and even more unmistakably so in some of the more celebrated, as the eagles and lions, than in the more humble species. They appear to personate a principle, if we may be allowed to use the expression, involving one of the most momentous and mysterious of problems, the existence of evil in the world. The prowling and treacherous lion, and the robber wolf, have unfortunately but too strong analogies in that race which is the head of the visible creation, and they and their kind everywhere present the same *intrinsic meanness* which is characteristic of violence and injustice, of vice and of crime among men."—Cassin, Birds of America, p. 159.

OWLS.

(Family Strigidæ.)

Nocturnal birds of prey. These are the cats of the bird tribe. Their whole structure is arranged for preying at night, ears to hear the cricket and mouse chirp, or bug under the leaf; eyes to see their minutest prey in the darkness; and soft downy feathers to glide like spectres in silence. There are but few species on the mountain.

SCOPS Asio, (Linn.) Red owl.—This is the little screech-owl found, according to Nuttall, from Greenland to Florida. It is friendly and familiar, approaching houses and sitting on apple-trees and bushes almost in contact with the dwelling. He preys only at night, feeding on mice and small birds, even beetles and moths. "Color, brown, ash, and rusty-red, mixed with black; length, ten to eleven inches."—Nuttall.

BUBO Virginianus, (Gm.) Great horned or cat owl.—This large night-bird, "king of the nocturnal tribe of American birds," is found on the mountain. His startling hoot, or strange and melancholy boo-hoo, is heard at night in almost every wood of any extent, and being loud and sonorous, it is audible at a great distance. He is found from Hudson's Bay to Florida. Color, mixed, brownish and black; he is twenty inches long. Prey, young rabbits, birds, squirrels, mice, etc. In a dark, silent night, nothing can be more ominous and unearthly than the notes of this gloomy bird. Mr. Cassin has described four varieties, showing quite a difference of plumage in the species, which has given rise to much trouble among ornithologists.

OTUS Wilsonianus, (Lesson.) Long-eared owl.—Nuttall represents this bird as "almost a denizen of the world, being found from Hudson's Bay to the West Indies, throughout Europe, in Africa, Asia, and China." Color, "mottled black and brown, ear-tufts long; length, fourteen inches."—Nuttall. Rarely seen on the mountain. Cassin says, "This is one of the commonest species of owls in the Northern and Eastern States on the Atlantic."

SYRNIUM Nebulosum, (Foster.) Barred owl.—This owl has a continental range. Color, " grayish-brown, with transverse whitish spots, beneath whitish, with longitudinal spots of brown."—Nut. Length, sixteen to twenty inches. This owl is sometimes seen in numbers on the mountain.

OTUS Brachyotus, (Foster.) Short-eared owl.—This is a northern bird, breeding at Hudson's Bay, where it goes in May. Between September and May it sometimes visits the mountain. Color, ochreous, blackish-brown spots; length, thirteen to fifteen inches; feeds on mice, and is a daring and courageous bird.

STRIX Pratincola, (Linn.) White, or barn owl.—This species, although a cosmopolite, is but rarely seen on the Alleghany. Color, "yellowish, with darkish zigzag lines, small spots of white, beneath whitish."—Nut. Length, fourteen inches. This is the unhappy representative of his family so "hooted at," maligned, and bedeviled by superstitious poets and the small singing birds that he eats.* He devours mice, birds, rats, and moles, and, like the rest of his wise brotherhood, says very little, as all fellows do who have very little to say, and of consequence is reckoned very knowing and sharp by common consent. He is a poor prophet, and consequently, as a bird of either good or evil omen, is a humbug. Mice and rats he is after, but has not time to appear as herald of the angel of death, except at the death of his own victims.

OMNIVOROUS BIRDS.

LARK.

STURNUS Ludovicianus.—This is the American meadow lark, and is a common bird, being found wherever the sur-

* When the owl appears in daylight he is attacked by the whole crowd of the birds of the wood in concert, and most villainously maltreated by all.

face is cleared into fields, but having a special love for meadows. He is a summer visitor, although the snows sometimes catch him. Nuttall remarks, "Wilson even observed them in the month of February, during a deep snow among the heights of the Alleghanies, gleaning their scanty pittance on the road in company with the small snowbird." This is not unusual. He is familiar to all, is a beautiful bird, and has always been much admired for his thrilling notes, which he utters on the wing.

ICTERUS Baltimore, golden robin, or hanging bird, passes its summers on the Alleghanies, and breeds there, but is not very abundant. He is seen occasionally in the forests, but seems to prefer a nearer approach to the residence of man. His bright and beautiful form, however, flashes through the denser woods, the golden sheen of his brilliant plumage startling the eye of the traveler. He is well known to all, and his melodious notes hailed as a voice of the spring. His pensile nest, woven out of stolen thread, flax, hair, and feathers, and hanging like a bag from some pendent branch, is one of the most interesting objects in nature. His biographers ecstasize over him, being seduced by his beauty and intelligence, and captivated by his song. He possesses powers of mimicking quite remarkable.

ICTERUS Spurius, (Bon.) Orchard oriole.—This is a much plainer species, and not so large as the golden robin. It comes to the mountain during the first part of May. This species has many of the interesting elements of character which mark the Baltimore oriole: the same deep bag-nest, same social instincts, etc. Of this bird, Nuttall remarks, "It appears to affect the elevated and airy regions of the Alleghany Mountains, where it is much more numerous than the Baltimore." This will not apply to the Pennsylvania Alleghanies, where the other oriole is much more numerous certainly.

ICTERUS Phœniceus, (Daud.) The red-winged blackbird is a very common species of the genus. This oriole is found on the mountains, in every swamp and meadow, and the summer is made noisy by him wherever the surface is cleared of forests, and there is water, bushes, and tall grass. It is a familiar and much-admired bird, inhabiting North America from Nova Scotia to Mexico. They travel north with the purple grakle, ferruginous blackbird, and cowbird, in the latter part of April, leaving for the south in November.

ICTERUS Icterocephalus, yellow-headed troopial.—In character and habits much like the red-winged blackbird. This bird, Nuttall says, "ranges from Cayenne to Missouri, and is wholly confined to the *west side* of *Mississippi*, beyond which *not even a straggler has yet been seen.*" A flock of this species appeared on the western side of the mountain in the fall of 1857, notwithstanding the statement of the illustrious Nuttall. On the eastern side of the mountain its appearance has been noticed but rarely. We must, consequently, catalogue the yellow-headed troopial as an occasional visitor of the mountain.

ICTERUS Pecoris, (Temm.)—This is the cow troopial, and is seen often here, but not in large numbers. In its migrations it takes the range of the valleys parallel to the mountain. It does not breed here, but passes along on his journey, being found accidentally with other birds in migratory troops. A thief and scavenger, parasite and outlaw, even as a traveler he cannot be concealed, but sneaks about the fields, sometimes approaching barns, and indulging in his fancy to associate with cattle.

BIRDS RELATED TO THE CROWS.

QUISCALUS Versicolor.—This is the common crow blackbird, an inhabitant of the whole continent. He is found here in his usual abundance as a regular resident, and in crowds or migrating parties as a visitor, fall and spring. He is a noisy and troublesome bird, and here, like every place else, is one of the commonest birds. It breeds from Nova Scotia to Louisiana.

QUISCALUS Ferrugineus, occasionally stops for a time on

the mountains, in its hurried migrations, but does not breed here, and is rarely seen at all except en route for the north, where it nests and establishes "civic relationships."

TRUE CROWS.

CORVUS Corax, is the raven. It is not an abundant species, but its gaunt, ugly, black form may occasionally be seen perched on a tall hemlock, or his discordant croak heard, as he heavily wades his way through the air. In all regions a bird of ill omen, he is the special aversion of many "on account of his indiscriminate voracity, sombre livery, discordant croaking, ignoble, wild, and funeral aspect."

The raven is an interesting bird, from his long association in the imagination of man with superstitious fears and prophecies of disasters, and if his biographers the ornithologists do not romance, he is really quite wonderful in his instincts and habits. Nuttall remarks, "Though spread over the whole world, they are rarely ever birds of passage, enduring the winters even of the arctic circle, or the warmth of Mexico, St. Domingo, and Madagascar." The raven is patient and devoted in its attachment, and lives to be a hundred years old.

CORVUS Americanus, crow.—This rascally species occurs in numbers through the whole range of the mountain. He is found in flocks, at certain seasons of the year, more or less numerous, and sometimes in hundreds, almost darkening the air, and filling the region where he is either flying or roosting, with his noisy cawing. A hardy wretch, he braves the fiercest storms of the Alleghanies, passing his winters in great numbers in the forests. Large flocks collect together and go through certain ranges of country, seeming to have favorite places for roosting. These are generally in dark woods of hemlock and pine, or in deep, sequestered ravines. Flocks are often seen pursuing their flight in the midst of the roughest storms, with the whole air full of flying snow, their jet-black bodies spotting the clouds. They may often be seen stalking over the snow-drifts in search of food, or strutting along roads, gleaning a miserable pittance. Like the raven, the crow is a bird of evil omen, and, like that bird, celebrated for "unrestrained natural affection," accompanying, protecting, and succoring its young until grown to the adult stage. They are considered destructive birds, and are condemned and destroyed in great numbers on that account. Great wit and wisdom is attributed to the crow, great cunning and wiliness. This is somewhat fabulous, for it is not so cunning or cautious even in the wildest parts of the mountains at any time but that it may be shot or taken by stratagem. The range of the crow is world-wide. It is found in Siberia, New Holland, the Philippine Islands, and United States. It breeds every place, and it is said the "conjugal union once formed, continues for life."

CYANURUS Cristatus, or blue jay.—This is a common species on the mountain. He is a brilliant, exquisite bird, imposing in his form, and with an extreme profusion of ornament in his dress. Sporting a fine erectile crest upon his head, and a graceful train of tail, his plumage mixed with azure, white, black, gray, and "vinaceous," all of the brightest tints and clearest hue, he would seem rather to belong to the tropics, the region of highly-colored birds, than to the cold mountains of the north, and would certainly never be suspected to be related to the sombre brotherhood of crows. He is found in numbers at all seasons, with the exception of partial migrations or "predatory excursions," and bears, like the common crow, often the coldest winter weather, seeming to delight in the wind and snow with "wild uproar." A noisy and garrulous chatterer, he soon announces his presence to all the inhabitants of the woods by a variety of discordant notes. His gay, bright form, gleams like a gem through the forest, and is sure to attract attention by his strange and foreign aspect. He has an extensive range of habitations and habits, and is a general favorite with lovers of birds, for his beauty of plumage, peculiarity of instincts, and style of movement, possessing a talent for mimicry, docility, and great cunning.

ÆGITHALI.

PARUS.

The two species of Parus, bicolor and atricapillus, visit the mountain. The first of these species is not common, but the second, the black-capped titmouse, or chickadee, is found in greater numbers. This restless, hardy little bird is said to "winter around Hudson's Bay, and to have been met with at 62° on the northwest coast." Its peculiar notes, tshe-de-de, tshe-de-de-deait, may be heard almost at any time in the woods.

SERICATI.

BOMBYCILLA.—Of this genus the species Carolinensis, or cedar-bird, is common on the Alleghanies. A graceful and beautiful bird, it is seen in small flocks whirling around through the air, or sitting, quietly and sedately, in rows upon the branches. A lover of cherries and berries, he may be seen slily dodging about where these fruits are to be found. His biographers tell some interesting stories about him.

BOMBYCILLA Garrula. Waxen chatterer.—This is only a visitor of the mountain.

INSECTIVOROUS BIRDS.

LANIUS, butcher-birds.—The species of this genus, "septentrionalis, or American shrike," is seen sometimes on the mountain. A bold little savage, he may occasionally be observed pursuing his depredations with his usual impertinence and temerity. Wilson remarked that it did not migrate farther south than Virginia. In March and April he seeks the forests of the mountains of Pennsylvania, and goes as far as new England for a summer residence. This is a bird of interesting habits.

FLY-CATCHERS.

TYRANNUS Intrepidus. — This species, the king-bird, is rather rare on the Alleghany, compared with other parts of the State, where he is *common*. A quarrelsome, crusty, and pugnacious bird, he may be seen carrying on his usual sparrings with almost everything that flies. A type of the now fashionable fillibuster, his quarrels have generally some gain to himself in prospective, a *fight* of *some kind*, but would prefer one that he will be the gainer after the fight is over. A redeeming trait is his "courage and affection for his mate and young," dwelt upon by his biographers, who also delight to array this little tyrant with many wonderful attributes, which are generally supposed to belong to the human species alone. Geographic range, from Mexico to Canada.

TYRANNUS Crinitus, (Linn.)—This species is rarely seen on the mountains.

TYRANULA Fusca.—This is the well-known pe-wee, or pewit fly-catcher. It is as common as the chipping sparrow, and is found everywhere, near caves, barns, bridges, and rock-ledges along streams. Its few notes are known to all, and its habits familiar to every one. An innocent catcher of flies, he sits silently near his nest watching for his winged prey, which he catches by a sudden whirl in the air, then quietly resumes his perch. His few plaintive notes are always welcome as announcing spring.

TYRANULA Virens, wood pe-wee.—This species is found in the forests of the mountain, as also the species "acadica." They are shy, solitary birds, and may be seen sitting quietly in the dark woods watching for their prey, which they take with great dexterity by quick circles in the air, returning to the spot from which they started. The wood pe-wee has a few peculiarly plaintive notes of a tender, touching strain, which, in the silent woods, come upon the ear with a strange, unearthly charm, awaking thoughts and emotions that perhaps no other sound could bring to the soul. Plain in form, solitary in habits, it seems to *brood*, and the recollection alone of its position on the dry branch of a tree, in the deep forest, brings pictures of cool retired shades, solitude, and silence.

Setophaga Ruticilla, (Wil.) American Redstart.—The redstart is an interesting and beautiful bird, appearing about the first of May, and retiring in October. It is a quick, active little creature, having some musical notes.

Icteria Viridis, (Bon.) Yellow-breasted icteria.—This bird is said by Nuttall to be a "summer resident of the United States, and to pass the winter in Tropical America, being found in Guiana and Brazil." It is rare on the mountain.

WARBLING FLY-CATCHERS.

Vireos.—This genus is related to the orioles, in nidification, eggs, color of young, and females, song, and notes of the young. It is a peculiarly American group. They live on insects one part of the season, and mix berries with their food, as that kind of fruit ripens. They confine their hunting of insects to the branches of trees and bushes, rarely coming to the ground for that purpose.

Of the vireos, an ancient friend has some interesting and clever remarks. "On account of their modest attire and sylvan habits, the birds of the group (vireos) to which the present species (vireo atricapillus) belongs, are seldom noticed by the general observer, though some of them are to be met with commonly during the summer in nearly all parts of the United States. But though inconspicuous in appearance, they make ample compensation by the loudness of their notes, which, after the early love-songs of the thrushes, and others of our songsters of spring, have subsided into the more serious duties of parental responsibility, are to be heard above those of any other of our resident birds. They are active insect-catchers, and may be seen at nearly all hours of the day patiently searching among the leaves and branches of the trees in almost every woodland, hopping from branch to branch, or sometimes making short sallies in pursuit of fugitive moths or butterflies, and occasionally pausing to refresh themselves with a rather quaint but very melodious warble, lengthened in the spring into a cheerful and agreeable song."*

VIREO Flavifrons, yellow-throated vireo.—This lively little bird is found in the forests of the mountain. He arrives in May, and is soon seen, a restless hunter, hurrying busily around the twigs of the trees in pursuit of his prey, which at this season is principally composed of insects and worms. His voice is soon heard, and his notes form one of the most peculiar and exquisite of the songs of the woods. In the words of one of his biographers: "In the warm weather, the lay of this bird is indeed peculiarly strong and lively; and his usually long-drawn, almost plaintive notes are now delivered in fine succession, with a peculiar echoing and highly-impressive musical cadence; appearing like a romantic and tender reverie of delight." Toward the middle of September he leaves for the south. He is an exceedingly interesting little musician, and his song silenced, one of the sweetest attractions of the grove is gone. Their curious pendent nests, woven with great skill from the branch of some forest tree, may be seen in numbers when the leaves have fallen. The workmanship of these frail air-baskets or sacks is quite wonderful. "It is attached firmly all round the curving twigs by which it is supported; the stoutest external materials, or skeleton of the fabric, is formed of interlaced folds of thin strips of red cedar (any flexible) bark, connected very intimately by coarse threads and small masses of the silk of spider's nest, and of the cocoons of large moths; these threads are moistened by the glutinous saliva of the bird. Among these external materials are also blended fine blades of dry grass. The inside is thickly bedded with this last material and fine root-fibres, but the finishing layer, as if to preserve elasticity, is of rather coarse grass stalks. Externally the nest is coated over with green lichens, attached very artfully by slender strings of caterpillar's silk,

---

* Birds of America, Cassin.

and the whole afterwards tied over by almost invisible threads of the same, so as to appear as if glued on; and the entire fabric now resembles an accidental knot of the tree grown over with moss."*

Vireo Solitarius, (Vieill.) Solitary vireo.—This is a rare species, but is sometimes seen. It has been observed from Georgia to Pennsylvania, but has been regarded as a straggler in the latter State.

Vireo Noveboracensis, (Bon.) White-eyed vireo, or fly-catcher.—This agile, industrious, and interesting little songster visits the mountain regularly in the summer season. His plain, diminutive form would scarcely be observed or attract attention but for a series of striking notes to which he gives utterance. These are especially eccentric and whimsical in their character, changed with great quickness, and he is affirmed, by some of his biographers, to possess a range of imitative combination quite surprising. He arrives in April, and leaves in the latter part of September, often later. The pensile nests which seem to characterize the family of vireos is also constructed by him. His food is the same as the rest of the vireos, consisting of different kinds of berries and of insects, of which he is a most vigilant hunter. Of this species, Nuttall observes, "The present species retires no farther for winter quarters than the southern part of the United States, where many also breed, as *would appear* from the concomitant circumstance of their music."

Vireo Gilvus, (Bon.) Warbling vireo.—This is the most highly endowed musical genius of the family, indeed of the whole woods almost. As a songster, he is richly gifted with variety and compass of notes, and for melody and sweetness, touching tenderness, and exquisite delicacy of intonation, no vibration of art can offer a parallel. He arrives on the mountain from Tropical America about the first of May, leaving the last of September. He is like the rest of the genus in all his habits. Nuttall states that "he is

* Nuttall.

wholly confined to towns, and even cities." The warbling vireo is certainly found on the Alleghany Mountain.

Vireo Olivaceus, (Bon.) Red-eyed vireo, or fly-catcher.—This bird arrives on the mountain in April. It is a busy and tireless songster, possessed of a variety of beautiful notes, which have been attempted to be imitated in words by a number of enthusiastic bird observers. It is a common species, and has a range of towns as well as forests. It has also the general habits of the vireos. He leaves with the crowd of retiring songsters in October. Great admiration is shown for him as a singer. Of this species Cassin remarks, "The red-eyed fly-catcher (V. olivaceus) is the most numerous, and not only is constantly to be met with in the woods, but ventures confidently into the public squares or parks, and the yards and gardens of the cities. In many such localities in Philadelphia, several of which are in the densest parts of the city, this little warbler rears its young, and pipes out his sprightly song in entire security, and apparently feeling himself as much at home as if in the recesses of the most remote forest. The warbling fly-catcher (V. gilvus) is another pleasing singer, though, in our opinion, but an indifferent performer compared with the preceding."

THRUSHES.

This is an interesting family, some of which are the most familiar and universally admired of our birds.

Mimus Polyglottus, (Linn.) Mocking-bird.—This bird is *said* to inhabit the "whole continent from the State of Rhode Island to equatorial regions." It is a plain bird, "cinerious, beneath white, with some white on wings and tail." His powers are wonderful. Although the Alleghany is within the geographic range given to this bird, it has not been seen there yet.

Mimus Rufus, (Linn.) Ferruginous Thrush.—This is a large thrush of a light-brown or reddish color, beneath whitish, with black spots, tail feathers long. It is found from the Gulf of Mexico to Canada, and breeds through all that region, coming north in April and May, and retiring in October to the Southern States. The Thrasher is a songster of rich and rare musical endowments. It is sometimes called the "mocking-bird," but does not seem to possess powers of imitation. Its musical faculties are very little inferior to those of the mocking-bird, and many of its combinations for depth of pathos and emotion are even superior. Mounted on the topmost twig of a tree or bush, his "full heart laboring with instinctive feeling," he pours out his loud, clear notes, in sweet and trilling warbles, or mingled with low, plaintive, and tender tones. They arrive in pairs on the mountain, and their beautiful song is soon heard at the dawn of the morning.

MIMUS Felivox, (Vieill.) Catbird.—This is a plain bird, of a dark-bluish, or slate color, paler beneath, with a black crown and tail. It is a very common and familiar species, having a migratory range from the Gulf of Mexico to Canada, and perhaps farther north. It arrives at the mountain early in April, and is soon actively engaged in nuptial preparations for the coming season of love. It is quick and restless, almost in perpetual motion, darting about the thickets and fences with ceaseless eagerness. It has many fine combinations in its song, occasionally getting up a strain of inimitable sweetness, whose enchantment is sometimes broken by its peculiar cat-squall, a noise which has given the bird its name. It possesses something of the faculty of mimicking other birds, and is often heard using notes of their songs mingled with its original lay. On this subject, Nuttall remarks: "A very amusing individual, which I now describe, began his vocal powers by imitating the sweet and low warble of the song sparrow, as given in the autumn; and from his love of imitation on other occasions, I am inclined to believe that he possesses no original note of his own, but acquires and modulates the songs of other birds." The catbird leaves the mountain early in September.

MERULA Migratoria, (Linn.) American robin.—This is

a common bird, and a universally welcomed visitor. A graceful and comely creature, with kind and friendly affinities for man, he is almost domestic in his habits. He approaches frankly and fearlessly houses and barns, building his nest often in the most exposed situations, on a fence or in the fork of an apple-tree, seeming by a gallant confidence to appeal to the generosity and magnanimity of man for protection. As a destroyer of noxious insects his services are invaluable, and the number of worms, slugs, and bugs devoured by him is incredible, as he vigorously bolts enormous quantities from morning till night. He has a sweet and touching song, which, however, has not much variety. A delightful enchanter of the field, his name carries the dreaming soul to sights and sounds of the country,—the flowery meadow, the running brook, the blossoming orchard, all made divine by the song of the beautiful robin. His range is the "continent, from Hudson's Bay, in the fifty-third degree, to the table-land of Mexico." He is among the first arrivals on the mountain, and appears often before the snows have gone, in flocks, with other birds, on the northward passage. The young and old both return to the same summer haunts visited in previous migrations.

MERULA Mustelina, (Gm.) Wood thrush.—This is a plain little brown bird, beneath white, "spotted with blackish." He is solitary and shy, retreating to the depths of wildernesses, far from human habitations and noise of towns. His song is one of the most attractive and melodious sounds of the forest, and is frequently the only voice heard in the deep, silent expanse of the woods. "The prelude to this song resembles almost the double-tonguing of the flute, blended with a tinkling shrill and solemn warble, which re-echoes from his solitary retreat like the dirge of some sad recluse who shuns the busy haunts of life." These strange, wild, liquid flutings, rising from the depths of leafy recesses, possess a peculiar power of exciting delicious and melancholy emotions which, once having thrilled the heart, leave forever the memory of solitudes sacred to thought and feeling, of retreats where beauty, overshadowed by gloom, inspires awe, and has become holy, while nature, from her tenderest depths, breathes a touching sob of that "melody which is the voice of the universe, whereby it proclaims its scheme and inmost essence." The wood thrush inhabits the continent from Hudson's Bay to Florida. It arrives at the mountain early in April, and migrates in October.

MERULA Minor, (Gm.) Little Hermit Thrush.—The hermit is "olive-brown on back, with rufus tail, beneath brownish-white, with dusky spots," and is a shy, wild little bird, with some of the habits of the wood thrush, and full of sweetest music. It affects also dark, solitary places, where its melodious notes, in "silver cadence," often mingle with those of the wood thrush. Range, New Hampshire to Florida. It remains but a short time on the mountain.

MERULA Wilsonii, (Bonap.) Wilson's thrush, or Veery. "Tawny-brown, beneath whitish, dusky spots on throat, tail short." This thrush has many habits in common with the wood and hermit thrushes, coming to the mountain the latter part of April, and leaving in October. His notes are singular and striking, monotonous and quaint, but frequently truly musical.

SEIURUS Noveboracensis, (Nutt.) New York thrush.— Rarely seen in Pennsylvania except as a wanderer to more northern or southern regions. This bird is peculiar and interesting in its habits, which are aquatic.

SEIURUS Aurocapillus, (Wilson.) Golden-crowned thrush, or oven bird.—This bird is remarkable for its oven-shaped nest and strange habits.

WARBLERS.

SYLVIA, (Lath.) This genus has many species widely extended. They are small, sprightly birds, perpetually busy in pursuit of the insect prey on which they live. They approach in their habits several other families of birds with which they are really allied. Some of them live almost entirely on berries part of the year, but their general food is insects. Of this genus, Cassin remarks: "Of the smaller birds of North America, no group exceeds that of the warblers, in variety and richness of color. It is, too, one of the largest of the groups of our birds, embracing not less than forty species, besides several which are South American" They are highly musical birds, and are somewhat allied to flycatchers, vireos, thrushes, saxicolas, and wrens. The nightingale and robin red-breast of the Old World belong to this party of vocalists.

SYLVICOLA Coronata, (Wilson.) Yellow-crowned warbler. This species arrives here in the end of April, proceeding north.

SYLVICOLA Œstiva, (Lath.) Summer yellow-bird, or warbler.—This is a handsome bird, ranging from the arctic circles to Florida. It arrives in Pennsylvania in April, and returns south at the end of September.

SYLVICOLA Maculosa, (Lath.) The spotted warbler.—Breeds far north at Hudson's Bay, and is only seen a short time as a traveler.

SYLVICOLA Virens, (Lath.) Black-throated green warbler.—This sylvicola sometimes stays the season on the mountain, but is a rare bird. It comes in April and leaves in October.

SYLVICOLA Blackburniæ. Blackburnian warbler.—A rare species, and only a visitor, on its way to boreal regions. It is a beautiful bird.

SYLVICOLA Icterocephala, (Lath.) Chestnut-sided warbler.—Only seen on the mountain for awhile, on its northern journey. It is said, however, by Nuttall, to rear young in the Northern States.

SYLVICOLA Striata, (Lath.) Black-poll warbler.—Sometimes arrives in the middle of April, remaining but a short time. It extends its migrations to Newfoundland.

MNIOTILTA Varia, (Lath.) Black and white creeper.—Perhaps only rests on its journey, as its nest has not been seen. It is a remarkable and interesting bird.

Sylvicola Pinus, (Lath.) Pine warbler.—Arrives at the mountain early in April; color, bright-yellow, tinged with green beneath, yellow wings, with whitish bands. It is a quick, sprightly little eater of insects, is found in the pine forests, and is musical to a certain extent, withal an interesting bird.

Parula Americana, (Lath.) Parti-colored warbler.—Perhaps only a visitor. It winters at St. Domingo and Porto Rico.

Trichas Agilis, (Wilson.) Connecticut warbler.—Only a visitor.

Trichas Marilandica, (Lath.) Maryland yellow-throat.—Comes to the mountain early in April and nests. It is a sprightly little yellow-olive bird, with black patch about eye and side of head.

Sylvicola Canadensis, (Bon.) Pine-swamp warbler.—Frequents hemlock swamps.

Sylvicola Azurea, (Steph.) Cœrulean warbler.—An occasional visitor.

Helenæa Solitaria, (Wilson.) Blue-winged yellow warbler.—Arrives on the mountain at end of April, retires to Tropical America in autumn; remarkable for its peculiar nest.

The following species of the old genus sylvia are frequently seen on the mountain, namely, Vermivora, Worm-eating Warbler; Wilsonii, Green Black-capped Warbler; Sphagnosa, Swamp Warbler; Philadelphia, or Mourning Warbler; and Parus, or Hemlock Warbler.

REGULUS, CRESTED WRENS.

These are small birds, hardy and active, enduring winter, but migrating as the cold increases. They penetrate the arctic spaces, living on insects, and having the style and action of the titmouse. They inhabit both continents, and are allied to the sylvias.

Regulus Calendulus, (Steph.) Ruby-crowned wren.—A

handsome little bird; only a visitor on his journey to Hudson's Bay and Greenland.

REGULUS Cristatus, (Vieill.) Gold-crested wren.—Comes south early in April on its journey far north. Sometimes seen in winter along the sides of the mountain.

WRENS, TROGLODYTES.

These are small quick-motioned musical birds, hopping and darting about near the ground, through log heaps, brush piles, holes, and crannies, after their prey of spiders, worms, and bugs. They have rapid and agreeable notes, and are general favorites.

TROGLODYTES Fulvus, (Bon.) House wren.—This perpetual-motion, this capricious atom of a bird, is well known to all. It has the general habits of the family, and may be seen darting about with such restless activity that the eye can scarcely follow its motions at all. Log piles, board piles, thick bushes, even stone heaps, he shoots through in every direction, his little saucily-cocked tail always in the same defiant attitude. Notes agreeable; habits and spiritual demonstrations interesting. Comes to the mountain in May, and leaves in October.

TROGLODYTES Bewickii, (Aud.) Bewick's wren.—This comely little bird is found in the Central Alleghany in the summer.

TROGLODYTES Hyemalis, (Vieill.) Common, or winter wren.—This wren sometimes winters on the Alleghany, and, as Audubon has remarked, breeds in the pine forests. It is a sprightly little bird, with an agreeable warble.

TROGLODYTES Palustris, (Bon.) Marsh wren.—This species is found about sedgy and willowy marsh spots. It comes in April, and leaves the last of September.

TROGLODYTES Ludovicianus, (Bon.) Great Carolina, or mocking wren.—This is the most illustrious of the wrens. A musician, a mimic, a busy, courageous worker, he is a special favorite of all bird lovers. His powers are wonderful beyond description, and there seems to be no end to the fanciful stories about him. He is an occasional visitor.

SIALIA Wilsonii, (Swain.) Blue-bird.—This universal favorite is continent wide in its range. He is a hardy bird, breeding from Labrador to Mexico. A constant friend of man, his presence is always hailed with delight, as he brings with him thoughts of the summer, butterflies, and flowers, and all the bright, vernal visions of country life. A beautiful, gentle creature, everybody loves the blue-bird.

ANTHUS Spinoletta, (Bon.) Brown lark.—This is a bird of passage in Pennsylvania, and rarely seen on the mountain.

EMBERIZA Nivalis, (Linn.) The Snow-bunting is a bird of high arctic regions, and sometimes in his southern winter-rovings visits the mountain.

EMBERIZA Americana, (Wilson.) Black-throated bunting.—This bunting sometimes comes to the mountain in May, leaving for Mexico in September.

PYRANGA Rubra, (Linn.) Scarlet tanager.—This brilliant blood-red bird, with black wings, frequently startles the explorer of the mountain forests with the vivid flash of his crimson plumage. He passes his winters in Tropical America, coming to Pennsylvania the first part of May, and retiring south the first of September. A gaudy and distinguished bird, he looks like a tropical product. His biographers endow him with the rare and transcendent elements of tenderness in love, and fidelity in affection.

FINCHES.

This is a numerous family. They live on seeds and grain; sometimes on insects. Many of the species are musical and easily domesticated.

SPIZA Cyanea, (Wilson.) The Indigo-bird is a small but bright and beautiful species. He passes his winters in Tropical America, and visits the mountain in the middle of May, retiring in September. He is a regular charm, styled by the venerable Nuttall, "the azure celestial musician." As his name indicates, he is a fine blue color, with greenish tinges.

ZONOTRICHIA Pennsylvanica, (Lath.) White-throated sparrow.—This is a large and handsome sparrow, whose natal region is the north. He visits the Alleghany in the winter months, going sometimes a little farther south in very inclement weather.

PASSERELLA Graminea, (Gm.) Grass finch.—This is a plain gray and brownish bird, a regular inhabitant of the mountain. It is very common around orchards and fields.

ZONOTRICHIA Melodia, (Wilson.) The song sparrow.—The song sparrow is common, familiar, and generally numerous. It arrives with the blue-bird in March, and is soon heard piping his agreeable but somewhat peculiar strain. He leaves late in the season, only retiring when compelled by the storms of winter.

PASSERCULUS Savanna, (Wilson.) Savanna sparrow.—This is not so abundant as the melodia. It has some pleasant notes, and the general habits of the sparrows. Times of migration, April and November.

JUNCO Nivalis, (Linn.) Common snow-bird.—This species is said to be common to both continents. It is a very hardy bird, braving the coldest Alleghany storms, large flocks appearing, with vivacious movements, in the midst of roaring winds and drifting snows. Large numbers nest and permanently occupy the mountain.

SPIZELLA Canadensis, (Lath.) The tree sparrow is a winter bird, his natal home being in the region of Hudson's Bay. He comes to the mountain with the snow-bird, retiring to his far northern summer range early in the spring.

SPIZELLA Socialis, (Wilson.) Chipping sparrow.—This plain little bird is almost domestic, certainly social, as his name indicates. It is a great pet with children, who feed it on door-sills and porches. Wide geographic range.

SPIZELLA Juncorum, (Nutt.) Field, or rush sparrow, is a small species like the chipping sparrow, but is wild and shy. It comes to the mountain in April, and leaves in October.

CHRYSOMITRIS Tristis, (Linn., Wilson.) Yellow-bird, or American goldfinch. — The goldfinch inhabits the whole United States, and goes as far north as the forty-ninth parallel. It is common, and generally gregarious, being frequently found in migrating crowds of other sparrows. Its habits are rather peculiar, being a vagrant and wanderer, with erratic movements.

PIPILO Erythrophthalma, (Linn.) The ground-robin, or Tow-wee finch, inhabits wild, dry, vacant spaces, especially barren tracts covered by bushes. He stays near the ground, hopping around, and scratching among the leaves, uttering all the time his monotonous notes, "tow-ee, tow-ee," or, as frequently pronounced, "che-wink, che-wink."

CARDINALIS Virginianus, (Bon.) This is the cardinal grosbeak, or red-bird, a royal prince of the finch family. His splendid form is sometimes seen, and his loud whistle heard for a time in the mountain woods. His general range is from New York to Florida, having a taste rather for the south. His visits to the mountain are short, although he remains nearly the entire year in the eastern and southern part of Pennsylvania.

AMMODROMUS Palustris, (Lath.) Swamp sparrow.—This bird, as its name indicates, is somewhat aquatic in its habits, living among reeds, rushes, and water-grasses. Not common on the mountain.

CHRYSOMITRIS Pinus, (Wilson.) Pine finch.—This is a northern species, visiting the mountain late in autumn, and retiring north early in spring.

PASSERELLA Iliaca, (Mer.) Ferruginous finch.—This is a handsome finch, larger than most of his brethren, and breeding in the north. He is a cold-weather visitor of the mountain.

GUIRACA Ludoviciana, (Bon.) Rose-breasted grosbeak. This is a large and beautiful finch, one of our noblest-looking birds, and a fine songster. He is a frequent visitor of the mountain, and may breed in the wilder parts, although Nuttall says " it is rare and accidental in the Atlantic States." He goes as far north as forty-nine degrees.

CARPODACUS Purpureus, (Gm.) Purple finch, or American linnet.—This bright and sprightly singer is found in the evergreen woods of the mountain, coming in April and leaving for the south in September.

CORYTHUS Enucleator, (Tem.) Bullfinch.—This is a hardy species, dwelling in the arctic regions, and only coming as far south as the mountains of Pennsylvania in the most inclement seasons. It is a fine bird, and is found on "northwest coast of North America, Lapland, Russia, Siberia, and Scottish Highlands."

CROSS-BILLS.

The cross-bills are northern birds, and have many habits of the bullfinches and grosbeaks. They frequent the forests of pines and firs, feeding on the seeds of those trees, and other trees and shrubs.

LOXIA Americana, common cross-bill.—This bird is found from Pennsylvania to Greenland, but inhabits and breeds generally in the arctic regions. It visits the pine woods of the Alleghany from September to April.

LOXIA Leucoptera, white-winged cross-bill.—This is a beautiful bird; habits same as Americana. Nuttall suggests that it may breed on the mountains of Pennsylvania.

CUCKOOS.

COCCYZUS Americanus, (Bon.) Yellow-billed cuckoo, or the rain-crow.—The American cuckoo comes to the mountain in April, leaving for Louisiana and Mexico in September. His strange notes may be heard often from the shady recesses and secluded thickets in which he delights to secrete himself. This bird is remarkable for certain peculiar parasitic habits. It is a constant resident in

Southern States, but has a geographic range from Mexico to Labrador and Columbia River.

Coccyzus Erythrophthalmus, (Wilson.) Black-billed cuckoo.—This species is closely related to the yellow-billed. It is permanent in the Southern States, having, however, a range from Texas to Labrador. It comes to the Alleghany in May and leaves in September.

WOODPECKERS.

Picus, (Linn.) This is a family of regular climbers, composed of shy, rough, unmusical birds, living on the larvæ of insects, which they obtain from decayed bark and wood, also eating berries, etc. Some of them are peculiar birds, all are useful as destroyers of noxious worms and insects.

Colaptes Auratus, (Linn., Wil.) Flicker, or golden-winged woodpecker.—This is a handsome and common species, found all over the continent, from 25° to 63° north latitude. It comes to the mountain in April and leaves in October. According to Dekay, "it sometimes remains in New York all the year." It is a useful bird, with very unsavory flesh, which fact leaves the fowler without excuse for the common practice of shooting it as a game bird.

Picus Pileatus, (Linn., Wil.) Pileated woodpecker, or log-cock.—This is the largest and most imposing of the woodpeckers that visit the mountain. Dekay gives him a range from Texas to the sixty-third parallel. He remains all the year in the United States, and although said to be an annual resident of Pennsylvania, and really a common bird in the hidden forests of the mountain, he is not often visible in the winter. This is the large, well-known black woodpecker, with red crest and mustache.

Melanerpes Erythrocephalus, (Linn., Wil.) Red-headed woodpecker.—The commonest of his tribe, he is found every place, from Mexico to the fiftieth parallel; arriving on the mountain in May, and departing in September. He is so familiar and common that we have forgotten, or ceased to remark, that he is really a beautiful and interesting bird.

Picus Carolinensis, (Linn., Wil.) The red-bellied woodpecker is a fine, handsome bird. Range, Florida to Canada, and the Island of Jamaica, in all which regions it breeds, making partial migrations from the colder parts. It is a wild, roving species, living in the solitudes of the woods. It is a constant resident from Texas to South Carolina. Visible on the mountain from May until November, and occasionally seen in the winter.

Picus Varius, (Wilson.) Yellow-bellied woodpecker.—This is a continental species, ranging from Mexico to sixty-first parallel, and a permanent resident from Maryland, south. Lives like the rest, on worms, insects, and berries, and is a frequent bird on the mountain.

Picus Villosus, (Wilson.) Hairy woodpecker.—Range of this species, from Texas to sixty-third parallel, and said, by Dekay, to remain all the year in New York. It is comon the mountain, and may be seen pursuing his prey in snows and the storms of winter. These last two birds, with the following, are called on the mountain "Spotted Flickers."

Picus Pubescens, (Wilson.) Downy woodpecker.—This is the smallest species, called also the sap-sucker; range, Texas to 58° north latitude; said, by Dekay, to remain in New York all the year. May be seen in coldest weather on the mountain, busy in pursuit of food. Nests in May.

The Three-toed Woodpecker (Picus tridactylus) was seen by Audubon on the Pokono Mountain, Pennsylvania. It has not been seen on the Central Alleghanies.

TENUIROSTRES, (Slender-billed Birds.)

This order is related to many of the woodpeckers or climbing zygodactili.

NUT-HATCHES.

Sitta Carolinensis, (Briss.) White-breasted American nut-hatch.—This is a common little bird, seen creeping around the trees in all directions after insects and worms.

He is a permanent resident from Hudson's Bay to Mexico. In the winter, hunger drives him from the woods into the neighborhood of barns and houses.

SITTA Canadensis, (Linn., Wil.) The red-bellied nut-hatch comes to the mountain in April, returning south in October. It is a smaller bird than the white-breasted nut-hatch, and seems to be wild and shy, preferring the recesses of pine woods as a residence.

CREEPERS.

CERTHIA Americana, (Linn., Wil.) The brown creeper is related to the nut-hatchers, is a climber, nests in holes in trees, and feeds on insects. It is a rare bird on the mountain as elsewhere. He makes extensive wanderings, like the nut-hatch, in search of food.

HUMMING-BIRDS.
(Family Anthomyzi, Vieill, Bon.)

TROCHILUS Colubris, (Linn.) Ruby-throated humming-bird.—This is the only individual of the genus which comes north. It is an exclusively American family, and very extensive in numbers, there being some three hundred species within the tropics. Nature seems to have sported an infinite extravagance, and almost exhausted the element of variety, in this group of birds. Every shape, style, tint, and line, every conceivable form of dress and ornament, is found in this exquisite family of brilliant eaters of nectar. The ruby-throated humming-bird is the plainest of the genus, although he is considered a beautiful little bird. It comes to the mountain in May, leaving in September, breeding there in numbers.

KING-FISHERS.
HALCYON, (Alcyones, Tem.)

CERYLE Halcyon, (Linn., Wil.) Belted king-fisher.—This strange, eccentric-looking bird, a regular angler, comes to the mountain in April, departing in October. His range is the borders of fresh-water streams, from Hudson's Bay to the tropics. His style of capturing his finny prey is an interesting process, being altogether an exciting feat.

SWALLOW TRIBE.
(Chelidones, Vieill.)

Hirundo Purpurea, (L. Wilson.) Purple martin.—The purple martin arrives about the middle of April, leaving in September. This beautiful and agile eater of insects is a great favorite, having almost domestic habits, and being associated in the thoughts and affections of men with the promises of spring and the enjoyments of summer.

Hirundo Rufa, (Gm.) The barn swallow is a common species, arriving in numbers in the early part of April, leaving the first part of September. Range, from latitude 50° to tropics. They are skimmers of the wind, taking their food on the wing, the air being their proper medium of existence, as of the whole family.

Hirundo Lunifrons, (Vieill.) Cliff swallow.—This species, formerly a Western bird, now extends his migrations over the Atlantic and Middle States. His peculiar jug-like nest is common on houses and barns on the Alleghany. He comes with the other swallows and leaves with them; habits the same.

Hirundo Bicolor, (Vieill.) White-bellied swallow.—This is an extensive traveler, continuing his journeys from the tropics to latitude 53°. Comes to the mountain about the middle of April. It lives about houses, and is a familiar species.

Cotyle Riparia, (Linn., Wil.) The sand martin is not a common species on the mountain. It is found, however, along the streams on both sides. Comes in April and leaves in October.

SWIFTS.

(Cypselus, Illig.)

CYPSELUS Pelasgius, (Tem.) Chimney swallow.—This bird comes in April, leaving in August. It is a common species, breeding in chimneys and hollow trees. They are seen in large numbers in the evening, whirling and circling through the air in pursuit of their prey, which consists of winged insects.

NIGHT-HAWKS.

ANTROSTOMUS Vociferus, (Wilson.) Whip-poor-will.— The melancholy and peculiar voice of this bird of the night may be heard in all the wilder parts of the mountain. He comes in April and leaves in September, passing his winters in Tropical America. They are said to migrate as far north as 49°.

CHORDEILES Virginianus, (Briss.) Night-hawk, or night-jar. Americanus, (Wilson.)—This bird comes north in April, leaving the mountain in August. They breed from the Southern States to Hudson's Bay. Numbers may be seen floating around through the air, the spots of white on their wings being visible at a great height, and the whirring sound of their large, open, bristly mouths being heard at a great distance, as they dart after their prey of winged insects.

PIGEON TRIBE.

(Columbini, Illiger.)

ECTOPISTES Carolinensis, (Linn., Wilson.) Turtle-dove, (Carolina pigeon.)—The dove is a constant resident south of Pennsylvania, and remains on the mountain from April until October. It has a range from Mexico to Massachusetts, and along the Pacific to Columbia River. It is a sweet, gentle bird, beloved by all.

ECTOPISTES Migratoria, (Linn., Wilson.) Passenger

pigeon.—Vast flocks of this pigeon stop on the mountain spring and fall. They are said to breed, from latitude 32° to 51°, around Hudson's Bay. Their range is the continent, from latitude 25° to 62°. Stragglers remain on the mountain through the summer season, but do not breed there. The supply of food seems to determine the movement of the myriads of these birds, which sometimes stream through the air, and not the ordinary migrating instinct which impels other birds to travel.*

COLUMBIA Livia.—This is the common domestic pigeon, an introduced species.

GALLINACEOUS BIRDS.

(Gallinæ, Linn., etc.)

MELEAGRIS Gallopavo, (Linn., Bon.) Wild turkey.—This bird is rarely seen on the Alleghany, although abundant on the parallel chains of the Appalachian range. Its geographic distribution extends from Mexico to Canada. It is not migratory in its habits, only making foraging expeditions in search of food. This magnificent bird is peculiar to North America. Of the turkey tribe, Cassin remarks: " Of the turkeys, two species are known, the most numerous of which is the wild turkey of North America. The other, even more handsome in its plumage than the former, has as yet only been found in Central America, and is known as the Honduras Turkey. It is by no means well established that the Domestic Turkey is descended from the wild species of North America. Its origin probably has not yet been discovered."†

---

* "Birds essentially tropical are known to migrate to different distances on either side of the equator, so essentially necessary is this wandering habit to almost all the feathered tribe."—Nutt.

† "Since the above was written, the distinguished English ornithologist, Mr. Gould, has introduced to the notice of naturalists what he considers a third species, under the name of Meleagris Mexicana, and which he regards as the parent stock of the domesticated turkey.

Of other gallinaceous birds, we have,—

PAVO Cristatus, (Linn.) Peacock.—This is an introduced bird, and belongs originally to India.

NUMIDA Meleagris, (Linn.) Guinea fowl.—This is an African species, long introduced.

GALLUS Domesticus, (Briss.) Common cock.—The original stock of this bird is supposed to be from Java.

PARTRIDGES.

(Perdix, Lath.)

ORTYX Virginiana, (Aud.) American partridge, or quail. The partridge is not abundant on the Alleghany. Having greater fondness for fields than forests, he does not find in that range an attractive residence. Geographic range, from Honduras to Massachusetts.

GROUSE.

(Tetrao, Linn.)

TETRAO Umbellus, (Linn., Wilson) Ruffed grouse.—The pheasant, as this grouse is called in Pennsylvania, is abundant on the Alleghany, where it breeds, and is found at all seasons. It has a wide range, from Mexico to the fifty-sixth parallel, and across the continent to the Pacific.

TETRAO Cupido, (Wilson.) Pinnated grouse.—Of this species, Dekay remarks: "It is still found in a few districts of the State, (New York,) in a few islands on the coast of Massachusetts, and in the mountainous regions of Pennsylvania." Said by Wilson to be found, in his day, on Pocono Pine Hills, Northampton County, Pennsylvania. It has not been seen on the Alleghany recently, although its range is said to be from Texas to Maine.

It differs, however, from the turkey of North America only in a few slight and apparently hardly sufficient characters for a distinct species, but may be, as supposed by Mr. Gould, the parent stock."—*Note from Cassin.*

WATER BIRDS.

It has been already stated that but few water birds either visit or reside on the mountain. The reason of this is obvious, as the medium in which the aquatic species are constituted to exist is, to a great extent, wanting there. In the valleys east and west, through which the streams pass and their waters accumulate in pools, there are a number of birds of this division.

Grallatores, (Tem.) Wading birds.—These are birds with long, extremely thin legs, stilting them up in an extravagant and ridiculous manner from ludicrous disproportions in length and extreme tenuity; bills cunningly-devised and of mechanical structure fitted to capture their prey, and spiritual endowments relating them harmoniously to their habitats.

Charadrius Vociferus, (Linn.) Kill-deer plover.—This is a noisy well-known bird, found every place between the twentieth and fifty-ninth parallels, breeding from Texas to Massachusetts, and extending his range as far west as the Rocky Mountains. He has nocturnal habits, feeding at twilight, and flying around on moonlight nights making great noise with his usual cry of kill-deer.

Charadrius Helveticus. Black-bellied, or Swiss plover. This plover breeds in Pennsylvania, but is not often seen on the Alleghany. Its geographic range is nearly the extent of the continent. It is seen on the eastern and western sides of the mountain in the cleared portions, and in neighborhood of the streams. It breeds, according to Nuttall, "from Pennsylvania to the very extremity of the arctic regions."

CHARADRIUS Semipalmatus, (Bon.) The semipalmated ring plover breeds far north, being seen often in the icy regions of Greenland. It is a small species, but much esteemed as game, being well flavored, and generally fat. It passes along the mountain in April north, returning south in September.

HERONS.

ARDEA Herodius, (Linn.) Great blue heron.—The great heron is occasionally seen on the mountain, but is rare. It is a traveler, and only seems to alight in the swampy spots and around the mill-dams for temporary repose or food. It is a large bird, being four feet six inches in length, and is quite an imposing form, either on the wing or wading in the swamps, and are voracious and stupid, feeding on reptiles and fish.

ARDEA Virescens, (Linn.) Green bittern.—This is the most common species in the United States. It comes to Pennsylvania early in April and leaves in October. Range, from Canada to the Gulf of Mexico, visiting Hayti and Jamaica. It is an abundant species on the mountain along all the streams and marshy places.

SANDPIPERS.

(Tringa, Briss.)

These are wandering and gregarious birds, frequenting marshes, rivers, lakes, and living on larvæ, worms, insects, small shell-fish, etc. They migrate in mixed crowds, breed generally in the north, are wild in their habits, and found in every part of the world.

TRINGA Alpina, (Linn.) Dunlin, red-backed sandpiper.— The Dunlin has a wide range, even the northern hemisphere. It penetrates the arctic circle, and breeds, according to the ornithologists, "on the wintry shores of Melville Peninsula." It is thus a regular hyperborean, only stopping rarely on the mountain in May and October, on its journeys from Greenland to Cayenne.

TRINGA Wilsonii, (Nutt.) Wilson's sandpiper. — The little "Peeps" is a northern bird, its breeding resorts being within the arctic circle. It passes through the State of Pennsylvania, north and south, in May and October, to and from its natal region. It is a well-known sandpiper, but its visits to the mountain are extremely brief, unless from stragglers who have become loafers.

TRINGA Solitaria.—The green swamp tatler comes to the Alleghany early in May, retiring in September. According to Nuttall, "it breeds in the marshy solitudes of the mountains of Virginia, Kentucky, and Pennsylvania, but a great part of the species proceeds to boreal regions, even as far as the extremity of the continent."

TRINGA Semipalmata. Semipalmated sandpiper.—This species is spread over the continent from the arctic circle to the southern extremity and West Indies. It is recognized by its familiar notes of "to-weet, to-weet." It is found along the streams in the valleys at base of mountain.

TOTANUS.—This genus is close to the snipe, god-wit, tringa, some of the species having high northern range, even to the $69\frac{1}{2}°$ of parallel.

TOTANUS Semipalmatus, (Tem.) Willet. — This is a large snipe, and said to inhabit "almost every part of the United States, from the coast of Florida to the distant shores and saline lakes in the vicinity of the Saskatchewan, up to the fifty-sixth parallel." It may breed on the mountain, but is rare.

TOTANUS Flavipes, (Vieill, Bon.) Yellow-shanks tatler. This is said to be "the most common bird of the family in America, its summer residence, or breeding station, extending from the Middle States to the northern extremity of the continent." It rarely appears on the mountain, notwithstanding this statement. This is no doubt accounted for from its preferring the rivers, marshes, and lakes near the ocean. It has been seen in small migratory flocks of upland plovers and peets.

Totanus Macularius, (Tem.) Spotted tatler, or peet-weet.—This is the most common and familiar species of the genus. In the middle of April it is found on all the shores of the rivers of Pennsylvania, leaving in October. It breeds in the "Middle States and to the confines of the St. Lawrence," and does not penetrate remote frigid regions. It wanders from the sea into the remotest interior, however. It is well known by the peculiar balancing of its body and tilting of its tail, and its notes of "weet, weet, weet."

Totanus Bartramius, (Linn.) Bartram's tatler. It is called also upland plover, and "breeds from Pennsylvania to the fur countries of Upper Canada." It is not abundant on the mountain, although common in other places. It comes in May and goes in September.

Scolopax Wilsonii.—The range of this snipe is from Hudson's Bay to Cayenne, numbers wintering in the Southern States. It comes north in March and lingers until December. As a game bird it has exquisite flavor, and is in great demand among sportsmen. It has nocturnal habits, is shy, wary, and not easily taken. Food, like others of this order of birds, worms, insects, larvæ, which are obtained by boring in the mud with its long bill. This is the bird which is supposed by some ornithologists to make a strange and peculiar sound, sometimes heard late in the evening in the regions it frequents. This noise is variously represented by those who attempt to describe it, as a "whistling," "flickering," "singular, tremulous murmuring," "humming, somewhat wailing," "whirring, quailing" sound, and is produced by the bird as it mounts in gyratory ascent through the air in the approaching shades of the evening twilight. It is generally invisible when making the sound, which is supposed to be produced by the wings, also by an "undulatory motion of air in the throat," etc. From the circumstance that the bird is generally invisible when the sound is made, it has been enveloped in mystery, even mixed with superstition. It is heard frequently on the mountain, although the bird is not abundant here, and is said to be made only during the pairing season. It is generally found in pairs or small parties, and is nearly allied to the European snipe.

RUSTICOLA Minor, (Nutt.) American woodcock.—The lesser woodcock is confined to the south side of the St. Lawrence, breeding in the Middle States, which it leaves in the winter, although it is said to winter sometimes in Pennsylvania, where it arrives in March. It closely resembles the European woodcock, and has also, like Wilson's snipe, nocturnal habits, and is much esteemed as a game bird, its flesh possessing extreme delicacy, and the finest flavor. It is said, by some of the ornithologists, to possess notes that are musical, and has the same habit as Wilson's snipe during incubation, of mounting up in a spiral whirl through the air, and making the whistling or whirring noise generally attributed to Wilson's snipe. Do *both birds* produce this sound? The woodcock most certainly does. It is not abundant on the mountain.

PINNATIPEDES.

(Lobe-footed Birds.)

FULICA Americana, (Lath.) Coot.—The American coot is said to "dwell and breed in every part of the North American continent, over a range of probably more than fifty degrees of latitude." It is occasionally seen on the mountain as a traveler in spring and fall, but does not remain there during the summer.

GREBES.

(Podiceps, Lath.)

PODICEPS Cornutus, (Lath.) The Dobchick, or dipper, like the rest of his family, is a far northern bird, breeding in the regions about Hudson's Bay. This grebe is sometimes found resting for a time in the mill-dams and streams of the mountain in its journeys north and south. Common in Europe and Asia.

PODICEPS Carolinensis, (Lath.) Pied-bill dobchick.—This is an American species exclusively. It is said to be the "commonest species in the United States." It is only seen here on its journeys north and south, to and from its breeding region in the far north.

PODICEPS Minor, (Lath.) Little grebe, or dobchick.—This is the smallest of the grebes, and said to be "common to the colder parts of both continents, having been seen around Hudson's Bay, though hitherto unknown even as a visitor within the limits of the United States." This is certainly a mistake, as stragglers have been seen on the Alleghany, and captured in ponds.

GEESE.

(Anser, Briss.)

ANSER Canadensis, (Vieill.) Canada goose.—This goose is a bird of passage only in the United States. It breeds between 50° and 67° north latitude. The breeding range of this goose is said to extend through thirty degrees. The great rallying regions of the north are the shores of Hudson's Bay. It sometimes alights on the ponds and dams of the mountain in its vernal and autumnal flights.

ANSER Cinereus, (Meyer.) This is the common or domestic goose, introduced from Europe.

SWAN.

CYGNUS Americanus.—The Swan visits the arctic regions for the purpose of executing the great function of reproduction, in "the short but brilliant summers which there prevail," passing over Pennsylvania early in spring and late in the fall, on its return south. It sometimes rests on ponds and streams for a short time on its journeys.

DUCKS.

(Anas, Linn.)

ANAS Boschas, (Rich.) Common duck, or mallard.—This duck, the original of the domestic species, has a range from the Gulf of Mexico to the sixty-eighth parallel, and is said to breed as far south as Pennsylvania. It is found also in many parts of Europe.

ANAS Discors, (Linn.) Blue-winged teal.—This duck passes the mountains of Pennsylvania in April, northward bound, returning south late in September. Range, from Guiana and West Indies to fifty-eighth parallel. These observations will also apply to the Buffel head.

ANAS Sponsa, (Linn.) The Bride, or summer duck.—A species peculiar to America, and a constant resident in the United States. Range, 45° north latitude to Mexico and Antilles. This is the most beautiful of the ducks; indeed, few of the whole feathered tribe are so elaborately and exquisitely ornamented as this bird.

COLYMBUS Glacialis, (Linn.) Loon.—This large water bird has also a northern range. It stops on the mountain in its migrations, and sometimes remains for several days, slily slipping around the mill-dams and ponds. It is a handsome bird, and has a voice which is one of the most remarkable sounds in nature.

CLASS III.—REPTILIA.

Order I.—Testudinata, (Turtles.)

The order of Chelonian reptiles has been a troublesome chapter in the herpetology of North America. An elaborated synonymy of genera and species, with a history of the same in this, and many other departments of natural science, would be literary and scientific curiosities.

Is the magnificent monograph of Louis Agassiz the ardently hoped for finality on this subject, and is the student of the testudinata henceforward to have cleared fields, and beaten paths, and to forget immediately agonizing columns of effete synonyms, monuments of the struggles of ambitious hunters of new species, and rejoice over the absolute fixation forever of generic and specific forms? As the learned professor has brought the old "order into doubt," it is but reasonable to expect, that after a profound and laborious exploration of the whole ground, with an innumerable menagerie of living turtles, already drilled and catalogued by an illustrious group of scientific predecessors, together with the assistance of the whole contemporary lay or uncanonical world, he shall surely arrange it that "chaos shall never come again."

The classification of the "Contributions" will no doubt be safe for cataloguing the few chelonians of the mountain for the present.

The Alleghany in Pennsylvania is embraced within Agassiz's northeastern division of the chelonian faunæ of North America. This extends northeast beyond the forty-fifth isotherm, west to Lake Erie, and south to North Carolina, being protracted "along the Alleghanies even as far south as Georgia." According to Agassiz, the boundary of this turtle fauna is the range of the Chrysemys picta, and the characteristic genera are Nanemys, Glyptemys, Calemys, Ptychemys, Cistudo, Chelydra, Ozotheca, Thyrosternum, Malacoclemmys, Emys, and Graptemys, rare, also Aspidonectes. Several families of testudinata are found on the mountain, some on the mountain proper, others in the streams cutting through the range and flowing from it. These are the Tryonychidæ, Chelydroidæ, Cinosternoidæ, Emydoideæ.

TRYONYCHIDÆ.

This family is aquatic in its habits, and called soft-shell fresh-water turtles. They inhabit muddy-bottomed streams, and not much is known of their habits. They live upon shell-fish, the larvæ of insects, and other substances which they find in the mud. In mill-dams and stagnant pools their sharp-pointed snouts may be seen above the surface of the water, mere dots, the animal being suspended below. These turtles are found rarely on the eastern side of the mountain, but are regular inhabitants of the slow, tortuous, and sluggish streams which descend from the broken plateau of the western side of the range. According to Holbrook, "the flesh of some of these turtles is the most delicate food, surpassing that even of the green turtle." Agassiz enumerates two genera of Tryonichidæ that are found in the waters of Western Pennsylvania.*

---

* "The soft-shelled tortoise was not generally known as an inhabitant of New York until after the completion of the Erie Canal, connecting the great lakes with the ocean. Previous to that period, it was *supposed* to belong exclusively to *Southern* and *Western* waters. The description given above was taken, several years since, from a specimen obtained in the Mohawk River. Subsequently, several individuals, as I understand, have been taken from the Hudson River, near Albany."—DEKAY, *New York Fauna*.

According to Holbrook, "it abounds in the great chain of Northern lakes, both above and below Niagara Falls, and is common in the Mohawk, a tributary of the Hudson River, but is not found in any other Atlantic streams for a distance of nearly eight hundred miles."

The first, AMYDA Mutica, (Fitz.,) was obtained by Baird from the Alleghany River.

ASPIDONECTES Spinifer, is the other soft-shelled turtle, which is said to be "common in the western part of New York and Pennsylvania."

These turtles are not abundant high up the mountain streams, but in the Ohio Tributaries of Western Pennsylvania, where there are large dams and pools, they abound, and are sometimes of larger size than represented by Agassiz.

Family CHELYDROIDÆ.

CHELYDRA Serpentina, (Schw.) The Snapping-turtle follows the streams of the mountain to a great height. In saw-mill dams, even on small runs, he grows to his largest dimensions. These large individuals are very old, as, according to Agassiz, "specimens, 12 inches long by $9\frac{1}{4}$ wide, are thirty-eight years old, and a specimen, marked forty-five years old, only increased an inch in that time." High up in the range they are frequently much larger than this, and, consequently, must be patriarchs of the race whose longevity no doubt has been insured by the salubrity of their alpine home. They are hideous in their form, savage in their habits, like other carnivorous animals, and from the ferocity of their style of defence, mode of attacking their prey, their ugly heads, with powerful jaws like the edges of a sharp-cutting vice, protruding from the shield of a rough, rocky shell, and accompanied by a long spinous tail like that of the alligator, they present an appearance to the last degree revolting.* They feed upon fish and water-rats, young ducks and geese, attacking even full-grown ducks

"This originally *Western species* passed from St. Peter's River through Red River to Lake Winnipeg, giving a passage for the Trionyx feror to Lake of the Woods; also, the Upper Illinois communicates with the waters of Lake Michigan, and thus reaches the chain of lakes that open into the St. Lawrence River."

* The fights of these reptiles are fierce and deadly, often protracted for hours.

and geese. Instances are known of their seizing upon the noses of mules and horses that stooped to drink where they were concealed watching for their prey. They are extremely tenacious of life, and are endowed with such intense organic or vegetative vitality that the heart, dissected from the body and laid upon a plate, will pulsate for a day and a half, and the decapitated head will bite for several hours after being separated entirely from the body. This reptile is eaten, and considered a delicacy. Its range is the eastern side of the continent from Maine to Florida and Louisiana, and west to the Missouri River.

Family CINOSTERNOIDÆ.

This is an exclusively aquatic family. They are small turtles, according to Agassiz, "the average size of the representatives of this family being smaller than in any other family of the testudinata." They are fierce and wild, living upon animal food. Two genera are found on the mountain.

Sub-Family of OZOTHECOIDÆ.

OZOTHECA Odorata, (Ag.) Range, from New England to South Carolina, Georgia, West Florida, Missouri, and Louisiana. Occurs on the mountain.

Sub-Family of CINOSTERNOIDÆ.

THYROSTERNUM Pennsylvanicum, (Ag.) This species "occurs from Pennsylvania to Florida, and westward to Mississippi Valley." Sometimes seen at base of mountain.

Family EMYDOIDÆ.

This is an extensive family, including, according to Agassiz, "sixty well-known species, and presenting the broadest ranges of differences in habits, size, and structure." This varied organization gives a wide habitat. Most of them live in or near water in pools or marshes, or on the edges of streams, being part of the time in the water and part on land. One genus is exclusively terrestrial in its habits. The size of the different species of this group varies from fifteen to four inches in length, the largest species being aquatic. In this family the "terrapenes," so much esteemed as articles of food and luxury, are embraced. Inoffensive and harmless, they do not capture their prey, and only show combative elements when attacked. They live on animal and vegetable food, the terrestrial species feeding on vegetables alone. "They lay their eggs upon dry land like all other turtles, the terrestrial laying the fewest eggs."

PTYCHEMYS Rugosus. Found at eastern base of mountain.

Sub-Family of NECTEMYDOIDÆ.

GRAPTEMYS Geographica, (Ag.) Not common on the mountain, but is found along its eastern base, and is said to be "common from Pennsylvania and New York to Michigan, Tennessee, and Arkansas."

CHRYSEMYS Picta, (Gray.) This is the old Emys picta, painted terrapene. It is described as a common species in every part of the geographic fauna of which its range is the limit. It is not common on the Alleghany, but very abundant near it. It is a beautiful turtle, and generally attracts attention by its ornamental box.

Sub-Family of CLEMMYDOIDÆ.

NANEMYS Guttata, (Ag.) This species is represented to occur in New England, New York, Pennsylvania, and North Carolina. Not abundant on the Alleghany.

CALEMYS Muhlenbergii. Muhlenberg's terrapene is said to be "entirely limited to New Jersey and the eastern part of Pennsylvania." (?)

Sub-Family of CISTUDININÆ.

CISTUDO Virginea. North American box-turtle.—This species of box-turtle is found on the highest parts of the mountain, and is as common on the lower part of the range as elsewhere. "Range, New England, west to Michigan, south to Carolinas."*

Order II.—Sauria. Family Agamidæ.

Tropidolepis Undulatus.—The brown swift is the only representative of this order on the mountain.† It is a grayish-brown lizard, beneath greenish and white; from five to eight inches long, and has the power to change its color. It lives on insects, frequenting pine woods; called sometimes pine lizard, and brown scorpion. It is quick in its motions, moving with incredible celerity, and is an ugly creature, but not venomous. Range, from Gulf of Mexico to 43° north latitude.

Order III.—Ophidia, (Serpents.)

The Ophidian, or snake tribe, have a number of genera and species on the mountain. In Baird and Girard's catalogue of well-ascertained North American serpents in the Smithsonian Institution, thirteen genera and eighteen species are recorded as belonging to Pennsylvania. Many of

---

* Agassiz states that a map showing the geographical distribution of North American turtles would exhibit "the whole table-land between the Sierra Nevada of California and the Rocky Mountains, as well as the eastern slope of the latter, down to the great American desert, without a single species of turtle over this extensive tract." He continues: "It would be a mistake, however, to infer, from this fact, that these animals are excluded from mountainous regions. In the range of the Alleghanies there are many species which ascend to the height of several thousand feet, and among those that reach the greatest height are Cistudo Virginea, Chelydra serpentina, and a species of Aspidonectes, probably Asp. nuchalis, (Com., p. 406;) but I regret that I am unable to give the absolute height with any degree of accuracy."—*Contributions*, vol. i. p. 452.

The great Central Railroad of Pennsylvania perforates the Alleghany 2200 feet above tide-water level. Several species are found above this line on the mountain, as the Snapper, the Virginia Boxturtle, Ozotheca odorata, and Chrysemys picta.

† This is a numerous order of reptiles in the torrid zone, there being found some three hundred species.

these snakes are found either on the Alleghany, or near the eastern and western bases of that mountain within the State.

Family I.—CROTALIDÆ. Serpents "with poison fangs in front, which are erectile, and few teeth in upper jaw. A deep pit between the eye and nostril; tail with a rattle."*

CROTALUS Horridus.†—This is the banded, or common rattlesnake of the mountain. It is exceedingly venomous and malignant, and found of large dimensions on that range. It is somewhat numerous on the highest knobs and ridges, especially on their southern and southeastern slopes. On the northwestern side and northern slopes it is not often seen. It appears to avoid the cool shades and moist places of the deep forests of the western declivity and table-lands, even the dense laurel thickets in which it is so much dreaded. On the summits of the highest knobs and their southern slopes, where the rocks and earth are heated by the sun, and where the huckleberry, blackberry, and grape abound, which attract birds and other small animals, their regular prey, it makes its haunts, and lives to a great age. Length, frequently, more than four feet.

AGKISTRODON Contortix. Copperhead. Tail without a rattle.—This is a poisonous serpent, possessing extremely dangerous habits and qualities. The rattlesnake is a regular fiend, occasionally, perhaps for his own protection, giving a peculiar style‡ of warning on the approach of any animal except its legitimate prey, a caveat which generally secures perfect freedom from all molestation. The copperhead, on the contrary, is silent, combative, and vicious, and where he frequents must be looked

* Baird and Girard.

† Major Le Conte has clearly determined this to be the Crotalus horridus, and not durissus. (Vide Proceedings of the Academy of Natural Sciences, vol. vi., 1852–53, p. 415.)

‡ The sound of his rattle, once sprung between the feet of the huntsman, will be remembered with a thrill of horror for the rest of his life.

for with extreme vigilance, or his death stroke may be the first notice of his presence. But few individuals of this species are found on the mountain, fortunately for its inhabitants. Like the rattlesnake, he obtains possession of his prey by striking it with his erectile poison fangs, waiting until the unfortunate squirrel or bird drops dead, which is generally but a few moments, then slowly swallowing it. The bite of these two serpents is generally fatal, "a complete solution of the blood in the whole body being the immediate cause of death." Length, sometimes attaining to thirty-four inches.

Family II. — COLUBRIDÆ. "Both jaws provided with teeth fully. No anal appendages."*

EUTAINIA Sirtalis, (B. and G.) The striped, or garter snake, is abundant. It preys on toads and frogs, which it seizes and swallows entire. These frogs, when recently swallowed, may be liberated alive by killing and opening the snake soon after the frog has been bolted. When this is done, the frogs generally hop off with as much vivacity as they exhibited before their capture and abdominal imprisonment; no doubt to be ever afterwards delighted by the same order of beautiful reminiscences which entertained Jonah after a like experience. This snake, according to Dekay, is found in the northern part of New York at the height of 2000 feet above the level of the sea. In Pennsylvania it is found on the highest spurs of the Alleghany, near 3000 feet above tide level.

Dekay quotes the EUTAINIA Ordinata as a New York species.

NERODIA Sipedon, (B. and G.) Vernacular "water-snake." As its name indicates, its habits are aquatic. It is an abundant species throughout the State, but not so common on the mountain. Length, generally two feet; preys upon fish and frogs.

REGINA Leberis. (?)

---

* Baird and Girard.

HETERODON Platyrhinos.—This is the snake commonly called "blowing viper." When approached it makes a hissing sound, swells its head, and flattens out its body, and assumes altogether a threatening aspect, but is harmless. Length, two feet.

HETERODON Niger, (Troost.)—This is the "black viper," a snake frequently found on the mountain. It has the same habit of spreading and swelling when approached or attacked, as the blowing viper, making up what it wants in venom by threatening attitudes and ugliness of expression. General length, from two feet to thirty inches. Major Le Conte thinks this a variety of platyrhinos, having seen specimens showing the transition to the black color. It seems to attain to greater dimensions than the light-colored viper assumes.

SCOTOPHIS Alleghaniensis, (B. and G.) COLUBER Alleghaniensis, (Holbr.) This is the common "big black snake" of the mountain, the slim Bascanion being called "racer." On the subject of its common name, Dekay remarks: "It is manifestly the snake which has been frequently described to me of great length and prodigious velocity, and to which they gave the name of 'Racer,' or 'Pilot.' As these names are frequently applied to the black snake, I had supposed that species to have been intended by their description."* In Pennsylvania it does not receive this name, both species being abundant, and generally recognized as different; the Bascanion, from its greater thinness and delicacy of style and more marked celerity of action, being exclusively styled the "Racer."

The "big black snake" grows to a great size, as its common name indicates; sometimes attaining to the length of eight feet, and is strong, quick, and violent in its motions, frequently presenting a truly formidable appearance. It is said to be tamable, and to become familiar and friendly.

OPHIBOLUS Eximius, (B. and G.) COLUBER Eximius,

---

* Fauna of New York.

(Dekay.)—This is the milk, house, and chicken snake. Not abundant high up in the mountain. It frequents out-houses, and is said to drink milk from the farmer's pans in his spring house.

BASCANION Constrictor, (B. and G.) (?) COLUBER Constrictor, (Linn., Syst. Nat.)—This is the black snake, or "racer." It is a very long, thin snake, graceful and comely, but exceedingly wild and unapproachable. It is quick and swift in its motions, gliding over the surface more rapidly than any other snake.

CHLOROSOMA Vernalis, (Wagl., B. and G.) COLUBER Vernalis of Dekay, Holbrook, Storer, etc. Vulgo, green snake. This handsome little snake is common on the Alleghanies. It is a harmless species, and can be handled with impunity.

DIADOPHIS Punctatus, (B. and G.) Ring-necked snake. COLUBER Punctatus of Linn., Gm., Harl., Holb., Stor.— This is rather a common species on the Alleghany. "Body bluish-black above; yellowish-orange beneath; a yellowish-white occipital ring." It is a comely little reptile, harmless and innocent, but, like the rest of his family, continues to suffer from the heel of the great tyrannical "seed of the woman."*

CELUTA Amœna, (B. and G.) COLUBER Amœnus, (Say.) BRACHYORRHOS Amœnus, (Holb.) etc.—"Above, chestnut-brown uniform; opalescent, bright salmon-color beneath." This little creature is positively pretty, (incarnations of evil frequently are!) and has nothing of the repulsive characters of the "snake" about it. It frequently occurs on the Alleghany.

STORERIA Dekayi, (B. and G.)—This species is rare, but is found occasionally at the eastern and western base of the mountain.

---

* The killing of inoffensive, harmless animals, even if they are serpents, is no very noble or exalting business. It seems rather an outlet (popular and right, of course!) to certain old instincts of prejudice and infernalism belonging to the domain of total depravity.

FROGS. 371

STORERIA Occipito-maculata, (B. and G.)—Occurs on the mountain, but is rare.

ORDER IV.—AMPHIBIA.

This is a division of the old class Reptilia adopted by some naturalists.

BATRACHIANS.
(Family Ranina.)

There are several species of frog on the mountain. In the seventh volume of the Proceedings of the Academy of Natural Sciences of Philadelphia, 1855, Major Le Conte has given a corrected catalogue of this genus. In this he asserts the identity of several of Holbrook's different species, and rearranges the group, discarding certain variable characters, ("frogs changing their color at will,") and establishing others that are constant.

RANA Catesbiana, (Linn.)—This is the common bullfrog, or blood-an'-owns. It has an extensive geographic range, the tadpoles, or undeveloped young, being found in almost every stream, and the full-grown frog in numbers in every pool of water of any size. It grows large, and is much esteemed by many as an article of food. This frog-taste is of Gallic origin, and was imported no doubt with some other etherially sublimated nonsense of the race that seems determined to rule the world, not only in ribbons and flummery, but in the department of powder and ball. The sound of the voices of ancient individuals of this species partakes of the sublime, and heard at twilight or night in the deep pools of the gorges of the mountain, constitutes the thorough-bass of nature's thousand-toned orchestra.

RANA Fontinalis.—This is the Horiconensis and Fontinalis of Holbrook, the first of which he confines to Lake George, while he gives to the latter a range common from Maine to Virginia. Major Le Conte says "it inhabits from one end of the country to another." In the streams of the mountain.

Rana Pipiens, (Halicina of Holbrook,) water-frog.—This frog abounds in the streams, ditches, and pools of the mountain. It makes a well-known piping noise, and is one of the harbingers of spring, waking up from his muddy doze, and adding his voice to the concert which announces the vernal resurrection. The accumulated piping of multitudes of this frog is sometimes deafening.

Rana Palustris.—Range, according to Holbrook, "Atlantic States from Maine to Virginia." Found on the mountain.

Rana Conspersa.—Ponds and ditches of the State. This species is common.

Rana Sylvanica. Wood-frog. Harlan's Pennsylvanica. Holbrook gives a range to this frog from New Hampshire to Virginia, Ohio, and Michigan. The wood-frog is found in all the forests of the mountain. It is a beautiful and exceedingly agile species, making long leaps when disturbed, and quickly concealing itself in the leaves and moss.

Bufo Americanus. Common American toad.—This reptile is well known to all, although its habits, which are interesting, are known to few. It first grows like the frog, a tadpole in water, and afterwards assumes terrestrial relationships. It has nocturnal habits, destroying many noxious insects, is harmless and wise, and said to be susceptible of domestication. Its beautiful eyes and style of capturing its insect prey are much admired.* It has a wide geographic range.

Hyla Versicolor, (Le Conte.) Tree-frog.—This is an

---

* The family Ranina feed on flies, worms, and the larvæ of insects, and will only take their prey when *alive*. They hybernate, burying themselves in the mud during winter. On an occasion, in midwinter, a bushel of torpid frogs were taken out of one hole under a mass of roots beside a spring, near the summit of the mountain. The water of the spring having the mean temperature of the earth here, which is far above the freezing point, kept them from being destroyed. They gave no signs of life when exhumed and thrown into the snow.

interesting animal, with peculiar habits and organization, possessing, like his brotherhood, the powers of the chameleon to a certain extent. It has a wide range, and is common on the mountain.

HYLA Pickeringia. Pickering's tree-frog.—This frog is found from Massachusetts to Pennsylvania.

These batrachians live upon trees, which they climb with great facility by a special structure of the toes, which terminate by adhesive balls, enabling them to stick to any surface, even the most polished. They can adhere to glass upside-down, suspending themselves like flies to the ceiling of a room. They feed on insects, and their croaking voices are well known to all.

TAILED BATRACHIANS.

LAND SALAMANDERS.

(Family Salamandridæ.)

In the Journal of the Academy of Natural Sciences of Philadelphia, October, 1849, Spencer F. Baird has given a revision of the North American Tailed Batrachians. In this he suggests the identity of several species described by other authors, and changes the arrangement of the group. His synonyms will be given in the following catalogue:—

SALAMANDRA, (Brong.) They are sometimes in water, all at first being aquatic, and breathing by external gills.

SALAMANDRA Salmonea, (Storer.) PSEUDOTRITON Salmoneus, (Baird.) Salmon-colored salamander.—Localities, quoted by herpetologists, Vermont, New York, South Carolina, and Pennsylvania. (?) Color, brownish-red, sides salmon-colored, with bright salmon-colored stripe from eye to snout. Length, six to seven inches.

SALAMANDRA Rubra, (Daud.) PSEUDOTRITON Ruber, (Tsch.) The red salamander.—This is a beautiful salamander of a red or crimson color, with minute spots of black. It is a common species, living under decayed logs, piles of leaves, etc. Holbrook gives it a range of the Atlantic States from Massachusetts to Florida, but not west of the Alleghany. It is certainly an abundant species on the Alleghany and the western slope of that mountain. Length, four to six inches.

SALAMANDRA Coccinea. The scarlet salamander.—"Scarlet, with two or more ocellated spots on the sides. Length, two to six inches." This vermilion-colored species is common; said to be "most abundant after showers," of course because it comes out, and is more easily observed at that time.

SALAMANDRA Glutinosa, (Green.) Blue-spotted salamander.—This species is "bluish-black, with minute white spots on the back and tail." It is a widely-distributed species, one of the most common of the family of North American salamanders, being found from 43° north latitude (Holbrook) to the Gulf of Mexico. It abounds on the mountain, frequenting moist places, under decaying timber and loose flat stones. Length, six inches.

SALAMANDRA Erythronata, (Green.) PLETHODON Erythronata, (Bd.) Red-backed salamander.—This is a common "wood-lizard," said to be the most abundant in the Northern States. Color, "head brownish above, white below, sides dull-white with brownish spots, a broad red stripe from snout to end of tail, on the young crimson. Length, 3 to 3·5 inches; range, from 44° to 39° north latitude."

SALAMANDRA Quadrimaculata, (Hol.) DESMOGNATHUS Fuscus, (Bd.) This is a handsome species, but rare on the Alleghany. Holbrook gives it a range of the Atlantic States. He obtained specimens from Pennsylvania.

SALAMANDRA Jeffersoniana, (Green.) AMBYSTOMA Jeffersoniana. First locality, Chartiers Creek, Washington County. (Holbrook, Green.) Dekay suspects this species to be a variety of Glutinosa. Found on Western Appalachian range. Habits, terrestrial, "feeds on insects, earth, worms," etc.

SALAMANDRA Bilineata, (Green.) SPELERPES Bilineata,

(Bd.) Striped-backed salamander.—This is a small, smart species, of a brownish-yellow color, with two or three black lines on its back. Length, three inches. "Found in shallow water, beneath stones, and moist places."—Dekay. Wide range, Massachusetts, Jersey, Pennsylvania, Ohio, North and South Carolina.

SALAMANDRA Symmetrica, (Harlan.) NOTOPTHALMUS Miniatus, (Bd.) Yellow-bellied salamander.—This is a beautiful species of "brownish-red" and bright pink and salmon color, with "brilliant vermilion spots" in two rows on the back. This species is common on the mountain, and has a wide geographic range. It is represented as being found from the Green Mountains of New Hampshire to Virginia, Carolina, Florida, and Alabama.

SALAMANDRA Longicauda, (Green.) SPELERPES Longicauda, (Bd.) Long-tailed salamander. — Characteristics, "yellow, with handsome black spots and bars; body half as long as tail; length, six inches; aquatic habits."—Dekay. Range, Eastern Pennsylvania, Massachusetts, New Jersey, and Pittsburg, west of Alleghany.

SALAMANDRA Subviolacea, (Bar.) AMBYSTOMA Punctata, (Bd.) Violet salamander.—"Bluish-black, with yellow spots." Range, Northern United States, Vermont, Massachusetts, Ohio, Maryland, Pennsylvania. Length, five to seven inches.

SALAMANDRA Fasciata, (Green.) AMBYSTOMA Opaca, (Bd.) The blotched salamander.—Color, gray, with blackish blotches. Length, five inches. Range, Jersey, Massachusetts, Ohio, and South Carolina.

AQUATIC SALAMANDERS.

TRITONS, Water-Newts.

This division of the salamander family is aquatic in its habits, soon dying when taken from the water, although it cannot breathe under water, coming up for air. A remarkable fact concerning this animal is its power to restore destroyed and removed limbs in a year; the leg being restored again and again if destroyed. Even in the case of an entirely extirpated eye, the whole organ, with all its multiplexity and delicacy of anatomical structure, is reproduced in less than eighteen months. Palatine teeth, transverse series, tongue adherent, tail compressed, fingers four, toes five, more or less palmated at root.

TRITON Dorsalis, (Harlan.) NOTOPTHALMUS Viridescens, (Bd.) Millipunctatus of Dekay. Crimson-spotted triton.—This is a hardy newt, "full of life in winter, even swimming under ice as lively as in summer, and only torpid in extremely cold weather." (Holbrook.) It is found in almost every pool, spring, and stream of water in its range, which "extends from one end of the Atlantic States to the other." It feeds on insects, and casts its skin in June, (Storer.) Color, olive, with crimson spots bordered with black; length, three to four inches.

TRITON Nigra, (Hol.) DESMOGNATHUS Niger, (Bd.)— The dusky triton is entirely aquatic in its habits. Color, blackish, with small white spots on sides, tail much compressed, (the tails of all the tritons are compressed.) Length, four to six inches; range, Atlantic States from latitude 43° to Gulf of Mexico. A rare species in the waters of the mountain.

TRITON Porphyriticus, (Green.) PLETHODON Glutinosum, (Tsch.) The gray-spotted triton. Black, with grayish spots; length, seven inches. Only locality Western Pennsylvania. (?)

The gelatinous ropes and coiled globular bunches of the spawn, containing the eggs and young of the salamanders, are found in all pools, puddles, or spots containing water, and which have no fish in them. Where there are fish, the eggs and young, with their enveloping mass, are destroyed. The precaution of the salamander is so great on this point that its eggs are frequently deposited in the drains and ruts, or wheel-tracks of roads, or any accidental puddle which may for the time contain water, but *inaccessible* to the regular inhabitants of water. These places drying up, millions are destroyed. Their reproductive power, however, seems incomputable.

Tribe Immutabilia. — The Crypto Branchiadæ have no gills, but breathe by exposed spiracles or branchial orifices at the neck.

Protonopsis Gigantea, (Barton.) — This is commonly called the Alleghany Hell-bender. It is the large water-newt of Western Pennsylvania, the Ohio, and Mississippi. It is "slate-colored, mottled with dusky." This enormous newt, which sometimes attains to thirty inches or nearly three feet, lives entirely in the water, eating fish, worms, shell-fish, etc. It is one of the most revolting creatures in existence, resembling Milton's sin, its sprawling, flabby, slimy, and almost amorphic outlines suggesting some "fortuitous concourse of atoms," presided over by the genius of deformity and disgust, rather than the clearly demarked structure of a regularly-organized animal. The euphonious name of hell-bender, which is commonly applied to this newt, seems exceedingly appropriate. It is constantly seizing the boy-angler's hook, and when landed with gaping mouth and wicked gestures, is generally left in the quiet possession of rod, line, hook, and all, the terror-stricken lad retreating with precipitation and fear from what he calls the "*poison alligator.*" The Protonopsis follows the streams of the western side of the mountain as high up as there are any considerable volumes of water. It is almost confined to Western waters;* abounding in streams which contain the soft-shelled turtles, (Tryonix,) and seeming, like that animal, to have an original natural affinity for that region.†

The Alleghany, being the eastern line of the great cen-

* It has been found in the Susquehanna, near Columbia.—Baird.

† See Dekay, Holbrook, etc., on Eastern appearance of the Tryonix.

tral North American zoological region, would seem, notwithstanding Dr. Binney's suggestion that it presents no barrier to the spreading of species, (see one of the leading extracts,) to exhibit some actual limits to the general diffusion of some of the reptiles and fishes at least.

MENOBRANCHUS Maculatus, (Harlan.) The spotted water-newt is a striking and interesting form of reptile. It has a handsomely-mottled body, with pleasant colors, and breathes by a group of fimbriated persistent branchiæ or spiracles, which project from the sides of the neck like a blood-red fringe. This lung of the animal is kept moving backward and forward in the process of oxygination of its blood. It is found in the Alleghany River, but does not get up high into the mountain.

MENOBRANCHUS Lateralis, (Say.)—This species was found by Say at Pittsburg. It does not pursue the waters of the Alleghany to great heights. These two animals are also Western species.

CLASS IV.—FISHES.

"ALL life is from the sea, none from the continent. All mucus is endowed with life. The whole sea is alive. It is a fluctuating, ever self-elevating and ever self-depressing organism. Where the sea-organism by self-elevation succeeds in attaining unto form, there issues forth from it a higher organism. Love arose out of the sea-foam. The first organic forms, whether plants or animals, emerged from the shallow parts of the sea. The first men were the literal and mountainous inhabitants of warmer countries, and found, therefore, at once reptiles, fishes, fruit, and game for food."—*Physiophilosophy*.

The ripple-marked sand-rock of the mountain's brow, a miniature sea embossed in original stucco, a miraculous medallion of a most antique regime, the agitated waters chiseled in stone by the artistic sculptor of the globe, now high in the air, "plays glad with the breezes as once with the waves:" "old play-fellows meet." So the cloud stoops and nods to his brother, has the old friend the ocean along with him, and cannot be severed, must meet in the great waltz again, "by one music enchanted;" thus by ancient affinity they approach: down comes the rain, and the sand and the wave meet. Strange ! but here is the sea, and here is its ever-accompanying life, for all "life is from the sea."

Under the shadow of that rock, poised in the crystal medium that has just sprung from its heart, hangs the mountain trout, true brother of the illustrious sailor of the seas, the navigator of the ocean, the grand salmon, (Salmo salar,) whose armies, by a wondrous instinct, as true as the needle to the pole, traversed weary wastes of water, silent, sure, and steadfast as the planets in their starry spaces. "Born in the fresh water, it grows in the sea; during winter takes refuge in the ocean; it passes the summer in rivers, and ascends to their sources. It traverses with facility the whole extent of the longest rivers."

"As soon as a river is freed of ice, the salmon enter it, and always seem by nature impelled to enter those streams in which they were born; an invisible power traces the route they are to follow, brings them back exactly to the place of their birth, and all of them, reassembled without tumult, appear to follow its guidance with implicit respect, just as we see the swallows every spring return to the nest of the preceding year." The season of fresh-water festivities passed, the pilgrimage to the original shrine of love, and the scenes of youth, rock, waterfall and tree, performed, the enchantment of his birth-place in the far-off hill and mountain river-bed realized, the summer ended, this great fish, attenuated and exhausted, quietly returns for a season of repose to the caverns of the sea. So his smaller brother of the distant rivulet, the brook-trout, born in the dance and roar of the rocky torrent, or in the play over pebbly bed of rushing spring-flows, has still an inextinguishable longing to go to the sea again, and will go when he can, forming new characters and affinities, almost to the loss of his identity. Mighty sounding Sea! Venerable Mother of life! ancient abyss of organic mucus! thou wrappest the world as a mantle; "an ever-fluctuating, ever self-elevating, ever self-depressing organism," like the infinite Brahma, thou givest life forever, but will not be defrauded; thy children still long to go to thee, still pray to be absorbed again, and the trout of the mountain-top, whose home is made by the droppings of the cloud, and the wandering salmon of the deep,—

> "The seeds of land and sea
> Are atoms of *thy* body bright,
> And *thy* behest obey."

Fishes are distributed into two great divisions, Bony and Cartilaginous, the first group containing very much the largest number of species. It is a numerous class of animals, supposed to consist of between eight and nine thousand species. The streams which take their rise in the Alleghanies and flow east and west, present a variety of fishes, a few only of which can be named here.

BONY FISH, (Spine-rayed.)

Family Percidæ.

PERCA Flavescens, (Mitch.) The yellow perch is a widely-distributed species. The almost universally-diffused "American yellow perch" is found in the larger streams flowing from the mountain. Small young ones occasionally penetrate the higher streams, rarely if ever the extreme spring-run or last rivulet. Being a rough, savage eater, bold and tough, he takes an extensive range.

PERCA Nebulosa, and Minima of Haldeman are inhabitants of the Susquehanna River, whose tributaries flow from the Alleghany Mountain. These species are found sometimes high up those streams.

LUCIOPERCA Americana, (Cuv. et Val.) Yellow pike-perch.—This fish is extensively distributed both east and west. It has many names in different parts of the country, and is called *salmon* in the Western waters. It sometimes ascends the streams into the mountain range, and is esteemed an excellent fish for the table, and being voracious, is easily taken.

POMOTIS Vulgaris, (Cuv. et Val.) Pond-fish, sun-fish.— The genus Pomotis is American, and composed of fresh-water fish. The vulgaris has a wide range, as Eastern States to North Carolina, and west to Lake Huron. This brilliant little gem of a fish is found in the mountain waters. It abounds, especially in the larger creeks and rivers, lower down, and does not seem to be much of a climber or mountaineer. Rarely seen in the extremely high runs, it prefers the deeper streams with pools and eddies. Here he may be seen poised under the floating water-plants, splatter-docks, and potomogotons, near the edge of the stream, looking up familiarly as if he wished, for variety, to leave his watery medium for a time and make a still more flashy display of the rays he has stolen from the sun. Thus, with quivering fin, motionless body, and great staring eyes, he fills the fisher-boy with the delicious perturbation that Campbell or Gerhard might feel in the presence of the king of the desert, the lion.

Pomotis Appendix. Black-eared sun-fish.—This species is found in the ponds at eastern base of the mountain.

Family Triglidæ.

Cottus Gracilis, (Heck.) Uranidea Quiescens, (Dekay.) Little star-gazer, Miller's thumb.—This strange little fish attains only to the length of a few inches. It lies still on the bottom of the streams, under stones, moving quickly when disturbed, and darting off to a new hiding-place.

Cottus Viscosus, (Hald.) This species penetrates the mountain streams.

"West of the Alleghany we know of the existence of two species, one C. Bairdii, in the northern, the other, C. Wilsonii, in the eastern tributaries of the Ohio."—(Girard.) Do these species penetrate high into the Alleghany range?

SOFT-RAYED FISHES.

(Family Siluridæ.)

Pimelodus Catus. The common cat-fish has a wide range, New Hampshire to Florida. Two or three species of the genus Pimelodus are found in the waters flowing from the mountain. Only the smaller species penetrate the higher streams, and these never get very near the spring-heads.

With regard to the fish called by Dekay Pimelodus catus, Girard remarks, in Proceedings of Academy of Natural Sciences of Philadelphia for 1859, p. 160, "The true Pimelodus catus is a Southern species, widely distinct from the above." He suggests that "it might be called the Dekai." He proposes the name of Pimelodus lynx for a species "furnished by the hydrographic basin of the Chesapeake." This fish is found in the streams, and ponds communicating with them, up to the eastern base of the Alleghany Mountain.

PIMELODUS Furcatus, (Cuv. et Val.) This fish grows in the Ohio to the enormous length of $4\frac{1}{2}$ to 5 feet. Large individuals are never found high up the streams among the mountains.

PIMELODUS. (?) A little cat-fish, called the stinger, or stony-batter, is found in the waters at the eastern base of the mountain. It is a quick-motioned fish which inflicts quite a severe wound by a spine concealed in the pectoral fin. Hence its name of "stinger." It lives much under stones in the streams it frequents, and never attains more than a few inches in length.

Family CYPRINIDÆ.

CATOSTOMUS.—Of the sucker family a number of species are found in the mountain streams. They are the most common fishes, and found in nearly all waters.* It is said by the icthyologists to be an exclusively North American group.† Descending from the mountain into the rivers, the old sucker attains to respectable dimensions, sometimes becoming a large and powerful fish. In the small and shallow runs higher up, they swarm in numbers, but are of diminutive size. The flesh of these fish is not much esteemed as an article of food, as it is soft, insipid, and at certain seasons entirely unpalatable. They abound

* Wherever water exists, except in dead puddles, this numerous family assume the privilege of going.

† M. Lesueur long since described seventeen species of American suckers, and figured nine of them. (See Cuvier, Pisces, p. 380.)

in bones, which are sharp and hard, and, altogether, the eating of this fish is not much unlike the mastication of a pincushion.

Catostomus Communis, (Les.) Common sucker.—This species abounds in the larger streams. It has a wide geographic range.

Catostomus Tuberculatus, (Les.) The horned sucker is said to be found in New Hampshire, Massachusetts, Connecticut, New Jersey, and Pennsylvania. (?)

Catostomus Maculosus, (Les.) This fish is commonly called the "mall head sucker" from its large, angular, and peculiar head. It climbs in the smallest streams high up on the mountain. It is the spotted sucker which lies still and motionless on the bottoms of the streams, clinging closely to the stones.

Catostomus Duquesnii, (Les.) White, or Pittsburg sucker.—This is a handsome fish, and in the larger rivers grows to a great size.

Catostomus Elongatus. Long sucker.—This species is commonly called the "winter sucker," and follows the runs to their springs in the mountain. Both the last species have a wide range.

Hylomyson Nigricans. Black sucker. (?)

Stilbe Crysoleucus. New York shiner.—There are a number of synonyms for this fish, as Cyprinus crysoleucus, Leuciscus Crysoleucus, Leucomosus Americanus, etc. It is a beautiful little bright silvery fish, sometimes attaining to five inches in length, and looks like a miniature shad. It is in all the streams of Pennsylvania, and has also a wide extralimital range. Said to be "found all over the temperate regions of North America."

Leuciscus Cornutus. The Plargyrus cornutus, red fin horn chub, abounds in all clear streams with trout and other species of the genus. It is a beautiful fish, and easily taken, being voracious, and biting at everything. Length, six to seven inches.

Leuciscus Pulchellus. Roach dace, cousin trout.—This

species is sometimes found fourteen inches long. It is found in the Susquehanna, but not high up the mountain streams.

LEUCISCUS atronasus. ARGYREUS atronasus. Black-nosed dace. (?) Dace, running chub, is common all over the State. Length, $3\frac{1}{2}$ inches.

LEUCISCUS argenteus. Silvery dace. (?)

LEUCISCUS nitidus. White dace, shiner. (?)

LEUCISCUS pygmæus. Pigmy shiner.—This is said to be the smallest of the American cyprinidæ, its length being only one inch.

LEUCISCUS rutilus. Roach.—This beautiful, familiar, almost friendly and domestic little fish, is common in all the runs of the mountain. It infests every brook, playing in their smallest beds without shyness, and darting and seizing as food almost anything that falls into the water. Every boy will remember him as his first trophy with string and pin-hook, his first Waltonian dream, when

"Sauntering 'long and listless,' as Tennyson has it,
   Long and listless strolling, ungainly in hobbadiboyhood."

Length, four or five inches.

HYDRARGYRA. Minnow.—This, and some of the preceding genera, are extensively distributed. They crowd the streams, and are the "shiners" of the boys' sport, being small, graceful fish, with a variety of metallic reflections. The mountain waters abound with them up to the spot where the springs boil up from the sand. Every little rivulet is alive with them, of every dimension, from the almost invisible fish-shaped atom, to individuals of three or four inches in length. They are tame and fearless, and can be seen at all times in shoals through the transparent ice, even in the coldest weather as lively as in August or July. Their bright-polished sides, tinged with silver and bronze, flash in every pool, and their delicate forms glide from every grass-tuft and overhanging bank of the mountain brooks. They are very prolific. Dekay enumerates three species belonging to New York.

SEMOTILUS atro-maculatus. The spotted shiner is one of the commonest "chubs." He flourishes every place on the mountain range.

EDOGLOSSUM masilingua. The wry-mouth dace is abundant on the mountain.

ETHEOSTOMA. (?) Darter.—One species of this genus is found on the mountain.

Family ESOCIDÆ.

Esox estor, (Les.) Pike, pickerel, muskellunge.—Length, one to three, or nearly four feet.

Esox reticulatus, (Les.) Common pike.—Length, one to two feet. Range, Eastern and Middle States, "being abundant in the waters of the Ohio River." Of the pike or pickerel family, the streams which flow from the mountain are supposed to have but this one species. It is rarely found high in the mountains, and never in the small spring-runs near their summits. Lower down, on both sides of the Alleghany range, where the streams are larger and there are natural and artificial pools, it is found of a large size. This seems to be one of the causes of the brook-trout pushing its residence to the smaller streams and springs, rather than remain in the lower larger waters to be devoured by pikes and perches. This is the species said to be common "throughout the United States except in extreme Western and Southern waters," extending from New England to the western limits of Pennsylvania, and found in every river, pond, and streamlet. It is represented not to grow larger than from six to seven pounds, although it is at the same time alleged that individuals have been taken weighing sixteen pounds. It has been also stated that the two large species, the Esox estor and Esox lucioides, are not found in any other part of the continent except the great lakes and waters of the St. Lawrence Basin. These fish, especially the Esox estor, grow to an immense size; by Dr. Richardson said to be often twenty-eight pounds. From the dimensions of some described by Dr. Dekay, more than four feet long, it has been suggested that this species may sometimes attain the weight of fifty pounds. The other species, the northern pickerel (Esox lucioides) sometimes attains the weight of seventeen pounds. The reticulatus being restricted to six or seven pounds, the range of the larger species must be more extensive than that assigned to it by some writers for the following reason : in the dams or slack-water pools of the Conemaugh River on the western side, and within the Appalachian range, a pike is often taken weighing thirty pounds, and very frequently twenty and twenty-eight pounds. The head is enormous, and the fish is considered the greatest delicacy, and not like the common pickerel, "coarse, watery, and of small value for the table." Is this the great St. Lawrence Basin Muskellange Esox estor or another Esox?

Family SALMONIDÆ.

SALMO fontinalis, (Mitch.) Brook-trout. — Range, all clear running streams in the Northern and Middle States. Length, said to be eight inches, but often much larger.* Far up in the mountain rivulets, even to the spring as it escapes through the fissures of the rock, this species climbs. Wherever fresh water, especially cold spring-water, is found in sufficient quantity to immerse their bodies, they abound in hole and eddy, in pool and rapid, and it is wonderful how they thread their way up the mountain side through the swift-rushing streams, over falls boiling through rocks, roots, and drifts. Where the smallest rill or little spring remains permanently fresh throughout the year, this species, in some shape of growth, is found in proportion to the quantity of the water, either as smallest troutlet or adult fish. The latter, or full-grown trout, is generally found in the larger waters some distance from the mountains, while the young fry in quantities find their way up to the springs, and live and

* "A trout, measuring fifteen inches in length, and weighing two pounds two ounces, was caught in Piney Creek, near the base of the Alleghany, July, 1859."—M.

grow in spaces that would not conceal the body of the full-grown trout. Off the mountain, where the springs form creeks and rivers, the trout attains frequently a very large size, even the fullest dimensions attributed to him by the naturalist. These large individuals are supposed to be extremely old. It has been suggested that there is a smaller form of the adult brook-trout adapted to the smaller streams which they inhabit, and that he is susceptible of still greater development under conditions more favorable to an enlargement of his body. In the clear, bright spring-runs of the mountain, the trout is generally thought to attain his greatest perfection of coloring, sporting his handsome figures and brilliant tints in perfection. Although he is spawned, lives, and dies in the mountain streamlet, it is maintained that he still retains his migratory instinct, and has a tendency to return to the sea, and that individuals do succeed in returning again through the larger rivers to the main, where, under the new conditions of the new medium, he develops new and altered attributes, to the perplexity and confusion of the fish-fancier, and even of the scientific observer. The flesh of this exquisite fish is considered one of the greatest luxuries of the gourmand.

Another member of the family of salmons is said to be found in the larger streams which flow from both sides of the Appalachian chain. This is commonly called the white salmon, and is a plain fish with a graceful form, but without brilliant coloring, and the clear prominent characters of the salmon. It is found in both branches of the Susquehanna and Juniata rivers in the East, and the Alleghany, Conemaugh, and Youghiogheny rivers in the West. The flesh of this fish is much esteemed.

Family ANQUILLIDÆ.

ANQUILLA vulgaris, (Mitch.) Common eel.—The eel is found in the streams both sides of the mountain, but not abundantly, high up. The Western waters are especially destitute of this fish, although it is said to be common, and a cosmopolite. The common eel is very abundant in the eastern waters, particularly low down in the larger streams or rivers, but it also ascends the mountains to a great height, small ones being occasionally found in the last rivulets of the springs. They say the eel spawns in the ocean, and never in lakes and rivers. The journeys from the estuaries of the ocean to the summits of the mountains must be full of adventure, and the biography of an eel would, no doubt, be the record of a varied experience. Leaving the "salt and slimy sea," however, for the pure and limpid streams of the mountain, is certainly excellent taste in the eel family, and the philosophy of the migrations of the Anadrom is a revelation of the infallible wisdom of instinct. In the clear, cold fresh waters of the large streams, this fish grows to an enormous size; the flesh is white, fat, and of delicious flavor. The habits of the family are well known.

Family SUCTORII, or PETROMYZONIDÆ..

PETROMYZON fluvialis, (?) Americanus. The lamprey is rather a rare fish, living in the larger streams, and never found high up in the mountain. It is peculiar, and its habits and organization are an interesting subject to the naturalist. Dekay enumerates three species of Petromyzon, two small, one large, which he calls the sea lamprey. The lamprey of the Juniata River is a large eel, and would fill his description of the sea lamprey or Americanus.

INVERTEBRATA;

OR,

SECOND, THIRD, AND FOURTH GREAT DIVISIONS OF THE ANIMAL KINGDOM.

The limits of the present work on the mountain being fixed quite in disproportion to the magnitude of the subject-matter, painful restraints, distressing hobbles, and troublesome bars, have hedged in the field of labor. Pause and ponder over this "daring of the impossible,"—creation to be squeezed into a nut-shell; the world precipitated into a thimble; still more insane, the mountain concentrated and preserved in a gallipot? Painful reflection! unheard of audacity! immeasurable folly! May the disgust and indignation of the gods be averted.

This shadow of the "bill of fare;" this inkling of the opulence of the ineffable promises of blessedness to body and soul from the mountain as a habitat, would be still more meagre, imperfect, and vain, without some representation from the invertebrates; for here is the region where the mysterious bond of animality commences; here is an organic realm of wonder and fable; here is a world of eccentric and anomalous FORMS; and here is the tragic union of the ponderable and imponderable in the lowest media, and under every possible condition of time and space, and in the most doleful and repulsive domains of absolute brutism.

"Life is a vortex more or less rapid, more or less complicated, the direction of which is invariable, and which always carries along molecules of similar kinds, but into which individual molecules are continually entering, and from which they are continually departing; so that the *form* of a living body is more *essential* to it than its *matter*." Perfection being the *end* proposed, all bottles were to be filled, all nooks and crannies of nature occupied, all things were to live, and "work in endless motion;" that celestial loaferdom, that far-off paradise of all men's dreams and prayers, where there is eternal repose and nothing to be done, having no prototype in the plan of the universe. Hence the tyrannic law of form must be revealed, its instrumentality was inevitable, the *adaptation* to *the condition, for a purpose*, and hence this endless variety, this countless diversity of organic beings.

But this is a strange relationship, vertebrata, invertebrata—brain and no brain.

Still stranger is the no-brain's relationship to the no-brain. What possible nexus can exist between this huge mollusk* with his fleshy body, and house of rock, and that ephemeral insect, with winged, etherial, and transparent body? What element of sameness could ever be found between the infernal arachnida, or spider, full of poison, in his trap-den of insidious ropes, and that winged, floating gem, the butterfly, innocent eater of nectar and lover of flowers? What bond of organic affinity could come between that hideous crustacean, with sprawling legs, satanic claws, spines, and bristles, and that strange protozoon, whose "simple organization is reducable to the type of a cell?" Only from the bond of that essential *law*, only from the resistless despotism of the powers which reign in the world of *matter* and the primordial necessities of "life, substance, and *form*." The element of generalization is, they are animals *without* vertebral columns, brains, or spinal cords. Wondrous vortex! miraculous cell! With symmetry and beauty, the circulation through the imperial structure of mammal, bird, reptile, and fish being accomplished, we arrive in a descending grade at the consideration of an anomalous and peculiar series of "*vortices*," real fantastic tricks, no back bone, no brain

---

* Chama gigas. "Specimens have been taken that weighed upward of three hundred pounds."—CUVIER.

or spinal cord, but mantles of stone, wings of purple and gold, gauze and silk, indurated skin-skeletons outside, crusty hides of lime and leather, with strange articulations, hardest shells, or mucous films, in short, of mollusk, lobster, butterfly, and polypus. Is there no end to this whirl? where do these animal vortices stop? On dances the enchanted cell, down, down through crawling worm and writhing zoophyte, to the inconceivable protozoa, "organization, type of a cell,"* where the animal shakes hands with the vegetable, and it is asked, which is the plant and which is the animal, while the microscope stands aghast over a hideous simplicity, a fearful unity, and that bridge, sharper a thousand times than the finest sword, is passed between "man and nothingness," and creation stands her last trick detected, her last joke confessed, "*infinitude within, infinitude without.*"

Siebold remarks: "The invertebrate animals are organized after various types, the limits of which are not always clearly defined. There is, therefore, a greater number of classes among them than among the vertebrates. But, as the details of their organization are yet but imperfectly known, they have not been satisfactorily classified in a natural manner."

The arrangement of the invertebrates in the Animal Kingdom of Baron Cuvier, is the classification which has been in general use, and is familiar to all. This is the distribution into divisions of Animalia mollusca, or soft animals, Animalia articulata, or articulated animals, and Animalia radiata, or radiated animals.

This generalization has been used by the greater number of writers on the subject, and its clever nomenclature has become mingled with most of the literature of that department. The microscope, and more recent scientific observers, have given more elaborate generalizations in this division

---

* "Siebold, Kölliker, and others, have taken the ground that individual animal forms may be unicellular; or, in other words, that an animal may be composed of only a single cell."—*Burnett's Introductory Note to the Infusoria.*

of science. This instrument (the microscope) is destined to realize the dream of the naturalist, in the registering of organic forms, and now stands the great sub-soil plough in the realms of knowledge intelligible to the senses of man.

The following classification of invertebrate animals is used by Von Siebold and Stannius in their "Comparative Anatomy of the Invertebrata," translated from the German by Waldo I. Burnett, of Boston.

ANIMALIA EVERTEBRATA.
INVERTEBRATE ANIMALS.

Brain, spinal cord, and vertebral column, absent.

FIRST GROUP.
PROTOZOA.

Animals in which the different systems of organs are not distinctly separated, and whose irregular form and simple organization is reducible to the type of a cell.

> CLASS I. INFUSORIA.
> CLASS II. RHIZOPODA.

SECOND GROUP.
ZOOPHYTA.

Animals of regular form, and whose organs are arranged in a ray-like manner around a centre, or a longitudinal axis; the central masses of the nervous system forming a ring, which encircles the œsophagus.

> CLASS III. POLYPI.
> CLASS IV. ACALEPHÆ.
> CLASS V. ECHINODERMATA.

THIRD GROUP.
VERMES.

Animals with an elongated, symmetrical body, and whose organs are arranged along a longitudinal axis; so that right and left, dorsal and ventral aspects may be indicated.

The central nervous mass consists of a cervical ganglion, with or without a chain of abdominal ganglia.

Class VI.   Helminthes.
Class VII.   Turbellarii.
Class VIII.   Rotatorii.
Class IX.   Annulati.

FOURTH GROUP.
MOLLUSCA.

Animals of a varied form, and whose bodies are surrounded by a fleshy mantle. The central nervous masses consist of ganglia, some of which surround the œsophagus, and others, connected by nervous filaments, are scattered through the body.

Class X.   Acephala.
Class XI.   Cephalophora.
Class XII.   Cephalopoda.

FIFTH GROUP.
ARTHROPODA.

Animals having a perfectly symmetrical form, and articulated organs of locomotion. The central masses of the nervous system consist of a ring of ganglia surrounding the œsophagus, from which proceeds a chain of abdominal ganglia.

Class XIII. Crustacea.
Class XIV. Arachnida.
Class XV.   Insecta.

By inspecting the above classification some conception may be had of the extent of this division of the animal kingdom. From Infusoria to Insect is a vast range of organization, and all possible modification of type and form would seem to have been called into requisition.

INVERTEBRATA. 395

The very imperfect catalogue of the first great division of the animal kingdom, the Anamalia vertebrata, or vertebrated animals, having occupied so much space, it has become necessary to postpone, for the present, any recitation of the *Invertebrata*. This is to be regretted, as it is a most interesting department of nature, full of suggestions to the contemplative mind, and fraught with never-failing attractions to the scientific observer. The mountain is furnished with a goodly array of species of invertebrates, the catalogue of which will be published in another form at another time.

A few words on each separate department of this great division of animals must suffice for the present. And first, of Malacology, and the relationship of the Mollusca to the preceding division of vertebrates, and the world.

Condensed from the illustrious Cuvier, the Mollusk stands, anatomically, thus,—No articulated skeleton, or vertebral canal; nervous system not united in brain and cord, but in nervous masses in different parts of the body, principal of which called brain, surrounds the œsophagus; organs of sensation and motion not uniform as in vertebrates; viscera more irregular, even in structure, as heart and respiratory organs; some respire air, others water, salt and fresh; external and locomotive organs generally on two sides of an axis; circulation double; blood white or bluish, with little fibrine; veins are absorbents; muscles attached to skin, resulting in harder tissues; motions, contractions, inflexions, are "prolongations of different parts" thus, creeping, swimming, seizing; no levers, or articulations in limbs; move slowly, and never per saltum; irritability great, even when divided; skin naked, covered with secretion; no olfactories. Acephala, Brachiopoda, Cirrhopoda, some Gasteropoda and Pteropoda have no eyes. Cephalopoda have them, also organs of hearing, and something like brain in a cartilaginous box; most have a folding of skin, *i.e.* mantle, sometimes a disk, pipe, sac, fin. Naked mollusks have mantles, membranous or fleshy, most have laminæ of harder substances in them, increasing in extent. This substance, which is concealed in mantles in the animal, styled naked mollusk, when it goes on to form a shell for use and protection, is called Testaceous. The "variety in form, color, substance, brilliancy of shells, is endless." All styles of mastication and deglutition exist in mollusks; stomachs simple, multiple, or provided with special instrumentalities. As animals, they are but slightly developed, have little industry, and only preserved from annihilation by "fecundity and vital tenacity."

By referring to the classification of Siebold, it will be seen that he distributes the Mollusks into three classes, namely, Acephala, Cephalophora, and Cephalopoda.

Cuvier separated the Mollusca into six classes, namely, the Cephalopoda, Pteropoda, Gasteropoda, Acephala, Brachiopoda, and Cirropoda.

CLASSES I. and II., or Cephalopoda and Pteropoda, exist only in the sea.

CLASS III.—Gasteropoda. ORDER I.—Pulmonea. Some of this order are terrestrial, others aquatic, the latter of "which are required to come to the surface of the water they inhabit to breathe." Of the terrestrial Pulmonea the mountain has many representatives. By consulting the beautifully-elaborated monograph of Dr. Binney, on the "Terrestrial Air-Breathing Mollusks of the United States," in three volumes, and still not finished,* some conception may be formed of the extent of this group of animals. The following is his tabular classification of the Pneumobranchiate Mollusca:—

* It will give the naturalists of the United States much pleasure to be assured that this splendid work is to be continued, and it is hoped finished, by the industrious and accomplished son of Dr. Binney, Wm. G. Binney, of Burlington, New Jersey.

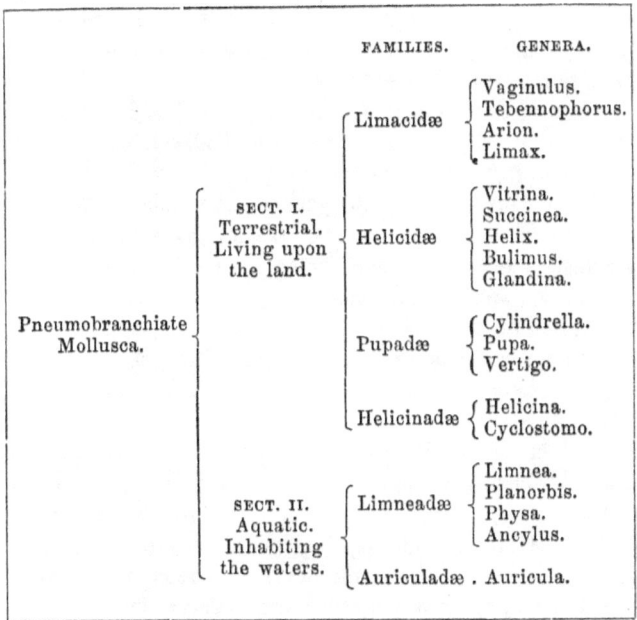

TERRESTRIAL MOLLUSKS.

The Alleghany in Pennsylvania is within Dr. Binney's geographic distribution, Section No. 4, or the "northern interior section," which "includes the country between the Ohio River and the Great Lakes, and between North Carolina and New York and Vermont. It extends west of the Mississippi River." This region, from its geology, climate, soil, and vegetation, would seem to be extremely favorable to the existence and increase of terrestrial mollusks. Dr. Binney says, volume first, page 124, of this section, "Vaginulus, Glandina, Helicina, the larger species of Bulimus, and Cyclostoma, restrained by climatal influences, have disappeared; but the majority of the species of Helix, Succinea, Pepa, and Vertigo, flourish in great numbers, and all the naked slugs, both native and introduced, with the exception of Vaginulus, are found. It would seem to be the *great central focus* of all these genera, from which they radiate into the other sections."

Some of the Helices are universally diffused, as labyrinthica, from Florida to Maine, also Helix minuscula, and Pupa contracta, rupicola, and exigua.

In the distribution of the genera and species of this geographic section, page 129, Dr. Binney gives the following synopsis, the foreign species being printed in italics:—

"Tebennophorus carolinensis.

"Arion *hortensis*.

"Limax *agrestis*, campestris, *variegatus*.

"Succinea avara, aurea, obliqua, ovalis, *putris*.

"Bulimus *lubricus*, fallax, exiguus.

"Helix albolabris, alternata, appressa, arborea, *cellaria*, chersina, clausa, concava, demissa, dentifera, electrina, elevata, exoleta, fallax, fuliginosa, hirsuta, *hortensis*, indentata, inflecta, inornata, interna, intertexta, labyrinthica, ligera, limatula, lineata, *lucida*, minuscula, monodon, multidentata, multilineata, palliata, pennsylvanica, perspectiva, profunda, *pulchella*, sayi, solitaria, striatella, suppressa, thyroidus, tridentata.

"Pupa armifera, badia, corticaria, contracta, rupicola.

"Vertigo decora, gouldii, milium, ovata, pentodon."

Most of these animals are inhabitants of forests; some of gardens and houses, even towns and cities.

Family I.—LIMACIDÆ. Slugs.—These are the slugs, or snails without shells, as they are commonly called. They do not go very far north or south, but abound in the temperate latitudes. Their slimy trails are found over logs, stones, walls, fences, etc. Many of them are injurious and destructive in gardens, having nocturnal habits, and being extremely difficult of detection in their devastations. They endure much cold, but do not hybernate like the snails. Wonderful stories are told of slugs and snails, of their varied qualities and strange powers of instinct. They have been used as food, medicine, agents of telegraphic communication, and stand as the general symbols of utter beastiality in the doleful region of ⸻.

Of the family of Lamacidæ, Binney makes four genera, namely, Vaginulus, Tebennophorus, Arion, and Limax, and affirms, "we have, then, not even one genus which is unquestionably *indigenous* to our territory." The mountain has the following genera and species:—

TEBENNOPHORUS caroliniensis, (Bosc.)—This is a very common slug in the deep forests on decayed wood and bark, where it is often four inches long.

LIMAX campestris, (Bin.)—Found in the forests and among rocks and logs. Binney remarks: "From its wide distribution, it would seem to be indigenous."

Family HELICIDÆ. Snails.—The animals of this group have shells, are herbivorous and carnivorous, and are found within the tropics, as well as temperate regions, but are more abundant in hot climates, decreasing in frequency in temperate and frigid regions. Some of the genera are northern, some southern exclusively. The family incline to forest residences, domiciliating on fallen leaves, trunks, branches, and rocks.

SUCCINEA.—Small shells like snails, but shorter, "ovate conic, generally amber-colored, thin, translucent," and they are found over every part of the temperate zone. Habits, like the genus Helix. Succinea obliqua, (Say.) Wide range. S. avara, (Say.) Common. S. ovalis, (Gould.) (?)

HELIX.—These animals have been called cosmopolite, from the universality of their diffusion. They occupy every part of the United States, and are abundant in Pennsylvania. They inhabit the forests of the mountain in great numbers; live on vegetables, hiding under logs, bark, leaves, stones, and grass, and affecting darkness and dampness.

The following species are found in Pennsylvania, and many of them on the Alleghany, including its eastern and western bases:—

Helix albolabris, multilineata, (not east of Alleghany,) pennsylvanica, thyroidus, dentifera, palliata, appressa, monodon, hirsuta, concava, pulchella, profunda, sayi, tridentata, labyrinthica, intertexta, alternata, fuliginosa, inonata, cellaria, arborea, indentata, interna, suppressa, lineata.

BULIMUS.—General character, like Helix. Most of them belong to the tropics.

BULIMUS lubricus, (Mul.)—Of this shell Binney remarks: "This little species, which is hardly larger than a grain of wheat, is certainly identical with the European shell. It has a vast range, being found on the bark and leaves of decaying trees in forests and groves." It is recognized by its "peculiarly brilliant reflections."

BULIMUS exiguus, (Say.)—The "length of this species is one-fifteenth, breadth, one-fortieth of an inch." This exceedingly minute shell has a wide range, "being common in all the Northern and Middle States." "Found under stones, wood, and moss, in damp places."

BULIMUS fallax, (Gould.)—A very small shell; "length, one-fifth, diameter, one-fifteenth of an inch." Wide range. These are the only species noticed on the Alleghany.

PUPA.—"Shells elongated, cylindrical or accuminate with numerous whorls," etc. This genus is widely distributed over the globe. Many of these little shells are very beautiful when examined closely, but from their minuteness, require great care to find or examine them. They live under fallen leaves, branches, and bark that is decaying, also on stumps and logs in forests; others on moss, stones, etc. in fields; others about water and swamps, seeming to require much moisture for their comfort. "They feed on decaying vegetables, keeping in the shade and hidden." "In winter they bury themselves in the earth or under the leaves."

PUPA armifera, (Say.)—"Length, three-sixteenths of an inch; diameter, half of the length." This the largest species, though a small shell, and common.

PUPA contracta, (Say.)—"Length, one-tenth, diameter,

one-twentieth of an inch." This is the commonest species of Pupa.

PUPA pentodon, (Say.)—Length, one-twelfth of an inch. This is a widely-distributed shell. It lives in woods, under leaves, and on the roots of trees. These three species inhabit the mountain.

VERTIGO ovata, (Say.)—"Length, three-fortieths, transverse diameter, one-twenty-fifth of an inch." Wide range. "It is somewhat aquatic in its habits."

PUPA corticaria, (Say.)—Length, one-tenth, diameter, one-twentieth of an inch. These minute shells are found on the Alleghany, and its eastern and western slopes.

FRESH WATER PULMONATA.

(Family Limniadæ.)

This family is wholly fluviatile.

PLANORBIS, (Lamarck.)—"Shell discoidal sinistral; spire depressed or concave, exhibiting the whorls above and below;" fresh water. Dekay reports, as belonging to New York, and probably Northern and Middle States, the following list of species: Planorbis trivolvis, bicarinatus, lentus, megastoma, (thin, delicate shell,) parvus, corpulentus, deflectus, dilatatus, which "occurs from Massachusetts to Maryland and Ohio." Several of this genus are on the mountain.

LIMNEA, (Lam.)—"Animal spiral, elongated, or oval." Dekay has catalogued the following species: Limnea catascopia, ("from Massachusetts to Delaware and West,") fragilis, umbrosa, caperata, pallida, megasoma, gracilis, humilis, reflexa, columella, emarginata, (a boreal species extending South,) desidiosa, juglaris, appressa.

PHYSA, (Drap.)—"Animal *oval*, more or less *spiral*." Of this genus Dekay reports species heterostropha, planorbula, cylindrica, elliptica, plicata, obesa, ancillaria, glabra, aurea, elongata.

In the monograph of S. S. Haldeman on the Limniadæ and other fresh-water univalve shells, we have the following mollusks registered as belonging to the geographic range of Pennsylvania, some quoted only in the eastern part of the State.

PHYSA heterostropha, (Say.)—Range, from latitude 31° to St. Lawrence and Great Lakes.

LIMNEA desidiosa, (Say.)—Range, latitude 35° to 45°, and from New England to Mississippi River. In fresh-water streams and lakes.

LIMNEA carperata, (Say.)—Eastern Pennsylvania.

LIMNEA columella, (Say.)—Pennsylvania.

PLANORBIS bicarinatus, (Say.)—New England to Georgia and Tennessee.

PLANORBIS parvus, (Say.)—Eastern, Middle, and Western States.

PLANORBIS armigerus, (Say.)—Eastern, Middle, and Western States.

AMNICOLA decisa, (Hald.)—In "streams connected with the Susquehanna."

AMNICOLA limosa, (Say.)—Maine to Pennsylvania and Ohio.

AMNICOLA lapidaria, (Say.)—East and west of Alleghany Mountain.

VALVATA tricarinata, (Say.)—New England and Middle States.

Many of these species are found on the mountain, or in the waters at the eastern or western base, as already remarked.

Dekay's catalogue of the Limniadæ of New York is a much more extensive list than Haldeman has given to Pennsylvania. It should be borne in mind, however, that the monograph of Haldeman was published in 1840, and Dekay's in 1843.

The next order of Gasteropoda is the PECTINIBRANCHIA.

Family TURBINIDÆ.

PALUDINA disscisa. — Dekay quotes this as "the commonest species in New York;" and extra-limital species lapidaria, subcarinata, as belonging to Pennsylvania.

MELANIA.—This genus abounds in Western and Southern States. Dekay recites ninety-two extra-limital species, and but few Northern species. A few of this family exist in the waters of the mountain. This ends the list of Gasteropoda.

CLASS IV.—ACEPHALA.
(No head.)

This class are all aquatic.

ORDER I.—ACEPHALA TESTACEA.

Embraces all bivalves and some multivalves.

Family I.—OSTRACEA. Marine.*

Family II.—MYTILACEA. Muscles.

ANODENTA, (Brug.) Inhabit fresh water.

UNIO, (Brug.) Inhabit fresh water. Now belonging to the Family Naiades, (Lamark.) This family, in the details of its organization, has been elaborated with wonderful perseverance and zeal by Mr. Isaac Lea, President of the Academy of Natural Sciences of Philadelphia. His synopsis of the Family of Naiades is one of the most perfect monographs, on natural science, in existence, and like all products of enthusiasm, bears upon it the stamp of devotion and love to the subject. His extensive catalogues illustrate the results of the confusion of interminable syn-

---

* Some eighty species of oysters have been described. Lamark gives three species, borealis, virginica, and canadensis, to the American coast, and Dekay "confesses his inability to find more than one, and that, under certain forms, cannot distinguish from the common oyster of Europe." The oyster flourishes best (Dekay) between the 36° and 42° of north latitude. It is said to live "twelve or fifteen years, and to be in best condition from the fourth to the sixth year."

onomies, and the endless propagation of names by naturalists ambitious to pile up new species. The gauntlet which one shell (the Anodonta cygnea) has run, is a curious comment upon this subject. This single species has been described and catalogued under five different genera, with seventy-five specific names, by seventy-six different authors. The following table will show the present disposition of the family as arranged with great labor by Mr. Lea:—

FAMILY NAIADES.

I. GENUS MARGARON:

1. Subgenus Triquetra,
    Having a cardinal and lateral tooth, and furnished with two siphons.

2. Subgenus Prisodon,
    Having a cardinal and lateral tooth transversely striate, and furnished with two siphons.

3. Subgenous Unio,
    Having a cardinal and lateral tooth.

4. Subgenus Margaritana,
    Having one tooth (cardinal.)

5. Subgenus Monocondylœa,
    Having a simple callus.

6. Subgenus Dipsas,
    Having a linear tooth under the dorsal margin.

7. Subgenus Anodonta,
    Having no teeth.

II. GENUS PLATIRIS:

1. Subgenus Iridina,
    Having a granulate dorsal margin, and furnished with two siphons.

2. Subgenus Spatha,
    Having a dorsal margin non-crenulate, and furnished with two siphons.

3. Subgenus Mycetopus,
    Having a straight, smooth, dorsal margin, and furnished with a long extensile foot.

INVERTEBRATA. 405

Some conception of the extent of this group of shells may be formed, when the statement is made, that one of the subgenera, Unio, has nearly four hundred species on the continent of North America.* Many species of this subgenus are found in the fresh waters of the mountain slopes, but they do not ascend to the highest runs near the summit.

Subgenus Anodonta has forty-three North American species, and subgenus Margaritana sixteen North American species. These have representatives in the mountain streams.

Family CYCLADÆ.

CYCLAS, (Lam.)—Dekay enumerates several species of Cyclas as belonging to New York. The similis is found in ponds and streams of every part of the State of New York, also dubia. The Partumeia in swamps and sluggish streams, also in every part of the State. He enumerates the rhomboides, elegans, and edentula.

CLASS V.—BRACHIOPODA.

This class contains but few shells, all of which are marine.

CLASS VI.—CIRROPODA.

This last division of the mollusks contains the smallest number of species. They belong to the ocean.

---

* These facts are taken from Mr. Lea's Synopsis, third edition, 1852. Since then he has described over one hundred species of Unionidæ indigenous to our country, and added greatly to the foreign synonomy, all of which he will publish in the fourth edition, now in preparation.

THIRD GREAT DIVISION OF THE ANIMAL KINGDOM; or, ANIMALIA ARTICULATA.

Of this division Cuvier observes: "This third general form is as well characterized as that of the Vertebrata; the skeleton is not internal as in the latter, neither is it annihilated as in the Mollusca, the articulated rings which encircle the body, and frequently the limbs, supply the place of it, and as they are usually hard, they furnish to the powers of motion all requisite points of support, so that here, as among the vertebrata, we find the walk, the run, the leap, natation, and flight."

The Articulata are distributed into four classes. These are the Annulata, Crustacea, Arachnides, and Insecta.

CLASS I.—ANNULATA.

Only Invertebrates with red blood. Nearly all inhabit water, the earth-worms excepted. This class is divided into three orders, based on organs of respiration.

Order I.—Tubicola.

Mostly inhabit tubes. Breathing arrangement, tufts or arbusculæ attached to head. These sea-worms are numerous, living in mud or sand, and making tubes of lime and other substances.

Order II.—Dorsibranchiata.

Branchiæ or breathing organs distributed along the body, arborescent, or tuft-like in shape, "ramified in laminæ or tubercles." They swim in the ocean or live in the mud, rarely with tubes. This is an extensive order, and has many genera over the world.

Order III.—Abranchiata.

No visible branchiæ, respire "by the surface of skin or internal *cavities.*" Live in water, mud, and moist earth. This order has two families. The first embraces the common earth-worm, Lumbicus terrestris, known to all; and the second, the genus Hirudo, or Leeches. One species of Hirudo is found in the waters of the mountain.

The next three classes of animals, form the fifth division of Siebold, or Arthropoda.

Class II.—Crustacea.

This class is separated into two sections, the Malacostraca and Entomostraca.

First Division.—Malacostraca, group *a*, "eyes placed on a movable and articulated pedicle."

Order I.—Decapoda, (Ten-footed.)

This order embraces the large, and some of them useful crustaceans. They usually inhabit water, and are carnivorous and voracious.

Family I.—Brachyura, short tailed. This family embraces but one genus of crabs.

Family II.—Macroura, long tailed. Cuvier, with De Geer and Gronovius, fixes this group into a single genus, Astacus. There are several subgenera, which contain the common hermit crab, (Cancer bernhardus, Linn.,) the common lobster, (Astacus marinus,) Homerus Americanus, and the fresh-water crabs, or craw-fish.

Astacus bartonii. Fresh-water lobster, craw-fish.—This crustacean is common in all the streams of the mountain. It is said to have "nocturnal habits, concealing itself by day," etc. This does not seem to be exclusively his habit;

he, as may be seen at almost any time, groping around on the bottom of runs, or sliding, head or tail first, as best suits him, along the edges of stones and roots, or in the mud. He is rather pugnacious, and very quickly seizes on anything that falls in the water. It has a wide geographic range, and is exclusively fluviatile. Length, $3\frac{1}{2}$ inches.

Order II.—Stomapoda.

This is divided into two families, Unipeltata, Bipeltata, and into genera and species, all of which are marine.

Malacostraca, group *b*, eyes sessile and immovable. This division of crustaceans is small. They inhabit the sea-coast, also fresh water, and some are terrestrial and parasitical.

Order III.—Amphipoda.

Most of this order inhabit salt water; some, however, are found in springs and rivulets. Some of this group, belonging to the sea, are the most ferocious and ravenous of the crustaceans.

Gammarus minus. Fresh-water shrimp.—This is a common animal in fresh-water streams under stones and roots. "It is quick and lively in its motions, and altogether an interesting creature."

Gammarus fasciatus is quoted as a Pennsylvania species.

Order IV.—Lœmipoda, (Throat-footed.)

This order is exclusively marine.

Order V.—Isopoda, (Equal-footed.)

Most of this order are aquatic, some terrestrial, and some are parasitical. Among the terrestrial are the species of the genus Oniscus, or wood-lice.

Asellus communis.—This is a little fresh-water crustacean, common in runs and found under stones.

Oniscus asellus. The sow-bug, or, as it is commonly

INVERTEBRATA. 409

called, the wood-louse, is found every place, in cellars and gardens, under stones, logs, etc. Its food is decomposing vegetable matter. "The female carries her eggs in an oval sack beneath, where they are hatched."

PORCELLIO spinicornis.—This is also called the sow-bug. It has the same habits as the Oniscus.

SECOND DIVISION.—ENTOMOSTRACA, called by the older naturalists, insects with shells. This group of animals is aquatic, inhabiting fresh water, and is generally microscopic. They have peculiar organizations, and sometimes possess a hundred feet.

ORDER I.—BRANCHIOPODA, (Gill-footed.)

Mostly microscopical. The old genus Monoculus, Linn., belongs here.

ORDER II.—PŒCILOPODA, (Various-footed.)

Their habitat is said to be on aquatic animals, and generally on fishes. This order is divided into two families— First, Xiphosura, in which is the genus Limulus; and second, Siphonostoma. There are two genera of this order, and they are parasitical; one, the Caligus, is called the Fish-louse.

This is the old Cuvierian arrangement of the crustaceans. The area of knowledge in this department has been immensely enlarged since this classification was made.

More recent classifications of the crustaceans place a new group between Brachyura and Macrura of the first order Decapoda, called Anomura; also, next to Pœcilopoda, an order Phyllopoda, Lophyropa, Branchiopoda, (old,) which contains Branchipus stagnalis, "common in most stagnant pools of fresh water," and lastly, order Ostrapoda, many of which are also found in fresh water pools.

New and vigorous laborers are now in the field with the enthusiasm of youth,[*] with culture and genius, and the hope of the science of the hour is, that this wonderful world of

[*] The accomplished and ingenuous youth, Wm. Stimpson, is doing good work in this department. Long and successfully may he labor.

curious and extraordinary animals will be finally explored, and rendered accessible to all students of nature. The mountain has but few crustaceans. They are, however, of great interest, and their story will hereafter be told.*

CLASS III.—ARACHNIDA.

"This class includes the various articulate forms known as spiders, mites, and scorpions, the characters of which place them between the Crustacea and Insecta. In general, the head is not distinct from the thorax, but intimately connected with it, forming a large segment named the cephalo thorax, which is followed by the abdomen, and this is either distinct or united in a single piece with the former. These animals are not subject to a perfect metamorphosis, but they have, in some cases, a partial one. They have neither wings, antennæ, nor upper lip; feet, eight, affixed to the sternum; mouth provided with a pair of mandibles or chelicera; eyes simple, two to eight, position and number much used as generic characters. Most of the Arachnida feed upon fresh animal food, as insects, which they take alive either in nets, or by running or suddenly leaping upon them. Some are parasitic, others live in meat, cheese, figs, and flour. They are mostly oviparous, and, like the crustacea, moult or change their integument from time to time."†

The class Arachnida is divided into two orders, Pulmonariæ and Trachearie.‡ The first is characterized as having "pulmonary sacks, and six or eight simple eyes." The second respire by "tracheæ, have no organs of circulation, or incomplete ones; the tracheæ divide into branches, which, unlike the insect, do not run parallel to each other, the whole body receiving air from various points by stigmata; ocelli four at most."

* Heck, pp. 118, 119, vol. ii.

† According to Heck, the class is divisible into three sections, Aporobranchia, Trachearia, and Pulmonaria.

‡ The ancient order of fossil crustaceans, called Trilobites, belong here. Many localities of this interesting fossil are found near the eastern base of the Alleghany Mountain.

Family I.—ARANEIDES.
ORDER V.—DIMEROSOMATA. (Heck.)

This is the family of spiders, or the genus Aranea of Linnæus. In their anatomy, their natural association with other animals, their physiological peculiarities, and special characteristics, no division of zoology is more attractive, *scientifically*. Devilish, for they possess venom ; ugly, for who does not hate a spider, (except the true naturalist or lover of God ?) and repulsive from their habits, for who does not abhor the idea of a trap, and of the keeper of a trap,—whether baited with jewelry or rags, brandy or green turtle, corsets or crinoline, satin or the slimy silk of the spider's web ? still, as filling "a yawning need of nature," to the eye of science, the Araneides are as wonderful and attractive as the animals over whose structure taste and beauty preside.

They have "two cords of a nervous system, and ganglions which distribute nerves to the various organs." Their eyes, simple ocelli, according to Dufour, "shine in darkness like those of the cat, and most probably enjoy the faculty of both nocturnal and diurnal vision." There may be some large economy in giving to spiders the control of both worlds, "night and morning," but to possess them also of the fiendish and cowardly element of *venom*, in poisoned swords and spears, and supply them with argus eyes having nocturnal and diurnal vision, together with the power of weaving invisible snares for capturing the innocent, unsuspecting inhabitants of the air, must trouble much the dreams of the optimist, whose solution of obscure points comes from the plane of the natural alone. Cuvier remarks : "I have ascertained that a single wound from a moderate-sized spider will kill the common fly in a few minutes. It is also certain that the bite of those large ones of South America, which are there called crab-spiders, and are placed by us in the genus Mygale, kills the smaller vertebrated animals, such as humming-birds, pigeons, etc., and produce a violent fever in man ; the sting of some species in the south of France has even occasionally proved fatal. We may, therefore, without believing all the fabulous stories of Baglivi and others respecting the bite of Tarantula, mistrust spiders, and particularly the larger ones." Various animals in turn prey on spiders as part of their food, as birds, wasps, etc. Their cocoons, or the sacks which contain their eggs, are familiar to all. "The texture and form of these sacks are variously modified, according to the habits of the race. They are usually spheroidal; some of them resemble a cap or tymbal, some of them are claviform. They are sometimes partially enveloped with foreign bodies, such as earth, leaves, etc.; a finer material, a sort of tow or down, frequently surrounds the eggs in their interior, where they are free or agglutinated, and more or less numerous." Spiders generally die in winter, but some survive several years, as the Mygales, Lycosæ, etc. Notwithstanding the revolting and ferocious character of the spider as generally estimated, touching illustrations of the action of the most sacred of all instincts, the maternal, have been observed and described by naturalists.*

The family Araneides is divided into a number of genera: the Mygale, Crab-spiders, the Aranea, including the rectigrade and sedentary spiders; the Clotho, a peculiar group; the Tetragnatha, Uloborus, Linyphia, and Epeira, with Lycosa, the common field or ground spider, familiar to all among the clods. There are a number of this family on the mountain. The species that weave their webs† on the trees and bushes abound, as may be experienced always by passing through the woods where their invisible ropes, stretching across large spaces, constantly tickle the face of the traveler. The Lycosa are abundant in field and forest.

* For example, see observations of Bonnet, on the Lycosa saccata, referred to by Kirby and Spence, p. 204.

† "Leuwenhoeck has calculated that it would require four millions of the strands of the spider's web to form a thread as thick as a hair of his beard."

Family II.—PEDIPALPI.

This group is composed, according to Cuvier, of two satanic genera, Tarantula and Scorpio. The species of these genera are described as malignant and venomous; but they do not exist in temperate or northern latitudes.

ORDER II.—TRACHEARIÆ.

This order differs in organs of respiration and circulation from the foregoing. It is divided into those "furnished with chelicera, two fingers of which are movable," and into those in which "these organs are replaced by simple laminæ, or lancets, which, with the ligula, constitute a sucker." These animals are very small.

First family of Cuvier, Pseudo-Scorpiones, is terrestrial, and composed of two genera, Galeodes and Chelifer.

Second family, Pycnogonides. These are marine animals. "They are found among marine plants, sometimes under stones near the beach, and occasionally also on the cetacea."

Third family, Holetra. This consists of two tribes, the Phalangium and the Acarus. The first "live on the ground at the foot of trees, and on plants, and are very active; others conceal themselves under stones and moss." The second, Acarides, is composed of genera Acarus, Trombidium, and Ixodes. The first, small microscopical, includes the itch insect,* the "arcari of the human psora," and the mites, which are "excessively prolific." The second, Trombidium, contains the subgenera Erythræus, Gamasus, Cheyletus, Oribata, Uropoda, etc. This is the group to which the common Tick belongs, or the subgenus Ixodes. Of the Ixodes, Cuvier remarks: "They are found in thick woods, abounding in brush, briars, etc. They hook themselves to low plants by the hind legs, keeping the others extended, and fasten to dogs, oxen, horses, and other quadrupeds, and even on the tortoise, burying their suckers so completely in their flesh that they can only be detached by force."

* Sarcoptes scabiei. "Itch is caused probably by different species of Sarcoptes."—H.

The Arachnides are repulsive creatures, but interesting to the naturalist.*

CLASS MYRIAPODA.

This class of articulata is extensively distributed, and has many representatives on the mountain. They are commonly called centipedes and millipedes, or hundred and million footed worms. The real number of feet is from "twelve to upwards of three hundred pairs." The class contains two orders: Chilognatha, (lip formed from jaws,) and Chilopoda, (lip formed from feet,) the first order containing twenty-one, and the latter sixteen genera. The first order contains six families, Glomeridæ, Polyxenidæ, Polydesmidæ, Iulidæ, Polyzonidæ, and Siphonophoridæ. The genus Iulus is the type of the order, and is widely distributed.† The second order includes four families, Scutigeridæ, Lithobiidæ, Scolopendridæ, and Geophilidæ. Some of these are large and poisonous, one being a foot long, but they are only found in warm latitudes. The myriapoda are terrestrial, living in dark, damp places, among moss, or under bark and stones, some feeding upon animal food, and others upon fungi, fruits or decaying vegetable matter. Some of the species are luminous at night at certain seasons, and some secrete a pungent, penetrating, and disagreeable material, with acid scent, but with neither acid nor alkaline qualities.‡

CLASS IV.—INSECTA.

It has been asserted that more than one hundred thousand species of insects exist. This fact suggests a range of natural affinities that would appear endless, between this class and the surrounding world, and reveals an order of final causes that would seem infinite in its complexity. Are

* For spiders of the United States, see Professor N. M. Hentz's papers in the Boston Journal of Natural Sciences.

† See Say, Journal of Academy of Natural Sciences, vol. ii., 1821.

‡ Heck, p. 130.

all, indeed, "but parts of one great whole?" Each form being an indispensable integer, amazement unspeakable is the only emotion which seizes the mind upon contemplating this endless chain of organisms. The patterns of Plato's cave were surely exhausted here; mechanism in every possible form was certainly made bankrupt in this series of structures. All the elements are inhabited by them; old earth, and air, and water are full of them. They infest all plants, all animals, and each other. As the ancient herb-eating monster had a flesh-eating brother to devour him in turn, so has the microscopic insect a sure and steadfast friend sticking closer than a brother—a microscopic dragon that is certain at last to swallow him. This compensative system is a happy one for man, who is so often the victim of the depredation of insects in various ways, as they divide the world with him, being carnivorous, herbivorous, and omnivorous. Thus is it, that this eternal devouring throughout nature is rendered harmonious in the silent clock-work of the world; by a Divine equation each open mouth has something to fill it, and is sure to know what has been arranged for it; and thus comes the terrific formula of all existence,—that the universe is a stomach and intestine, in which circulate peristaltically palpitating particles, still crushed and consumed, and whose destiny in the system of uses is to serve a purpose, fill an end, in short, eat and be eaten.

On what may be styled the personal relationship of insects to man there are many curious chapters, most of which are troublesome and offensive, from fleas and itch-insects to the pediculus humanus and the inhabitants of unclean beds. Many bite venomously; others inflict poisonous wounds by stings; while others revel in his blood, constituting the most execrable torments of existence. Of these are hornets, yellow-jackets, and "infernal furies;" also wasps, gnats, and flies, not forgetting that beautiful and musical friend of man, the charming mosquito, a word upon whom will illustrate the most interesting relationship of insect and man, or of "insects which make man their food."

This universally-admired and beloved insect belongs, according to entomologists, to the family Culicidæ and genus Culex; order Diptera; the numerous species of which are said to "cover the globe from pole to pole, and from east to west, through both hemispheres." The Culex pipiens is the common mosquito of America. He derives his specific name from the music he makes, (particularly attractive in serenade;) which piping is produced by vibrations of his "immaculate wings," executed at the rate, according to Baron C. de Latour, of three thousand per minute. This is a great fact to meditate upon at midnight, when his touching song is performed, with all its variations, simply for one's amusement. The mosquito was noticed early by naturalists: by Aristotle and Pliny, who, according to Kirby, "distinguishes well between Hymenoptera and Diptera, when he says the former have their stings in the tail, and the latter in their mouth; and that to one this weapon is given as the instrument of vengeance, and to the other of avidity." The interesting sting in the mouth of this sweet singer is said to be of exceeding ingenuity as a mechanical implement, not to speak of certain venomous qualities beside. "The instrument of avidity is even more terrible than that of vengeance in most insects thus armed with it; like the latter, also, as appears from the consequent inflammation and tumor, it instills into its wounds a poison; the principal use of which, however, is to render the blood more fluid and fitter for suction. This weapon, which is more complex than the sting of hymenopterous insects, consists of five* pieces besides the exterior sheath, some of which seem simply lancets, while others are barbed like the spicula of a bee's sting, is at once calculated for piercing the flesh and forming a siphon adapted to imbibe the blood."†

* The rostrum is very long and slender, apparently simple, but composed of seven organs."—H.

† Kirby and Spence.

Again, this mouth-sting and its possessor are described:
"They (the mosquitos) are provided with a long, horny, stiff, and perpendicular proboscis, with antennæ consisting of fourteen joints, feathered on the males, and with two wings covered with small scales. Every part of this insect, when magnified, presents not only a beautiful and wonderful appearance, but cannot fail of exciting contemplation of the most serious (certainly) kind. Indeed, one has no idea of the *amazing beauty* of these diminutive creatures until he has observed them through a microscope."* The microscope is not required to discover the "amazing beauty" of this lovely little creature; when he soars off, upon his "immaculate wings," filled with your blood, it is visible to the naked eye. The biographers of the Culex, and travelers, generally tell wonderful and hideous stories of him, from the tropics where he flourishes vastly, to the region "where the polar winter extends its icy reign."

In the Crimea, Russian soldiers are required to sleep in sacks; the "case-hardened cuticle of the Laplander" is required to be daubed with unguents of tar, fish-grease, or cream, "or wear nets steeped in fetid birch-oil to protect him from bites of these blood-suckers." Travelers in warm countries represent them as "demons," that the sound they make is "fearful," that "men die of mortification of the skin" from their bites, or if they recover; look as if they had had the small-pox. Among Cossack herdsmen they are veritable plagues, "thousands of these insatiate monsters entering the nostrils, ears, eyes, and mouth of the cattle, who shortly after die of convulsions, or of secondary inflammation, or from absolute suffocation." In certain countries men are required to travel with their heads in bags and hands in leather gloves. Weld relates the fact from Washington himself, "that at one place the mosquitos were so powerful as to pierce through his boots;" and Humboldt informs us "that between the little harbor of Higeurote and

---

* Jaeger.

the mouth of the Rio Unare the wretched inhabitants are required to stretch themselves on the ground, and pass the night buried in the sand three or four inches deep, leaving out the head only, which they cover with a handkerchief."

It appears the female mosquitos are the fiercest depredators (only,)* "attacking with most avidity the softer sex, and trying their temper by disfiguring their beauty!"†

The Culex deposits its eggs in stagnant water, and is most numerous in wet seasons. It is said that "six or seven generations take place in one season, each female depositing about three hundred eggs, which, in three or four weeks, become perfect flies, which again deposit eggs," etc. From the eggs the larvæ come out in two days and swim around, coming to the surface to breathe. "In two weeks they change into the pupa, which still remains on the surface of the water, and, after a week, bursts open, and the perfect mosquito flies out as if shot from under the water." Trees generally harbor gnats and mosquitos, but it is said the horse-chestnut, planted about a house, will drive them away.

---

* "The male, which *does not sting*, can be readily distinguished by the feathery antennæ."—HECK.

† Kirby and Spence.

Wonderful is this unity in the midst of diversity; fearful is this law of identity in the domain of instinct. What now of the doctrines of the "Feminine Soul," of the angelic instrumentality of "Feminicity" as the refining and saving influence of the world? It appears that woman, and the female mosquito, are under the dominion of the same barbarous necessities, and held by the same terrible stinging proclivities, "attacking with avidity and disfiguring the softer sex, trying their temper and beauty." There is one vast difference: mosquito never stings mosquito; and of course it was no form of the play of this instinct that Byron divined,—

> "Gayer insects fluttering by,
> Ne'er droop the wing o'er those that die,
> And lovlier things have mercy shown
> To *every failing but their own*,
> And every woe a tear may claim,
> Except ———."

The mountain districts, of temperate latitudes, are not so obnoxious to the infliction of mosquitos as flat or low countries abounding in water. There are but few species of the genus Culex on the mountains of Pennsylvania.

The Midge, or Tipulidæ family, is also an interesting group of diminutive insects who have friendly leanings toward man.*

Of the spiritual manifestation or the play of the faculties of instinct of insects, many astonishing records are made by entomologists, under the chapters of "Affection of insects for their young;" "Stratagems employed by insects in procuring food;" "Habitations of insects for their young and for their own use;" "Habitations of insects living in society;" "Perfect and imperfect societies of insects," etc. These seem heads of chapters, not of insects, but of *men*. To read the chapters is to doubt and wonder, for the fancy seems alone to have created them; and yet, these great facts are now the common property of science, and naturalists assert them as the most familiar things. An example is found in the wonderfully-organized kingdom of the honey-bee, known to all, but however familiar, seeming forever an incredible romance, for human society has thus far failed in any comparative organization. Was it not a vain and shortsighted flash of the poet, that the "*only study* of mankind is man"? The fact that Tumble Beetles will leave their work and go and help a brother in trouble to roll his ball when his hill is too steep for him to do it alone, was no doubt the origin of the clever custom of log-rolling among Congressmen. Many of the family Formicæ, or Ants, live in societies, or commonwealths, in burrows of their own construction, or mounds,† or regular nests on trees and rushes.

* The Hessian fly belongs to this group.

† The large mounds of the yellow American ant abound on the highest summits of the Alleghany. They seem to be filled by great numbers of ants, and are sometimes three or four feet in diameter,

From the observations of Dr. T. Savage, there are three or four grades of ants, namely, "neuters, soldiers, workers, and carriers." "The genus Polyergus make predatory excursions to the nests of other species and take young workmen in the pupa state. These captives assume their perfect state in the domiciles of their captors, and become the slaves of the community. All labor of building, collecting food, and taking care of the young falls upon them."* St. Forgeau thinks the Polyergus (ant) exhibits the "perfection of instinct, being capable of laboring, but *preferring idleness;*" while Huber asserts they have no talent but for war, and that they would starve to death but for the working formica. This " perfection of instinct" in the ant has a terrible analogue in a larger ant called man, on a larger ant-hill called the earth, and who is supposed to be its arbiter and king, under the divine endowments of intellect, morality, and religion.

Insects are also related to man through friendly qualities, as luxuries, necessaries, and in the arts, medicine, and economies. Witness cantharides and cochineal, honey, the emblem of luxury and plenty, and silk, the badge of wealth, extravagance, and, unhappily, of pride and folly.

The biography and morphology of insects is a department of perfect enchantment in nature, so entirely wonderful that it seems incredible, and even absurd. In many, the change of entire organization, justly called *metamorphosis,* is one of the order of perpetual miracles, and is without parallel in any other department of organic bodies. A wise prophecy it would appear to the uninitiated, that that loathsome, crawling worm, formless and disgusting, in mud and slime eating filth and corruption, should ever soar through

and two or three feet high. This ant is said by Heck to "make slaves of the black ant, both being true Formica, and both working."

* See Iconographic Encyclopedia of Science, Literature, and Art, by J. G. Heck, translated by Baird, p. 174.

the ether an object of absolute beauty, a form in which all excesses of ornamentation seem perfected, and whose dainty appetite can feed only upon the nectar of flowers. The recitations of interesting and strange things in this department would be endless. Reflect! Science has recognized more than one hundred thousand insects; patient naturalists have watched and worked, and the microscope has lifted the veil of mystery from their private lives, organization, and habits, and entomology stands one of the most extensive and curious dominions of knowledge possessed by man. Of the classification or manner in which this knowledge is arranged, a number of systems have been adopted by different entomologists. The general observations of Heck on the anatomical elements of the Articulata embrace, of course, the structure of the insect. He says: "The Articulata are named from having the various parts of the body and limbs articulated to each other. The nervous system is composed of ganglions united by a double cord, and there is usually a kind of outside skeleton composed of a series of rings protecting the interior parts, and serving as points of attachment for muscles. In some classes respiration is affected by means of branchiæ, and in others by tracheæ, or air tubes. When limbs are present, they are never fewer than six."

Cuvier, after an extended dissertation on the anatomy and physiology of insects, remarks, on their classification: "All general systems or methods, relative to insects, are reduced essentially to three. Swammerdam based his on their metamorphoses; that of Linnæus was founded on the presence or absence of wings, their number, consistence, superposition, the nature of their surface, and on the deficiency or presence of a sting. Fabricius had recourse to the parts of the mouth alone. In all these arrangements the Crustacea and Arachnides are placed among the Insects, and in that of Linnæus, the one generally adopted, they are even the last." He then proceeds with his own classification:—

"I divide this class into twelve orders, the three first of which are composed of Apterous Insects, undergoing no essential change of form or habits, merely subject to simple changes of tegument, or to a kind of a metamorphosis, which increases the number of legs, and that of the annuli of the body. The organ of sight in these animals is usually a mere (more or less considerable) assemblage of ocelli resembling granules.

"Certain English naturalists have formed new orders, based upon the wings; I see no necessity, however, for admitting them, that of the Strepsipter excepted,—the name of which appears to me to be erroneous,[*] and which I call Rhipiptera.[†]

"In the first order, or the MYRIAPODA, there are more than six feet—twenty-four and upwards—arranged along the whole length of the body, on a suite of annuli, each of which bears one or two pairs, and of which the first, and in several, even the second, seem to form a part of the mouth. They are Apterous.[‡]

"In the second, or the THYSANOURA, there are six legs, and the abdomen is furnished on its sides with movable parts, in the form of false feet, or terminated by appendages fitted for leaping.

"In the third, or the PARASITA, we find six legs, no wings, and no other organs of sight than ocelli; the mouth, in a great measure, is internal, and consists of a snout containing a retractile sucker, or in a slit between two lips, with two hooked mandibles.

"In the fourth, or the SUCTORIA, there are six legs, but no wings; the mouth is composed of a sucker inclosed in a cylindrical sheath, formed of two articulated portions.

"In the fifth, or the COLEOPTERA, there are six legs and four wings, the two superior of which have the form of cases, and mandibles and maxillæ for mastication: the inferior wings are simply folded crosswise, and the cases, always horizontal, are crustaceous. They experience a complete metamorphosis.

"In the sixth, or the ORTHOPTERA, there are six legs, four wings, the two superior in the form of cases, and mandibles and jaws for mastication, covered at the extremity by a galea; the inferior wings are folded in two directions, or simply in their length, and the inner margins of the cases, usually coriaceous, are crossed. They only experience a semi-metamorphosis.

"In the seventh, or the HEMIPTERA, there are six legs, four wings, the two superior in the form of crustaceous cases, with membranous extremities, or similar to the inferior, but larger and firmer; the

---

[*] Twisted wings. The parts taken for elztra are not so. See this order.
[†] Wings folded like a fan.
[‡] Destitute of wings and scutellum.

mandibles and jaws are replaced by setæ forming a sucker, inclosed in a sheath composed of one articulated, cylindrical, or conical piece, in the form of a rostrum.

"In the eighth, or the NEUROPTERA, there are six legs, four membranous or naked wings, and mandibles and jaws for mastication; the wings are finely reticulated, and the inferior are usually as large as the superior, or more extended in one of their diameters.

"In the ninth, or the HYMENOPTERA, there are six feet, and four membranous and naked wings, and mandibles and jaws for mastication; the inferior wings are smaller than the others, and the abdomen of the female is almost always terminated by a terebra or sting.

"In the tenth, or the LEPIDOPTERA, there are six legs, four membranous wings, covered with small, colored scales resembling dust; a horny production in the form of an epaulette, and directed backward, is inserted before each upper wing, and the jaws are replaced by two united tubular filaments, forming a kind of spirally-convoluted tongue.

"In the eleventh, or RHIPIPTERA, there are six legs, two membranous wings folded like a fan, and two crustaceous movable bodies, resembling little elytra, situated at the anterior extremity of the thorax; the organs of manducation are simple, setaceous jaws, with two palpi.

"In the twelfth, or DIPTERA, there are six legs, two membranous extended wings, accompanied, in most of them, by two movable bodies or halteres, placed behind them; the organs of manducation are a sucker composed of a variable number of setæ inclosed in an inarticulated sheath, most frequently in the form of a proboscis terminated by two lips."

The following is the Linnæan arrangement, as rendered by Jaeger in his Life of North American Insects:—

I. Coleoptera. *Beetles or Chafers.*—All Insects with horny bodies, six legs, and four wings, of which the upper ones are horny, and the lower ones parchment-like, as the Stag-beetle, May-beetle, etc.

II. Hemiptera. *Bugs.*—All Insects with four parchment-like wings, six legs, and who obtain their nourishment by sucking with a movable proboscis, as the Cicadar, Plant-lice, Bed-bugs, etc.

III. Orthoptera. *Straight-winged Insects.*—Insects with four parchment-like wings, of which the upper ones overlap on the back, and the two under ones are thin and folded together like a fan. They differ from those of the preceding order in that they have strong jaws instead of a movable probocis, as, *e.g.*, the Grasshopper, Cricket, and many others.

IV. Lepidoptera. *Butterflies, Hawk-moths, and Moths.*—Insects with four expanded wings, covered with colored farinaceous scales.

V. Neuroptera. *Net-winged Insects.*—Those which have four transparent, net-woven, or lattice-like wings, as the Dragon-fly, etc.

VI. Hymenoptera. *Vein-winged Insects.*—With four transparent, veined wings, and generally provided with a venomous sting, as Bees, Wasps, etc.

VII. Diptera. *Two-winged Insects.*—As Flies and Mosquitos.

Following are two other systems used by entomologists:—

CLASSIFICATION OF STEPHENS.

His first general division of insects is into two sub-classes.

First Sub-class.—*Mandibulata.*

Order 1. Strepsiptera.
" 2. Orthoptera.
" 3. Neuroptera.
Order 4. Dermaptera.
" 5. Trichoptera.
" 6. Hymenoptera.

Second Sub-class.—*Haustellata.*

Order 1. Hemiptera.
" 2. Homoptera.
" 3. Lepidoptera.
" 4. Diptera.
Order 5. Homaloptera.
" 6. Aphaniptera.
" 7. Aptera.

WESTWOOD'S CLASSIFICATION.

First Sub-class.—*Dacnostomata.*
(Mouth with Jaws.)

Order 1. Hymenoptera.
    (?) Osculant Order, Strepsiptera.
Order 2. Coleoptera.
    Osculant Order, Euplexoptera.

Order 3. Orthoptera.
    (?) Strepsiptera. (?)
Order 4. Neuroptera.
    (?)
Order 5. Trichoptera. (Phryganea alone.)

    Second Sub-class.—*Anthostomaia.*
      (Mouth with a Sucker.)

Order 1. Diptera.
    Osculant Order, Homaloptera.
    Osculant Order, Aphaniptera.

Order 2. Heteroptera, (including the water-bugs.)
" 3. Homoptera.
" 4. Lepidoptera.

For reasons already stated, the catalogue of insects of the mountain, with some notices of their habits, cannot be admitted here.

FOURTH GREAT DIVISION OF THE ANIMAL KINGDOM; or, RADIATED ANIMALS.

This division embraces animals of simple or uncomplicated organization, not the less wonderful on that account, rather the more so, as executing complex functions with the most rudimentary instrumentalities; and is the region of trouble, surprise, and doubt, where the plant and animal contest their respective fields, and the naturalist has attempted a compromise by calling the forms Zoophytes, which means animal-plants. It includes a vast range of structures and "variety of degrees," all of which, however, agree on one point, namely, "their parts are arranged around an axis, and on one or several radii, or on one or several lines extending from one pole to the other," and, with a few exceptions, affecting the radiating form, however shadowy or far off. It is a world of creatures that seem doomed on the question of cunningly-devised mechanisms eliminating thought through material organs alone,—for the "*nervous system is never very evident,*" there is *never any true circulating system,*" and "in the great number of Zoophytes there are *no vessels whatever.*" Some Zoophytes have regular stomachs and the rudiments of an intestinal canal; others have a mere intestinal sack without any opening, and in others there is a "mere excavation in their substance without any opening," and there are those which "can only be nourished by porous absorption." Sex is sometimes distinguishable; and they are said to be oviparous, while others are "reproduced by divisions or buds."

The Radiata are divided into five classes, namely: Echinodermata, Entozoa, Acalepha, (or sea-nettle,) Polypi, including the sponges and Infusoria, or the "microscopic inhabitants of stagnant waters." Among this group are the single-cell animals, to which allusion has been made as the simplest form of animal. The mountain has many representatives of this great division of the animal kingdom, from the order Nematoidea, of more complicated structure, to the simple Infusorial orders, Rotifera and Homogenea.

CLIMATE;

OR,

METEOROLOGY OF THE MOUNTAIN.

"Add to this a fickle and variable sky, an atmosphere alternately very moist and very dry, very misty and very clear, very hot and very cold, and a temperature so changeable, that in the same day you will have spring, summer, autumn, and winter, Norwegian frost and an African sun. Figure to yourself these, and you will have a concise physical sketch of the [climatology of the] United States."

VOLNEY'S "View," 1800.

"The influence of climate on animal life constitutes the end for which a physician studies the meteorology of the country in which he labors. To understand this influence, it is not sufficient to consult his thermometer, hygrometer, and other instruments of science, but he must also look at the species and habitudes of animals which live on its surface, or in its seas, lakes, rivers, and atmosphere. In doing this he will find that climate, in addition to its direct, has an indirect effect on the distribution of animal forms; through its influence on the growth and dissemination of plants, which constitutes the food of the greater number of animals, especially those which are the prey of the carnivorous."

DANL. DRAKE, M.D.

"The whole of organic nature is found to be in dependence upon meteorological phenomena. The influence of climate is very powerful over the existence and development of vegetables and animals."

M. CH. MARTINS.

"The air also changes the electricities while it roams over the earth. This wandering motion is a contact of different polarized tracts of the earth. Every mountain, valley, and river, every meadow is differently polarized; from each the air derives another electricity. Through this ceaseless alternation of polar exchange, its activity becomes so elevated, that at last the electricity makes its appearance in a manner cognizable by the senses. The production of electricity by *friction* admits of a similar explanation. Friction is, in miniature, what the sweep of air is over the earth. Were the earth quite level, and composed of homogeneous matter, the air would not become electrical by motion."

OKEN.

"To be bathed in the light and heat of a new sun, and washed with the winds of a fresh sky, to feel the steam of an unwonted surface of earth and the tension of a different magnestism and electricity to that to which we are accustomed, are *important elements in the recovery of health*, particularly where moral circumstances also are favorable. The hygienic map of countries gathered, as it might be, from the physical character of the inhabitants, or from susceptible temperaments on the spot, would be a guide worth having in the directions of patients to localities of specific benefit. In this respect, we require something more precise than the guide-books which have been written by the climatic physicians."

WILKINSON.

"Marvelous are the offices, and wonderful is the constitution of the atmosphere. Indeed, I know of no subject more fit for profitable thought on the part of the truth-loving, knowledge-seeking student, be he seaman or landsman, than that afforded by the atmosphere and its offices. Of all parts of the physical machinery, of all the contrivances in the mechanism of the universe, the atmosphere, with its offices and its adaptations, appears to me to be the most wonderful, sublime, and beautiful."

M. F. MAURY.

CHAPTER VI.

CLIMATE OF THE MOUNTAIN.

> "Do not all charms fly
> At the mere touch of cold philosophy?
> There was an awful rainbow once in heaven:
> We know her woof, her texture; she is given
> In the dull catalogue of common things.
> Philosophy would clip an angel's wings,
> Conquer all mysteries by rule and line,
> Empty the haunted air, and gnomed mine—
> Unweave a rainbow, as it erewhile made
> The tender-personed Lamia melt into shade."

ONCE, men talked of the mysteries of the deep, of the "dark, unfathomed caves of ocean," and thought that the blue water was as bottomless as the blue ether; while the poet even dreamed of

> "Where the isles of perfume are,
> Many a fathom down in the sea,
> To the south of sun-bright Araby;
> Where ocean spreads
> O'er coral rocks and amber beds;"

indulging also in visions of

> "Dark, green solitudes,
> Where shades, beautiful and bright,
> Amid sweet sounds across the deep would sweep,
> Like swift and lovely dreams, that walk the waves of sleep."

Now it has come, that

> Maury's head and Brooke's lead
> Have changed the "isle" and "amber bed"
> To doleful caverns of the dead;

"cemeteries for families of living creatures that outnumber the sands of the sea-shore for multitude," and have arranged it that the "physical geography of the sea" is almost as familiar as the physical geography of the land.

So, once, men spoke of the mysteries of the air-ocean above, and beheld with awe the wondrous meteor of the storm, and the motions of the winds were secrets of the heavens; for "the wind bloweth where it listeth, and thou hearest the sound thereof, but *canst not tell whence it cometh and whither it goeth;*"* and "the wind goeth toward the south, and turneth about unto the north; it whirleth about continually, and the wind returneth again according to his circuits." A special Providence was supposed to hold the wings of the whirlwind in his fingers, and man bowed to an inexorable death as to the wrath of an avenging Deity. It was a natural instinct of the barbarous man to personify the winds, and endow them with attributes profoundly allied, either in friendly attachment *to* him, or with anarchic and destructive force, *against* him. The air-currents of the spring hours were supposed to inspire hope, and carry with them the promises of the coming world of life; having to

---

* What follows is not meant as an impiety, or a fling even at John, because he was not a meteorologist, for undoubtedly he has expressed and fixed, in the above beautiful words, the limitation of his knowledge in that department of physics, but merely an intimation that the science of meteorology was not cultivated much in those days. Neither is *ignorance* by any means *imputed* to the more ancient and venerable author of Ecclesiastes, for in the next verse to the one above quoted, (viz., verse 7 of chap. i. Eccles.,) we have recorded what is now a familiar stereotyped formula of science. Thus, "All the rivers run into the sea; yet the sea is not full; *unto the place from whence the rivers come, thither they return again.*" The face of nature is veiled until science lifts that veil, and beholds her eye to eye.

sow the earth with flowers. The summer wind was said to be genial, kind, and maternal, nursing and perfecting a growing and expanding world. The autumnal wind was thought beneficent and good, when it showered down the ripened fruits of the globe in plenty upon all creatures, as from the hand of a loving parent. Fierce and stern the winter winds rushed from their homes in the cloud-chasms, hurrying the life-forms to silent sleep, and giving the earnest of a temporary death to nature, again to be relieved by the promises of resurrection and life by the returning airs of spring. The fabulous cave of Æolus was not a mere creation of the poet, but a significant symbol in the minds of men that there were laws for the winds, and that intelligent and intelligible forces determined the phenomena of the air.

This was all beautiful and well before the arrival on the planet of the systematic meteorologist, and before the scissors of philosophy had commenced "clipping the wings of angels," and it had come to pass that the poet's talk about the "waste airs pathless blue" was more poetical than true, and the secrets of the "viewless winds" were fixed "among the dull catalogue of common things."

Ruthless science, with her army of explorers, has navigated, as it were, and sounded, this air-ocean of fifty miles depth; has penetrated its mysterious phenomena; has wrestled with and exhausted its secrets. She now understands and has fixed its currents and motions; has arranged its cataracts, and defined its eddies and roaring maelstroms; its death-trails of the tornados; its circling arena of the trade-winds; its fiery tracks of the monsoon, harmattan, and sirocco; its chimneys of aspiration, and vortices of gyratory respiration; its dances of electricity and magnetism, and its boilings and surgings of caloric.

The beautifully-systematized and harmoniously-arranged machinery of the atmospheric sea has been made the subject of scientific analysis, and its laws announced and been demonstrated to the understanding of man, as plainly as the school-boy's rule of three.

Meteorologists have discovered that there are regular and irregular winds, regular and irregular rains, regular and irregular storms and electrical phenomena. Of this category of movements the regular winds, rains, and storms, with accompanying electrical manifestations, are those most generally found in activity. In other words, there is a system in the action of all these meteoric elements, the constant operation of which produces a series of constant results. These have been made the subject of scientific observation for some time by different meteorologists. The great causal forces at work, of all atmospheric movements, are differently designated and explained by different theorists and observers, but the general results, the catalogue of visible outward facts, are accredited and acknowledged by all.

Thus the details and facts of the trails of the storms which have integrated themselves as great individual meteors, worthy of separate histories, and which have been followed for thousands of miles and traced out as minutely as the movements of armies of men, and their operations as critically analyzed, are generally admitted by all; and thus the registration of visible phenomena is nearly identical, as given by Kamtz, Dove, Espy, Loomis, Redfield, Reid, Butler, and Blodget. What the primum mobile may be, whether caloric or electricity, whether those same gyratory aspirations, or heat respirations, whether magnetic stratifications and transfusions with positive attractions and negative repulsions, the disputants each arranges the facts, and marshals them under the order and drill of the polarity of his theory. In the mean time, the great facts that are obvious to all of the movements of air-currents, clouds, and electrical manifestations, which occur within the distance of a few miles of the surface of the earth, have been ascertained and recorded, and now stand the material and rudiments of what will soon be a beautiful, wonderful, and, it is to be hoped, an absolutely positive science.

Of the movements of the atmosphere in the mountain ranges of Pennsylvania, the general laws of the climatology of the eastern side of the continent must of course prevail, while their special influences are markedly visible.

WINDS AND STORMS.

Of the class to which the winds of the mountain belong, we are presented with the following universally admitted general statement of facts and laws of action :—

"Beyond the limits of the trade-winds in the temperate climates of both hemispheres are the regions of the southwest and northwest currents, called *Prevalent Winds.*"—JOHNSTON.

"The mean direction of the prevailing currents of air or winds for North America, is south. 86° west."—KAMTZ.

"The counter-trade, after leaving the northern limit of the surface-trades, curves to the eastward, and gradually assumes an E.N.E. course, and becomes a W.S.W. current where it crosses the line of no variation, and continues on until it passes over the Atlantic; and this course and curve is analogous to what may be found true of the counter-trade everywhere. It is best illustrated by the course of all the storms (in the American sense of the word, as distinguished from thunder showers and other brief rains) which have been traced north or south of the limits of the trades. It was found by Mr. Redfield in most of the storms investigated by him, which originated within or north of the tropics. Doubtless it was the actual course of the others, and that the investigation was imperfect. All the great autumnal, winter, or spring storms which have traversed the whole or any considerable portion of the territory of the United States, east of New Mexico, which have been investigated by Professors Espy, Loomis, Redfield, or others, have been found to follow this course.

"Messrs. Espy and Redfield, recognizing the existence of a '*prevailing*' S.W. current, but considering the surface-winds beneath it as the principal actors in producing the atmospherical conditions and changes, have attributed no office to that current, except that of giving direction and progression to our storms. This is their great mistake. It plays no such unimportant part in the philosophy of the weather, as we have already incidentally seen, and will proceed still further to consider.

"*All our storms originate in it.* This we may know from analogy.

"*Where there is no counter-trade, outside of the equatorial belt of rains, and within influential distance of the earth, there are neither storms nor rains.*"—BUTLER.

These prevalent winds blow with constantly varying strength and velocity, the register of the normal and abnormal month range is very extensive, and in certain seasons they are quite tempestuous in their transit of the Alleghany range. This occurs even when there is no storm in existence, and comes from the mountain heights stretching up through the surface-winds, and catching the regular streams of the S.W. winds unbroken by the local interference of the surface. This journeying of the higher strata of air, or streams and currents of regular winds, is clearly declared by the roar of the forests on the higher mountain peaks and ridges. This sound for hours, sometimes days, precedes the large regular storms, and is heard for miles, like the regular boom of the ocean in a tempest. This far-resounding boil or roar of the mountain-tops is one of the grandest phenomena of the atmosphere in the mountainous regions. It is well known even to common observers: "a storm is coming, the mountain roars," being a fixed fact of general apprehension. The greatly predominating, or regular winds of the mountain summits, belong to the western segments of the horizon, while those from the eastern side of the circle are only found to prevail in great atmospheric perturbations, such as accompany the larger storms, and are vastly the exception.

During regular storms, and even when *no* storm prevails, the higher cirrus-stratus clouds are often seen careering aloft, borne swiftly on by these air-streams, while below, the surface-winds are shifting about to almost every point of the compass, and frequently are found traveling rapidly in a direction *opposite* to that of higher currents. These higher currents are the channels through which are borne the constant supply of waters which form what are called the zones of regular extra-tropical rains, or that belt which is perpetually liable to precipitation, consequently this region is the best watered part of the earth. This is clearly shown by the splendid system of rivers or conduits for the meteoric waters back to the ocean whence they came; for as "all the rivers run into the sea, yet the sea is not full, so unto the place from whence the rivers come, thither they return again."

"This constitutes one vast, wonderful, connected, and regular system, coëxtensive with the globe, necessary to the return of moisture from the oceans upon the most inconsiderable portion of it, and to the condensation of the local moisture of evaporation; and by it the waters are returned from the oceans, as regularly and bountifully upon the far interior of the great continents in the same latitudes as upon the 'isles which rest in their bosoms.'

"From what ocean and by what machinery do our rivers return? Not wholly or mainly from the North Atlantic, although it lies adjacent to us, and they often seem to do so; for, first, all storms, showers, and clouds, which furnish, *independently*, any appreciable quantity of rain to the United States, and even adjacent to the Atlantic itself, come from a westerly point and pass to the eastward. This is a *general, uniform*, and *invariable* law, although there is in different places, and in the same place at different times, some variation in their direction; ranging in storms from *W. by S. to S.S.W.*, *and in showers between S.W. and N.W. to the opposite easterly points of the compass; the most general direction, east of the Alleghanies being from W.S.W. to E.N.E.*"—BUTLER.

The rush of N.N.E. winds to meet the S.W. storms, carried on by the higher currents to the N.E., are said by some meteorologists to be most observable on the S.E. side of the Alleghanies, on the Atlantic plane. There are also S.E. and southern winds, which flow under the larger storms, if the axes of the storms are some distance north of the place of observation, or if the axes are south of the observer these winds will be even N.N.W., flowing into the same. On the Alleghany range these winds have as much violence as on the S.E. side of the mountain barrier, and are accompanied by nearly the same order of phenomena. These winds are sometimes of long duration, and have great force and velocity; striking the sides of the mountains, they produce something of the ocean sound or roar of the higher rushing currents. They also carry clouds, sometimes full, dark, and heavy, in the strata of the storm-fog and storm-scud, in the region within a mile and a half of the earth's surface, and have all the characteristics of the principal actors of the storm performance.

It is easily perceived that the Huttonian, or caloric school, can, in these phenomena, get a visible and almost tangible confirmation of their views. These rushing streams of air, carrying fogs or scuds, or low clouds, in volumes toward the centre of the annulus, or the mid-axis of the storm that is coming from the southwest, present all the appearance of regular water-carriers to the advancing chimney or vortex of suction or uprushing.

It would seem, from the statements of observers, that approaching the warmer Atlantic Ocean coast this scud-mass is greater, and loses much of its water, as suggested by Butler and Blodget, before it arrives at the Alleghanies; the lofty cirrus and stratus clouds still floating onward, as can easily be observed in the line of the regular counter-trade, and dropping or pouring out their water, as may be, through these terrestrial fogs and vapors

There is nothing especially peculiar in the phenomena of the transit of the great storms over the Alleghany range. The largest storms, or those having axes of several hundred of miles in extent, with corresponding annuli, are perhaps more violent, and exhibit the whirling, twisting, and combating of the irregular under-currents in a more exaggerated manner than the eastern or western planes ever witness. The winds from the eastern segment, on the approach of the vast vortices of the continental storms, are extremely violent, and their arrival and persistent blowing is the sure precursor of a great meteor striding over the continent from the western segment. In the winter, these eastern winds, sometimes heavily charged with moisture, clothe the forests on the highest knobs or summits of the mountain with a mantle of ice or hoar-frost, while a few hundred feet below, on the east and west sides, there is no such appearance. The mountain reveals its highest expression of grandeur and sublimity when seized and in full possession of one of these magnificent storms.

The tornados march across the mountains, as elsewhere,

mowing their swathes of death. The tracks of many of them are visible for years in the form of narrow avenues of fallen and crushed timber (called fallen-timbers) torn through the dense forests. They observe the same laws of progress in their passage of the mountains, and occur at the same periods of the year, as at other places.

The smaller storms, or circumscribed meteors, from a single cloud, dropping its contents, to the regular thunder storms several miles in circumference, are accompanied by winds from all quarters, more or less violent, from moderate breezes to almost the tornado's force. In the mountains these small storms show their usual character, as elsewhere, perhaps a little more noisy from their battling with the forests. There is nothing peculiar except that the low scud or fog-clouds often envelop the whole mountain-top in a silver mantle, while the region below is clear

CALORIC.

It would appear, as the result of the concurrent evidence of meteorologists, physical geographers, and writers on climate in general, that the climate of the continent of North America is *peculiar* in its caloric developments, and has characters quite its own, being separated widely in its leading features from that of the Old World. This is soon visible by comparing the American climate with that of Europe and Africa. It will be seen that the range of the thermometer is more extensive, that the changes are quicker and greater, that the *heat* in summer is more excessive, and the *cold* in winter more intense, in the same parallels of latitude, on the shores of America than in those of Europe. It is also stated that the Western Atlantic is much more stormy than the Eastern. Buffon placed the climate of North America in the class of "*excessive climates*,"—excessively hot in summer, and excessively cold in winter,—thus exhibiting a great extent of the annual range of temperature.* In Clarke, "On the Sanative Influence of Climate," we have the following table of comparison of mean annual temperature of a number of places nearly the same on the eastern and western hemispheres, and of the difference of this range:—

PLACES.	Mean Annual Temp.	Temp. of Summer.	Temp. of Winter.	Dif. of Winter and Summer.
Paris..........................	51·4°	66·0°	38·0°	28·0°
Cambridge, America	50·4°	70·5°	34·0°	36 0°
St. Maloes.....................	54·5°	66·0°	42·0°	24·0°
Cincinnati	53·7°	72·9°	32·9°	40 0°
Nantes.........................	55·6°	70·7°	42·2°	28·4°
New York......................	53·8°	79·2°	29 8°	40·0°
Bourdeaux	56·5°	70·7°	42·1°	28·6°
Philadelphia	54·9°	73·9°	32·2°	41·7°

A number of causes have been assigned for this, and a number of explanations and suggestions made of the rationale of the universally acceded facts in this department.

In the Physical Atlas of Johnston, we have this suggestion:—

"The permanent and drifting ice of the arctic regions essentially contributes to depress the isothermal lines on the east coast of North America to such low latitudes, and to increase the difference of the seasons; for, while on the European side of the Atlantic Ocean, between the isothermal lines of 40° and 32°, the difference between winter and summer amounts to 36° and 40°, on the other side, on the coasts of the New World, it amounts to 52° and 54°. There is here 14° and 16° difference on the different sides of the Atlantic under some lines of latitude."

Dr. Drake remarks:—

"On the western side of the continent the high range of the Sierra Nevada cuts off the genial influence of the Pacific Ocean."

Thus, he supposes the equalizing influence of large bodies of water is prevented from reaching the eastern side of the

* See one of the leading quotations from Volney; a rather sharp observation for sixty years ago.

continent, as borne by the prevalent winds, by the wall of mountains.

Lorin Blodget describes the climate approaching the western side, and far interior of the continent, as "singularly mild and warm," compared with the range of the eastern coast. "On the Upper Missouri an extensive region was as mild in climate as St. Pauls in Minnesota." Wheat grows on Mackenzie's River nearly to the sixty-fifth parallel.

"The comparison of climates for the United States shows a rapid increase of heat in going westward, on any line of latitude from points in Minnesota, and this even when the elevation *increases*. It is warmer at Fort Benton on the Missouri, in longitude $110\frac{1}{2}°$ west, and latitude $47\frac{1}{2}°$ during every season, than at St. Pauls, Minnesota. The isothermal lines, even for winter, curve very largely northward over this space, indeed they curve *most* for this season, making there more difference in the temperature than in any other part of the year. At Sitka, on the Pacific coast, in Russian America, at $57°$ north, the winter temperature is $33\frac{2}{10}°$, which is as warm as at St. Louis, Washington City, and Philadelphia. Beginning at the coldest side of the continent, we have not yet ascertained the value of the west side. If the *mountains* were *removed*, the whole area would correspond in climate to the west of Europe, very nearly at least; at the latitude of St. Petersburg it would be as habitable as that part of Russia is," etc. etc.

From all of which statements of Mr. Blodget it appears that the isothermals on the east side of the continent make a most singular and rapid declension southward.

On the subject of the causes of fluctuations of temperature on the eastern side of the continent, Mr. Butler has the following suggestions as to the *magnetic causes* of the same phenomena:—

"To the difference in the magnetic intensity of the eastern portion of this continent, compared with Europe and our western coast, very much of the difference of climate, so far as temperature is involved, may be attributed. We have seen in what manner the isothermal lines surround these areas of intensity. So the most excessive climate, that is, the climate where the greatest extremes alternate, other things being equal, is upon, or near, the line of area of *greatest magnetic* intensity. I say other things being equal, because large bodies of water modify climates by equalizing the seasons,—making the summers cooler and the winters warmer than the mean of the parallel.

"Thus, our great interior lakes modify the climate in relation to temperature in their vicinity. Their summers are cooler and their winters warmer; but westward of them the same line of equal summer temperature, or isothermal line, rises with considerable abruptness; and the winter, or isocheimal line of equal temperature, falls in a similar manner; thus, the range of the thermometer, from the highest elevation to the lowest depression, for the year, is very great, while in the tropics the range is comparatively small.

"From observations made at the military posts of the United States, Dr. Forrey deduced summer and winter lines of equal temperature, starting from the vicinity of Boston and running west, which showed most remarkably the rise of the summer lines as intensity increased, and the fall of the winter lines in like manner. The influence of the lakes was also most obvious. The elevation of the earth increases, going west, to about 700 feet at the surface of the lakes, and to nearly 4000 feet at the eastern base of the Rocky Mountains, and, although temperature does not decrease to as great a degree when the elevation above the level of the sea is *gradual*, yet some allowance should doubtless be made for that elevation on this line. When that allowance is made, the ascent of the summer line to the north, over the area of the greatest intensity, is strikingly apparent."

He further remarks :—

"The effect of this difference of magnetic intensity upon the climate of Europe is marked. There, the excessive summer heat, which our greater magnetic intensity and larger volume of counter-trade give us, is unknown. Hence, while we can grow Indian corn (which requires the excessive summer heat) over all the Eastern States, up to 45°, and in some localities, east of the lakes, to 47° 30′, and to 50° west of them, to the base of the Rocky Mountains, and, notwithstanding the increase of elevation, they cannot grow it except over a limited area, and with limited success."*

Magnetism and *Thermalism* it would seem, then, are intimately associated in the phenomena of the surface of the earth; and, on the point now under consideration, the former exerts, according to Mr. Butler, great influence in

* In thermometric range, the western side of the eastern continent is the same as the western side of the western continent.

depressing the temperature of the eastern side of the continent. Whatever may be the cause, whether from topographic agency in modifying atmospheric movements, or deeper geological and magnetic forces, or the "permanent and drifting ice of the arctic region," etc., the great fact is universally acceded.

Speaking of the arctic fauna, Agassiz observes:—

"It has already been said that the arctic fauna of the three continents is the same; its southern limit, however, is not a regular line. It does not correspond precisely with the polar circle, but rather to the isothermal zero; that is, the line where the average temperature of the year is at 32° Fahrenheit. The course of this line presents numerous undulations. In general, it may be said to coincide with the northern limits of trees, so that it terminates where forest vegetation succeeds the vast arid plains; the barrens of North America are the tundras of the Samoyides. The uniformity of these planes involves a corresponding uniformity of plants and animals. On the North American continent it extends much farther southward on the eastern shore than on the western. From the peninsula of Alaska, it bends northward toward the Mackenzie, then descends again toward the Bear Lake, and comes down nearly to the northern shore of Newfoundland."

On this subject Butler makes also the following statement:—

"Take the isothermal line of 0 or zero, that is, the line where the mean or *average* height of the thermometer *for the year* is at zero. At Behring's Straits this line is a little below the arctic circle, or the parallel of 66° 30′ north latitude. Passing east over North America, it descends into Canada, almost to Lake Superior, and to about the fiftieth parallel; that is to say, it is on an average during the year as cold as our continent at the fiftieth parallel as it is at Behring's Straits at the sixty-fifth parallel. Passing east, the line of zero rises again over the Atlantic Ocean until, in the meridian of Spitsbergen, it reaches, within the arctic circle, up almost to the seventy-fifth parallel. So, too, the isothermal of 5° below zero, which is below the sixtieth parallel in Siberia, rises in the North Sea, above Behring's Straits, to the parallel of 75°, descending on the continent in North America to the fifty-fifth parallel, and rising again almost to the pole at Spitzbergen, to descend again in Siberia, while the isothermals of 10° and 15° below zero, which in North America are but just above the latitude of 60° and 75° respectively, ascend abruptly *surrounding the magnetic pole, and falling short of the geographical one.*"

Of the isothermal curves in the interior valley, Dr. Drake indites:—

"The curves of equal mean temperature, which traverse the Interior Valley, cannot yet be delineated, for the want of a sufficient number of observations. In the west, from the cooling influence of the Cordilleras of Mexico, and the Rocky Mountains, extending into the polar circle, and to the east from a *similar* though *smaller influence* of the same kind *exerted* by *the Appalachian* chain, from the latitude of 33° to 48° or 50° north we know that the curves of equal mean temperature cannot lie parallel to the lines of latitude, except for a certain distance in the middle of the valley. East of the Mississippi, as they approach the Appalachian Mountains, they must bend to the south; west of that river, as they ascend the great inclined plane, they must come in the same direction, and, on reaching the Rocky Mountains, must of necessity extend along their slopes, rising gradually as the latitude lessens, but not attaining the summits of these mountains until we come within the tropics. It results from these data that the isothermal lines of the valley are nearly parallel to those of one side of a compressed ellipsis or long oval with their eastern curved extremities much shorter than their western. Where they intersect the trough of the Mississippi they have their highest latitude."

It has been clearly demonstrated that the climate of the State of Pennsylvania, in its thermometric oscillations, is the most equable of the whole Atlantic range. This comes from its mediate latitudinal position, also its being saddled over the two planes of the Atlantic and Ohio water-sheds, and over the Appalachian range, its territory extending from the lakes to the arms of the ocean; one cause of its distinctive climate thus being the well-known equalizing influences of large bodies of water. A region of agreeable equilibrium of climate, that happily-located State enjoys a most desirable temperature; removed from the chilling northern and northeastern Atlantic and lake sweep of currents, also from the hotter southwestern and southeastern streams of air, it exhibits less of the excessiveness of climate described by meteorologists than any other of the United States. Its mean temperature is 47°, or nearly the same as that of Great Britain, whose mean latitude is about 54°, *while that of Pennsylvania is not* 41°.

Mr. Blodget gives the mean average temperature of the spring months of the whole State as 47°, or its mean *annual* temperature.* The mean temperature of summer is thus stated by observers: from tide to mountain range, $72\frac{1}{2}°$; mountain belt, 67°; western end of State, 70°, or $2\frac{1}{2}$ of difference between the east and west plains. The climate of the mountains, then, it seems, gives an average summer temperature of 67°. On the heights of the Alleghanies it is much less. The autumnal mean of the State is 50°, the Atlantic side 54°, and the western slope 52°. The winter mean of the mountain group is 24°, the western slope 28°, and the eastern 30°. The maximum summer temperature of the whole State is 74°, the summer minimum 65°. The low mean summer temperature of 67° gives a delightful climate to the mountain district of the State, and constitutes it one of the most attractive regions on the continent. That belt of mountains, as will be seen from the above data, has a calorical range, from mean winter to mean summer temperatures, of 42°.

The climatal vibrations of the State exhibit of course the general extremes of temperature which characterize the eastern side of the continent. This statement applies to annual, monthly, and diurnal changes, also to those dependent upon accidental atmospheric vicissitudes, which often amount in a short time to enormous thermometric ranges. The regular *diurnal changes* are, perhaps, the most considerable in the mountain regions, the surfaces of the mountains being more covered with forests, thus preventing uniform and extensive heating of the surface by the direct rays of the sun. This range of protected surfaces has over it a stratum of cold air, which, as soon as the sun declines

* "Pittsburg has a summer mean of 71·4°, and Marietta, Ohio, 71·3°, while Philadelphia is 72·5° to 73·7°."—BLODGET.

beneath the horizon, pours out into cleared spaces, ravines, and valleys, rivers of cold air. This strikes all travelers through the mountains, especially among the higher ranges, and is the cause of the sudden diurnal change of those regions. The extremes, monthly and annual, above alluded to are, however, from all authorities, less in Pennsylvania than any other State of the Union, thus giving that State, as already remarked, a more equable and salubrious climate than is exhibited in any other part of North America. Speaking of the great general uniformity of the Eastern United States, Lorin Blodget remarks, in his admirable work, the "Climatology of the United States," p. 128 :—

"The district embraced by this uniform climate is very large. Excepting the points of local influence at the coasts and near the great lakes, it may be said to include all the continent east of the one-hundredth meridian; at which line the arid and extreme character of the plains sets in. Of this district nearly the whole surface may be practically regarded as level, and very little elevated. The mountains which occur do not break in upon the climate except by reduction of temperature simply, or by changes caused by altitude alone. They do not shelter or expose either side, nor cause any contrasts in the character of productions respecting them. Western and Eastern Virginia differ little, and probably not at all, from the influence of the intervening range of mountains. It is still more decisively so in Pennsylvania, and at the southern extremity of the Alleghany ranges, where Tennessee may be contrasted with North and South Carolina and Upper Georgia. This *absence* of *interruptions* of the *general condition*, even where *mountains* of considerable *height* occur, is one of the most distinguishing features of the North American climate, and that which, more than any other, requires it to be treated as a separate district for the area east of the plains."

Still, as has been observed, there is a difference between the climate of the Atlantic slope and the Appalachian range of mountains, and the western or great valley slope, which constitutes the basin of drainage of the Alleghany and Monongahela Rivers. This gives three minor shades of climate in Pennsylvania, each with its distinctive characteristics.

The climate of the Alleghany Mountain range through

CALORIC. 449

the State presents the same general laws, as already stated, and characteristic features of the climate of the eastern side of the continent. Through this portion of their range they are embraced between the isothermal lines of 50 and 45. At this point the lines correspond with the lines of latitude of 39° 40′ and 42°.

By following these isothermal lines around the globe, as we have already seen, we will discover, that after leaving the Alleghany summits and making the transit of the Atlantic plain, and leaving the continent to cross the ocean, there is a great deflexion north approaching the eastern shore or continent of Europe. It has been suggested that the lines in the Atlantic Ocean are carried north by the vast river of hot water, whose liberated caloric modifies to so great an extent the rivers of air of the ocean above. This flowing sea is the Gulf Stream rushing north through the bed of the Atlantic from the boiling heats of the tropics. It will be seen that the lines of latitude which correspond with these isothermals are, on the west of Europe, 50° and 60°; thus showing the difference of 10° to 18° of latitude between the two continents. As a direct conclusion from this, it is evident that this range of mountains through the State of Pennsylvania has an extremely low mean annual temperature, *lower than any other corresponding* latitudinal point, with a few exceptions, on the surface of the globe; in other words, is cooler than any other corresponding point on the earth.

The range of the thermometer must not necessarily, from this fact, exhibit the exaggerated extremes or excesses of the special climates of the continent. There may be, in uncultivated wilderness extents, some difference in the thermometric changes from the same parallels of the lower surfaces of cultivated districts, or spots of particular local influences. Observation will prove this, no doubt, and establish the places. The elevation of the mountain, and its parallel collateral ridges above the level of the sea, gives also a greater range of caloric depression. As there is a fall of one degree for every three hundred feet (Espy) of ascent into the air, and, under certain circumstances, very much less than that, as, according to Drake,* it is two hundred feet in steep ascents, and four hundred on gentle acclivity as on the Rocky Mountain plains, this cause alone would give diminished temperature on the same line of latitude, as many of the peaks of the range are from three thousand to six thousand feet above the ocean. These high knobs or ranges of elevations, extending as we have seen into the higher currents of air, and catching the counter-trade as it pours down from the heights from which it is deflected from over the tropics, must of necessity be subject to vicissitudes from sudden changes, also extremes of depression from local causes. These are the causes of the great coolness of the mountain and its winds, also the shortness of its seasons, there being sometimes, in latitude 40°, at an elevation of 2000 feet, frost in all months of the year.

At Cresson, on the Alleghany Mountain, latitude 40° 30′ 1″ north, longitude west 1° 30′ 6″, and 2000 feet above the sea, there was frost in every month of the year 1859. This is rather a rare occurrence on the central Pennsylvania range. An absence of frost for two or three months is the most general character of summer.† Thus the Indian corn, whose range is to the sixty-fifth degree of mean temperature for the three months of summer, approaches its limit of cultivation here, only one or two varieties being at all sure crops, as already noticed.

RAIN.

Among hydrometeors, rain forms the most important climatic element, hence an inquiry into the different quantities

---

* "So peculiar is the vertical distribution of heat, that an elevation of 4000 feet, in some parts of the Rocky Mountain plateau, does not reduce the temperature even one degree."—BLODGET.

† The mean duration of winter at New York, according to Dekay, "is five months, while in the interior northern counties there is frost nearly every month."

precipitated in different parts of the globe, and its distributions among the different seasons, has an important bearing on many departments of physical science. The life of plants and animals depends as much on moisture as on temperature, and their development is greatly modified by the dryness or humidity of the atmosphere. Rain is very unequally distributed over the different regions of the globe. It is generally most abundant in those latitudes where evaporation takes place most rapidly; yet there are exceptions to this rule. In many parts of the earth it almost never rains, because, as Kamtz remarks, the greatly heated atmosphere does not contain sufficient moisture to admit of precipitation even during the greatest decrement of temperature. The temperate zone of the New World gives an annual amount of thirty-seven inches in the United States, according to Johnston, and forty inches according to Butler and Blodget.

Rain is most abundant at the equator, and decreases toward the poles, in some lines of observation, from 150 to 13 inches. The amount of rain decreases, ascending from low plains to elevated table-lands; on the contrary, increases from plains and slopes of mountains, if those are steep and rugged, as shown by the annual fall at Paris being twenty inches, while at great St. Bernard it is 36·13 inches. Steep and rugged mountains promote, through partial currents of air, the formation and increase of clouds, such mountains being more cloudy than those with uniform summits and smooth slopes. The quantity of rain *decreases*, receding from coasts to the *interior* of continents, from the greater amount of evaporation on sea than land, and because of greater interchange of heat between land and sea, consequently greater movement of arial currents than between different parts of a continent. This rule is apparent in the interior of the United States of North America, in the centre of the plains of Orinoco, in the Steppes of Siberia, and in the interior of Australia. There are exceptions to this rule from the geographic position of countries in relation to regions of winds, and the direction of mountain chains, which produce moisture in one country and drought in another in its vicinity, the former, when the country is on the side of the mountain against which the rain-winds blow, and the latter, when the country is on the opposite side of those mountains.

In Johnston's Hyetographic, or Rain Map of the World,* we are presented with a division into the three important zones of precipitation. The first is the zone of the periodical rains, extending both sides of the equator to the tropics of Cancer and Capricorn. This includes the subordinate zone of "frequent, almost constant, precipitation, always accompanied by electrical explosions." This is a narrow belt of from 5° or 6° width, near the equator. The greatest precipitation occurs in this belt, amounting, according to Johnston, at one point on the western coast of Africa, to "upwards of 300 inches, or twenty-five feet, which frequently falls during one season alone."

The other two are the *northern* and *southern* zones of constant precipitation.

"The zones of *constant precipitation* are so named in order to distinguish them from those of periodical rains. In the former, it does or may rain during every day in the year, whereas, in the latter, during many months, not a drop of rain falls."—JOHNSTON.

These northern and southern zones of constant precipitation extend to the arctic and antarctic circles. There are *rainless districts* in all these zones; stretching around the earth in different latitudes, they are generally, however, within or near the tropics. Within these zones of precipitation there are, as suggested in the quotations from Johnston's Physical Atlas, various causes for irregular distribution of the quantities of rain in different parts of the earth's surface.

On this subject, Schouw, of the University of Copenhagen, has the following remarks:—

"Another principal cause of the increased quantity of rain, lies in the inequalities of the earth's surface. Mountains *increase the*

---

* Johnston's Map is VERY far from correct for the American continent.

amount of rain; it increases in proportion as we approach toward them, and the higher and steeper they are. The reason is obvious here also: the strata of air over the mountains are colder than those over plains, and a constant reaction takes place between these different strata. Sometimes the warm air of the plains rises up the sides of the mountains, or through the valleys, sometimes the masses of cold air flow down from the mountains into the plains; these strata, possessing different temperatures, meet above and below; cooling is thus caused, and the vapors are precipitated as rain. When we inquire into the amounts of rain upon the great plain which is bounded on the north by the Alps, and toward the south by the Apennines, we find that they increase toward the Alps. Southward of the Po, the annual quantity of rain amounts, on an average, to twenty-six inches; northward of the river, to thirty-eight inches; immediately at the foot of the Alps to sixty inches. There are particular places in the southern part of the plain where the quantity of rain amounts only to twenty-one inches, and isolated points in the Alps where it amounts to one hundred inches. We meet with similar conditions when we follow the Rhine or the Rhone upward, or when we compare the quantities of rain in the mountains of Germany and France with those presented by the plains."

Again, he observes, that the

"Influence of mountain chains, in the increase of rain, is greater than that of the ocean; where, however, a range sinks down precipitously toward the sea, the increase of the rain is especially striking. This is seen on the east and west side of Scandinavia, on the mountains on the west side of England, and of the south side of the Northern Apennines, which extend down to the Mediterranean, where there is sometimes a hundred inches of rain. The relation of the various winds to rain is just as simply and readily explained. In North America the *east wind* is the principal source of rain; it *comes from the Atlantic Ocean.*"

From which last opinion, and some others, many American meteorologists entirely dissent.

On the subject of the amount of rain which falls on the summits of the Alleghany Mountains, there have been but few observations made by actual measurement of the aggregate of precipitation.* The observations made would point

---

* It is with extreme regret that the statement must be made, that the Observatory of the Alleghany Mountain Health Institute has not yet been completed and furnished

to a confirmation of Blodget's views, given in an important communication to the Scientific Association, in 1853, on the annual fall of rain in the United States. The showing on this point now stands with the following conclusions: The amount of absolute moisture or water in the air diminishes, leaving the surface of the Atlantic at the foot of that plain, and ascending the Appalachian steps or waves until the summit range of crests is reached, where there is great demonstrable decrement of humidity. After passing that range, and descending into the Valley of the Mississippi, the moisture increases, until the surface of the Mississippi River is reached, where the *greatest* amount of moisture is found. A diagram of the great atmospheric sponge would thus show increased and intensified shading or regular increase of the quantity of moisture from the summit of the Alleghany to the surface of both waters.*

In Butler's "Philosophy of the Weather"† we have the following statements, made from facts furnished by Blodget:—

"The northern portion of the continent lies beneath the zone of extra-tropical rains, and north of the northern limit of the northeast trades is never uncovered from it, and has no distinct rainy or dry season, although more rain falls at certain periods, and in certain localities, than at others. The climate of that part of Oregon which lies upon the Pacific, and the character of its rains, resemble those of Northwestern Europe, and will be further explained hereafter.

"Coming to the portion of the continent which we occupy, the United States, we find it different, still a most favored region. Portions of it, Eastern Texas, for instance, are upon the same parallels

with a regular set of meteorological instruments. It is hoped, however, that this much-desired object will soon be achieved, when results of the highest interest and significance may be expected. Located on the rim, or eastern margin of the great continental basin, and some 2000 feet above the sea, it is inevitable that results highly important to science must be accomplished.

* One cause of the general impression that more water falls on the Alleghany than east or west is, that during the winter months the mountain summits are generally white with snow, while there is no snow at eastern or western base or the sides of the mountain. Of course, the height of the mountain, stretching up into colder spaces, and preventing the melting of the snow, will explain this, without any increase in the quantity of water falling in the form of snow.

† This is an interesting and suggestive book, and one of the best contributions made recently to the science of meteorology.

of latitude as the rainless regions of Northern Mexico, etc. Eastern Texas, however, is not rainless. Other portions are upon the same parallels as California, etc., yet have no distinct rainy and dry season. We repeat, this section is a most favored region, without a parallel upon any portion of the earth's surface, except in degree, in China and some other portions of Eastern Asia.

"It is not only without a distinct rainy and dry season, but it is watered by an average, annually, of more than forty inches of rain, while Europe, although bounded on three sides by seas and oceans, and apparently much more favorably situated, receives annually an average of only about twenty-five inches, if we except Norway and one or two other places, where the fall is excessive. The distribution of this supply of moisture over the United States is, in other respects, wonderful. Iowa, in the interior of the continent, far away from the great oceans, on the east or west, or the Gulf of Mexico on the south, receives *fif'y inches*—some ten or fifteen inches more than fall upon the slopes east of the Alleghanies, and contiguous to the great Atlantic, (*from which all our storms are*, ERRONEOUSLY, *supposed to be derived!*) and the average over the entire great interior valley is about forty-five inches, falling at all seasons of the year."

On the views of the combating theorists as to the particular oceanic origin of the waters falling on these mountains, there might be an interesting critique.

While Maury and Redfield contend that our southwest currents, with their freight of moisture, come from the Pacific Ocean, Butler assumes that they come from the *South Atlantic*, and Espy and the school of Huttonians generally talk of the warm streams of moisture from the North and East Atlantic Ocean, the forty-five annual inches of water do actually fall upon the United States, minus ten inches on the Alleghany heights, on the authority of Mr. Blodget. At the same time we have seen, from the authority of other meteorologists, that mountain ranges catch, condense, and precipitate, controlling and modifying the whole supply of water to those portions of the earth.

From Butler we have the following statements:—

"Everywhere currents passing from the ocean, *over mountain ranges*, part with a large share of their moisture."

Again,

"The influence of mountains in extracting the water from the atmospheric currents which pass over them is *well known* and *readily explainable.*"

Blodget, however, found that whatever might be the source of our rains, when the water-carriers reached the Alleghanies they were so far exhausted of their moisture that those mountains extracted less from them than fell to the westward, by some five or ten inches annually; and that the fall of rain upon them was *less* than *upon the Atlantic slope eastward of them to the ocean.* This last announcement does not accord with observations elsewhere made, but is easily explained.

As the storm approaches the ocean, it attracts in under it the surface atmosphere of the ocean, loaded with vapor, condensing in the form of fog and scud as it becomes subject to the increasing influence of the storm. Although the scud or fog would *not* of *itself make rain,* it aids materially in increasing the quantity of that which falls *through it.* "The drops, by attraction and contact, enlarge themselves as they pass through, in the same manner as a drop of water will do in running down a pane of glass which is covered with moisture. The small drop which starts from the upper portion of a fifteen-inch pane will sometimes more than double its size before it reaches the bottom." It is by this power of attracting the surface atmosphere, which contains the moisture of evaporation *under it,* and inducing condensation *in it,* that the moisture of evaporation, which rarely rises very far in the atmosphere, is made to fall *again* during storms and showers.

This attraction of a moist atmosphere from the ocean, accounts for the excess of rain on the east of the Alleghanies compared with its fall *upon them.* So the great Valley of the Mississippi is comparatively level, and less of its water runs off than of that which falls upon the Alleghanies, and there is, therefore, more moisture of evaporation in the atmosphere of the former to be thus precipitated and add to the annual supply of rain upon that valley, and it therefore *exceeds* that which falls upon the Alleghanies.

Those mountains, too, are elevated but about 1500 feet above the table-lands at their base, and do not exert great influence on the *counter-trade.* If they were 6000 or 8000 feet high, a different state of things would exist.

Again, Mr. Blodget found the quantity of rain which fell in Iowa, and to the south and west of the lake region, to be *greater* than *fell over the lake region itself.*

This, he thinks, is doubtless in part owing to the same cause. The counter-trade, in a stormy state, attracts the *surface atmosphere from the lake region,* with its evaporated moisture, before it arrives over it, and, therefore, more rain falls *southwest* of the lake region than upon it. This power of attracting the surface-wind of the ocean in under it, produces the heavy gales which affect our coast, and which are rarely felt west of the Alleghanies to any considerable degree; and a storm coming from the W.S.W., extending a thousand miles or more from S.S.E. to N.N.W., may have the wind set in violently at southeast on the *southern coast first,* and at later periods, successively at points farther north, and thus induce the belief that the storm traveled from south to north.

Of the influence of the Alleghanies, as atmospheric modifiers, Dr. Drake records:—

"The mountains bounding the Mississippi Valley on either side deserve great consideration. To the east, or rather southeast, the Appalachians stretch, in many parallel or coalescing ridges, from Alabama to the region north of the Gulf of St. Lawrence, rising from 2000 to 5000 feet above the sea. They no *doubt contribute to some extent to give direction to certain winds.* When an easterly wind prevails, they deprive it by *condensation* (?) of a *portion* of the *moisture* with which the *warm Atlantic Ocean* had imbued it, and reduced its temperature, and hence, on the banks of the Ohio, and in other central portions of the valley, a *southeast wind* never *raises* the *temperature* as high as a *southwest.*"

Aside from the general laws of atmospheric phenomena on the Appalachian Mountains of Pennsylvania, there are local and special causes of meteoric manifestations. The higher ridges, and especially the great culminating range called the Alleghany Mountain, show this in an eminent degree. Their height alone above the level of the sea would give a modified meteorology. Another cause of special character in the surface or local influences, is the condition of that surface, its soil, rocks, etc. We have already seen, in the chapter on the soil of the mountain, that it is composed principally of sand and clay, the *sand predominating*, and without much superficial detritus.

From the rocky heights, terraced slopes, and precipitous ravines, the meteoric waters flow off quickly by surface conduits and subterranean drainage through the fissured strata. Thus, there is no intense or protracted soaking of the soils, as occurs in regions of extensive diluvial deposits, or flats without natural drainage, and in the composition of which the clay element is the predominating ingredient. There are few* ponds of water, but the very few lakes or tarns that do exist near the mountain proper, are of a highly interesting character. They are small, limpid bodies of water, inclosed within folds of the ridges and hills, gleaming jewels upon the bosom of the landscape. Of this character are Lewis and Hunter's Lakes, in Lycoming County. They have been, till within a few years, surrounded by native forests, and are pools of perfectly pure water, and of exceeding beauty.

As would be expected, there are but few bogs, morasses, or swales of any extent, and very rarely pools of stagnant water. Thus, from evaporating surfaces of bodies of water, there is

---

* In the northeastern and northwestern corners of Pennsylvania there are many interesting lakes and ponds, forming striking features in the landscapes of those parts of the State, so long celebrated for the beauty of their scenery. Southwest of the waters of the West Branch of the Susquehanna there are no lakes on the Alleghany range, or either side of it, for long spaces extending through the Southern States. There is a geological solution of this fact which is an interesting scientific deduction.

but little supply of moisture to the atmosphere. Dense, native forests, and extensive wastes of shrub and bush-growth, cover the greater part of the surfaces of the higher ranges of knobs and slopes. This, of course, prevents the sun's rays and winds from acting on the water of the soil, and therefore quick surface evaporation, to the extent which occurs in cleared and cultivated regions, cannot here take place. The springs and streams of the mountain show this by their volume and freshness, the creeks and rivers, in the cultivated portion, drying up in the summer months. The constant prevalence of the regular air-currents, always of some degree of intensity, from gentle breezes to rushing streams, carry off to the northeast most of the moisture which they drink up from the surface of the mountain. This occurs almost constantly, except during the prevalence of regular storms of precipitation, or local cloud-falls. The meeting streams from the northeast, running as under-currents in a direction opposite to the regular marching of the storm, then, of course, drop their local additions or feedings from local evaporation. In fact, the air-currents, from far distant spaces of the air-ocean, are the regular *water-carriers* of the Alleghany Mountains; while constantly prevalent winds, or gentle air-streams take up the moisture of the surfaces, to be precipitated in distant spaces of the earth or ocean of water again. The presence of any undue humidity in the atmosphere of the mountain heights is proved, moreover, by recorded observation, not to exist.

From this whole condition of things it follows that the exact hygrometric range of the mountain's atmosphere is nearly the same as at corresponding latitudinal points at its base below, with the unexpected difference only that the air is dryer; leaving to be explained by the local influence already described—of large forests in a state of nature, receiving and retaining in their cool shades the water supplied by the clouds, uninfluenced by the evaporating power of the sun and winds coming in contact with the earth's surface—the *appearance* of excessive dampness beneath the canopy of branches and leaves.

There are really upon the mountain no special local phenomena on this point visible or demonstrable except those directly dependent upon this "boundless contiguity of shades." To the influence of this cause is due the growth of the vast number of lichens and mosses, which are here found investing, as parasites, the bodies of trees, logs, and rocks, through the deeper and more protected parts of the forests, *seeming* to indicate an undue amount of moisture, while, as already remarked, experiments demonstrate it not to be the case. The dew and rain precipitations, which, falling upon a cleared and open soil permanently heated by the direct rays of the sun, are speedily driven off, remain, on the contrary, in these impenetrable shades, prevented from exhaling by the mantle of trees and bushes, ferns and mosses, and pass off by slower evaporation, but principally underneath, giving origin to the numerous springs with which the mountain abounds.

As a direct consequence of this, the formation of large bodies of low fog is unusual, and the dense masses of vapor, resting for hours in the valleys and lowlands, is of unfrequent occurrence in the mountain ranges. Occasionally a silver veil of snow-white fog is seen overhanging the deeper valleys, ravines, or gorges, but it is as evanescent as a wandering cloud, and looks often, in the distance, like a sheet of water or mountain lake sleeping in repose among the hills. Like the mirage of the desert, these white clouds, settling in the depressions of the mountain, *simulate, to absolute perfection, bodies of water reflecting the light of the sky*, and the pictures are so artistically elaborated that the captivated beholder cannot disenchant himself from the beautiful illusion. Preceding and following the storms, *low* fog often envelops the spurs of the mountain; as also the regular storm-scud, occasionally, when the overhanging mass, heavy and low, sinks down to the stratum of the storm, or high-fog, embraced within a half mile of the surface.

The connection of electricity with the hygrometric state of the air is a subject of interest, and exhibits sanitary relations of vital moment.

Local electrical phenomena also occur on the mountain ranges. The higher currents, with differently charged clouds, or masses of air holding water in a state of suspension, in passing through the mountain heights, bristling with forests, which are constantly-acting conductors, as might be expected, give rise to varied electrical demonstrations.

The volumes of air in the forest spaces are constantly more or less highly charged with electricity from the friction of the rolling masses above. This explains the vivid and etherial nervous exaltation always experienced upon entering a mountain wood, and which is as real and tangible, even to an unimpressible person, as the *earth* on which he walks.

INDIAN-SUMMER.

The meteor of the Indian-summer is of exceeding beauty and interest on the mountain. The causes of this peculiar condition of the atmosphere have been variously estimated and rendered by different writers on the subject. The phenomenon is most striking on the high range of knobs of the summit. They seem to repose in the light of a new heaven, and to be arrayed by the genii for the advent of some rare and unexpected pageantry. The air is pervaded by a generally diffused haze of an azure or smoky hue, resting upon the earth like a translucent fleece, imparting to the sunlight, as illuminating objects, a variety of tints, violet and gold. At times, the setting sun, half veiled with ruddy glow, descends a globe of fire, while the landscape assumes the strange, disastrous aspect of the surface under the shadows of the eclipse. The charm of the still, hushed, almost perpetual twilight of the Indian-summer days, brings the world into the finest pictures of quietness and sweetness, contrast and surprise. A dreamy opium-trance steals upon the senses; the atmosphere is no longer an invisible element of power, the terrible stream of a viewless river, or even a gently flowing current of azure air, but the crystalline wave is now *visible* and tangible in a new sense and attitude, and lies against the hill a glowing cloud of purple light, or bends over the mountain-top like a regal mantle that you could lift, as the "babe thinks it can play with heaven's rainbow." The enchantment is permeating, dissolving, and ecstatic; that *invisible* and *wonderful air* is *visible;* the great storm-king, from uprooting forests, destroying cities and navies, lies down upon the mountain slope, like a weary lion, to sleep. Nature, glad with his repose, and sympathizing with the drowsy giant, hushes all her voices, and he dreams,

> "Als still is his luke, and als still is his e'e,
> Als the stillnesse that lay on the emerant lee,
> Or the myst that sleips on ane waveless sea."

SANITARY RELATIONS.

"It would be no new thing to insist on the influence which climate exerts upon the health; but the continually increasing facilities for traveling, and the locomotive spirit of the present age, invest the subject, every day, with a fresh interest. Along with this, we find the enlightened views of modern medical practice, enlarging the basis of its curative means, and putting its trust not in the employment of drugs only—often, indeed, assigning to them but an ancillary value—but calling in the aid, without regard to its nature, of any adjuvant that reasonably promises relief. And so it has recognized in the change of air and scene, and in those moral and social influences which go along with them, to a degree far beyond what our more immediate ancestors would have been prepared to admit, a *most powerful agent* in the treatment of actual disease, and of those numerous lesser ailments, the diffusion of which seems to advance with the advance of civilization. To this end the admirable work of Sir James Clark, the first, I believe, in which anything like a system of sound principles was advanced for our guidance in the selection of localities, has very much contributed."*

"*Physical causes* lie at the bottom of whatever differences the maladies of different portions of the earth may present; and hence the region which a medical historian selects, should have well-defined, *natural*, and not merely *conventional* boundaries."†

"These hydrographical facts (viz. of the Basin of the Alleghany River) show that Chestnut Ridge and Laurel Hill are not boundary mountains of our great valley, but are really included in it. Its true limits are, in fact, the Alleghany Ridge in Pennsylvania and Northern Virginia, while, in the southern part of the latter State, and in North Carolina, the Blue Ridge is its actual terminus or rim. The medical etiologist of the Interior Valley has, then, within his own jurisdiction, a broad, alpine region, running through eight degrees of latitude, with a mean elevation of fifteen hundred feet above the bed and banks of the Mississippi, to which it is parallel; and the time will come when a comparison of the two belts, in the physiology and

---

Francis, "Change of Climate." † Drake.

diseases of their inhabitants, will be regarded as a work of deep interest.

"Unable to visit any part of the region lying between the Alleghany River and Alleghany Mountain-crest, or to meet with publications illustrating its medical topography or diseases, I must content myself, at this time, with indicating it to others, as a field comparatively unexplored by the physician."*

In the invaluable work of Dr. Drake, on the "Diseases of the Interior Valley of North America," from which so many quotations have been made, we are presented with the following general views on "Climatic Etiology :"—

"CLIMATE OCCASIONS DISEASE.—As no fact in etiology is more universally admitted, than the influence of climate in the production of disease, it follows that he who would understand the origin and modifications of the diseases of a country must study its meteorology. The effects of climate are both predisposing and exciting. Thus, the long-continued action of a particular kind or condition of climate may bring about such changes in our physiology as to incline us to some particular form of disease; while sudden changes often act as exciting causes to other diseases, to which we may be inclined, from agencies not connected with climate. Again, the influences of climate are both direct and indirect. The former results from the immediate action of the atmosphere on our systems; the latter from its action on the matters which are accumulated on the surface of the earth, which are thus made to send forth agents of an insalubrious character. Thus, the same state of the earth's surface which in one climate may prove highly pernicious, in another may be altogether harmless.

"CLIMATE CURES DISEASE.—But climate must not be studied with a reference to etiology *only;* for it can *cure* as well as *occasion* disease. It modifies the effects of blood-letting, medicines, and regimen; and, although it maintains some diseases against the united powers of the most active and appropriate articles of the materia medica, it cures others in the absence of the whole. Considered as a therapeutic agent, it is, when skillfully ordered, entitled to *great confidence.* Its *action* is *not often speedy*, but the *certainty* of its *salutary effects*, in general, compensates for their slow development.

"DEFINITIONS OF CLIMATE.—In physical geography, the word climate expresses a zone of the earth, running parallel to the equator, of such width that the longest day at its northern limit is half an

---

* Drake, pp. 275, 276.

hour longer than that of its southern limit, supposing we are in the northern hemisphere; but, in etiology and therapeutics, the term is used in a different sense, and simply expresses states of the atmosphere. These states involve, or consist in varying quantities or qualities of certain elements of the air itself—its caloric, light, and electricity; its aqueous vapor, fogs, mists, and clouds; its dews, rain, hail, frost, and snow; its weight and density; its movements or winds; its factitious gases and mechanical impurities; all of which may be very different in different times or places of the same geographical climate, and nearly the same in different zones.

"ELEMENTS OF CLIMATE ON THE GLOBE.—The crust of the earth is not uniform in chemical composition or surface; it abounds in mountains, plains, and valleys, distributed in a very irregular manner; portions of it are densely overshadowed, while others are destitute of forests; the larger part is covered with oceans, lakes, rivers, and swamps; an elastic atmosphere rests upon the whole; and every part—solid, fluid, or aeriform—is permeated by electricity. Were the earth, with this surface removed from the influence of the sun, the phenomena of climate would be annihilated; in that luminary, then, reside the dynamics on which they depend; and the rays of light and heat are the efficient agents by which its quickening influence is exerted on the earth.

"THE ELEMENTS OF CLIMATE NOT THE SAME IN DIFFERENT PARTS OF THE EARTH.—It results from what has been said, that the elements of climate are not precisely the same in any two regions of the globe; and, therefore, that the climate of every region, even in the same latitude, must possess *some peculiarities;* the causes of which are to be sought in the physical geography and hydrography of the *region itself*, and of those by which it is *immediately* surrounded."*

This brings us to the therapeutics of climates, special and general.

On climatic therapeutics we have the following universally-accredited statements and opinions of one* fully recognized as uttering the voice of the science of the times:—

"The influence of climate over disease has long been established as a matter of fact, and physicians have, from a very early period, considered change of climate and change of air as remedial agents of great efficacy. This opinion is supported both by reason and experience: it is reasonable, for example, to believe that a change of

---

* Drake, "Diseases of the Interior Valley."
† Sir James Clark, "Sanative Influence of Climate."

residence from a crowded city to the open country, or from a cold, exposed part of the country to a warmer and more sheltered situation; from a confined, humid valley to a dry, elevated district, or the reverse, would produce very sensible effects upon the human body; and we find by daily experience that such *is* the case.

"The marked improvement of the general health, effected by the transition from the city to the country, even for a short period, is matter of daily remark; and the suspension, or even cure, of various diseases by a removal from one part of the country to another, is an occurrence that must have come within the observation of every one. It may suffice to mention here, in reference to this fact, intermittent fevers, asthma, catarrhal affections, hooping-cough, dyspepsia, and various nervous disorders. These diseases are often benefited, and not unfrequently cured, by simple change of situation, after having long resisted medical treatment; or they are found to yield, under the influence of such a change, to remedies which previously made little or no impression upon them. If such marked effects result from a change of so limited a nature as has just been noticed, it might be expected that a complete change of climate, together with the circumstances necessarily connected with it, should produce still more important results in the improvement of the general health, and in the alleviation and cure of disease. In this expectation we are also borne out by experience.

"My own experience has been sufficient to satisfy me, that, for the prevention and cure of a numerous class of chronic diseases, we possess, in change of climate, and even in the more limited measure of change of air in the same climate, *one of our most efficient remedial agents;* and one, too, for which, in *many cases,* we *have no adequate substitute.* Again, in dyspepsia, and disorders of the digestive organs generally, and in the nervous affections and distressing mental feelings which so often accompany these; in asthma, in bronchial diseases, in scrofula, and in rheumatism, the beneficial effects of climate are far more strongly evinced than in consumption. In cases also of general delicacy of constitution and derangement of the system in childhood and in youth, which cannot be strictly classed under any of these diseases; and in that disordered state of the general health which so often occurs at a certain period of advanced life, climacteric disease, in which the powers of the constitution, both mental and bodily, fail, and the system lapses into a state of premature decay, change of climate becomes a most invaluable remedial agent."

This comes indorsed by the wisdom of ages. Hippocrates and Galen are here, and much that the tireless efforts of

CLIMATE—SANITARY RELATIONS. 467

men, for hundreds of years, have established as to the influence of climate on disease, is here, simply and with common sense, stated.

The profession has, from time immemorial, been satisfied on this point, and catalogued a multitude of phenomena by careful analysis, grouping together a series of influences under the names of sanitary powers of climate, alterative influence of change of air, etc. What are they? They must embrace the whole order of existences that surround and impress the animal economy, as ponderable or imponderable.

Man walks upon the earth like a locomotive plant, sucking his blood from its surface. The rock, the soil, the vegetable, the river, the animal, build up the temple of his soul; for, is he not " a complex of all that surrounds him, namely, of element, mineral, plant, and animal ?" The computation of all the influences which surround man in this medium of his existence, is a large field of labor, and necessarily involves the science of every object which he touches, or which in any way comes in contact with the great vital surfaces through which his body is sustained in existence.

Extensive and learned volumes have been written on climate as a remedial agent. In the first dawn of the intellect of the profession we have seen that the attention of its most gifted mind, Hippocrates, was directed to its investigations, and the great problem of climate, as a physiological and pathological modifier, received a splendid thesis on "Airs, Waters, and Places," from the hand of the Father of Medicine. Since those ancient days, the profession has never lost sight of this rich and beneficently fruitful subject, nor ceased to give assiduous attention to this department of knowledge, so important to the vital and all-absorbing interest of health to mankind. Traveling physicians have constantly made their observations on the influence of the different climates, localities, springs, and health retreats, in all places with all peoples. Surgeons of the armies and navies of the different nations have been registering, by government authority, all facts observed of value for the profession. The accounts of common travelers have been collected, and sifted severely for any elements of the science of sanitary climatology which they might contain in their collected facts. Faith in the change of air, as a sanative influence, has become extra-professional, and is now the ground of ordinary experience, so that it is constantly suggested to the valetudinarian by his friends, to visit foreign countries, to take a sea *voyage* for sea *air*, to go to the mountains for mountain air, or even to go a few miles into the country for *country air*. So general a series of conclusions must have its origin in the natural constitution of things, and the great problem of change of air, as a curative resource, stands with the verdict of approval from the human race. This general faith is valuable, as enabling the profession to apply its science and skill to vast ranges of diseases amenable to the power of change of locality and the therapeutics of special habitats. From the gross, glaring facts of the wonderful power of even a few miles, to change and cure extensive chains of morbid symptoms, the conviction was forced upon the mind, that the medicine, and poison of airs and places, was an important region of knowledge demanding rigid scrutiny, patient investigation, and vigilant observation. The regular profession, ever awake to the highest interests of humanity, has labored hard in this field, and with results, as ever, signal and honorable, significant and wise. The literature of medicine, in this department, has expanded largely, and the well-educated physician's library now contains volumes and essays, learned and precise, on the "Sanative Influence of Climate,"[*] "Change of Climate Considered as a Remedy in Dyspeptic, Pulmonary, and other Chronic Affections,"[†] "Geography of Health and Disease,"[‡] "Systematic Treatise, Historical, Etiological, and Practical, on the Principal Diseases of the Interior Valley of North America,"[§] "General Sanitary Relations of the United

[*] Sir James Clark, Bart., M.D.
[†] D. J. T. Francis, M.D.
[‡] A. K. Johnston.
[§] Daniel Drake, M.D.

CLIMATE—SANITARY RELATIONS. 469

States Climate," etc.,* "Influence of Tropical Climates on European Constitutions,"† "Change of Air, or the Philosophy of Traveling,"‡ "Mountain Climate Considered in a Medical Point of View,"§ "Diseases of Heights,"‖ "Morbid Affections among the Alps,"¶ "Meteorological Characteristics of Mountain Climates,"** "Dissertations and Suggestions on Alpestine Pathology,"†† with numerous treatises on the climate of places, hygienic maps and charts of the distribution of disease, and reports on the specific powers of localities.

This great question of the Geography of Health and Disease introduces the mind into a prolific arena of medical dynamics. "Man is a cosmopolite." He modifies the agency of the elements upon himself,—but those agencies modify *him*. They have rendered him, in his organization, different in different regions, physiologically, pathologically. The great physical formula of natural elements, called "*climate*," is, as far as man is concerned, only the generalized synthesis of the great librations or internecine warfare of *ponderable and imponderable*.

Reflect on the vastness of the problem—the indigenous diseases of climates! It embraces the physiology and pathology of geographic zones: as, the calorical boilings and roastings of organs and tissues, of malarial poisons of such intensity that they destroy tigers and snakes, and produce congestive and quickly-destructive diseases in man, metamorphosing healthy organs into pools of disorganized and dissolved blood, followed by infectious emanations, which characterize the tropics; also of plastic inflamma-

* Lorin Blodget.
† James Johnson, M.D., and James Ronald Martin, Esq.
‡ James Johnson, M.D.
§ H. C. Lombard, M.D., of Geneva.
‖ Dr. Von Tschudi.
¶ Dr. Albert, of Briancon.
** Professor Plantamour.
†† Professor Bertrand, of Grenoble, Dr. Meyer, of Zurich, Dr. Michaux, of Chamounix.

tions of temperate zones, strange equipoise in the contest of conservating and dissolving powers, life, tough, tenacious *life*, in the tissue and organ slowly eaten and consumed by the death of the molecule, the furor of combustion being the agonizing surrender of the painfully worried and exhausted cell. Add to this the morbid galvanics of frigid zones, frosty rheumatisms, writhing neuralgies, with the deadening arrestation of development of electrical and vital organs, etc. etc., in short, diseases of continents, diseases of islands, diseases of heights or mountains, diseases of depths or valleys, diseases from heat, diseases from cold, from dryness, from moisture, from light, from darkness, and all the powers and qualities of *localities* alone. This is a wide field for scientific zeal and benevolence to exhaust.

That there are positive and demonstrable laws of habitats with reference to this climatal and specific power, is proved by numberless observations. An example of special climatal influence is seen and felt in the effects of certain winds. These, in different regions, have their names—sirocco, solano, autun, monsoon, mistral, northeaster, norther—associated in common parlance with positive states and conditions of the body, and are well known to produce most characteristic physiological and pathological effects. In this connection, many localities of specific poisons, also sites of hygienic and therapeutic powers, might be mentioned. As the natural history of the special powers of climate has been ascertained, more specific results have accrued in rendering the catalogues of diseases of which they are curative or to which deleterious—in other words, of conditions of media, either hygienic, therapeutic, or lethiferous. Leaving out these specific elements, the points fixed and established have been geographic, or relationship to latitude; topographic, or to the place or site as related to oceans and continents, lakes and mountains, as in the question of altitude and mere vertical elevation above the sea; also, of relationships purely meteoric, as in the motions of bodies of air, their electrical and hygrometric states, with calorical conditions, revealing the force of the imponderables, as of heat, the great life element, the

CLIMATE—SANITARY RELATIONS. 471

great vitalizer, the great creator and destroyer of organisms; of light, the incomputable, the illimitable power, "offspring of heaven, first-born," and electricity, his brother, rather himself again, dread, wonderful agent,—all of which belong to the kingdom of the air, and are represented in the climates of places, and of which record has been made. The relationship of purely mechanical or physical conditions of the air, its *rarity* and density, and barometric vicissitudes; as also of its *medical constitution*, with sanative power or seeds of death, are more or less pre-established by geography, topography, and geology. The influence of surface, of valley, mountain, gentle slope, or precipitous declivity, sheltered or exposed situations, characters and composition of soils, with vegetable covering, as of trees, shrubs, grass of savanna, or naked sands of the desert, winds or calms thereon, with annual and diurnal thermometric and hygrometric changes, also their relationships to gastronomics, æsthetics, including morals and religions, have all been cognized and united, more or less accurately, with physiological states and conditions, and their consequent pathological and psychological infirmities. The connection of health and disease with all these elements, the state and condition of original diathesis of bodies subjected to them, of organs and tissues submitted to them, of form or type of disease, style and stage of development brought under their influence, have, to a certain extent, been established.

Other more recondite researches have been made into the existence and nature, or specific qualities of a certain principle in the air, called ozone, discovered by Schönbein. It is said to be an "irritant principle," a "powerful oyxdizer, at once destroying those poisonous gases composed of hydrogen united with sulphur and phosphorus, and the presence of which renders the air irrespirable. The various gaseous products of the decomposition of animal and vegetable matters which are being incessantly evolved, especially in great towns, seem, according to the experiments of Schönbein, to yield no less completely to the destructive influence of ozone. Hence it is viewed as the *great purifier* of the atmosphere."* This principle in the air has been the subject of much speculation, but its laws of action and special sanitary qualities are still conjectural, and "although the constant existence of the principle in the open air of the country and the sea is ascertained, the proportions in which it exists in different localities is found to be subject to great variation."†

Dr. Charles Smallwood, of St. Martin, Isle Jesus, Canada East, the accomplished professor of meteorology in the University of McGill College, Montreal, has been making constant observations on ozone for twelve years. His contributions in this department of science are of a most interesting character, and as he is one of the *extremely few* observers on the continent, his labor possesses great value. His publications may be found in the "Transactions of the American Association," for 1857, also in numbers of the "Canadian Naturalist and Geologist," 1859. In a letter recently received from Dr. Smallwood, he says:—

"I use the formula of Schönbein; but instead of paper I find calico or fine muslin, soaked in the solution of starch and iodide of potassium, better than paper, and I am now observing the constant variations of the amount by an instrument that is worked by clockwork, and keeps constantly moving the prepared test one inch per hour. I wish to ascertain the connection of ozone with the usual barometric fluctuations, and also with the humidity of the atmosphere. I have also subjected the tests to different colored rays of light, and also to polarized light; and I have also investigated the effects of vegetation on its amount.

"The daily continued observations are taken at ten P.M. and six A.M., at the height of five feet from the surface of the soil; besides this, I have observed at an altitude of eighty feet above the ground, and in all possible situations on the ground, between the rows of vegetables, potatoes, Indian corn, etc.

"I would very concisely sum up thus:—

"Ozone does exist in the atmosphere; varies in quantity; moist weather favors its development; northeast and southeast winds favor its development; snow and rain also increase its amount; and

* British and Foreign Medico-Chirurgical Review, 1852.
† Francis, "Change of Air."

I am led to believe that the amount attains two maxima and two minima in twenty-four hours corresponding to the barometric oscillations, and also to the degrees of humidity. It has been largely developed for some years during the potato rot, the weather being moist, and with a hot sun, a state peculiarly fitted to show ozone present. I do not find it at all connected in amount with the electrical state of the atmosphere; sea breezes seem to favor its development, such as a northeast wind. I have noted its presence, with a thermometer, 36° below zero, and as high as 90° above. Temperature does not seem to influence the amount so much as the humidity of the atmosphere."

In the "Canadian Naturalist and Geologist" for December, 1859, he further remarks:—

"The psychrometer always indicates presence or absence of ozone; it is never in *dry air;* is decomposed by heat when formed by means of phosphorus; light has, in its development, not much influence upon ozonized paper; polarized light has least influence; influenced by luminous, heating, and actinic rays; the influence of colored media are proportioned, having a grade of power from orange, maximum, to green, minimum; east and south winds ozonic; westerly and northerly not; rain and snow, large amount; northeast land wind not ozonic; sea breezes, with moisture, ozonic; dry northeast wind, with high barometer, no ozone. Its effects on animals and man will require a system of registration.

"During cholera, amount diminished, but *humidity* was also diminished; it is highly deleterious to lower class of animals, its well-known poisonous properties being turned to advantage, when produced by slow combustion of phosphorus. As a therapeutic agent, it can scarcely be said to have been administered. Oil of turpentine, exposed to light, has acquired a pungent taste like peppermint, owing to formation of ozone, and proved poisonous to small animals. It has been advised as a *local application* in rheumatism, and *internally* in chronic discharges from mucous membranes of man. He (the doctor) is prosecuting investigations of effects of vegetation on amount of ozone; also effects from *germination of plants*. The continent of Europe is full of observers, but on the continent of North America but little attention has been given to it. A constant, systematic form of observation is necessary, and it is hoped soon to take its proper place in the annals of true science, and become alike interesting to the chemist,* physician, and meteorologist."

---

* "The chemical composition of ozone is defined to be a compound of oxygen, analogous to the peroxide of hydrogen, or that it is oxygen in an allotropic state, that is,

Medical climatologists have given classifications of climates from their effects upon the human body; as "Tonic" or dry, bracing and exhilarating, possessing the qualities of tonic medicines; "*Atonic,*" moist, relaxing, even sedative, indicated in conditions requiring those influences. There are also "Irritant Climates," etc.*

Nosological tables, or catalogues of diseases curable by climates have also been given, with the connection of places and their airs, with organs and their conditions. These details belong to the special domain of the physician, and are much too extensive to attempt to recite them here. They will be more fully discussed in the "Supplement to the Mountain," which will contain an extended treatise on climate as a remedy for disease, as also the special claims of the Alleghany Mountain as a locality of great power in the cure of a long list of maladies.

It may not be amiss, in this connection, to quote a few conclusions of the illustrious Drake, whose authority is unquestioned. Following the declension of the malarial plain north, toward the geographic line of perpetual exemption from malarial diseases, he says:—

"We find, then, that in the latitude of 42° north, the topographical conditions which originate autumnal fevers, are nearly overcome by a mean altitude of 1400 feet; but we have previously seen that, in the basin of the Kenawha, among the mountains of Virginia, at an elevation of 1800 feet, Professor Rogers saw many cases of intermittent fever. This is to be ascribed to the difference of latitude, that locality being about 4° farther south than the table-land in the vicinity of Chautauque Lake."

This lake is in Chautauque County, New York, the extreme southwest corner of the State, bounded on the north by Lake Erie, and on the south by Pennsylvania. It is a

---

with the capability of immediate and ready action impressed upon it. It is a great oxydizer and destroyer of the miasma arising from the decomposition of animal and vegetable substances. It is colorless, possesses a peculiar odor resembling chlorine, and, when diluted, cannot be distinguished from the electrical smell. Its density is said to be four times that of oxygen."—SMALLWOOD.

* Francis, "Change of Air."

CLIMATE—SANITARY RELATIONS. 475

few miles from the northern line of Pennsylvania. Of this region as an alpine summer residence for invalids, Dr. Drake remarks :—

"When describing the sources of the Alleghany River, including Chautauque Lake, we were brought, by a southern route, upon the water-shed which we have now ascended from the north. It may be regarded as the great salient terrace, or projecting table-land of the Appalachian Mountains; that portion which advances farthest to the northwest, from the central axis of the chain,—that which approaches nearest to the great lakes. Its tabular yet undulating or hilly surface results from its resting on a broad outcrop of Devonian shale or sandstone, in which the former greatly predominates."

Then follows a description of the region; after which, he thus proceeds :—

"Here, then, are all the requisites for a comfortable and *curative summer residence*. I will mention a few classes of patients to whom it would be likely to prove beneficial.

"*First*. Those who are inclined to tubercular consumption, or in whom the disease, although fatally established, is not so far advanced as to confine them to the house. To which may be added, children affected with scrofula in the external lymphatic ganglia, the skin, and the eyes.

"*Second*. Those who have had their livers and spleens deranged in structure or function, or their constitutions otherwise shattered, by repeated attacks of autumnal fever, in low and hot situations.

"*Third*. Dyspeptics, from any and all causes; hypochondriacs, and those subject to chronic hysteria, or any other form of morbid sensibility."

Then follows a flash on the fallibility of drugs, and the immense power of "simple diet," "new scenery," "active exercise," and the "*disuse of medicine*," with kindly guide-book information as to comfortable localities. To this succeeds some indications of the summer climate of the region: fires at night acceptable in July and August; Indian corn frost bitten in August; peaches ill at ease; "wheat and hay harvest in August." He then adds :—

"It may be said that the *Virginia springs* are *more elevated*, and, therefore, better fitted for summer sojourn. But their greater elevation of five hundred feet, would, in the reduction of temperature, only equal a degree of latitude, while this region is four degrees farther north. Nor can Saratoga be compared, in its summer climate, with this mountain platform; for, although a degree farther north, it lies twelve hundred feet nearer the level of the sea. The celebrated springs of Virginia and New York are, moreover, places of *amusement for the healthy, not rural retreats for the infirm;* to some of whom, it is true, the *mineral waters might prove beneficial; but all other* circumstances would combine to counteract their salutary influence. The enlightened physician* who conscientiously desires to redeem his patient, for three months of the year, from the deleterious agency of *heat* and *malaria,* or to countervail the debilitating effects of a protracted summer in others, in whose lungs the fatal work of tubercular excavation is going on, will, I trust, not *regard* the business-like details which I have been giving, with *disfavor;* but patiently read on until he qualifies himself for overcoming the scruples of such valetudinarians as may fear or fancy that, in going to the mountain terrace for the summer, they would languish for want of scenes and objects of interest. These are quite as numerous, diversified, and striking as in almost any other portion of the Interior Valley; and I will briefly enumerate the most important."

The benign and indefatigable Drake then proceeds:—

First. "This region comprehends the great pine forests of the Alleghany Mountain," etc. etc.

He continues to describe, with sentiment and cleverness, the resources of the region, sanitary and pleasurable. This poetical doctor,† with rhubarb and lancet in his pocket, recites routes to famous shrines, enchanting journeys, excur-

---

* "It is not sufficient for the physician to advise his patient, laboring under a chronic infirmity, to leave off medicine and depend on travel. When he prescribes the former, he directs where it can be obtained; and, in like manner, when he recommends the latter, he should be able to lay down the appropriate and practicable route; in doing which, he should draw his information from the books of the profession, and convince his patient that he is familiar with what he recommends, or but little confidence will be reposed in his advice."— DRAKE.

† Why should doctors not sometimes be poets? In constant scientific and sympathetic contact with the great realities and tragicalities of the world, and the human body, no man is so *real* and *alive,* if earnest and spiritual, as the *true* and *manly* physi-

CLIMATE—SANITARY RELATIONS.

sions innumerable and beautiful to "falls of rivers" and "minor cascades," "pleasant roads," "romantic paths," "hunting grounds," "trout streams," "grouse roosts;" in short, all that men want or pray for, sick or well, including, as climax, the great Falls of Niagara. In that beautiful region of extreme Western New York and Northwestern Pennsylvania he discovers a desideratum long sought, a great *alpine sanitary resort* for the sick, above the malarial plain, and possessed of all desirable physical prerequisites and climatal elements for the transformation and rejuvenescence of the diseased, exhausted, and weary laden.

And here the statement may be made, that the whole range of knobs of the Alleghany Mountain in Central Pennsylvania is several hundred feet above this line of malaria, as indicated by Dr. Drake, and possesses *all the advantages* enumerated as belonging to the Chautauque Lake region, which he indeed affirms is *but a "salient terrace,* or projecting table-land *of the Appalachian Mountains."* Being a degree farther south, and a thousand feet higher, the Pennsylvania Alleghany combines *all the* physical elements, and *greater sanitary advantages*, than the *plateau* described by Dr. Drake. It also extends above the line of "alpine climate," as established by Dr. Lombard, which, at latitude 40° north, is 2000 feet above the level of the sea.

Thus the illustrious Drake, who had studied with zeal and genius for thirty years the whole climatal relations of the great valley and its elevated boundary lines, or geographical rim, and had hunted a healing (asylum) retreat for its sick,

---

cian. As there is "poetry in *man* and *every* object that *surrounds* him," and as the chief end of the doctor is to study man and cure him perpetually, who of the elect of heaven has a better right, with star-woven toga, to walk the heights of Parnassus? Dr. Camillo Brunori, the "Physician a Poet," under the divine afflatus, indited lovely idyls on purgatives, celestial rhymes on blisters, and "one hundred and seventy-two sonnets on all *Diseases, Drugs,* and *Parts* of the *Body, Functions,* and curative means." Honor to the doctor-poet! *all honor* to Camillo the brave!

discovered, and appears an ardent advocate for, and enthusiastic indorser of, the Alleghany Mountain plateau as a place with "all the requisites for a *comfortable and curative summer residence*," and a "*rural retreat for the infirm*," far "from the *deleterious agency* of *heat* and *malaria*," and possessing more essential elements of a perfect summer resort than any other part of the continent of North America.

Hence the solemn import of the words, on the streamer of the flag-staff of the next book of the "Mountain," Æsculapius, namely,—The significance of the Alleghany Mountain as the site of a Sanitarium, or retreat for the sick, arranged by Infinite Wisdom. And hence, also, arrives the grand corollary from all the foregoing arguments and demonstrations, the inevitable "Doctorial uses of the Mountain!"

END OF BOOK ATLAS.

This ends the Book Atlas, or Natural Science of the Mountain. Why dive so deep in rocks, or soar so high in air? Only to make good the promise to try to dovetail some knowledge of the mountain, a protuberance of the venerable spheroid, into universal science. The natural objects (sciences) of a spot are its furniture as a medium of existence or habitat for living creatures. A hurried invoice has been made of some of these effects, exhibiting so much for the body. Natural history contains supernatural history, for "*Nature is the spirit* analyzed and at *rest*," and the final cause of any existence being the object or end for which created, much has also been indicated for the soul, who, with queenly power, will make out her own case. But who was Atlas, and what of him? The brawny-backed Titan was, according to Hesiod, (Theog., 507, etc.) "a son of Japetus and Clymene, and a brother of Menœtius, Prometheus, and Epimetheus; according to Apollodorus, his mother's name was Asia; and, according to Hyginus, he was a son of Aether and Gaea." Other accounts are given of his genealogy. Hesiod says "he bore heaven with his head and hands." From the Homeric poems: "Atlas knows the depth of the sea, and bears the long columns which keep asunder, or carry all around, earth and heaven; or of the columns which keep asunder heaven and earth, which columns are the mountains." The Homeric description was a "superhuman or divine being, with a personal existence, and blended with the idea of a mountain."

"The idea of heaven-bearing Atlas is, according to Letronne, a mere personification of a cosmographic notion, which arose from the views entertained by the ancients respecting the nature of heaven and its relation to earth."—(L. S.) Again, he led the Titans in their fight with Zeus, and "being conquered, he was condemned to the labor of bearing heaven on his head and hands." Another version is, "he was a man who was metamorphosed into a mountain." Again, Perseus, by the "Medusa's head, changed him into Mount Atlas, on which rested heaven and all its stars."

This mythico-cosmical origin of mountains, embracing every imaginable formulæ, gives a sure and steadfast baseline for the chapters on the natural science of the mountain, by getting as near to the bones or skeleton of the old structure as possible; or, in other words, of what is under, in, and on the mountain, namely, its geology, upon which must repose its soil, its organized bodies, its waters, and downy ocean of air above.

ÆSCULAPIUS.

"ÆSCULAPIUS, ($Ασκληπιός,$) the god of the medical art, in the Homeric poems, not considered a divinity, and without descent, is mentioned as the father of Machaon and Podaleirius. (Il., ii. 731, iv. 194, xi. 518.) But Homer also calls those who practice the healing art descendants of Paeëon, and, as Podaleirius and Machaon are called the sons of Æsculapius, it has been inferred that Æsculapius and Paeëon are the same being, and consequently a divinity. As in Homer's opinion all physicians were descended from Paeëon, he probably considered Æsculapius in the same light. This is corroborated in later times by the fact that Paeëon was identified with Apollo, Æsculapius being *universally described* as a *descendant* of Apollo. The two sons of Æsculapius, in the Iliad, were the physicians in the Greek army, and ruled over Tricca, Ithome, and Oechalia. The more common tradition was that the god himself was a son of Apollo and Coronis, the daughter of Phlegyas, a descendant of Lapithes." (Apollod., iii. 10, § 3; Pind. Pyth., iii. 14, with the Schol.)

For the story of the babe Æsculapius, saved from the flames by Hermes, of the vengeance of Apollo, and the tragical death of his mother Coronis, and her lover, see Pind., Ov., Hom., Paus., Hygin., Apol., Strab., etc. Hermes gave the boy to Cheiron, (the Centaur,) who instructed him in the art of healing and in hunting. The shepherd Aresthanes saw the boy surrounded by a lustre like that of lightning, and from his dazzling splendor, or from his having been rescued from the flames, he was called, by the Dorians, $αιγλαηρ$. Of his youth and the wonderful power of his manhood, until the full-developed divinity assumed the proper functions of his sphere, saving life and raising the dead, many astonishing traditions fill the records of classical history, from the gift of Athena in the blood of Gorgo, to the secret of the serpents in the house of Glaucus.

"These legends, about one of the most important and interesting divinities of antiquity, are full of significance. Various hypotheses have been brought forward to explain the origin of his worship in Greece; and, while some consider Æsculapius to have been originally a real personage, whom tradition had connected with various marvelous stories, others have explained all the legends about him as mere *personifications* of certain ideas. The serpent, the *perpetual symbol* of *Æsculapius*, has given rise to the opinion that the worship was derived from Egypt, and that Æsculapius was identical with the serpent Cnuph, worshiped in Egypt, or with the Phœnician Esmun. (Euseb. Præp. Evang., i. 10; comp. Paus., vii. 23, § 6.) But it does not seem necessary to have recourse to foreign countries in order to explain the worship of this god."

"Æsculapius was worshiped all over Greece, and many towns claimed the honor of his birth. His temples were usually built in healthy places, on hills outside of towns and cities, and near wells or springs, which were believed to have healing powers. These temples were not only places of worship, but were frequented by great numbers of sick persons, and may, therefore, be compared to modern hospitals. (Plut. Quaest. Rom., p. 286., D.)

"The principal seat of his worship in Greece was Epidaurus, where he had a temple, surrounded with an extensive grove, within which no one was allowed to die, and no woman to give birth to a child. His sanctuary contained a magnificent statue of ivory and gold, the work of Thrasymedes, in which he was represented as a handsome and manly figure, resembling that of Zeus. (Paus., ii. 26.)

"He was seated on a throne, holding in one hand a staff, and with the other resting upon the head of a dragon, (serpent,) and by his side lay a dog. (Paus., ii. 27, § 2.)

"Serpents were everywhere connected with the worship of Æsculapius, probably because they were a symbol of prudence and renovation, and were believed to possess the power of discovering herbs of wondrous powers, as is indicated in the story of Æsculapius and the serpents in the house of Glaucus. (Paus.)

"After Æsculapius had grown up, reports spread over all countries that he not only cured all the sick, but called the dead to life again. Several persons, whom Æsculapius was believed to have restored to life, are mentioned by the Scholiast on Pindar, (Pyth., iii. 96,) and by Apollodorus, (C. 6.) When he was exercising this art upon Glaucus, Zeus killed Æsculapius with a flash of lightning, as he feared lest men might gradually contrive to escape death altogether, (Apol., iii. 10, § 4:) or, according to others, because Pluto had complained of Æsculapius diminishing the number of the dead too much. (Diod., iv. 71; comp. Schol. Pind., Pyth., iii. 102.) But, on the request of Apollo, Zeus placed Æsculapius among the stars." (Hygin. Poet. Astr., ii. 14.)—*From Dictionary of Greek and Roman Biography and Mythology.*

1. "Honor a physician with the honor due unto him for the uses which ye may have of him: for the Lord hath created him.

2. "For of the Most High cometh healing, and he shall receive honor of the king.

3. "The skill of the physician shall lift up his head, and in the sight of great men he shall be in admiration.

4. "The Lord has created medicines out of the earth, and he that is wise will not abhor them.

5. "Was not the water made sweet with wood, that the virtue thereof might be known?

6. "And he has given men skill that he might be honored in his marvelous works.

7. "With such doth he heal men, and taketh away their pains.

12. "Then give place to the physician, for the Lord hath created him: let him not go from thee, for thou hast need of him."—ECCL.

"The intelligence denoted by the leaf, which shall be for the use of the celestial man, is called Medicine. A.C. 57."

SWEDENBORG.

BOOK II.

CHAPTER I.

ÆSCULAPIUS.

"Man is God wholly manifested. God has become Man, zero has become $+\ -$. Man is the whole of arithmetic, compacted, however, out of all numbers; he can therefore produce numbers out of himself. Man is a complex of all that surrounds him, namely, of element, mineral, plant, and animal."—OKEN.

THE regular profession of medicine, called the "Faculty," "Hippocratic," or "Old School," boasts a genealogy time-honored and ancient as the earth. From its present noonday splendor of light and science it goes into the obscurity of the past for more than two thousand years of authentic history, and still on through realms of myths and dreams, until, in the mists and shadows of primeval worlds, it mingles its exegesis with the fables of the gods. These stories of the ages, these legends of the sages, have nothing in them accidental, arbitrary, or factitious; for myths are but shadows of more transcendent facts, having necessary and immortal existence in the depths of nature and the soul.

The profession of the healing art, divine in its origin, grave and grand in its scientific evolution, sacred and sublime in its ultimate functions, stands as a necessary part of the order of things, *old* as *humanity*, and inseparable from its existence upon earth; for when did not man suffer, and when did not his brother try to relieve him? Synchronous with man's advent upon the planet, the chronicles of this art, inaugurated by the oracles of Fate, are as absolutely a part of the inevitable, and as *genuine* a *fragment* of the *universe*, as the beautiful "song of the stars." As the creation of the human body is the first significant fact of its history, its *protection* and *preservation* from the agencies of change and destruction about it must certainly be the *second* consideration of importance, scarcely less in its grandeur, surely equally solemn in its *end*. The soul, incarnated once, demands immortality as a right of its own being, and would *ask it, also*, for the body. What art so grand, then, as the art of preserving and prolonging life, and what so godlike in aspiration as the effort to restore man to the splendor of his unfallen youth, and save him from the tortures of pain and suffering, of disease and death?

All the races of men, but especially the *cultivated* and *dominant*, have ever had a clear perception of this great fact; and through the darkness and ignorance of barbarous tribes, and the light, culture, and science of the illuminated and progressive nations, the *professor* of the art of healing has ever been regarded as the *possessor* of the secrets of life and death, and held in veneration and love, allied to the worship of the supernals.* The scriptures of the races, sacred and profane, record his achievements, and the history of his miracles is embalmed in ejaculations of ceaseless wonder and admiration. Their monuments of art have registered the highest tidal waves of the progress and intellectual growth of man, by associating his entire spiritual unfolding, the advancement and perfection of his nature, *with the deities* which preside over the *fate* and *destiny* of the *material world*, and the *physical salvation* of humanity. The wondrous intellect of the Greek has filled the horizon of human vision for hundreds of years. With a physical conformation perfect, and rendered godlike by a habitat in

* Priest and physician were originally united in one functionary, and should still be one. "The Asclepiadæ were also regarded as an order or caste of priests, and for a long period the practice of medicine was intimately connected with religion."

which the perfection and splendor of nature were revealed and the beauty of the world exhausted, he has, in all his creations, made the *ideal real*, by an eternal production of himself, "his body *absolutely expressing his soul.*"

In his highest efforts, forever captivated by truth and beauty, he became the prophet, priest, and king of nature, making his artistic or reproduced world bright with the immortal stars of thought, redolent of Olympian airs, aromatic shades, haunts and bowers of the gods. The muses, the heavenly nine, hover around his path of progress, and the glory of an undebauched, unfallen world is shadowed forth in "shapes whose beauty is truest and rarest, in visions, in soul, the grandest that crowd on the tear-dimmed eye," in the prophetic oracles of Delphi, in the whispering of the groves of Dodona. In all his intellectual manifestations true; true in the symbolism of the world embodied in his poetical mythology; true in the instincts of his mind in the path of science; perfect in the world of the senses and understanding, his genesis of the healing art is the embodiment of wisdom. What but a Grecian hand could chisel an Apollo of Belvidere, the ideal physical? and what but a Grecian head could create the magical romance of the son of Zeus and Leto, the ideal spiritual?—both worlds united in the form of the God of Medicine, Divination, and Poetry.

> "Mine is the invention of the charming lyre;
> Sweet notes and heavenly numbers I inspire.
> Medicine is mine; what herbs and simples grow
> In fields, in forests, all their powers I know,
> And, am the *great physician* called below."

Thus muses the charmer of high Olympus, and thus the ethereal god of the gods announces the duties of his transcendent sphere, and profers the sympathies of heaven to sufferers in the gloomy realms of pain, uniting, in his blessed form, the spirituality of thought and intellect, with the beneficence and grandeur of love and mercy.

"Whatever we may think of the modes of explaining the

origin and nature of Apollo, one point is certain, and attested by thousands of facts, that Apollo and his worship, his festivals and oracles, had more *influence* upon the *Greeks than any other god.* It may be *safely asserted,* that the *Greeks would never have become* what they *were,* without the worship of Apollo; in *him the brightest side of the Grecian mind is reflected."* This radiant Olympian, proudest in his power of the supernals, the proper creator of Grecian thought and art, was accounted the *father* of *Æsculapius,* the *special God* of Medicine. That his temple, at Delphi in Phocis, should be situated on the hill Parnassus, "umbilicus orbis terrarum," *the centre of the world,* at once reveals the fact, "that deep wisdom lies under these fables of time," that the ancient *poet* was a *seer,* and, in giving a *supernatural origin* to an art the most honored and useful of the callings of men, he but uttered the voice of that "necessity which is the mother of the world." Let all honor be given to the ancients; all veneration to the gods of Olympus.

From this proud height of thought and art; from this ancient Eden of Grecian poetry and philosophy, *itself stretching into still more* venerable and primeval solitudes of time, comes the regular profession of medicine of this hour. Down to this moment it has struggled through ages of the soul's travail; through time-honored battlings with worlds of night and chaos, ignorance and darkness; through dawnings of light; through manifold tribulations and difficulties; through the ceaseless efforts of the best brains and hearts the races have ever produced; still on, until, in the blaze and splendor of the inductive process of reasoning, the *absolute* of *medical* science was *revealed,* and now stands, with its granite peaks of "positive philosophy," in the light and glory of an everlasting day.

Still, while we gaze with awe into the past, and reverence with filial veneration the old—following that magical river into the charmed land, where fact and fable dance in the dawn of thought and reason, and men and gods interact—

we must not forget that the "past is death's," the present only is our own; that *progress* and *growth* are written on all things; that a flowing river, a seed-filled field, is this time; that there are no *ends* or beginnings, but only arrestations and continuations; that there is nothing erect or fixed, but only leanings and slidings everywhere—no rest even for the rock,* which *will* be a plant; the plant, "struggling to become a different and to attain the light," *must* be an *animal*, while the animal stirs in its somnambulism and dreams, and would fain be a man. Let us accredit this revelation of the growth and development of the universe revealed by science, and, while with sentiments of gratitude and joy we celebrate the achievements of the mind in the past, and glorify its wonderful power, recorded in the written word, or books of the world, "its monuments more enduring than brass," we must not forget that "in all scriptures, the *letter* kills," the *spirit* alone is *alive, growing, reproductive, immortal.* With sadness, then, we must also arrive at the conclusion that a painfully servile subjugation of the soul has been achieved; that the *old*, with dogmatism and tyranny, has always demanded an agonizing humility and worship, *because it is old;* that the lessons of the ancient schools, assuming the overwhelming prestige of an-

* The ordinary apprehension that the rock reposes in eternal stillness in its geological fastness, is erroneous. (See note at end of chapter Æsculapius, page 534.) One extravagant dreamer, Evan Hopkins, (on connection of geology with terrestrial magnetism and the general polarity of matter,) has made it out clearly (he thinks) that the epidermis, or stone mantle of the globe, is in perpetual motion, creeping north, and turning within itself by a stupendous galvanic devouring, and has also fixed the rates of its progression by lines in thousands of years. As the continents and most of the bodies of land visible above the watery envelope of the planet have their heads or larger extremities north and their tails or terminating points south, it comes that the tadpole-theory of development holds good in the movements of worlds as well as the growth of frogs. Onward toward the north star crawl the continents and islands, and onward to the north is progress and the watchword of development. Advance, Hopkins, with your rhinoceros hide of the world!

tiquity and the "*past*," have robbed, and dispossessed us of aboriginal and filial consort with the fountains of influx from the equally divine present. This wretched tribute is extorted at the fearful cost of the total integrity of man, and the emasculation of the profoundest attributes of his being. Why pay the word by an unqualified surrender of its own *life?* Why capitulate on the fatal condition of the *annihilation* of the spirit? The book or word is only a bridge over a yawning gulf of the past; a floating raft of logs it may have been, or a rainbow-arch sublimely spanning the heavens, but *still* a *bridge*. Shall we dwell perpetually on the bridge? The word is a ladder; when the height is achieved, shall we stay to glorify the ladder alone? The word is a scaffold. When the spiritual edifice is constructed in symmetrical proportions, shall the scaffold, once essential, *now useless*, stand a persistent deformity? The word is a fountain of inspiration. If the waters have shrunken away, of what value is the fountain?

But the total record or word of the world, it may be affirmed, is the greatest fact of the world's history. As an *exponent* of the world it stands, then, a tropical mountain, stretching through all depths and heights, all times and spaces, revealing the spiritual growths of the ages, the Andes of the soul. At its base, warm, genial, intense, a world of light and life, exhaustless in its fullness, illimitable in its profusion, stunning and bewildering in its excessive brilliancy, blooms a sempiternal youth. Here sport and babble the *babes* of the senses; here glow with warmth and ardor the first fiery thoughts of the children of the sun. Higher upon the mountain is the belt of umbrageous (deciduous) woods, with foliage waving in the winds of temperate climes, and whose cool, sequestered shades invite to contemplation and dreams. Here, in "academic groves," have wandered the men of thought and reflection, the philosophers of the intellect, the *seekers* of truth, and talked to unborn millions. Still higher, the solemn evergreen forest stands, cold and dark; and here the brave preachers of righteousness, the grave reformers of truth, the earnest seekers of holiness, have chiseled their stern edicts on stone; and here, also, amid deepening shadows, have sung the "pensive muses, whom dismal scenes delight, frequent at tombs, and in the realms of night." And yet still higher, looms the snow-capped summit, lofty and lonely, cold and silent as eternity, where the inspired few have spoken the words of life. Here, in "infinite but incomprehensible solitude, yet in the boundless self-sufficiency of their blessed natures," the martyrs and prophets have uttered their oracles, and, in love and worship, brooded in loneliness, with the silent stars, over the depths of God.

Endless seem the attractions of the word, and beautiful continually are the first songs of joy when the soul has found its symbol. Is it strange that myriads of thoughtful, cultivated human spirits, should thus cling to the word, and, like happy children, play with the toy when its meaning was long forgotten? Touching, sadly touching is this awe and veneration for the garments and bones of the saints,—this worship of the wood of the true cross; and melancholy is this reverential retrospection into the past, the dreary domain of night and silence. Still sadder is the *backward longing*, and still more fatal is the backward looking, as the only rest of the spirit. Especially is this reliance on the past *alone*, in science, fatal to future growth and development; this backward looking alone is bad, and worse than it seems, in *all departments* of thought and *knowledge*. An ingenuous criticism of the regular profession of medicine of this hour is, that it *demands* a deeper philosophy, and *needs a higher faith*. It asks a philosophy that has come into the world unembarrassed by mortgages to the thought and intellect of the dead, and uncumbered by the mouldy formulæ of departed generations, and without the oppressive details of a too painful genealogy. The *Faith* which it deeply needs is not a blind, indiscriminate worship of *traditional power;* no veneration for the "*word* of the master;" no uninquiring acceptance of the imaginative fables of other days, or the waning fancies of departed races, but a living and abiding conviction and trust, that the world is still in the rosy light of its dawn; that the "days of inspiration" are not passed; that the wise man who exclaimed, in anguish, "I have lost a day!" was a "king without a crown;" that the world is really not faded, spent, and gone into dotage, and near its final deliration. This flimsy garment of a theory is only a fact, so far as nature indorses it, and no farther.

In medicine, as in other departments of knowledge, it is, and ever has been, that "Genius is always sufficiently the enemy of genius *by over-influence.*" The word of the inspired man, instead of becoming warm life-blood in the veins, or growing seed in the soil, has always hardened into a fossil, and made a stumbling-*stone* for long ages to come. Shakspeare is born, and having scaled the heavens of poetry, henceforward, the riders of Pegassus must hobble the celestial steed with *his yoke*, having first constituted him the great ideal artist in the realms of imagination and fairie. Hunter, Stahl, and Broussais are born, and the human race bleed rivers of blood for ages, the world having resolved itself into a hospital for the cure of inflammations alone— phlogiston ($\varphi\lambda o\gamma i\sigma\tau o\varsigma$) being their sole morbific power—under the plenary inspiration of the "Fundamental Principles of Inflammation," and the divine ægis of "Physiological Medicine." Each age, in superstitious veneration, turns its eyes to the past, and being sorrowfully indigent in the possessions of the present, it contents itself by magnifying the claims of the dead, and reciting with veneration the *record* of *their achievements.* Each of its new books is but a votive leaf on the altar of the "worship of genius." Still lingering around the fires of departed worlds, it would "roast its eggs with the cinders of extinct volcanoes." With its eye fixed on the distant mountain-tops of the *past,* it hopes for the dawn *there* "when it is *really* sunset, and night is coming fast." With mournful assiduity it stirs the dead embers of lights gone by, having hopes of illumination and heat, when *life has* departed and death *has come.* It hangs with devotion and love over the dust of departed greatness, and delights to glorify the voices of antiquity by building monuments of wonder and admiration to their greatness. It writes endless commentaries upon *what has been done* in the past, but has no hopes or aspirations for the future, or what may be done in the hour that now is, or that is to come. In the shade and darkness of long and mournful eclipses the races have wandered. Some colossal man came upon earth and scored the surface of the planet with his name, attributes, and works, and, for hundreds of years, his form arises, darkening the sun of truth and casting a baleful shadow, in the deep darkness of whose night whole races have reposed and slept. They have ever said, "in the shadow of this rock in the wilderness we will rest." The sleepless vigilance, the never-tiring exertion essential to growth, the *travail* of *thought*, they will not endure. The *search* for *truth demands toughness* of *fibre of heart and brain*, and few men have either *will* or *power* to work in the rugged ways leading to the mountain-top, whose head is in the light of the day of knowledge and thought.

In medicine, as in other departments of human knowledge, the *past* has hobbled and chained the human mind, and postponed the revelation of the future or time to come by a superstitious veneration for the "old." Too *much faith in tradition,* too *much reliance* on the *authority* of *other days*, is the sickness of the schools of medical science, as of all other schools whose history goes into the past. The "word of the master" has always been the *oath*, and inertia and torpidity of spirit prevailed, the last ripple-mark of the advancing wave rising and hardening into a mountain of rock, and constituting for the time the horizon or visible line of union of earth and heaven. And this perception brings at once the staring fact to the mind that the medical science of this hour, through drowsiness and inappetency, through indolence and want of courage to investigate, is too *grossly material* in its philosophy. With eye and scalpel constantly groping after *material processes* and functions only, it reveals facts of the senses and understanding alone, giving an interpretation of nature which leaves the mind in the mire. Gravity and the affinities of chemistry, pathology or the gross *outward results of disease*, it recognizes with sufficient precision. It does not believe that the fall of an apple could introduce the mind of man to the mysteries of the mechanism of the heavens, and reveal the miraculous dance of the worlds in time and space; it does not believe that a flash of the soul in the darkness of the night called life, may illume the celestial mountaintops of undiscovered continents of knowledge; that gleams or great intuitions of the mind, may let us as deeply into the laws of nature as the anatomist's knife or chemist's crucible. It forgets that nature is but a *name* for an *effect, whose cause is the absolute and infinite spirit;* assiduously and devoutly acquainting itself with *external results, material phenomena merely*, it does not reflect that the "visible is but the *terminus* of *the invisible;*" that what we *see* and *touch* is *dead;* that "the body is itself but the drowsy brute that the Eternal hath yoked to the chariot of life to urge man across the finite."

The constantly recurring mistake of the profession, in its phantasmal dance of theories, has always been *infinite faith in matter*. From earliest dreams of atomists, humeralists, and solidists, mechanical laws, and powers of polarity, with elixirs of life and philosophers' stones, to the modern swarm of drugs whose name is legion, the profession has been blundering over its *mountains of matter*, and had its faith *only* in *heroic doses* of *heroic remedies*, and in the most *absolute* of "*material aids.*" Its theory of nature is gross and mechanical, an hypothesis accounting for the universe on the purely physical laws of natural philosophy, architecture, and chemistry. Thus, in its conception of *diseases* also, it is like the *medicine-man* of the Thibetans; believing and calling the destroying powers material devils, it would scare them into cages with gourds and calabashes, and *destroy* them with the *sword*.

This is mournful, and profanely closes the avenues to higher and better light; for, although "matter may be one of the grandest facts that a *finite intelligence* can *know*," yet can it also cognize with true *spiritual precision* and *absolute knowledge*, other existences, powers, and forces of the world. "The business of philosophy is to discover *truths* which, as *first principles*, are to give *intelligibility*, and which, therefore, *cannot* be *deduced from* the *facts* of *experience* which they are *intended* to *explain*, and to which they are to give *unity* and *connection; they are truths supersensuous*. We demand, and the *rational* mind *cannot be satisfied with less*, that the *facts, phenomena*, and *changes which form the sphere of our sensible experience*, and, *collectively, are* called *nature*, shall be rendered *intelligible to*, and *rationally accounted for, by our mind*. The *instincts of reason* lead us to *investigate what the realities are* of which the *phenomena* are but the *outward signs*." What are the true moving forces of the universe ? through what miraculous causes does this multiform phenomenal perform the dramaturgy of nature ? Around us is a fullness of life and power, and the endless procession goes forward with ceaseless regularity, pointing to the net of golden threads of living connection in all things, and asserting through all the kingdoms of being the tyranny of law. We arrive at last, in our investigations, in the dread presence of a range of forces in whose fingers the *material universe*, or matter with *gravity* and *attraction*, is as *clay* in the *potter's hands*. They have nothing in common with the sixty ponderable, elementary bodies, recognized and catalogued by chemistry, or any of their combinations, constituting the multifarious forms of outward existences, but antagonize in *every single attribute* this world of *matter* with *sensible qualities*. One class seeking, as if by the instincts of a blind and drowsy soul, to rest and sleep, holding globes and atoms safely together in concreted masses and revolving spheres; the other, essentially *active, alive*, and *quick*, without an element of sameness or affinity with ponderable bodies, but dissolving, rending asunder, and separating all things as by a fearful instinct of *dissolution,* having neither *weight, form,* nor *any* quality, primary or secondary,* *appreciable* to the senses, making iron fluid as water, and, with irresistible *energy,* metamorphosing the granite into grass and ether. These agents or invisible powers of existence have ever attracted the attention of men, and invited to investigation, and theories of the *imponderables* and of *life* have long been recorded. The *imponderables* and *vital powers* are the true *moving forces,* the *real dynamic agents* of existence.

In the plastic fingers of these dread creatures all matter reels and dances. Nature seems but a masquerade of these miraculous wonder-working powers, now dreadful in the thunder-storm, now beautiful in the gentle wind, now majestic in the animal and tree, now magical and lovely in the flower, insect, and bird, and without whose perpetual play the organic world would soon become a reeking corpse. How long shall it be before the atomic philosopher, with his system of *dead particles* performing the *pantomime* of *life* as fatal machinery, shall be superseded by a *real philosophy* of the dynamics of the world ? The hour demands a rational philosophy of the imponderables; also a more searching and critical recognition of the laws and action of the *vital forces.* It likewise asks the true hygienic and therapeutic powers of the imponderables, as of all influences that bear upon the phenomena of life in health and disease. This will surely come. Chemistry has, with a precision that seems wonderful, told the story of the sixty ponderables, and left a catalogue of elemental bodies and their laws of relationship, or powers of combination, which promises, at last, that, by vigilance and patience, absolute knowledge will be attained, and nature reduced to a familiar laboratory. That this is demonstrable, can easily be seen by comparing the present precise and profound works on chemistry with even the comparatively recent dreams of the alchemists and the older chemists. The vitalist, or student of organized

---

* *Primary,* extension and divisibility. *Secondary,* color, taste, smell, etc.

matter, has also expanded his domain immensely, and the microscope appears in triumph with its beautifully-exhausted and subjugated *cell*, whose *last phantastic* phase it has discovered, whose deepest secret of structure and combination it has told. For the expansions in the department of organized bodies, consult the works of the physiologists and anatomists, vegetable and animal. For profound and rational dissertations on the vital powers, see the extensive literature of the medical profession, the philosophers, and physiophilosophers. Surely in the wake of all this light must follow the exhaustive analysis, and true philosophy of the imponderables, and their connection with the ponderables, both in the worlds of organic and inorganic matter! Then, also, must come the greatest consummation, the true *end* of science, the answer to the long and agonizing prayer of the intellect, the *philosophy* and *practical* application of the imponderables as *protective* and *curative* agents, or *real hygienic* and *therapeutic* powers of the world.

In the mean time there are not wanting systems full of pretenses and impertinent affectations of philosophies of all things, and, multitudinous as the world is in many things, it is not least productive in *dreams of vital powers, theories of imponderables*, "philosophies of spiritual manifestations," "mesmerisms," and nothingisms,—*mushrooms of the night*, with medical theories built thereon, that affect to have unlocked the secrets of Nature, and hold the keys to the "realms of shade." And here, as ever, in the thick darkness, "birds of evil omen are upon the wing; the dead walk, the living dream." The problem to solve for the genius of the history of medical science of the present time, is the true significance, the positively philosophical exposition of the pompous pretenses that have assumed the names of new medical systems or theories, and new philosophies of spirit and matter. The regular profession, coming from antiquity, hoary-headed with years, wise according to the ancients, and having the intellect and conservative forces of the *whole past* to indorse it, is now beset by legions of parasites, monsters of night and chaos; "mumblements from the lake of eternal sleep." This swarm of gad-flies, like the plagues of Egypt, the curses of Pharaoh, are ceaseless in their efforts to scare the college from its proprieties, and to alarm the toga and tripod in their sanctity.

In steep and sour antagonism to the ancient formulæ of medical philosophy, the fruit of that highly respectable old tree rooted in the *actual*, with all nature to defend her, comes this party of innovators, constituting the category of fashionable and impertinent quackeries of the hour. Some of these, ignoring matter as *matter* with fixed and unalterable laws, addressing the senses and intellect of man, try to make it *spirit* with *omnipotent power* by dilution and trituration; others, profanely setting aside the time-honored division, that venerable classification of all things into the four sensible old elements, namely, earth, air, fire, and water, aver that man is a fish, and requires only *one* of them for his medium of existence, and that he ought to live, move, and have his being in water; while others, dropping entirely the sensible universe, appeal directly to the supernals, and, through heaven-directed influxes and divinely-inspired media, summon the spirits from the "vasty deep" to reveal the hidden secrets of disease, to dispatch the dirty chores of the body, and abolish its nasty obstructions.

Of these heterodox and belligerent schisms, (for schools, their crude, heterogeneous, and inconceivable agglomeration of dreams cannot be called,) some are quite hydra-headed and formidable, armed with the true poison-fangs of the serpent Error, and thus, being real agencies of death, and *clearly* belonging to the *devil's* department of strategies, lies, and baleful enchantments, eternizing evil, legitimating murder, and forming true vampirisms on earth. Others wane away into the confines of inanition and stupidity, constituting the lowest systems of vulgar and fraudulent deceits and old-womanish delusions, until, in the limbo of absolute fatuity, they terminate in the "sound and fury of the idiot's story, signifying nothing," noise and smoke overclouding the splendors of the heaven of human reason and common sense.

In the van of this army of innovators, comes the German dreamer and mystic, Hahnemann. From the land of visions and seers, from the charmed realm of metaphysical figments and poetical fables, the true home-world of spiritual sea-serpents, mermaids, "gorgons, hydras, and chimeras dire," comes this portentous shape, "form of the formless," this inconceivable being.

> "The shadow came! a tall, thin, gray-haired figure,
> That looked as it had been a shade on earth;
> Quick in its motions, and with an air of vigor,
> But naught to mark its breeding or its birth.
> Now it waxed little, and again grew bigger,
> With now an air of gloom or savage mirth;
> But, as you gazed upon its features, they
> Changed every instant—to what none could say.
> The more intently the ghosts gazed, the less
> Could they distinguish whose the features were;
> The devil himself seemed puzzled even to guess;
> They varied like a dream—now here, now there;
> And several people swore, from out the press,
> They knew him perfectly; and one could swear
> He was his father, upon which another
> Was sure he was his mother's cousin's brother;
> Another that he was a duke, or knight,
> An orator, a lawyer, or a priest,
> A nabob, a man-midwife; but the wight
> Mysterious, changed his countenance at least
> As oft as they their minds: though in full sight
> He stood, the puzzle was increased;
> The *man was a phantasmagoria* in
> Himself,—he was so *volatile and thin*."

This shadow, like the heroes of Ossian, cloudy, vague, and indefinite, comes surrounded by mists and inarticulate mutterings, a true son of the realm of transcendental ecstasy and dreamy philosophy. With Thor-hammer in hand he tried to crush the skulls of the past, essayed to pulverize to infinitesimal powder the labors of the intellect of man for six thousand years, to dissipate and dilute into an ocean of nothingness the records and monuments of his honest work, and ceaseless spiritual growth for ages of vigilance and effort, to reverse the poles of the world, and, riding supreme upon "the wings of blarney," and the virtue and omnipotence of the infinite divisibility of matter, and the medical virtues thereof, to be carried on the trumpet-blast of common fame, that "always most impudently lies," within the sphere of imaginative women and sickly-souled men.

Wonderful Germany! thou art turning the heads of the human race with thy deep-musing professors! "For strange is it, nay, not without some touches of awfulness, to reflect on what is every day achieved in those dim chambers in high attics of learned Jena, Heidelberg, (Meissen,) and the rest, by those skin-dried anatomies who inhabit the same, to outward appearance not without some *vague resemblance* to humanity, especially such of them as occasionally shave, but, in fact, not being *men at all*, except in their faint outline and similitude, but actually intellectual or full-brained spiders, weaving ingenious webs, intricate, almost invisible in their separate lines, but forming altogether a reticulated mesh-work, (say rather cloud-grating,) through which but dim and indistinct glimpses can be caught by eyes of hieroglyphic deciphering Champollions, but *darker than midnight Erebus* to the great mass of mankind."

A desperate sportsman was this Hahnemann. Like the swallow-fishers on the towers of the Alhambra, flinging their flies to the wind for winged prey, he cast his lines into the vacuities of infinitude, flung out his world-wide nets of spiritual cobwebs, and, after divers hopeless rakings of the seas of space, returns with his basket crowded with shining prey; the *world's riddles* read, the sphinx's story told, mankind physically redeemed by spiritualized sugar-molecules under the divine guidance of a newly-invented force of the universe called "similia similibus curanter."

Hail, thou blessed wing-power of the imagination, creating epics and idyls, dreams and fables, long hast thou troubled the waters of theologies and histories, philosophies and literatures; thou hast now at last gotten thy tail into the mush-pots of science, and henceforward the bread of the understanding must be eaten with the "cud of sweet and bitter fancies," while the spectacles of demonstration must be taken from the learned nose, and their place supplied by thine infernal kaleidoscope! With all deference and love for the order of poetical minds, "misled by fancy's meteor ray," whom this seductive system has warped from the normality and light of reason, and seduced by the rainbow-tints of its "sailing foam-bells," or swallowed by the inarticulate and hazy infinitude of its suggestiveness, an enlightened criticism brings the fatal verdict: "thou hast been weighed in the scales, and found wanting." Lacking the positive in science, wandering in the wilderness of distractions belonging to the metaphysical or transition period, or phases of development of the human mind, and lacking every single element of the fatal and absolute, constituting true science with eternally fixed and definitive laws; lacking the *one thing* needful for the life of a theory, or system, thou lackest *all things*, and hast failed. The Ajax of this hallucination, a poet by the ordinance of Nature, and true son of the morning, winged and heaven-aspiring, but sadly cut loose from the moorings of sound sense and the ballast of logical reasoning, has the following set of oracular utterances: "I suppose it impossible to *overrate* the consequences of Hahnemann's life. Even the negative results are vast for our future well-being. I think of medicines now as curative personalities who take upon them to battle in us with our ills. He made the true experiment of *doing relatively nothing* in medicine, and found it abundantly *successful and humane.* Purgatives were one *nasty superstition* which he banished. Bleeding was another of these vampires," etc.* A man and a system who make the awfully-daring and significant ex-

* "Negatives tend to annihilation; affirmations are precious; negative results might be affirmative consequences, and medicines, as curative personalities, might have a good time battling in the bowels of a man; but 'ex nihil nihil fit.' "—ROBERT SMITH.

periment of "doing nothing" in medicine, and discover it to be abundantly *successful and humane*, are, of course, both divine, and, although the results are "*negative*," yet is it "impossible to *overestimate* the consequences of such a life." Hahnemann being the great zero in medical philosophy, plus and minus must necessarily spring from his bosom. The historic muse of science must chuckle vastly over this nut for the sages to crack, and be rejoiced to find this only absolutely pure spiritual intelligence of the ages, through whom God's ray shines without smut or varnish, at last saddling himself upon the meek and assinine formula, the mournful skeleton of a theory of an infinite fountain of all diseases, a ghastly "mother of dead dogs," incarnated in three diabolical forms: syphilis, sycosis, and psora, which last, being vernacularized, means common itch, or Scotch fiddle. Unspeakably grand is this explanation and solution of the whole multifarious world of diseases, at the same time *simple* and *sublime*. This old-fashioned, dirty, school-boy itch, is the great sin-fountain of *seven-eighths* of *all* the diseases of man. Let us thank God it was not the first of his eternal, all-embracing crotchets that was selected as the last, and that each innocent toothache pang, or harmless scab, must necessarily come from that infamous French ——. Beneficent itch, all hail! a good mother art thou, and Pandora's box held thee almost alone. And here the sinner, fallen in soul and broken in body, is left with a gleam of hope and consolation inspiring and unexpected. This itch, being the veritable origin of evil, perhaps the ancient devil himself, has a magical specific, a "similia similibus curantur," and hell is left full of comfort and glory, for there disease cannot enter, as it is destroyed in the egg by a divine specific, brimstone.

Shade of Aureolus Philip Theophrastus Bombast de Hohenheim Paracelsus, with thine immortal "two hundred and fourteen secrets," rise! What now of the infinite Archimedes' lever of all the world of diseases, the powder of the boar's tusk taken in the act of —————————, the irresistible virtue of "pigeon's" and "virgin's" milk, of the perfectly infallible "calcined hen's feather's," which will "mundify, mollify, cicatrize, and incarnate any ulcer whatsomever?" What of all the divine revelations concerning the *Rose-Solis* and the "herb-Robert"? Like "baseless fabrics" swept into the dust of the past, the splendor of thine escutcheon is tarnished by thine illustrious followers, Crollius and Hahnemann, the sage of Meissen. The vis-medicatrix having made up her mind that her golden key is "similia similibus," henceforward there is to be no more "swilling down of whole beakers full of gross and filthy drinks," her favorite formulæ being, "the conditions on which the remedy which produced the disease in the healthy body, already sick, are the following : first, the sick person must adhere to the most rigid diet, so that the effect of harmful food may not disturb that of the medicine ; second, the *medicine itself must be entirely simple*, or mixed only with perfectly indifferent substances, such as water, sugar of milk, etc. ; third, the medicine must be taken in the smallest, infinitesimally-microscopic portions, *because* the operation, in virtue of its quality, increases in the same proportion that its *mass* diminishes in *quantity.* This is *all the magic of homeopathy* expressed in a few words. There is nothing *unintelligible, nothing unseemly, nothing mysterious,* nothing *extraordinary,"*—Simply, O profound and erudite sage, because its nett result is simply *zero,* is *simply nothing!* Nothing from nothing and nothing remains. Go on registering the eternal chapter of "*post hocs,*" and pass them for sun-clear "*propter hocs,*" and nothing is extraordinary, nothing is impossible. And here it is refreshing to reflect, that this party of ethereals have bored no new artesian-wells, have struck no new leads of gold, undreamed of in the philosophies. Crollius holds the absurd idea that those remedies that externally resemble the symptoms of disease, in *color, form,* and *smell,* are the *safest:* saffron for jaundice, quaking asp for ague, and tea of the skin of a toad's back for small-pox. But, ridiculous as this is, it is but a short step from this theory to homeopathy.

"External resemblance" would only have to be new-christened "*internal.*" "But it is remarkable that his *physiognomical* remedies are often, in fact, *really homeopathic*, where external resemblance actually accompanies an internal one." Thus mutters a homeopathic oracle. Thus it is that the *new* is ever *old;* the *old* ever *new.* Hence everybody understands the matter, and is struck by its simplicity and probability; and hence everybody is a philosopher and doctor, and knows as much, or more than *everybody else*, whether philosopher *or* doctor. Progress, thou insane crab of a world! (head or tail foremost) where men with entrails (slimy tubes thirty or forty feet long) and solid viscera, (livers three and a half pounds normal, to twenty abnormal,) with bodies hundreds of weight avoirdupois, do nothing, think of nothing, believe in nothing, trust in nothing, get sick on nothing, and, "similia similibus curantur," take nothing, and get well on nothing.

In the Chaldean oracles of Zoroaster we find the following sublime saws. The unlettered may find obscurity and smoke in these flashes of the primitive soul, but to the initiated they are as the splendor of the noonday sun.

Oracle 75.

"Irrational demons derive their subsistence from the aerial rulers; wherefore, the oracle says, being the charioteer of the aerial, terrestrial, and aquatic dogs."

Oracle 76.

"The aquatic, when applied to the divine natures, signifies a government inseparable from water, and hence the oracle calls the aquatic gods water-walkers."

Oracle 80.

"The paternal mind has sowed symbols in the souls."

Oracle 98.

"Moisture is a symbol of life, hence Plato and the gods before

ÆSCULAPIUS. 505

Plato call it (the soul) at one time the liquid of the whole of vivication, and at another time a certain fountain of it."

ORACLE 103.

"The fontal nymphs, and all the aquatic spirits, and the terrestrial, aerial, and glittering recesses are the lunar riders and rulers of all matter, of the celestial, the starry, and that which lies in the abysses."

ORACLE 117.

"He makes the whole world of fire, and water, and earth, and all nourishing ether."

ORACLE 118.

"Placing earth in the middle, but water in the cavities of the earth, and air above these."

ORACLE 94.

"O man, of a daring nature, thou subtile production!"

With awe, like unto the ravishment which once seized upon the trembling priest, when voices from the depths of the inscrutable revealed the mysteries of eternity, and the as yet unborn future threw its shadow before, let us accept these oracles of the inspired ancients. Somewhat inarticulate, somewhat of the vastness of the unspeakable, looms out through the shady, evanescent, and transcendental imagery of the Oriental seer; but still the eye of faith can discover the infallible finger of prophecy in the hazy diffuseness of its cloudy terminology, and feel assured that the inevitable, with unerring precision, has here cast its shadows on the dial of time. It was clearly the triumphs of the new gospel of salvation by water alone, the symbols of which the paternal mind had sown in the soul of Zoroaster, touching "the prophet's hallowed lips with fire," that were thus vouchsafed by revelation in love and mercy to the sons of men. From the region of shades and mysticisms comes also this portentous humbug of the times, the cure of all diseases by water alone, this thing called Hydropathy. The modern author of this revelation is one Priessnitz, a peasant, who, being a seventh son of a seventh son, and born on Christmas night, was thus, by an eternal edict, or law of foreordination, made the recipient of that rarely-condescended compliment of the supernals, creative genius. Entirely innocent of the crime of any species of knowledge, having never tasted of the apples of any forbidden trees, and consequently left to wander in unprofaned paradises, on "the high hills and sunny lawns where men and angels meet," his sacred mission was to reveal the unspeakable virtue and amazing power of cold water. Gods of waters there had been in the old mythologies—Neptune and Triton—and goddesses of brooks and rivers—Nymphs and Naiades—but the secrets of hidden springs and rivers were still kept, and the gods and naiads maintained an unbroken quiet. At last the old silences brooding over the faces of the waters were broken, and the new evangel, the glad tidings of great joy, the doctrine of physical regeneration for man through cold water alone, was proclaimed, and the German peasant stood, the wonder of the hour. Just what the primordial idea of the water-cure was, deep down in the soul of Priessnitz;* just what he finally announced as the scientific basis of his system of medication, and gave as the rock of safety, around which should be left the floating chaos of destroyed medical theories, or the Ararat upon which obsolete Noah's-arks of systems must finally repose, being wholly surrounded by water, the sages have yet to declare, the happy initiated have yet to reveal. Taking certain doctrines of anatomy, physiology, and pathology to be true, namely, that the human creature is an amphibious animal, a magnificent frog or lizard, a water-biped without feathers or scales, and necessarily aquatic from his organization, requiring, like ducks and sponges, zoophytes and fishes, the constant application of water to live at all; that all diseases are simply an extensive variety of dirts, bodily pollutions, stickings and stuffings-up of tissues and organs; that man, being an absolute water-walker, all you have to do, is to pass him through a sufficiently diversified series of washings and soakings, dashes and splashes,

* See note, page 535.

flomixings and pourings of the all-healing specific water, and finally, like the miracle of soap and water upon soiled linen, he should be clean, and consequently well, starched up by the "stimulation of cold water." Shade of Zoroaster, behold the splendid world that has sprung from the power of the aquatic gods, or water-walkers! Thine oracle, with a divinely-directed instinct of the spirit, has thus prophesied that final consummation so long and ardently prayed for, even the achievements of the "Maine Liquor Law" and Hydropathy, "with a government inseparable from water."

And here exclusiveness is impertinence again, and the assumption of an absolute originality on the part of Priessnitz is an affectation of the most egregious intensity. The value and importance of water has been self-evident since its creation. The glory of water has always been known and appreciated by all men, and its real significance was long since revealed to them by the science which discovered that their bodies were made principally out of water; that four-fifths of the world were covered with water; that without this element of Nature all animals and plants must perish from off the earth's surface; that water was infinitely beautiful, the symbol of spirit, and of Deity; that without it, the poet could not make a song, the painter could not make a landscape, and God could not make a world. But it has been reserved for these modern days to make out the sublime demonstration, that all disease and human infirmity were to be specifically cured and readjusted by water, especially dropsy, diabetes, and the reduction of important inflammations; in short, that all the virtues of all medical agents, and all curative processes, reside in simple water. This quiet putting aside of the science of the times, this slapping the mouths of the anatomists, physiologists, and pathologists, in their supposed discovered laws of the body in the present habitat of man, is a contemptible insult to some of the best heads that have visited this planet, and argues great thickness of skin, and a verdancy not expected in the author of a system pretending to be an emanation from the human mind indorsed by human reason. However, being a German peasant, acknowledged by all to be profoundly ignorant of everything, error or inapprehension as to what the world had been doing, or dreaming, and trying to do, for six thousand years, in the shape of sciences and literatures, was to be expected.

But is it expected that the New World will indorse this hallucination of an ignorant serf? Undoubtedly cleanliness is akin to godliness; the virtue of washing is infinite, and there is no end to the glory of water; but that hydropathy is an "art and science among established things," was reserved for the poet of the "isms" to sing or say. The North American continent takes up the rusty hoaxes of the Old World, makes them run the gauntlet of Yankeedom new varnished and patched up in decayed and gone parts, never, however, touching them until exploded in the country where they rose, and "courteously declining to take up a German theory until the Germans had quite done with it and thrown it away for something new." The hopeful and aspirant have thus been disappointed continually. When the genius of history recorded the discovery of a new hemisphere, and hailed with joy the new-born giant's smile, the heart of man was glad with hopes for the dawn of light upon some undiscovered continents of the soul, commensurate in their boundless exuberance and exhaustless profusion, with those which Nature had provided as the theatre of untried colossal physical experiments and expansions of the races. With mournfulness and despair, behold the result! In their migration, with superstitious veneration, they carried the ashes of the dead with them, and with sedulous fear imported the mouldy skeleton-forms of departed polities, religions, literatures, and philosophies, and when men of prayer and hope, men of progressive instincts and faith in the onward growth and beneficent advancement of all things, looked to find that the old and effete skins had been sloughed off by a new expansion, and cast aside, the narrow and stony shells cracked and burst asunder by a new growth, lo! "men and beasts and worms crawled on the same." The swarm of liliputians and dwarfs donned the dusty rags of the dead, and the New World, rich in the splendors of a virgin bride, full of unspeakable promises for the future, appeared under the incubus of a fossil church and state, a fossil literature and philosophy, imported in decrepitude and decay from the Old. For what can be wiser and safer than the laws of England, deeper and more universal in its formulæ than the philosophy of Germany, or more exhaustive of the depths of the infinite than the visions and dreams of Judea? "The new must have its radicals in the old." Certainly, erudite savant; but demonstrate the problem: if the old be good wheat, whence, in the devil's name, come these infamous crops of cheat? Do you believe in univocal, or equivocal generation?

The glimpse just taken at the Priessnitzian formula, or water-cure, brings us into the presence of another imported delusion, long since exploded in the land of its birth, dead, buried, and almost forgotten there, that has found a fat and nourishing asylum, a soil of strength and richness, in this land of new inventions. Mesmer, of Suabia, collected a multitude of the eccentric and anomalous manifestations of the life of the nervous system, recording all obscure and mooted facts, all morbid and inexplicable phenomena under the name, style, and title, of the "Science of Animal Magnetism." This hallucination has given birth to whole races of monsters in the New World, a family of hydras which has grown more heads a thousandfold than the fabled monster.

In the first moment of contemplation this is incomprehensible and overwhelming. But we need not be surprised with anything from the country that has the honor of giving birth to Miller, the man milliner of ascension robes; to Jo Smith, the true evangelical representative-man, the authoritative exponent of the spirituality of the New World, say the veritable Mohammed of the North American continent, whom it has murdered, and consequently glorified;

not forgetting the quondam world-renowned Connecticut Count Cagliostro, the illustrious arch-quack of quacks of the western hemisphere, and grand Mogul of humbugs, the famous Nimrod of mooncalves, and whom the North American continent has *not* murdered, as he does not belong to the order of radical blasphemers, sinning unpardonably against its popular faiths, but is rather, in his own person, a sort of monkey deity astraddle of his woolly horse, a veritable representative spirit of the mermaid order from the realm of twaddledom, a kind of "Grand Lama" of Yankee Buddhism, or rather, perhaps, a satanic scene-shifter in the contemptible theatricalities of a rotten mammon-worshiping world. A soil that could give birth and grow such a creature as the once illustrious proprietor of the "Ivy Island," elevate him to the dignity of a niche in the temple of heroes, installing him in a golden house of Nero, and give twenty-five thousand dollars (whisper low!) for the most flagrant, nauseous and diabolical confession of sin, made off the scaffold of a common malefactor, on record: the finikin, cynical, and would-be smart exposé and dissection of a tissue of cunningly-devised fables, by which thousands of hard-earned dollars were extracted from the human race by a brutal invasion and assassination of the best element of man, the disposition to believe, or faith, through the instrumentality of a series of tricks and juggleries of a common showman,—a soil which can grow such a man will grow all the humbugs of perdition. In this rich mould the genius of Mesmer soon struck root and flourished, and consequently the world has been shown the spectacle of a crop of Jonah's gourd follies and delusions springing from the mire of that dismal swamp, human gullibility. Transcended and cast aside in his native land, this obsolete progenitor of innumerable absurdities has sown a crop of bold and noxious weeds, "an enemy of man who, while he slept, came and sowed tares among the wheat," that have grown into a harvest of wretched deceits, which, fortunately however for humanity, die of their own inanition, and still, from their dust, come the weeds of hallucinations and quackeries, until the earth groans, and is wearied with her myriad births of monsters. To the vague and diffuse mumblements of clairvoyance, with its profane babbling of spirits, and direct unvailing of the mysteries of the "abysses where God's eternal secrets lie," must succeed the order of the "darlings of Providence, fond Fate's elect," in the shape of especially-inspired healing media, whose precious privilege it is permitted to be, to wash their subjects in the "Pools of Siloam," to galvanize the dead as the corpse of Lazarus was raised, to heal the cold and stiffened tenements of the grave as the daughter of Jairus was healed. In their own cant, "their practice is similar to that which was prevalent in the days of miracles." This is the last achievement of folly, this is the catastrophe of sin made perfect. The readers of the "Spiritual Telegraph" behold each day, as if in positive earnest, without a wrinkle of mockery and derision, the following advertisement of a "Healing Medium:" "Behold, the sick are healed! Mrs. ——, of ——, Psychical Physican and Medium, would respectfully offer her services—assisted by her husband—to the diseased, particularly those with *cancerous* afflictions, and such diseases generally as have baffled the skill of the 'faculty.' Examinations of persons at a distance will be promptly attended to on the receipt of five dollars and a *lock of hair or other relic*, with name and the residence of the patient. Rooms, ——. Address ——." It is well not to omit the magical "V" in calling on these ethereal doctors. Wonder of wonders! in these days of porcelain teeth and East India hair dyes, incomparable lustres and gossamer wigs, that by a lock of hair or some "relic," say an artificial tooth, sent to ——, the spirits will soon hocus-pocus out what part of the bowel is obstructed and the genus and species of cancer afflicting the sufferer, and abolish them both; the distance off of the sick man presenting no difficulty to spiritual influence,—for where cannot spirits go? what cannot spirits know? why shall not spirits pick all God's locks as easily one way as another, and from a "lock of hair or relic," divine everybody's ills a thousand miles away. A common ghost still in the mud, in the shape of an old-fashioned terrestrial doctor, smelling loudly of assafœtida and ether, with pill-box and scarificator in his pocket, makes himself extremely disgusting by actually looking into his patients' mouths, at their tongues, and feeling pulses, occasionally (say it softly for ears refined) putting his hand on the sinner's bowels to know his ailments, not forgetting a few exploratory squints at the contents of ———. This race of leeches is becoming effete, frosty, and fogy, too slow for Yankee go-it-while-your-young-ness, with its "two-seventeen" horses, locomotives, and telegraph wires. Now, a Healing Medium—what a beautiful and euphonious name!—(which, being rendered into English in common use, means a windy gasconader of the genus quack) perpetrates, under this name and title, the infamous impiety of attempting to don the God-mantle of Jesus the Christ, and transact miracles as he would the every-day business of vending cheese or patent medicines. A letter containing five dollars, it seems, is the golden key, or irresistible fiat for the issuing of the saving force required, of course using no medicines in any case whatever, but "relying on the remedies used in the days of miracles," "guided by a secret though invisible intelligence." The radiant recipient of celestial influxes gets himself, particularly herself, as the sex of the vessel is a subject of indifference to spirits, (the feminine gender being generally preferred however,) into a state of supernatural ecstasy, a celestial furor or trance, cuts short his acquaintance with the body, and its five old donkey senses, floats off upon angelic wings into heaven, stirs up the whole Shanghai roost of spirits, produces his "lock of hair or relic," demands a cure for the troubled mortal who has been coloring his hair with East India dye, (who has honestly sent the five dollars with a lock of it,) asks a flash of lightning to amputate the cancerous mass, in a dream, without suffering to the patient, or to open his bowels without glyster-pipe or castor oil, simply by the good old practice which prevailed "in the days of miracles."

Speak of the days of miracles, will you! it is a mark of true wisdom to discover, in the commonplace, the miraculous. The spiritual medium simply becomes a vessel or tub recipient of the higher influx, the secrets of eternity are laid bare by the tousel of hair, the disease destroyed by an "invisible intelligence," and the faculty is requested to take a back seat, being essentially floored. No spirits about, no ghosts these days, pshaw! everybody is a spirit, everybody is a ghost; "ere thy watch tick, a million pop up from the dark; ere thy watch tick again, a million bob down into the dark." And here the reflecting mind, the soul of sympathy and meditation, is brought to a dead halt, a bolt-upright stand in the presence of a world of ghastly suggestions, partaking of the nature of hair-starting or true terror horripilations, the trouble which spirits in the clay always have with spirits out of the clay, that ghosts in one sphere have with ghosts in another sphere. Once we thought that the grave surely had rest for us all, and when the "mortal coil was shuffled off," that the Silences and the Infinite claimed us by right eternal.

> "Peace waits us on the shores of Acheron:
>   There no forced banquet claims the sated guest,
>   But silence spreads the couch of ever-welcome rest.
>   Yet if, as holiest men have deemed, there be
>   A land of souls beyond that sable shore,
>   To shame the doctrine of the Sadducee
>   And sophist madly vain of dubious lore;
>   How sweet it were in concert to adore
>   With those who made our mortal labors light!
>   To hear each voice we feared to hear no more!
>   Behold each mighty shade revealed to sight,
>   The Bactrian, Samian sage, and all who taught the right!"

So muttered the dreaming bard; alas, but dreaming! Peace no longer waits us on the shores of Acheron, and silence no longer spreads for us a couch of rest; sweet, no doubt, it would be "in concert to adore," "with those who made

our mortal labors light;" but these infernal rappers, he and
she media, have other work than the sweets of adoration on
hand for us; for saint or sinner, whether in heaven or hell,
whether drinking of the "rills that sparkle in the bowers of
bliss," or gulping with sorrow the flames of "that fire the
angels shudder but to name," are both alike subject to
the wills and caprices of souls still in the bitterness and
bonds of the clay, and may be summoned, as lackeys
in a theatre, to the most ignoble services, galloping up
stairs with tables on their backs, passing through the human
intestine to count its ulcers and warts, or conjure
out by the legerdemain known only to spirits, from a lock
of dyed hair, the philosophy and cure of cancer and "diseases
in general that have baffled the skill of the faculty."
No longer are we to hold ourselves in readiness, with "best
bib and tucker," for awful judgment days, or settlement of
doomsday books, or sleep till the second coming; no longer
is the "horn of Monker, waking up the dead," required; but
Tom Johnson and Sallie Jones pile their hands upon a table,
and lo! rap, wake snakes, the grave is opened, the gates of
heaven fly back with a golden sound, while those of Pandemonium
"grate harsh thunder;" the dead walk, the shades of
Plato and Zoroaster, of Hahnemann and Paracelsus, are summoned
to the bar to testify in cases pending: Conniption
Fits *vs.* Jemima Flint; Stone in the Bladder *vs.* John
Smith; Worm in the Liver *vs.* Hobensach; or Ghost of
Woolly Horse *vs.* Barnum. Vast are the abysses through
which the soul blunders in the darkness of this sorrowful
delirium. And here a spirit whispers a suggestion: these
rappers, by invading the sanctity of the grave and calling
the spirits of the departed back from that "sable shore" to
perform the functions of leech and lancet, ignore the wisdom
of one grand man of inspiration who has appeared on the
planet since the days of cloven tongues—Emanuel Swedenborg.
In the "Angelic Wisdom" concerning Divine Providence
(114) it is recorded "that evils in the external man
cannot be removed *by the Lord* except by means of *man.*"

Diseases of all orders not being material, (cancer pumpkins, hypertrophied livers large as a mule's head to the contrary notwithstanding,) but spiritual and dynamic existences, it appears among the things seen and heard in the seventh heaven, as revelations of supernatural wisdom, that the only means even the *Lord* himself has to remove the evils of the external man, is the instrumentality of man himself. Progressive, and slightly ahead of the Lord, then, ye wise, ye learned, "like superstitious thieves YOU think the light of DEAD MEN'S marrow guides YOU best at night." If it is true that the Lord cannot remove the evils of man except by means of man, then why would ye summon the souls of the dead, why trouble the departed who sleep well after "life's fitful fever," to return and vex themselves again with the infirmities of those frail and weary weeds, the bodies of other men? Surely they had trouble enough with their own colic spasms, toothaches, itches, scald-heads, and diarrhœas during their stay upon earth, and should not to all eternity be open to intrusion upon the sweet rest of the grave, and dragged, it may be, from heaven and the raptures of singing the 119th Psalm, long meter, to rectify the intestinal obstructions of brutal sinners, still imprisoned in bodies stuffed with mackerel and whisky. This seems an offense to the sentiment and law of justice which pervades the universe. That a soul, after being tortured through the hell of the finite with a cancerous stomach, should be liable to be summoned from the everlasting silences to dose through all eternity cancerous stomachs, is a revelation of the infinite torments of perdition, compared with which, the bigot's common hell would be heaven, and the old-fashioned brimstone lake as sweet as a bed of roses. Oh, lugubrious rappers! let them sleep; ye are investing the grave and eternity with horrors yet undreamed of in the armory of God's eternal wrath.

In remote spaces of hopeless inanity and stupidity there loom still others of the flock of ill-starred birds of prey, or quackeries of the times. Many of them are so phantasmal, shadowy, and unreal, so clearly fictions of the dream-world, such plainly-marked satanic stratagems, that the common sense of the race cannot tolerate even a hearing with court and jury, but dismisses them at once to the shades. When the two startling and peculiar names, "Kinesipathy" and "Hypnotism," arise before us and ask our consideration as modes of curing disease, what shall we say? There is magic in a name, certainly, and magic has been a powerful force in the world in days gone by, why not now? Ling, the author of the "Swedish Medical Gymnastics," was a poet who failed to take cold after exposing himself, half naked, on a frosty day, for the purpose of committing suicide; and, rapping himself with a ruler on a rheumatic part, discovered that it relieved the pain, and thus was revealed to him a new system of medical suggestions which he called Kinesipathy,—a name, beyond a doubt, which means the curative virtues of rubbing, snubbing, nudging, and kneading, scratching and pounding, (which, of course, includes the art of pugilism, which has always been known to be good for weak eyes,) the philosophy of shampooing and poking, dancing and wriggling, jerking, squirming, and fumbling. Two thousand sublime movements, of all orders imaginable, cure the whole catalogue of chronic diseases, constituting a system of organic sanitary exercises or drillings. It has been practiced in Sweden for more than thirty years. The time it seems for Yankeedom to take it up, revamp, and trot it out, has now arrived.* We propose the health of the Swedish poet Ling, with all the honors.

Hypnotism was discovered by James Braid, of Manchester. The oracular bard of the sciences calls it "one of a number of arts to which we shall give the generic name of Phrenopathy, for it produces its effects principally as actions of mind upon mind." "The heart's wounds are immedicable, and canst thou minister to a mind diseased." Hypnotism pours physical salvation into the animal man through his soul. This is done by

* There are practitioners of this system at several places in the United States.

intense contemplation, by excessive abstraction, holding the intellect in thumb-screws, a cast-steel rivet through the centre of the mind; a kind of "double internal squint" being the most potential direction of the eyes for the purpose. "Abstraction tends to become more and more abstract, narrower and narrower; it tends to unity, and *afterward to nullity.*" Sound! Of *course to nullity*. All films are thus cast aside from organs and tissues; exaltation in impressibility is the achievement; "the body trembles like down with the wafts of the atmosphere; the world plays upon it as upon a spiritual instrument finely attuned;" ("Harp of a thousand strings and sperets of just men," including the "voice of the turtle;") angels of mercy descend, touch the raw and agonized surfaces with balmy kisses of healing; and the patient, in the sanitary embraces of a hypnotic trance, is redeemed from the horrors of disease, and is carried blissfully back to the harmonious circulation of health and life. This idea is supposed to be a full forty-second cousin of that highly respectable phantom of the human brain, called Animal Magnetism.

Beside these fanciful and suggestive systems of medication which seem to bring in arcs of the circle, and serve to complete the whole sphere of the possible in this realm of imaginative and ideal healing, there are others scarcely worthy of notice, while some are positively filthy, noxious, and insane, mere beggarly insults to the good sense of humanity; for, to speak or allude to Uroscopy or Thompsonianism in the presence of decent persons, is to be vulgar and ridiculous. Add to this list the "grape cure," the "goatswhey cure," the "hunger cure," the "beer cure," the "rest cure," and there would seem to be no end to the cures or systems of healing in this department of strategies and wiles, of humbugs and horrors. Still is it wonderful how the swarms of delusions acknowledge the same venerable author of lies for their illustrious sire, and have even a similarity of detail, a family resemblance most obvious; the end proposed by ALL their efforts being to humbug and swindle the world.

In these latter times we have heard much of commercial feudalisms and merchant princes, an order of men who, by handling commodities alone, creating *no* particle of *value* in the world, but simply by huxtering and swapping garlic and soap-fat, have come to handle the helms of financial worlds, and, like the steeds of the ancient barbarians, become installed in the palaces of the Cæsars. But it has been reserved as the peculiar glory of the North American continent to breed a new race of saurians of the commercial deeps, a *new order* of *colossal lizards* and *flying dragons*, whose food is human flesh, and whose coprolites in a thousand years will show only the presence of human bones.

This calls to the bar a host of parasites that infest the medical profession in the shape of vendors of patent medicines.

Of course, "Hobensach" is infallible and sound, for everybody takes his vermifuge, whether wormy or not. Retire, "Hobensach!" one worm you forgot in your catalogue of murdered victims—maggot in the head. It was well, however, to let him flourish as grand generator of crotchets, else how otherwise could it come about that *everybody would take* "Hobensach?"

Swaim has retired to the shades. Rappers notify him that he left the earth too soon, that the sublime panacea of scrofula and cancer has found a place in a sphere of uses undreamed of by its illustrious discoverer.*

And then there have been dukes of sarsaparilla, and almost * * * * * . Shades of Webster and Clay! creators of nostrums, vendors * * * * * grabbing for the mantles you so sadly and hurriedly dropped. O tempora, O mores! * * * * * anything for the vainglorious flash of the hour. Feejee Island cannibals on the thrones of the world not half so anomalous, not half so lost.

* See Robert Smith's story of Aunt Katy's sweetening her cakes with Swaim's panacea. AUNT KATY—It *was* a *panacea*, else how could it help the old man's cough, and make the best cakes in the world?

ÆSCULAPIUS.

A stranger, walking the streets of American cities, and elevating his eyes in view of certain august granite and marble masses, might suppose he had gotten into the presence of palaces of proud old monarchs, huge men, kings by consent of the earth.

By what magical incantation, by the music of what Orpheus have the iron and marble, the sandstone and granite danced to these cities, and arranged themselves in such artistic piles? The guardian angels of humanity must weep over these monuments of sin, these sublime Choctaw wigwams, made hideous to the spirit's eye by the scalps of murdered gullibles. It is certainly the age of a new order of miracles. Those imperial towers—what mountains of congealed human sweat! what tallyboards of years of human agony! the sad inheritance of the fall and fearful curse of a wrathful Deity, in an *expiatory struggle* of *twelve dismal hours of work*, represented by the dollar! Touch those marble and granite blocks, they bleed and shriek like the trees in "Dante's Hell," alive with the torments of suffering souls, and this calamity from those cunningly-devised institutions of the devil, quack nostrums, the *meanest* and most murderous mode of assassination of the fraternal instincts of humanity, abhorrent to men and angels both. Unhappy creators of shams and Yankee vulturizations, gas, puff, sell the waters of the rivers of the earth, diluted with simples, constituting a series of infamous hoaxes, and insult humanity by building from their revenue palaces to the stars. Say to the human race, with the Veiled Prophet of Khorassan: "Yes, ye vile race, for *hell's* amusement given, too mean for earth, yet claiming kin with heaven; is it enough, or must we, while a thrill lives in your sapient bosoms, *cheat you still?*"

There is in heathen mythology a goddess of revenge, whose special function it is to see that retribution, swift and sure, shall seize delinquent sinners. Unhappy fabricators of nostrums, she is after you all even now, with her sharpest stick. The granite and marble, the iron and sandstone are but *dust;* they must crumble and vanish under the teeth of Time. Until which consummation shall arrive, let those feudal towers stand, like infernal gallows, from which hang the bones of malefactors that rattle in the winds of the ages, more loathsome to heaven than that spectacle of horror of "the shaggy demon of the wilderness," the Tartar Khan's pyramid of ten thousand human skulls.

Inspecting this dismal catalogue of nostrum-makers who are a *poisonous mixture of quack and felon*, and wandering through the disastrous dance of this chaos of medical systems and theories of healing, what is the wretched victim of the maladies of the body, who seeks relief for his sufferings from the interference and assistance of the skill of man, to believe? especially what is he TO DO? Is this array of doctors all a mournful army of Sangrados, a party of "knights of the rueful countenance," on fantastic errands, and victims of Quixotic hallucinations; mournful ravens croaking delusive make-believes over the sick man's couch? Is poor, sick, and sorrow-stricken humanity thus ever to be deluded and made the sport of a mocking and wicked fate, wretchedly victimized by a villainous order of infatuations and deceits terminating only in the despair and torments of death? Is the proverbial uncertainty of all medicine an inevitable conclusion from a critical survey of the different fields of its operations, and the analysis of its scriptures, canonical and uncanonical? A synopsis of even the most fantastic "ism," with a nett result of man's endeavors in this sphere, would be a desirable achievement. What can the common sense of the hour fix as the absolute result, the clean, scientific sediment from the boiling pots of each of these portentous systems, prominent in the day in which we live? First of the fashionable quackery of the German mystic Hahnemann, what do we know as real substance? what as most absolute shadow?

The doctrine of "similia similibus curantur" puts in requisition the protective and conservative sanitary instinct of the organism called "vis medicatrix naturæ," the essential curative efforts of tissues and organs; and by diluting into annihilation and nothingness its famous similia, it leaves said healing plus-forces to battle unobstructed with the ills of the organization. Falling back into a "masterly inactivity," the absurd ultimatum of the expectant method, the sublime of the system of "laissez-faire," or let alone, it hands the patient into the motherly care of Nature. In short, it inculcates the wholesome, though not very pleasant doctrine to the sinner, that Nature is really a forgiving and kind mother, but that she requires penitence and perfect virtue, to restore him to health, and that *diet, temperance, self-denial*, and *nothing* (except faith) are terrible agencies in curing disease, and have a power almost infinite over the body and the soul to save them both; that in the reliance of homeopathy upon its inconceivable abstractions beyond the reach of reason, or mathematics in its efforts to metamorphose matter into spirit by infinite dilutions, triturations, and mechanical comminutions, it may thus become a spiritual and dynamic agent among diseases which it asserts are spiritual and dynamic entities which must be vanquished by powers of the same order; and withal, constantly producing an array of alleged "post hocs" which it can in no conceivable manner demonstrate to be "propter hocs," but which *can* be clearly shown to be the result of the action of known laws of organic life, it is clear that it trusts veritably and absolutely to nothing. The system has value as a rebuke and pronuncimento against the arrogance and self-sufficiency of the Old School, with its unfaltering faith in *drugs*, and has real significance as a criticism upon the regular routine art, with its fossilizing pharmacopœias, its elaborate prescriptions, peck-measure pill-boxes, and enormous dosing of nauseous medicines. It has also value as a demonstration of the influence of mind over matter, imagination over the body, or man upon man spiritually. By singing its song of incomprehensible abstractions, and reiterating its earnest promises of healing, the patient is flung into the arms of an all-cherishing Nature, and, in the slumber-draught of her charmed goblet, with the angels of faith and hope watching over it, it must come that the body will be deserted by its ills, they being finally expelled by the conservative life-forces which originally build it up with miraculous architecture out of the wheat field and the orchard. Dream on, sorrowful dreamer, there may be healing in your dreams. Believe in your brother man even if he does delude you with a song, for, according to an ancient formula, *there is salvation in faith alone.* There is one other aspect in which homeopathy, unfortunately for itself, is valuable to the world and the profession, namely, as an indorsement of the Old School of medicine itself. Wholesale drugging has long since been abandoned by sensible men; but the rational, judicious, and intelligent administration of medicine is an art indorsed by science.

These homeopathic worthies have discovered no new drugs or elements of materia medica, but, by an astonishing coincidence, have adopted the old substances in toto, only using them microscopically, and after the new law of like curing like, at the same time retaining their faith in the accredited dragon forces of the world; and, unless those scoundrels the druggists slander them foully, they still, notwithstanding their twaddle about infinitesimals, drive the venerable stage horses in the same style that the regular profession have been in the habit of driving them.

Secondly, that Hydropathy, maugre its impertinence and affectation in calling itself a medical system, particularly *cure*, and especially new system, has done one thing for the good of humanity, namely, assisted somewhat in the exaltation of water to the position of one of the most beneficent gifts of the supernals. Cleanliness being really a species of holiness, water, an element high in the catalogue of the good things of the Lord, may, in divers applications to dirty, jaded, and gone bodies, to burnt-out crucibles and fire-eaten bread-baskets of stomachs, accompanied with brandy-boiled brains, and nerves corroded with intensity of galvanic action, in short, that have grown diseased, and are paying the penalties of sin in a medium of sensuality and luxury in different shapes of such derangements, remove obstructions of the emunctories, and wash out or deterge the abominations of the body, especially if, as is always the case, the water be "accompanied with absolute diet, and exercise in the open air with uncovered head." They call it *Hydropathy*, and take, with the good sense of the world in all ages and in all systems, such aphorisms as this: An essential law of life is activity; without exercise or some shape of motion no animal can be healthful or live; things are so constituted, and not otherwise; and that cleanliness and diet are powerful helps to nature in every shape of disease or morbid condition of the bodies of men or animals.

Let us honor Priessnitz with the honor due unto him, as the great apostle of cold water, in an age whose history will be redolent of whisky for a thousand years, and among a people whom it has become necessary to muzzle with the strong arm of the common law, and whose lips it has been deemed advisable to close with padlocks, only giving the keys to courts and juries.

Thirdly, look for a moment at the sediment of the rappers. In the far East, the region of the cradle of the races, and, of course, the fountain of light and knowledge to all the world, the Oriental spiritualists or doctors, whose interpretation of disease is, that each one is a bad spirit or devil, rap on hollow trees and drums, blow with horns, and roar with gongs, to frighten them away. This is the whole medical treatment. The spirit rappers, by giving no medicine, "being guided by a secret though invisible intelligence," may also, by calling in the ghosts of the dead, alarm the ravens of disease and resuscitate the sick and dying by fear or faith.

Send a lock of your hair to *Mrs.* ——, and suddenly be made whole, thou colicky sinner!

It is written, "man shall not live by bread alone." Being half an angel, he must have some pabulum for his soul; being half spirit, he must, to be sound, have some food from heaven; why shall not the spirit medium, practicing with trans-grave ideas and remedies, say, man shall not die by medicine alone? As they give "no medicines in any case whatever," but rely solely upon Nature's remedies, neither attempting to advance or arrest the procession of things, by the way the safest position to take for final judgments is surely to leave the sick man to get along alone, to live or die by "Nature's remedies."

The schools stand vis-à-vis on the question of death, as on the question of life.*

Mrs. B—— has lost her only daughter, and is broken-hearted.† * * * * *

To conclude this currente calamo splash on the subject of some of the most prominent of the satanic strategies, wiles, and charlatanries assuming the prerogatives and powers of the regular profession of medicine which are now at work hoaxing the world, it might be true, that spring fever, gout, calculous concretions of the joints, pathological obesity or morbid fatness, dyspepsia, blue devils, and common mulligrubs, and all diseases connected with incorrigible laziness and soggy immobility, with indiscriminate stuffing of cavities, would be essentially benefited by the "Lingian formulæ" of medical gymnastics. Of course, many things might be done by *two thousand movements,* by the therapeutic virtue of kicking and cuffing, nudging and snubbing, etc., especially by the drill of the muscles of arms and legs in some useful operation in the creation of value, as in the highly-curative gymnastic movement of ploughing the earth, or splitting wood; that good may come of this medicine of the muscles, "from the muscles of medicine," there is not the least doubt; also, that hypnotism may cure hypochondriacism and vaporism, and that hocus-pocus may medicate successfully "conniption fits" and the whole range of diseases which may be classified under the genus of "lackadaisical fancies." "The unit of hypnotism is intense attention, ab-

---

* See Robert Smith's story of the death of Mrs. T.'s son for want of the twenty-fifth bleeding in bilious fever.

† See Smith's story of the death of her daughter in the *natural way,* or without the assistance of any kind of doctor at all.

straction, the personal *ego* pushed to nonentity. The unit of Mesmerism is the common state of the patient, caught as he stands, and subjected to the radiant ideas of another person: it is mediate; or both personal and impersonal. Neither sleep nor hypnotism can exist in the presence of a second person, without partaking more or less of Mesmerism. The sleep brain is fluid, the hypnotic brain movable-pointed, and the Mesmeric brain elastic. Sleep = influx; hypnotism = efflux; Mesmerism = afflux."* This is as crystalline as mud, and must be clear even to the uninitiated and unlettered; transparent and glorious as the splendors of an October morning, the "ideas sticking out like asses' ears." Consummation; "the virtue of hypnotism, where it succeeds, is just this, that for the moment, it unweeds the human soil so completely, that whatever faith is impressed, can work and grow."

Some faiths will grow in almost any soil, weeded or unweeded, and work too; but most faiths grow best where there are most weeds. But wherever it does grow, it is a good thing, and may cure. Thus, hypnotism, by pushing the personal ego to nonentity, may work and grow, and thus cure and save by faith.

What is the scientific solution of the phenomena of apparent curing by nostrums, quacks, and delusions in general?

Various forms of revelation of the optimism or overflowing goodness of Nature have been made to divers inspired souls; and to all men in whom perception is at all awake it must be apparent, that a good principle, a conquering energy of benevolence and love, a constantly-acting recuperative power predominates in the order of things. "The universe is a system of divine ends, organizing and executing itself, under the influence of divine love, directed by divine wisdom." All created beings dwell in the full exuberance of this boundless nature, this overwhelming goodness, this unspeakable beauty, live, move, and have their being in the bosom of an infinite intelligence, held tenderly in the lap of an infinite love. Like little children, drawing life and strength

* Wilkin

from a cherishing mother, fed and clothed by invisible fingers, nursed and caressed by invisible hands, we grow. The quackeries of the world "sing the song of sixpence," and get "a pocket full of rye," "betting" on the triumph of this beneficent power, this strong will of nature, this plus fullness, this exuberant vitality and strength, which battles in us with the destroying powers, quarrels with, and resists toughly death in every shape, and says, even to the body of man, thou shalt live forever. As a centre of all organic forms there exists this budding and expansive life-force, which, by a miraculous centrifugal tendency, seeks a full pronunciation somehow, even through difficulties insuperable, of the proper sphere of being of the creature, through consummation or finishing of its form, life, and power, as facts in the divine economy of uses, of which the universe of matter is the perpetually unfallen, also glorified and transcendent symbol. This is the real philosophy of the world of post hocs, which, by satanic cunningness, get themselves passed for propter hocs, assuming the relationship, the absolute golden nexus of cause and effect, instead of mere apparent antecedent and consequent.

Nature walks her own paths, makes and keeps, works and sleeps. Assailants of all orders come; she says, nay! Nostrum and quack watch, like the eagle for the fish-hawk, pounce, and away with the prey; antecedent—sugar globules, cold water, Swaim's panacea, or Hobensach; consequent—normal poise of restoring powers and all safe; hands of death off; soundness is restored. Recuperative sanitary ecstasy of nature says, never mind the nostrum, the cabalistic sign, the nothingness of Hobensach & Co.; I will make you well, notwithstanding your scabs and scratches, your childish whinings and querulous complainings, your sufferings and distractions; disease is an impertinence and intrusion into the charmed realm of life in which I am Queen. Your simples and water, your treacle and peppermint, do not hinder me seriously in my work, which is to grow a new universe every moment, keeping the apples and cabbages of Eden freshly on hand each instant of time; for, "ever forth the broad creation, a divine improvisation, from my heart proceeds." The heinous offense of the quack is, that he steals; does not "render unto Cæsar the things which be Cæsar's, and unto God the things which be God's," but would feloniously rob the altar of life of its sacred fire, to melt his gold and roast his potatoes. Taking his ideas, (when he has any,) his language, his intellectual conceptions, of which his stock is meagre enough, from the regular scientific profession, he would assume an originality and newness which cannot appertain to *shams* and *appearances*, which are at best but *beggarly imitations* of something which has an honest and earnest existence. He would *varnish* the *false* and *accidental*, into the appearance of the absolute and real. Living and moving in a world of insincerities and lies, he howls of *persecution* and monopoly, privileged orders, and learned professions, steals the prerogatives of *all*, and, bowing obsequiously, assumes, without shadow of right, the immunities, privileges, and emoluments pertaining to the same, and thus is perpetually a felon, serving the devil with *all* the "liveries of heaven" upon his back.

This is the cardinal confession of sin. Why the quack's perpetual abuse of the regular profession? Why this imitation? Why this continued stretching to and affectation of the possession of the achievements of science? Why does each fashionable quack profess *once* to have been of the regular profession and *old school?* Why this inward fealty to an authority which they outwardly ignore? The regular profession, in reliable history, stretches back hundreds of years. Conservative as to what it has found with alembic and microscope, crucible and dissecting knife, it questions with intensity of earnestness every innovation, and asks of all propositions in the art of healing, are they true? have they "quod erat demonstrandum" affixed to them? Why the honest new or rational progressive should quarrel with venerable conservatisms, and surely-rooted truisms, and be impatient under the asking of sound questions, is surprising. The *honest, earnest,* and *sensible new,* has always

appealed to the sympathy for weakness and infancy, asking
consideration for the tender, fresh-*budding*, and *undeveloped;*
while the rational *old*, on the score of generosity and disinterestedness, has been required to apologize for its tyranny
in the consciousness of the superiority of force, in the simple
possession of power. The quarrel of the regular profession
with quackery comes from a profound and undying antagonism. It is the ancient war of truth and error, light and
darkness, knowledge and ignorance. As regular exponents
of the powers of evil, the *quackeries of the world* have ever
had, and will ever have to meet the *honest and sane realities*
of science in an eternal attitude of hostility and opposition.
Books have been written upon the philosophy of magic and
witchcraft, the explanation of hallucinations and delusions,
but we still wait to see an exposition of the diabolical
essence of quackery. An historical delineation of the modus operandi of the devil in this his favorite department
of stratagems and tricks, his most authentic and material opposition to the final ascendency of truth and goodness, and
the quick arrival of the kingdom of heaven, would be a gift
of the gods to humanity.

Turning with sickness and sorrow from the nauseous recitation of the quackeries of the world, this dreary waste of
infatuations, this "fantastic chase of shadows after shades,"
where is suffering humanity to look for relief? Wounded,
wearied, and riven, what is the haggard victim of pain to do
to be saved from despair and destruction ? Are all systems of medication phantoms and follies, with nothing of
truth or light in them, only disappointment and ruin to offer
to the deluded faith of mankind ?

"Grand on her pedestal, as urn-bearing statue of Hellas,"
stands the regular profession, the *ark of safety*, the *rock of
ages*, the *hope of the world*. The god of medicine was
represented as seated on a throne, holding in one hand a
staff, and with the other resting upon the head of a dragon-
(serpent,) and by his side lay a dog. The interpretation of
this beautiful fable surely the simplest man is able to

make. The staff* is the emblem of assistance and help; the profession standing steadfastly as a support or prop to tottering man, giving eyes to the blind, limbs to the lame, and saving the weary foot-sore traveler from fainting on the journey of life. With the other hand he rests upon the head of a dragon (serpent.) This shadows forth with artistic precision and beauty the triumphs of the art of healing. This serpent is a type of the prudence and wisdom which control the demon of disease and pain, fallen man's most fearful foe. The hand of Æsculapius rests upon its head, thus typifying his godlike sphere, even the full and perfect control of the powers which so fatally environ man in his strange imprisonment in the body, and his struggles with the elements of darkness and death.

Contemplate the singular analogies, poetic justice, and propriety of the myth, in the detailed opotheosis of this divinity. The gloomy god of Tartarus was dissatisfied with the labors of this shining conservator of humanity, fearing that from his cures and resurrections hell was not being filled fast enough, and he must suffer the fate of all the gods who have perished for others, and, by a divine self-sacrifice, a splendid murder, through the jealousy of the highest divinities of Olympus, and the envy and hatred of the miserable superintendent of the infernal regions, be killed by a "flash of lightning and placed among the stars."

And by his side lay a dog. In the symbolical representation of things among all nations, the dog is the emblem of fidelity. Thus the deity who presides over the well-being of humanity, true to the law of love and fidelity, has by his side a dog. Let the earth fail, and the perishing man be hunted to the brink of the grave, with all terrestrial relationships crumbling to nothing about him, yet will he find by his side, sure and steadfast in his hour of agony and suffering, the *Physician*, his hope in life, his consolation in death.

Waiving the poetries and symbolisms, what has the regu-

* Life-preserver.

lar profession to offer to fulfill the dream of the Greek in his conception of the god of medicine? "In the thick darkness are there gleams of a better light?" What promise has the profession made to men that it cannot redeem? What hope has it excited that it cannot realize? What faith has it inspired to be met by disappointment? What can the profession emphatically *do*? What *has it done and rendered fixed and established immutably as law*, by principles of the *positive* and *absolute in philosophy?* And here it must be said, that a systematic and logical recitation of what it *has* done, a catalogue of its unquestioned and demonstrable elements, would be a treatise on the philosophy of medical science, a serious and profound recapitulation of which, together with a historical account of the order of sequence of development, with the unalterable laws of affinity or alliance which chain them together in nature, is a desideratum that can in no way be supplied by a hurried flash, or popular story. An enumeration of a few obvious achievements of the regular profession comes spontaneously and irrepressibly, and must here be made without any effort at organic plasticity, or logical cohesion.

The profession has built a science of Anatomy, or a perfect demonstration of the most intimate molecular structure of the body as a machine, subsequently introducing the mind to a sublime reading and analysis of the great series of organic forms; "for the human form is the grammar of every school which gives real instructions to mankind." It has also, by a carefully-conducted succession of experiments and observations on the vital actions of the same machine under the influence of powers within itself, a series of forces that seems to use the body, with its congeries of organs, as instruments of its use and will, cognized the laws of life of the organs and tissues, or created *a science of physiology*. With patience and assiduity in the dead-house, it has explored the results of disease in its action on the body, has critically appreciated the after-death appearances, connecting them with the antecedent living language of suffering, or the voice of organs in the process of change and destruction, together *with the alteration incompatible* with life, and constructed the science of pathology, with its sister science semiology, or the philosophy of the natural language of disease. By carefully-conducted experiments upon the whole category of created things, all substances possessing properties which influence the organization, it has discovered a class of agents, called medicines, with which its power is absolute over many conditions of the body in disease, or it has produced the science of materia medica. By a never-intermitting series of observations upon the effects of different substances upon the body in all states and conditions, and by the discovery of the uniform chemical elements that give medical qualities to these agents, there has been constructed a demonstrable science of therapeutics, or an account of the modus operandi of medical substances upon the body. By nicely-conducted experiments, under the influence of every-day agents about us, the *power of climate*, or special localities, chemistry of diet and digestion, with the influence of habits of life, it has elaborated a system of perfect details, constituting the laws for the preservation of health, or the science of hygiene; in short, from the mere mechanical achievement of a surgical operation, or scientific cutting of the living body, directed by an absolute knowledge of every fibre of its organization, or from the gross outward phenomenon of the transit of epsom salts or castor-oil through the intestine, to the more hidden and recondite doctrines of the antiplastic and deobstruent virtues of calomel, or the alterative and metamorphic properties of iodine, the regular profession has catalogued every fact of importance, has achieved every result of vital significance to man, with regard to the laws of his body, in health and disease, and does really *know* what *it assumes* to *know*, and has a *sensible account to render of itself before any tribunal*. With solemnity and grandeur, with dignity and earnestness, with serene wisdom and a perfect intellectual superiority, stand the rational principles of the old school of medicine, in savage rebuke, in bitter contrast with the foolish systems which assail them, and with noise and clamor fill the ears of a gullible world, insulting the *science* of the *moment* with the pretensions of a host of infamous and preposterous empiricisms.

In the light of a benignant and blessed hope, the regular profession stands the *only rock of safety* for humanity, full of promises of health and well-being; the dragon-serpent under the hand of Æsculapius being the veritable serpent of brass, "the symbol of *prudence* and *renovation*," upon which the disease-stricken tribes of the earth have but to look in order to be saved. Sublime in its exalted heights, pure and benevolent, but stern and solemn in the possession of an irreproachable purity and strength, it looks with complacency and pity upon the sweltering sea of foamy charlatanries and empty bubbles that float around it, feeble and impotent. The shining path of its progress, from the first dawnings of the intellect of man to its present exalted position as an inductive science, has been rendered illustrious by the labors of a *lofty brotherhood* of the genius of the race, an order of men in whom great powers of thought were revealed, and the enthusiasm and sympathy of man for man consecrated and embalmed for all time. The literature of the profession stands the indestructible monument of the best endeavors of the most gifted souls of the world, made aromatic and immortal by a spirit of love and angelic self-sacrificing devotedness; for, through ages, with a quiet, heavenly self-reliance in its labors after the good and the true, it has kept its eye on the possibly perfect and absolute while beset by legions of intrusive follies at each moment of its radiant progress.

Slow induction, through irresistible growth and progressive perfection, has been the law of development, with occasional disposition to postponement and arrestation or fossilization, as in every department of knowledge it would seem, by the ultimation of some fatal law of the mind. Still its march has been *onward* by slow *but sure advances*. Essentially eclectic, although respecting and holding to the conservatism of the past with wisdom and sobriety, unseduced by the flashy radicalisms of the moment it has maturely estimated each suggestion of the new, and read with reflection and respect each critique of the present, at all its stages of growth, and adopted whatever of truth or fresh revelation each original phasis of the advancing waves of light brought to the intellect of man. Ceaselessly experimenting, dissecting bodies of animals, bodies of men, reading, interpreting the language of the organism in health and disease, ransacking nature's warehouse, and torturing all the elements, every created form of matter, for its secret power over the body, to save from suffering, to save from death, the *genius of the art* has always been characterized as one of endless seeking and endeavor after the absolute of truth.

What is the body of man, and what are its laws in health and disease, and what agents and powers control these conditions of the same, has the spirit of man demanded from immemorial time, with a zeal kindled upon the altar of science to burn with freshly-renewed splendor until the divine end shall be achieved and disease appear on earth no more.

Where, then, shall suffering humanity turn for hope in this gloomy world of disease? Where shall the tortured body, held in the fatal folds and dark environment of the destroying powers, look for relief from agony and despair, and the wretched instincts, startled at the appearance of destruction, seek the soothing of promised safety?—where, but to the brotherhood who have struggled for thousands of years in ceaseless efforts to save? Earth has no stone, plant, or animal, the air no saving qualities, the waters of the earth no healing virtues, chemistry has no combination of elements, and the mechanical forces of the world no powers which have not been exhausted by the profession in her vigilant search to alleviate the condition of humanity, and save the suffering from pain and dissolution. "Under all these means, coworking for good, shall not the body be redeemed, and evil begin to lose the footing that sickness gives it? By heaven's law the sick have claims which the healthy have not, and there is more joy over one man cured than over ninety and nine who are sound. This is a *test of every society,* how it *speeds,* or how it *lags, in administering to the sick.* They are the weakest parts of our common body, and care and thought turn to them with longings that are the flesh of the physician's heart. And the more that are healed the more concentrated is the love upon those who suffer still; so that at length the world's whole skill and tenderness shall surround, with arts and healing tears, the bed of the *last sick man.*" "Then give place to the physician, for the Lord hath created him: let him not go from thee, for thou hast need of him."

(NOTE TO PAGE 489.)

For real demonstrable motion of considerable extents of rock, see works on geology, as the rising and subsiding of coasts, the appearance and disappearance of volcanic islands, oscillations of earthquakes, etc.; also, for clearly ascertained vibrations in natural and artificial masses of rock, see "Annual of Scientific Facts" for 1859, on Conducting Power of Rocks, Altitude of Mountains not Invariable, by Charles Maclaren, page 310. It appears from actual observation, that the "entire mass of rock and hill on which the Armagh Observatory is erected, is slightly, but to an astronomer quite perceptibly, tilted or canted at one season to the east, at another to the west. This was at first attributed to the sun's radiation, to the hydrostatic energy of water, and afterwards to conducting power of rocks from heated nucleus below. The hill upon which the Armagh Observatory is situated is at the junction of the mountain limestone and clay-slate, one leg on the former, the other leg on the latter. Absorbent rocks are best conductors, and consequently in wet seasons will expand most, and tilt the hill to one side, in dry seasons subside most, and tilt the hill in the opposite direction." So mountains and hills swing, like the pendulum, in the waves of heat from above, of heat from below. Bunker Hill Monument, supposed to be a fixed fact, is as uncertain as any other Yankee notion, and vibrates in the brush of the sun, as the pine-tree rocks in the waves of the wind.

ÆSCULAPIUS. 535

(SEE ANTE, PAGE 506, AT *)

In the Hydropathic Encyclopedia of R. T. Trall, we are presented with the following lucid statement of the modus operandi of water:—

"Contrary to the teachings of the standard medical books of Allopathy, Homeopathy, and the Eclectic Schools, *we must ever bear in mind that disease is never a positive entity*, [tumors ten pounds avoirdupois, colic, cholera, enlarged spleen, lock-jaw, *nonentities!*] but always a *negative result;* it is the *absence* of health, [a stick of timber present is never a positive thing, but always a negative result, it is the *absence* of NO STICK of TIMBER!] or of the state, circumstances, and actions which constitute the balance of *functional duty we call health.* [Causes of these nonentities!] Abuse of hygienic agencies produce abnormal causes of disease, bad air, improper light, impure food and drink, excessive or defective alimentation, indolence or over-exertion, unregulated passion—in three words, *unphysiological voluntary habits.* General indications—remove obstructions, *wash away* impurities, supply healthy nutriment, regulate temperature, *relax intensive and intensify torpid action; and what but water, with its concomitants air, light, food, temperature, can answer these indications?*"

How clear and bright, luminous and heavenly, in the mind of Priessnitz, must have shone the vision of the power of the infallible panacea, *water!*

> "Water, water everywhere,
> And all their throats did shrink;
> Water, water everywhere,
> And forty barrels to drink."

HYGEIA.

HYGIEIA ('Υγίεια,) also called Hygea or Hygia, the goddess of health, and a daughter of Asclepius, (Æsculapius.) (Paus. i. 23, § 5; xxxi., § 5.) In one of the Orphic hymns (66–7) she is called the wife of Asclepius; and Proclus (ad. Plat. Tim.) makes her a daughter of Eros and Peitho. She was usually worshiped in the same temples with her father, as at Argos, where the two divinities had a celebrated sanctuary (Paus. ii. 23, § 4; iii. 22, § 9) at Athens, (i. 23, § 5; 31, § 5;) at Corinth, (ii. 4, § 6;) at Gortys, (viii. 28, § 1;) at Sicyon, (ii. 11, § 6;) at Oropus, (i. 34, § 2.) At Rome there was a statue of her in the temple of Concordia, (Plin. H. N., xxxiv. 19.) In works of art, of which a considerable number has come down to our time, she was represented as a virgin dressed in a long robe, with the expression of mildness and kindness, and either alone or grouped with her father and sisters, and either sitting or standing, and leaning on her father. Her ordinary attribute is a serpent, which she is feeding from a cup. Although she is originally the goddess of physical health, she is sometimes conceived as the giver or protectress of *mental health*, that is, she appears as Mens sana, or υγίεια φρενῶν, (Æschyl. Eum. 522,) and was thus identified with Athena, surnamed Hygieia, (Paus. i. 23, § 5; comp. Lucian, pro Laps., 5; Hirt. Mythol. Bilderb., i. p. 84.)—*Greek and Roman Biography and Mythology.*

L. S.

"Man is a link in nature, but his intellectual faculties enable him to rise above her, to battle with and acquire influence over her.

"But that nature affects mankind as a part of herself in manifold ways in material respects, rests on experience so abundant and clear, and opinions so unanimous, whether we refer to single men or to entire races, that we need only give a brief indication of it.

"The varied character of nature in the different regions of the earth in a great measure determine the food, the dress, the dwellings, the means of intercourse, and the *diseases* of the races."

Schouw,
Earth, Plants, and Man.

CHAPTER II.

HYGEIA.

Of the father of Hygeia, Æsculapius, many accounts and interpretations have been given by classical writers, as we have seen. Leonard Schmitz announces his critique of the fable thus :—

"His story is undoubtedly a *combination of real events* with the results of thoughts or ideas, which, as in so many instances in Greek mythology, are, like the former, considered as facts. The *kernel*, out of which the whole myth has grown, is perhaps the account we read in Homer; but gradually the sphere in which Æsculapius acted was so extended, that *he became the representative* or the personification *of the healing powers of nature*, which are naturally enough described as the *son* (the effects) of Helios, Apollo, or the Sun." Epione, the wife of the god of medicine, had a number of children who were highly gifted and distinguished, "most of whom are only personifications of the powers ascribed to their father," and among whom was the radiant daughter, "goddess of health."

Here, then, appears Hygeia, a "virgin, dressed in a long robe, with the expression of *mildness* and *kindness*," "the goddess of *physical health*, also the giver or protectress of *mental health*," the "*mens sana*," (in corpore sano,) giving her name ('ὐγίεια health,) to the "department of medical science which treats of the *preservation of health*." Being the "mens sana," or sound mind, on this subject, she must, of course, preside over the following fields of labor, or differently-named fields of the same labor: "The Art of Prolonging Life,"* "The Philosophy of Living,"† "The Laws of Health,"‡ "Life and Health,"§ "Human Health, or Elements of Hygiene,"‖ "Elements of Health,"¶ "Physiology Applied to Health and Education,"** "Physical Education," and the whole domain of "Human Physiology," etc.

Grand in thy niche, great, kind, and brooding Prophylactic, "What shall I do to thee, O thou preserver of men?"†† Surely not make thee *superior* to thy *father?* See the grace and fitness of the classical myth; the *mild maid*, with flowing robes, *leans upon* her father. Being only a "personification" of *one of the "powers"* ascribed to him, is it justice in poetry or science to exalt *her* at the sacrifice of the dignity and supremacy of her sire, the venerable god?

Hear the sage Mayo, from Boppard on the Rhine, (1851,) more than fifty-five years after Hufeland, of Jena, had published "The Art of Prolonging Life:" "In the Greek medal which furnishes the device for the title-page, [of his book 'Philosophy of Living,'] Hygeia is represented with emblems of greater efficiency than the healing god. Her snake is three times as big as that of Æsculapius, and could evidently eat half-a-dozen such at a meal. Besides, she handles it with familiar dexterity, while the god's is carelessly twined round his life-preserver. Even so, in the advance of knowledge, *hygiene*‡‡ is found to be an *art more important than medicine—prevention* is recognized to be something *better* than *cure*. The tons of medicine which were annually swallowed by the British public are already sensibly reduced. *Physicians* and *apothecaries* begin to look anxiously around for protection; and society, at this pace, is not unlikely soon to adopt the sage custom of the court of China, which consists in paying its medical adviser

---

* Hufeland, a philosophic physician and professor of medicine in the Universty of Jena. † Mayo. ‡ Beale.
§ Alcott. ‖ Dunglison, Smith, Johnston, and others.
¶ Tilt. ** Combe. †† Job, vii.
‡‡ The italics are our own except a few.

as long as the sovereign is well, and withholding his salary during the term of the royal illness. Accordingly, although it seems hard to expect those who *live* by *curing* disease to co-operate in preventing it, the *enlightened few* see which way the wind sets, and are already lending their efforts to promote hygienic knowledge.

"*But I am no renegade to my profession. No one knows better*, [modest!] or would argue more stoutly, *than myself*, that the *common basis* of *hygienic* and of *medical knowledge is an enlightened study of disease*, [one would think so, extremely sharp!] and that *physicians and surgeons* have *honestly* [clever!] *done their best for the real* interests of *both*, in their *long* and *elaborate researches, which have resulted in modern physiology and pathology.* For the *first step* to be realized was, the determination of *what it is that* is to *be cured, or prevented*, of what *are the causes*, what the *intimate nature*, and what the *spontaneous course* and *progress of disease*. Thus much, I repeat, this *necessary initial* achievement has been worthily accomplished by the labors of *physicians* and *surgeons. The science*, so to speak, has been done ample justice to; *not so the art*, at *least* the *medical part of the art of healing*. Not that efforts on the part of *physicians* in this direction have been *wholly wanting* or erroneous. [They have been in active existence and successful progress for more than two thousand years: witness Hygeia and her '*big snake*,' which he so much admires.] Not to speak of the noble *half-hygienic* [only half?] invention of Jenner for the *extirpation* of small-pox, the *realization* of the *efficiency* of bleeding, of *calomel*, of tartar emetic in various forms of *inflammation*, of opium, colchicum, iodine, in other *specialities*, [specialties?] are *valuable points* in the *art. But still* the *art* is a *world behind* the *science.*" (Compare with Hufeland, fifty-five years before, on the origin of ideas!) Next to this follows an ignominious insult to "nineteen cases [gentlemen] out of twenty" of the profession to which he, of course, is "*no renegade.*"

By consulting the preface to Prof. Mayo's work, we find the following statements: "The Philosophy of Living, of which I am now preparing a *third edition*, was written at the suggestion of an eminent publisher, [a book to order,] *who desired to have a book to the title. I gladly acceded* to a *proposal* which *offered* me an *opportunity* of *using up some odds and ends* of *physiological reflection*, and *involved the necessity* of *referring* to their sources for various curious and valuable facts *hitherto only vaguely known to me*. The book is, accordingly, a *superficial compilation of facts and principles*, which *any one, without previous physiological reading*, may understand." He further says of his book: "It is to be viewed, therefore, rather as *ancillary* to the *advice* of the *fashionable physician*, than as *conveying lessons of sanatory regulation and provision* for the *poorer classes*." Thus "The Philosophy of Living" appears, a book to order, made up of "odds and ends of physiological reflection;" acknowledged by its author to be a "*superficial compilation of facts and principles*," "*ancillary* [subservient] to *fashionable physicians*," without much "*provision* for the *poorer classes*."

The author of "The Philosophy of Living" is Herbert Mayo, M.D., "formerly Senior Surgeon to the Middlesex Hospital, and one of the Professors of Anatomy and Surgery of the Royal College of Surgeons," etc. etc. His broad generalization is that "Hygiene is found to be an *art more important than medicine*." What does he mean by the "*art of medicine?*" The physician prescribing, (supposed to be in close communication with the *science* of *man*,) the *druggists compounding* doses, (posology,) or *nurse administering* remedies? Webster's definition of *Hygiene* is "*that department of medicine* which treats of the *preservation of health*." That it is a *very* "*important* department of medicine" there can be no doubt; but why such division into two arts that are only *departments* of *one*, with an address to the popular mind which is an injustice to the profession from which he says he is, of course, "*no renegade?*"

One glance at the table of contents of the book *will show its connection* with medical science.

DIVERSITIES OF CONSTITUTION.—1. Temperament; 2. Habit; 3. Diathesis.

CHAP. I. OF DIET.—1. Digestion; 2. Food, (whole story of alimentation;) 3. Quantity of Food; 4. Intervals between Meals; 5. Conditions which strengthen or weaken the Digestive Powers; 6. Of Food at Different Ages; 7. Social Relations of Food.

CHAP. II. OF EXERCISE, (as Exercise of Muscles.)—Exercise of Boys; Physical Education of Girls; Exercise proper for Adults; Exercise of the Aged.

CHAP. III. OF SLEEP.—(Whole story as far as recorded.)

CHAP. IV. OF BATHING.—(Whole story, including Preservation of Teeth.)

CHAP. V. OF CLOTHING.

CHAP. VI. OF AIR OR CLIMATE.—1. General Properties of the Atmosphere; 2. Noxious Agencies of Air and Climate generally considered; 3. Malaria, (whole story;) 4. Climate suited to the *Strumous* Diathesis.

CHAP. VII. HEALTH OF MIND.—(Habits of Mind favoring Health of Body;) 1. Of Self-control; 2. Of Intellectual Culture and Occupation.

"This necessary *initial achievement* has *been worthily accomplished* by the *labors of physicians and surgeons.*" So much for an "*art more important than medicine;*" so much for the confounding of words and the effort at mere *abstractions* in science.

Hear, also, the great Hufeland, at Jena, 1796, fifty-five years before Mayo: "The life of man, physically considered, is a peculiar chemico-animal operation; a *phenomenon effected by a concurrence* of the *united powers* of *nature* with matter in a continual state of change. This, like every other physical operation, must have its defined laws, boundaries, and duration, so far as they depend on the sum of the given powers and matter, their application, and many other external as well as internal circumstances; but, like every other physical operation, it can be promoted or impeded, accelerated or retarded. By laying down just principles respecting its essence and wants, and by attending to observations made from experience, the circumstances under which this process may be hastened and shortened, or retarded and prolonged, can be discovered. Upon this may be founded *dietetic* rules and a *medical* mode of *treatment for preserving life;* and hence arises a particular science, the MACROBIOTIC, or the art of prolonging it, which forms the subject of the present work.

"This art, however, must not be confounded with the *common art of medicine* or *medical regimen;* its objects, *means, and boundaries are different.* The object of the *medical art is health;* that of the macrobiotic, *long life.* [Long life and health are supposed to be somewhat connected; but it seems here that 'dietetic rules' and a 'medical mode of treatment for preserving life,' 'health,' and the 'macrobiotic art,' are 'different,' although the latter *'arises'* from the former!] The means employed in the medical art are regulated according to the *present state* of the body and its variations; [case, head and stomach sick from rum and tobacco; one 'means of medical art,' *take no more!*] those of the *macrobiotic* by *general principles.* [Case, head and stomach *not sick* from rum or tobacco; on the prolongation of life question, what has the macrobiotic art to say?—take rum and tobacco, or take *no more?* But it seems the *'object, means,' of the two arts are 'different'!*] In the first it is sufficient if one is able to restore that health which has been lost; [but it is no art of *'prolonging life'!*] but no person thinks of inquiring whether, by the means used for *that purpose,* life, upon the *whole,* will be *lengthened* or *shortened;* [every *physician* does;] and the latter is often the case in many methods employed in medicine. [A play upon crotchets.] The medical art must consider every disease as an evil which cannot be, too soon, expelled; [as by a blister, sound!] the macrobiotic, on the other hand, shows that many diseases [a blistered surface is not normal but *diseased*] may be the means of prolonging life. [Sound! But are the 'medical' and 'macrobiotic' arts so entirely 'different'?] The 'medical art,' by *corroborative* and *other remedies*, [by every conceivable influence, force, or power of the world which makes it, the medical art, a perfect and limitless formula,] to *elevate mankind* to the *highest* degree of *strength* and physical *perfection;* while the 'macrobiotic' proves that here, even, there is a maximum, [in mathematics, greatest quantity attainable,] and that strengthening, [elevating *mankind* to *highest perfection*] *carried* too *far*, [? ? !!] may tend to accelerate, and consequently, to shorten its duration. The *practical part* of medicine, therefore, ['all science has but one aim, to find a theory of nature, and to a *sound judgment* the most *abstract truth* is the *most practical;'* the *only* evidence, therefore, of the profundity and validity of a theory being its *applicability to nature*, it is clear that 'the only part of medicine' which men hold to be of *any consequence*, is the '*practical*,' or *true* and *only science of medicine*,] in regard to the macrobiotic art, is to be considered only as an *auxiliary science* which teaches us *how* to *know diseases*, [of course, their opposite, health, and thus, *physiology and pathology*, the only *two conditions* it is possible to conceive of the body existing in at all,] the *enemies* of life, and how to prevent and expel them, but which, however, must *itself* be SUBSERVIENT to the *higher laws* of the *latter*."

It would be natural to inquire what is meant by the "practical part of medicine?" Is it the mere art of drugging (posology) by *routine*, or the application of the dead letter of the Pharmacopœia to the dead letter of the nosological table, or the art, which, with all the light of the moment, cognizes and treats with scientific precision, prophylactically and therapeutically, all normal and abnormal conditions of the human body?

Whence did the art of macrobiology obtain a knowledge of the "*higher laws*" to which the "*art of medicine*" *must be* "*subservient?*" Whence its knowledge of man? There is but one key to all knowledge of man: the anatomy and physiology of the human body, the *foundation* of the "*art of medicine.*" Whence its knowledge of the "life of man as a "*chemico-animal phenomenon?*" There is but one source of the knowledge of the laws of "life," namely, the science of "physiology," which is the foundation of all vital operations of the body, normal or abnormal, or in health and disease. These are the elements of the "art of medicine," the noblest of all arts, "auxiliary" to no other science, and "subservient" to no other art—*itself the true macrobiotic art* of all arts, called, from of old, the "*healing art,*" or the true "art of prolonging life."

The sage of Jena, in his chapter on "Preventing Diseases, Judicious Treatment of them, and Proper use of Medicine and Physicians," says: "The *business of medicine* is to *guard against these* [diseases] *as well* as to *cure them; and so far* medicine *may be considered* and *employed* as a *means for prolonging life.*" Again, he asks "How does the practice of physic contribute to the prolongation of life? Can one consider it absolutely as a means for prolonging our existence? *Without doubt we can,* so far as it cures disorders that might *destroy us, but not always* in *other respects.*" He then attempts to *show* that to *restore health* and *prolong life are not the same.* He proceeds to answer questions which concern those who are not physicians. "By what means can disease be prevented? How ought those, which have already appeared, to be treated? and, in particular, how ought physicians and the medical art to be employed in order to contribute in the highest degree possible to the support and prolongation of life?" Following which is a dissertation upon this subject and an answer also to the question — "In what manner should a disease, which has already taken place, be treated, and what *use ought* to be *made* of *physicians* and of the *medical art?*" This is arranged under fourteen "rules," embracing his conceptions of the connection of the medical with the macrobiotic art.

An inspection of the table of contents of Hufeland's book will give some apprehension of the domain over which reigns the goddess of health; also, Æsculapius, god of medicine;

in other words, the inseparability of the parts of one great art, the indivisibility of one great science into major or minor, *subservient* or *ancillary* departments, and the impossibility of one existing without the other.

Part First. Chap. I.—State of the science of prolonging life among the ancients; state in middle ages, and on down to Mesmer.

Chap. II.—Of the vital powers; whole problem of life, its essential nature, laws, etc.

Chap. III.—Duration of life of plants; the laws thereof, etc. etc.

Chap. IV.—Duration in animal world; general view, etc.

Chap. V.—Duration of life of man; general recitation of the facts thereof, etc.

Chap. VI.—Results of above observations; influence of the world on its life; states and conditions of inhabitants on the same; relative duration of; tables of, etc.

Chap. VII.—Special examination of human life; definition of operation of; condition of laws, without, within; history of.

Chap. VIII.—Signs of long life in individuals; dissertation on the organs, their laws, and portrait of a long liver.

Chap. IX.—Examination of methods of prolonging life; recitation from elixirs down to proper means and modifications of the same, etc.

Part Second.—Practical art of prolonging life. 1. Means which shorten life.

Chap. I.—Delicate nursing and treatment in infancy.

Chap. II—Physical excess in youth.

Chap. III.—Overstrained exertion of the mental faculties.

Chap. IV.—*Diseases;* injudicious manner of treating them; sudden kinds of death; propensity to self-murder.

Chap. V.—Impure air; men living together in large cities.

Chap. VI.—Intemperance in eating and drinking; refined cookery; spirituous liquors.

Chap. VII.—Passions and dispositions of mind which shorten life; peevishness; too much occupation and business.

Chap. VIII.—The fear of death.

Chap. IX.—Idleness; inactivity; languor.

Chap. X.—Overstrained power of the imagination; imaginary diseases; sensibility.

Chap. XI.—Poisons, physical as well as infectious.

Chap. XII.—Old age; premature engrafting of it on youth.

PART THIRD. MEANS WHICH PROLONG LIFE.

CHAP. I.—Good physical descent.

CHAP. II.—Prudent physical education.

CHAP. III.—Active and laborious youth.

CHAP. IV.—Abstinence from physical love in youth, and too early assumption of the married state.

CHAP. V.—Happy married state.

CHAP. VI.—Sleep.

CHAP. VII.—Bodily exercise.

CHAP. VIII.—The enjoyment of free air; moderate temperature of warmth.

CHAP. IX.—Rural and country life.

CHAP. X.—Traveling.

CHAP. XI.—Cleanliness and care of the skin.

CHAP. XII.—Proper food; moderation in eating and drinking; preservation of the teeth.

CHAP. XIII.—Mental tranquillity; contentment; dispositions of mind and employments, which tend to prolong life.

CHAP. XIV.—*Reality of character.*

CHAP. XV.—Agreeable stimulants of the senses and of sensation moderately used.

CHAP. XVI.—Preventing diseases; judicious treatment of them; proper use of medicine and physicians.

CHAP. XVII.—Relief in cases where one is exposed to the danger of sudden death.

CHAP. XVIII.—Old age; proper treatment of it.

CHAP. XIX.—Cultivation of the mental and bodily powers.

From this table of contents it would appear that the "Art of Prolonging Life" involves every relationship of man to the world, and thus a recapitulation of the resources and implements of that art would be a schedule or periscope of the whole domain of both outward and inward existences.

Chapters of this department of medical science have been bravely labored out by different writers and observers, and *partially finished;* and it appears upon the records of that literature that mere catalogues of the implements of prevention, belonging to the domain of Hygiene, fill volumes. Illustrious names are recorded in this department, and the race would do well, in its mad rushing, to pause, and hear the lessons of wisdom from a Hufeland, Comb, Johnston, Smith, Dunglison, Tilt, Beale, or a Mayo, and the whole school of human physiologists.

The extent of the literature or bibliography of the medical profession in this department is surprising. Some of the works are of a popular character, addressing the comprehension of all; others are of a more technical and scientific structure, belonging to the order of strictly professional books. However popularized or familiarized, the knowledge belongs to the department of medical science which takes cognizance of the instrumentality of prevention (prophylactics) as well as implements of cure (therapeutics) of disease. The *strictly professional books* are significant and wise, but are not accessible to all, and it has now become the imperative duty of every physician to be a preacher (he is a high-priest in the temple of Apollo) of the gospel of life and the laws of health, if he has any exalted apprehension of the aims and ends of his calling, or realizes the high and noble functions of his sphere as the destroyer of pain and suffering, and the creator of health and happiness.* Sacred is his calling, sublime are the duties of his mission, but vast is the extent of his field of labor, and fearful are the responsibilities of his vocation.

"Man is in little all the sphere." The wonderful extent and variety of his relations come from the universality of his connection with the world, and his total circularity, rather *sphericity*, of organization. Having "more points of contact with the whole of nature by which he is surrounded," than any other creature in existence, it has been arranged that the microcosm (little world) has all the macrocosm (great world) to consult for his health, as nothing exists that is not in connection with him, physiologically, pathologically. This embraces his highest bonds of affiliation, as well as the

---

* "A Greek philosopher and physician had so just an appreciation of the nobility of his mission, that he called the physician 'the hand of God.' Are we Christians to have a less exalted notion of our duties than the pagan Hierophilus?"—EDWARD JOHN TILT.

lowest details of his merely animal nature, even to the most forlorn exigencies of his brutehood.

Hence, it must strike the serious observer, how simple and familiar to the open eye are the greater number of the sources of power of the art of hygiene. Here are no far-off attainments in arts and sciences, no recondite abstractions, or special medical formulæ, but commonplace and vulgar things, every-day-by-the-roadside influences on the bodies we have; what we eat, and especially how fixed up; the water we drink, as necessary, medicinal; the air we breathe; how, when, and where we sleep; what we wear, and how we wear it; what we *do*, and how we do it; to all of which may be added the influences from the side of the soul. And first, a word on the

BODIES WE HAVE.

Before the problem of hereditary disease, and hereditary *proclivity* to *certain* diseases, the mind stands aghast, especially on the abysmal question of justice and compensation between the Finite and Infinite.* "Sour grapes" have been consumed, and tubercle and cancer, the "children's teeth set on edge," are the crop in this harvest of woe. The bitter results of ignorant and lawless generation realized, what can be done by science and art in this inalienable entailment of despair?

The mild goddess offers immense consolation and solace in the habits of a well-regulated life, and in the vast resources of temperance and virtue; but especially is the result to be achieved by the prevention of the issues of profane genesis in congenital taints, malformations, and infirmities. Shall the end surely come soon, in the ineffable beneficence of the promise,—"As I live, saith the Lord, ye shall not have *occasion* any more to use this proverb in Israel." The body, with transmitted adaptation or hereditary tendency to disease, is under the special protection, and belongs to the de-

* Concerning the origin of evil, optimism of Nature, and "God in Disease," see Benedict Spinoza, William Godwin, and James F. Duncan.

partment of medicine which prevents disease; but all bodies of all men are under the same power, whose resources are endless.

WHAT WE EAT.

"Make the sin of intemperance, popularly so called, great as you please,—as great even as God makes it,—and it falls short, *very far short*, of the sin of *intemperance*, as connected with the use of food."* Gastronomy has come to be a science,† an *art* rather, higher than a science, and there have been inspired cooks, men of genius who were cooks.‡ The gastronomic "fine art" has become a part of the religion of the "dominant race," and will soon demand separate temples of worship. Great is the "belly," much greater than the "members."

The stomach of man is the base of the pyramid man, the living foundation of his high and glorified form. Heavy and cumbrous, but broad and firm, it rests upon the bosom of the earth, and in the repose of Gizeh, Sachara, or Cholula, it says, I am planted forever. It is the bond of universal alliance with all nature and created things, from the lowest to the highest. The animal and vegetable kingdoms are its

---

* A——t.

† Elaborate works have been written on gastronomy. A General History of Cooking was published at Leipsic in 1835, "in ten portly volumes," 8vo., and other works on that beautiful and attractive science had appeared before, and have since, so that they now constitute a library of gastronomy.

‡ Vatel, the maître d'hotel of Condé, was a man of genius. He committed suicide because he had made a blunder in the preparation of a breakfast. "Who was ever more worthy of the respect and gratitude of true gourmands, than the man of genius who would not survive the dishonor of the table of the great Condé? who immolated himself with his own hands, because the sea-fish had not arrived some hours before it was served? So noble a death insures you, venerable shade, the most glorious immortality! You have proved that the fanaticism of honor can exist in the kitchen as well as the camp, and that the spit and the saucepan have also their Catos and their Deciuses."—*Almanach des Gourmands.*

reservoirs of life, and its consanguinity is absolute with all the creatures of the earth, sea, and air.

"For there is nothing more general in animal life than the digestive apparatus, because matter is the largest, if not the *greatest fact* in the universe. Every creature which is here must be made of something, and maintained by something, or must be landlord of itself. Every part and every faculty of every being inhabiting the planet must be duly clothed, and ballasted, with stuff derived from the earth, or it would have no operation in the body, or upon the body, much less upon the external world.

"Hence, the *stomach* is an organ of the first importance to *all mortals*. You may take away brain or nervous system and leave their places to be supplied by the fluxions and imponderables of Nature; you may take away the lungs and consign their office to the circumambient, lifeless atmosphere; you may abstract the heart with its blood-vessels, and commit the dull, gluey circulation to the almost mechanical and chemical laws of affinity that obtain in vegetables, and, notwithstanding all this, you may still have an *animal being* remaining. In short, there are animals which are nothing but stomachs, but there are *no animals* which are *nothing but brains.* In the human race, also, the stomach is of the same paramount importance; its existence and due impletion are the first or last conditions of the existence of the individual; they are the basis of humanity, and nothing is so sublime but it rests upon them, and must perish out of this world if they cease, and otherwise follow their vicissitudes. The assured *feeding* of the nations is a question that involves in its settlement *all other questions*, and postpones sublimities until *necessities* are complied with. Jeweled goblets there are besides, but this earthen cup must be satisfied before the other vessels of the man can begin to be filled."

This intimate alliance or physical affinity with all earthly beings must necessitate or preordain a general dominion; also, a subjugation to universal law, for every form of every animal is but a man in disguise. Hence the grandeur of this "earthen cup," the stomach and its laws, and from the universality of its affinities, comes the multitudinous world of horrors in the shape of diseases, to which the infraction of those laws introduce the unhappy creature, man. Is this humble earthen-cup the veritable vessel of Pandora? "When Prometheus had stolen the fire from heaven, Zeus in revenge caused Hephaestus to make a woman out of earth, who by her charms and beauty should bring misery upon the human race. Aphrodite adorned her with beauty, Hermes gave her boldness and cunning, and the gods called her Pandora, as each of the Olympians had given her some power by which she was to work the ruin of man. Hermes took her to Epimetheus, who forgot the advice of his brother Prometheus, not to accept any gift from Zeus, and from that moment the fatal vessel of gifts of the gods was opened, and all miseries came down upon men, the blessings having escaped irrecoverably." Mournful consummation! And have the gifts of the Olympians *all* escaped on the wings of the wind, through disease and infirmity, only the fatal power remaining "to work the ruin of man?" Is this cave of the vital forces wholly surrendered to the destroyers? Once the magical grotto from which the golden currents of life rushed to the remotest atoms of the body, is it now a baleful lake of Avernus, over whose dismal waters the birds dare not fly, and in whose poisonous bosom the fabulous Proteus alone can swim?

Catalogues of diseases of the stomach, their causes and treatment, make volumes. Alas! for the *base* of the *Pyramid Man!* Alas! for the magazine of his powers, the fountain of the rivers of his body! Tantalus is no fable: it means the impossibility of eating anything that will not nauseate and rebel; for your stomach is diseased, "broken the goblet and wasted the wine."* This great substratum of

* "The mind is its own place, and in itself can make a heaven of hell, a hell of heaven." Not so while in the body, which also "is its own place." Thus the man diseased, makes his clay a colored

man from whose vital surface all the radicles of the miraculous tree of life suck nourishment, is poisoned and foul. The Cadmus sin has sown it with dragon teeth, and the harvest is death.*

THE WATERS WE DRINK.†

That the habitual use of water surcharged with earthy salts is productive of disease, there is not the least doubt. *Pure water* is the great *hygienic water*. It is a generally received impression that the influence of climate, and other agents, in the prevention (as *well as cure*) of many diseases, is effectually promoted by the use of what are called "mineral waters." Many places, like the fabulous wells and enchanted springs of Eastern romance, have, by common consent, been made shrines and places of holy pilgrimage to the world of invalids. Like the belief in charms and witches, this faith has, as have many others, come to be accepted *without challenge* by multitudes of unreflecting minds. How just and rational, how near to science and demonstration, this impression is, unassisted *common sense alone* can answer. The unintelligent, indiscriminate flocking to watering-places, or "going to the springs" as it is called, is essentially absurd.

The diseases in which mineral waters have been supposed to possess their most energetic action, preventive and curative, are those of the digestive, or great assimilative function.

In joint, nervous, skin, and uterine diseases, the efficacy of a change of water, or the supposed specific benefit of a particular water on those diseases, is wholly referable to the

---

medium, or glass, through which he looks upon the world. Suppose an inflamed stomach, or an ulcerated intestinal tube, the optical instrument through which he contemplates the earth and its glories, the heavens and their majesties. Would nature or the stars bloom with celestial beauty to one in the horrors of gastritis or pains of the bowels? Is not the "mens sana in corpore sano" the end of all science?

* See note, page 564. † See note, page 564.

impression made upon the digestive machinery, and the re-energizing power of the *large new functional impression*, made by *all surrounding influences, water included.*

That a perfectly adapted regimen and suitable climate, assisted by the *novel impression* of a change of water, will modify the action of morbidly inclined, or even morbidly impressed and seized mucous membranes, skin, and viscera of splanchnic cavities, and induce a *new action* in chronic cases of vicious habitudes of organs, is not questionable. But the application of *one mineral water* to diverse and various derangements of complexly-mixed, and often different states, or diseased conditions, or impending diseases, as specially *preventive* or *curative* of them *all*, is *simply*, in the present state of science, preposterous. That certain *new impressions* made by whatever causes upon the organism about to be diseased, or that is diseased, in various ways further the efforts of the great guardian sanitary forces of complaining parts, and facilitate their return to a state of normality, there can be no doubt.

But that in the indefinitely-complicated derangements of a number of differently-diseased persons, with *diversity of temperaments, ages, habits of life*, and *idiosyncrasies*, all, or any number of them, shall be specifically relieved by *one* and the *same water*, of one and the same spring, savors of the *scientific absurdity* of the quack's specific cure-all nostrum. "*A well-directed course of mineral waters*" would be a well-directed course of pure water, rationally mineralized, or medicated and adapted to the special conditions of the case, by an intelligent medical man. It is conceded that many forms of stomach disease are positively (caused) injured by what are called mineral waters. In many cases of highly irritable, morbidly *impressible*, and *diseased conditions* of the *stomach, (and lungs,)* mineral waters are *poisonous*. Efforts have been made, with vaunted results, to refer special conditions of particular organs to special waters: Ems, Vichy, and Plombieres, to this or that organ or condition; Marienbad, Carlsbad, Kissingen, Bedford, and Saratoga, to others, etc. The great things, almost altogether overlooked, but which should be most emphatically dwelt upon, are *change of place, climate, whole environment of the patient*, with *pure water*, and *what medicine an intelligent physician* directs to be mixed therein. Pure water alone gives the proper base or menstruum for different shapes of medical combinations.

Dr. Struve, of Dresden, has demonstrated the fact, that factitious mineral waters, made by chemical imitation, *have all the demonstrable effects of the natural.** The great advantage is, that the factitious waters may be *changed* to suit the *varying circumstances* of cases developed by the progress of diseased conditions, *new complications and phases of advancement.* Of deobstruent, alterative, prevent-all, cure-all waters, more than enough of fables have been told; at the same time, it is true that certain springs do possess over the body clearly-marked adjuvant powers to prevent and cure morbid conditions of the same, but not *specific virtues over entire diseases.* Thus there are springs said to possess specific powers over bronchial diseases. Here the *direct* stroke of the hammer is clearly questionable; but that

---

* From the grave statements of the advocates of the *inexplicable powers* of their particular springs, one might be led to suppose that the chemist was incapable of making exact analyses of their waters, and that they possess some occult virtues that science cannot discover or understand. In this day of light and knowledge, suspicion is naturally attached to all charmed fountains of the world which are represented to possess *inexplicable* qualities and powers which cannot be stated. Any *change* of *water* is generally followed by results of some kind, but the question will constantly arise, are they morbific or sanitary? When we reflect upon the philosophy of springs and the *origin of their mineral contents*, the conviction must come, that the waters of mineral springs must be constantly changing in quality and quantity of contents, and, in different seasons and kinds of seasons, be *very* different. As these waters all fall from the clouds and percolate the soil and rocks, dissolving the mineral elements which give character to the springs, it must follow, that a rainy or dry season will decide the precise proportion of contained matter, and the constantly varying qualities of the waters.

diseased mucous membranes of lungs connected with vicious conditions of other mucous surfaces, may be benefited by change of water through sympathetic action of allied organs, there is no doubt, but not as specific agents. Bronchial diseases, with grave, morbid complications in the abdominal cavity, especially the upper part of the digestive tube, may undoubtedly be benefited by a change in the great menstruum, or mixing material from which the streams of blood are made. Here, again, *pure water* is the desideratum, mingled with what science says is required by particular cases in particular conditions. Of asthma, rheumatism, gout, and nervous derangements, there are stories connected with particular springs and their powers, unassisted by any other great sanitary force, all of which come in an apocryphal shape. Pure water, mineralized for the case by an intelligent and wise physician, is the great agent, of course, all the more efficient when accompanied by the sanitary powers of *change of scenery, locality, climate,* etc.

THE AIR WE BREATHE.

Volumes have been written on the "use and abuse of air," the "powers of fresh air to prevent disease," the necessity of pure air to health, the preventive and curative powers of air, etc., from which it is obvious that *pure air* is the greatest prophylactic power of the world, and, therefore, one of the favorite agents of Hygeia in the preservation of health.

HOW, WHEN, AND WHERE WE SLEEP.

> "How wonderful is death,
> Death and his brother sleep!
> One, pale as yonder waning moon,
> With lips of lurid blue;
> The other, rosy as the morn
> When, throned on ocean's wave,
> It blushes o'er the world;
> Yet both so passing wonderful!"

The range between rosy red and lurid blue is the scale of life and death. One of the most powerful agencies in the prevention of disease is the proper management of *sleep*. The "preserver of men" has a special favorite in this beauful brother of death, and insists upon it that we shall be wary and wise *how*, *when*, and *where* we sleep.

"This inner part of the process of rejuvenescence may be rendered more clearly comprehensible by sleep, for this also is a phenomenon of periodical rejuvenescence, the rejuvenescence of the consciousness. In sleep the mind is relaxed from the tension in which it is held toward the outward world while awake. Thus sleep, a necessary recreation for the mind, is equally required by all the powers of the body immediately serving the mind. The inner formative processes, on the contrary, through which the body is preserved, do not rest during this time of retreat; they rather act the more undisturbedly and concentratedly. Hence the rejuvenescing power of sleep also over the *body*, which appears so wonderful."*

WHAT WE WEAR, AND HOW WE WEAR IT.

The philosophy of clothes is of profound interest to the "biped without feathers," and "Sartor Resartus" is exhaustless in suggestions as a critique on the divine rights of the only universally-acknowledged kings and queens of the present time, namely, tailors† and mantua-makers; and the doctrine that "spiritual idiosyncrasies reveal themselves in the style and color of clothes," and that the external husk of the monkey man, is all-powerful in the "table of forces" of the world, the flesh, and the devil, even belonging to the abysmal necessities which superintend the developments of peacocks and parrots, fashionable ladies, fops, and Indian chiefs, ("with stripes of red and yellow,") have a sublime significance in the publication of the outside of things as a mode of "visualizing the ideas of the eternal mind."

* Braun.

† "The Tailor is not only a man, but something of a creator or divinity. With astonishment the world will recognize that the Tailor is its hierophant, and hierarch, or even its god."

SARTOR RESARTUS.

On the subject of clothes, as preventives of disease, volumes might be written, as it embraces considerations of the entire organization of man, and its connection with all elements of the external world. On the true philosophy of clothes the race is profoundly asleep, in an ignorance of Egyptian blackness; but in the ordinary stupid and besotted worship of fashion in dressing, it is so entirely insane, that the guardian spirits of the earth have forsaken it in disgust. Its fearfully destructive and tragical bearing, not only on the passing generation, but on the health and destiny of unborn millions, is not to be computed by mathematics.

Profoundly, very profoundly we must penetrate to exhaust the hygienic significance of dress; and to a very exalted height we must soar, to transcend entirely the influence of the mud-swamp in which we wriggle like polliwogs, on the subject of clothes; and long, very long, it is to be feared, we must "gnaw at this slave's chain," and pray to God for deliverance from ignorance and barbarism, before what we wear, and how we wear it, shall be arranged by science, reason, taste, and health and comeliness shall appear as the shining consummations of the achievements of the soul, and "*Use be the suggestor of Beauty.*"

WHAT WE DO, AND HOW WE DO IT.

This must embrace the hygiene of work, the whole chapter of exercise, physiological, pathological, or the *work*, the *calling*, how we do it. This will suggest the *law* of *work* for the life of the organ, and also the *lesson;* that is, never to *use* a *defective* bolt or screw; never work with an imperfect implement; never tax a diseased organ, or overwork an organ threatened with disease. The reason is obvious without a dissertation. The power of work to prevent disease is almost limitless. And here the gymnastics of human industry take their attitudes as life preservers by a divine polarity. "We are created by the craft of nature to be ourselves *workers*, by Him whom nature clothes, vails, and manifests, to be workers. To *work, to do, was that for which we were called forth to be.*" Cease to dream, O man! thou gorgeous loafer, of celestial lubber-lands where eternity shall be dozed away with cigars, and *nothing to do.**

On the specially preventive and curative powers of particular *kinds of work* over special states and individual organs, much has been suggested, and an essay of the most significant import might be written from facts already on record, in connection with the physiology of organs, on the prophylactics and therapeutics of *exercise*. Estimate by critical analyses the life-giving processes of ploughing and sowing, digging and delving, wood-chopping and fence building, with the ambrosial recreation of making hay, together with the useful mechanical arts that are making the earth comfortable, and civilized life endurable, and see the result. Then, there is wonderful virtue in the *walk*, the great voluntary act of locomotion; man, the sublime, with upturning immortal eyes, ($ανθρωπος$,) moving in the erect attitude. Is there not sanitary significance in the dreamy stroll of the philosopher and poet, the soul erect also, and walking in thought; in the enchanting excursion of the botanist collecting plants, and the "tug and tussle" of the geologist, hammer in hand, climbing and dissecting his mountains? Of the exercise and gymnastic virtues of swimming, too high a commendation cannot be given; it is bold work and purifying ablution combined. Are there not positive and absolute powers in the hunt, man's return again to the original game of life and death, with the animal kingdom about him?

Long have the refreshing and life-renewing influences of the fishing, or piscatorial art, been celebrated and sung; and Izaak Walton was a poet, and a prophet of health. Then we are presented with the great passive forms of exercise—the sail, the drive, the horseback ride. In horseback traveling is achieved the highest results of passive motion, the last issues of jactitation, or churning of viscera, of pounding

* Idleness is the largest gate of perdition now open.

and friction of cavities and their contents, with passivity of voluntary muscles, and the simple fillip of concussion and vibration, or exercise of whole body without use, or active drill of organs in a state of threatened, or actual, disease. On this account horseback exercise has had many advocates in the medical profession, in diseases of the *lungs*, digestive organs, nervous system, etc. Thus, from stern labor of loins and wrists in the battle of life, to the walk, or sail, or horseback or carriage ride of the weakened valetudinarian, the preventive power of work, or exercise, over disease, also the curative power in disease, are almost without bounds.

On the side of the soul, or order of moral and spiritual influences, as hygienic forces, there is a world of great resources.

This closes both segments of the circle man, on the question of preventing disease, and brings into play all the surroundings of the human being, and hence common, familiar things, every day and hour's experiences, gastronomics, bodily habitudes, manners and customs, work, philosophy, æsthetics, and morals, confirm the great announcement to the body and soul, that physiological and pathological laws preach the gospel of the ten commandments, and the doctrines of Hygeia, the goddess of health. As *she* represents but *one attribute* of the divinity who presides over the *whole domain* of the healing art, the extent of the resources of that art may be inferred from the representations just made, and so it comes that all nature stands as waiting-maid to the great god who is a "personification of all the healing powers of the world."

It seems, from this critical rendering of the beautiful evangel of prevention, that the mere mending and patching-up business, the cobbling and darning of humanity, when torn and defective, not to speak of the operation of chunking and daubing the walls of the "house we live in," when worn and dilapidated, are not the *only* end and *function* of the "medical art," narrowly limited to the physician administering drugs. Undoubtedly it is a great and wonderful thing, allied to the labors of the gods, to *cure a disease*, (that is, of course, to lend a help to nature, which she could *not do without*,) and to stoop, with the power of an angel's wing, to snatch a perishing mortal from the grave. And here it occurs to the reflecting mind, that if the *making* of *man* was to God the infinite, the crowning of his creation, the finishing of his work, and the perfection of his glory, surely the *saving from destruction* of his "heaven-labored form, erect, divine," is the crowning of *all human art*, and stands the perfection and splendor of *all man* the finite's *creations* or works. It appears, then, that while it is obvious that the prevention of disease is *one* of the highest and noblest efforts of man,—the *curing* of a *disease already* in *existence*, the saving from pain and death, and the resurrection, as it were, of the body from the grave, is certainly the grandest revelation of human power, and that art the *most exalted of all arts*. Wonderful is it that the spirit and far-reaching prophecy of the classical myth has become a revelation of truth in the sanitary department of this mundane sphere, and the god of medicine stands arrayed in the full grandeur of his attributes and proper function, namely, the publication of the life of man *free from disease* and infirmity in all its terrestrial relations, with the possibility of patriarchal longevity and soundness; while the mild maid, with flowing robes, representing "*one of his attributes*," that of preserving health when given by a higher power, and guarding with care the restored sick, or essaying to *prevent* the calamities which only her sire, the great god Æsculapius himself, can certainly avert, must forever *lean upon* her beneficent parent. To prevent disease, if possible, is blessed and great, but to *cure it*, when in existence, is *heavenly* and *divine*.

Hand in hand stand the elements of the great science of man, Anatomy, Physiology, Pathology, Hygiene, not separate sciences, (at the bedside of the diseased sufferer SURELY *not separate*,) not dissevered members, not merely "*subordinate*" or "*ancillary*," not simply "*auxiliary*," not "*en-

tirely initial" to each other, but as pillars of one great temple, parts of one grand whole, over which presides that unity of design, that oneness of spirit which is the mind and majesty of the world.

(NOTE TO PAGE 555, AT *)

The education of the stomach is one of the great accomplishments of the civic state. 'Tis not the brain, but stomach, that represents thee truly, multifarious man! In the hot-bed of metropolitan life, behold how faithfully, hand in hand, go the graces with the fell disgraces; how quickly luxury and vice dethrone the soul, and sin "that high face defaces!"

(NOTE TO PAGE 555, AT †)

In the Philadelphia edition, published by J. B. Lippincott & Co., 1859, of Dr. Moorman's "Virginia Springs," there is a note, page 209, referring to a quotation made from a former edition of his work, in *The Mountain*, page 161. This quotation is verbatim, and, for the satisfaction of any hope inspired by it, the consumptive reader was simply referred to Dr. Moorman's book for anything it might contain on the "cure of confirmed consumption."

That quotation is certainly an indorsement, to a certain extent, of the fact advanced, "confirmed consumption" being included in the list of diseases for the cure of which one of the waters he describes had "peculiar and distinguished reputation." In the second, or Richmond edition, we find the following words, page 153, which are republished in the Philadelphia edition, page 208: "The *peculiar* and *distinguishing reputation* of this water (Red Sulphur Springs) as a medical agent, is for diseases of the *thoracic viscera*, and, by some it has been considered remedial in *confirmed tubercular consumption*. Without *affirming* or *controverting* this high claim for the water as a remedy in confirmed consumption, our observations," etc. etc. The following is the note referred to in the Philadelphia edition of Dr. Moorman's book: "In a work [he should have said the *first part* of a work] just issued from the Philadelphia press, entitled *The Mountain*, our volume is referred to as showing that this water *cures confirmed consumption*. We need scarcely say to our *careful readers* that it is a mistake to ascribe such an opinion to us; and that we never held or taught that this or any other sulphur water should be regarded as curing that, as *we believe, incurable affection.* We are satisfied that the error on the part of the author of *The Mountain* was entirely unintentional." It appears that Dr. Moorman "*believes consumption an incurable* affection," and yet will not *affirm* or CONTROVERT the high claims of one of his waters as a *remedy in that disease.* The above note is a most emphatic CONTROVERSION of the "high claim for the water;" but it must be apparent to the "careful reader," from an inspection of the quotation, that the "mistake," or "error," of the author of *The Mountain*, although "*entirely unintentional,*" is not so *obvious after all.* Entertaining the highest respect for Dr. Moorman, and faith in his orthodoxy, also having much admiration for the zeal he has shown in laboring for the springs of Virginia for twenty-three years, nothing at all derogatory was intended in the *Mountain's* reference to his work. Might not the "controverting" have been in the *text* as well as in a note, and his "belief that the affection *was incurable*" been "affirmed" there also, as well as in a mere marginal reference? The unwillingness to "affirm or controvert" the claims of a certain water as a "remedy for confirmed" consumption is followed by the direct "affirmation" of his *belief* that it is an "*incurable affection.*" So now, in justice, we will only say on the subject of this water "curing confirmed consumption," *do not see* Moorman.

ANTAEUS THE GIANT.

Antaeus (*'Ανταῖος*) was a son of Poseidon and Ge, a mighty giant and wrestler in Libya, whose strength was invincible so long as he remained in contact with his mother earth. The strangers who came to his country were compelled to wrestle with him; the conquered were slain, and out of their skulls he built a house to Poseidon. Heracles discovered the source of his strength, lifted him up from the earth, and crushed him in the air. (Apollod., ii. 5, § 11; Hygin. *Fab.*, 31; Diod., iv. 17; Pind., *Isthm.*, iv. 87, etc.; Lucan, *Pharsal.*, iv. 590, etc.; Juven., iii. 89; Ov., *Ib.*, 397.) The tomb of Antaeus, (*Antaei collis*,) which formed a moderate hill in the shape of a man stretched out at full length, was shown near the town of Tingis, in Mauretania, down to a late period, (Strab., xvii. p. 829; P. Mela, iii. 10, § 85, etc.,) and it was believed that whenever a portion of the earth covering it was taken away, it rained until the hole was filled up again. Sertorius is said to have opened the grave, but when he found the skeleton of sixty cubits in length, he was struck with horror, and had it covered again immediately. (Strab., *l. c.;* Plut., *Sertor.*, 9.)—*Greek and Roman Biography and Mythology.* [L. S.]

"Man is the summit, the crown of Nature's development, and must comprehend everything that has preceded him, even as the fruit included within itself all the earlier developed parts of the plant. In a word, Man must represent the whole world in miniature.

"The universal spirit is *Man*. In the human race the world has become individual. Man is the entire image or likeness of the world. His language is the spirit of the world. All the functions of animals have attained unto unity, unto self-consciousness, in Man."

PHYSIOPHILOSOPHY.

"Man, without doubt, is the highest link, the crown of the visible creation; the last, the most finished production of the plastic power of Nature; the highest degree of its self-representation which our eyes are capable of seeing, our senses of comprehending. With him our sublunary prospect is closed; he is the extreme point with which and in which the sensible world borders on a higher spiritual world. The organization of man is, as it were, a magic band, by which two worlds of a totally different nature are connected and conjoined; an eternally incomprehensible wonder, by which he becomes, at the same time, an inhabitant of these two worlds, the material and the intellectual.

"One may, with propriety, consider man as a compendium of Nature; as a master-piece of conformation, in which all the active powers scattered throughout the rest of nature, all kinds of organs and forms of life, are united in one whole, act in concert, and, by these means, make him, in the strictest sense, a little world; a copy and epitome of the greater, as he was so often called by the ancient philosophers.

"His life is the most expanded; his organization the most delicate and best finished; his juices and component parts the most ennobled and best prepared; and his intensive life and self-consumption are, therefore, the strongest. He has, consequently, *more points of contact with the whole of* nature by which he is surrounded, and likewise more wants; but he has, also, a richer and more perfect restoration than any other being.

"The inanimate mechanical and chemical powers of nature; the organic or living powers; and that spark of divine power, the power of thought, are here united and blended together in the most wonderful manner, to form that godlike phenomenon which we call the life of man."

HUFELAND.

BOOK III.

ANTAEUS THE GIANT.

CHAPTER I.

> "Man is all symmetry,
>   Full of proportions, one limb to another,
> And all to all the world besides.
>   Each part may call the farthest brother:
>   For head with foot hath private amity;
>   And both, with moons and tides."—HERBERT.

THUS sing the birds of the heavens, and some "old poet's grand imagination is imposed on us as adamantine and everlasting truth, and God's own word!" Is it the man of history, the man of the past, wrapped in the inarticulate mutterings of fable, the man of the present hour, intensated, pungent, and wickedly real, or the man of the future, the ripened fruit of the ages, the *possibly perfect* man, who, like the man of the past, is "made of such stuff as dreams are made of," that the poets have thus embalmed in the "amber of song?"

Surely they do not describe with artistic accuracy the skulking scavenger that now infests this planet,—the mournful victim of disease and pain that now ghosts it through the world, with heart devoured by the cares of a sensual life, with a brain seethed by the fires of excitements that never die, and a stomach which is a ghastly museum of all the eccentric and heterogeneous forms of matter in existence, for "nothing has got so far, but man hath caught and kept it as his prey." With this stomach, which the last revelations of science declare to be omnivorous, and "organs of reproduction that take hold on eternity," and each part calling the farthest brother, what poet has yet sung him truly? Another bard by the wayside has a different lay:—

> "But man crouches and blushes,
>   Absconds and conceals;
> He creepeth and peepeth,
>   He palters and steals;
> Infirm, melancholy,
>   Jealous glancing around,
> An oaf, an accomplice,
>   He poisons the ground."

Can this be the "man," "all symmetry, full of proportions, one limb to another, and all to all the world besides?" Why is he now dethroned and debauched, his light of mind darkened, while his body wallows supinely in the mire of the earth? They say the "foundations of man are not in *matter*, but in *spirit*," and that the "element of spirit is eternity;" that "the universal spirit is man," and call him "Little World." A deeper and more ingenuous criticism of the man of this time is, that he has failed and fallen, and continues perpetually to fail and to fall; that he has sunk from the exalted stature of demigods and Providential men whom history delights to make and to honor, and that his ancient garments fit him not. They even say his antique portrait so illy resembles him now, that he calls it fable, and believes, and solemnly affirms it to be *supernatural*, for so only are the gods. Now he is shrunk almost to annihilation, and approaches the confines of that abyss of gloom, total depravity. "The ground supports him in vain, and his feet kill his purpose; herbs feed him, and beasts clothe him for disgrace; his frame puts costliest energy into play to be manufactured into sloth, and his soul hovers, uninhabiting, over his slime. This is the final shape of unhappiness, the lot of apoplexed men and societies, whose curse it becomes that they are lashed to the halberds of use, upside down, which cleaves with poison to their human forms. For the human form is the divinity either of Nemesis, or of God." Can this be him of whom the mystical winds of the ages whisper so grandly? History mutters his story with a genuflection, and points with awe-struck hand to the heights of Sinai, where he met the supernals in manly communion, and his days were not like the "flower and the grass, which springeth up in the morning and are cut down in the evening time." Once he "strode the earth like a Colossus." Venerable legends come down to us from primeval worlds, that he erst communed with the Infinite, and, in the divine circle of charms of his beautiful mother, Nature, was held entranced for a thousand years; that he carried the fires of life in that charmed alembic of a body of his for ages, the angel of death having almost forgotten that his title to its possession in perpetuity was not valid. "For all the days of Methuselah were nine hundred and sixty and nine years, and he died." Why should the welling-up of those deep founts of physical immortality ever have ceased, and man become the mushroom of an hour? With an absolute balance of forces, mechanical and chemical, ponderable and imponderable, why should not his body be as the Sequoia-tree of three thousand years existence, which is a mere bottling of earth and gas? With a perfect organization, "with head and foot in private amity, and both with moons and tides," why should not life be longer, and man wander the earth a glorified and immortal being, and not be forced to pass into the eternal state by an agonized awakening as from a troubled dream?

> "Nothing that is good *can die;*
> Souls, that of His good life partake,
> He loves as his own self; dear as his eye
> They are to him; he'll never them forsake.
> When they shall die,—then God himself shall die:
> They live, they live in blest eternity."

Why death should ever have arrived in those happy patriarchal days is a subject of continued surprise to the philosophic mind. But they say, also, that if it had not been for

ANTAEUS THE GIANT.

his fascinating and seductive brother sin, who prepared the way, that man could surely have laughed at his dart and scythe, and defied them both. Sad is his fate *now*, born out of time. Like a mournful and solitary traveler he gropes his way through this valley and shadow of a youthful and premature death. The inexorable curse of threescore and ten now holds him by the hair, and irremediably reaps him home to the harvest of everlasting rest. The flames of that ancient and divine fire have long since died out of human clay; for very few men possess, in these degenerate days, half the vitality of Methuselah, or at all contemplate remaining upon earth a thousand years, or seriously think of perpetuating their species* at the good old age in which it seems that venerable patriarch was in the full vigor of his youth. "For Methuselah lived after he begat Lamech seven hundred and eighty and two years, and THEN begat sons and daughters." Science and philosophy will hang long and sadly over this problem of the ages, (on the question of the dead letter alone,) and regret that a chapter of dietetics was not also written to accompany and somewhat explain the chapter of "begats." Were the stomachs of men

---

* Something after the style and power of the venerable Methuselah has occurred in modern days, thus giving hope to those ancient gentlemen of the present hour who are in the horrors of the rapidly approaching period called grand climacteric. "A certain Baron Baravicino de Capellis died in 1770, at Meran, in Tyrol, at the age of 104. He had been married to four wives: the first he married in his fourteenth, and the last in his eighty-fourth year. By his fourth wife he had seven children, and when he died (at 104!) she was pregnant with the eighth. The vigor of his body and mind did not forsake him till the last months of his life. He never used spectacles, and, when at a great age, would walk frequently a couple of miles. His usual food was eggs; he never tasted boiled flesh; sometimes he ate a little *roasted*, but always in very small quantities; and he drank abundance of tea with rosa-solis and sugar-candy."

Another example: "A Frenchman, named De Longueville, lived to the age of 110. He had been married to ten wives; his last wife he married when in his *ninety-ninth* year, and she bore him a son when he was in his hundred and first."—HUFELAND.

in those days made as they are now, with three, four, or five coats?* and were they supplied with the same arrangement of fountains of gastric solvents which they reveal to the patient eye of the naturalist, in these profane days of scalpels and microscopes? Was the bread of the primal fathers perpetually sweet; were their steaks constantly well cooked; were they habitual drinkers or cold water men; and had they books written on "*protracted indigestion?*" Here are quarries to dig in, and the devoted sage may gaze into the dim distance long and ardently, before the anatomy and physiology of the stomach and loins of that wonderful man Methuselah shall be clearly made out, and scientifically arranged with pictorial illustrations, for the edification of school-boys. Shall a truer philosophy and a more profound science yet explain the longevity of the patriarchs, and restore the purple light of this early dawn of the world, whose story comes to us embalmed in heavenly fragrance? Does deep wisdom lie concealed in the sacred myths of departed races? Is the letter of their legend absolute fact, or fable, flesh and blood verity, or symbolical shadow? The history of the immortal youth of the primeval man, the story of his soundness and strength, his happiness and purity, does not belong exclusively to the wondrous race of prophets and poets.

The constant presence of these traditions in the early life of all nations is a most significant fact. For all the tribes of men have had dreams and fables of golden ages departed, of paradises they had somehow lost, of *falls* from *higher* and *better worlds*. They have all inherited sad and mournful legends of regions of purity and bliss from which ruthless and tyrannical powers had driven them, days of innocence and joy, whose light and glory had forever departed. These stories of heaven, these visions and dreams of the celestial, are shadowed forth in the dim dawn of the world in all religions, in all poetries. They are the first spring

---

* Malpighi divided the stomach into three coats, Winslow into four, and Heister into five.

flowers of man's heart and brain; they are the first stretching forth of his baby hand toward the sceptre of the spiritual kingship of this world; they are the first auroral glimmerings of his intellect gilding the distant mountain-tops of the past, and flinging around the earth a wreath of sacred lustres, giving life, blood, and aroma to all primeval histories. Why do men hang with such worship and veneration upon these hoary chronicles, stories of glories departed, of gardens of blessedness passed away, with only prophecies of *heavens to come*, postponed until their arrival in other worlds? The poverty and sorrow of the dwarfish *actual* perpetually present to them, pressing with pain upon eye, heart, and brain, give a sad and tender earnest to these seductive romances which imagination, with retrospective vision, delights to place in the past. Unsatisfied and crushed with the *present*, the toils of this Egypt of the REAL have only sadness for them, and a longing to wander to the ideal of some happy and blissful Canaan haunts them forever. This dim instinct, this dumb prayer of the soul has its origin in reason and nature. For now if man be really "an angel in disguise," and scarcely "less than archangel ruined," it may be but the memory of "joys he has tasted," or "the light of other days," and the hallowed recollections of the past, which shape themselves from his inarticulate sorrow into the forms of a Garden of Eden closed, a Paradise lost, a holiness that knew no sin, with a fall and the curse of death, since he is held constantly by longing and hope of regaining his immortal state; for even in his ruin he cannot forget his Father's kingdom, or forego the hope of a restoration to his crown. "The earth waits for her king;" "the world prays for a *man* to be born." How many ardent souls long for that wonderful second coming! Is the genius and majesty of man an impalpable tradition? Is that prophet's garment of the ages a harlequin mockery? Is sin that Himalaya mountain that rises before him constantly; that Upas that springs at his side with every bleeding footprint? Are the dim prophecies of inspired souls delusive dreams? Must the ideal man remain *ideal?* Is the present possessor of the planet lost without hope of salvation, and are the poet's forebodings, the seer's visions, figments and follies?

Why speak of the flaming sword over the gate of that mournful garden of Jehovah? Why talk of the golden age *as a tradition?* Why say that "Urim and Thummim keep their glory hid? that our days *must be* dark, and our nights *must be* visionless?" Is man certainly that broken giant; is he really that fallen splendor; is he surely that disconsolate Adam whose doom it is to wander endlessly over a world accursed, with only a tradition of the happiness of a past heaven from whose aromatic shades he has been extruded, and the remote hope of the joys of a paradise in some future world, to soothe him in the sorrows of this? Will his deep sleep of sensuality never be broken? Will the thick night hang around him perpetually, and the earth turn its darkened side to him in his lethargy and trance of death forever? Has science struggled for six thousand years in vain to sever the bars of this prison of pain and suffering in which he groans? Is he destined constantly to be the occupant of his diseased body, and this ball of rocks they call the earth to roll through space a hospital of incurables? These are dogmas of that fearful fatalism which now overshadows the earth, and calls in a special Providence who is author, as separate edicts of his arbitrary will, of all the ills which are the consequence of man's infraction of the laws of his organization. These are the doctrines of a bitter revenge, or a savage retaliation, incompatible with the beautiful and sublime spirit of benevolence and love that shines so grandly throughout every part of the world.

As disease had its entrance into the human body through sin, must it really have its exit through human suffering?*

---

* "I maintain the principle, that diseases are not direct visitations, but almost always the result of inattention to Nature's teaching; and, as far as they are punishments for our own indiscretions or vices, should act as warnings. The majority of diseases are produced by our own imprudence or ignorance; observation of the laws of health would enable us to prevent some altogether, to modify

Whole libraries are made of books that scarcely serve to catalogue man's infirmities; temples of learning are erected, and proud professorships are endowed, whose whole function it is to recite the bill-of-fare for the angel of death, and repeat the list of wines of the grave. The best medical treatise has been styled "a Dissertation upon Death," and the best physician a "blind man with a club." This mournful pessimism is a cloud of that gloomy despondency which characterizes the hour, giving a science without faith or worship, a philosophy without hope or holiness, and a religion without love or charity. But "man's misery is his grandeur in disguise, and discontent is immortality."

If he is the "entire image or likeness of the world," whence have shrunk the rivers of his life? whence have withered away his verdant savannas? Why do salt deserts and arid mountains fill the horizon? Is he a broken-hearted god, mourning with infinite grief over the solitude of a bankrupt and dead Universe? One green oasis of a living soul in long thousands of years, one spot of flowers in weary, endless leagues, and he rolls a pathless waste! Is the world a school-house for the education of angels, or a den of torment for the excruciation of demons? Many of the dogmas of fatalism and despair of the past make it a howling wil-

---

others, and to alleviate the effects of all. Disease is much more frequently the result of our own conduct than the direct infliction of Providence, the necessary result of climate, or other external influence."—BEALE.

Different philosophers have given different origins of the evil called disease: first, it comes from man himself as a consequence of the infraction of the laws of his physical and moral constitution; again, the devil has been made the inventor of disease; or the genius of accident has been supposed to preside over this department; and it has also been impiously suggested that God himself is the author of this, as of all other evil. We need go no further than *man*, and the wonderful laws of his organization, for this whole list of horrors: diseases are the invariable consequents of the violation of the laws of his body, the laws of his soul, and are "schoolmasters' rods" for the reformation and education of both soul and body.

derness of barbarism, a Sahara of death. Let us be thankful that the oases exist; that *brave living souls have been here, are here,* and *will come again;* that the fight with the dragons goes on; that the pythons of the past, the saurians of the ancient slimes of the soul, still extant, must perish, and the "new man," and the "new world," redeemed from the chaos of antagonistic elements, shall be indeed the "entire image and likeness" of each other. Sorrowful is his present attitude, and full of despair, for now he dwells among dust, shrouds, and grave-stones, and turns from the living world, which, with gentle, kindly invitations and smiles, importunes him to *explore,* to *interrogate,* to *grow,* promising incalulable expansions and perfections beyond his hopes. Is he sane to make the past a millstone around his neck, instead of a stepping-stone under his feet for progress into the future? Will the milk-founts of the venerable mother never be dry? While change and growth are written upon all things, and the new condition asks to develop the new man, and the expanding future invites him to untried manifestations, and with infinite hope promises that "*all things* shall be added to that kingdom," why must the soul still cling for nourishment to this ancient bosom, and seek there alone for nourishment where all is withered and dry? The procession of the ages has called forth a few souls to whom the *past* was "the dead burying the dead," who used the present to *work in,* and to whom the *future* offered a fresh living and promising harvest. Ignoring the *past,* this order of transcendent spirits have fixed all its hopes and efforts in the future. Vast, prophetic men, the *only real* lovers of the race, with souls genial and expansive, these transcendent beings, striding whole ages before the rest of their kind, have always either located *their heavens* in other *worlds,* or in the *future* of this. With instincts of finest love, with hopes so golden in their riches, with faith so childlike in its trust, and a self-reliance so divine in its imperturbable quiet, these angelic natures, the great radical reformers of humanity, have held their eyes on the *future,* or world to come, with no goal but the infinite heavens, and no end proposed but the final assumption of the splendors of deity. Shall the words they have uttered, the thoughts they have planted, grow till the earth is filled with life and sweetness, and the harmonious relationship of man to nature, of man to man, and of man to Deity, be no longer the foreshadowing of blessedness for the illuminated spirits of the divine few, but will come to be the common inheritance of the whole race, and health of body, purity of heart and sentiment, and holiness of soul, be the *law*, as now the exception, and the diseased, vicious, and insane shall no longer cumber the earth?

Leaving the inspired ones, the prophets of regeneration, and their dreams of salvation for man, to the coming ages to arrange, what has the present time to say of the present man? what is the science of the now-existing representative of the venerable "gardener of earth uncorrupted?" is he plus, minus, or zero? is he fulfilling the divine economy or playing the devil? At the rapid gait of 2·17, his ideal of progress, he has rushed into the possession of a beautiful "heritage of woe," in the shape of a catalogue of diseases amounting to several thousand, more or less, among which are greasy and hypertrophied liver, (Dead Sea fruit of whisky and heaven of alcoholic diathesis,) cancerous and ulcerated stomach, (cachexy and gluttonous abuse,) effete blood, (result of soggy immobility and laziness,) gouty feet, (celestial harmony of gastronomy,) tuberculated lungs, (horrors of profane generation, bad air, and defective nutrition,) lock-jaw, (general spasmodic clutch of dissolving powers,) and hydrophobia, (commonest affliction of Young America,) not forgetting the benevolent Yankee institutions of the bowie knife, revolver, and "*improved American rifle*," which, in nosological and etiological tables, belong, of course, to the causes of sudden and violent death. Having arrested him for a moment under the first shade-tree in his "desert of life," and having thoroughly performed his ablutions by friction with sand, as per recipe of Koran, let us interrogate his present vital connection with the great benevolent cow, Nature, his cherishing mother.

What are his relations to her now? A lover of leeks and flesh-pots, hurried on to hideous morbid growths in hot-beds of vice and luxury, and boiled in the caldrons of towns and cities, has his back been so long turned upon God, that the flaming sword is inexorably fixed between him and the heaven of physical soundness? Can he never enter again the Paradise of sound digestion, and taste the sensuous joys of hilarious youth? Is the divine crucible, that body of his, broken, and does the world, with mountains of the golden ore of health and happiness, gleam in mockery around him, torturing to phrenzy?

The first critical question, the truly essential problem, is, has the human race actually degenerated physically* in modern times, for, morally and spiritually, it seems to be admitted, that it has wilted and withered almost to death.

"For many centuries past we have had numerous writers and *preachers* on the moral degeneracy of mankind, and many still are asserting, on spiritual grounds, the increasing laxity and gradual decline of morals, and the growing disregard of strict principles of religion and rectitude. But it must strike us forcibly, that though PHYSICAL DEGENERACY *has also been making equally rapid strides*, and *progressed hand and hand* with *moral decay*, it was not until very lately that those who are the properly constituted guardians of health, have raised their voices, or taken up their pens, to arrest its progress. That this degeneracy (*physical*) *actually exists, and is still progressive*, is not *a subject of controversy, but capable of easy demonstration*. A glance back at the history of the world, and the contrast that presents itself between the mental, moral, and physical condition of society in ages long past, and its con-

---

* "Two-fifths of all who are born die under five years of age, the remainder all die prematurely,—a fearful mortality. Half die of fevers; one-fourth of consumption and scrofula; the rest of other diseases,—all die of *violence*,—no such thing known, in modern days, as natural death, a death from mere old age. But is not the length of human life increasing? It was so till recently; chronic diseases are multiplying," etc. etc.—ALCOTT.

dition as regards these relations now, is met by a sudden and humiliating conviction of the *awful dilapidation* that has taken place in the social fabric. *It is impossible* for the present age to *flatter* itself into the *contrary* opinion. As the accumulation of literature, which is stored up in the huge intellectual magazine into which the world has grown, and the multiplied facilities of modern education, which a long experience has secured, are no proofs that we are relatively increasing in *strength of mind;* so our concentrated facilities and stupendous triumphs of bodily labor are no proofs that we are relatively increasing in *physical energy.* On the contrary, when we look back with an impartial eye on the severity and unbending morality, the refinement in taste and sentiment, the mental and physical vigor, so common among the ancient Egyptians, Athenians, and Romans, as evinced at the present day, in monuments that have defied the wreck of time and the vandalism of ages, and then make allowances for our advantages, we are penetrated with an *irresistible sense of relative inferiority*, and can no longer boast of our march of intellect and our splendid achievements. Under these circumstances, it is clearly the duty of every member of society to exert any influence he may happen to possess to avert this impending calamity, and if he have a *mite* of information on its removable causes, to give it free publicity."*

The comparative longevity of the ancients and moderns thus becomes a question of vital interest. Passing the fables of primitive giants, we come to the recorded word on the longevity of man, and Methuselah and Jared, Noah and Adam, stand the great plus affirmations. "Haller and Buffon both admit the possibility of long life *before the deluge.* The fact admitted, Buffon hastens to *explain it by a system.* Haller limits himself by quoting the system of Buffon and some others. We are acquainted with the system of Buffon. Before *the deluge*, the earth was less solid and compact than at present, *because* gravity had

* Griscom, "Uses and Abuses of Air."

only been a short time in operation, all its productions had less consistency. Man's body, especially, was more pliant, supple, and more susceptible of extension; it could then grow a longer time; man arrived at *puberty only upon attaining one hundred and thirty years*, instead of fourteen. With this, other things are reconciled, for in multiplying these two numbers, one hundred and thirty and fourteen, by the same number, *i.e.* seven, 'we perceive,' says Buffon, 'that the life of man being now-a-days ninety-eight years, it *must then have been* nine hundred and ten years.'* It is singular that Buffon here states this view seriously, because he gives it as his own, although he sneers at it in Woodward, *from whom he has taken it.*"† Hufeland cleaves the knot of the standing joke on this point, namely, the age of Methuselah, by adopting the views of Hensler. He says: "Acute theologists have shown that the chronology of the early ages was not the same as that used at present. Some, particularly Hensler, have proved, with the highest probability, that the year, till the time of Abraham, consisted only of three months; that it was afterwards extended to eight; and that it was not till the time of Joseph that it was made to consist of twelve. These assertions are, in a certain degree, confirmed by some of the Eastern nations, who still reckon only *three months to a year;* and besides, it would be altogether inexplicable why the life of man should have been shortened *one-half immediately after the flood*. It would be equally inexplicable why the patriarchs did not marry till their sixtieth, seventieth, and even hundredth year; but this difficulty vanishes when we reckon these ages according to the before-mentioned standard, which will give the twentieth or thirtieth year; and consequently, same periods at which people marry at present. The whole, therefore, according to this explanation, assumes a different appearance. The sixteen hundred years before the flood will become four hundred and fourteen; and the nine hundred years (the highest recorded) which Methu-

* Vol. xi. p. 76. † Flourens, "Human Longevity."

selah lived, will be reduced to *two* hundred, an age *which is not impossible*, and to which some men in modern times have *nearly approached.*"*

So Methuselah appears on the record, not as a fable, but as a possible and actual fact. He (Hufeland) then adduces the facts of "profane history, the account of many heroes and Arcadian kings of those periods who attained to the age of several hundred years; but these *pretended instances of longevity* can be explained in the same manner. With the period of Abraham, a period when *history* seems first to be established on more certain grounds, we find mention of a duration of life which can still be attained, and which no longer appears extraordinary, especially when we consider the *temperate manner* in which the patriarchs lived; and that as they were *nomads*, or a *wandering people*, they were much exposed to the FREE OPEN AIR."†

He then recites the Hebrew record. Abraham, a "man of great and resolute mind, fortunate in all his undertakings," lived 175 years; Isaac, "a chaste, peaceable man, and fond of tranquillity," 180; Jacob, "a lover of peace, crafty and cunning," *only* 147; "Ishmael, a warrior, 137;" "Sarah, the only female of the ancients with whose duration of life we are acquainted, lived 127 years;" Joseph, with whose history all boys are acquainted, lived 110 years; Moses, a "man of extraordinary strength and spirit," but a murderer, weathered it 120 years. He complained of the *shortness of life, as everybody does now.* "His eye was not dim, nor his natural force abated." Joshua, "the warlike and active," was 110; while "Eli, the high-priest, a corpulent, phlegmatic man, of a resigned disposition, lived only 90 years;" and Elisha, the austere, attained to 100; whereas Simeon, a "man full of hope and confidence in God," survived only 90 years. The Egyptians, notwithstanding the immortality of the pyramids, were not extremely long livers, "the

* Hufeland, "Art of Prolonging Life." Many quotations are made here from this interesting work.

† Hufeland.

longest reign of any of their kings being 50 years." The Chinese are said to exist forever, (probably fabulous!) *tea* being the saving principle. The Greek, supposed by ethnologists to be very closely allied to the *modern gentleman*, was not distinguished for longevity. They say Epimenides of Crete lived to be 157; Democritus, "the *friend and searcher of nature*, a man also of good temper and serene mind," 109; Georgias of Leontium, orator, traveler, and teacher of the young, 108; Diogenes, the tub man, 90; Zeno, the Stoic, 100; Solon, the wise, 80; Protagoras of Abdera, an orator and traveler, 90; Isocrates, a man of great temperance and MODESTY, 98; Plato, the immortal, 81; and Pythagoras, to be "very old." This philosopher, (Pythagoras,) always sound, gives us a fine schedule of human life. He used to divide the life of man into four equal parts. "From the first to the twentieth year he called *him a child, a man begun;* from the twentieth to the fortieth, a *young man;* from the fortieth to the sixtieth, A MAN; from the sixtieth to the eightieth, an *old, or declining man;* and after this period he reckoned *him no more among the living, let him live to whatever age he might.*"*

Among the Romans, fast livers, the instances of longevity are not numerous or extraordinary. M. Valerius Corvinus, "bold and courageous, extremely popular, and *always fortunate*," lived over 100 years. Orbilius, the pedagogue and soldier, made his 100. Hermippus, "the instructor of young maids," lived long; while Fabius the slow, and Cato, the "man with iron body and iron *mind*, fond of country life, and an enemy to physicians, each lived to be 100." Roman ladies, it appears from the record, often lived long. "Terentia, the wife of Cicero, notwithstanding her many misfortunes, cares, and THE GOUT, with which she was tormented, lived to the age of 103; and Livia, the wife of Augustus, an imperious and passionate woman, lived 90 years." Roman actresses, it seems, lived long; one Luceja, who came on the stage very young, performed a *whole century*, and even made her

* "Xenophilus lived 106 years, and Demonax above 100."

appearance publicly when in her 112th year. "Galeria Copiola, an actress and dancer also, was 90 years old *when she first performed in the theatre;* and she was again brought foward as a wonder, in order to compliment Pompey. But even this was not the last time of her acting; for she appeared once more, to show her respect for *Augustus.*"

"A very valuable collection in regard to the duration of human life, in the time of the Emperor Vespasian, has been preserved by Pliny from the records of the Census, a source perfectly true and worthy of credit." (See Hufeland's Synopsis.) He proceeds: "The bills of mortality of the celebrated Ulpian agree in a most striking manner with ours, and in particular with those of great cities. From these it appears that one might, with great propriety, compare Rome with London, in regard to the probability of the duration of life. We have sufficient reason, therefore, to believe that the duration of life in the time of Moses, the Greeks, and the Romans, was *invariably* the same as at present; and that the age of the earth has no influence on the longevity of its inhabitants, that difference excepted which may be produced by the cultivation of its surface, and the difference of climate that may thence arise. The result of this research will therefore be, that man may still attain to the *same* age *as ever.* The difference only is, *that more* attained to old age formerly than at present."*

Flourens presents us with an interesting periscope on the subject of longevity.† Examining and quoting a large number of authorities, all of accredited testimony, he asks, "what is the natural, usual, and normal life of man?" and concludes, from a critical survey of the field, that "a first century of *ordinary life,* and almost a second century, or *half a century* [at least?] of *extraordinary* life, is *then the prospect science holds out to man.* It is quite true, to speak like the ancients, that science offers us great store in life,

* "Art of Prolonging Life."

† See "Human Longevity and the Amount of Life on the Globe," by P. Flourens.

more in power than in act, 'plus in posse, quam in actu;' but were it given to us to offer it in act, would the complaints of man cease? It is a fact, a *law* that is to say, from general experience in this class, (the mammifera,) that *extraordinary* life can be prolonged to *double* that of *ordinary life*."

Buffon says, "The man who does not die of accidental causes, reaches, everywhere, the age of ninety or a hundred years."* He asserts this to be true irrespective of varieties of races and external conditions, "duration of life depending solely on *internal constitution, or intrinsic virtue of organs*."

Haller places man among the animals which live the longest, and thinks "he *might* live not less than *two centuries*." He says, "Man should be placed among the animals that live the longest; how very unjust, then, are our complaints of the brevity of life!"† He collected a great many instances of extreme old age, the two oldest being 152 and 169. The first, Thomas Parr, of Shropshire, comes indorsed by Harvey. Charles I. killed him by feasting him. "Harvey dissected him; all the viscera were *perfectly healthy;* the cartilages were not ossified, etc. He might have lived many years; he *died of an accident*"‡

Hufeland gives a particular account of Thomas Parr: "He was a poor farmer's servant, and obliged to maintain himself by daily labor. When above 120 years of age he married a widow for his second wife, who lived with him twelve years, and who asserted that during that time he never betrayed *any signs* of *infirmity* or *age*. Till his 130th year he performed all his usual work, and was accustomed even to thrash. Some years before his death, his eyes and memory began to fail; but his hearing and senses continued sound to the last. In his 152d year the king sent for him, and he was treated at court in so *royal a manner* that he

* Vol. ii. p. 76.
† Elementa Physiologiæ, vol. viii. lib. xxx. p. 75.
‡ Flourens.

died soon after, at London, in 1635, being 152 years and nine months old, and having lived under nine kings of England. His body was opened by Dr. Harvey and found to be in the *most perfect state*. His great grandson died at Cork a few years ago, at the age of 103, [and another of his descendants at 120,] showing the great fact of transmissible stamen vitæ."

The other instance adduced by Haller has, from Hufeland, a more special notice, from which it appears that both these modern patriarchs were Englishmen. He says: "In the year 1670 died Henry Jenkins, of Yorkshire. He remembered the battle of Floddenfield in 1513, and at that time was twelve years of age. It was proved, from the registers of the Chancery and other courts, that he had appeared, 140 years before his death, as an evidence, and had an oath administered to him. At the time of his death, he was, therefore, 169 years old. His last occupation was *fishing*, and when above the age of 100, he was able to swim across rapid rivers."*

Hufeland presents us with a most interesting list of veterans, which he says is taken chiefly from Bacon's "Historia Vitæ et Mortis." Draakenberg, a Dane, born in 1626, lived to be 146 years old. He was a seaman till his 91st year, and suffered slavery in Turkey for 15 years. At 111 he married a woman of threescore, whom he outlived, and "at 130 years fell in love with a young country girl, who, as may well be supposed, rejected his proposal. He made, unsuccessfully, several other attempts in this line, but concluded to finish his life alone." "In the year 1757, J. Effingham died in Cornwall in the 144th year of his age." Born *poor*, he was brought up to labor, and served as a soldier and corporal. He ended his days as *day-laborer*, had been temperate, and "in his youth had never drank *strong* and *heating liquors*." "In the 1792 died, in the Duchy of Holstein, an industrious day-laborer, named Stender, in the 103d year of his age." He lived on oatmeal and buttermilk, mostly ate flesh much salted, seldom drank, was fond of

* "Art of Prolonging Life."

smoking, was old before he used tea and coffee, lost his teeth early, was never sick, "or *out of humor*," and had "his chief dependence always in the goodness of God." "An old soldier, named Mittelsted, died in Prussia in the year 1792, in the 112th year of his age; was born 1681, lost at a gambling table, entered the army, and was a soldier 67 years, being in seventeen general engagements," in the campaigns of Frederick I., Frederick William I., and Frederick II. After all these adventures he married three wives, the third in his 110th year. H. Kauper, of Neus, Cologne, was 112. "He was a strong man, and accustomed to walk every day." Helen Gray was 105 years old. "She was of small stature, exceedingly lively, peaceable, and *good tempered*, and a few years before her death acquired new teeth." Thomas Garrick lived to be over 108 years; "had an extraordinary appetite, and had not been sick for twenty years." "Anthony Senish, a farmer of the village of Puy, in Limoges, died in 1770, in the 111th year of his age." He labored till within a few days of his death; had his teeth, hair, and eyesight; his food, chestnuts and Turkish corn; had never been bled nor used any medicine."

R. Glen, a shoemaker, lived at Tacony, near Philadelphia, was 114 years old. He was a Scotchman; had seen King William III., had a keen appetite, and was married three times, his last wife being thirty years old, and "with whom he *lived happily*." Notwithstanding the conclusions of some learned ethnologists that the present composite race of Anglo-Americans can never become thoroughly acclimatized, or assume the prerogatives of an indigenous variety on this continent, many instances have been adduced of extreme or extraordinary old age. For a contradiction of a number of statements on this subject, see Dunglison's "Human Health," and other tables of longevity, mortality, etc. Of the negro race on this question of longevity, he says: "Throughout the United States the number of colored persons, who are reported to attain the age of one hundred and upwards, bears a large ratio to the whites." See also Prichard on longevity of negroes. At St. Andrew's, Jamaica, Robert Lynch, the property of Sir Edward Hyde East, died, aged 160. At St. John's, Antigua, a black woman died at 130. Numerous instances are given of the great age of this race in the United States. It appears that the most refined and polished nations have not much pre-eminence in longevity over savage tribes, leaving out a few causes of destruction inseparable from the habitudes of barbarous races, and that Africans and Indians often attain extreme old age. Humboldt gives native American Indians long lives. Hilario Savi died at Chiguata, aged 143, while Humboldt was at Lima. Her husband, Andrea Alexis Zar, was 117 years old. He also knew a Peruvian, of 130 years, who walked daily three or four leagues.

After enumerating cases of extreme longevity, Hufeland remarks: "These are all the instances of great age in modern times with which I have been acquainted. Persons of 100 I omit, for these are more common." He concludes on the problem, "how long can man live as an individual, and what is the relative duration of human life?" "We may, therefore, with the greatest probability, assert that the *organization* and *vital* power of *man* are able to support a duration and activity of TWO HUNDRED *years.*" This, as we have seen, is the conclusion of Haller. On the question of what class of men, employment, temperament, etc. live longest, see the tables of Madden, Hufeland, Flourens, Wilson, and ethnologists and physiologists generally. The following would seem to be the general conclusions: "The most extraordinary instances of longevity are to be found *only among* those classes of mankind who, *amidst bodily labor, and in the open air, lead a simple life agreeable to nature,* such as *farmers, gardeners, hunters, soldiers, and sailors. In these situations man still attains to the age of* 140 *and even* 150 *years.*"

The general results further seem to be these: kings and emperors are not characterized as long livers. "From Augustus till now, out of two hundred Roman and German emperors only four lived to be eighty, namely, Gordian, Valerian, Anastasius, Justinian." This holds good of the great ecclesiastical representatives; of over three hundred Popes only five having arrived at eighty. Monks and hermits, on the contrary, by temperance and rectitude, strict regimen and prayer, including the saving virtues of starvation and devout contemplation of the umbilicus, have arrived at the patriarchal numbers. St. David survived 146; Paul, the hermit, 113; St. Anthony, 105; John, the apostle, 93; Theodore, of Canterbury, 88, and Athanasius and Jerome, 80. Philosophers profound, it seems, attain great age, especially such as are "occupied with the study of nature, and the discovery of new and divine truths." This is true from the Greek to the present time. From the recitation of records, it would seem that poets and artists have long leases from their "occupation, which leads them to be conversant with the sports of fancy, and self-created worlds, and whose whole life, in the *roperest sense,* is an *agreeable dream.*" It appears, from the tables, that doctors are the shortest livers of all; "for, at any rate, mortality *is greater among practical physicians than perhaps among men of any other profession.*" "Physicians, who so abundantly dispense to others the means of health and life, ought to claim here a distinguished place. But, unfortunately, this is not the case. It may be said of them in general: 'Aliis inserviendo consumunter; aliis medendo moriuntur.' In serving others they are consumed; in healing others they are destroyed."

By consulting the highly-interesting table of Erasmus Wilson,* of the ages of medical philosophers, it will be seen that from Hippocrates to Boerhaave the range has been from seventy to ninety-three; Hippocrates only attaining 109, which, in the "venerable predecessor," was achieved by "his whole life being employed in the study of nature, in *traveling,* and in visiting the sick; passing more of his time in small villages and in the country than in great cities." It would also appear from the tables that miners, and those exposed to poisonous effluvia, are among the shortest livers.

* See page 605.

The countries most favorable to longevity are Sweden, Norway, Denmark, England, Scotland, Ireland, France, Greece, Hungary, and Germany. General conclusions from chapters on longevity synopsized are: age of world no influence on man; "people may still become as old as in the time of Abraham;" at periods men lived longer, not *from the world*, but man *himself*. "When men were in a savage state,* simple, laborious children of nature, *and much exposed to the open air*, as shepherds, hunters, and *farmers*, great age was very common among them; but when they despised the dictates of *nature*, studied *refinement*, and indulged in luxury, the duration of life became shorter. The same people, restored to a rude state and manner agreeable to *nature, may regain their ancient longevity.*" May attain to great age in almost all climates. High situations, with pure air, favorable; *too great height not* favorable; nothing more unfavorable to duration of life than very *sudden changes;*† "in cold climates men older than in warm," except in extreme cold; uniformity as to gravity and lightness, heat and cold, therefore small variations of barometer and thermometer, favorable; too dry or too moist unfavorable; life on islands and peninsulas favorable; they are "cradles of old age;" thus, "longer life on islands of Archipelago than near countries of Asia; in Cyprus than Syria; in Formosa and Japan than China; in England and Denmark than Germany." Much depends on *ground* and *soil;* cold soil unfavorable; where all these favorable elements exist combined, men of course attain the greatest age.

"The more a man follows *Nature*, and is *obedient* to her *laws*, the *longer he will live;* the further he *deviates from*

---

* Diderot and Rousseau advocated a return to the savage state as the surest way of attaining the macrobiotic life.

† "The zone which presents this inconstancy in the highest degree is that comprised within the 34th and 44th parallels, having mean temperatures varying from 60° to 45°. This, however, is the zone of densest population and greatest activity; *demonstrating* that vicissitudes of temperature are *not* unfavorable to human development."— DRAKE, p. 485.

these, the shorter will be his existence. This is one of the *most general of laws*. In the same district, therefore, as long as the inhabitants lead a *temperate* life, as shepherds or hunters, they will attain to old age; but as soon as they become civilized, and by these means sink into luxury, dissipation, and corruption, their duration of life will be shortened. It is, therefore, not the rich and great, not those who take gold tinctures and wonder-working medicines who become old; but country laborers, farmers, mariners, and such men as, perhaps, never in their lives employed their thoughts on the means which must be used to promote longevity. It is among these people ONLY that the most astonishing instances of it are to be found. The most terrible mortality is to be found among West India slaves and hospitals for foundlings," etc.* Final conclusion from experience, condensed from authorities: *moderation in everything*, and in a certain *mediocrity* of *condition, climate, health*, temperament, constitution, employment, spirits, diet, etc., lies the *great secret* for becoming old. All extremes shorten life. There are also other elements of longevity: the married state is favorable; there being not *one instance* on *record* of a *bachelor having* attained to a great age, (although there are so many *old bachelors!*); labor in youth; avoidance of immoderate use of flesh in diet; cultivation; life in country and small towns extremely favorable; in large towns and cities, extremely *unfavorable*. More women than men become old, but fewer *reach* the *extreme* old age of men.

For many interesting particulars, see tables of Hufeland, Wilson, Dunglison, and others; see also instances of renovation of teeth and hair in extreme old age. The following

* To which Dunglison replies: "This estimate, (namely, that the proportion of slaves that reach the age of one hundred and upwards, is to that of the free in the ratio of 14·1 to 1·02,) coupled with the unquestionable fact, that the slaves in the principal slaveholding States double their number in something less than twenty-eight years, is a sufficient answer to Hufeland, who, without the possibility of having data to guide him, affirms that 'the most terrible mortality reigns among them,'" etc.

tables from Hufeland and Haller give their results of observations on the relative duration of human life:—

HUFELAND.—Of a hundred men born, 50 die before the tenth year.
20 between 10 and 20
10 " 20 " 30
6 " 30 " 40
5 " 40 " 50
3 " 50 " 60
Six only live to be above 60.

HALLER.—Of men who lived from 100 to 110 years the instances have been 1000.
110 to 120 60
120 " 130 29
130 " 140 15
140 " 150   6
     169   1

For interesting particulars, see tables of the physiologists and writers on hygiene already quoted.

Haller and Buffon treat the question of human longevity in two ways: historically and physiologically. The historical side of the question would embrace the recitation of all facts known of the natural, ordinary, and extreme duration of life. The physiological aspect of the problem involves the contemplation of the great natural phases of development of the species, as of gestation, period of growth, etc.

Buffon's formula of the duration of the lives of animals is, they exist six or seven times as long as they are growing or attaining perfect adult development. He adduces the examples of man, the dog, the horse, etc.

Hufeland asserts: "One may lay it down as a rule, that an animal lives eight times as long as it grows. Now, man in a natural state, where the period of maturity is not hastened by art, requires full twenty-five years to attain his complete growth and conformation; and this proportion will give him an absolute age of 200 years, although not above one in a thousand attain to the age of 100 years."

Flourens admits that the "real physiological problem is stated." He proceeds: "One thing only was unknown to Buffon, namely, the *certain sign* that marks the term of growth. I find this sign in the *union* of the *bones with their epiphyses:* as long as the bones are not united to their epiphyses, the animal grows; when once the bones and their epiphyses are united, the animal grows no more. This union in man is effected at 20 years; in the camel at 8; horse 5; ox 4; lion 4; dog 2; cat 18 months; rabbit 12 months; guinea-pig 7, etc. Now man lives from 90 to 100 years; the camel 40; horse 25;* ox 15 to 20; lion 20; dog 10 to 12; cat 9 to 10; rabbit 8; guinea-pig 6 to 7, ete. etc. The relation pointed out by Buffon is very near the truth. He says that every animal lives nearly six or seven times as long as the term of its growth. The true relation is *five*, or very nearly. Man being twenty years growing, lives five times twenty, that is to say, one hundred years; the camel being eight, lives forty, etc. We have, then, finally, a *precise characteristic* which gives accurately the duration of growth; the duration of growth gives us the duration of life. All the phenomena of life are united by the following chain of relations: the duration of life is given by the duration of growth; the duration of growth is given by the duration of gestation; the duration of gestation, by the height, etc. etc. The larger the animal the longer is the time of gestation. The gestation of the rabbit is thirty days; that of man is nine months; that of the elephant is nearly two years."

Such being the finally-arranged scientific biological results of ages of observation, why this great scarcity of patriarchs of even a century, and extreme rarity of octogenarians, while the regular, never-failing harvest of threescore and ten arrives, and Death and his dart appear so often before half a score, and such multitudes never see onescore and five? How does it come that nearly everybody (two-fifths!) dies before five years of age; very many before they are born, (for the percentage of still-births, see tables,) and multitudes in their youth, while not one in a thousand lives to be one hundred years old, as originally arranged by the structure of his bones in an ordinary physiological minimum,

* As an example of "extraordinary" life in animals, the horse has attained to fifty years.—See FLOURENS.

not to speak of the historical, and extraordinary maximum, of two hundred years? Is man, the giant Antaeus, thus lifted and crushed in the air by the habits and vices of civilized life? Let him touch the earth again, and the dreams of the prophets, the promises of inspired souls, and nature, shall be realized, and the original contract with God upon bones will be kept inviolate.

On granite in place, then, we walk in demonstrating the interesting problem that great human longevity is within the "province of pure reason," and practically attainable. Refreshing, invigorating, really inspiring, it is to find that there is a possibility and hope, even a critical rendering of feasibility of the undertaking to live to be "as old as Methuselah"—of course, as the story is modernized by accredited theologians. The historical side of the great question clearly makes out the case, which it is enchanting to reflect upon, that a man (why not *any man*, possibly *every man?*) may live to be two hundred years old, the interpreted age of Methuselah and Jared, enjoying all his faculties to the *last*.

The physiological and scientific side of the subject give nearly the same cause of jubilation to the mortal who wishes to remain in the prison of the flesh for a few hundred years, by establishing the conclusions, that by *demonstrable laws of nature*, on the question of the life of bones and their connection with the animal economy, 100 years of *ordinary*, and 200 of *extraordinary* life, *ought* to be enjoyed by every man *accepting, under any circumstances*, the common boon of existence.

While history and science stand hand in hand grandly united (a rather rare occurrence on any subject) on this question of human longevity, it becomes imperative to ask for a rendering of the *conditions* upon which these results are to be achieved. This is justice to both history and science (a *very* rare occurrence to either) on one of the most important subjects engaging the mind of man.

Gratifying, rather beatifying, it is to know, then, the means by which this end or answer to the prayers of all men is to be consummated, and the result, the *extreme* of *macrobiotic* life, or ultimate longevity of the patriarchs, achieved. Here the poet takes time by the forelock, and philosophy and physiology by the nose. Antaeus, the mighty giant and wrestler, was invincible as long as he remained an integral and perfectly sound part of the world, and by organic and celestial harmony filled an indispensable need in the instrumentality of a divine organization, as long as some shape of ultimate filial life-bond united him with his mother, the earth; but a feeble infant in the arms of any brutal Hercules, (demon of vice,) who could detach and easily crush him in the air, when his foot had left the maternal contact.

Starting with ancient records, where things are somewhat dim in the fields of the prophetic telescopes, and coming down to the present time, where the knife and microscope appear, and records of common courts testify, who lived the longest, who fulfilled the sum-total of all prophecies, of all philosophies, of all religions, all sciences, natural, supernatural, and made the body of man a sound implement, and plastic clay in the fingers of the pure, intelligent soul, and told the secret of the universe on this point of longevity? First, the patriarchs were clearly the longest livers, because they "*were nomads, passing most of their time in the open air*, were temperate, and conformed to the dictates of nature." Methuselah, of course, heads this list, attaining to upwards of 200 years, the orthodox interpretation of the "acute divine" Hensler, or to near a thousand, old style, verbal rendering. In either case he is a precious fact, and stands as the great hope of humanity. Then follow the rest of the patriarchs, in order of longevity, Jared, 962; Noah, 950; Adam, 930; Seth, 912; Cainan, 910; Enos, 905; Lamech, 777, etc. etc.

Very nearly approaching the ages of these men of centuries, interpreted as already stated, profane history has many records of longevity with interesting examples.

The following table has striking points, not only in long life, but as representing a variety of types of the different bloods or races, showing that long life is not a *characteristic* of *any* one original *race* or compound race:—

Table of Longevity of Mr. Easton, Salisbury, England.

	A.D.		
Appolonius, of Tyana, died in	99	aged	130
St. Patrick died in	491	"	122
Attila* died in	500	"	124
Leywarch Hêw died in	500	"	150
St. Coemgene died in	618	"	120
Piastus, King of Poland, died in	861	"	120
Thomas Parr died in	1635	"	152
Henry Jenkins died in	1670	"	169
Countess of Desmond died in	1612	"	145
Thomas Damme died in	1648	"	154
Peter Torton died in	1724	"	185
Margaret Patters died in	1738	"	137
John Rovin and wife died in	1741	"	172 and 164
St. Mougah, or Kentigern, died in	1781	"	185

Coming down to the time of courts and post-mortems, we find the testimony is pointed on one side, that is, the order of men who lived the longest, and reasons why. Henry Jenkins lived to the age of 169 years, "as proved by the registers of Chancery and other courts where he had appeared as an evidence," etc. He was a fisherman, and consequently passed most of his life in the open air in the exercise of the Waltonian art. He was a close observer of nature, and no doubt learned from the fishes the art of swimming well, for "when above 100 years old he was *able* to *swim across rapid rivers.*"

Thomas Parr, we have seen, lived to be 152 years and nine months. He died by the "accident" of overgorging his stomach, an *accident* that has killed many a younger man. Harvey's post-mortem showed him to be perfectly sound, except the gorged stomach, and from all after-death appearances he might have lived to the age of Methuselah, *i.e.* nine hundred sixty and nine years, as "his cartilages were not

* Attila succeeded his father, King of the Huns, in 434, died in 453, reigned 19 years. What Attila is the above?

ossified," and "there was not the least symptom of decay to be discovered," and his wife, a widow when he married her, and consequently a woman of knowledge and experience, testified that until his 132d year, when *she* died, "he had never betrayed any signs of infirmity or age." He was poor, and "maintained himself by daily labor," being "accustomed to *thrash*," and continued to work to the last.

Draakenberg was a "*seaman*," and "spent fifteen years as a slave in Turkey." This sailor was a powerful man, and had the grit in his 130th year to "fall in love with a young country girl," who was foolish enough to reject his proposals. "He tried his fortune *with several others*, but had no better success." This boy of near a century and a half had come in contact with the world, as slave and sailor, and carried the fires of love freshly in his heart till near 150, as his death occurred in his 146th year.

Effingham died in his 144th year. He was born poor, and brought up to *labor* from infancy. He was "soldier and corporal," and present at many battles, but "was a day-laborer till his death."

Stender was 103 at his death. "He was a *day-laborer till his death, drank seldom*, his food for most part being oatmeal and buttermilk," and "his chief dependence always was in the goodness of God." The list of these ancient men is quite extensive, and their habits of life, original organization, or blood and bone stock, but especially the causes of their longevity, as shown by their modes of existence, are subjects of great interest to the student of man.

From a critical reading of this hopeful record, we discover that the physical conditions necessary to extreme longevity are an absolute contact with the earth,—*i.e.*, sane, rational, physical bond with nature; that long life is only attainable by man's becoming a *sound conduit* of the perpetually rejuvenizing forces of the world, and that bodily labor, existence in the open air, as of nomads, or wandering shepherds, hunters, and fishermen, soldiers and sailors, farmers, gardeners, day-laborers, and the habits of all who

ANTAEUS THE GIANT. 599

lead a "*simple life agreeable to nature*," are the true powers of physical regeneration, prevention, cure of and exemption from disease. Man, in sound contact with the earth, seems to be the great problem solved of a long, healthy, and happy life. So much from the *material* and *earthy side* of the question, and the giant of Libya is the Earth-son, a mighty wrestler, as long as his body is a prime-conductor of the recuperative forces of the earth. But he was a son also of Poseidon, the "god of the Mediterranean Sea," who was also "the god of the fluid element of the world." Of this divinity, Heroditus (ii. 50; iv. 188) states "that the name and worship of Poseidon was imported to the Greeks from Libya, but he was probably a divinity of Pelasgian origin, and originally a personification of the *fertilizing power of water*, from which the transition to regarding him as the god of the sea was not difficult." "His palace was in the depth of the sea, near Aegae in Euboea, (xiii. 21; Od., v. 381,) where he kept his horses with brazen hoofs and golden manes. With these horses he rides in a chariot over the waves of the sea, which become smooth as he approaches, and the monsters of the deep recognize him and play around his chariot. He was further regarded as the *creator of the horse*, [symbol of genius,] and was accordingly believed to have taught men the art of managing horses by the bridle, and to have been the originator and protector of horse races."

Poseidon, the "god of the fluid element," the creator of the horse, thus stands the mythical representative of genius and virtue. The horse in all symbolisms represents the *intellectual principle*, genius,* power, force of thought, and thus his achievements herald the triumphs of the mind. But water (fluid element) is the great "fertilizer," great cleanser, *washer*, *baptizer*, and hence, is the symbol of *virtue* and regeneration,†

* The horse signifies genius; the ass, stupidity; the mule, (a doleful cross between them, cursed with barrenness,) common sense.

† Water signifies the spiritual things of faith. A.C. 680. To give water (Gen. xiii. 24) signifies the common influx of truth; such influx is the illumination which gives the faculty of apperceiving and un-

and so is revealed the perfection of this beautiful myth. The "sacrifices of Poseidon were the bridled horse, wild boars, and rams, white and black bulls." Antaeus, the son of Poseidon, we thus discover, also represents the side of spirit, (the soul,) as from his mother, the earth, he represents *matter*, (the body,) and thus represents thee, "oh rich and varied man!" What have we, then, on the side of *spirit*, from this son of the earth—what has the fable to say on the influences *from above?*

Physicians and philosophers, physiologists and moralists, have, from the most ancient times, been earnest and eloquent in announcing virtue and happiness inseparable, vice and misery constant companions; "golden rules of health," temperance and rectitude; mode of attaining a long life, exercise or work, moderation in all the appetites, and a life in conformity to both man's higher and lower nature. All this is simple as the air we breathe; simple as the water we drink; simple as the sleep that bathes us in its life-renewing trance. Charming is the discovery of the unity of thought, the oneness of conviction on this subject, all adjusted by the finest spiritual gravitation; and Moses and Hippocrates, Socrates and Sydenham, Plato and Hunter, Bacon and Boerhaave, Cornaro and Hufeland, shout the same song, that *physical regeneration is only possible* through temperance and virtue, that absolute rectitude is a certain and invaluable preventive of disease, and that man's life may be much sounder, happier, and longer. Witness their recorded words, many of them embalmed in everlasting sweetness.*

derstanding truth; this illumination is from the light of heaven, which is from the Lord, which light is no other than the divine truth. A.C. 5668.

* Especially is the crowing of the juvenile chanticleer, Ludovico Cornaro, at 100 years, beautiful, brave, and refreshing. He was a Venetian of a patrician family, which gave the republic three doges, besides some females, poetical and learned. He was a dissipated man till he was 40 years old, and, from some accounts, lived to be 104, others giving only 90 years for his life. When near 100, Cornaro composed his celebrated song to sobriety, or a treatise on the "sure and certain

Thus, from both worlds, represented in the elements of the mournfully-ruined and crushed members of the mangled giant, from natural, from supernatural, come the stern

methods of attaining a long and healthy life." In this little treatise we are presented with an ecstatic series of encomiums, or half lyrical jubilations, or hymns, to his golden panacea for all sorrow, infirmity, and disease of humanity, his formula of elements being, that earthly soundness, contentment and happiness, and a long life, are only attainable through *a rigid adherance to the laws of temperance, sobriety*, exercise, and the cultivation of the household virtues of good temper, regular hours, cheerful spirits, including sentiment and music. Hear an apostrophe of the venerable youth of 100 in a moment of exhilaration:—

"O holy, happy, and thrice blessed temperance! how worthy art thou of our highest esteem! and how infinitely art thou preferable to an irregular and disorderly life! Nay, would men but consider the effects and consequences of both, they would immediately see that there is as wide a difference between them as there is betwixt light and darkness, heaven and hell."

Again, the pious old disciple of the doctrine of physical regeneration through personal holiness and cleanness alone, proceeds:—

"But from these two evils, (sickness and death,) so dreadful to many, blessed be God, I have but little to fear; for, as for *death*, I have a joyful hope that that change, come when it may, will be gloriously for the *better;* and besides, I trust that He, whose divine voice I have so long obeyed, will graciously support and comfort his aged servant in that trying hour. And as for *sickness*, I feel but little apprehension on that account, since by my divine medicine TEMPERANCE, I have removed all the causes of illness; so that I am pretty sure I shall never be sick, except it be from some intent of Divine mercy, and then I hope I shall bear it without a murmur, and find it for my good. Nay, I have reason to think that my soul has so agreeable a dwelling in my body, finding nothing in it but peace and harmony between my reason and senses, that she is very well pleased with her present situation; so that I trust I have still a great many years to live in health and spirits, and enjoy this beautiful world, which is indeed beautiful to those who know how to make it so, as I have done, and likewise expect (with God's assistance) to be able to do in the next.

"Now, since a regular life is so happy, and its blessings so permanent and great, all I have still left to do (since I cannot accomplish my wishes by force) is to beseech every man of sound under-

edicts of physical despotisms and moral laws, and the voice of mercy still pleads: "repent ye, and surely there is a kingdom of heaven at hand," for there is no soundness of body without soundness of soul, and no soundness of soul without soundness of body.

Sin, weariness of being, disease and death, have thousands of doors to enter humanity: on the side of the body, on the side of the soul, obscure gateways of the body, sublime portals of the soul. Long has the prodigal wandered from home, long has he blundered and deeply fallen, but his pathway through swine husks and suffering becomes brighter, and his return to realms of peace and love is sure, for sound-

standing to embrace, with open arms, this most valuable treasure of a long and healthy life: a treasure which, as it far exceeds all the riches of this world, so it deserves above all things to be diligently sought after and carefully preserved. This is that divine sobriety so agreeable to the Deity, the friend of nature, the daughter of reason, and the sister of all the virtues. From her, as from their proper root, spring life, health, cheerfulness, industry, learning, and all those employments worthy of noble and generous minds. Excess, intemperance, superfluous humors, fevers, pains, gouts, dropsies, consumptions, and the dangers of death, vanish in her presence, like clouds before the sun. She is the best friend and safest guardian of life, as well of the rich as of the poor; of the male as of the female sex; the old as of the young. She teaches the rich modesty; the poor frugality; men continence; women chastity; the old how to ward off the attacks of death; and bestows on youth firmer and securer hopes of life. She preserves the senses clear, the body light, the understanding lively, the soul brisk, the memory tenacious, our motions free, and all our faculties in a pleasing and agreeable harmony.

"O most innocent and divine sobriety! the sole refreshment of nature, the nursing mother of life, the true physic of soul as well as of body. How ought men to praise thee for thy princely gifts, for thy incomparable blessings! But as no man is able to write a sufficient panegyric on this rare and excellent virtue, I shall put an end to this discourse, lest I should be charged with excess in dwelling so long on so pleasing a subject. Yet, as numberless things may still be said of it, I leave off, with an intention to set forth the rest of its praises at a more convenient opportunity."

ness of both body and soul *is the indefeasible birthright of his being*, and cannot be stolen from him by hollow delusions of sin. All has been heralded by the sublimity of the laws of his genesis; all foretold by the grandeur of his *birth*. The perfected splendor of material nature, the production of his body alone, seems to have exhausted antecedent worlds; and when the celestial flames of an immortal spirit burned upon the humble altar of his clay, and thought, love, conscienciousness, devotion, and truth were added to the miracle of organization, and the cell was arrayed with the halo of strength and the spells of beauty, the end had surely come, "and God saw everything that he had made, and behold, *it was* very good."

"The first creation of the organic took place where the first mountain summits projected out of the water; and thus, indeed, without doubt, in India, (?) if the Himalaya* be the highest mountain.

"The first organic forms, whether plant or animal, emerged from the shallow parts of the sea.

"It is possible that man has only originated on one spot, and that indeed on the highest mountain.

"It is even possible, that only one favorable moment was granted, in which men could arise.

"The first men were the littoral and mountainous inhabitants of warmer countries, and found, therefore, at once, reptiles, fishes, fruit, and game, for food."†

In the scientific genealogy of things, the mountainous summits must have been the *first shores* in the universal waters, and consequently the first organic life-theatres, and this because the sun first kissed, dawn first bathed, the mountain heights, (poetical, divine genesis of life!)‡ and the imponderable broke the deep slumber of the ponderable,

* Dwalagiri, 28,000 feet; Kunchinginga, 28,173 feet.

† Organogeny, L. O.

‡ The æther imparts the substance, the heat the form, the *light* the *life*. (Oken first started this opinion in his work, "Die Zeugung," Frankfurt, Wesche, 1805.)

galvanism* and the rock being the first victims of an erotic trance, and the "Goddess of Love arose from ocean's foam." Mountains are still the shores of the ocean of *true* life,† the life of body and soul; for the sun must still first kiss their summits, the dawn must bathe them with her first golden beams, and the beatitude of being, the truest and purest raptures of consciousness, there spring in the immortal freshness and beauty of Venus rising from that rosy sea.

Lo! for the son of man there is hope in the return to perennial fountains of vitality; he may share the undying youth of Nature by placing himself, an immortal babe, with humility and faith, in contact with his mother's bosom, and thus, by temperance and rectitude, virtue and holiness, commune again in love and worship with God and the universe.

This is the coming day, the morn of health and life for the body; this is also the coming day of true life for the soul, when, throned on ocean's wave, *her "dawn* is also blushing o'er the world."

---

* "Galvanism is the principle of life. There is no other vital force than the galvanic polarity. The heterogeneity of the three terrestrial elements in a circumscribed individual body is the *vital force*. The galvanic process is one with the vital process. Electrism has a basis; it is the air. Magnetism has a basis; it is the metal. Chemism has a basis; it is the salt. So has galvanism a basis; it is the *organic mass*."—BIOLOGY, L. O.

† Large extents of the earth's surface are still covered by the malarial sea for many months of the year. The mountains, in these regions of "bad air," often stretch up through and above the surface of this sea, and are the only places of safety for the inhabitants of the valleys at their bases. To a certain degree of N. latitude, the Atlantic Plain and Interior Valley of North America are vast gulfs of this ocean of malaria, and the mountains bounding them, *i.e.* the Appalachian and Rocky chains, where their summits extend above the plains or surfaces of these poisoned gulfs, are the natural and only places of refuge for the inhabitants of that plain and valley. Thus are mountains not only poetically and philosophically, but literally (littorally) and scientifically, the true shores of the ocean of life.

ANTAEUS THE GIANT.

(NOTE TO PAGE 590, AT *)

The following list embraces a few distinguished names of medical philosophers who have attained an advanced age:—

Boerhaave	70
Haller	70
Tissot	70
Gall	71
Darwin	72
Van Swieten	72
Fallopius	72
Jenner	75
Heister	75
Cullen	78
Galen	79
Spallanzani	79
Harvey	81
Mead	81
Duhamel	82
Astruc	83
Hoffman	83
Pinel	84
Swedenborg	85
Morgagni	89
Heberden	92
Ruysch	93
Hippocrates	109

ERASMUS WILSON.

PAN A SYMBOL OF THE UNIVERSE.

PAN, (Πᾶν,) the great god of flocks and shepherds among the Greeks; his name is probably connected with the verb πάω, Lat. pasco, (to feed,) so that his name and character are perfectly in accordance with each other. There are later speculations, according to which Pan is the same as τὸ πᾶν, or the universe, and the god the symbol of the universe. He is described as a son of Hermes, by the daughter of Dryops, (Hom. Hymn., vii. 34,) or as the son of Hermes, by Penelope. Some, again, call him the son of Aether and Oeneis, or a Nereid, or a son of Uranus and Ge. From his being a grandson or great grandson of Cronos, he is called χρόνιος. (Eurip. Rhes. 36.) *He was, from his birth, perfectly developed, and had the same appearance as afterwards*—that is, he had his horns, beard, puck nose, tail, goat's feet, and was covered with hair, so that his mother ran away with fear when she saw him; but Hermes carried him into Olympus, where all (πάντες) the gods were delighted with him, and especially Dionysus. (Hom. Hymn., vii. 36, etc., comp. sil. Ital., xiii. 332; Lucian, Dial. Deor 22.) He was brought up by nymphs. (Paus., viii. 30, § 2.) The principal seat of his worship was Arcadia, and from thence it spread over other parts of Greece. In Arcadia he was the god of forests, pastures, flocks, shepherds, and huntsmen, dwelling in grottoes, and wandering on the summits of mountains and rocks. As the god of everything connected with pastoral life, he was fond of music, and invented the shepherd's flute. He was possessed of prophetic powers, and instructed Apollo in this art. Fir trees were sacred to him; and the sacrifices offered to him consisted of cows, rams, lambs, milk, and honey. (Theocrit., v. 58; Anthol. Palat., ii. 630, 697, vi. 96, 239, vii. 59.)—*Greek and Roman Mythology.* L. S.

The fame of Democritus in modern times rests on his extraordinary prevision of the *Atomic*, or modern physical theory of the *Universe*. Rising above the confined idea of the Ionian school, that all things are modifications of one element or principle, he broached the conception that bodies are made up of *ultimate atoms*, and that in the *character* of these *atoms* must be sought the explanation of the *qualities* of what we call *body*. He went off at once from all barren lagomachies about the *Plenum*, and, indeed, *more* than any other thinker of antiquity, achieved the privilege of laying down the ground of just speculation in physics. His doctrines prevailed widely, and were afterwards enshrined in noble verse by Lucretius. Democritus was certainly a materialist: the *mind*, he thought, *like fire*, consisted of *finer atoms*. He had *no notion of life apart from the body;* and the gods he deemed delusion. He had grand views of the universe. In the milky way, first of *all*, he saw the light of innumerable worlds; but he had a correspondingly mean opinion of the nature and destiny of *Man*. Nay, he treated Man, his evanescent works, and feeble struggles, so lightly, that we find his effigies always with a jeer on the lip, and himself with the appellation of the *laughing philosopher*. Democritus is not the only thinker who, in the intensity of his contemplation of material nature, has overlooked a *Force* infinitely more enduring and grand.

The loss of his writings is that, perhaps, among all calamities to ancient monuments, which we ought most to deplore. The titles of his works relate to Logic, Ethics, Physics, Mathematics, Astronomy, Medicine, Poetry, Music, Grammar, and even Strategy. Cicero tells us, that in style Democritus might be the rival of Plato—he wrote so clearly, and so adorned what he wrote. During his youth and manhood he traveled through India, Ethiopia, Chaldæa, and Persia; spent several years in Egypt, and seems to have visited the schools of Pythagoras and Zeno. It is said also that he heard Socrates, and communed with Anaxagoras concerning the phenomena of Astronomy and the physical structure of Nature.

J. P. N.
Cyc. of Biog.

Democritus (*Δημόκριτος*) was a native of Abdera, in Thrace. His birth was fixed by Appolodorus 460 years before Christ. He spent a great inheritance in traveling over the world, to satisfy his extraordinary thirst for knowledge. He visited all the distinguished men of science of the times, and his wealth enabled him to purchase the works they had written. His investigations embraced all departments of human knowledge, especially such as related to *natural history*. He excelled, in the extent of his knowledge, all the earlier Greek philosophers, among whom Leucippus, the founder of the atomic theory, is said to have had the greatest influence upon his philosophical studies. It is said that he was on terms of friendship with Hippocrates, and some writers even speak of a correspondence between Democritus and Hippocrates. He was a contemporary of Plato, and may have been acquainted with Socrates, and Plato also, although Plato does not mention him. Aristotle describes him and his views as belonging to the ante-Socratic period; but modern scholars, such as the learned Dutchman, Groen van Prinsterer, assert, that there are symptoms in Plato which show a connection with Democritus; and the same scholar pretends to discover in Plato's language and style an imitation of Democritus. (Persop. Plat. p. 42.) Many anecdotes about Democritus are preserved, especially in Diogenes Laërtius, showing that he was a man of the most sterling and honorable character. His diligence was incredible: he lived exclusively for his studies, and his disinterestedness, modesty, and simplicity are attested by many features which are related of him. Notwithstanding his great property, he seems to have died in poverty, though highly esteemed by his fellow-citizens, not so much on account of his philosophy as because, as Diogenes says, "he had foretold them some things which the event proved to be true." This had probably reference to his knowledge of natural phenomena. His fellow-citizens honored him with presents in money and bronze statues. Even the scoffer Timon, who, in all his silli, spared no one, speaks of Democritus only in praise. He died at an advanced age, (some say that he was 109 years old,) and even the manner in which he died is characteristic of his medical knowledge, which, combined as it was with his knowledge of nature, caused a report, which some persons believed, that he was a sorcerer and a magician. (Plin. H. N., xxiv. 17, xxx. 1.) His death is placed in Ol. 105.4, or B.C. 357, in which year Hippocrates also is said to have died. (Clinton, F. H., ad ann. 357.) There was a tradition that he had deprived himself of his sight to be less disturbed in his pursuits, an invention of a later age, which was fond of piquant anecdotes. He probably lost his sight by severe study. This loss did not disturb the cheerful disposition of his mind and his views of human life, which was to look at the cheerful, comical side of things, which *later* writers took to mean that he always laughed at the follies of men. (Senec. de Ira., ii. 10; Aelian, V. H., iv. 20.) His knowledge was universal, from mathematics and natural science to philosophy and poetry. Aristotle wrote a work on his problems, and Cicero praised his works for poetic beauties and liveliness of style, comparing them with the *works of Plato*. Unfortunately, his works have not come down to us, or only in fragments considered spurious. He carried out Leucippus's theory of atoms, especially in his observation on nature. [For explanations of this theory, see Adolph Stahr's account of Democritus, in *Greek and Roman Mythology*, from which these notices are excerpted, exhibiting the first dawn of the theory of atoms, or obscure gropings of the mind, which ultimated, now stand the sublime formulæ of science.] In his ethical philosophy, Democritus considered the acquisition of peace of mind the end and ultimate object of our actions. (Diog. Laërt., ix. 45; Cic. de Fin., v. 29.) This peace, this tranquillity of mind, and freedom from fear and passion, is the last and fairest fruit of philosophical inquiry. The noblest and purest ethical tendency is manifested in his views on virtue and on good. Truly pious, and beloved by the gods, he says, are only those who hate that which is wrong. The purest joy and the truest happiness are only the fruit of the higher mental activity exerted in the endeavor to understand the nature of things, of the peace of mind arising from good actions, and of a clear conscience.

The titles of the works which the ancients ascribe to Democritus may be found in Diogenes Laërtius. [They almost form a system of Pantology.] A. S.

Greek and Roman Myth. and Biog.

Cuvier believed it his duty to call Democritus the first Comparative Anatomist.—*Hist. des Sciences Naturelle*, p. 103.

There are only two kinds of generation in the world—the creation proper, and the propagation that is sequent thereupon, or the *generatio originaria* and *secundaria*.

No organism has been consequently created of larger size than an infusorial point. No organism is, nor has one ever been, created, which is not microscopic.

Whatever is larger, has not been created, but developed.

Man has not been created, but developed. So the Bible itself teaches us. God did not make man out of nothing; but took an elemental body then existing, an earth-clod, or carbon; moulded it into form, thus making use of water; and breathed into it life, namely, air, whereby galvanism, or the vital process, arose.— *Organogeny*.

L. O.

"Animals are only the persistent fœtal stages or conditions of man. Malformations are only persistent fœtal conditions, or animal formations in individual animal bodies. *Diseases are vital processes* in *animals*. *Pathology* is the *physiology* of the *animal kingdom*. A human fœtus is a whole animal kingdom." Death is only a continuous growth through *retrogression* into the organic primary matter or *Infusoria*. Death is an organized decomposition. Decomposition is a forming of seeds, ova, and fœtuses. Dying is a multiplication of *self*. No individual organism is eternal, because it is only a changing pole of the world-organism. There is no constancy in the individualities; change only is *persistent*. Death is no annihilation, but only change. One individual emerges out of another. Death is only a transition to *another life*, not unto death.—*Biology*.

L. O.

Rejuvenescence appears, in the first place, as a return to an earlier condition of life, whereby is obtained a point of departure for renewed progress; or, in the extreme case, as a retrogression to the commencement of the entire course of development, to attain the aim in a repetition of the development.

Inquiring into the causes of the phenomena of Rejuvenescence, we recognize that external Nature, amid which special life displays itself, acts in calling and awakening through the influences which the seasons of the year, nay, even the hours of the day, bring forth; but the proper internal cause can only be found in the tendency toward completion, which is present in every existence according to its kind, and drives it to subordinate to itself ever more completely the foreign and external world, to shape itself within it as independently as the specific Nature allows.

The mind which becomes developed in Man is not fitted together, with the physical organism, *from without,* for we behold its evolution indicated in the *lower stages of natural life,* especially in the *animal kingdom;* the spiritual life is rather the purest and most refined representative of the fundamental life, which we meet as natural life in the preceding stages. We may say of Mind, that it is the *youngest,* and yet the *oldest,* existence in nature, destined to attain, in its last age, its *eternal youth,* the *freedom fittest to its essential nature.* Rising from the groundwork of Nature bearing and supporting them, the spiritual Rejuvenescences in the history of Man strive toward this aim of internal vital emancipation, driving the mind out of every senility, every fetter of time, to soar upward in a new flight of life.

Nature points to Man from step to step, ever more distinctly throughout her entire series; and Man again cannot be considered without that which itself constitutes his humanity, the development of *Mind.* The development of Mind cannot be separated from its substratum, *Nature,* since although Mind itself is destined to rise victorious over all the obstructions of physical life, it must also penetrate backward through all the stages of that life, and give them a spiritual signification. Only by starting from this standing-point, fixing the aim of the entire development in Nature, can we find the true internal connection of all the gradations of natural life; and by the very conjunction with the course of development of Man, Natural History acquires its highest import. Nature, without man, presents externally the image of a labyrinth without a clue. The aim to which the infinite Rejuvenescences throughout all Nature strive, is the progressive development of the Human Race.

DR. ALEXANDER BRAUN.

The cell is, therefore, the IMMEDIATE FOCUS of REJUVENESCENCE, the POINT from whence come all the phenomena of Rejuvenescence in the building up of the articulated (or complex) organism of the plant.

Thus have we completed our design of subjecting to minute inspection, in the example of the development of the Vegetable Organism, the phenomenon of Rejuvenescence, a phenomenon profoundly connected with the essence of natural life, and lying at the base of all progressive movement of life and development, with its multifariously complicated ascending and descending vibrations, in the largest as in the smallest circle of Nature, *since this movement is sustained in every case only by renovation.*

Is it not here again the recollection of the original destination of created life, which carries up step by step the development of nature, from the first stirrings of life, through infinitely numerous links of Rejuvenescence, to the appearance of Man? Finally, is it not this which impels even humanity to rejuvenize itself from race to race in even more deeply-searching recollection of its high purpose, comprehending that of all Nature, and connecting it with the Eternal Source whence all internal Law and Force of Life derive their origin?

BRAUN.

CHAPTER II.

PAN A SYMBOL OF THE UNIVERSE.

"The true recognition of the organism of Nature and its composition of members or links, as objective facts expressed by Nature itself, is essentially necessary to the higher shaping of Natural History as a unit."

THE atomic theory of Leucippus, elaborated by Democritus twenty-three hundred years ago, and its connection with modern science, or the theories of atoms or scientific minima, which now prevail, do not demand a critical or minute analysis here. As it is impossible for the rational intelligence to conceive of an *accident, the apparent coincidence* of the doctrine of antiquity—that "bodies are made of ultimate atoms, and that in the character of these atoms must be sought the explanation of the qualities of what we call body,"—with the present announcement of the microscope, that "no organism has been created of larger size than an infusorial point;" and that "no organism is, nor has one ever been created, which is not microscopic;" and that the "organism of nature and its composition, of members or links, as objective facts expressed by nature itself, is essentially necessary to the higher shaping of natural history as a unit,"—will appear as the revelation of a sublime law of the intellect, its prophetic instincts, and patient searching, under the dread powers which preside over the worlds of matter and mind.

What has the Understanding, in its efforts to solve the mystery of creation, and climb the ladder between the finite and infinite, done, but tramp in ceaseless iteration upon the steps of the majestic treadmill of a system of grand but identical propositions? For more than two thousand years it appears upon the record, that the mind of man has been after the molecule of matter; and although the *last* step has not been taken, the *last* question answered,* or the *last* analysis executed, still, what wondrous strides have been made on the trail of the atom, from Leucippus to Malpighi and Dalton, and from Democritus to Leuwenhœck, Hook, Grew, Ehrenberg, Schawn, Kutzing, and Schleiden, what a world has sprung into existence! Had not that ancient philosopher, (Democritus,) who said that "he preferred the discovery of a *true cause* to the possession of the kingdom of Persia," a worthy successor and fruit of the centuries, in the genius of the youthful Rector† of Kendal school, (Dalton,) who preferred the unambitious labor of teaching mathematics at Manchester, and the discovery of the atomic theory of chemistry, to the throne possibly of a bishopric of England.

Gifted and profound souls herald and announce gifted and profound souls, through the desert wastes of long hundreds of years, with an understanding that seems the identity of inspiration; and although there is a vast difference between the story of the primeval atom of the ancient philosophers and the modern atom of chemistry, or the doctrine of definite

---

* "The origin of the cell is by no means yet quite clearly made out; only this much is certain, that a peculiar little body appertaining to the primordial utricle, and called the cell-nucleus, plays a very important part in it."—*Structure of Plants.* M. J. SCHLEIDEN, Prof. of Botany to the University of Jena.

† Dalton succeeded to the Rectorship of a school at Kendal in his nineteenth year, and, after remaining there for eight years, retired to Manchester, and preferred leading the "unobtrusive life of a scientific member of the Society of Friends," and advancing the world by one of the most splendid discoveries of science, to advancing *himself* in a worldly point of view, although a gold medal by the Royal Society and a statue by Chantrey came at last.

proportions, and the cytoblast and vesicle of the modern animal and vegetable physiologist, yet there is here revealed the intellectual laws by which minds act through aboriginal necessities of spiritual beings, demonstrating that the great intuitions of the analytic and synthetic powers of the soul are held in leading strings by the unalterable logic of the plan of nature and the essential elements of the structure of things. Thus grow the spiritual edifices of man by an architecture whose laws are grave and sublime, grand and beautiful as the soul itself, and the plans of the temples are all arranged by antecedent mathematics or geometry of thought, and have their everlasting prototypes scored upon the tablets of the mind.

Strange is the enchantment, fatal the chain, of that remorseless basilisk atom; wonderful, but fell, is the power of despotism of that ideal minimum. Why do the most majestic seekers, the most subtile and exhaustive minds, gravitate toward this gyratory maze? Why have so many of the finest spirits incarnated, so many profoundly attuned souls, brooded in solitude and prayer over the secret of the atom, and made the terrible analysis of the ultimate monad the dream of existence, the criterion of intellectual power? Leucippus, Democritus, Kepler, Descartes,* Malpighi,† Lewenhœck, Ehrenberg, and Schleiden, have held to the ultimate exploration of the logical details of all things, knowing that *thus only* could the laws of the universe be discovered, and the last mystery solved. Can the maximum be conceived

* "Kepler and Descartes were much indebted to the ancient doctrines of these masters (Leucippus and Democritus) for the explanation of the planetary vortices. Bacon remarked that Democritus and Leucippus were so much taken up with the *particles* of things, as to forget or neglect their structure." Very stupid in Bacon, who could not construct the "Organon" without the same science of analysis, laws of necessary induction, and logical relations of all structures in the "method" of nature.

† "Malpighi had early in life learned the necessity of making experiment the foundation of true philosophy, and was the *first* to use the microscope in anatomical observations." W. B.

without the minimum? Give us the minimum, and we will project for you the maximum. So have they meditated through laborious lives, so have they struggled through solitary and desolate worlds, and thus have they stoutly battled with stern reasoning through brave analyses, from the chaos of necessary initial logomachies of the "quantitative or qualitative relations,"—"primary, secondary, or infinite number of particles, homogeneous in quality, heterogeneous in form,"—"necessary reality of vacuum or space and motion;" that "all phenomena arise from the infinite variety of form, order, and position of the atom in forming combinations," "motion being the eternal necessary consequence of the original variety of atoms in the vacuum or space, *the atom being impenetrable*," until they have emerged into the clear sunlight of inductive science; that nature consists of minima; that the crystal and the globe are but masses of atoms; and that all organized bodies are cells or organic points; that the protococcus floating through the heavens and falling with the rain or snow, and the stately elephant and ponderous whale are but magical representations of that strange atom, the protoplastic cell,* held under the

* For interesting information with regard to an order of wonders far outstripping the powers of the imagination, and suggesting matter for profound reflection concerning the ultimate structure of organic bodies, made through the discovery of the microscope by modern naturalists, see the following dissertations:—

Reflections on the Phenomenon of Rejuvenescence in Nature, Especially in the Life and Development of Plants. By Dr. Alexander Braun, Professor of Botany in the University of Berlin. Leipsic, 1851. Translated by Arthur Henfrey.

Animal Nature of Diatomeæ: with an Organographical Revision of the Genera Established by Kützing. By Professor G. Meneghini. Translated from the original Italian edition. Venice, 1845.

On the Natural History of Protococcus Pluvialis. By Ferdinand Cohn. (Abstracted from the "Nova Acta Acad. Caes. Leop. Carolin. Naturæ Curios. Bonn.," tome 22, pp. 605–764; 1850.) By George Busk, F.R.S.

Reports and Papers on Botany, consisting of—I. Mohl on the Structure of the Palm-stem. II. Nägeli on Vegetable-cells. III. Nä-

yoke of the stern, absolute law, that "no organism is, nor has one ever been, created, which is not microscopic;" that "whatever is larger has not been created, but developed;" that the "first organic points are vesicles;" that "the whole world of organic forms originates from infusoria." To Descartes, the starry spaces of ether were vortices in which whirled the molecules of powdered fire, called planetary and sidereal systems, suns, and worlds, and thus must be developed the "mechanical theory of planetary motion," and the "architecture of the heavens." To the genius of Cuvier, "life is a vortex, into which individual molecules are continually entering, and from which they are continually departing;" and thus must arrive the theory of cell-formation and the doctrine of "utricles." Fatal, beautiful, divine despotism! and so at last it is demonstrated that no organism has been or *can be* created, which is not microscopic; that the whole organic world originates from infusoria; and that throughout the realms of vitality the first organic is a point, a vesicle.

Strange is this whirl and flow, strange this vibration and libration of the cell! Life is a perpetual wonder, a constant miracle, an eternal becoming and ceasing, a wasting by decomposing powers, a reproduction by recomposing forces— fresh arrivals from all the kingdoms of nature, with as constant surrender of exhausted particles again passing away under the irresistible affinities of chemistry and the quick and nimble

geli on the Utricular Structures in the Contents of Cells. IV. Link's Report on Physiological Botany for 1844–45.—*Ray Society*.

The British Desmidieæ. By John Ralfs. The drawings by Edward Jenner.

Manual of British Algæ. Harvey.

British Diatomaceæ. Smith.

Berkley's Cryptogamic Botany.

Also, Queckett on the Microscope, and the works of the animal and vegetable physiologists generally. "Hither has the whole new direction of science turned, and names like Robert Brown, Brisseau, Mirbel, Amici, and Mohl mark the commencement of a new and richly-blessed epoch."

forces of plastic vitality. This is the tragic dance of the inorganic assuming organic, and side by side move animation and exhaustion, activity and corruption, quickness and death. Thus is never-ceasing change written on every form—"Naught may endure but mutability." An invisible influx of atoms, with a synchronous efflux of atoms, and the solidest creature with life stands a phenomenon as evanescent as a changing cloud, as unreal as a vanishing shadow. What is it? A momentary grasp of the outward, fleeting as a vision, an instantaneous appropriation by assimilation under chemical and vital forces in a specific form, with definite organic attributes—matter in the trance and exaltation of life— then comes a change: the momentary grasp relaxed, the ghastly transfiguration arrives, and death, the most inexorable despot holds, in a stillness that seems everlasting, the form of light and life. But this ghastly corpse, this sacred dust, is also a quickly rushing shadow; for nature, with a never-intermitting parsimony, makes demand of the loaned particle, whether it has been circulating in the lip of beauty or the ragged ulcer, and by a relentless requisition breaks the sequestration which once appeared to be endless, but now, by dissolution, gives new life and motion. This payment and separation must be made, and the required atom returned again to the grand reservoir of consumed, exhausted, or effete matter, either through secretion, excretion, or death. And this phantasmal whirl goes on and on; each organ of the complex organisms seizes on its prey, makes its substance and use in the divine arrestation of whizzing currents, and the equipoise called life, exists; but the used particle must again be thrown broadcast to the elements—and so this endless circulation goes on. Wonderful organ! still more wonderful function! from low excretion, offensive and revolting, to high revelation of thought and spirit, or sacred attributes of love and affection!! Wonderful organ! wonderful function! still more wonderful essence behind the organ, artificer of the organ, creator of the function, which scalpel cannot find, which microscope looks for in vain!! Is the organ a prophet? and are his mechanism and life secrets of God? The great functions and metamorphoses of nature stand surrounded by halos of sacred mystery, aureolas of divine awe.

"Child, youth, and man, caterpillar, chrysalis, and butterfly, are not to be *conceived* from *external appearance*, but only in consequence of their *immaterial essence*, as *one* and the *same being.*" Natural history—supernatural history—the atom, the soul, stand mysteries incomprehensible, miracles divine. Of the natural history of the soul, what do we know? Nothing. Of the supernatural history of the atom, what do we know? Nothing. Through dark vortices silently glides the atom, brave servitor of the Eternal—while aloft, on wings of celestial beauty, soars the soul, high minister of his imperial will, bright child of his holy love.

But there is a tragic attitude of the atom and the soul. What is disease? What is infirmity? What are care and sorrow? Especially, what is pain? What is physical anguish? What is death?

The philosophers plainly show that the "first organic points are vesicles;" that the organic world has for its basis "an infinity of vesicles;" and that the "organic fundamental substance consists of infusoria;" so must the "whole organic world originate from infusoria." "Plants and animals can only be metamorphoses of infusoria." In the presence of this dread monad, this "organic fundamental," this salient point of vitality, this vesicle, this protean "cell," this protoplastic (germ) substance, which is the origin and basis of all organic forms, the philosopher of life, of organization, of health and disease, stands. Leaving to the mere abstractionist the problems of vitality, the physician asks: What is health? What is disease? What are the sciences of physiology and pathology? Is it normal cell formation, or *abnormal protoplastic* substance; the elements perverted, or specifically distinct? Here is this fearful tubercle, this hideous cancer—here is a loathsome monstrosity of form, a malignant degeneration of tissue, and what is this turgid, burning rock of pained and perishing fibres, this slow and corrosive wasting of finely-organized transparent membranes—what is this terrible withering and wilting, this shrinking down to revolting skin and skeleton, this irresistible marasmus, this ghastly consumption?

Leaving out of consideration all the splendid circles of healthy life, where the majestic wheels turn in silence and the endless gyration of organic vortices goes on in harmonious stillness, and the cell, with mute but resistless impetus, wanders through its duration rapidly, the pathologist, or philosopher of morbid vitality, turns to the jarred, dislocated, creaking, shrieking, groaning, dying molecule—the cell-abortive, malignant, fatal, venomous, belligerent, constituting the world of disease, or the suffering organization disappearing from dying cells—murdered cells—the cell arrested in development or being redissolved by the dread power of inorganic matter—the cell perverted, morbific, the cryptogamic spore of evil, (smallpox, scarlatina, hooping-cough,) the cell, the instrument of death.

What is health? what is disease? ask the ponderable, ask the imponderable. What is this heritage of joy and sweetness, also of bitterness and ashes, which has come from their vicious love-kiss—blissful results, or vengeful consummations of the fatal covenants of ancient Eros and Anteros*—"fruit of that forbidden tree whose mortal taste brought death into the world, and all our woe"?

What has the cell to do with the gloomy operations of the death-forces in the tragical processes of disease? What is its instrumentality in the category of great physico-vital

---

* "We must especially notice the connection of Eros with Anteros, with which persons usually connect the notion of "Love returned." But originally Anteros was a being opposed to Eros, and fighting against him. (Paus., i. 30, § 1; vi. 23, § 4.) This conflict, however, was also conceived as the rivalry existing between two lovers, and Anteros accordingly punished those who did not return the love of others; so that he is the *avenging Eros*, a *deus ultor*." (Paus., i. 30, § 1; Ov. Met., xiii. 750, etc.; Plat. Phœdr., p. 255, d.)

hydraulics, or specially vital lesions of circulation—forms of hyperæmia, forms of anæmia? What is the *modus operandi* in its poise and strange momentary arrestation by the nutritive function, or in lesions of nutrition, as by the irregular arrangements of anatomical elements; number of molecules—hypertrophy, atrophy, ulceration; consistence of particles—hardening, softening; nature of architectural alteration by distribution of molecules, as in transformations of cellular, serous, mucous, cutaneous, fibrous, cartilaginous, and osseous structures or tissues? What is its duty or work in the troublesome and peculiar lesions of secretion—modifications of quantity, situation, quality, essential nature? What agency has it in the terrible lesions of the blood, vitally subversive, metamorphic, poisoned, or specifically tainted by heterogeneous and vicious seeds of contagious diseases? What part does it play in the mysterious, ponderable, imponderable, galvanic, vital lesions of innervation? "Old mole of the ground!" art forever here—substance and shadow, ubiquitously present still? On the wings of the rosy morning of health, life, and joy, thou art with us, and in the anguish and despair of the midnight of disease and death thou never forsakest us.

The actor at play in this dreary domain of abnormal phenomena, called disease, is still the *cell*, under the grasp of the imponderable, for "the æther imparts the substance, the heat the form, the *light* the *life*." "The formative nutrient process is the principal process of the organic world;" but "death is only a continuous growth through retrogression into the primary matter of infusoria." An organ *tending to death* can thus only be in a stage of "continuous growth, through retrogression, into the primary matter or infusoria." Hence, in the calamitous forms of vital phenomena, which are classified as diseases, we can only be presented with the "æther the substance, the heat the form, the light the life;" and when the æther resumes the substance, and the heat surrenders the form, and the light gives up the life, it is but a *continuous growth* through the retrogression of death. Alas! that this should be through pain to the soul. Stupendous joke of nature! tyrannous law of unity!—to the eye of science there are no fixtures, no specialties, no abysses or secrets, no novelties or wonders, no high, no low, no new, no old—only *despotic law*, eternal change, everlasting motion, and *death* itself, but a "multiplication of self!!"

As this perfected instrument, this summit of nature's organic developments, the wondrous body of man, is itself but a bag of water, a sack of fluids, quivering with million vibrations, whirling with million vortices—churnings of ponderable and imponderable, flowings of organic mucus, heat, light, and galvanism—all possible conditions of that structure, from first salient point of life to retrogression into primary infusoria again, or death, *health, disease*, normal symmetry, abnormal deformity, and dissolution, can only be the tragical dance of identical ponderable and imponderable, identical inorganic, organic, and identical cell, in the tissue, the organ, the organism. But this movement and progression of the organic, "*with its multifariously complicated ascending and descending vibrations, is sustained in every case only by renovation,*" *which renovation is the phenomenon of rejuvenescence,* "*profoundly* [*inseparably!*] *connected with the essence, and lying at the base of all natural life.*" There is thus no possible rejuvenescence in nature, except that which *commences with the cell*, or the *only point* from which it is possible for any organism to exist at all. The cell is the divine focus of renovation, the cell is the sempiternal fountain of rejuvenescence. The philosophy of rejuvenescence, which is the restoration (*renovation*) of the original vitality or expansive life-power of the cell, whether arrested, defectively developed, or morbidly endowed, whether injured by disease, or exhausted by old age, is the philosophy of the venerable and thrice-blessed Art of Healing. The body of man is sick, agonized by intense morbid action, (acute disease, phlogistic destruction of important organs,) or jaded and attenuated by long-continued morbid degeneration, (wilting out by chronic disease,) and gone by excesses in every shape of wasting or effete outpouring; nervous system run down like a clock, and tottering, rickety, on the verge of dissolution by exhaustion of life in a medium whose atmosphere is fire and poisonous gases; or the sack of water* which floats the organs is impure, filled with corrupt particles—terrible crop of specific disease, sprinklings from different pools of the Stygian River, involving, as they do, all possible injuries, as lesions of circulation, lesions of nutrition, lesions of secretion, lesions of blood, and lesions of innervation, and can only be relieved through centrifugal forces by the removal of abnormal and the substitution of normal elements. By what instrumentalities does the medical philosopher propose to execute the arrestation or the elimination of disease, the prevention of destruction, or expulsion of morbific or dead molecules, and the establishment of newly-vitalized or renovated atoms? *A full catalogue* of *all* his implements of cure or assistants of nature would be an entire schedule, or résumé of the principles and resources of the science of medicine in the treatment of the whole world of acute and chronic diseases, recorded in the extensive and painfully elaborated literature of that noble profession.

The vicious states, conditions, and habitudes of organs and tissues, called chronic diseases, being in existence, and the powers of the healing art being called into requisition, the pathologist has still only the tragical play of ponderable and imponderable, the æther imparting the substance, the heat the form, the light the life, modified by time. All interference of art in these conditions is often vain, in a certain medium or habitat, from the despotism of local causes. In an extensive range of diseased conditions in particular localities, it seems indispensable, to secure a sanitary change, that all the *relations*, as far as possible, of ponderable and imponderable, be modified, and that a new heat, light, and galvanism, also new moral and æsthetic surroundings, must

* "Life and organization without *water* are inconceivable."
SCHLEIDEN.

be brought to bear upon those conditions of the organism, to insure a return to the normal state. Especially does this involve an abandonment of the predisponent and exciting causes of chronic diseases, as of vicious and artificial habits, and violation of the laws of *nature.*

Thus, from all history, all science of man, from the depths of existence, in all his relations to the world, is heard the still small voice, the pleading prayer of nature, come to *me*— come back to the golden orient of your primal union with *me*—come back to the charmed realm of original life-fountains—come back from the wallows of sin—come back from the hot-beds of the artificial life—come back to the little child's simplicity and holiness, "for of such [only] is the kingdom of heaven," of health, the paradise of rejuvenescence of the body, and to such only shall be added the perennial raptures of the normal or sound soul. The stern command from the world of pain is, also, return to nature —let new life-currents stream through the weary and sickened body—let the cell, the original, the *only focus* of renovation or germ of rejuvenescence, be bathed in a new ocean of air, washed with purer, fresher water, startled by a new galvanism, and be made quickly, freshly alive by a new polarity of vital points. Bring all *new influences* to bear upon the body in the charmed power of the country life, the only medium of organic renovation. Go to the woods and fields; go into the fresh and dewy haunts of Pan; go to the rock, the roaring forest, the flowing river; go to the dream-grotto of the poet; go to the first temples of the gods, and your dust shall be renewed by a heavenly metamorphosis, and the enchantments of health shall play through your bones. Bring also the new influence to bear upon the soul; let a new world address the mind through the avenues of the senses, as by new objects of beauty, freshness, and sweetness; let a new murmur of the leaf, and voice of bird, and water-fall, charm the ear, whispering holy dreams; let the clouds float over the eye to the music of a new melody, and a fresh world be redolent of all that breathes a newness of life, or speaks of light and of deity—then must also this magical permeation reach your spirit, and a rejuvenescence by celestial transubstantiation of the whole man be achieved, and you shall be startled into the regenerate life as deliciously as you awake from a refreshing slumber.

And does all this laying down of the burdens of weariness, this heavenly awakening and beautiful resurrection to the consciousness of the joys of the plane of a higher and renewed life, the sound mind in the sound body, this rhythmical relationship to the world, this rapturous flow of milk and honey, come from the renewed infusorial point; all from the regenerated "primordial utricle and cell-nucleus;" all these fine results and stupendous ends from such *small details* of things? "We wonder, and ask ourselves, what does 'small' mean in nature?" The world is a bundle of small details; continents and islands, hills and mountains, are made of small microscopic organic remains; and forests and coal-fields are only accumulations of small vegetable cells. "The imagination halts in the attempt to realize these masses of organic life, when we remember that a single chalk-enameled visiting card forms a zoological cabinet of, perhaps, a hundred thousand shells. As Galileo, Kepler, Newton, and Herschel introduced us into an infinite world of huge magnitudes; as Columbus, Magellan, and their successors first unfolded to us one entire half of the earth, so, in the present day, has Ehrenberg, by his untiring industry, laid open to us a wonderful world of organic life, which—small as are the individuals composing it, invisible to the keenest eye when unassisted—through the inconceivable activity of development, through the number, vast beyond expression, of single beings, heaps up masses, before which man himself seems insignificant."* The inorganic exists only as a great substratum of the organic, and in the *minute mechanism* of things, and laws of vitality, alone can be found the philosophy of the world. The sublime brain of Shakspeare was but a congeries of organic points; and the most minute animal, the *Monas termo*, is presided

* Schleiden.

over by the same law of organic necessity. This majestic
simplicity carries the soul into a region of perpetual wonder,
demanding, as "the only condition of real insight, veneration
and love." Patient labor, and assiduous devotion in effort,
to explain the smallest minutiæ of the world, present the only
pathway to the secrets of nature, or mode of realizing our
connection with her great system of ends and uses. The
vaticination of the genius of the Greek comes then as a first
inspiration of science, and the myth of Pan is the song of
the "cell.*"†.

* "Primordial utricle" of Hugo von Mohl.

† As an instance of flagrant and reckless profanity of a would-be
philosopher, and sacrilegious disregard to the religious sentiments as
organized in the worship of the Gentile world for ages, and embodied
in the wonderful mythologies of the different nations, witness the
following extract; from which it may appear well enough for an impertinent theological Philistine, ensconced in the comfortable cocoon
of modern Christianity and smartness, to talk in this manner; but
to the true philosopher, the myth is really the higher world—seen
through the glass of nature, possibly, somewhat darkly:—

"Great latitude must be allowed on the score of poetry, and the
despotism of private opinion, in rendering all classics and classical
allusion, myths and Scriptures. As to profound philosophical and
philological interpretations of the Greek or any other myths, is not a
man his own horizon? or can a man lift himself up by his own ears?
and, looking from the obscure depths of the well of his own nature,
what can he see but its walls, upon which is written inscrutable mystery; or possibly extending his vision beyond those walls, he may
discern a spot of azure or a star gleaming in still more immeasurable
depths of the infinite heavens, upon which is written everlasting incomprehensibility and wonder. As is the man, so is his reading of
all myths, symbols, scriptures, men, and gods. A wise natural guess
would probably come as near to the gist or hidden meaning of many
of the fables which have occupied the world's solemn consideration
as the thousand-and-one interpretations of the most acute mythologists. Numberless are the ways through which the Infinite communicates with the finite, and numberless are the ways which the finite
has of reading the hieroglyphics of the Infinite.

"Human scribes and interpreters are infirm, and it is supreme
folly for one man to try to think for any other man; absurd for one
man to attempt to read or *interpret* anything for another man, or for

It was surely wise and well not to neglect, or leave entirely out of the councils of Olympus, even the smallest concerns of the world, to the last details of things; the mean and vulgar (these words have no defamatory significance or meaning in the science of matter and organization, but in sentiment and morals they have,) holding as actual existence as the elegant and divine, must be represented as departments under the jurisdiction of the pantheon of the gods. The great and imposing forms of matter, their laws and relations, would naturally suggest grand and dignified deities, as kingly Zeus, (Jupiter,*) "ruler of the heavens and upper regions, and father of gods and men;" queenly and motherly goddess of the earth, Gaea or Ge, "personification of the earth;" terrible god of the ocean, Neptunus, (Poseidon;) or gloomy "pater Tartarus" Pluto, god of infernal regions; but that all the kingdoms of being shall be ruled, including the forlorn abominations of the world, there must be supernals of less degree, humble and lowly deities. Hence the number of "beastly divinities and droves of gods" infesting the purlieus of the celestial mountain. It must also be a law and appear as a necessity that each Olympian should carry with him some prestige of his personality and power, and be announced without herald;

the rest of mankind. In all things, then, it behooves us, of course with great caution and circumspection, gravity and decorum, to proceed on our "own hooks"; and every man being his own philosopher, philologist, mythologist, and spiritual factotum, let him read the myths and scriptures of the dreamy and poetical races with whatever spectacles he sees proper to put on his nose, or read them, if he pleases, or can, without 'specks' at all. One thing he *must* do or *die*, as a rational being—stick to the *verdicts* of the *private judgment* in all his readings, thinking precisely what he pleases; or *must*, by the fatal laws of his constitution, of letter and spirit, internal, external meaning—primordial idea, or consequent material symbol, Boodh, Jupiter, Juno, Mars, Venus, Atlas, Esculapius, Hygeia, Antaeus, and Pan."
—*Robert Smith's Critique on Cicero's "De Natura Deorum,"* chap. xii. page 405.

* "The eagle, the oak, and the summits of mountains were sacred to this god."

hence his *form* must reveal or express his attributes, and be the impersonation or material and ethereal representation of the royalties and insignia of his own kingdom.

"Jupiter and Minerva have high foreheads and commanding brows, while Pan and Vulcan have narrow, small, and mean heads;" yet the procession of things and the guardianship of the great common essentials would stop, but for these ugly gods with "mean heads;" and Pan and Vulcan are indispensable, and the ascendants of the hour, for they manage the world and "shape us a home of refuge here." Without the flow of milk and honey, and the constant *renewal* of all things through this god of the woods and "guardian of flocks," this player "upon the pipe of seven reeds," whose "sheep-hook signifies the turning of the year into itself," this feeder ($πάω$, pasco,) of herds and filler of milk-sacks, this Pan, himself a symbol of the world, what were the earth, and the inhabitants thereof? Without the magical artifices of the stithy, and the cunning of the right hand of Vulcan and his forges, this "god of fire and furnaces," the prophet and evangelist of the times, (the ferruginous element, or iron, being the true implement of advancement, witness old mariner's needle, railroad bar, locomotive, and telegraph wire, etc.,) where would be the word *progress;* and what would become of the rushing and expansive spirit, which is the genius of the riotous hour in which we live? Blessed be the gods who have supervision and charge of the lowly details, the homely works, and repulsive chores, or actual things to be done, (which, after all, somebody *must* do)—blessed be the "beastly divinities" who preside over the ghastly secrets and wants of our bodies and the world—thrice blessed the stalwart, rugged Olympians who are making the earth habitable and heavenly, and necessities humble and obscure, the golden gates to undreamed-of paradises of the high and divine.

This Pan, the god of the woods, had a dismal exterior, and was at first the joke of the skies, although "all the gods were afterwards delighted with him." At his birth, his mother, as we have seen, fled in dismay from what seemed to be a monster—half-man, half-animal, having "goat's feet, beard, puck nose, tail, horns, and covering of hair." Representing the shrubs, wild beasts, trees, and rocks of the earth below, this drinker of the blood of wolves must superintend the low and common-place, the troublesome needs of the human body and of the world, microscopic horrors of man's mere animal nature, subserving the humblest functions, structures, and uses of the elements of his mechanism—not only the handsome and graceful, not only the sweet and beautiful, but the *homely and necessary*, the *absolute and indispensable*. "In his lower part he is shagged and deformed as beast of the earth," that fatal tail and hoof (cloven-foot) unlocking the secrets of the dreary domain, the dread kingdom of brutality. "But in his upper part he resembles a man," and that radiant face is "like the splendor of the sky;" those horns are "like the sun and horns of the moon;" while the "leopard's skin which he wears is an image of the starry firmament," for is not Pan also a symbol of the Universe? Let us rejoice with great joy that he is the "President of the mountains and of country life;" that when he blows his pipe all milk-founts are filled, cream drops from distended udders, and the honey-bee is busy. Shall he not play on the syrinx, and "wander on the summits of mountains and rocks, and in valleys, either amusing himself with the chase or leading the dances of the nymphs?" Surely let this rollicking god of pastures and groves, flocks, shepherds, and huntsmen, this increaser of herds, this "guardian of everything connected with pastoral life," and patron of bees, roam over the mountains and wander through the forests, piping, if he pleases, with noise and riot—let him instruct Apollo in prophecy, "sing and dance the lyric songs of Pindar," dreaming of Echo the beautiful, and Pitys the adored; and perpetual fires shall burn in his temples; and all who desire a renewal of their life-forces and constant return to the splendors of youth or rejuvenizing forever, will continue to offer to him his ancient sacrifices of "cows, rams, lambs, milk, and honey."

The god of the woods stands the great symbol of the "primordial utricle," the personification of the perfect "cell" or original "germ" of the organic world.

"Pan was, from his birth, *perfectly developed*, and had the same appearance as afterward."

"*No organism* has been created of larger size than an *infusorial point*."

"The *formative nutrient* process is the *principal process* of the *organic world*."

Thus is it that the great inspirations and prophecies of the Reason march whole ages before the perceptions and demonstrations of the Understanding, and the pipe of Pan, the hymns of Homer, and the ancient atom, herald the advent of the microscope, the doctrine of "cells," and the philosophy of development and rejuvenescence in Nature.

FINIS.

www.ingramcontent.com/pod-product-compliance
Lightning Source LLC
Chambersburg PA
CBHW031538300426
44111CB00006BA/93